PRAXIS II: ELEMENTARY EDUCATION: CONTENT KNOWLEDGE

Titles of Additional Interest

PRAXIS I

PRAXIS II: Parapro Test Prep (0755-1755)

Becoming a Teacher

Best Careers for Teeachers

PRAXIS II: ELEMENTARY EDUCATION: CONTENT KNOWLEDGE

NEW YORK

Library of Congress Cataloging-in-Publication Data:
Praxis II : elementary education: content knowledge.—1st ed.
p. cm.
ISBN-13: 978-1-57685-770-0 (pbk. : alk. paper)
ISBN-10: 1-57685-770-0 (pbk. : alk. paper)
1. National teacher examinations—United States—Study guides. 2. Teachers—Certification—United States. 3. Teaching—United States—Examinations—Study guides. I. Title: Praxis two. II. Title: Praxis elementary education.
LB1762.P753 2011
370.76—dc22

2010040777

Printed in the United States of America

9 8 7 6 5

First Edition

ISBN-10: 1-57685-770-0
ISBN-13: 978-1-57685-770-0

For more information or to place an order, contact LearningExpress at:
2 Rector Street
26th Floor
New York, NY 10006

Or visit us at:
www.learnatest.com

ABOUT THE AUTHOR

Russell Kahn is a developer, writer, and editor of educational publishing products. He has developed scores of test prep guides and authored products for both children and adults. He is currently working toward dual master's degrees in education from Montclair State University. He lives in Montclair, NJ, with his wife and two children.

CONTENTS

INTRODUCTION

The Praxis II: Elementary Education: Content Knowledge Assessment

Becoming a Teacher

Being a teacher is one of the most important and rewarding jobs a person can choose. However, becoming a teacher is no simple task. For most teaching positions, applicants must be well prepared before they can qualify.

Private schools and religious institutions can set their own requirements for hiring teachers. However, public schools must follow their state's guidelines for the necessary qualifications of teachers. The requirements to work at one of the nearly 100,000 public elementary and secondary schools are therefore set by the individual states. However, most states require that their elementary school teachers achieve both of the following objectives:

- earn a bachelor's or master's degree in education
- pass a state test or Praxis exam

A state's teacher certification requirements may change frequently. Your state's Department of Education's website should contain the specific and current requirements to becoming a teacher where you live. The University of Kentucky's College of Education has a website that links to the requirements for each of the 50 states. That page can be found at education.uky.edu/AcadServ/content/50-states-certification-requirements.

You can also visit the Praxis website directly to determine the testing requirements based on your state: www.ets.org/praxis/prxstate.html. For example, New Jersey residents who wish to teach elementary education (grades K through 5) must pass the Praxis II: Elementary Education: Content Knowledge assessment. The test code for this examination is 0014. Even certified teachers from other states who move to New Jersey must pass this Praxis exam.

Some states in need of teachers have allowed for certain candidates to become accredited through alternative—and much quicker—routes. Even those applicants, however, will likely need to pass a standardized test. The purpose of this book is to prepare you for that test and get you one step closer to becoming a full-time teacher.

Praxis II Background

The standardized tests used to determine whether teachers have the core knowledge necessary to do their jobs are mostly developed by a company called Educational Testing Service (ETS). This is the same company that creates the SAT Reasoning Test and many other assessments, such as the TOEFL and the GRE.

ETS's series of Praxis assessments are designed to be used in the teacher certification process. According to ETS's website, the Praxis II tests "measure general and subject-specific knowledge and teaching skills." There are more than 100 different Praxis II tests, ranging from agriculture to World and U.S. History: Content Knowledge.

As of 2010, all Praxis II tests are only offered as paper-and-pencil tests, meaning that you must register at a test center to take a Praxis II at a specific date and time. See page xi for specific registration instructions.

About the Praxis II: Elementary Education: Content Knowledge

One of the most popular Praxis II tests is the Elementary Education: Content Knowledge exam, designed specifically for aspiring elementary school teachers. As its name suggests, it covers the content that teachers will be expected to know to teach grades K through 5. According to ETS, nearly 100,000 examinees take it each year.

Test Content

The Praxis II: Elementary Education: Content Knowledge assessment covers four major subject areas. Each subject area will contain exactly 30 multiple choice questions. The four subject areas, as they will appear on your test, are as follows:

- Reading/Language Arts
- Mathematics
- Social Studies
- Science

In total, the test will be comprised of 120 questions. The approximate number of items in each subject area by subsection is shown below.

- Reading/Language Arts (30 questions in total)
  - Foundations of Reading (15 questions)
  - Language in Writing (10 questions)
  - Communication Skills (5 questions)
- Mathematics (30 questions in total)
  - Number Sense and Numeration (12 questions)
  - Algebraic Concepts (7 or 8 questions)
  - Informal Geometry and Measurement (6 questions)
  - Data Organization and Interpretation (4 or 5 questions)
- Social Studies (30 questions in total)
  - Geography, Anthropology, Sociology (9 questions)
  - World History (3 questions)
  - United States History (9 questions)
  - Government, Citizenship, and Democracy (3 questions)
  - Economics (3 questions)
  - Social Studies as Inquiry and Social Studies Processes (3 questions)

- Science (30 items in total)
  - Earth Science (9 questions)
  - Life Science (9 questions)
  - Physical Science (9 questions)
  - Science in Personal and Social Perspectives (1 or 2 questions)
  - Science as Inquiry and Science Processes (1 or 2 questions)

Test Timing

You are allowed two hours (120 minutes) to take the Praxis II: Elementary Education: Content Knowledge assessment. Because there are 120 questions on the test, that means you will have an average of exactly one minute to answer each question. The subject-specific sections within the test are not timed. That means you can spend more time on one section of the test than another. For example, if you need to spend 40 minutes on the 30 math questions, then you will simply need to spend 10 minutes less on the other sections.

You will not be allowed to leave the test center before the two hours are over. If you find that you have completed the test with time to spare, use the extra time to review your work. A valuable use of extra time is to check your calculations on the math problems again. Above all else, make sure that you have answered every question. You may have decided to skip a hard problem and come back to it later. Make sure you don't leave any question blank.

Test Scoring

Each multiple choice question has equal worth. There may be a few questions that won't count toward your score, but you won't know which those will be. There is no guessing penalty, which means you will not lose points for getting a question wrong. Therefore, you should always guess on a question, even if you are not sure what the correct answer is.

Even though there are 120 questions, the score is not based on 120 points. ETS counts the number of questions you answered correctly and then translates it into a scaled score from 100 to 200. The median score on the test is 164. According to ETS, the average student scores between 151 and 176.

The passing rate for the Praxis II: Elementary Education: Content Knowledge assessment varies by state. According to ETS's web site,[1] the states or territories with the lowest passing score in 2010 are South Dakota, Tennessee, and the U.S. Virgin Islands with a required score of 140. The state with the highest passing score is Mississippi with a required score of 153.

A score of 181 means that you rank in the top 15% of all test takers and, as a result, you will receive a special ETS Recognition of Excellence. If you achieve this high score and earn this recognition, the honor will be noted on all your official score reports, which are viewed by graduate schools and elementary schools. Therefore, even if you feel confident that you will achieve a passing score on the test, you should still strive to attain the special recognition.

You will receive your score online about a month after taking the test. You can get your test score a few days early by using ETS's Scores by Phone service, but this convenience will cost you an additional $30.

If you want to cancel your scores, you need to notify ETS within a week of taking the test. You will not be able to see your scores before canceling them. You will also not receive a refund. You will need to complete the score cancellation form on the Praxis web site, www.ets.org/praxis. Cancelling your score is not recommended unless you are certain that you did very poorly and were either unable to complete the test or got sick during it.

Registering for the Test

Praxis II: Elementary Education: Content Knowledge is offered about seven times per year, usually once every two months. You will need to register for the test about a month before the test date. While you *can*

[1]http://www.ets.org/Media/Tests/PRAXIS/pdf/09706passingscores.pdf

register for a Praxis II exam up to about ten days before the test, you will have to pay additional fees for the late registration.

To check test dates and test center locations, visit ets.org's Praxis site at www.ets.org/praxis. You can register on that site for the test using a credit/debit card. Make sure that you give yourself enough time to complete all the information on the site; the process can take nearly an hour.

What to Bring to the Praxis

You will need to bring identification and your admission ticket to your Praxis II assessment. Be sure to also bring several sharpened #2 pencils, erasers, pens, and a calculator that you are comfortable using. You will not be allowed to use a cell phone or other electronic device.

Special Accommodations for the Praxis II

ETS offers some accommodations for students with disabilities. For example, students may have extended time or additional rest breaks. Some students may take the ParaPro test in a large print, Braille, or audio format.

You can view the testing arrangements and registration procedures at www.ets.org/praxis/prxdsabl.html. To find out if you are eligible for the special accommodations, you can contact ETS Disability Services directly:

Phone: Monday through Friday 8:30 A.M.–4:30 P.M. Eastern Time
1-866-387-8602 (toll free) from the United States, U.S. Territories, and Canada
1-609-771-7780 (all other locations)

TTY: 1-609-771-7714
Fax: 1-609-771-7165
E-mail: stassd@ets.org
Mail: ETS, Disability Services, P.O. Box 6054, Princeton, NJ 08541-6054

How to Use This Book

Chapter 1 contains the LearningExpress Test Preparation System, tailored toward the Praxis II: Elementary Education: Content Knowledge test. Even if you feel confident about certain subject areas and don't feel that you need to read this entire book, make sure you read this chapter.

Chapter 2 contains a full-length Praxis II: Elementary Education: Content Knowledge diagnostic test. Set aside two hours to take this test when you are free from distractions. Turn off your phone, and take the test in one sitting. When you are finished, check your answers and read the explanations for the problems. You can use the results to determine which areas you need to spend the most time studying.

Chapters 3 through 6 contain subject-specific content reviews for the four major subject areas covered by the Praxis II: Elementary Education: Content Knowledge test. These chapters go into great detail about the type of content you will be expected to know for the test. Use your results from the diagnostic test in Chapter 1 to determine which of these chapters to spend the most of your time reviewing. If you struggled with the math and science sections of the practice test, for example, you may choose to spend more time working through chapters 4 and 6. Each of these chapters also includes a 30-question section designed like the respective section of the Praxis II: Elementary Education: Content Knowledge test. If you work through these chapters of the book carefully, you will be very prepared for the types of questions that will appear on your test.

Chapters 7 and 8 contain two full-length Praxis II: Elementary Education: Content Knowledge practice tests with explanations. Just as you did with the diagnostic test, take these practice tests in a similar environment to the actual test. Time yourself so that you have exactly two hours to take the exam. Remove all distractions so you can focus on the test for two hours. When you've completed each practice test, review the answers and read the explanations.

At that point, you may choose to go back to the content chapters (3 through 6) to review the specific skills that are still giving you trouble. The 240 questions in these chapters will provide thorough preparatory experience for the actual Praxis II: Elementary Education: Content Knowledge test, so be sure to take both practice tests in addition to the full-length diagnostic test in Chapter 2.

PRAXIS II: ELEMENTARY EDUCATION: CONTENT KNOWLEDGE

CHAPTER

1

THE LEARNINGEXPRESS TEST PREPARATION SYSTEM

CHAPTER SUMMARY

Taking any test can be tough. But don't let the written test scare you! If you prepare ahead of time, you can achieve a top score. The LearningExpress Test Preparation System, developed exclusively for LearningExpress by leading test experts, gives you the discipline and attitude you need to be a winner.

First, the bad news: Getting ready for any test takes work. This book focuses on the reading, math, social studies, and science skills that you will be tested on in the Elementary Education: Content Knowledge assessment. By honing in on these skills, you will take your first step toward achieving the career of your dreams. However, there are all sorts of pitfalls that can prevent you from doing your best on exams. Here are some obstacles that can stand in the way of your success.

- being unfamiliar with the format of the exam
- being paralyzed by test anxiety
- leaving your preparation to the last minute
- not preparing at all
- not knowing vital test-taking skills like:
  - how to pace yourself through the exam
  - how to use the process of elimination
  - when to guess

- not being in tip-top mental shape
- forgetting to eat breakfast and having to take the test on an empty stomach
- forgetting a sweater or jacket and shivering through the exam

What's the common denominator in all these test-taking pitfalls? One word: *control.* Who's in control, you or the exam?

Now the good news: The LearningExpress Test Preparation System puts *you* in control. In just nine easy-to-follow steps, you will learn everything you need to know to take charge of your preparation and performance on the exam. *Other* test takers may let the test get the better of them; *other* test takers may be unprepared, but not *you*. You will have taken all the steps you need to take for a passing score.

Here's how the LearningExpress Test Preparation System works: Nine steps lead you through everything you need to know and do to master your exam. Each of the steps listed here gives you tips and activities to prepare for any exam. It's important that you follow the advice and do the activities, or you won't be getting the full benefit of the system. Each step gives you an approximate time estimate.

Step 1. Get Information (30 minutes)
Step 2. Conquer Test Anxiety (20 minutes)
Step 3. Make a Plan (50 minutes)
Step 4. Learn to Manage Your Time (10 minutes)
Step 5. Learn to Use the Process of Elimination (20 minutes)
Step 6. Know When to Guess (20 minutes)
Step 7. Reach Your Peak Performance Zone (10 minutes)
Step 8. Get Your Act Together (10 minutes)
Step 9. Do It! (10 minutes)
Total time for the complete system is 180 minutes (3 hours).

You estimate that working through the entire system will take you approximately three hours, though it's perfectly okay if you work faster or slower than the time estimates suggest. If you can take a whole afternoon or evening, you can work through the entire LearningExpress Test Preparation System in one sitting. Otherwise, you can break it up and do just one or two steps a day for the next several days. It's up to you—remember, *you're* in control.

Step 1: Get Information

Time to complete: 30 minutes
Activities: Read the Introduction.

If you haven't already done so, stop here, go back, and read the introduction of this book. Here, you'll learn all about the Praxis II: Elementary Education: Content Knowledge assessment, such as the length of the test, the number of questions, and the way that the test is scored.

Knowledge is power. The first step in the Learning Express Test Preparation System is finding out everything you can about the types of questions that will be asked on the exam. Practicing and studying the exercises in this book will help prepare you for those tests.

After completing the LearningExpress Test Preparation System and the diagnostic test (Chapter 2), you will then begin to apply the test-taking strategies you learn as you work through practice questions in the topic areas covered in the test (Chapters 3 through 6). You can see how well your training has paid off in the two practice tests at the end of the book, which are based on all the topics covered in this book. (You can also check your training with the online test!)

Step 2: Conquer Test Anxiety

Time to complete: 20 minutes
Activity: Take the Test Stress Quiz

Having complete information about the exam is the first step in getting in control. Next, you have to overcome one of the biggest obstacles to test success: test anxiety. Test anxiety not only impairs your performance on the exam itself, but it can even keep you from preparing! In Step 2, you'll learn stress management techniques that will help you succeed on your exam. Learn these strategies now, and practice them as you work through the practice tests in this book, so they'll be second nature to you by exam day.

Combating Test Anxiety

The first thing you need to know is that a little test anxiety is a good thing. Everyone gets nervous before a big exam—and if that nervousness motivates you to prepare thoroughly, so much the better. It's said that Sir Laurence Olivier, one of the foremost British actors of the last century, was ill before every performance. His stage fright didn't impair his performance; in fact, it probably gave him a little extra edge—just the kind of edge you need to do well, whether on a stage or in an exam room.

On page 5 is the Test Stress Quiz. Stop here and answer the questions on that page to find out whether your level of test anxiety is something you should worry about.

Stress Management before the Test

If you feel your level of anxiety getting the best of you in the weeks before the test, here is what you need to do to bring the level down again:

- **Get prepared.** There's nothing like knowing what to expect. Being prepared will put you in control of test anxiety. That's why you're reading this book. Use it faithfully, and remind yourself that you're better prepared than most of the people taking the test.
- **Practice self-confidence.** A positive attitude is a great way to combat test anxiety. This is no time to be humble or shy. Stand in front of the mirror and say to your reflection, "I'm prepared. I'm full of self-confidence. I'm going to ace this test. I know I can do it."
- **Fight negative messages.** Every time someone starts telling you how hard the exam is, start replying to them with your self-confidence messages. If the someone with the negative messages is you, telling yourself you don't do well on exams and you just can't do this, don't listen.
- **Visualize.** Imagine yourself reporting for your first day on the job. Visualizing success can help make it happen—and it reminds you why you're preparing for the exam so diligently.
- **Exercise.** Physical activity helps calm down your body and focus your mind. Besides, being in good physical shape can actually help you do well on the exam. Go for a run, lift weights, go swimming—and do it regularly.

Stress Management on Test Day

There are several ways you can bring down your level of test anxiety on test day. To find a comfort level, experiment with the following exercises in the weeks before the test, and use the ones that work best for you.

- **Breathe deeply.** Take a deep breath while you count to five. Hold it for a count of one, then let it out on a count of five. Repeat several times.
- **Move your body.** Try rolling your head in a circle. Rotate your shoulders. Shake your hands from the wrist. Many people find these movements very relaxing.
- **Visualize again.** Think of the place where you are most relaxed: lying on the beach in the sun, walking through the park, or sipping a cup of hot tea—whatever works for you. Now close

your eyes and imagine you're actually there. If you practice in advance, you'll find that you need only a few seconds of this exercise to experience a significant increase in your sense of well-being.

When anxiety threatens to overwhelm you right there during the exam, there are still things you can do to manage your stress level:

- **Repeat your self-confidence messages.** You should have them memorized by now. Say them quietly to yourself, and believe them!
- **Visualize one more time.** This time, visualize yourself moving smoothly and quickly through the test, answering every question right and finishing just before time is up. Like most visualization techniques, this one works best if you've practiced it ahead of time.
- **Find an easy question.** Skim over the test until you find an easy question, and then answer it. Filling in even one circle gets you into the test-taking groove.
- **Take a mental break.** Everyone loses concentration once in a while during a long test. It's normal, so you shouldn't worry about it. Instead, accept what has happened. Say to yourself, "Hey, I lost it there for a minute. My brain is taking a break." Put down your pencil, close your eyes, and do some deep breathing for a few seconds. Then you're ready to go back to work.

Try these techniques ahead of time, and see whether they work for you!

TEST STRESS QUIZ

You need to worry about test anxiety only if it is extreme enough to impair your performance. The following questionnaire will provide a diagnosis of your level of test anxiety. In the blank before each statement, write the number that most accurately describes your experience.

0 = Never
1 = Once or twice
2 = Sometimes
3 = Often

______ I have gotten so nervous before an exam that I put down the books and did not study for it.
______ I have experienced disabling physical symptoms such as vomiting and severe headaches because I was nervous about an exam.
______ I have simply not shown up for an exam because I was afraid to take it.
______ I have experienced dizziness and disorientation while taking an exam.
______ I have had trouble filling in the little circles because my hands were shaking too hard.
______ I have failed an exam because I was too nervous to complete it.
______ **Total: Add up the numbers in the blanks above.**

Your Test Stress Score

Here are the steps you should take, depending on your score. If you scored:

- **Below 3:** Your level of test anxiety is nothing to worry about; it is probably just enough to give you that little extra edge.
- **Between 3 and 6:** Your test anxiety may be enough to impair your performance, and you should practice the stress management techniques in this section to try to bring your test anxiety down to manageable levels.
- **Above 6:** Your level of test anxiety is a serious concern. In addition to practicing the stress management techniques listed in this section, you may want to seek additional, personal help. Call your local high school or community college and ask for the academic counselor. Tell the counselor that you have a level of test anxiety that sometimes keeps you from being able to take the exam. The counselor may be willing to help you or may suggest someone else you should talk to.

Step 3: Make a Plan

Time to complete: 50 minutes
Activity: Construct a study plan.

Perhaps the most important thing you can do to get control of yourself and your exam is to make a study plan. Too many people fail to prepare simply because they fail to plan. Spending hours on the day before the exam poring over sample test questions not only raises your level of test anxiety, it is also no substitute for careful preparation and practice.

Don't fall into the cram trap. Take control of your preparation time by mapping out a study schedule. If you're the kind of person who needs deadlines and assignments to motivate you for a project, here they are. If you're the kind of person who doesn't like to follow other people's plans, you can use the suggested schedules here to construct your own.

Even more important than making a plan is making a commitment. You can't review everything you need to know for the Elementary Education: Content Knowledge assessment in one night. You have to set aside some time every day to study and practice. Try for at least 20 minutes a day. Twenty minutes daily will do you much more good than two hours on Saturday.

Don't put off your studying until the day before the exam. Start now.

Even ten minutes a day, with half an hour or more on weekends, can make a big difference in your score—and in your chances of making the grade you want!

Schedule A: The 30-Day Plan

If you have at least one month before you take your test, you have plenty of time to prepare—as long as you don't procrastinate! If you have less than a month, turn to Schedule B.

Day 1: Skim over any written materials you may have about the Elementary Education Content Knowledge assessment. Learn the specific content that you need to brush up on to prepare for the test. Read the introduction and the first chapter of this book.

Day 2: Take the diagnostic test (Chapter 2) and score yourself. Be sure to take the test during one 120-minute session, just like the actual test.

Day 3: Review any questions on the diagnostic test that you answered incorrectly. Note which chapters review the skills contained in these questions.

Days 4–6: Read Chapter 3, "Reading/Language Arts Review." Take care to review the skills you will be expected to know for this section of the test. Finally, practice these skills by working through the chapter's practice questions.

Day 7: Review any Chapter 3 concepts that you feel are necessary for you to brush up on.

Days 6–8: Read Chapter 4, "Mathematics Review." Take care to review math concepts and formulas you will be expected to know to answer the questions in the math section of the test. If you need to, make index cards for unfamiliar concepts and formulas. Finally, work through the practice questions.

Day 9: Review any Chapter 4 concepts that you feel are necessary for you to brush up on.

Days 10–12: Read Chapter 5, "Social Studies Review." Take care to review the different social studies subjects you will be tested on in this section. If you need to, make index cards for unfamiliar items. Finally, work through the practice questions and score yourself.

Day 13: Review any Chapter 5 concepts you feel are necessary for you to brush up on.

Days 14–16: Read Chapter 6, "Science Review." Take care to review the areas you will be tested on in the science section. If you need to, make index cards for unfamiliar items. Finally, work through the practice questions and score yourself.

Day 17: Review any Chapter 6 concepts you feel are necessary for you to brush up on.

Day 18: Take the first practice test at the end of this book. Be sure to take the test during one 120-minute session, just like the actual test. Score yourself.

Days 19–20: Review any incorrect answers from the practice test, and then go back to the chapters covering skills that you might have missed on the practice exam.

Day 21: Take the second practice test at the end of this book. Again, be sure to take the test during one 120-minute session, just like the actual test. Score yourself.

Days 22–24: Review any incorrect answers from the second practice test, and then go back to the chapters covering skills that you might have missed on the practice exam. Note improvement from the diagnostic test and the first practice test.

Days 25–26: Review any concepts that you feel are necessary for you to brush up on. Work through similar questions in the appropriate chapters.

Day 27: Take the online practice exam.

Day 28: Review any incorrect answers from the online practice exam, and then go back to the chapters covering skills that you might have missed.

Day 29: Continue to review the chapters that contain the topics you were weak on during the practice exams.

Day before the exam: Relax. Do something unrelated to the exam and go to bed at a reasonable hour.

Schedule B: The 14-Day Plan

If you have two weeks or less before the exam, you may have your work cut out for you. Use this 14-day schedule to help you make the most of your time.

Day 1: Read the introduction. Take the diagnostic test in Chapter 2.

Days 2–3: Read Chapter 3, and complete the practice questions.

Days 4–5: Read Chapter 4, and complete the practice questions.

Days 6–7: Read Chapter 5, and complete the practice questions.

Days 8–9: Read Chapter 6, and complete the practice questions.

Day 10: Take the first practice test at the end of the book and score yourself. Review all the questions that you missed.

Day 11: Review any concepts you feel are necessary for you to brush up on. Work through similar questions in the appropriate chapters.

Day 12: Complete the second practice exam and score yourself. Review all of the questions that you missed.

Day 13: Review topics as necessary, based on the questions you missed on the practice tests. Then, after reviewing the underlying concepts, look at the questions you'd missed and make sure you understand them this time around.

Day before the exam: Relax. Do something unrelated to the exam and go to bed at a reasonable hour.

Step 4: Learn to Manage Your Time

Time to complete: 10 minutes to read, many hours of practice!
Activities: Use these strategies as you take the sample tests in this book

Steps 4, 5, and 6 of the LearningExpress Test Preparation System put you in charge of your exam by showing you test-taking strategies that work. Practice these strategies as you take the diagnostic and practice tests in this book, and then you'll be ready to use them on test day.

First, take control of your time on the exam. The assessment has a time limit of 120 minutes, which may give you more than enough time to complete all the questions—or not enough time. It's a terrible feeling to hear the examiner say, "Five minutes left," when you're only three-quarters of the way through the test. Here are some tips to keep that from happening to you.

- **Follow directions.** If the directions are given orally, listen closely. If they're written on the exam booklet, read them carefully. Ask questions *before* the exam begins if there is anything you don't understand. If you're allowed to write in your exam booklet, write down the beginning time and ending time of the exam.
- **Pace yourself.** Glance at your watch every few minutes, and compare the time to how far you've gotten in the test. When 30 minutes has elapsed, you should be about a third of the way through the test (or completely through one 30-question section), and so on. If you're falling behind, pick up the pace a bit.
- **Keep moving.** Don't waste time on one question. If you don't know the answer, skip the question and move on. Circle the number of the question in your test booklet in case you have time to come back to it later.
- **Keep track of your place on the answer sheet.** If you skip a question, make sure you skip it on the answer sheet, too. Check yourself every five to ten questions to make sure the question number and the answer sheet number are still the same.
- **Don't rush.** Although you should keep moving, rushing won't help. Try to keep calm and work methodically and quickly.

Step 5: Learn to Use the Process of Elimination

Time to complete: 20 minutes
Activity: Complete the worksheet on using the process of elimination.

After time management, your most important tool for taking control of your exam is using the process of elimination wisely. It's standard test-taking wisdom that you should always read all the answer choices before choosing your answer. This helps you find the right answer by eliminating wrong answer choices. And, sure enough, that standard wisdom applies to your exam, too.

Choosing the Right Answer by Process of Elimination

As you read a question, you may find it helpful to underline important information or to make some notes about what you're reading. When you get to the heart of the question, circle it and make sure you understand what it is asking. If you're not sure of what's being asked, you'll never know whether you've chosen the right answer. What you do next depends on the type of question you're answering.

- Take a quick look at the answer choices for some clues. Sometimes this helps to put the question in a new perspective and makes it easier to answer. Then make a plan of attack to solve the problem.
- Otherwise, follow this simple process-of-elimination plan to manage your testing time as efficiently as possible: Read each answer choice and make a quick decision about what to do with it, marking your test book accordingly:
  - ✔ The answer seems reasonable; keep it. Put a ✔ next to the answer.
  - ✔ The answer is awful. Get rid of it. Put an **X** next to the answer.
  - ✔ You can't make up your mind about the answer, or you don't understand it. Keep it for now. Put a **?** next to it.

Whatever you do, don't waste time with any one answer choice. If you can't figure out what an answer choice means, don't worry about it. If it's the right answer, you'll probably be able to eliminate all the others, and if it's the wrong answer, another answer choice will probably strike you more obviously as the right answer.

- If you haven't eliminated any answers at all, skip the question temporarily, but don't forget to mark the question so you can come back to it later if you have time. Because the Content Knowledge assessment has no penalty for wrong answers, and you're certain that you could never answer this question in a million years, pick an answer and move on.
- If you've eliminated all but one answer, just reread the circled part of the question to be sure you're answering exactly what's asked. Mark your answer sheet and move on to the next question.
- Here's what to do when you've eliminated some—but not all—of the answer choices. Compare the remaining answers, looking for similarities and differences, reasoning your way through these choices. Try to eliminate those choices that don't seem as strong to you. But *don't* eliminate an answer just because you don't understand it. You may even be able to use relevant information from other parts of the test. If you've narrowed it down to a single answer, check it against the circled question to be sure you've answered it. Then mark your answer sheet and move on. If you're down to only two or three answer choices, you've improved your odds of getting the question right. Make an educated guess and move on. However, if you think you can do better with more time, mark the question as one to return to later.

Guess on Every Question

You will *not* be penalized for getting a wrong answer on the Content Knowledge assessment. This is very good news. That means you should absolutely answer every single question on the test. If you're hopelessly lost on a question and can't even cross off one answer choice, make sure that you don't leave it blank. Even if you only have 30 seconds left and 10 questions still to answer, you should just guess on all those last questions.

Of course, if you can eliminate even one of the choices, you improve your odds of guessing. If you can identify *two* of the choices as definitely wrong, you have a one in two chance of answering the question correctly. Either way, be sure to answer every question.

If You Finish Early

Use any time you have left to do the following:

- Go back to questions you marked to return to later and try them again.
- Check your work on all the other questions. If you have a good reason for thinking a response is wrong, change it.
- Review your answer sheet. Make sure you've put the answers in the right places and you've marked only one answer for each question. Remember, if you mark more than one answer on a Praxis item, that item will be marked wrong.
- If you've erased an answer, make sure you've done a good job of it.
- Check for stray marks on your answer sheet that could distort your score.

Whatever you do, don't waste time when you've finished a test section. Make every second count by checking your work over and over again until time is called. Try using your powers of elimination on the questions in the worksheet that follows called "Using the Process of Elimination." The answer explanations that follow show possible methods for arriving at the right answer.

Process of elimination is your tool for the next step, which is knowing when to guess.

USING THE PROCESS OF ELIMINATION

Use the process of elimination to answer the following questions.

1. Ilsa is as old as Meghan will be in five years. The difference between Ed's age and Meghan's age is twice the difference between Ilsa's age and Meghan's age. Ed is 29. How old is Ilsa?
   a. 4
   b. 10
   c. 19
   d. 24

2. "All drivers of commercial vehicles must carry a valid commercial driver's license whenever operating a commercial vehicle." According to this sentence, which of the following people need NOT carry a commercial driver's license?
   a. a truck driver idling his engine while waiting to be directed to a loading dock
   b. a bus operator backing her bus out of the way of another bus in the bus lot
   c. a taxi driver driving his personal car to the grocery store
   d. a limousine driver taking the limousine to her home after dropping off her last passenger of the evening

3. Smoking tobacco has been linked to
   a. increased risk of stroke and heart attack.
   b. all forms of respiratory disease.
   c. increasing mortality rates over the past ten years.
   d. juvenile delinquency.

4. Which of the following words is spelled correctly?
   a. incorrigible
   b. outragous
   c. domestickated
   d. understandible

Answers

Here are the answers, as well as some suggestions as to how you might have used the process of elimination to find them.

1. d. You should have eliminated choice **a** off the bat. Ilsa can't be four years old if Meghan is going to be Ilsa's age in five years. The best way to eliminate other answer choices is to try plugging them in to the information given in the problem. For instance, for choice **b**, if Ilsa is 10, then Meghan must be 5. The difference in their ages is 5. The difference between Ed's age, 29, and Meghan's age, 5, is 24. Is 24 two times 5? No. Then choice **b** is wrong. You could eliminate choice **c** in the same way and be left with choice **d.**

2. c. Note the word *not* in the question, and go through the answers one by one. Is the truck driver in choice **a** "operating a commercial vehicle"? Yes, idling counts as "operating," so he needs to have a commercial driver's license. Likewise, the bus operator in choice **b** is operating a commercial vehicle; the question doesn't say the operator has to be on the street. The limo driver in choice **d** is operating a commercial vehicle, even if it doesn't have a passenger in it. However, the cabbie in choice **c** is *not* operating a commercial vehicle, but his own private car.

USING THE PROCESS OF ELIMINATION (*continued*)

3. a. You could eliminate choice **b** simply because of the presence of the word *all*. Such absolutes hardly ever appear in correct answer choices. Choice **c** looks attractive until you think a little about what you know—aren't fewer people smoking these days, rather than more? So how could smoking be responsible for a higher mortality rate? (If you didn't know that mortality rate means the rate at which people die, you might keep this choice as a possibility, but you would still be able to eliminate two answers and have only two to choose from.) And choice **d** is not logical, so you could eliminate that one, too. You are left with the correct answer, choice **a**.

4. a. How you used the process of elimination here depends on which words you recognized as being spelled incorrectly. If you knew that the correct spellings were *outrageous*, *domesticated*, and *understandable*, then you were home free. Surely you knew that at least one of those words was wrong.

Step 6: Know When to Guess

Time to complete: 20 minutes
Activity: Complete worksheet on your guessing ability

Armed with the process of elimination, you're ready to take control of one of the big questions in test-taking: Should I guess? In the Praxis II: Elementary Education: Content Knowledge assessment, the number of questions you answer correctly yields your raw score. So you have nothing to lose and everything to gain by guessing.

The more complicated answer to the question, "Should I guess?" depends on you, your personality, and your guessing intuition. There are two things you need to know about yourself before you go into the exam:

1. Are you a risk taker?
2. Are you a good guesser?

You'll have to decide about your risk-taking quotient on your own. To find out whether you're a good gueser, complete the worksheet called "Your Guessing Ability" that begins on page 12. Frankly, even if you're a play-it-safe person with terrible intuition, you're still safe in guessing every time, because the exam has no guessing penalty. It would be best for you to overcome your anxieties and go ahead and mark an answer. But you may want to have a sense of how good your intuition is before you go into the exam.

Step 7: Reach Your Peak Performance Zone

Time to complete: 10 minutes to read; weeks to complete!
Activity: Complete the Physical Preparation Checklist

To get ready for a challenge like a big exam, you have to take control of your physical, as well as your mental, state. Exercise, proper diet, and rest will ensure that your body works with, rather than against, your mind on test day, as well as during your preparation.

Exercise

If you don't already have a regular exercise program going, the time during which you're preparing for an exam is actually an excellent time to start one. If you're already keeping fit—or trying to get that way—don't let the pressure of preparing for an exam fool you into quitting now. Exercise helps reduce stress by pumping

YOUR GUESSING ABILITY

The following are ten really hard questions. You're not supposed to know the answers. Rather, this is an assessment of your ability to guess when you don't have a clue. Read each question carefully, just as if you did expect to answer it. If you have any knowledge at all of the subject of the question, use that knowledge to help you eliminate wrong answer choices. Use this answer grid to fill in your answers to the questions. Bear in mind that while these questions do not resemble those you will find on the Praxis, they are a good indication of your ability to make an educated guess.

1.	ⓐ	ⓑ	ⓒ	ⓓ
2.	ⓐ	ⓑ	ⓒ	ⓓ
3.	ⓐ	ⓑ	ⓒ	ⓓ
4.	ⓐ	ⓑ	ⓒ	ⓓ
5.	ⓐ	ⓑ	ⓒ	ⓓ
6.	ⓐ	ⓑ	ⓒ	ⓓ
7.	ⓐ	ⓑ	ⓒ	ⓓ
8.	ⓐ	ⓑ	ⓒ	ⓓ
9.	ⓐ	ⓑ	ⓒ	ⓓ
10.	ⓐ	ⓑ	ⓒ	ⓓ

1. September 7 is Independence Day in
a. India.
b. Costa Rica.
c. Brazil.
d. Australia.

2. Which of the following is the formula for determining the momentum of an object?
a. $p = mv$
b. $F = ma$
c. $P = IV$
d. $E = mc^2$

3. Because of the expansion of the universe, the stars and other celestial bodies are all moving away from each other. This phenomenon is known as
a. Newton's first law.
b. the big bang.
c. gravitational collapse.
d. Hubble flow.

4. American author Gertrude Stein was born in
a. 1713.
b. 1830.
c. 1874.
d. 1901.

5. Which of the following is NOT one of the Five Classics attributed to Confucius?
a. the *I Ching*
b. the *Book of Holiness*
c. the *Spring and Autumn Annals*
d. the *Book of History*

6. The religious and philosophical doctrine that holds that the universe is constantly in a struggle between good and evil is known as
a. Pelagianism.
b. Manichaeanism.
c. neo-Hegelianism.
d. Epicureanism.

7. The third Chief Justice of the U.S. Supreme Court was
a. John Blair.
b. William Cushing.
c. James Wilson.
d. John Jay.

8. Which of the following is the poisonous portion of a daffodil?
a. the bulb
b. the leaves
c. the stem
d. the flowers

9. The winner of the Masters golf tournament in 1953 was
a. Sam Snead.
b. Cary Middlecoff.
c. Arnold Palmer.
d. Ben Hogan.

10. The state with the highest per-capita personal income in 1980 was
a. Alaska.
b. Connecticut.
c. New York.
d. Texas.

YOUR GUESSING ABILITY *(continued)*

Answers

Check your answers against the correct answers below.

1. c.
2. a.
3. d.
4. c.
5. b.
6. b.
7. b.
8. a.
9. d.
10. a.

How Did You Do?

You may have simply gotten lucky and actually known the answer to one or two questions. In addition, your guessing was more successful if you were able to use the process of elimination on any of the questions. Maybe you did not know who the third Chief Justice was (question 7), but you knew that John Jay was the first. In that case, you would have eliminated answer **d** and, therefore, improved your odds of guessing right from one in four to one in three.

According to probability, you should get two and a half answers correct, so getting either two or three right would be average. If you got four or more right, you may be a really terrific guesser. If you got one or none right, you may have decided not to guess. Remember not to leave any question blank, no matter how hard it may seem!

You should continue to keep track of your guessing ability as you work through the sample tests in this book. Circle the numbers of questions you guess at; or, if you don't have time during the practice tests, go back afterward and try to remember which answers were guesses. Remember, on a test with four answer choices, your chances of getting a right answer is one in four. So keep a separate guessing score for each exam. How many of your answers were guesses? How many did you get right? If the number you got right is at least one-fourth of the number of questions you guessed at, you are at least an average guesser—and you should always go ahead and guess on the real exam.

wonderful, good-feeling hormones called endorphins into your system. It also increases the oxygen supply throughout your body and your brain, so you'll be at peak performance on test day.

Half an hour of vigorous activity—enough to break a sweat—every day should be your aim. If you're really pressed for time, every other day is okay. Choose an activity you like, and get out there and do it. Jogging with a friend always makes the time go faster, as does listening to music.

But don't overdo it. You don't want to exhaust yourself. Moderation is the key.

Diet

First of all, cut out the junk. Go easy on caffeine and nicotine, and eliminate alcohol and any other drugs from your system at least two weeks before the exam. Promise yourself a special treat the night after the exam, if need be.

What your body needs for peak performance is simply a balanced diet. Eat plenty of fruits and vegetables, along with protein and complex carbohydrates. Foods that are high in lecithin (an amino acid), such as fish and beans, are especially good "brain foods."

Rest

You probably know how much sleep you need every night to be at your best, even if you don't always get it. Make sure you do get that much sleep, though, for at least a week before the exam. Moderation is important here, too. Extra sleep will just make you groggy.

If you're not a morning person and your exam will be given in the morning, you should reset your internal clock so that your body doesn't think you're taking an exam at 3 A.M. You have to start this process well before the exam. The way it works is to get up half an hour earlier each morning, and then go to bed half an hour earlier that night. Don't try it the other way around; you'll just toss and turn if you go to bed early without getting up early. The next morning, get up another half an hour earlier, and so on. How long you will have to do this depends on how late you're used to getting up. Use the "Physical Preparation Checklist" on page 15 to make sure you're in tip-top form.

Step 8: Get Your Act Together

Time to complete: 10 minutes to read; time to complete will vary
Activity: Complete Final Preparations worksheet

Once you feel in control of your mind and body, you're in charge of test anxiety, test preparation, and test-taking strategies. Now, it's time to make charts and gather the materials you need to take to the exam.

Gather Your Materials

The night before the exam, lay out the clothes you will wear and the materials you have to bring with you to the exam. Plan on dressing in layers because you won't have any control over the temperature of the exam room. Have a sweater or jacket you can take off if it's warm. Use the checklist on the worksheet entitled "Final Preparations" on page 16 to help you pull together what you'll need.

Follow Your Routine

If you usually have coffee and toast every morning, then you should have coffee and toast before the test. If you don't usually eat breakfast, don't start changing your habits on exam morning. Do whatever you normally do so that your body will be used to it. If you're not used to it, a cup of coffee can really disrupt your stomach. Doughnuts or other sweet foods can give you a stomachache, too. When deciding what to have for breakfast, remember that a sugar high will leave you with a sugar low in the middle of the exam. A mix of protein and carbohydrates is best: Cereal with milk or eggs with toast will do your body a world of good.

PHYSICAL PREPARATION CHECKLIST

For the week before the exam, write down (1) what physical exercise you engaged in and for how long and (2) what you ate for each meal. Remember, you are trying for at least half an hour of exercise every other day (preferably every day) and a balanced diet that is light on junk food.

Exam minus 7 days

Exercise: ______________ for _____ minutes

Breakfast: ___________________________________

Lunch: ___________________________________

Dinner: ___________________________________

Snacks: ___________________________________

Exam minus 6 days

Exercise: ______________ for _____ minutes

Breakfast: ___________________________________

Lunch: ___________________________________

Dinner: ___________________________________

Snacks: ___________________________________

Exam minus 5 days

Exercise: ______________ for _____ minutes

Breakfast: ___________________________________

Lunch: ___________________________________

Dinner: ___________________________________

Snacks: ___________________________________

Exam minus 4 days

Exercise: ______________ for _____ minutes

Breakfast: ___________________________________

Lunch: ___________________________________

Dinner: ___________________________________

Snacks: ___________________________________

Exam minus 3 days

Exercise: ______________ for _____ minutes

Breakfast: ___________________________________

Lunch: ___________________________________

Dinner: ___________________________________

Snacks: ___________________________________

Exam minus 2 days

Exercise: ______________ for _____ minutes

Breakfast: ___________________________________

Lunch: ___________________________________

Dinner: ___________________________________

Snacks: ___________________________________

Exam minus 1 day

Exercise: ______________ for _____ minutes

Breakfast: ___________________________________

Lunch: ___________________________________

Dinner: ___________________________________

Snacks: ___________________________________

FINAL PREPARATIONS

Getting to the Exam Site

Location of exam site: ______________________________

Date: ______________________________

Departure time: ______________________________

Do I know how to get to the exam site? Yes ____ No ____ (If no, make a trial run.)

Time it will take to get to exam site ______________________________

Things to Lay Out the Night Before

Clothes I will wear ______

Sweater/jacket ______

Watch ______

Photo ID ______

Four #2 pencils ______

Other Things to Bring/Remember

______________________________ ______________________________

______________________________ ______________________________

______________________________ ______________________________

______________________________ ______________________________

______________________________ ______________________________

Step 9: Do It!

Time to complete: 10 minutes, plus test-taking time
Activity: Ace your test!

Fast-forward to exam day. You're ready. You made a study plan and followed through. You practiced your test-taking strategies while working through this book. You're in control of your physical, mental, and emotional state. You know when and where to show up and what to bring with you. In other words, you're better prepared than most of the other people taking the test with you. You're psyched!

Just one more thing. When you're finished with the exam, you will have earned a reward. Plan a night out. Call your friends and plan a party, or have a nice dinner for two—whatever your heart desires. Give yourself something to look forward to.

And then do it. Go into the exam, full of confidence, armed with test-taking strategies you've practiced until they're second nature. You're in control of yourself, your environment, and your performance on exam day. You're ready to succeed. So do it. Go in there and ace the Content Knowledge assessment. And then, look forward to your new career.

CHAPTER

DIAGNOSTIC TEST

Praxis II: Elementary Education: Content Knowledge Diagnostic Test

You have 120 minutes to take the entire 120-question Praxis II: Elementary Education: Content Knowledge diagnostic test. The test consists of four sections: Reading/Language Arts, Mathematics, Social Studies, and Science. You can spend more time on one section than another. You can go back to any section of the test at any time. Take the diagnostic test with a timer or stopwatch so that you can get familiar with the 120-minute time limit. You may use a scientific or four-function calculator.

Use the answer sheet on the following page to record your answers to the 120 questions.

Reading/Language Arts

1.	ⓐ ⓑ ⓒ ⓓ		**11.**	ⓐ ⓑ ⓒ ⓓ		**21.**	ⓐ ⓑ ⓒ ⓓ							
2.	ⓐ ⓑ ⓒ ⓓ		**12.**	ⓐ ⓑ ⓒ ⓓ		**22.**	ⓐ ⓑ ⓒ ⓓ							
3.	ⓐ ⓑ ⓒ ⓓ		**13.**	ⓐ ⓑ ⓒ ⓓ		**23.**	ⓐ ⓑ ⓒ ⓓ							
4.	ⓐ ⓑ ⓒ ⓓ		**14.**	ⓐ ⓑ ⓒ ⓓ		**24.**	ⓐ ⓑ ⓒ ⓓ							
5.	ⓐ ⓑ ⓒ ⓓ		**15.**	ⓐ ⓑ ⓒ ⓓ		**25.**	ⓐ ⓑ ⓒ ⓓ							
6.	ⓐ ⓑ ⓒ ⓓ		**16.**	ⓐ ⓑ ⓒ ⓓ		**26.**	ⓐ ⓑ ⓒ ⓓ							
7.	ⓐ ⓑ ⓒ ⓓ		**17.**	ⓐ ⓑ ⓒ ⓓ		**27.**	ⓐ ⓑ ⓒ ⓓ							
8.	ⓐ ⓑ ⓒ ⓓ		**18.**	ⓐ ⓑ ⓒ ⓓ		**28.**	ⓐ ⓑ ⓒ ⓓ							
9.	ⓐ ⓑ ⓒ ⓓ		**19.**	ⓐ ⓑ ⓒ ⓓ		**29.**	ⓐ ⓑ ⓒ ⓓ							
10.	ⓐ ⓑ ⓒ ⓓ		**20.**	ⓐ ⓑ ⓒ ⓓ		**30.**	ⓐ ⓑ ⓒ ⓓ							

Mathematics

31.	ⓐ ⓑ ⓒ ⓓ		**41.**	ⓐ ⓑ ⓒ ⓓ		**51.**	ⓐ ⓑ ⓒ ⓓ
32.	ⓐ ⓑ ⓒ ⓓ		**42.**	ⓐ ⓑ ⓒ ⓓ		**52.**	ⓐ ⓑ ⓒ ⓓ
33.	ⓐ ⓑ ⓒ ⓓ		**43.**	ⓐ ⓑ ⓒ ⓓ		**53.**	ⓐ ⓑ ⓒ ⓓ
34.	ⓐ ⓑ ⓒ ⓓ		**44.**	ⓐ ⓑ ⓒ ⓓ		**54.**	ⓐ ⓑ ⓒ ⓓ
35.	ⓐ ⓑ ⓒ ⓓ		**45.**	ⓐ ⓑ ⓒ ⓓ		**55.**	ⓐ ⓑ ⓒ ⓓ
36.	ⓐ ⓑ ⓒ ⓓ		**46.**	ⓐ ⓑ ⓒ ⓓ		**56.**	ⓐ ⓑ ⓒ ⓓ
37.	ⓐ ⓑ ⓒ ⓓ		**47.**	ⓐ ⓑ ⓒ ⓓ		**57.**	ⓐ ⓑ ⓒ ⓓ
38.	ⓐ ⓑ ⓒ ⓓ		**48.**	ⓐ ⓑ ⓒ ⓓ		**58.**	ⓐ ⓑ ⓒ ⓓ
39.	ⓐ ⓑ ⓒ ⓓ		**49.**	ⓐ ⓑ ⓒ ⓓ		**59.**	ⓐ ⓑ ⓒ ⓓ
40.	ⓐ ⓑ ⓒ ⓓ		**50.**	ⓐ ⓑ ⓒ ⓓ		**60.**	ⓐ ⓑ ⓒ ⓓ

Social Studies

61.	ⓐ	ⓑ	ⓒ	ⓓ	**71.**	ⓐ	ⓑ	ⓒ	ⓓ	**81.**	ⓐ	ⓑ	ⓒ	ⓓ
62.	ⓐ	ⓑ	ⓒ	ⓓ	**72.**	ⓐ	ⓑ	ⓒ	ⓓ	**82.**	ⓐ	ⓑ	ⓒ	ⓓ
63.	ⓐ	ⓑ	ⓒ	ⓓ	**73.**	ⓐ	ⓑ	ⓒ	ⓓ	**83.**	ⓐ	ⓑ	ⓒ	ⓓ
64.	ⓐ	ⓑ	ⓒ	ⓓ	**74.**	ⓐ	ⓑ	ⓒ	ⓓ	**84.**	ⓐ	ⓑ	ⓒ	ⓓ
65.	ⓐ	ⓑ	ⓒ	ⓓ	**75.**	ⓐ	ⓑ	ⓒ	ⓓ	**85.**	ⓐ	ⓑ	ⓒ	ⓓ
66.	ⓐ	ⓑ	ⓒ	ⓓ	**76.**	ⓐ	ⓑ	ⓒ	ⓓ	**86.**	ⓐ	ⓑ	ⓒ	ⓓ
67.	ⓐ	ⓑ	ⓒ	ⓓ	**77.**	ⓐ	ⓑ	ⓒ	ⓓ	**87.**	ⓐ	ⓑ	ⓒ	ⓓ
68.	ⓐ	ⓑ	ⓒ	ⓓ	**78.**	ⓐ	ⓑ	ⓒ	ⓓ	**88.**	ⓐ	ⓑ	ⓒ	ⓓ
69.	ⓐ	ⓑ	ⓒ	ⓓ	**79.**	ⓐ	ⓑ	ⓒ	ⓓ	**89.**	ⓐ	ⓑ	ⓒ	ⓓ
70.	ⓐ	ⓑ	ⓒ	ⓓ	**80.**	ⓐ	ⓑ	ⓒ	ⓓ	**90.**	ⓐ	ⓑ	ⓒ	ⓓ

Science

91.	ⓐ	ⓑ	ⓒ	ⓓ	**101.**	ⓐ	ⓑ	ⓒ	ⓓ	**111.**	ⓐ	ⓑ	ⓒ	ⓓ
92.	ⓐ	ⓑ	ⓒ	ⓓ	**102.**	ⓐ	ⓑ	ⓒ	ⓓ	**112.**	ⓐ	ⓑ	ⓒ	ⓓ
93.	ⓐ	ⓑ	ⓒ	ⓓ	**103.**	ⓐ	ⓑ	ⓒ	ⓓ	**113.**	ⓐ	ⓑ	ⓒ	ⓓ
94.	ⓐ	ⓑ	ⓒ	ⓓ	**104.**	ⓐ	ⓑ	ⓒ	ⓓ	**114.**	ⓐ	ⓑ	ⓒ	ⓓ
95.	ⓐ	ⓑ	ⓒ	ⓓ	**105.**	ⓐ	ⓑ	ⓒ	ⓓ	**115.**	ⓐ	ⓑ	ⓒ	ⓓ
96.	ⓐ	ⓑ	ⓒ	ⓓ	**106.**	ⓐ	ⓑ	ⓒ	ⓓ	**116.**	ⓐ	ⓑ	ⓒ	ⓓ
97.	ⓐ	ⓑ	ⓒ	ⓓ	**107.**	ⓐ	ⓑ	ⓒ	ⓓ	**117.**	ⓐ	ⓑ	ⓒ	ⓓ
98.	ⓐ	ⓑ	ⓒ	ⓓ	**108.**	ⓐ	ⓑ	ⓒ	ⓓ	**118.**	ⓐ	ⓑ	ⓒ	ⓓ
99.	ⓐ	ⓑ	ⓒ	ⓓ	**109.**	ⓐ	ⓑ	ⓒ	ⓓ	**119.**	ⓐ	ⓑ	ⓒ	ⓓ
100.	ⓐ	ⓑ	ⓒ	ⓓ	**110.**	ⓐ	ⓑ	ⓒ	ⓓ	**120.**	ⓐ	ⓑ	ⓒ	ⓓ

I. Reading/Language Arts

1. In Robert Frost's poem "The Road Not Taken," the forked road represents choices in life. The road in the poem's title is an example of a
a. personification.
b. metaphor.
c. simile.
d. symbol.

2. George Orwell wrote *Animal Farm* in the style of a
a. comedy.
b. fable.
c. legend.
d. tall tale.

3. *First*, *later*, *immediately following*, and *soon after* are all signal words for expository text that
a. shows cause and effect.
b. compares and contrasts.
c. provides a description.
d. denotes a chronological order.

4. Read the following poem:

She walks in beauty like the night
Of cloudless climes and starry skies
Source: "She Walks in Beauty," Lord Byron

This passage uses what figurative speech technique?
a. hyperbole
b. simile
c. metaphor
d. personification

5. Which of the following attributes best describe concrete poetry?
a. the arrangement of words forming a visual effect
b. a five-line poem containing two, four, six, eight, and two syllables
c. the repetition of vowel sounds within the lines to create an internal rhyme
d. a three-line poem with five, seven, and five syllables

6. What is the primary purpose of a persuasive piece of writing?
a. to argue a specific point of view
b. to explain or explore an idea
c. to tell a detailed story
d. to describe a person, place, or thing

7. Identify the word or phrase in the following sentence that represents an error:

The three most preferred activities in gym class are basketball, gymnastics, and playing dodgeball.

a. most preferred
b. gym class
c. are
d. playing

8. Read the following sentence:

Did you know that it rained three inches last night?

This is an example of a(n)
a. imperative sentence.
b. exclamatory sentence.
c. interrogative sentence.
d. declarative sentence.

9. During the prewriting process, a student would do all EXCEPT
   a. complete a first draft.
   b. collect facts and data.
   c. find a topic.
   d. consider a thesis statement.

10. The best indicator of strong comprehension is when a student
   a. constructs meaning with the written language.
   b. uses phonics to recognize words.
   c. reads orally with clarity and expression.
   d. completes silent reading quickly.

11. Read the following:

Hickory Dickory Dock
The mouse ran up the clock
The clock struck one
The mouse ran down
Hickory Dickory Dock
Source: Mother Goose Nursery Rhyme

This nursery rhyme is an example of a(n)
   a. cinquain.
   b. elegy.
   c. limerick.
   d. lyric.

12. Read the following:

"Methods of Teaching," Jennifer Pollock, Teaching Society of America, 2008. Excerpted from Kim Gana, ed., *Education in America: A Modern Guide to the Classroom* (New York: LearningExpress, 2008), 97–101.

The preceding entry would most likely be found in which section of a book?
   a. bibliography
   b. glossary
   c. index
   d. table of contents

13. Which of the following does NOT include examples of narrative writing?
   a. Short story, novel, and epic
   b. Sonnet, ode, and ballad
   c. Essay, directions, and editorial
   d. Legend, elegy, and tragedy

14. Which stage of writing development is characterized by the first appearance of letters on a student's drawing?
   a. scribble writing
   b. random letter
   c. conventional
   d. transitional

15. Which of the following is an example of a simple sentence?
   a. Damien took the poster off his wall, and then he rolled it into a tube.
   b. After eating lunch, Lori waited 30 minutes before jumping into the pool.
   c. Because I am so incredibly tired.
   d. Christina worked 15 hours of overtime last week at the grocery store.

16. The reading process primarily occurs
- **a.** through the eyes.
- **b.** through the ears.
- **c.** in the brain.
- **d.** with the hands.

17. What is the study of word formation in a language, including inflection, derivation, and compound formations?
- **a.** etymology
- **b.** morphology
- **c.** metonymy
- **d.** orthography

Read the following excerpt, then answer Questions 18 and 19.

> DEAR SON: I have ever had pleasure in obtaining any little anecdotes of my ancestors. You may remember the inquiries I made among the remains of my relations when you were with me in England, and the journey I undertook for that purpose. Imagining it may be equally agreeable to you to know the circumstances of my life, many of which you are yet unacquainted with, and expecting the enjoyment of a week's uninterrupted leisure in my present country retirement, I sit down to write them for you. Having emerged from the poverty and obscurity in which I was born and bred, to a state of affluence and some degree of reputation in the world, and having gone so far through life with a considerable share of felicity, the conducing means I made use of, which with the blessing of God so well succeeded, my posterity may like to know, as they may find some of them suitable to their own situations, and therefore fit to be imitated. That felicity, when I reflected on it, has induced me sometimes to say, that were it offered to my choice, I should have no objection to a repetition of the same life from its beginning, only asking the advantages authors have in a second edition to correct some faults of the first. So I might, besides correcting the faults, change some sinister accidents and events of it for others more favorable. But though this were denied, I should still accept the offer. Since such a repetition is not to be expected, the next thing most like living one's life over again seems to be a recollection of that life, and to make that recollection as durable as possible by putting it down in writing.
>
> —Benjamin Franklin

18. In this excerpt, the most plausible writing to follow is a(n)
- **a.** autobiography.
- **b.** biography.
- **c.** letter.
- **d.** novel.

19. In the excerpt from his book, the author
- **a.** implies that he had a perfect life.
- **b.** regrets a few incidents along the way.
- **c.** would like to change his life and start over.
- **d.** wishes to return with his son to England.

20. Read the following:

> What are you able to build with your blocks?
> Castles and palaces, temples and docks.
> Rain may keep raining, and other go roam,
> But I can be happy and building at home.
>
> *Source:* Robert Louis Stevenson, "Block City"

Reading poetry to young children helps provide a strong language base. This first stanza illustrates the use of
- **a.** rhythm and rhyme.
- **b.** rhyme and repetition.
- **c.** repetition and alliteration.
- **d.** rhythm and alliteration.

21. Children with little exposure to print will have more difficulty with

a. hearing rhyming words.
b. discovering that letters represent phonemes.
c. homonyms and synonyms.
d. metaphors and similes.

22. Which of the following techniques is least helpful for a student who is unsure of the meaning of a word in a text?

a. reading several lines before the unknown word
b. looking for synonyms or antonyms within the text
c. looking for a homonym within the text
d. reading several lines after the unknown word

23. The author Samuel Clemens used the pseudonym Mark Twain. The prefix *pseudo-* in the word pseudonym means

a. magic.
b. temporary.
c. mistaken.
d. false.

24. What is the type of error in the following sentence?

The island of Midway, a 2.4-square mile territory of the United States, is best known for their military and geographic importance about halfway between Japan and California.

a. subject-verb agreement
b. verb tense
c. pronoun agreement
d. adverb form

25. Read the following:

Little brown baby wif spa'klin' eyes,
Come to yo' pappy an' set on his knee.
What you been doin', suh—makin' san' pies?
Look at dat bib—you's es du'ty ez me.

Source: "Little Brown Baby,"
Paul Laurence Dunbar

This is an example of

a. colloquialism.
b. dialect.
c. jargon.
d. slang.

26. A student identifies a favorite wildflower in a guidebook. Unfamiliar words like decumbent, hirsute, and orbicular appear in the description. Which section of the book would be most helpful?

a. bibliography
b. glossary
c. index
d. table of contents

27. A developing speller begins to use letters to match sounds. She spells the word *doorway* as DARTY and the word *mother* as MARR. In which developmental stage of spelling is the student?

a. invented spelling
b. scribble
c. random letter
d. transitional

28. Which is the best way to improve the comprehension of a speech for English language learners?

a. Avoid eye contact.
b. Speak more quickly.
c. Include a series of directions.
d. Include visual aids.

29. A student is confused by a series of directions given to him orally. Which of the following is the best strategy for him to complete the steps?
- **a.** Have him skip the step and come back to it at a later time.
- **b.** Have him ask a question to clarify the directions.
- **c.** Have him continue through the exercise.
- **d.** Have him draw a picture to interpret the directions.

30. In preparing your students for a writing assignment, you are encouraging them to form a clear thesis, find strong supporting evidence, find evidence to provide possible opposition to their thesis, and form a conclusion that will restate the thesis or provoke an action. Your students are engaged in
- **a.** narrative writing.
- **b.** expository writing.
- **c.** persuasive writing.
- **d.** technical writing.

II. Mathematics

31. Lefty keeps track of the length of each fish that he catches. Here are the lengths in inches of the fish that he caught one day:

12, 13, 8, 10, 8, 9, 17

What is the median fish length that Lefty caught that day?
- **a.** 8 inches
- **b.** 10 inches
- **c.** 11 inches
- **d.** 12 inches

32. Which of the following is the greatest common factor of 15 and 75?
- **a.** 3
- **b.** 5
- **c.** 15
- **d.** 75

33. The first four numbers of a pattern are $\frac{1}{2}$, $\frac{1}{4}$, $\frac{1}{8}$, and $\frac{1}{16}$. If the pattern is continued, what will be the denominator of the tenth term?
- **a.** 1
- **b.** 64
- **c.** 512
- **d.** 1,024

34. Which of the following number sentences shows the associative property?
- **a.** $(5 + 8) + 2 > 5 + (8 + 2)$
- **b.** $5 + 8 + 2 < 5 + 8 + 2$
- **c.** $5 + 8 + 2 = 2 + 5 + 8$
- **d.** $5 + (8 + 2) = (5 + 8) + 2$

35. If $x + 5 = 10$, then $x + 9 = ?$
- **a.** 5
- **b.** 14
- **c.** 17
- **d.** 19

36. What is the area of a square that has a perimeter of 8 inches?
- **a.** 4 square inches
- **b.** 16 square inches
- **c.** 32 square inches
- **d.** 64 square inches

37. Fishing regulations state that a sole caught in the ocean must be a minimum of 25 centimeters or it must be thrown back. A fisherman catches the following sole and measures it with a meter stick. The fisherman determines that the sole is about 20.5 centimeters long.

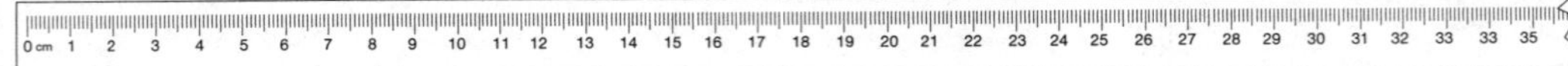

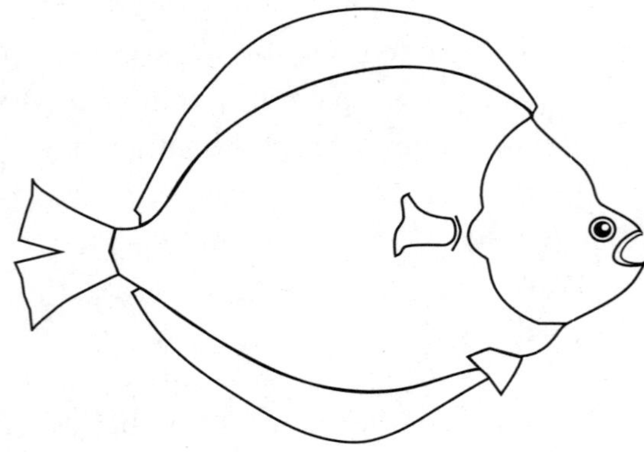

How much more does the sole have to grow, in millimeters, before it can be legally kept?

a. 4.5 millimeters
b. 45 millimeters
c. 55 millimeters
d. 205 millimeters

38. In the number 3,756.192, which number is in the hundredths place?

a. 2
b. 5
c. 7
d. 9

39. A local phone company offers a long-distance plan that costs $6.95 per month and includes 100 free long-distance minutes. After the first 100 minutes, each additional minute costs 5 cents per minute. If John uses 240 long-distance minutes in March, how much will his long-distance bill be?

a. $7
b. $12
c. $13.95
d. $18.95

40. Solve for n. $\frac{1}{2} = \frac{n}{4}$

a. $n = 2$
b. $n = 4$
c. $n = 6$
d. $n = 8$

41. What is the volume of a rectangular solid if its length is 2, its width is 3, and its height is 5?

a. 10 cubic units
b. 15 cubic units
c. 30 cubic units
d. 38 cubic units

42. A bag has 5 white gumballs, 4 polka-dotted gumballs, and 7 striped gumballs.

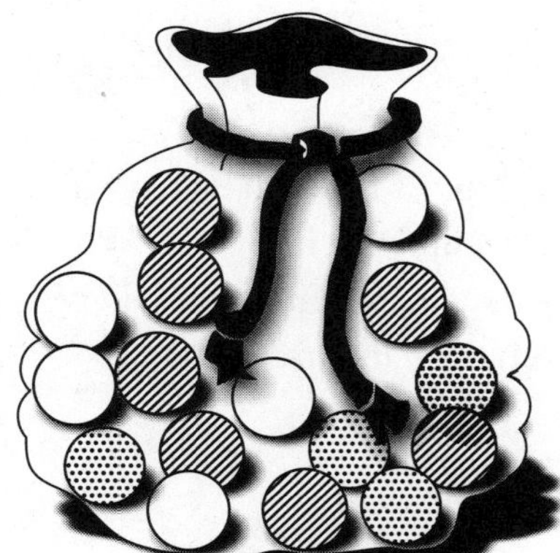

What is the probability of pulling out a striped gumball?

a. $\frac{4}{16}$
b. $\frac{5}{16}$
c. $\frac{7}{16}$
d. $\frac{9}{16}$

43. Which number below is the additive inverse of $-\frac{1}{2}$?

a. –2
b. $\frac{1}{2}$
c. $1\frac{1}{2}$
d. 2

44. Solve for x where $3(2x + 4) = 9$ using the distributive property.

a. $x = -\frac{1}{2}$
b. $x = 3$
c. $x = 6$
d. $x = 21$

45. Which of the following is NOT a multiple of 7?

a. 7
b. 27
c. 42
d. 77

46. What is the value of 3^5?

a. 15
b. 53
c. 81
d. 243

47. Which three-dimensional figure can be formed with the following net?

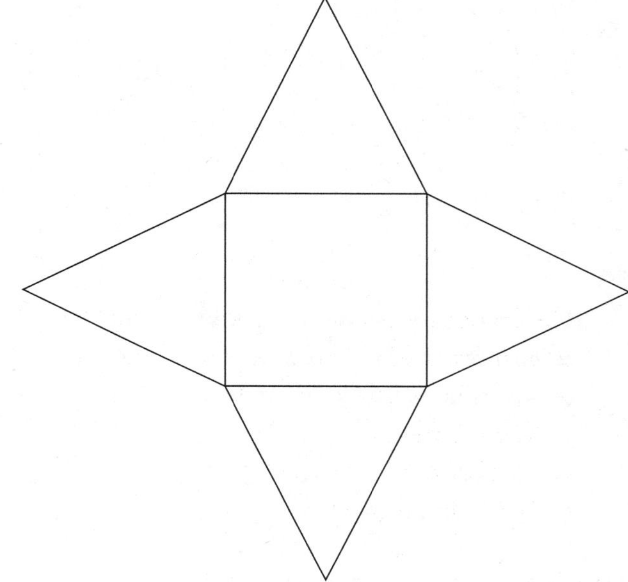

a. square pyramid
b. triangular prism
c. cube
d. triangular pyramid

48. Which number sentence below correctly illustrates the commutative property?

a. $4 + 5 > 3 + 5$
b. $2 + 5 = 5 + 2$
c. $2 + 5 = 3 + 4$
d. $2 + 5 \leq 2 + 5$

49. The following rectangle is rotated a certain number of degrees.

Which degree of rotation will NOT affect the orientation of the rectangle?

a. 100°
b. 270°
c. 540°
d. 600°

50. A florist calculates the number of different flowers that she sells during a week at her store. She creates the following circle graph to organize and display the results.

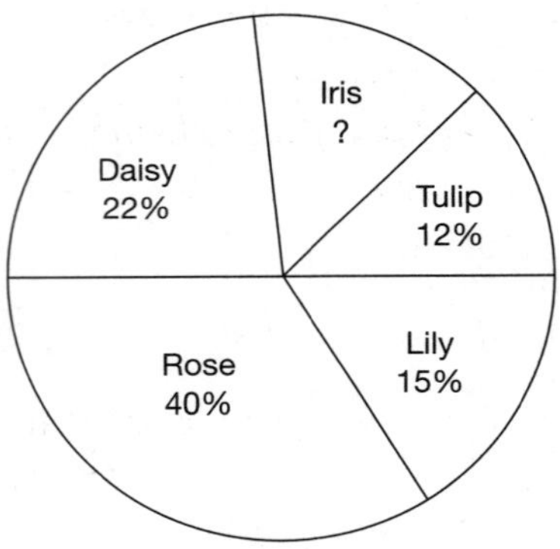

The florist sold a total of 500 flowers. Based on her circle graph, how many irises did she sell?

a. 11
b. 22
c. 55
d. 100

51. How many inches are there in a yard?

a. 3
b. 12
c. 30
d. 36

52. The integers from 1 through 9 are written on pieces of paper and put into a hat. What is the probability that an even number will be selected from the hat at random?

a. $\frac{1}{9}$
b. $\frac{4}{9}$
c. $\frac{1}{2}$
d. $\frac{5}{9}$

53. Which of the following is NOT a prime number?

a. 2
b. 11
c. 29
d. 51

54. Use the order of operations to find the value of the following expression.

$5 + 10 \times 2 - 4 \div 2$

a. 5
b. 13
c. 23
d. 28

55. Aubrey wants to wear an outfit based on a pair of shoes, a pair of pants, and a top. She has 4 different pairs of shoes, 5 different pairs of pants, and 8 different tops to choose from. How many possible outfits can she wear consisting of one pair of shoes, one pair of pants, and one top?

a. 17
b. 28
c. 80
d. 160

56. If $8n + 25 = 65$, then n is:

a. 5
b. 10
c. 49
d. 90

57. Which number, when tripled, is equal to the sum of the number and 4?

a. 2
b. 3
c. 8
d. 12

58. The value of a home in 2005 was $200,000. In 2010 the home had a value of $209,000. By what percentage did the value of the home increase from 2005 to 2010?

a. 4.3%
b. 4.5%
c. 9%
d. 45%

59. Which of the following represents the multiplicative inverse of 16?

a. -16
b. $\frac{1}{16}$
c. $\frac{16}{1}$
d. 61

60. Which of the following can NOT be expressed as a fraction with integers in both the numerator and denominator?

a. -25
b. 0
c. π
d. $5.\overline{5}$

III. Social Studies

61. The Sahara Desert is the largest desert in the world, so large that it splits the continent of Africa into two regions, which lie

a. in the countries of North Africa and South Africa.
b. east or west of the Sahara.
c. on opposite sides of the Nile River.
d. within and north of the Sahara or south of the Sahara.

62. The Indus River Valley and the Mesopotamia River Valley are alike in that they both

a. house tributaries of the Yellow River.
b. were inhabited by Pharaohs.
c. contain rivers that have not been dammed.
d. were home to ancient civilizations.

63. In a free-market economy, companies are allowed to produce whatever consumers will buy in the marketplace. A free-market economy is the opposite of

a. a command, or planned, economy.
b. a mixed economy.
c. a traditional economy.
d. a local economy.

64. Which event signaled the end of the War of 1812?

a. William Hull invaded Canada.
b. Andrew Jackson defeated the British in the Battle of New Orleans.
c. The Creeks surrendered to Andrew Jackson after the Battle of Horseshoe Bend.
d. The United States Senate ratified the Treaty of Ghent.

65. In the United States, citizens have to serve on a jury if they
- **a.** pay taxes.
- **b.** are selected to do so.
- **c.** are registered with the Selective Service System.
- **d.** vote in a local or national election.

66. In 1605, France established its first territory in North America, which extended from modern-day Quebec to Philadelphia. What was the name of this territory?
- **a.** Acadia
- **b.** New France
- **c.** Montreal
- **d.** Nova Scotia

67. The suppression of the Whiskey Rebellion in western Pennsylvania led to
- **a.** the first successful exercise of federal authority.
- **b.** the overthrow of Washington's Continental Army.
- **c.** the immediate repeal of the whiskey tax.
- **d.** an increase in the national debt.

68. A monetary union occurs when
- **a.** one country merges its denominations of notes.
- **b.** a die used to mint money melts into the coin it is creating.
- **c.** two or more governments decide to use the same currency.
- **d.** one country is under a state of war and creates a unique form of currency for internal use.

69. Which of the following strategies should a student first employ before gathering data for research?
- **a.** Clearly formulate the goals of the data-gathering process.
- **b.** Locate the greatest number of resources that could prove valuable.
- **c.** Develop a detailed time line of the events involving the data.
- **d.** Present a lecture based on the gathered data.

70. During the nineteenth century, China fought the First and Second Opium Wars to prevent
- **a.** the British from growing opium in China.
- **b.** the British from selling Chinese opium abroad.
- **c.** the British from requiring China to import British opium from India.
- **d.** the British from requiring China to import American opium.

71. As a result of the Mexican-American War, the United States gained the Mexican territories of Alta California and Santa Fé de Nuevo México through the
- **a.** Adams-Onís Treaty.
- **b.** Treaty of San Francisco.
- **c.** Treaty of Alliance.
- **d.** Treaty of Guadelupe Hidalgo.

72. A pollster is gathering data about an upcoming election by asking people who they intend to vote for. Which of the following would be the most effective location for the pollster to gather his data to get accurate and unbiased results?
- **a.** inside an elementary school
- **b.** on several random streets
- **c.** outside a political party's headquarters
- **d.** at a prestigious and expensive restaurant

73. In the 1870s, thousands of Chinese men were allowed into California and Nevada to build the Central Pacific Railroad. Yet in 1882, Chinese immigrants were prohibited from entering America by

a. Executive Order 9066.
b. California's new constitution.
c. the Chinese Exclusion Act.
d. the Geary Act.

74. During the 1950s, Joseph McCarthy, a U.S. senator, used prolonged investigations to question many members of the entertainment industry and political world about

a. their participation in the House Un-American Activities Committee (HUAC).
b. their service against the Japanese in World War II.
c. different rock-and-roll groups.
d. their suspected role in the Communist Party.

75. The right to vote was extended to American women with the ratification of the Nineteenth Amendment. In what year were the voting rights of the American citizens extended to female citizens?

a. 1848
b. 1944
c. 1920
d. 1756

76. How are regions for time zones defined across the world?

a. the prime meridian
b. lines of longitude
c. the equator
d. satellite images

77. A student uses the following topographical map to research an area of interest.

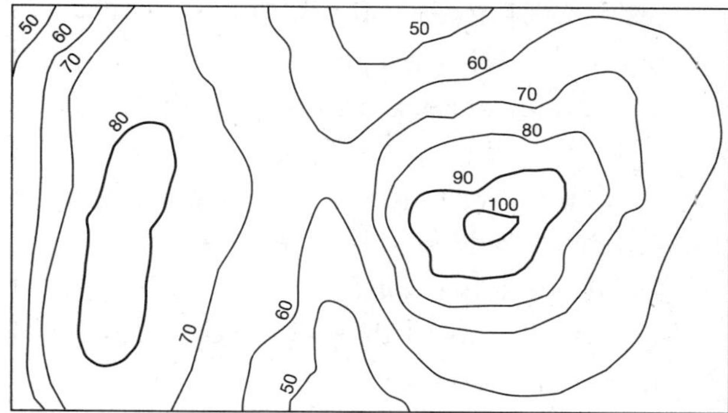

What do the curved lines on the student's topographical map represent?

a. changes in elevation
b. population growth
c. areas of natural resources
d. income disparity

78. The period of American history called the Gilded Age (1865–1893) earned its nickname for

a. the yellow journalism engaged in by many newspapers.
b. the great wealth displayed and obtained by American businessmen in the second industrial revolution.
c. the gold rushes that occurred in the Western states.
d. the abandonment of the gold standard.

79. After invading in 1066 CE, Duke William of Normandy introduced which of the following systems of land ownership to England?

a. communal property
b. land grants
c. cash tenancy
d. the feudal system

80. Mainland Europe's only active volcano, Mt. Vesuvius, has not had a major destructive eruption in nearly 2,000 years. How should residents of nearby cities, including Naples, best react to this inaction?
a. continue development up the slope of the volcano
b. improve warning and evacuation systems
c. seek out additional volcanoes near the European mainland
d. formally classify the volcano as inactive

81. Many poorer countries produce agricultural crops called cash crops with the help of foreign assistance that is most often in the form of
a. international drug enforcement teams.
b. bank loans.
c. donated medical supplies.
d. credit cards.

82. Frederick Douglass, a former slave and the publisher of the antislavery newspaper, *The North Star*, was most famous for his role as
a. the author of the Thirteenth Amendment.
b. an abolitionist.
c. a general under President Abraham Lincoln.
d. a slaveholder.

83. Cartography is best defined as the art, science, and technology of
a. creating maps and globes.
b. digital geographic information systems.
c. surveying the globe.
d. navigating the Seven Seas.

84. The Eighth Amendment to the U.S. Constitution does not allow cruel and unusual punishment, such as and including which of the following penalties?
a. capital punishment
b. a life sentence for fraud crimes totaling less than $500
c. deprivation of a natural-born citizen of his or her citizenship
d. a monetary fine

85. In what way did the Great Irish Famine most greatly affect the population of American cities during the mid-nineteenth century?
a. Large numbers of Irish citizens immigrated to large U.S. cities.
b. American populations dipped as a result of the hunger caused by the famine.
c. The hunger created by the famine caused many Irish workers to be too weak to perform manual labor in America.
d. American states sent billions of dollars in aid to Ireland, weakening the economy.

86. Which American state was created as a result of volcanic activity?
a. Florida
b. Alaska
c. California
d. Hawaii

87. West Germany and East Germany were reunified to form the modern-day nation of Germany as a result of which of the following twentieth-century developments?
a. the invasion of the Soviet Union
b. the rise of the Third Reich
c. the fall of Napoleon Bonaparte
d. the dismantling of the Iron Curtain

88. The well-developed Native American population that lives in the Arctic regions of North America, including Alaska, is given what collective name?
a. Inuits
b. Mound Builders
c. Anasazi
d. Iroquois

89. Which of the following is NOT a significant environmental concern of nuclear reactors for energy creation?
a. disposal of nuclear waste
b. creation of greenhouse gases
c. prevention of radioactivity
d. warming of local waterways

90. Which of the following best defines a peninsula?
a. a land area with access to ample freshwater
b. a series of islands formed tectonically
c. a land mass surrounded by water on three sides
d. a landlocked state or nation

IV. Science

91. Earthquakes are a process by which rock suddenly breaks along a flat surface called a fault. These events cause waves of vibrational energy to move throughout the rock. What is the study and measurement of sound vibrations within the Earth called?
a. geology
b. vulcanology
c. seismology
d. audiology

92. The Hawaiian Islands are considered a volcanic chain of islands. That means
a. they were created by the release of molten rock through volcanic eruptions.
b. they are created by volcanoes that are lined up precisely.
c. they are all linked together.
d. they stimulate volcanic activity.

93. Which of the following processes produces identical cells?
a. meiosis
b. mitosis
c. gamete formation
d. fertilization

94. Astronomers study radio waves, light, and the planets to understand the solar system and the universe. The instrument best suited to this task is the
a. microscope.
b. telescope.
c. gyroscope.
d. Geiger counter.

95. Which of the following processes does NOT represent a conversion of a substance from one state of matter to another?
a. neutralization
b. vaporization
c. melting
d. condensation

96. The northern lights, also known as the aurora borealis, are the result of which event?
a. meteor showers
b. the moon passing between the sun and Earth
c. the collision of high-energy particles with the gases in the atmosphere
d. wind acting on magnetic particles

97. Which of the following is a negatively charged subatomic particle that orbits the nucleus of the atom?
a. molecule
b. neutron
c. proton
d. electron

98. If a person needs a food source to provide short-term energy, he or she should eat foods that are high in
a. fat.
b. carbohydrates.
c. protein.
d. lipids.

99. In the following graph, the *y*-axis depicts the percentage of a population who are 15% greater than their recommended body weight.

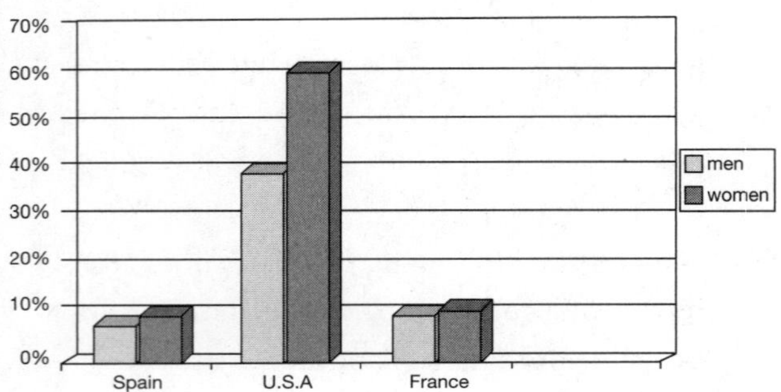

Which statement can be proven from the graph?
a. In Spain, a greater percentage of men are overweight as compared to women.
b. In the United States, women are overweight by a greater percentage of their recommended body weight than women in France.
c. Fewer men are overweight in Spain than in France.
d. In the United States, a greater percentage of women are overweight than men.

100. The mantle of Earth can be described as
a. the metallic core.
b. containing hot, melted rock.
c. the surface of Earth.
d. primarily mineral in content.

101. In genetics, what kind of diagram indicates all the possible genotypes in the F2 generation of a Mendelian cross?
a. Punnett square
b. flow chart
c. periodic table
d. test square

102. The state of Earth's atmosphere at a given time and place is known as
a. weather.
b. climate.
c. temperature.
d. pressure.

103. Which of the following is at the second trophic level?
a. cow
b. killer whale
c. lion
d. pine tree

104. Which of the following is a device that converts stored chemical energy into moving energy of electrons running through a wire?
a. telescope
b. gyroscope
c. battery
d. prism

105. Which process yields four gametes, each containing half the chromosome number of the parent cell?
a. morphogenesis
b. mitosis
c. metamorphosis
d. meiosis

106. Which of the following terms can be applied to a lion in terms of the way it gets its energy?
a. producer
b. consumer
c. herbivore
d. decomposer

107. Which information is generally NOT contained in a periodic table?
a. chemical notation for molecular compounds
b. the mass of an atom
c. the number of protons in the atomic nucleus
d. symbols for each known element

108. Diatomic oxygen gas, the breathable oxygen in the atmosphere, makes up more than 20% of the air in Earth's atmosphere. What is the chemical notation for the molecule?
a. O
b. O_2
c. H_2O
d. O_3

109. A person with a mass of 100 kg on Earth travels to the moon. Which is a true statement?
a. The person will have the same mass on the moon.
b. The person will have a greater weight on the moon.
c. The person will have the same weight on the moon.
d. The person will have a smaller mass on the moon.

110. Which process was most directly responsible for the creation of the Grand Canyon?
a. natural selection
b. plate tectonic shifting
c. magnetic striping
d. erosion

111. The kidneys are a major organ in which organ system of the human body?
a. digestive system
b. endocrine system
c. excretory system
d. circulatory system

112. According to current theory, about how many years ago was the planet Earth formed?
a. 4,500 years
b. 5 million years
c. 4.5 billion years
d. 13.75 billion years

113. Which of the following is a pure substance, as opposed to a mixture?
a. blood
b. soil
c. wood
d. copper

114. Many animal cells are somewhat permeable and can allow water molecules through the membrane. What is the most accurate name for this process?
a. osmosis
b. photosynthesis
c. mitosis
d. meiosis

115. Which of the following produces oxygen?
a. phytoplankton
b. amphibians
c. mammals
d. zooplankton

116. Which layer of Earth's atmosphere contains enough oxygen for human beings to survive?
a. exosphere
b. stratosphere
c. mesosphere
d. troposphere

117. Which of the following events represents an example of kinetic energy?
- **a.** A bike rider prepares to head downhill from the top of a slope.
- **b.** A cannonball is loaded into a cannon and loaded with gunpowder.
- **c.** An apple falls to the ground from an apple tree.
- **d.** A pair of shoes rests on the ground.

118. The clownfish protects the anemone that acts as its home by interfering with fish that would ordinarily eat the anemone. The anemone has stinging tentacles that do not affect the clownfish but protect it from predatory fish that might otherwise eat the clownfish. Which term best describes the relationship between the clownfish and the anemone?
- **a.** commensalism
- **b.** mutualism
- **c.** competition
- **d.** parasitism

119. A tsunami, one of the most destructive events on the planet, can be caused by which of the following events?
- **a.** tidal forces
- **b.** tectonic uplift
- **c.** low pressure
- **d.** extreme winds

120. Venus is often referred to as Earth's "sister planet" for each of the following reasons EXCEPT
- **a.** Venus also has exactly one moon.
- **b.** Venus also has a solid rock surface.
- **c.** Venus also has a dense atmosphere.
- **d.** Venus and Earth have nearly the same gravity.

READING/LANGUAGE ARTS KEY

ITEM	KEY	SUBSECTION	ITEM	KEY	SUBSECTION
1	D	Foundations of Reading	12	A	Foundations of Reading
2	B	Foundations of Reading	13	C	Foundations of Reading
3	D	Language in Writing	14	B	Communication Skills
4	B	Foundations of Reading	15	D	Language in Writing
5	A	Foundations of Reading	16	C	Foundations of Reading
6	A	Language in Writing	17	B	Language in Writing
7	D	Language in Writing	18	A	Foundations of Reading
8	C	Language in Writing	19	B	Language in Writing
9	A	Communication Skills	20	A	Foundations in Reading
10	A	Foundations of Reading	21	B	Language in Writing
11	C	Foundations of Reading	22	B	Foundations of Reading

READING/LANGUAGE ARTS KEY *(continued)*					
ITEM	KEY	SUBSECTION	ITEM	KEY	SUBSECTION
23	D	Foundations of Reading	27	A	Communication Skills
24	C	Language in Writing	28	D	Communication Skills
25	B	Foundations of Reading	29	B	Communication Skills
26	B	Foundations of Reading	30	C	Language in Writing

MATHEMATICS KEY					
ITEM	KEY	SUBSECTION	ITEM	KEY	SUBSECTION
31	B	Data Organization & Interpretation	46	D	Number Sense & Numeration
32	C	Number Sense & Numeration	47	A	Geometry & Measurement
33	D	Number Sense & Numeration	48	B	Algebraic Concepts
34	D	Algebraic Concepts	49	C	Geometry & Measurement
35	B	Algebraic Concepts	50	C	Data Org. & Interpretation
36	A	Geometry & Measurement	51	D	Geometry & Measurement
37	B	Geometry & Measurement	52	B	Data Organization & Interpretation
38	D	Number Sense & Numeration	53	D	Number Sense & Numeration
39	C	Number Sense & Numeration	54	C	Number Sense & Numeration
40	A	Number Sense & Numeration	55	D	Data Organization & Interpretation
41	C	Geometry & Measurement	56	A	Algebraic Concepts
42	C	Data Organization & Interpretation	57	A	Number Sense & Numeration
43	B	Algebraic Concepts	58	B	Number Sense & Numeration
44	A	Algebraic Concepts	59	B	Algebraic Concepts
45	B	Number Sense & Numeration	60	C	Number Sense & Numeration

SOCIAL STUDIES KEY					
ITEM	KEY	SUBSECTION	ITEM	KEY	SUBSECTION
61	D	Geography, Anthropology, Sociology	64	D	United States History
62	D	Geography, Anthropology, Sociology	65	B	Government
63	A	Economics	66	B	United States History

SOCIAL STUDIES KEY *(continued)*					
ITEM	KEY	SUBSECTION	ITEM	KEY	SUBSECTION
67	A	United States History	79	D	World History
68	C	Economics	80	B	Geography, Anthropology, Sociology
69	A	Inquiry/Processes	81	B	Economics
70	C	World History	82	B	United States History
71	D	United States History	83	A	Geography, Anthropology, Sociology
72	B	Inquiry/Processes	84	C	Government, Citizenship & Democracy
73	C	United States History	85	A	Geography, Anthropology, Sociology
74	D	United States History	86	D	Geography, Anthropology, Sociology
75	C	Government, Citizenship & Democracy	87	D	World History
76	B	Geography, Anthropology, Sociology	88	A	United States History
77	A	Inquiry/Processes	89	B	Geography, Anthropology, Sociology
78	B	United States History	90	C	Geography, Anthropology, Sociology

SCIENCE KEY					
ITEM	KEY	SUBSECTION	ITEM	KEY	SUBSECTION
91	C	Earth Science	102	A	Earth Science
92	A	Earth Science	103	A	Life Science
93	B	Life Science	104	C	Physical Science
94	B	Science Inquiry/Processes	105	D	Life Science
95	A	Physical Science	106	B	Life Science
96	C	Earth Science	107	A	Physical Science
97	D	Physical Science	108	B	Physical Science
98	B	Science in Personal/Social	109	A	Physical Science
99	D	Science in Personal/Social	110	D	Earth Science
100	D	Earth Science	111	C	Life Science
101	A	Life Science	112	C	Earth Science

SCIENCE KEY *(continued)*					
ITEM	KEY	SUBSECTION	ITEM	KEY	SUBSECTION
113	D	Physical Science	117	C	Physical Science
114	A	Life Science	118	B	Life Science
115	A	Life Science	119	B	Physical Science
116	D	Earth Science	120	A	Earth Science

Reading/Language Arts Answers

1. d. A symbol is a concrete object that represents an idea or concept. Choice **a** is incorrect because personification allows the writer to give animals, plants, and ideas the qualities of a human. Choice **b** is incorrect because a metaphor is a direct comparison of two objects without using any comparison words. Choice **c** is incorrect. A simile is the comparison of two unlike objects using the words *like* or *as*.

2. b. A fable is a story with a moral principle using animals or birds as the protagonists. Choice **a** is incorrect because a comedy takes the serious side of life and makes it light, humorous, or funny. Choice **c** is incorrect because a legend is a traditional story passed down through the ages, centering on a particular hero. Choice **d** is incorrect. A tall tale is a story combining history, myth, and fact.

3. d. Signal words for chronological order include *first*, *later*, *immediately following*, and *soon after*. Choice **a** is incorrect because cause and effect signal words include *because*, *since*, *so that*, *therefore*, and *as a result*. Choice **b** is incorrect because compare and contrast signal words include *however*, *but*, *unless*, *on the other hand*, and *similarly*. Choice **c** is incorrect because descriptive signal words include above, across, along, over, and beside.

4. b. A simile is the comparison of two unlike objects using the words *like* or *as*. Choice **a** is incorrect because a hyperbole is an exaggeration or overstatement. Choice **c** is incorrect because a metaphor is a direct comparison of two objects without using any comparison words. Choice **d** is incorrect because personification allows the writer to give animals, plants, and ideas qualities of a human.

5. a. Concrete poetry is defined by the arrangement of the words on the page. The shape that the words form have a significant visual effect. There is no requirement regarding the number of lines in concrete poetry, so **b** and **d** are not correct. The description in choice **c** describes assonance, a poetic device that can be used in any type of poem.

6. a. The purpose of a persuasive type of writing is to persuade the reader about something through an argument. Choice **a** is the best description of this. Choice **b** describes an expository type of writing. Choice **c** describes a narrative type of writing. Choice **d** describes a descriptive type of writing.

7. d. The items in a list must be consistent with each other. The list begins with "basketball, gymnastics, and." The third item in the list should be a game or sport. The verb *playing* is unnecessary and confuses the order of the activities. There are no errors with the words listed in choices **a**, **b**, or **c**.

8. c. An interrogative sentence asks a question. Choice **a** is incorrect. An imperative sentence makes commands. Choice **b** is incorrect because an exclamatory sentence expresses strong emotion or surprise, most often followed by an exclamation point. Choice **d** is incorrect because a declarative sentence makes a statement.

9. a. A first draft is written following the prewriting process. Choice **b** is incorrect because collecting facts and data is part of the prewriting process. Choice **c** is incorrect because finding a topic is part of the prewriting process. Choice **d** is incorrect because determining a thesis can be part of the prewriting process.

10. a. Comprehension is constructing meaning with the written word. Choice **b** is incorrect because recognizing words does not mean one comprehends them. Choice **c** is incorrect because being able to say words does not mean that one understands what she is reading. Choice **d** is incorrect. Unless there is some type of assessment, one does not know what the reader understands.

11. c. A limerick is a five-line, usually humorous, verse with the aabba rhyme scheme. Choice **a** is incorrect because a cinquain is a form of poetry containing five lines of two, four, six, eight, and two syllables, respectively. Choice **b** is incorrect. An elegy is a poem mourning the death of an individual. Choice **d** is incorrect because a lyric expresses the emotions of the poet and has a musical quality.

12. a. The bibliography is a section at the back of the book that lists books or articles used in preparation of the text. Some books include bibliographies as a guide for further reading. Choice **b** is incorrect because the glossary lists and defines the most specialized terms used in the text. Choice **c** is incorrect because an index alphabetically lists names, places, and subjects used within a text. Placed toward the end of the book, it also indicates the page where the information is found. Choice **d** is incorrect because the table of contents is the section of the book that indicates the major divisions of the book (units, chapters, topics). This section is placed before the body of the work.

13. c. An essay, directions, and an editorial are all examples of expository writing. Choices **a**, **b**, and **d** are all correct because they all list forms of narrative writing.

14. b. The scribble writing stage, choice **a**, includes only pictures or drawings with perhaps an oral story to go with them. It is not until the random letter stage when students begin to use letters—albeit random letters—with their work. The conventional and transitional stages come after the random letter stage.

15. d. A simple sentence has one independent clause and no dependent clauses. Only choice **d** includes this. The sentence in choice **a** includes two independent clauses, so it is a compound sentence. The sentence in choice **b** include a dependent clause, so it is a complex sentence. Choice **c** is a fragment and not a sentence at all.

16. c. The actual reading process occurs in the brain. Choice **a** is incorrect because while one uses the eyes to transmit the word images to the brain, it is the brain that begins the reading process. Choices **b** and **d** are incorrect. The ears and hands do not play a part in the reading process.

17. b. Morphology is the study of word formation in a language, including inflection, derivation, and compound formations. Choice **a** is incorrect because etymology is the study of history of words. Choice **c** is incorrect because metonymy is substituting one word for another that has close association to it. Choice **d** is incorrect because orthography concerns a writing system including punctuation, spelling, and capitalization.

18. a. In *Autobiography of Benjamin Franklin*, Franklin introduces the book with a note to his son. An autobiography is the author's account of his or her life. Choice **b** is incorrect because a biography is an account written about someone by another person. Choice **c** is incorrect because although this section has the appearance of a personal letter, the author states that he plans to write down his recollections or his life story. Choice **d** is incorrect because a novel is a story of fiction. This account is nonfiction.

19. b. The author indicates he had a few faults, but generally, life was pretty good. Choice **a** is incorrect because although the author had a good life, he does indicate a few faults. Choice **c** is incorrect because in spite of a few faults, he did have a pretty good life. Choice **d** is incorrect because there is no evidence to support this.

20. a. Rhythm is the order or free occurrences of sound. This stanza has a regular meter. The rhyme is the likeness or similarity of sounds in words. Rhyme occurs at the end of lines 1–2 and 3–4. Choice **b** is incorrect because although there is rhyme in the poem, we are not repeating words (repetition). Choice **c** is incorrect because there is neither repetition nor alliteration (same sounds at the beginning of sequential words). Choice **d** is incorrect because although there is a distinct rhythm in the poem, there is no alliteration.

21. b. Reading various forms of print to prereading students allows them to begin to understand that there is meaning in the text. The students see letters on the page as it is being read. Choice **a** is incorrect because it is an auditory-brain function. Choice **c** is incorrect because synonyms are words that have the same or similar meanings. Homonyms are words that sound and are spelled alike but have different meanings. Choice **d** is incorrect because metaphors and similes are figures of speech.

22. c. Context is one of the most useful tools for a student to determine the meaning of an unknown word. The context can appear before or after the unknown word, so choices **a** and **d** are not correct. Finding an antonym or synonym, **b**, would help identify the unknown word's meaning. However, finding a homonym, **c**, will not help identify the meaning.

23. d. Pseudo means false. The pseudonym of Samuel Clemens is Mark Twain. Choices **a**, **b**, and **c** do not fit the definition.

24. c. The subject of the given sentence is Midway Island, a singular subject. The correspon-ding pronoun in the sentence is *their*, which is plural. The pronoun should be *its* to agree with the singular nature of the subject. There is no error in subject-verb agreement, verb tense, or adverb form.

25. b. Dialect is the local language of the people. This includes the accent, vocabulary, grammar, and idioms. Some might also describe this poem as black dialect. Choice **a** is incorrect because colloquialism is an informal expression that is usually accepted in spoken and written language. Choice **c** is incorrect because jargon is language used by a specific group. All academic areas each have their own jargon. Choice **d** is incorrect because slang, language also used by specific groups, is generally coined to set themselves apart from others. It is ever-changing.

26. b. The glossary of a book lists and defines the most specialized terms used in the text. Choice **a** is incorrect because the bibliography is a section at the back of the book that lists books or articles used in preparation of the text. Some books include bibliographies as a guide for further reading. Choice **c** is incorrect because an index alphabetically lists names, places, and subjects used within a text. Placed toward the end of the book, it also indicates the page where the information is found. Choice **d** is incorrect because the table of contents is the section of the book that indicates the major divisions of the book (units, chapters, topics). This section is placed before the body of the work.

27. a. Students begin to use letters to match sounds during the invented spelling stage. They may only use the beginning letter to represent a word.

28. d. Eye contact improves a speech, so avoiding it, choice **a**, is not a good strategy. Likewise, speaking more quickly is not usually going to improve comprehension, especially for ELL students. The inclusion of visual aids can be incredibly helpful for all students, but especially for ELL students.

29. b. Skipping a step, choice **a**, is not the best strategy for following directions. When listening, it is acceptable to ask specific questions when appropriate, choice **b**. The strategies listed in choices **c** and **d** will not aid the student in following the directions if he does not initially understand them.

30. c. Persuasive writing seeks to influence or change one's opinion. Choice **a** is incorrect because narrative writing seeks to paint a vivid picture so that the reader is pulled into the writer's experience. Choice **b** is incorrect because expository writing seeks to inform, explain, clarify, or instruct. Choice **d** is incorrect because technical writing seeks to communicate clear information about a specific subject to a targeted audience.

Mathematics Answers

31. b. The median value is the middle value when the numbers are sorted in descending order. The answer here is 10 inches. The mode is 8 inches, choice **a**. The median is 11 inches, choice **c**.

32. c. The GCF, or greatest common factor, is the largest factor that divides two or more numbers evenly. The factors 3 and 5 are common to both 15 and 75. Multiply 3 by 5 to get the GCF of 15. Choice **d**, 75, represents the least common multiple of the two numbers.

33. d. Given the first four terms of the pattern, $\frac{1}{2}$, $\frac{1}{4}$, $\frac{1}{8}$, and $\frac{1}{16}$, notice that the denominators double as the pattern advances. There are four terms so far. The fifth term's denominator is 32, the sixth term's is 64, the seventh term's is 128, the eighth term's is 256, the ninth term's is 512, and the tenth term's is 1,024. So, the tenth term is $\frac{1}{1,024}$.

An alternate way of looking at the pattern is to notice that the denominators are powers of 2. The x term is $\frac{1^x}{2}$.

Therefore, the tenth term is $\frac{1^{10}}{2} = \frac{1}{1,024}$.

34. d. The associative property refers to grouping and states that $a + (b + c) = (a + b) + c$. Choice **d** correctly illustrates this property. Choices **a**, **b**, and **c** are incorrect because they do not show the associative property.

35. b. From $x + 5 = 10$, you can subtract 5 from both sides of the equation to determine that $x = 5$. This answer correctly completes the number sentence $5 + 9 = 14$. Choice **a** is the value for x, but you need to find the value of $x + 9$. If $x = 5$, then $x + 9$ is equal to $5 + 9$, or 14.

36. a. The perimeter of a square is 4 times the length of one side. So if the perimeter of a square is 8 inches, then the length of each side is $8 \div 4$, or 2 inches. The area of a square can be determined by squaring the length of one side. 2 inches squared is equal to 4 square inches, choice **a**.

37. b. The length of the sole is 20.5 cm, which converts to 205 mm. The fish needs to be 25 cm, which converts to 250 mm. The difference is 45 mm, which is why answer choice **b** is correct.

38. d. The hundredths place is two places to the right of the decimal point. Therefore, the digit 9 is in the hundredths place. The digit 2, choice **a**, is in the thousandths place. The digit 5, choice **b**, is in the tens place. The digit 7, choice **c**, is in the hundreds place.

39. c. Determine how many minutes John will be charged for by subtracting the free minutes from the total minutes: $240 - 100 = 140$. John will be charged five cents per minute for 140 minutes. Multiply to find the cost of the minutes: $140 \times \$0.05 = \$7$. Add the monthly charge to the cost of the minutes to find the total amount of the long distance bill: $\$6.95 + \$7 = \$13.95$. Choice **a** is incorrect because \$7 only represents the cost of the minutes; it does not include the monthly fee. Choice **b** is incorrect because \$12 represents the cost of all the minutes (including the free minutes) and does not include the monthly fee. Choice **d** is incorrect because it includes the cost of all the minutes (including the free minutes) and the monthly fee.

40. a. In this proportion, it is necessary to cross multiply to solve for n. This gives us $2n = 4$. Divide each side by 2 and the result is $n = 2$. Choice **b** is incorrect because only one side was divided by 2. Choice **c** is incorrect because 2 was added to 4 instead of being divided into 4. Choice **d** is incorrect because 4 was multiplied by 2 instead of divided by 2.

41. c. The volume for a rectangular prism is length $\times$ width $\times$ height. Choice **a** is incorrect because the sides of the prism were added instead of multiplied. Choice **b** is incorrect because this does not fit the formula. Choice **d** is incorrect because the squares of each number were added together, which does not fit the formula.

42. c. To find the probability of an event happening, divide the total number of possible outcomes by the total number of successful outcomes. The number 7 represents the number of striped gumballs, or the successful outcomes. The number 16 represents the total number of gumballs in the bag. Therefore, the probability of picking a striped gumball is $\frac{7}{16}$. Choice **a** is incorrect because this is the probability of pulling out a polka-dotted gumball. Choice **b** is incorrect because this is the probability of pulling out a white gumball. Choice **d** is incorrect because this is the probability of NOT pulling out a green gumball.

43. b. The additive inverse refers to that number that is needed to bring the result to zero. In this example, $-\frac{1}{2} + \frac{1}{2} = 0$; therefore, the correct answer is choice **b**. Choice **a** is incorrect because adding –2 will not bring the result to zero; –2 is the multiplicative inverse of $-1\frac{1}{2}$. Choice **c** is incorrect because adding $1\frac{1}{2}$ will not bring the result to zero. Choice **d** is incorrect because $-\frac{1}{2}$ plus 2 does not equal zero.

44. a. The distributive property of multiplication states that you can add two or more terms together and then multiply by a factor, or you can multiply each term by a factor separately and then add them. To solve the given equation using the distributive property, use the following steps:

$3(2x + 4) = 9$

$(3 \times 2x) + (3 \times 4) = 9$

$6x + 12 = 9$

$6x = -3$

$x = -\frac{1}{2}$

None of the other numbers in the answer choices satisfies the given equation.

45. b. The first multiple of 7 is 7 itself. The next four multiples are 14, 21, 28, 35, and 42. The number 27, choice **d**, is therefore NOT a multiple of 7. You can multiply 7 by the whole number 11 to get a product of 77, so choice **d** is not correct.

46. d. In an exponent, the base number is multiplied by itself the number of times shown in the power. In the case of 3^5, 3 is multiplied by itself 5 times. $3 \times 3 \times 3 \times 3 \times 3 = 243$, choice **d**.

47. a. A square pyramid has a square-shaped base and triangular faces, as shown below.

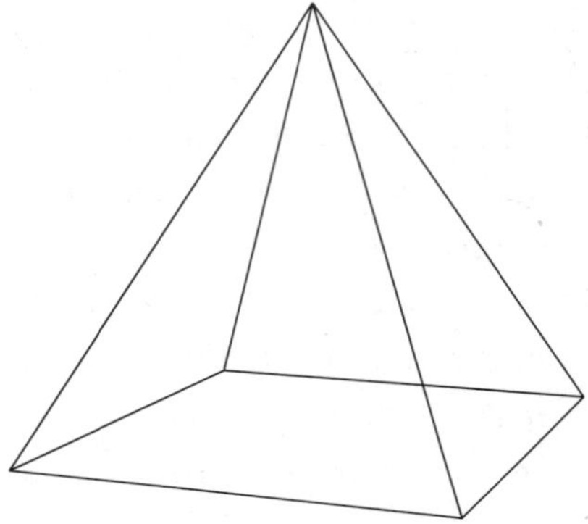

When the sides are laid flat in a two-dimensional representation (called a net), it looks like the figure shown in the question stem. A triangular prism, choice **b**, has two triangular sides and three rectangular sides, so this net does not represent a triangular prism. A cube, choice **c**, has six square-shaped sides, so the net does not represent a cube. A triangular pyramid, choice **d**, also has triangular faces, but its base is also in the shape of a triangle.

48. b. The commutative property states that $a + b = b + a$. Choice **b** properly illustrates this property. Choices **a** and **d** are incorrect because an inequality is not used to show the commutative property. Choice **c** is incorrect because, while the opposite sides of the equation are equal, it does not use the same numbers in reversed order.

49. c. If the rectangle undergoes a rotation of 180°, it will flip completely over—and it will look exactly the same as a result. A rotation of 360° will return the figure to its original orientation. A rotation of 540°, therefore, rotates the figure completely around and then halfway around again. It will look exactly the same, so choice **c** is correct.

50. c. The missing percentage in the florist's circle graph can be found by subtracting all the other percentages from 100%. 100 – (12% + 22% + 15% + 40%) = 11%. Therefore, 11% of the flowers sold by the florist last week were irises. But don't pick choice **a**; the question asks how many out of 500 flowers were irises. To find that, multiply the 11% of the circle graph that represents irises by the total, 500. A percentage of 11% is equivalent to 0.11. $0.11 \times 500 = 55$, choice **c**.

51. d. There are 12 inches in a foot. There are 3 feet in a yard. Therefore, to find the number of inches in a yard, you need to multiply 12 by 3. The product is 36, which is why choice **d** is correct.

52. b. There are nine numbers written on pieces of paper. Of those numbers, the even numbers are 2, 4, 6, and 8, so there are 4 even numbers. To find the probability of picking an even number out of the hat, you need to divide the number of even numbers by the total number of numbers in the hat, which is $\frac{4}{9}$, or choice **b**. If you picked choice **c**, you may have forgotten that there are not the same number of even numbers and odd numbers in the hat. Choice **d** represents the probability of picking an odd number from the hat.

53. d. A prime number is any whole number that has no other factor besides itself and 1. The numbers 2, 11, and 29 are each only divisible by 1 and themselves. The number 51, however, is a multiple of 3 and 17, so it is a composite number and NOT a prime number.

54. c. To follow the order of operations, perform the multiplication and division in the expression from left to right first. Then perform the addition and subtraction from left to right. See the following steps:

$5 + 10 \times 2 - 4 \div 2$

$5 + 20 - 4 \div 2$

$5 + 20 - 2$

$25 - 2$

23

55. d. To find the total number of possible outcomes in this scenario, you need to multiply the number of pairs of shoes by the number of pairs of pants by the number of tops. Aubrey has 4 different pairs of shoes, 5 different pairs of pants, and 8 different tops to choose from. Therefore, $4 \times 5 \times 8 = 160$, choice **d**.

56. a. You can simplify $8n + 25 = 65$ by first subtracting 25 from both sides. Thus, $8n = 40$. Then divide 40 by 8 to get the answer, which is 5. The value of n is 5.

57. a. The easiest way to solve this problem is to try the different numbers in the answer choices to see which one satisfies the given problem. Fortunately, every question on the Praxis II: Elementary Education Content Knowledge test will be multiple choice, so you will always have the ability to plug in the numbers from the answer choices. In this case, the first choice, 2, satisfies the problem. When 2 is tripled, the result is 6. This is equal to the sum of the number 2 and 4. Because $2 \times 3 = 2 + 4$, choice **a** is correct.

58. b. If you divide the 2010 home value, \$209,000, by the 2005 home value, \$200,000, you will get a quotient of 1.045. This shows that the 2010 value is 1.045 times the size of the 2005 value. In other words, it is 0.045 bigger. To translate a decimal into a percentage, move the decimal two places to the right; the new home value is 4.5% more valuable. Choice **b** represents this change in value.

59. b. The multiplicative inverse of a number is a number that, when multiplied by the original number, will provide a product of 1. Multiplying 16 by –16, choice **a**, will yield a product of –256. Multiplying 16 by $\frac{1}{16}$, choice **b**, will provide a product of 1. The numbers in answer choices **c** and **d** will provide products far too great for them to be the multiplicative inverse. Just remember that if the original number is greater than 1, its multiplicative inverse will need to be less than 1.

60. c. The number –25, choice **a**, can be represented as a the fraction $-\frac{25}{1}$. The number 0, choice **b**, can be represented with any fraction where the denominator is 0, such as $\frac{5}{0}$ or $\frac{1}{0}$. However, π cannot be expressed with integers in a fraction. That is why it is considered an irrational number—and it's why choice **c** is correct. The fraction $\frac{50}{9}$ would be equal to , so choice **d** is not right. Repeating decimals can always be represented by a fraction with integers in the numerator and denominator.

Social Studies Answers

61. d. The Sahara Desert divides Africa into two regions, one within and north of the Sahara, and one south of the Sahara. Choice **a** is incorrect because North Africa is a region and South Africa is a country. The Sahara Desert cannot be in North Africa because North Africa is not a country, and cannot be in South Africa because it is located very far from South Africa. Choice **b** is incorrect because the desert does not split the continent from east and west. This desert is bounded by the Atlantic Ocean on the west and the Red Sea on the east. Choice **c** is incorrect because the Sahara desert does not split the continent in the same way that the Nile River does.

62. d. The Indus River Valley in India and the Mesopotamia River Valley in Iraq were home to thriving cultures with hierarchical structures that also developed reading and writing systems. Choice **a** is incorrect because the Yellow River is located in China and both of these river valleys are in countries other than China. Choice **b** is incorrect because this description fits the Valley of the Kings in Egypt. Choice **c** is incorrect because both of these river valleys contain rivers that been dammed to generate hydroelectric power.

63. a. A free-market economy is one in which the consumers decide what to buy and producers are allowed to set their own prices. A command, or planned, economy is one in which the government decides how much consumers will pay for goods and services and how much of these items producers will produce. Choice **b** is incorrect because a mixed economy is an economy in which the consumers, the producers, and the government all have a say in how many goods and services will be provided, and what their prices will be. A mixed economy is not the direct opposite of a free-market economy. Choice **c** is incorrect because a traditional economy is an economy in which the government and consumers decide what actions to take based on what the economy has been like in the past. A traditional economy is not the direct opposite of a free-market economy. Choice **d** is incorrect because a local economy is the economy of a specific location, such as a city or state. A local economy is not the direct opposite of a free-market economy.

64. d. The war ended when the United States Senate ratified the Treaty of Ghent, which both parties to the war had signed. Choice **a** is incorrect because the war began, not ended, when William Hull invaded Canada in 1812. Choice **b** is incorrect because the War of 1812 did not end when Andrew Jackson defeated the British in the Battle of New Orleans. Jackson engaged in battle with the British in January 1815 because he was not aware that the two nations had already signed the Treaty of Ghent. Choice **c** is incorrect because the Creeks' surrender did not end the conflict between Great Britain and the United States.

65. b. Citizens must serve on a jury if the jurisdiction has selected them for that purpose. Choice **a** is incorrect because citizens do not have to serve on a jury because they pay taxes. Choice **c** is incorrect because citizens do not have to serve on a jury because they are registered for the Selective Service System. The Selective Service System refers to the system through which U.S. citizens who are males age 18 or over register to be part of the United States military. Choice **d** is incorrect because citizens do not have to serve on a jury because they vote.

66. b. The French territory as a whole in North America was known as New France. Choice **a** is incorrect because Acadia was only one of the colonies of the larger French territory. Choice **c** is incorrect because Montreal is a city in Canada, not the whole territory that the French colonized in North America. Choice **d** is incorrect because Nova Scotia is a Canadian province on the southeast coast of Canada, not the whole territory that the French colonized in North America.

67. a. Based on the suppression of the Whiskey Rebellion, George Washington was able to force distillers into paying the whiskey tax and fine persons involved in the rebellion. Choice **b** is incorrect because Washington's Continental Army defeated groups of rebel forces who did not want to pay the whiskey tax. Choice **c** is incorrect because the whiskey tax was eventually repealed in 1803, about nine years after the Whiskey Rebellion. Choice **d** is incorrect because the purpose of the whiskey tax was to reduce the national debt. When President Washington forced the Pennsylvania distillers to pay the whiskey tax, the national debt was not increased.

68. c. A monetary union involves two or more countries sharing the same currency. Choice **a** is incorrect because a monetary union involves two or more countries merging their forms of currency, not one country merging its own denominations of notes. Choice **b** is incorrect because the die creating a coin is an act that creates money, but does not have to do with the creation of a monetary union. Choice **d** is incorrect because a monetary union does not involve a country using siege money, a form of currency issued during wartime when the normal type of cash is no longer available.

69. a. Without setting up proper goals in advance of the data-gathering process, it can be overwhelming and difficult to find the appropriate information for research. While the strategies listed in choices **b** and **c** may be effective, the first step would be to set clear goals. The strategy for choice **d** sounds like something that would follow the data-gathering process.

70. c. Chinese officials were angered by Britain's success in importing opium into China from India. The act of importing and selling opium in China opened Chinese ports to the British. Choice **a** is incorrect because the Opium Wars centered on Britain's attempts to secretly import opium from British India into China. China was concerned that its citizens were becoming addicted to the drug, and resented Britain's intrusion into its economic affairs. Choice **b** is incorrect because the Chinese were not concerned with Chinese opium being sold abroad. Choice **d** is incorrect because the Chinese were not concerned with American opium entering China.

71. d. The Treaty of Guadalupe Hidalgo, which was ratified in 1848, involved the cession of these two large Mexican territories to the United States. This treaty completely ended the Mexican-American War. Choice **a** is incorrect because the Adams-Onís Treaty, ratified in 1819, allowed the United States to purchase Florida from Spain. Choice **b** is incorrect because the Treaty of San Francisco, ratified in 1951, was a peace treaty made between the Allied powers and Japan. Choice **c** is incorrect because the Treaty of Alliance, ratified in 1778, concerned the alliance of the colonies participating in the American Revolution with France.

72. b. A poll is going to be most effective if it poses questions to the broadest possible audience. It also must ensure that the people who are involved in the poll would be eligible to vote. That's why **a**, inside an elementary school, is not the best location. Asking the question on several random streets would ensure that there is a cross-section of people answering and no one particular location would skew the results too greatly. The location listed in choice **c** would greatly influence the results and create a potential for bias. A restaurant may seem unbiased, but if it is very expensive the only people who will answer the poll may be wealthy voters, which can also create bias in the results.

73. c. The Chinese Exclusion Act, a federal piece of legislation, is the pertinent act. It placed a significant hardship on Chinese immigrants already in the United States by limiting the growth of the Chinese-American community. Choice **a** is incorrect because Executive Order 9066, enacted in 1942, allowed President Roosevelt to intern Americans of Japanese descent during World War II. Choice **b** is incorrect because California's new constitution, approved by the state's voters in 1879, did not limit Chinese immigration to the United States. Choice **d** is incorrect because the Geary Act, passed in 1892, was a renewal of the Chinese Exclusion Act.

74. d. Joseph McCarthy used government hearings and intelligence agents to question many people as to whether they were members of the Communist Party. He was attempting to determine whether they were aiding the Soviets in the Cold War. Choice **a** is incorrect because the House Un-American Activities Committee was the government body that investigated many actors, directors, and politicians accused of being Communists. Choice **b** is incorrect because McCarthy questioned people about Communism, not their service in the military during World War II. Choice **c** is incorrect because McCarthy did not use government hearings to question people about popular music.

75. c. Women in all states won the right to vote when the Nineteenth Amendment to the United States Constitution was ratified in 1920. Choice **a** is incorrect because although the Seneca Falls Convention, an early women's suffrage convention, took place in 1848, this event did not award American women the right to vote. Choice **b** is incorrect because 1944 was the year that French women were granted the right to vote by an ordinance of the French provisional government. American women won the right to vote 24 years earlier in 1920. Choice **d** is incorrect because in 1756 Lydia Taft, a woman, voted in three New England town meetings, yet the majority of women in the region were not allowed to vote.

76. b. Lines of longitude set 15 degrees apart define the 24 time zones on Earth. Choice **a** is incorrect because the Prime Meridian in Greenwich, England, is only one of the lines of longitude that define time zones. Choice **c** is incorrect because the equator, like other lines of latitude, does not determine the boundaries of time zones. Choice **d** is incorrect because satellite images do not play a major role in defining time zones.

77. a. Topographical maps are drawn to show features of land. The curved lines on a topographical map, called contour lines, reflect changes in elevation. While topographical maps can include other data, such as population and natural resources, the contour lines represent the elevation of the land.

78. b. The exhibition of wealth earned the Gilded Age its nickname. Several businessmen who exemplified the period's "robber baron" were J.P. Morgan, Andrew Carnegie, and Henry Flagler. Choice **a** is incorrect because although many newspapers published sensational stories, which constituted the practice of yellow journalism, this practice had nothing to do with the nickname for the era. Choice **c** is incorrect because there were only gold rushes in California and Alaska. These occurred in 1849 and during the 1890s. The gold rushes provided many businessmen with the funds for bigger investments, such as the transcontinental railroad, but they were not the phenomenon that earned the Gilded Age its nickname. Choice **d** is incorrect because the federal government refused to abandon the gold standard in 1896 even in the face of aggressive speeches by Congressman William Jennings Bryan.

79. d. Duke William, also known as William the Conqueror, brought to his kingdom the feudal system from France. In this system, tenants were granted the right to live and produce crops on land by farming it primarily for the benefit of the landowner. Choice **a** is incorrect because communal ownership involves everyone who lives in the land possessing a right to the property. In medieval Europe, wealthy parties owned property under the rule of the king. Poorer farmers did not own the land on which they lived and worked. Choice **b** is incorrect because land grants are an institution common in Islamic countries, not a type of land ownership system in medieval Europe. With a land grant, or waqf, a charitable organization such as a school or mosque received an undetermined, continued right to use the land. Choice **c** is incorrect because cash tenancy involves renters paying a set amount for the land that they rent. This was not a system of land ownership in medieval England.

80. b. Mount Vesuvius is one of the most dangerous volcanoes in the world, with about 3 million people living in its vicinity. The volcano remains active, so residents should not continue development on the volcano, choice **a**, or classify it as inactive, choice **d**. They have no reason to seek out additional volcanoes, choice **c**. The best advice is to continue to monitor the volcano and improve warning and evacuation processes for an eventual eruption, choice **b**.

81. b. Bank loans, especially from institutions such as the World Bank, have often aided poorer countries in producing cash crops. Typically, such institutions lend money to a nation's government at a low commercial interest rate with strict conditions attached. The government then grants money to agricultural producers through various public and private channels. Choice **a** is incorrect because international drug enforcement teams do not assist poorer countries in producing cash crops. Choice **c** is incorrect because donated medical supplies do not directly assist poorer countries with producing cash crops. Choice **d** is incorrect because credit cards do not assist poorer countries with producing cash crops. This is because credit cards are usually given to individuals by banks. Typically, the banks of poorer countries do not have enough money to issue credit cards to people who might be unable to pay their bills.

82. b. Douglass became widely known for his denunciation of slavery and his assistance of those working to end it. During the 1840s, he made a series of speeches against slavery, wrote his autobiography, and traveled to England to make antislavery speeches there. Choice **a** is incorrect because Douglass was not the author of the Thirteenth Amendment. The Thirteenth Amendment, which abolished slavery, was coauthored by congressmen James Mitchell Ashley (R-OH), James Walconer Wilson (R-IA), and Senator John B. Henderson (D-MO). Choice **c** is incorrect because Douglass served as an adviser under President Lincoln during the Civil War. He did not serve as a general in Lincoln's Union Army. Choice **d** is incorrect because Douglass was never a slaveholder.

83. a. This is the correct definition of cartography. The field encompasses all methods of making graphical representations of Earth. Choice **b** is incorrect because the discipline of cartography involves maps of any type, such as paper, rock, and clay maps, as well as digital maps. Choice **c** is incorrect because cartography does not focus on determining official land, water, and airspace boundaries through measurements. This is the job of surveyors. Choice **d** is incorrect because cartography involves charting the seas, but is not solely about navigating the world's oceans.

84. c. In the case *Trop v. Dulles* (1958), the U.S. Supreme Court held that this punishment was cruel and unusual. Choice **a** is incorrect. The United States allows states to impose the death penalty. Choice **b** is incorrect. In 1980, the United States Supreme Court upheld a life sentence for fraud crimes for the amount of $230. Choice **d** is incorrect. The United States allows states to impose economic fines.

85. a. The Great Irish Famine devastated the Irish population between 1845 and 1852. As a result of the hardship to the Irish population, about a million Irish emigrated from the island nation. Many of those crossed the Atlantic Ocean to begin new lives in the United States, mostly in the large cities. There is no support for the statement in choices **b**, **c**, or **d**.

86. d. Hawaii was not only formed as a result of volcanic activity, but continues to be reformed and reshaped due to continual volcanic eruptions. The chain of islands that form the state of Hawaii is comprised of a series of volcanoes, many of which are still active.

87. d. West Germany and East Germany were reunified in 1990, following about 45 years of division. Hitler's invasion of the Soviet Union, choice **a**, occurred in 1941, before the division. The rise of the Third Reich, choice **b**, associated with the rise of the Nazi Party, occurred in the 1930s. Napoleon Bonaparte died in 1821, so his fall, choice **c**, was not responsible for the reunification of Germany in 1990. It was the dismantling of the Iron Curtain, the division between the two countries, in 1989, that led directly to the country's reunification.

88. a. It is the Inuit population that is known for being a unique and well-developed culture in the Arctic regions of North America. While many live in the Canadian territory of Nunavik, others still reside in the North Slope of Alaska and the Siberian Coast. The other three native populations listed in choices **b**, **c**, and **d** are not known for residing as far north on the continent: The Anasazi population culture was known for residing in the American southwest; The Iroquois lived in the northeastern United States; and the Mound Builders lived in the Great Lakes and Ohio Valley regions of the American Midwest.

89. b. Nuclear power is one of the most effective ways to generate energy. However, it has its drawbacks. The disposal and storage of the spent fuel, or the waste, remains an ongoing concern, so choice **a** is not correct. The release of radioactivity, choice **c**, is always a concern—even though there has not been a significant leak in the United States in many years. Nuclear reactors require large amounts of water for cooling, which has the effect of warming the local waterways, choice **d**. This is not an insignificant environmental concern. The creation of greenhouse gasses is not associated as a byproduct of nuclear reactors, so choice **b** is correct.

90. c. A peninsula is a land mass that is surrounded on water by three sides, such as Florida. The definition in choice **b** defines an archipelago. The definitions in choices **a** and **d** are not associated with peninsulas.

Science Answers

91. c. This question provides a definition of seismology. Geology, choice **a**, is the study of Earth, the materials of which it is made, and the processes acting upon them. Vulcanology, choice **b**, is the study of volcanoes, and audiology, choice **d**, is the study of hearing balance and related disorders.

92. a. The Hawaiian Islands are the result of hot spots, large isolated chimneylike columns of rising hot rock coming to the surface. Landmasses created by this process are known as volcanic islands. Choices **b** and **c** are incorrect as these are not characteristics that define this volcanic chain of islands. Choice **d** is incorrect, as the islands have no impact on the volcanic activity that creates them.

93. b. Mitosis, choice **b**, is cell duplication or reproduction that involves the production of two identical daughter cells from the division of one parent cell. Mitotic division occurs when an organism needs to grow more cells and/or repair or replace cells or tissues. Choice **a** is incorrect because meiosis is a special kind of cell reproduction that results in the production two non-identical daughter cells from a single parent cell. Meiotic division results in daughter cells that have half the genetic material of the parent cell. Gamete formation, choice **c**, which is the generation of male and female cells, is the result of meiosis and therefore incorrect. Choice **d**, fertilization, is the joining of two gametes, each of which is generated by meiotic division. This is therefore incorrect.

94. b. A telescope is a device that focuses and concentrates radiation from distant objects. A microscope, choice **a**, is designed to magnify objects smaller than the naked eye's detection capabilities in close proximity. A gyroscope, choice **c**, is a device with a spinning mass that can turn freely in multiple directions, thereby always maintaining its orientation. A Geiger counter, choice **d**, is an instrument that detects radiation and measures its intensity.

95. a. Neutralization does not represent the conversion of a substance from one state of matter to another. Neutralization refers to the reaction of an acid with a base to produce pure water. Choices **b**, **c**, and **d** refer to different changes of state. The three states of matter are solid, liquid, and gas. Choice **b**, vaporization, refers to the transformation of a substance from a liquid to a gas. Choice **c**, melting, refers to a solid-to-liquid transformation. Choice **d**, condensation, refers to a gas-to-liquid transformation.

96. c. These particles, emitted by the sun, start to glow and manifest as an array of colors in the sky. Choice **b** describes a solar eclipse, which occurs when the moon passes between the sun and Earth so that the sun is wholly or partially blocked. Choice **a** occurs when small pieces of ancient space debris fall into Earth's atmosphere. Choices **a**, **b**, and **d** have no contribution to the formation of the colors in the northern sky known as northern lights.

97. d. According to the Bohr model of the atom, an electron is a negatively charged subatomic particle that orbits the atom's nucleus. Choice **a** is incorrect because a molecule is not a subatomic particle; it is a group of atoms bonded together. Choice **b**, the neutron, is an uncharged subatomic particle that forms part of the atom's nucleus. Choice **c**, the proton, is a positively charged subatomic particle that forms part of the nucleus along with the neutron.

98. b. Carbohydrates are a class of molecules that play a central role in the way that living organisms acquire and use energy. Choices **a** and **d** are incorrect because fat, which is a type of the larger class of molecules called lipids, provide long-term energy storage. Choice **c** is incorrect because proteins are a class of molecules with various functions, but none of those functions involves their use as an energy source.

99. d. The graph compares only the relative percentage of the total population of the specific country who are overweight. It does not provide actual numbers of individuals. Therefore, choices **b** and **c** cannot be determined. Choice **a** is incorrect because the bar graph shows that fewer than 10% of Spanish men are overweight as compared to approximately 10% of Spanish women.

100. d. The core, choice **a**, which is the center of the earth, is comprised of the metals nickel and iron. The outer layer of the core, which is under less pressure than the inner core, but at a similar temperature, exists in a liquefied state, choice **b**. Choice **c** describes the crust, the outermost layer of Earth comprised of rock.

101. a. The Punnett square is a grid that represents all the possible genotypic combinations in the F2 generation produced by a male (gametes listed horizontally) and a female (gametes listed vertically).

102. a. This question provides the definition of weather. Climate, choice **b**, is the long-term average of weather for a given region. Temperature, choice **c**, reflects how vigorously atoms in a substance move and collide. Pressure, choice **d**, is the force on a surface divided by the area of the surface.

103. a. A trophic level reflects the sequential step in matter and energy in a food web. The steps move from producers to primary, secondary, and tertiary consumers. As the cow's primary source of nourishment is a plant (grass), it is the animal in this group that is at the second trophic level. Choices **b** and **c** are incorrect as both killer whales and lions are tertiary consumers. Choice **d** is incorrect because a pine tree is the producer, or first trophic level.

104. c. This question provides the definition of a battery. Choice **a**, a telescope, is incorrect because it is a device that focuses and concentrates radiation from distant objects. A gyroscope, choice **b**, is incorrect, because it is a device with a spinning mass that can turn freely in multiple directions, thereby always maintaining its orientation. A prism, choice **d**, is not known for the storage of chemical energy.

105. d. Meiosis results in four reproductive cells, each with half the number of chromosomes found in the parent cell. This is often confused with mitosis, the result of which is two daughter cells with the same number of chromosomes as the parent cell.

106. b. Producers, choice **a**, are organisms that produce their own food from sources like the sun, such as plants. A lion cannot produce its own food, so choice **a** is not correct. Consumers are organisms that consume other organisms for their food. This is how a lion creates its energy, so choice **b** is correct. An herbivore, choice **c**, does not specify how an organism creates its energy, but it specifies that it only eats plants—which is not true for the lion. A decomposer, choice **d**, is an organism that breaks down dead organisms or other waste. This does not describe a lion, so choice **d** is not correct.

107. a. A periodic table always lists the symbol for each known element, choice **d**, and the number of protons in the atomic nucleus, choice **c**. Most also include the atomic weight, choice **b**. However, the periodic table is about the individual elements—not the compounds formed by two or more elements. Therefore, choice **a** is correct.

108. b. Diatomic oxygen is a molecule comprised of two atoms of oxygen. This represented by O_2, the notation listed in choice **b**. The notation listed in choice **c**, H_2O, represents water. The notation listed in choice **d**, O_3, represents ozone.

109. a. The mass of an object does not change depending on a gravitational force acting on it. Even when there is no gravity, the mass of a 100-kg person would remain 100 kg. Therefore, choice **a** is correct and choice **d** is not correct. Weight, however, *is* influenced by gravitational forces. A person on Earth will have a greater weight than he or she would have on the Moon. Therefore, choices **b** and **c** are incorrect.

110. d. The Grand Canyon was formed in large part by dirt and rocks being removed by a combination of ice, water, and wind. The combination of these actions is called erosion, choice **d**.

111. c. The kidneys perform a vital role in the excretory system of the human body. The digestive system, choice **a**, includes organs like the stomach and the small intestine. The endocrine system, choice **b**, deals mostly with the glands that secrete hormones. The circulatory system, choice **d**, involved the flow of blood and includes the heart and arteries.

112. c. The most commonly accepted age for planet Earth is about 4.5 billion years, choice **c**. Choice **d**, 13.75 billion years, represents the approximate age of the universe, according to current theory.

113. d. Pure substances have a uniform chemical composition throughout, while mixtures are a blend of two or more substances. The only pure substance among the choices is copper, which is a single element. Choice **a**, blood, is a mixture of components, including plasma, red blood cells, and white blood cells. Choice **b**, soil, is a highly heterogeneous mixture of geological and biological materials. Choice **c**, wood, is a biological material that is also highly heterogeneous in physical and chemical composition.

114. a. The description from this question accurately defines osmosis, choice **a**. None of the other terms in answer choices **b**, **c**, or **d** involve the passage of water molecules through the membrane.

115. a. Any plant will produce oxygen. Phytoplankton are incredible small plants that produce immense amounts of oxygen. While they are too small to see with the naked eye, they are responsible for about half of the oxygen in our planet's atmosphere. The creatures listed in answer choices **b**, **c**, and **d** all represent a type of animal life, which consumes oxygen.

116. d. The lowest layer of Earth's atmosphere, which begins at the surface, is the troposphere. This layer contains most of the mass of the atmosphere, including the oxygen that human beings require. The exosphere, choice **a**, is the uppermost layer of the atmosphere. The mesosphere, choice **c**, is below that, and the stratosphere, choice **b**, is below the mesosphere. None of these other layers contain enough oxygen for human beings to survive.

117. c. Kinetic energy is energy that is being transferred from stored energy due to motion. Of all the events in the answer choices, only choice **c** represents a situation in which the energy is being released as a result of motion. The scenarios in choices **a** and **b** represent potential energy.

118. b. Commensalism, **a**, is a relationship where only one of the species benefits and the other neither benefits nor is harmed. Mutualism, choice **b**, describes the relationship of the clownfish and the anemone because both organisms benefit. Competition, choice **c**, describes a relationship between two species in which the population of one will go down when the other goes up; that is not the case in this scenario. Choice **d**, parasitism, describes a relationship in which one organism benefits and the other is harmed.

119. b. Tsunami may be referred to as tidal waves, but tides have nothing to do with them. Therefore, choice **a** is not correct. A tsunami may be caused by a disruption in the water, such as an earthquake or a landslide. Tectonic uplift, for example, would create a disturbance on the sea floor and release enough energy to produce a tsunami. Weather events do not play a role in the creation of a tsunami, so choices **c** and **d** are not correct.

120. a. Venus has many similarities to Earth. It has a solid surface, unlike some of the gaseous planets in the solar system, so choice **b** is not correct. It also has a very dense atmosphere, so choice **c** is not correct. Venus and Earth are nearly the same size and have similar gravitational forces, so choice **d** is not correct, either. Venus has no known moon, so that is one way that Earth and Venus are NOT alike, making choice **a** the correct choice.

CHAPTER 3

READING/ LANGUAGE ARTS REVIEW

The first section of the Praxis II: Elementary Education: Content Knowledge test is the Reading/Language Arts section. Of the 120 questions on the test, 30 will cover material from the Reading/ Language Arts section.

About the Reading/Language Arts Section

The Reading/Language Arts section of the Praxis II: Elementary Education: Content Knowledge test covers a variety of content-based and pedagogical-based knowledge. Test takers will be expected to be familiar with the structures of texts and the elements of literature, as well as the strategies, practices, and theories for students to build their literacy and communication abilities. In other words, the test ensures that future teachers not only possess the knowledge base that is required to be an elementary school teacher, but also the teaching methods to impart this knowledge to students at the elementary level.

About half of the questions on the Reading/Language Arts section will be based on a short passage. The passage may be given from a range of possible selections, including poems or children's literature.

The five major areas of the Reading/Language Arts section are as follows:

- understanding literature
- text structure and organization for reading and writing
- literacy acquisition and reading instruction
- language in writing
- communication skills

The elements of each major area are explained in detail in the following five sections.

Understanding Literature

As an elementary-level educator, you will be working with students who are beginning to understand a variety of texts. Young students should be exposed to a wide range of literature. It is therefore critical that you have knowledge of the different types of literature and their various purposes.

This section focuses on four different types of literature, each of which students will be exposed to at the elementary level.

- narrative
- nonfiction
- poetry
- resource and research material

Each type of literature is explained in the following four sections. The **elements** of literature will be explained later.

Narratives

A **narrative** is a type of literature that tells a story. Narratives are associated with fictional writing, which means that the story is invented, with made-up characters and an imaginary plot. (You can read about nonfictional literature beginning on page 64.) There are many types of narrative literature, including many examples of popular children's literature. On the Content Knowledge test, you may be given an example from a type of literature and be asked to identify the genre it represents.

A novel is a popular type of narrative, but there are many others. The following list defines more than a dozen different types of narratives. Read through the list and be prepared to recognize samples on the test.

Adventure fiction provides a great deal of action (often violent). A fictional military-based narrative may be considered adventure fiction.

A **fable** is a story that uses animals or plants to provide a moral lesson. The animals, which can include mythical creatures, are anthropomorphized, meaning that they have human characteristics.

Fantasy fiction involves an invented world, such as J.R.R. Tolkien's Middle Earth in the *Lord of the Rings* series.

Fairy tales are a type of folk tale that contain elements of magic or magical beings, such as a fairy or dragon. As such, they usually contain far-fetched stories. They often contain a moral.

A **folk tale** is a traditional story that can date back many centuries. Many folk tales were originally passed down orally.

Historical fiction includes fictional stories based around historical events. A made-up love story that occurs during the Civil War or on the Titanic would be representative of historical fiction.

A **legend** is a story that, while based on a supposed event in human history, is most likely a fictional tale. Legends do not contain unbelievable events, such as magic, but that does not mean they should be believed.

A **myth** is like a fairy tale, but instead of including magical elements such as fairies, it usually includes a god or hero to explain a phenomenon.

Mystery fiction involves stories where the characters attempt to find information. The discovery occurs at the climax of the book. Detective mysteries are the most common type of mystery books.

A **novel** is a lengthy narrative that only includes fictional context. The novel is usually considerably longer than other types of narratives.

A **play** is a type of literature that is intended to be interpreted on the stage by actors. Examples of literary plays include comedies and tragedies written by William Shakespeare. Plays may be acted out as **story theater** for children, or even as **puppetry**.

Science fiction is a type of narrative that takes place in the future. As a result, the setting plays a large role, as do the science and technology of the future.

A **short story** has the same structure as a novel but is much shorter, as its name suggests.

There are seven major elements of a story that you should consider for the Praxis II: Elementary Education: Content Knowledge test: the plot, characters, setting, tone, point of view, perspective, organization, and theme. You may see questions about any one of these elements on the test.

Plot

Plot refers to the series of events in a story—the order in which the actions take place. A story's plot always revolves around some kind of *conflict*. The conflict may be between two characters, between the main character and an idea or force (e.g., nature or racism), or between the character and him- or herself.

Plot is often arranged **chronologically** (in time order), but authors sometimes vary the order of events to help build suspense and to control how much we know about the characters. For example, an author may use **flashbacks** to describe events that took place earlier in the time line of the action—events that might help us understand the character and his or her traits or motivations.

Plots usually follow a five-part "pyramid" pattern, though the pyramid should be lopsided, since the climax typically occurs near the end of the story.

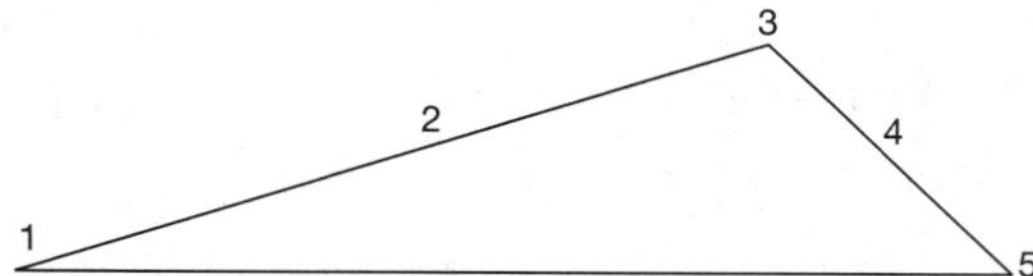

1. **Exposition** introduces readers to the people, places, and basic circumstances or situation of the story.
2. **Complication** (sometimes referred to as "rising action") is the series of events that complicate the story and build up to the climax.
3. **Climax** is the high point of the story, the moment of greatest tension (the peak of the pyramid). This is often the turning point of the story, when a character must make a difficult decision or take some kind of action.
4. **Falling action** occurs when the missing pieces of the puzzle are filled in (for example, secrets are revealed, mysteries solved, confessions made). The story settles down.
5. **Resolution** or **denouement** is the conclusion of the story, in which conflicts are resolved (at least to some degree), questions are answered, and characters are set to move on with a new understanding or under new circumstances.

Characters

Characters are the people created by the author to tell the story. They perform the actions, speak the words, and convey the ideas of the story. As readers, we see what the characters think, do, and say, and we try to understand why they think, do, and say these things. Characters can be round or flat. **Round characters** are fully developed, complex, three-dimensional creatures. They are dynamic characters who embody contradictions and undergo change or growth of some sort throughout the story. **Flat characters**, on the other hand, are one-dimensional, undeveloped, and static. They are typically defined by one main characteristic and do not change. They are often *stereotypes* or *symbolic*. Just as every story has a conflict, every story has a protagonist and an antagonist. The **protagonist** is the hero or main character of the story, the one who faces the conflict and undergoes change. The **antagonist** is the person, force (such as a disease or natural disaster), or idea (such as prejudice or crippling self-doubt) that works against the protagonist.

In fiction, characters reveal themselves through **dialogue** and **action**. In dialogue, characters tell us what they think, feel, and believe. Dialogue may include the use of a specific **dialect** or **slang**. How a character talks can provide information about the character's background (for example, a Southern dialect may mean that a character grew up in the South) and education (for example, a character who speaks with a highly sophisticated vocabulary may have spent several years in an institution of higher learning). Action undertaken by characters moves the story forward while creating dynamic, rounded characters.

Setting

The **setting** is the *time* and *place* in which the story unfolds. This gives the story a particular social and historical context. What was happening in the world at that time? What was happening in that particular place at that time? The setting of a narrative can be described through details of not only the visual scenery but also the smells and sounds, among other things.

Remember that the setting of a piece of fiction is not the same as the publication date. Many stories written during contemporary times have settings dating back hundreds of years. When considering the setting, we should consider the political, social, and overall historical contexts of the time and place. For example, if a story takes place in 1762 in Boston, there are certain historical expectations. You can expect tensions to be high between Americans and the British. You can expect certain details of daily life, such as carriages, torches, and outhouses. If the story does not meet those expectations (if, for example, a character rides into town in a convertible), you need to consider why the author has broken those expectations. Setting can be specific or universal. Some stories, for example, can take place anywhere and any time; the plot and characters are not unique to any historical circumstances.

Other stories, like a story of the American Revolution, must take place in a certain place and time. Some of the story's themes (e.g., the importance of freedom) are considered universal.

Tone

Setting is often important in creating the tone of the story. **Tone** is the mood or attitude conveyed in the writing. For example, notice how Edgar Allan Poe uses setting to establish an appropriately gloomy tone for his horror tale *The Fall of the House of Usher*:

> During the whole of a dull, dark, and soundless day in the autumn of the year, when the clouds hung oppressively low in the heavens, I had been passing alone, on horseback, through a singularly dreary tract of country; and at length found myself, as the shades of the evening drew on, within view of the melancholy House of Usher.

Poe's word choices—*dull, dark, soundless, oppressively, alone, dreary, melancholy*—work together to create a dark and somewhat mysterious tone for the story.

Often the most important tone in fiction is irony. **Situational irony** occurs when there is incongruity between what is expected to happen and what actually occurs. For example, in Guy de Maupassant's classic short story "The Necklace," Madame Loisel spends ten years of her life struggling to pay off the debt she owes for a necklace she bought to replace the one she had borrowed from a friend and lost. In the last lines of the story, Madame Loisel runs into that old friend and learns that she sacrificed in vain:

> "You remember the diamond necklace you lent me for the ball at the Ministry?"
>
> "Yes. Well?"
>
> "Well, I lost it."
>
> "How could you? Why, you brought it back."
>
> "I brought you another one just like it. And for the last ten years we have been paying for it. You realize it wasn't easy for us; we had no money. . . . Well, it's paid for at last, and I'm glad indeed."
>
> Madame Forestier had halted.
>
> "You say you bought a diamond necklace to replace mine?"
>
> "Yes. You hadn't noticed it? They were very much alike."
>
> And she smiled in proud and innocent happiness.
>
> Madame Forestier, deeply moved, took her two hands.
>
> "Oh, my poor Mathilde! But mine was imitation. It was worth at the very most five hundred francs! . . ."

Point of View / Perspective

Point of view refers to the person who is telling us the story. All stories have a **narrator**—the person who describes the characters and events. Note: The author is NOT the narrator. In fiction, the narrator is always a character created by the author to tell the tale.

A **first-person narrator** tells the story from his or her own point of view using *I*. With this point of view, you see and hear the story from someone directly involved in the action. This is a very subjective and personal point of view. Here's an example:

> I wiped my eyes and looked in the mirror. I was surprised at what I saw. I had on a beautiful red dress, but what I saw was even more valuable. I was strong. I was pure. I had genuine thoughts inside that no one could see, that no one could ever take away from me. I was like the wind.
>
> —Amy Tan, *The Joy Luck Club* (1989)

In a story told from the **second-person point of view**, the writer uses the pronoun *you*, and thus the reader becomes a character in the story, thinking the thoughts and performing the actions of the main character:

> Moss Watson, the man you truly love like no other, is singing December 23 in the Owonta Opera production of *Amahl and the Night Visitors*. He's playing Kaspar, the partially deaf Wise Man. Wisdom, says Moss, arrives in all forms. And you think, Yes, sometimes as a king and sometimes as a hesitant phone call that says the king'll be late at rehearsal and don't wait up, and then when you call back to tell him to be careful not to let the cat out when he comes home, you discover there's been no rehearsal there at all.
>
> —Lorrie Moore, "Amahl and the Night Visitors," from *Self Help* (1985)

With a **third-person narrator**, the author uses the pronouns he, she, and they to tell the story. This narrator is removed from the action, so the story is more objective. Third-person narrators are often **omniscient**: They know everything about the characters and tell us what the characters think and feel. Here's an example:

> To tell the truth, he found it at first rather hard to get used to these privations, but after a while

> it became a habit and went smoothly enough—he even became quite accustomed to being hungry in the evening; on the other hand, he had spiritual nourishment, for he carried ever in his thoughts the idea of his future overcoat. His whole existence had in a sense become fuller, as though he had married, as though some other person were present with him, as though he were no longer alone, but an agreeable companion had consented to walk the path of life hand in hand with him, and that companion was no other than the new overcoat with its thick wadding and its strong, durable lining.
>
> —Nikolai Gogol, "The Overcoat" (1842)

Third-person narration can also be **limited**. This means the author still uses the third-person pronouns (*he, she, they*), but only imparts the thoughts and feelings of one character in the story. In this way, third-person limited point of view is very similar to first-person narration, but it does not give as intimate a feeling as first-person narration does.

The point of view of the story may also include the **perspective**, which can be considered the narrator's attitude throughout the story.

Organization

The many different ways that text is organized are explained in the section "Text Structure and Organization for Reading and Writing." The list of organizational structures for both nonfiction and fiction texts will be found on page 73.

Theme

All these elements add up to express the story's **theme**. To determine a theme, you have to evaluate the whole and consider the questions the story has raised, the points it has made, and the positions it has taken. Indeed, stories can have several themes. The key is to ask yourself what the story adds up to in the end. What seems to be the message the writer wants to convey through all that has occurred? What ideas can you take away from the characters and events you just experienced?

In *Frankenstein*, for example, you might state the themes this way:

- People must be responsible for what they create.
- We should not play God and attempt to control or overrule nature.
- Everyone needs to be loved, and we bring destruction on ourselves when we reject others.

All three of these themes and more come from the story—from all elements of fiction working together in the novel to convey the writer's ideas.

Nonfiction

Nonfiction literature is defined by a truth-based recount of actual events. Nonfiction texts deal with real people and real events. In nonfiction, there is no narrator, so there is no filter between the author and the reader. In a nonfiction text, the author is speaking to the reader directly, expressing his or her point of view. Thus, the voice in a nonfiction text is the unique voice of the author.

Common types of nonfiction literature include biographies and autobiographies, though they may also include essays, news articles, research papers, editorials, and reviews, as well as directions and manuals. You may be tested on the different types of essays and their purposes. The following section describes the different types of essays and also tells about the other common nonfiction text, autobiographies and memoirs.

There are many different types of **essays**. The four most common types are:

1. **descriptive:** describing a person, place, or thing
2. **narrative:** telling a story or describing an event
3. **expository:** exploring and explaining an idea or position
4. **persuasive:** arguing a specific point of view

There are essays about every imaginable topic, from what it is like to grow up poor (or rich, or bilingual) to why we should (or should not) clone human beings.

One type of writing that you may see in essays (as well as other forms of literature) is satire. **Satire** is a form of comedy in which the writer exposes and ridicules someone or something in order to inspire change. Satires rely heavily on **verbal irony**, in which the intended meaning is the opposite of the expressed meaning. Satirists also use **hyperbole**, which is extreme exaggeration, as well as sarcasm and understatement in order to convey their ideas.

Jonathan Swift's 1729 essay "A Modest Proposal" is one of the most famous examples of satire. In the essay, Swift proposes that the Irish, who are starving, eat their own children to prevent "the children of poor people in Ireland from being a burden to their parents or country." Here's a brief excerpt:

> I have been assured by a very knowing American of my acquaintance in London, that a young healthy child well nursed is at a year old a most delicious, nourishing, and wholesome food, whether stewed, roasted, baked or boiled; and I make no doubt that it will equally serve in a fricassee or ragout.

Of course, Swift is not really suggesting that the Irish become cannibals. He is using this ridiculous proposal to criticize the British for oppressing the Irish, especially poor Irish Catholics, who often had many children. The outrageous nature of Swift's proposal reflects his feelings about the absurdity of British rule in Ireland at the time and the British government's inability to find a satisfactory solution to the Irish famine.

In an **autobiography** or **memoir**, the author will—very subjectively, of course—tell the story of his or her life. The difference between autobiographies and memoirs is that memoirs tend to be less comprehensive and more exploratory—they will cover less ground and spend more time examining the impact of people and events. Authors may write to clarify an experience, teach a lesson, or make a statement about a historical event or social movement. As you read an autobiography or memoir, look for what the author feels has shaped him. Why has he chosen to relate these particular events, describe these particular people? For example, here is a brief excerpt from Frank McCourt's best-selling 1996 memoir, *Angela's Ashes*:

> Next day we rode to the hospital in a carriage with a horse. They put Oliver in a white box that came with us in the carriage and we took him to the graveyard. They put the white box into a hole in the ground and covered it with earth. My mother and Aunt Aggie cried, Grandma looked angry, Dad, Uncle Pa Keating, and Uncle Pat Sheehan looked sad but did not cry and I thought that if you're a man you can cry only when you have the black stuff that is called the pint. I did not like the jackdaws that perched on trees and gravestones and I did not want to leave Oliver with them. I threw a rock at a jackdaw that waddled over toward Oliver's grave. Dad said I shouldn't throw rocks at jackdaws, they might be somebody's soul. I didn't know what a soul was but I didn't ask him because I didn't care. Oliver was dead and I hated jackdaws. I'd be a man someday and I'd come back with a bag of rocks and I'd leave the graveyard littered with dead jackdaws.

Journal writing, or **journaling**, is a personal type of writing that requires a student to write down his or her thoughts with a degree of regular frequency. This free form of writing provides a student a terrific opportunity to translate his or her experiences to paper.

On the Praxis II: Elementary Education: Content Knowledge test, you may be given a short nonfiction passage and be asked about one of the following attributes of the nonfiction literary text:

- inferences/conclusions
- main idea/primary purpose
- information clarity/organization
- point of view/perspective

You may see questions about any of these attributes of a nonfiction literary text. Each is explained in the following sections.

Inferences/Conclusions

Inference questions on the Praxis II: Elementary Education: Content Knowledge test will ask you to make an inference, or draw a logical conclusion, about what you read. Sometimes a writer does not explicitly state the main idea or offer a conclusion. The reader must infer the writer's meaning. To make an inference, you need to look for clues in the context of the passage.

The trick to making inferences on passages on the test is finding the answer choice that is supported. The exact answer will not be spelled out exactly, but the author's position should be clear.

Inference questions may ask you to identify the author's assumptions and attitudes and evaluate the weaknesses and strengths of the author's argument or logic. To determine a writer's underlying assumptions or attitude, you need to look for clues in the context of the passage. One revealing clue to the writer's meaning is his word choice.

Word choice, also called **diction**, is the specific language the writer uses to describe people, places, and things. Word choice includes these forms:

- particular words or phrases a writer uses
- the way words are arranged in a sentence
- repetition of words or phrases
- inclusion of particular details

Writers can reveal their attitude toward a subject through the use of positive or negative expressions. Additionally, an author's style can alert you to his or her underlying message. **Style** is the distinctive way in which a writer uses language to inform or promote an idea. Lastly, writers who want to persuade a reader of something may rely on emotional language. **Emotional language** targets a reader's emotions—fears, beliefs, values, prejudices—instead of appealing to a reader's reason or critical thinking. Just as advertising often uses emotional language to sell a product, writers use emotional appeals to sell an idea.

Try the following inference question, based on a passage about Jane Austen.

> Jane Austen died in 1817, leaving behind six novels that have since become English classics. Most Austen biographers accept the image of Jane Austen as a sheltered spinster who knew little of life beyond the drawing rooms of her Hampshire village. They accept the claim of Austen's brother, Henry: "My dear sister's life was not a life of events."
>
> Biographer Claire Tomalin takes this view to task. She shows that Jane's short life was indeed tumultuous. Not only did Austen experience romantic love (briefly, with an Irishman), but her many visits to London and her relationships with her brothers (who served in the Napoleonic wars) widened her knowledge beyond her rural county, and even beyond England. Tomalin also argues that Austen's unmarried status benefited her ability to focus on her writing. I believe that Jane herself may have viewed it that way. Although her family destroyed most of her letters, one relative recalled that "some of her [Jane's] letters, triumphing over married women of her acquaintance, and rejoicing in her freedom, were most amusing."

1. The passage suggests that Jane Austen
- **a.** never left the comfort of her Hampshire village.
- **b.** may have enjoyed being unmarried.
- **c.** did not get along with her brothers.
- **d.** wished that she had married the Irishman.

To solve this inference problem, you need to choose the answer choice that is most supported by the passage. Because the passage mentions that Jane Austen had "many visits to London," it is not true that she never left her village, choice **a**. There is nothing in the passage to support the idea that she did not get along with her brothers, choice **b**. The relative mentions at the end of the passage that Austen wrote letters "triumphing over married women" and "rejoicing in her freedom." You can infer from those statements that she may have enjoyed being unmarried, choice **b**—and that she did not wish to marry the Irishman, choice **d**.

Main Idea/Primary Purpose

Even if the writer is describing an experience in a nonfiction text, he or she has a reason for telling that story, and that reason—why the writer thinks the story is important enough to tell— is the main idea. Essays will often make their main idea clear in a **thesis statement**. This statement is likely to come at the beginning of the essay. Notice here how the author states his thesis at the end of the opening paragraph of his essay.

> When you think of former president Bill Clinton, what's the first thing that comes to mind? Unfortunately, for many people, the first thing they think of is Monica Lewinsky. Like millions of people around the globe, I was horrified by how much the Whitewater investigation delved into Mr. Clinton's private affairs. No one needed to know the sort of details that were revealed by Ken Starr's investigation. But while I don't want to know the details, *I do believe we have a right to know what sort of lives our politicians are living. I believe their behavior in private is a reflection of their true values and how they will behave in office.*

The purposes of a nonfiction text can vary. It may simply be to inform the reader of some knowledge or to analyze some data, but it may be more biased than that. A political speech, a letter to the editor, and a newspaper editorial are common examples of nonfiction texts. Those have very specific purposes. The author of those texts will likely appeal to the reader's reasoning or emotions in order to persuade him or her to share the same beliefs.

Informational Clarity/Organization

For a nonfiction text, organization can play an important role in getting the information across. If the structure isn't easy to understand, then the reader can end up confused. Test questions may ask you for ways to improve the clarity of a nonfiction passage. For example, the passage may introduce a term but not define it; a definition would improve the clarity of the passage's message.

See page 73 for the list of organizational structures and a more in-depth look at the types of common organizational structures for both nonfiction and fiction texts.

Point of View/Perspective

Point of view is important in nonfiction. Remember, point of view establishes a certain relationship with the reader. First-person texts are more personal but also more subjective. Third-person texts are more objective but less personal. The point of view an author chooses will depend on his or her purpose and audience. For example, an annual report would likely use the third person, which is appropriate for a formal business document, while an essay about a personal experience would probably use the first-person point of view and explore the impact of that experience on the writer.

Poetry

Poetry is often easy to recognize but not as easy to define. Poems are usually short, and often rhyme, but not always. The beauty (and, for many, the difficulty) of poetry is its brevity. The writer must convey an idea or emotion in a very short space. Because there are so few words in a poem, every word counts, and poems are often layered with meaning. That's where a poem gets its power.

One fundamental difference between poetry and prose is structure. Poems, of course, are written in verse. They are meant to be *heard* as well as read. The meaning in a poem comes not just from the words, but also from how the words *sound* and how they are arranged on the page.

While poems are often categorized by structure, a more fundamental way to classify poems is by their general purpose. Poems can be emotive, imagistic, narrative, and argumentative. They can also mourn or celebrate. Here is a list of 15 different types of poems, which are defined in the following pages. You should expect to see at least one of these types of poems on the Praxis II: Elementary Education: Content Knowledge test.

- argumentative
- ballad
- concrete/visual
- couplet
- elegy
- emotive
- free verse
- haiku
- imagistic
- limerick
- lyric
- narrative
- ode
- sonnet
- villanelle

The definitions of these types of poems fall into specific categories, such as rhythm of structure. Therefore, be sure to read through this entire section to be sure you are familiar with all these possible forms of poetry.

An **emotive** poem aims to capture a mood or emotion and to make readers feel that mood or emotion. Here is an untitled poem by the Russian poet Alexander Pushkin:

> I have loved you; even now I may confess,
> Some embers of my love their fire retain
> but do not let it cause you more distress,
> I do not want to sadden you again.
> Hopeless and tongue-tied, yet, I loved you dearly
> With pangs the jealous and the timid know;
> So tenderly I loved you—so sincerely;
> I pray God grant another love you so.

Short, emotional poems that are personal from a single speaker are referred to as **lyrical** poems.

An **imagistic** poem aims to capture a moment and help us experience that moment sensually (through our senses). Here is a powerful two-line imagistic poem by Ezra Pound:

> **In a Station of the Metro**
> The apparition of these faces in the crowd;
> Petals on a wet, black bough.

Narrative poems tell stories, while **argumentative** poems explore an idea (such as love or valor). Here's a poem by Robert Frost that does both:

> **The Road Not Taken**
> Two roads diverged in a yellow wood,
> And sorry I could not travel both
> And be one traveller, long I stood
> And looked down one as far as I could
> To where it bent in the undergrowth;
> Then took the other, as just as fair,
> And having perhaps the better claim,

Because it was grassy and wanted wear;
Though as for that the passing there
Had worn them really about the same,
And both that morning equally lay
In leaves no step had trodden black.
Oh, I kept the first for another day!
Yet knowing how way leads on to way,
I doubted if I should ever come back.
I shall be telling this with a sigh
Somewhere ages and ages hence:
Two roads diverged in a wood, and I—I took
the one less traveled by,
And that has made all the difference.

An **elegy** is a poem that laments the loss of someone or something. An **ode**, on the other hand, celebrates a person, place, thing, or event. Here are a few lines from John Keats's (1795–1821) famous "Ode on a Grecian Urn":

Ah, happy, happy boughs! that cannot shed
Your leaves, nor ever bid the spring adieu;
And, happy melodist, unwearied,
For ever piping songs for ever new;
More happy love! more happy, happy love!
For ever warm and still to be enjoy'd,
For ever panting, and forever young;

WORD CHOICE IN POETRY

Because of their brevity, poets are especially careful about word choice. They often rely on figurative language to convey larger ideas, allowing images to convey ideas, rather than sentences. Poets will also often use words that can have multiple meanings or associations. See pages 94–95 for a more in-depth look at figurative language terms.

Elements of Sound

Although not all poems use rhyme, this is the most recognized element of sound in poetry. A **rhyme** is the repetition of identical or similar stressed sounds at the end of a word. Rhymes create rhythm and suggest a relationship between the rhymed words. There are several different types of rhymes:

- **Exact rhymes** share the same last syllables (the last consonant and vowel combination). Examples are *cat, hat; laugh, staff; refine, divine.*
- **Half-rhymes** share only the final consonant(s). Examples are *cat, hot; adamant, government.*
- **Eye rhymes** look like a rhyme because the word endings are spelled the same, but the words don't sound the same. Examples are *bough, through, enough, though.*

Alliteration is another important element of sound, and one that is often used in prose as well. **Alliteration** is the repetition of sounds. The sound is most often found at the beginning of words but can also be found throughout words. For example, the words *pitter patter* use alliteration at the beginning (repetition of the *p* sound), in the middle (repetition of the *t* sound), and at the end (repetition of the *r* sound).Notice the alliteration of the *k* sound in the first line and the *l* sound in the second line of "The Eagle" by Alfred, Lord Tennyson:

He **c**lasps the **c**rag with **c**roo**k**ed hands;
Close to the sun in **l**onely lands,

Some sounds, such as *l, s, r, m, n,* and vowel sounds (*a, e, i, o,* and *u*) are soft and create a pleasant, musical effect. Other sounds, such as *b, g, k,* and *p,* are much harder sounds, less pleasant and more forceful. Writers will use sound to help create the right tone and reflect the theme of the poem. By using the *k* and *l* sounds together in the first two lines, Tennyson suggests the duality of the eagle: its serene beauty and its awesome power.

Onomatopoeia is another element of sound. **Onomatopoeia** is a word that sounds like its meaning; the sound is the definition of the word. *Buzz, hiss, moan*, and *screech* are a few examples. These two lines from Robert Frost's 1916 poem "Out, Out," for example, use onomatopoeia:

> And the saw snarled and rattled, snarled and
>   rattled,
> As it ran light, or had to bear a load.

Assonance is the repetition of vowel sounds within a sentence or a phrase to create an internal rhyme. For example, read the last line of William Wordsworth's poem, "The World is Too Much with Us; Late and Soon":

> **O**r hear **o**ld Triton bl**o**w his wreathed h**o**rn

The /o/ sound is repeated within the line from the poem and is assonant.

Rhythm

One of the most important ways poets establish rhythm in their poems is through meter. **Meter** is the number of syllables in a line and how the stress falls on those syllables. In **iambic meter**, one of the most common metrical patterns, the stress falls on every other syllable, creating a steady *da-**dum***, *da-**dum***, *da-**dum*** rhythm to the poem. Each drumbeat (da-**dum**) is called a **foot**. Here is Robert Frost again to demonstrate iambic tetrameter (four feet per line). Read these lines from "Stopping by Woods on a Snowy Evening" out loud to hear how the rhythm works. The stressed syllables are in bold type.

> Whose **woods** these **are** I **think** I **know**.
> His **house** is **in** the **vill**age, **though**;
> He **will** not **see** me **stop**ping **here**
> To **watch** his **woods** fill **up** with **snow**.

Elements of Poetry's Structure

Knowing the poetic forms and techniques can help you better understand the poems you read. In poetry more than any other type of literature, form is part of the poem's meaning. Line breaks, stanzas, and punctuation therefore play an enormous role in defining a poem.

Because poems are written in verse, poets must decide how much information belongs on each line and when those lines should be broken into **stanzas** (poetic "paragraphs"). First, it's important to remember that when you read a poem out loud, you should pause only when **punctuation** tells you to pause. Do not pause at the end of each line or even at the end of a stanza unless there is a comma, period, or other punctuation mark that requires pause. That way, you can hear the flow of the words as the poet intended.

When you *look* at a poem, however, you need to take into consideration the important visual element of line breaks and stanzas. Line breaks and stanzas have two purposes: (1) to call attention to the words at the end of each line, and (2) to set aside each group of words as a distinct idea. Thus, while poetic sentences sometimes cut across line breaks and even sometimes stanzas, the visual separation of words within those sentences helps poets set off particular words and ideas for emphasis. Any word at the end of a line, for example, will stand out. And poets can space words in various ways as in the following example.

> **Sleeping**
> Sleeping, and it was
> dark
> outside. Inside,
> I was
> wondering
> alone,
> wandering
> in a dream
> of you.

Notice how the spacing here ties the words *dark*, *wondering*, and *wandering* together, pairs the words *inside* and *outside*, and sets off *alone*.

In fact, the arrangement of the words within a poem can be as important as the meaning of the words themselves. This type of poetry is referred to as **concrete poetry** or **visual poetry** because the words create a visual effect. For example, e.e. cummings's well-known poem "l(a . . . (a leaf falls on loneliness)" is an example of concrete poetry:

l(a

l(a
le
af
fa
ll
s)
one
l
iness

Rhymed and Metered Verse

Poems can be **rhymed verse**, **metered** (or **blank**) **verse**, or **free verse**. Rhymed and metered/blank poems are very confined by their structure; the lines must follow a rhyme scheme or metrical pattern (or both, if the poem is both rhymed and metered).Word choice (diction) is especially controlled by rhyme scheme and metrical pattern. Poets must find words that convey just the right idea, have the right ending to fit the rhyme scheme, *and* have the right number of syllables and the right stresses to fit the metrical pattern.

Three common types of rhymed and metered verse include the **sonnet**, the **ballad**, and the **villanelle**. These forms all have specific rhyme schemes and metrical patterns that poets must follow.

A **sonnet**, for example, is composed of 14 lines usually written in iambic pentameter (five groups of syllables known as feet per line). The rhyme scheme will vary depending on the type of sonnet. An Italian sonnet, for example, will divide the poem into two stanzas, one with eight lines, the other with six, using the following rhyme scheme: **abbaabba cdcdcd** (or *cdecde* or *cdccdc*). A Shakespearian sonnet, on the other hand, separates the lines into three **quatrains** (a quatrain is a stanza of four lines) and ends with a **couplet** (a pair of rhyming lines) with the following rhyme scheme: *abab cdcd efef gg*.

A **ballad** is a poem that usually tells a story and is often meant to be sung. The rhyme scheme is typically *abcb defe ghih*, and so on. Ballads tend to emphasize action rather than emotions or ideas and often have a steady, sing-songy meter.

One of the most complex rhyme schemes is the villanelle. A **villanelle** has five three-line stanzas with an *aba* rhyme scheme and a final quatrain with an *abaa* rhyme. There are only two rhymes in the poem, and line one must be repeated in lines 6, 12, and 18 while line three must be repeated in lines 9, 15, and 19.

Blank or metered verse is guided only by meter, not rhyme. Thus, the lines have a set number of syllables without any rhyme scheme. A haiku is an example of blank verse.

A **limerick** is a five-line poem with the rhyme scheme *aabba*. The content of a limerick is usually funny and occasionally obscene. Here's an example of well known limerick about pelicans:

A wonderful bird is the pelican,
His bill will hold more than his belican,
He can take in his beak
Enough food for a week
But I'm damned if I see how the helican!
—Dixon Lanier Merrit (1879–1972)

Haikus are unrhymed poems of three lines and 17 syllables. Line 1 has five syllables; line 2 has seven; and line 3 has five. Here is an example:

The Falling Flower
What I thought to be
Flowers soaring to their boughs
Were bright butterflies.
—Moritake (1452–1540)

Free Verse

Free verse is poetry that is free from the restrictions of meter and rhyme. But that doesn't mean that free verse poems are haphazard or simply thrown together. Rather than fitting a traditional metrical pattern or rhyme scheme, free verse poems often use a thematic structure or repetitive pattern. "Sleeping" on page 70 is one example, setting off words to isolate some and associate others. A more structured free verse poem is Kenneth Fearing's 1941 poem "Ad." The poem is structured like a help wanted ad designed to recruit soldiers for World War II.

> ***Wanted:* Men;**
> Millions of men are *wanted at once* in a big new
> field
> Wages: *Death.*

The last line of the poem sums up the compensation for the soldiers. Thus, the structure of the poem helps reflect its theme: The absurdity of running an advertisement for men to kill and be killed, of calling war "a big new field" to make it sound exciting, reflects the poet's feelings about the war—that it, too, is absurd, and that it is absurd to ask men to kill each other and to die.

Resource and Research Material

Students will use a variety of resource and research materials to gather information. Each resource has a unique purpose, as well as advantages or disadvantages over the other resources. It is important, therefore, to not only recognize examples of each resource but to be able to understand when and how students should use each one.

Reference Materials

Five basic reference works are standard in most elementary school classrooms, whether in book or online format.

An **almanac** is an annually published resource that contains basic information concerning the calendar, such as weather predictions, eclipses, tides, sunrises, and sunsets.

An **atlas** is a geographical resource that is full of maps. An atlas can cover a region, such as southern Florida, or the entire Earth—or even other planets.

A **dictionary** contains definitions for all the words of a language, listed alphabetically. Most dictionaries also include other information for the word, such as phonetics, pronunciation, and etymology.

An **encyclopedia** is a reference work that provides information about a wide variety of subjects from all branches of knowledge. Articles in a general encyclopedia, listed alphabetically, provide information about everything from biographies to scientific theories.

A **thesaurus** provides synonyms and antonyms for the words of a language, listed alphabetically.

Other Materials

Elementary school students in the twenty-first century will frequently be working on the Internet. Even very young students should be able to perform keyword searches effectively to locate information about a topic. They can also access databases and even online bulletin boards and message boards as helpful resource materials for specific tasks.

Students will use a variety of other resources, in addition to the aforementioned basic reference works and the Internet. While newspapers and magazines no longer play as big a role in learning, they still provide a terrific resource for specific information. Similarly, professional journals can provide very specific information for students who are looking to dive deeper into a subject. Newspapers, magazines, and journals also provide time-specific information; a student who is doing research on a specific event in the past can locate these materials to see how it was addressed at the time. This perspective can be very valuable for a student, since time can have an altering effect on the perception of an event.

Primary sources are materials that are generated from direct witnesses of an event. For example, autobiographies, diaries, and personal letters are primary sources. Given that these materials provide a direct link from the observer to the student, they can provide a unique advantage in that their information is not filtered by any third party.

When considering a resource material for a student, be sure to consider its appropriateness. For example, certain websites are more trustworthy than others for the accuracy of their information. And while a newspaper editorial may give an interesting perspective for a political debate, it is not an unbiased source of information—so it may not be applicable for the student's purposes.

Finally, there are parts of the resource and reference materials that students will be using—and that you will be expected to know about. A **footnote**, usually a note of explanation or reference, appears at the bottom of a page in a document. It can be a comment about the topic that may be a digression from the topic of the text. **Endnotes** are similar to footnotes but are listed at the end of the chapter or work. The **bibliography** is a list of works cited, usually at the end of a resource. The bibliography should reference all of the sources that are used to create the work. Sometimes an abbreviation of the reference is used within the text as a **citation**.

Text Structure and Organization for Reading and Writing

Organizational questions on the reading section of the Praxis II: Elementary Education: Content Knowledge test may ask you to identify how a passage is structured. You need to be able to recognize organizational patterns, common transitional phrases, and how ideas relate within a passage. Understanding the structure of a passage can also help you locate concepts and information, such as the main idea or supporting details.

The organization of a passage may be centered around powerful thesis statements. Therefore, recognition of the thesis statement and the concluding statement—as well as the supporting evidence for the thesis in a passage—is also critical to understanding the organization of a passage.

Organizational Patterns

To organize their ideas effectively, writers rely on one of several basic organizational patterns. The five most common strategies are:

1. chronological order
2. order of importance
3. comparison and contrast
4. cause and effect
5. problem and solution

Chronological order arranges events by the order in which they happened, from beginning to end. Textbooks, instructions and procedures, essays about personal experiences, and magazine feature articles may use this organizing principle. Passages organized by chronology offer language cues—in the form of transitional words or phrases—to signal the passage of time and link one idea or event to the next. Here are some of the most common chronological transitions.

first, second, third, etc.	before	next	now
then	when	immediately	suddenly
soon	during	meanwhile	later
in the meantime	eventually	finally	afterward
then	when	immediately	suddenly
at last	after	as soon as	while

Order of importance organizes ideas by rank instead of by time. Instead of describing what happened next, this pattern presents what is most, or least, important. The structure can work two ways: Writers can organize their ideas either by increasing importance (least important idea to most important idea) or by decreasing importance (most important idea to least important idea).

Newspaper articles follow the principle of decreasing importance; they cover the most important information in the first sentence or paragraph (the *who*, *what*, *when*, *where*, and *why* about an event). As a result, readers can get the most important facts of an event without reading the entire article. Writing that is trying to persuade its readers or make an argument often uses the pattern of increasing importance. By using this structure, a writer creates a snowball effect, building and building on the idea. "Saving the best for last" can create suspense for the reader and leave a lasting impression of the writer's main point. Just as a chronological arrangement uses transitions, so does the order of importance principle. Look for the following common transitional words and phrases.

first and foremost	most important	more important	moreover
above all	first, second, third	last but not least	finally

Comparison and contrast arranges two things or ideas side by side to show the ways in which they are similar or different. This organizational model allows a writer to analyze two things and ideas and determine how they measure up to one another. For example, this description of the artists Pablo Picasso and Henri Matisse uses comparison and contrast: The grand old lions of modernist innovation, Picasso and Matisse, originated many of the most significant developments of twentieth-century art (comparison). However, although they worked in the same tradition, they each had a different relationship to painting (contrast). For example, Picasso explored signs and symbols in his paintings, whereas Matisse insisted that the things represented in his paintings were merely things: The oranges on the table of a still life were simply oranges on the table (contrast).

Writers use two basic methods to compare and contrast ideas. In the **point-by-point** method, each aspect of idea A is followed by a comparable aspect of idea B, so that a paragraph resembles this pattern: ABABABAB. In the **block** method, a writer presents several aspects of idea A, followed by several aspects of idea B. The pattern of the block method looks like this: AAAABBBB. Again, transitions can signal whether a writer is using the organizing principle of comparison and contrast. Watch for these common transitions:

TRANSITIONS SHOWING SIMILARITY		
similarly	in the same way	likewise
like	in a like manner	just as
and	also	both

TRANSITIONS SHOWING DIFFERENCE		
but	on the other hand	yet
however	on the contrary	in contrast
conversely	whereas	unlike

Cause and effect arranges ideas to explain why an event took place (cause) and what happened as a result (effect). Sometimes one cause has several effects, or an effect may have several causes. For example, a historian writing about World War I might investigate several causes of the war (assassination of the heir to the Austro-Hungarian throne, European conflicts over territory, and economic power), and describe the various effects of the war (ten million soldiers killed, weakened European powers, and enormous financial debt).

Key words offer clues that a writer is describing cause and effect. Pay attention to these words as you read:

WORDS INDICATING CAUSE	
because	created by
since	caused by

WORDS INDICATING EFFECT	
therefore	so
hence	consequently
as a result	

A writer might also describe a **contributing** cause, which is a factor that *helps* to make something happen but can't make that thing happen by itself. On the opposite end of the spectrum is a **sufficient** cause, which is an event that, by itself, is strong enough to make the event happen. Often an author will offer her opinion about the cause or effect of an event. In that case, readers must judge the validity of the author's analysis. Are the author's ideas logical? Does the author properly support the conclusions?

Read the following excerpt and answer the practice question.

> When Rosa Parks refused to give up her seat to a white person in Montgomery, Alabama, in December 1955, she set off a train of events that generated a momentum the Civil Rights movement had never before experienced. Local civil rights leaders were hoping for such an opportunity to test the city's segregation laws. Deciding to boycott the buses, the African-American community soon formed a new organization to supervise the boycott, the Montgomery Improvement Association (MIA). The young pastor of the Dexter Avenue Baptist Church, Reverend Martin Luther King, Jr., was chosen as the first MIA leader. The boycott, more successful than anyone hoped, led to a 1956 Supreme Court decision banning segregated buses.
>
> *Source:* Excerpted from the Library of Congress papers in the exhibit, "The African American Odyssey: A Quest for Full Citizenship."

2. The author implies that the action of Rosa Parks directly resulted in

a. the 1956 Supreme Court decision banning segregated buses.

b. Martin Luther King, Jr.'s ascendancy as a civil rights leader.

c. the formation of the Civil Rights movement in Montgomery, Alabama.

d. the bus boycott in Montgomery, Alabama.

The correct answer is choice **d.** According to the passage, Rosa Parks's action directly inspired local civil rights leaders to institute the Montgomery bus boycott. Although Rosa Parks's action may have been a *contributing* factor to King's emergence as a civil rights leader, choice **b** and the Supreme Court's later decision to ban segregated buses, choice **a**, it was not the *direct* cause of these events, according to the passage. Choice **c** is incorrect because the passage makes clear that a local civil rights movement already existed and was not the result of Rosa Parks's refusal to give up her bus seat. Rosa Parks may have furthered the national Civil Rights movement, but she was not its direct cause.

Problem and solution presents an issue at the beginning of the text and then attempts to resolve it throughout the text. This type of format is common with persuasive types of writing, such as editorials or speeches. For example, a political candidate may write that our taxes are too high; he or she will (or should) then present a detailed explanation that demonstrates how this problem will be solved.

As you begin to read a short text, pay special attention to the first few sentences or the main idea of the first paragraph. More than likely, if the text is structured with a problem and a solution, the problem will be evident early on in the text.

Structural Elements

In addition to the overall organizational pattern, there are several specific elements to consider when reviewing a text.

The element of a text that best defines its structure is the **thesis statement**. While the thesis statement usually appears at the beginning of a text—sometimes even in the first sentence—it can show up a bit later. It's even possible for the thesis statement to show up at the very end of a short passage. In answering organizational questions on the Praxis II: Elementary Education: Content Knowledge exam, you may be asked to identify the thesis statement of a text. Look for the sentence that best sums up the main idea of the passage.

If the thesis statement of a text tells the main idea, then the rest of the text should serve to support the thesis statement. Recognizing the different ways that the thesis statement can be supported is critical to understanding the way a text is structured. **Support of a thesis statement** can be provided with quotes, examples, or information from a research source that backs up the thesis. Writers also often paraphrase an expert to support the thesis; this means that they reword the quotes to put thm in their own language while still providing the same information.

Keep an eye out for **transitional words** that help change the direction of the text. In a short excerpt that may appear on the Praxis II: Elementary Education: Content Knowledge exam, these transitional words are critical elements that point to not only the pattern of the organization but also the direction of the argument. A list of helpful transitional words to look for can be located in the previous section about organizational patterns.

In addition to recognizing the thesis statement and its support in a text, you will be expected to recognize the conclusion statement on the Praxis II: Elementary Education: Content Knowledge exam. The **conclusion statement** restates the thesis statement at the end of a text, drawing on all the reasoning that was used as support throughout the text.

Literacy Acquisition and Reading Instruction

As an elementary-level educator, you will be working with students during a pivotal time in their reading and literacy development. While they are in the elementary grades, students will go from learning to read to reading to learn. Helping emerging readers through the process of becoming literate requires being familiar with the foundations of literacy, including the concepts and current theories of language acquisition. Educators must also be familiar with children's literature, including criteria for evaluation and appropriateness. Lastly, an elementary-level educator must be familiar with the myriad strategies for students to improve their word recognition and comprehension abilities.

Foundations of Literacy and Reading Instruction

The term *emerging readers*, used to describe students encountering print in an early developmental stage, refers to the continual process by which students learn to read. There is no one point in which literacy begins for a student; rather, young students often enter kindergarten with some knowledge of printed language, and the process of becoming literate is a constant developmental process. It is also worth noting that current research shows that reading and writing abilities develop together and are much more related than once thought.

There are many ways to support emergent readers through a myriad of strategies. This section lists some of the most common and efficient strategies to use with students to support a student's development as an emergent reader, as well as factors that will help determine a reader's success. You should become familiar with each of these terms, listed in alphabetical order, and you should know how to apply the strategies in the classroom with your students.

The **alphabetic principle** states that letters represent the sounds of a language. Every written language depends on the alphabetic principle. Even though it sounds simplistic, students need to make the connection that a combination of letters represent a series of sounds based on a relationship between the letters and the corresponding sounds. This relationship is predictable and based on a system of rules.

Direct instruction, as its name implies, is a straightforward method of passing information from a teacher to a student. It is highly scripted, and many literacy programs rely on direct instruction from the teacher to his or her students. Probably the most common style of instruction, it is important to note that direct instruction is not the *only* way to way to teach. Some material should be taught this way, of course; for example, a student may be unable to decode the /tch/ sound in the word *hatch* and will require direct instruction to determine its sound. But while the teacher has control of the timing and content of the lesson during direct instruction, some students miss out on the purpose of the lesson with this way of learning.

Independent reading requires students to read on their own. A certain amount of time each day allotted for independent reading has several advantages. It can help a student improve comprehension and learn vocabulary, as well as develop a passion for reading and learning. Beyond that, however, it can give the educator time to monitor each student's development during individual conferences.

Scaffolding, a critical concept in pedagogy for all subjects and all grade levels, provides support for students to help them move toward literacy independence. Scaffolding is a process by which teachers initially provide the reading assistance, and then gradually shift the responsibility of the learning to the students. The end result is a confident learner who has the ability to reach his or her full potential.

Shared reading involves students reading along while an expert reads fluently. By modeling the reading, the expert (usually the teacher) demonstrates what it is that good readers do. The observer witnesses the aspects of the reader's reading process in a powerful way. Combining the instruction with shared reading aloud, students can be engaged through participation as well. Importantly, it can build confidence in struggling readers who may not have the self-assurance to lead a reading by themselves.

Students can also practice shared reading while working with their peers to read collaboratively. Teachers must model and encourage successful shared reading, of course, but if done properly it has the potential to be a lot of fun for students and give them the opportunity to practice successful independent reading. Although more common at the very early grades, shared reading can become a very important part of every reading program, regardless of the grade.

Shared writing is a composition of a text created by the teacher and the students. The teacher generally writes the story while the students piece together the students' ideas. The text can be published when it is completed.

Sight words are words that students should be able to recognize as soon as the student sees them in print. These words may not be easily decodable, but because they include the most commonly used words in print, they are critical to the success of emergent readers. For example, "the," "where," and "you" are all sight words at the earliest levels.

The **social interaction** theory stresses the importance of the surrounding environment in literacy development. Relying on feedback, the social interaction model states that language acquisition is not an innate ability but must be fostered with context from the cultural environment. The social interaction theory requires support from both peers and adults alike.

The **reader response** theory puts the focus on the reader of a text and his or her experience with it. Its intention is for students to find meaning in the process of reading itself. Readers must use **metacognition** to think about how the text affects them directly—armed with the knowledge that the text exists in their minds when activated by the reader's thoughts.

Text innovation, also called **rewrites**, is a strategy to help struggling readers with existing text materials that may be too challenging for them. Using text innovation, a teacher—or, more likely, a group of teachers over a period of time, rewrites a text so that the readability level is low enough for the struggling reader.

A **word wall** is a collection of words organized in a system and displayed visibly in a classroom. Word walls foster reading skills by providing a reference for young students. The system of the word wall can help students make connections between the words and their characteristics. While supporting the teaching of the principles of words, a word wall can also help develop a student's growing vocabulary.

Literacy and Reading Instruction for ELL Students

About one out of every nine students in American classrooms is an English Language Learner (ELL).[1] This presents a unique challenge for educators to help a population of their students. ELL students have the difficult task of learning a new language while also attempting to understand the content of the specific subject. A variety of strategies and factors should be considered with these students. There is disagreement about the best ways to promote higher levels of reading achievement for ELL learners, but you should be prepared to answer questions about support for these students. Keep in mind that regardless of the techniques used, educators who work in English with both English speakers and ELL students must modify their instruction to consider the ELL students' language limitations.

Note that the terminology for ELL students may differ; they may be called second-language learners or students who are learning English as a Second Language (ESL).

Children's Literature

The type of books that a young student reads has a gigantic influence on his or her reading success. An overly difficult book may frustrate a young reader. A series of unchallenging books has the potential to stagnate a student's reading abilities. A low-quality book can bore a student and stunt any enthusiasm he or she has for reading. Knowing all this, it is the educator's responsibility to choose a "just right" book for each student in his or her classroom. The following sections provide some methods to inspire children's literacy through literature.

Create a Superior Classroom Library

Every classroom should have its own area dedicated to a large collection of books. The library should be inviting, accessible, comfortable, and well lit. More important, it should be stocked with a great number of appropriate and high-quality books. According to Regie Routman's *Reading Essentials*, "an excellent library will have more than a thousand" books." The books should be displayed in a way that makes them appealing to the students; for example, the covers for many of the books can face out, like best sellers in a bookstore.

Get students involved in the creation and organization of the classroom library. Discover what types of books the students like to read, as well as who their favorite writers are. The more students feel that they are responsible for the collection, the more they will use it.

[1]http://www.netc.org/focus/challenges/ell.php, *American Educator*, Summer 2008, pages 8–15.

Include All Types of Books

Most classroom libraries are stuffed with fiction titles. Students are drawn to these titles, of course, and they should remain a focus of a classroom library. However, an educator must be willing to expose students to a wide range of different books—fiction and nonfiction alike. Students who read more nonfiction titles tend to write more informational writing. This leads directly to higher reading achievement.

It should go without saying, but there is simply no substitute for excellent books. The task of ensuring that students are only provided with quality books rests on the shoulders of their teachers. The stories should be engaging. The stories should relate to the interests of the students. They should also address the needs of the specific school curriculum.

Students should have access to books on a wide range of levels covering a wide range of topics. Students should never be limited to seeing only books at their level; being able to pick a book that is appropriate for a student is an important skill.

Strategies for Word Recognition

Phonology is the system of sounds in a language. Each of these single sounds is called a **phoneme**. Each phoneme does not necessarily correspond exactly to a letters in the English alphabet. For example, /ch/ and /sh/ are both unique phonemes. In the English language, there are approximately 44 phonemes. (There has been disagreement about the exact number, but 44 is the most commonly accepted tally.) By determining the phonemes in a series of letters, students can begin to determine the words in a text.

Sound segmentation requires students to separate the sounds in a word by speaking each of the sounds separately in the order in which they appear in the word. While this phonemic task may sound simple, students occasionally struggle with the ability to isolate the sounds from the word. The skill is important, so students can begin by identifying the initial phonemes before breaking down all the components of the word.

A **syllable** is a unit that is larger than a phoneme. Syllables have at least one vowel sound. The word *syllable* has three syllables, *syl*, *la*, and *ble*. Sounding out the individual syllable in a multisyllabic word can help a student recognize the word's meaning. The process of splitting a word into its separate syllables (or putting syllables together to form new words) is called **syllabication**.

The Running Record

One of the most common and efficient tools to track a student's ability to recognize words is a **running record**. In a running record, a student reads aloud from a selection no more than 250 words long. The teacher follows along with the text and notes whether the student has read the word properly. If the word is spoken correctly, the teacher denotes it with a check mark above the word. If the word is not spoken correctly, the teacher writes the misspoken word above the actual word in the text. The results of the running record help form a very useful assessment of the student's reading competence.

The **accuracy rate** is used to determine whether the text is easy enough or too frustrating for the reader. Expressed as a percentage, the rate can be calculated using the formula: accuracy rate = (total words read – total errors) ÷ total words read × 100%.

Using the student's accuracy rate, you can determine whether a text is at the reader's level. If the accuracy rate is between 95% and 100%, the student can read the text on his or her own and the text is called **independent**. If the accuracy rate is between 90% and 95%, the student can read with help, and the text is called **instructional**. If the accuracy rate is below 90%, the student can't read the book yet, and the text is called **frustrational**.

The **error-frequency rate** gives an approximation for the number of words read correctly compared to the number of incorrectly read words. The error rate can be found by dividing the total number of words read by the total number of errors made.

The rate shows how many words are read correctly for each word read incorrectly.

If a student corrects him- or herself during the course of the reading, the original miscue is not counted as an error.

The following excerpt from *The Adventures of Tom Sawyer* provides an example of a running record. The text in regular font represents the words in the book. The bolded words above those words show the mistakes that the student made while reading the text aloud.

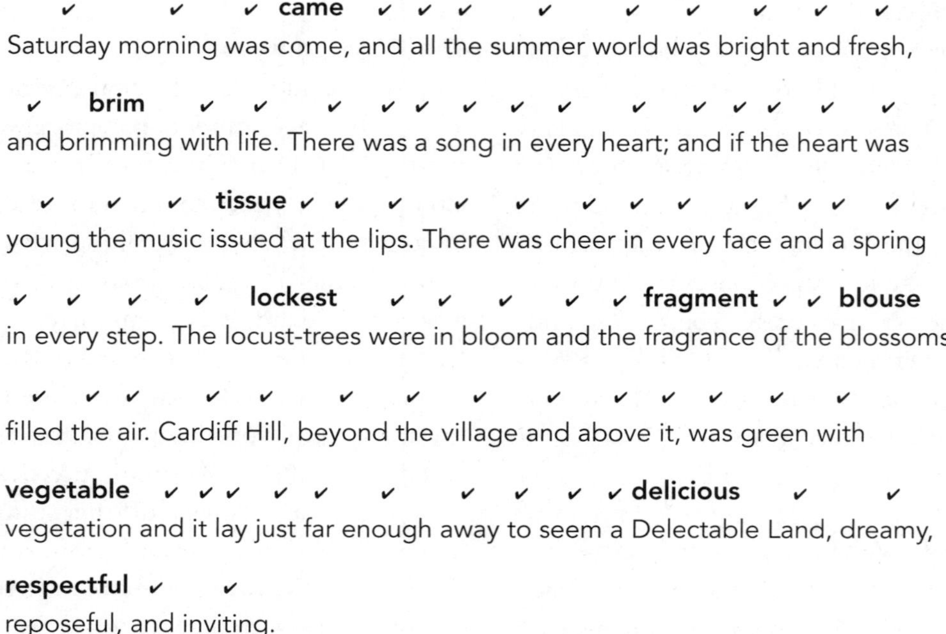

There were 90 words in the passage. The student made 9 errors. Therefore, the accuracy rate is (total words read – total errors) ÷ total words read × 100% = $\frac{81}{90}$ × 100, or 90%. The text is therefore considered instructional. The error-frequency rate is 90 ÷ 9, or 10.

While a running record is a very powerful tool to determine whether a student is able to correctly decode a text, it does not by itself demonstrate a student's level of comprehension. Additional comprehension assessments should be included to fully determine whether a student understands the text.

Strategies for Comprehension

Students spend so much of their time in the very early grades learning how to decode. They are taught about the importance of fluency and understanding the words. As a result, many students struggle with the comprehension of a text—even if they can read it smoothly. However, comprehension is not a matter of merely sounding competent while reading, since reading does not prove any in-depth comprehension from a student. After all, what is the point of reading without comprehension? As such, it is recommended that students are not simply taught comprehension once they have mastered decoding; by that point, they may not be able to understand the true purpose of reading. Reading should *begin* with comprehension.

The following common and useful reading strategies can aid a student with his or her comprehension of a text.

As a comprehension strategy, **rereading** (also called **repeated readings**) is helpful for readers of every age. Rereading a text has a very pronounced effect on improved comprehension. Teachers can model the effectiveness of rereading by reading a challenging text aloud, attempting to decipher its meaning, and then reading the text again and seeing how the comprehension was increased.

Making connections is one of the most proficient ways to improve comprehension of a text. It helps engage readers to see how reading is not an autonomous experience. There are three basic ways a student can make a connection with a text.

- **Text-to-self** connections require students to apply the information in the book to their own personal experiences in their lives. For example, students can consider how the book relates to events that they have encountered, people they know, or their own culture.
- **Text-to-text** connections require students to relate the text that they have read to other texts. Comparisons can be made by stories from the same author or about the same topic, for example, or perhaps they can relate a character from one text to a character in another text.
- **Text-to-world** connections require students to think about how a text relates to the world in a larger context. A text about science, for example, should connect events or experiences in a student's world.

Prior knowledge has been proven to be a critical element for a student's comprehension. For example, students are much more likely to understand a story about a topic that they're familiar with and have some experience with. Students are similarly going to enjoy a book much more if it touches on their background, knowledge, and prior experiences. Therefore, teachers should be sure that the subjects of the texts they are selecting are appropriate for the interests of their students.

Having a student **retell a story** in his or her own words is one of the most basic methods to ensure comprehension of the story. Ask a student to consider the details of a story, in addition to the big-picture concept of the book. Retelling the story has the added benefit of requiring a student to process the text that he or she has read.

Throughout a story, students should be given opportunities to **make inferences** about what is happening. For example, a student can be asked to make a prediction about what he or she thinks will happen next in the story. This can occur at any point within the text or even after it is over. Either way, students will be assessing the situation in the text and engaging in an active thought process that requires them to think critically about the text—and, in fact, *beyond* the text.

At the end of a book, teachers should be asking comprehension-related questions of their students. In fact, many leveled readers include a list of comprehension questions at the end of each chapter or at the end of the book. However, helping students to **ask their own relevant questions about comprehension** is a skill that will help students consider comprehension in an in-depth way while reading. By requiring students to construct their own open-ended questions from the text—which can be used in future discussions—they are forced to analyze the text in a way that aids significantly in comprehension. Additionally, students who come up with questions to ask about the text are forced to think about the way that they think about reading. This important process—thinking about thinking—is called **metacognition**.

Guided reading involves a student or students reading a book that was carefully and thoughtfully selected for their level by the teacher. This reading is generally silent, and the teacher can support and evaluate the student as necessary.

The **K-W-L (Know, Want to Learn, Learned) Chart** is an incredibly effective study tool to aid in a student's comprehension. Before reading a text, students activate their prior knowledge by filling out the

K column of the table, representing what they know already about the topic. They then fill out the W column, representing what they want to learn. Students should then consider the results of these steps while reading the text. When the reading is complete, students will then work to fill out the L column, representing what they learned. Not only does this useful chart require students to consider their knowledge about a topic outside of the book, it then engages them as they search for information in the book for the chart.

Graphic organizers also provide students with a tool for comprehension. They can be used in many ways, from helping a student map out the main idea and supporting details of a passage to helping them visualize the time line of events from a text. An idea web, for example, is a graphic organizer that shows how concepts and ideas within a text are interrelated.

The **Survey, Question, Read, Recite, Review (SQ3R)** strategy is intended to help a student's comprehension of a text using five steps. First, students will survey, or skim, the chapter before reading it, looking for headers, subheaders, or any other structures that can help identify the main idea or content of a chapter. Second, students should briefly ask what information the chapter is trying to provide to the reader—or determine what questions should be answered by the text. Third, students should read through the text, making sure to answer the questions posed in the question section, if possible. During the fourth step, recite, student say (or write) their own phrase that sums up the section and answers the questions posed earlier. Last, the fifth stage, review, gives students a few minutes to remember the key phrases from the section.

Language in Writing

The Praxis II: Elementary Education: Content Knowledge exam will test you on a variety of elements of the English written language. This includes everything from the proper use of commas and semicolons to the types of sentences. For example, you may be given a sentence and be asked to define what type of sentence it is. Or you may be given a sentence and be asked to identify the type of error that it contains. The following list shows the several aspects of language in writing that you may be tested on.

- components of language, including the parts of speech, grammar, and word usage
- sentence types
- orthography and morphology
- semantics
- vocabulary in context
- figurative language

Components of Language

Parts of a Sentence

There are only two basic parts of a sentence: the subject and its predicate. For this question type, you need to be able to identify the parts of a sentence. For example, a question may ask you to find the simple predicate in a given sentence.

The **subject** is the person, place, or thing in a sentence that is performing the action. The subject can be a noun, like in the sentence "The chair is black." It can be a pronoun, such as "He is the vice president." It can even be a group of nouns or a phrase, such as "Audrey and Anna went to the store" or "The last sip of coffee is the best."

The **predicate** is the action that is being done by the subject in the sentence. Read the following sentence.

Emma watches the sunrise from her porch.

The subject of the sentence is Emma. The action she is doing is watching the sunrise from her porch. That entire phrase, "watches the sunrise from her porch," is called the **complete predicate**. It tells you about Emma. Usually you won't need the complete predicate; the **simple predicate** is the main verb in the sentence that tells what Emma is doing. The simple predicate is "watches."

Parts of Speech

A sentence is made up of words. Each word is considered a part of speech. These parts include a handful of common terms that you must be able to recognize on the Praxis II: Elementary Education: Content Knowledge test: noun, verb, adjective, adverb, pronoun, preposition, and conjunction. You will also be expected to recognize different types of phrases and clauses.

Nouns

A **noun** is a person, place, thing, or idea. For example, the word *noun* is itself a noun. The words *doctor*, *bedroom*, *computer*, and *love* are all nouns as well because they represent a person, place, thing, or an idea.

A **proper noun** is a noun that names a specific person, place, thing, or idea. Proper nouns always start with a capital letter. For example, *Roger*, *Arizona*, and *Empire State Building* are all proper nouns.

Verbs

A **verb** is the action word of a sentence. The three basic verb tenses—present, past, and future—let you know when something happens, happened, or will happen. Verbs can appear in many different tenses. For example, *talk*, *ran*, *was raining*, and *have slept* are all verbs in different forms.

As ironic as it may seem, a verb takes on an *s* if the subject that is doing the event is singular. If the subject is plural, the verb does not have the *s*. For example, look at the following sentences with the verbs underlined.

> **Singular:** Madeline <u>helps</u> her friends with their homework.
> The policeman <u>protects</u> the community.
> **Plural:** Bob and Janet <u>mow</u> the lawn together.
> Her grandparents <u>own</u> the house on the hill.

Adjectives and Adverbs

Adjectives and adverbs add spice to writing—they are words that describe, or modify, other words. However, adjectives and adverbs describe different parts of speech. Whereas adjectives modify nouns or pronouns, adverbs modify verbs, adjectives, or other adverbs.

> We enjoyed the *delicious* meal.
> The chef prepared it *perfectly*.

The first sentence uses the adjective *delicious* to modify the noun *meal*. In the second sentence, the adverb *perfectly* describes the verb *prepared*. Adverbs are easy to spot—most end in *ly*. However, some of the trickiest adverbs do not end in the typical *ly* form. The following are problem modifiers to look out for:

Good/Well. Writers often confuse the adverb *well* with its adjective counterpart, *good*.

> Ellie felt *good* about her test results. (*Good* describes the proper noun, *Ellie*.)
> Ruben performed *well* on the test. (*Well* modifies the verb, *performed*.)

Bad/Badly. Similarly, writers confuse the function of these two modifiers. Remember to use the adverb *badly* to describe an action.

> Henry felt *bad* after staying up all night before the exam. (*Bad* describes Henry.)
> Juliet did *badly* in her first classroom presentation. (*Badly* describes the verb form, *did*.)

Fewer/Less. These two adjectives are a common pitfall for writers. To distinguish between them, look carefully at the noun modified in the sentence. *Fewer* describes *plural* nouns, or things that can be counted. *Less* describes *singular* nouns that represent a quantity or a degree.

The high school enrolls *fewer* students than it did a decade ago.
Emilia had *less* time for studying than Maggie.

Adjectives that follow verbs can also cause confusion. Although an adjective may come after a verb in a sentence, it may describe a noun or pronoun that comes before the verb. Here is an example:

The circumstances surrounding Shakespeare's authorship seemed strange.
(The adjective, *strange*, describes the subject, *circumstances.*)

Take special note of modifiers in sentences that use verbs that deal with the senses: *touch*, *taste*, *look*, *smell*, and *sound*. Here are some examples of sentences that use the same verb, but different modifiers:

Sarah felt sick after her performance review.
(The adjective, *sick*, modifies *Sarah.*)

The archaeologist felt carefully through the loose dirt.
(The adverb, *carefully*, modifies *felt.*)

The judge looked skeptical after the witness testified.
(The adjective, *skeptical*, modifies *judge.*)

The judge looked skeptically at the flamboyant lawyer.
(The adverb, *skeptically*, modifies *looked.*)

Pronouns

A **pronoun** is a word that takes the place of a noun or another pronoun. For example, the word his in the following sentence is a pronoun: Mark loves his dog. Without the pronoun, you would have to say "Mark loves Mark's dog," which is redundant. The pronoun *his* stands for *Mark's*.

More examples of pronouns are shown in the following table. Note that some of these words can be used as nouns or pronouns.

PRONOUNS				
All	He	Mine	Somebody	We
Another	Hers	My	Someone	Which
Any	Herself	Myself	Something	Who
Anybody	Him	Neither	Their	Whoever
Anyone	Himself	No One	Theirs	Whom
Anything	His	Nobody	Them	Whomever
Both	I	Nothing	Themselves	Whose
Each	It	Other	They	You
Either	Its	Ours	This	Yours
Everyone	Itself	Ourselves	Those	Yourself
Everything	Many	She	Us	Yourselves
Few	Me	Some		

Some pronouns are considered **personal pronouns** because they are taking the place of a noun. The pronouns can replace the subject or object in a sentence. Some pronouns are considered **possessive pronouns** because they are simply referring to the noun. See the examples of both types of pronouns in the sentences below. The pronouns are underlined.

Personal Pronouns
Chase grabbed the microphone and gave it to me.
She ran the marathon in under 4 hours.

Possessive Pronouns
Jacqueline read her book in a week.
Mine is the fastest computer in the class.

Prepositions

Prepositions are words that express the relationship in time or space between words in a sentence. They are generally short words, such as *in*, *on*, *around*, *above*, *between*, *beside*, *by*, *before*, or *with*, that introduce prepositional phrases in a sentence. See the examples of prepositions in the sentences below. Some sentences have two or more prepositions. The pronouns are underlined.

The girl ran to her room.
I cannot sleep before 10 o'clock.
Please go to the store with her.
The mouse ran through the hole in the wall.

Conjunctions

A **conjunction** is a part of a sentence that joins two words, such as *and* or *or*. Not every sentence will have a conjunction, but most compound sentences require it. (See page 91 for an example of a compound sentence.)

Clauses

Dependent clauses are part of a sentence that has its own subject and verb, but cannot stand by themselves as a sentence. These clauses are generally represented with a special word that can change an independent clause into a dependent clause. Some examples of dependent clauses are listed here in italics with those special words, called dependent markers, underlined. Notice that none of these clauses can stand alone as a sentence.

After Josie walked to the store, she visited her grandmother.
When Jackson takes a nap, we should play a game of chess.
Because he was the last person to show up for the class, Martin had to clean the blackboard.
Unless she gets at least an A– on her next quiz, Tina won't be able to do better than a C+ for the class.

Other examples of dependent markers are *although*, *as*, *before*, *even though*, *when*, *whether*, and *while*.

Independent clauses are part of a sentence with their own subject and verb; they can stand by themselves as sentences. Some examples of independent clauses are listed below in italics. The underlined words represent coordinating conjunctions or independent markers, which can either connect an independent clause or begin a new one. Notice that these clauses can stand alone as their own sentences.

Nina didn't practice before her basketball game, *but she still scored 19 points.*
Eduardo chopped up three apples, *and he mixed some cinnamon into the concoction.*
Zoey jogged to the nature preserve; *however, she didn't have time to stop and look for animals.*

Other examples of coordinating conjunctions and independent markers include *also*, *for*, *nevertheless*, *nor*, *so*, *therefore*, and *yet*.

Phrases

A **phrase** is a group of two or more words that cannot stand by itself as a sentence, but adds to an existing sentence. There are three ways that a phrase can act as a noun, adjective, or adverb.

A **participial phrase** is a short descriptive phrase at the beginning or end of a sentence. This type of phrase is set off from the main clause in the sentence with a comma. For example, "howling at the moon" in the following sentence represents a participial phrase that is set off from the rest of the sentence.

> Howling at the moon, Rover sat alone in his master's yard.

A **prepositional phrase** is a short phrase that helps describe a verb or adjective within a sentence. For example, the prepositional phrase "with the yellow cover" in the following sentence describes which book was written by the uncle.

> The book with the yellow cover was written by my uncle.

An **appositive phrase** is a short phrase that modifies a noun or pronoun using other nouns. It usually follows the noun or pronoun directly, but it can come before it as well. In the following sentence, the appositive phrase "a beautiful green convertible" describes the noun "car" with other nouns.

> My brother's car, a beautiful green convertible, was damaged by the recent storm.

Grammar

For the Reading/Language Arts section of the Praxis II: Elementary Education: Content Knowledge test, you must be able to identify problems in the grammar of a sentence. Fortunately, you don't need to be a grammar expert. There are only a few aspects of grammar that will likely be tested. For example, you need to be on the lookout for the incorrect use of subject-verb agreement, pronoun agreement, and shifting verb tenses. You should also understand how to use participles and infinitives.

Subject-Verb Agreement

They goes together, or *they go together*? You probably don't even have to think about which subject goes with which verb here—your ear easily discerns that the second version is correct. Subject-verb agreement means that the subject of a clause matches the verb *in number*. Singular nouns take singular verbs; plural nouns take plural verbs. However, some instances of subject-verb agreement are tricky. Look out for the following three problem areas.

Phrases Following the Subject. Pay close attention to the subject of the sentence. Do not be misled by phrases that may follow the subject. These phrases may confuse you into selecting a verb that does not agree with the subject. Try this practice question:

3. Which word represents an error in the following sentence?

> Betty Friedan's 1963 book, an exposé of domesticity that challenged long-held American attitudes, remain an important contribution to feminism.

a. exposé
b. challenged
c. remain
d. contribution

The correct answer is choice **c**. The singular subject, *book*, needs a singular verb, *remains*. Don't be confused by the plural noun *attitudes*, which is part of a phrase that follows the subject.

Subjects Following the Verb. Be sure to locate the subject of the sentence. Test makers use subjects that come after the verb to confuse you. Sentence constructions that begin with *there is* or *there are* signal that the subject comes after the verb.

4. Which word represents an error in the following sentence?

> Although the Australian government protects the Great Barrier Reef, there is environmental factors that continue to threaten the world's largest coral reef ecosystem.

a. Although
b. protects
c. is
d. continue

The correct answer is choice **c**. The plural subject *factors* requires a plural form of the verb, *are*. Nothing is wrong with the word "Although," so choice **a** is incorrect. The plural verb *protects* matches the singular tense of the word *government*, so choice **b** is incorrect. The verb *continue* is in the correct tense to match the plural subject *factors*, so choice **d** is incorrect.

Special Singular Nouns. Some words that end in *s*, like *measles*, *news*, *checkers*, *economics*, *sports*, and *politics*, are often singular despite their plural form, because we think of them as one thing. Watch for collective nouns—nouns that refer to a number of people or things that form a single unit. These words, such as *audience*, *stuff*, *crowd*, *government*, *group*, and *orchestra*, need a singular verb.

5. Which word represents an error in the following sentence?

> That rowdy group of drama students were labeled "the anarchists," because they took over the university president's office in a protest against the dress code.

a. rowdy
b. were
c. because
d. protest

The correct answer choice is **b**. The collective noun *group* is the singular subject of the sentence. Notice how the position of the prepositional phrase *of drama students* following the subject is misleading.

Pronoun Agreement

Pronouns are words that take the place of nouns. Just as subjects and verbs must agree, pronouns and their antecedents must match. If a noun is singular, the pronoun must be singular. If a noun is plural, the pronoun must be plural. Pronouns also need to match their antecedent in case. Remember that a pronoun can also take the place of another pronoun. In those cases, the pronouns must agree as well.

A pronoun that takes the place of the subject of a sentence should be in the nominative case (*I*, *we*, *he*, *she*, *they*), whereas a pronoun that takes the place of the object in a sentence should be in the objective case (*me*, *us*, *him*, *her*, *them*). Here are some examples.

> Matteo is funny, but *he* can also be very serious. (subject)
> Bernadette hired Will, and she also fired *him*. (object)

In most cases, you will automatically recognize errors in pronoun agreement. The phrase *Me worked on the project with him* is clearly incorrect. However, some instances of pronoun agreement can be tricky. Review these common pronoun problems:

- **Indefinite pronouns** like *each*, *everyone*, *anybody*, *no one*, *one*, and *either* are singular.
  <u>Each</u> of the boys presented *his* science project.
- **Two or more nouns joined by *and*** use a plural pronoun.
  <u>Andy Warhol and Roy Lichtenstein</u> engaged popular culture in *their* art.
- **Two or more singular nouns joined by *or*** use a singular pronoun.
  <u>Francis or Andrew</u> will lend you *his* book.

- **He or she?** In speech, people often use the pronoun *they* to refer to a single person of unknown gender. However, this is incorrect—a singular noun requires a singular pronoun.

  A person has the right to do whatever *he or she* wants.

The following lists some pronouns that are commonly confused with verb contractions or other words. Look out for these errors.

CONFUSING PRONOUN	QUICK DEFINITION
its	belonging to it
it's	it is
your	belonging to you
you're	you are
their	belonging to them
they're	they are
there	describes where an action takes place
whose	belonging to whom
who's	who is *or* who has
who	refers to people
that	refers to things
which	introduces clauses that are not essential to the information in the sentence and do not refer to people

Try this practice sentence correction question:

6. What is the error in the following sentence?

A child who is eager to please will often follow everything that their parents say.

a. who
b. will
c. their
d. say

Choice **c** is the correct answer. The subject, *a child*, is singular. Even though you don't know the gender of the child, the possessive pronoun should be *his* or *her* in order to agree in number.

Pronoun Problem—Unclear Reference

When a pronoun can refer to more than one antecedent in a sentence, it is called an unclear, or ambiguous, reference. Look carefully for this error; a sentence may read smoothly, but may still contain an unclear reference. Look at this practice usage question:

7. What is the error in the following sentence?

A regular feature in American newspapers since the early nineteenth century, they use satirical humor to visually comment on a current event.

a. since
b. they
c. visually
d. on

The answer is choice **b**. Who or what uses satirical humor? You don't know how to answer, because the pronoun *they* does not have an antecedent. If you replace *they* with *political cartoons*, the sentence makes sense.

Verb Tense

Verb tense should be consistent. If a sentence describes an event in the past, its verbs should all be in the past tense.

> *Incorrect:* When Kate visited Japan, she sees many Shinto temples.
> *Correct:* When Kate visited Japan, she saw many Shinto temples.

Past Tense for Present Conditions. It's incorrect to describe a present condition in the past tense.

> *Incorrect:* My sister met her husband in a cafe. He was very tall.
> *Correct:* My sister met her husband in a cafe. He is very tall.

Incomplete Verbs. Test makers may trick you by including the *-ing* form, or progressive form, of a verb without a helping verb (*is*, *has*, *has been*, *was*, *had*, *had been*, etc.). Make sure that verbs are complete and make sense in the sentence.

> *Incorrect:* The major newspapers covering the story throughout the year because of the controversy.
> *Correct:* The major newspapers have been covering the story throughout the year because of the controversy.

Subjunctive Mood. The subjunctive mood of verbs expresses something that is imagined, wished for, or contrary to fact. The subjunctive of *was* is *were.*

> *Incorrect:* If I was a movie star, I would buy a fleet of Rolls-Royces.
> *Correct:* If I were a movie star, I would buy a fleet of Rolls-Royces.

Now practice answering this usage question.

8. Which word contains an error in the following sentence?

Unhappy about the lack of parking at the old stadium, season ticket holders considering boycotting next week's game.

a. Unhappy
b. of
c. considering
d. boycotting

The correct answer is **c.** *Considering* needs a helping verb to be complete and to make sense in this sentence. The clause should read *season ticket holders are considering boycotting next week's game.*

Participles and Infinitives

A **participle** is a word that is usually associated as a verb but is used as an adjective. Because participles act as adjectives, they modify nouns or pronouns. Most of the time, a participle will end in *–ing* or *–ed.* The italicized word in the following example demonstrates a type of participle because it is acting as an adjective although it is in a recognizable form of a verb.

> The *crying* baby had not had a bottle in six hours.

An **infinitive** is a verb in the form *to* + *verb*, such as *to live*. You can then change a verb from the infinitive form to a different tense, depending on when the auction occurred or whether one or more things are involved in the action. These words may look differently; the following list shows several common verbs in their past, present, and future tenses.

Infinitive Form	Past	Present	Future
to fall	fell	falls/fall	will fall
to jump	jumped	jumps/jump	will jump
to study	studied	studies/study	will study
to tell	told	tells/tell	will tell
to write	wrote	writes/write	will write

Usage

A misused word can significantly alter the meaning of a sentence. That's why the Praxis II: Elementary Education: Content Knowledge test may check your ability to recognize misused words. The following list contains some commonly confused words. If you find some that you frequently confuse, study them and practice using them correctly in a sentence.

CONFUSING WORD	QUICK DEFINITION
accept	recognize, receive
except	excluding
affect (verb)	to influence
effect (noun)	result
effect (verb)	to bring about
all ready	totally prepared
already	by this time
allude	make indirect reference to
elude	evade
illusion	unreal appearance
all ways	every method
always	forever
among	in the middle of several
between	in an interval separating two
assure	to remove doubt
ensure	to make certain (an outcome)

CONFUSING WORD *(continued)*	QUICK DEFINITION
insure	to make certain (financial value)
beside	next to
besides	in addition to
complement	match
compliment	praise
continual	constant
continuous	uninterrupted
disinterested	lacking a strong opinion
uninterested	uncaring
elicit	to stir up
illicit	illegal
eminent	well-known
imminent	pending
farther	beyond
further	additional
incredible	beyond belief, astonishing
incredulous	skeptical, disbelieving
loose	not tight
lose	fail to keep
may	indicates possibility or probability
maybe	perhaps
overdo	do too much
overdue	late
persecute	to mistreat
prosecute	to take legal action
personal	individual

CONFUSING WORD *(continued)*	QUICK DEFINITION
personnel	employees
precede	go before
proceed	continue
proceeds	profits
principal (adjective)	main
principal (noun)	person in charge
principle	standard
stationary	still, not moving
stationery	writing paper
than	in contrast to
then	next
to	on the way to
too	also
weather	climate
whether	if

Sentence Types

A sentence can be defined based on its structure or its purpose.

Sentence Structure

There are four different ways that a sentence can be structured, depending on whether it includes dependent clauses, independent clauses, or both. There are also sentence fragments, which are occasionally used in literature.

A **simple sentence** has one independent clause and no dependent clauses. For example, the following sentence is a simple sentence.

> I enjoyed taking a walk with you.

A **compound sentence** combines multiple independent clauses in the sentence, but it has no dependent clauses. The following sentence is a compound sentence.

> Abby looked into the mirror, and she did not like what she saw.

A **complex sentence** has one independent clause and at least one dependent clause. The following sentence is a complex sentence.

> After sitting in the airplane for eight hours, Maryanne realized that she desperately needed to stretch her legs.

A **compound-complex sentence** combines multiple independent clauses in the sentence, as well as at least one dependent clause. The following sentence is a compound-complex sentence.

> Franklin D. Roosevelt is often considered one of the country's greatest presidents; because he served during World War II, Roosevelt's leadership was critically important to the future of his nation.

A **sentence fragment** is, as its name suggests, an incomplete sentence. Fragments may represent clauses that are disconnected from a main clause. In many cases, a sentence fragment represents an error; in some practices, however, it is used for literary effect. The second sentence below is an example of a sentence fragment.

> At some point, I'm going to have to find a new job. Because the one I have now is driving me crazy.

Sentence Purpose

A sentence has four major purposes. Those purposes help define the type of sentence that it is. Here are descriptions of each of these sentence types.

A **declarative** sentence makes a declaration. Every declarative sentence ends in a period. This is the most common type of sentence. In fact, the four sentences in this paragraph are declarative sentences.

An **interrogative** sentence asks a question. As a result, every interrogative sentence ends in a question mark. The following sentence is an example of an interrogative sentence.

What is for dinner?

An **exclamatory** sentence includes an exclamation. Every exclamatory sentence ends in an exclamation mark. The following sentence is an example of an exclamatory sentence.

I told you to wash the dishes!

An **imperative** sentence gives a command. It can end with a period or an exclamation mark. The following sentence is an example of an imperative sentence.

Please enjoy my homemade soup.

Orthography and Morphology

Orthography describes the proper way to use a written system of language, including proper spelling. **Morphology** describes the structure of words and their parts, including morphemes. A **morpheme** is the smallest unit of sound with meaning. While the Praxis II: Elementary Education: Content Knowledge test is not a spelling test, it will ensure that you are familiar with the following four elements of orthography and morphology.

Affixes

An **affix** is a morpheme that is attached to the stem of a word, creating an entirely new word. There are two types of affixes: prefixes and suffixes.

A **prefix** is the beginning part of the word that helps identify its meaning. For example, the prefix in the word *tripod* is *tri-*, meaning three. Many words do not have a prefix.

A **suffix** is the ending part of the word that helps identify its meaning. For example, the suffix in the word *jobless* is *-less*, meaning that the subject is without a job. Many words do not have a suffix.

Roots

The **root** of a word is the main part of a word that gives it the meaning, without any prefixes or suffixes. For example, the root of *disinterested* is *interest.* For a student struggling with vocabulary, the identification of the root of a word is a critical skill.

Semantics

Semantics represents the specific meaning, or meanings, of a word in a written language. For the Praxis II: Elementary Education: Content Knowledge exam, the aspects of semantics that you need to know include the following topics.

An **antonym** is a word that has an opposite meaning. For example, *tall* is an antonym of *short.* It may help to remember the meaning of this word if you consider that *ant-* is a prefix that means *opposite*, just as *Antarctica* means *the opposite of the Arctic.*

A **synonym** is a word that has the same meaning as another word. For example, *use* and *utilize* mean the same thing and are synonyms.

An **idiom** is a word or group of words that cannot be interpreted literally. For example, an author may say that something was "as easy as pie." Students who are unfamiliar with a particular idiom may struggle with trying to identify its meaning. As an educator, you should be able to determine whether a word or phrase is being used figuratively or idiomatically.

A **homonym** is a word that sounds like another word but has a different spelling and meaning. Here are some of the most common homonyms:

accept	to take or receive
except	leave out
affect	to have an influence
effect *(noun)*	the result or impact of something
all ready	fully prepared
already	previously
bare	uncovered *(adj)*; to uncover *(verb)*
bear	animal *(noun)*; to carry or endure *(verb)*
brake	to stop *(verb)*; device for stopping *(noun)*
break	to fracture or rend *(verb)*; a pause or temporary stoppage *(noun)*
buy	to purchase
by	next to or near; through
desert	dry area *(noun)*; to abandon *(verb)*
dessert	sweet course at the end of a meal
every day	each day
everyday	ordinary; daily
hear	to perceive with the ears
here	in this place
know	to understand, be aware of
no	negative—opposite of *yes*
loose	not tight; not confined
lose	to misplace; to fail to win
may be	might be (possibility)
maybe	perhaps
morning	the first part of the day
mourning	grieving
passed	past tense of *pass* (to go by)
past	beyond; events that have already occurred
patience	quality of being patient; able to wait
patients	people under medical care
personal	private or pertaining to the individual
personnel	employees
presence	condition of being
presents	gifts
principal	most important (*adj*); head of a school (*noun*)
principle	fundamental truth
right	correct; opposite of *left*
rite	ceremony
write	produce words on a surface
scene	setting or view
seen	past participle of *see*
than	used for comparison (*he is taller than I*)
then	at that time, therefore
their	possessive form of *they*
there	location; in that place
through	in one side and out the other; by means of
threw	past tense of *throw*
to	in the direction of
too	in addition; excessive
two	number

waist	part of the body
waste	to squander *(verb)*; trash *(noun)*
weak	feeble
week	seven days
weather	climatic conditions
whether	introducing a choice
which	what, that
witch	practitioner of witchcraft

Vocabulary in Context

Elementary-level students are constantly building their vocabularies. While you won't likely be asked to use vocabulary in context to define the meaning of a word yourself, you will be expected to know how to help students who come across an unfamiliar word in a text. While a student could grab a dictionary or go online and look a word up, it can be more powerful for a student to use a number of strategies to figure out what a word means on his or her own.

Understanding vocabulary is one of the most primary and essential reading comprehension skills for students, which is why the ability to determine the meaning of a word from its **context** is so critical.

The first strategy that students should employ to determine the meaning of an unknown word is to read the sentence with the word in it—as well as the sentence before and after that sentence. While the meaning of the word by itself may remain a mystery, the surrounding words often offer important clues about its meaning. For example, the surrounding words and sentences may contain synonyms or antonyms that point to the meaning of the unknown word. Keep in mind that many vocabulary words, especially those that may appear on ETS's standardized tests, contain multiple meanings; therefore, just because a student knows one possible meaning of a word does not necessarily mean that he or she understands the meaning of the word in the context of the sentence.

Figurative Language

Authors use figurative language by using words that cannot be taken literally. Figurative language is especially popular in poetry, but it is used in all types of literature.

A **simile** makes a comparison using *like* or *as*: *Your eyes are like shining sapphires.*

A **metaphor** is more powerful. It makes the comparison directly: *Your eyes are shining sapphires.*

Personification is the attribution of human characteristics to animals or objects. For example, in the following poem, the eagle is described as "clasp[ing] the crag with crooked hands."

> **The Eagle**
> He clasps the crag with crooked hands;
> Close to the sun in lonely lands,
> Ringed with the azure world, he stands.
>
> The wrinkled sea beneath him crawls;
> He watches from his mountain walls,
> And like a thunderbolt he falls.
> —Alfred Lord Tennyson, "The Eagle" (1851)

Eagles do not actually have hands. Tennyson gives human characteristics to his subject, the eagle. This is personification.

Imagery is the representation of sensory experience through language. Imagery helps us see, hear, taste, smell, and touch in our imaginations. Notice the powerful imagery and the similes in the passage below, from Sandra Cisneros's *The House on Mango Street* (1984):

> Everybody in our family has different hair. My Papa's hair is like a broom, all up in the air. And me, my hair is lazy. It never obeys barrettes or bands. Carlos' hair is thick and straight. He doesn't need to comb it. Nenny's hair is slippery—slides out of your hand. And Kiki, who is the youngest, has hair like fur. But my

> mother's hair, my mother's hair, like little rosettes, like little candy circles all curly and pretty because she pinned it in pincurls all day, sweet to put your nose into when she is holding you, holding you and you feel safe, is the warm smell of bread before you bake it, is the smell when she makes room for you on her side of the bed still warm with her skin, and you sleep near her, the rain outside falling and Papa snoring. The snoring, the rain, and Mama's hair that smells like bread.

In fiction, writers often use **symbolism** to help convey the themes of their stories. A **symbol** is a person, place, or thing invested with special meaning or significance. It is a person, place, or thing that is both itself and a representation of something else (usually an idea). Flags are an everyday example of symbolism. A flag is a decorated piece of cloth, but it is also much more than that; it represents a group of people and the ideas that hold those people together. Colors are also highly symbolic. White may be used to represent purity or innocence, red to represent passion or bloodshed, purple to represent royalty. Birds often represent freedom, and an olive branch represents peace.

In "The Necklace," the necklace Madame Loisel loses becomes a symbol of what happens when we want desperately to be something or someone we are not, of what we can suffer when we are too proud to tell the truth to others.

Style is more than just figurative language. It is the overall manner of writing, including sentence structure and the level of formality, which is managed through word choice. It is also a matter of how much description and detail the author likes to provide. Notice, for example, the drastically different styles of the two science fiction writers in the next example. One uses very long sentences and sophisticated, formal vocabulary. The other is much more casual, with shorter sentences and more everyday vocabulary.

From Mary Shelley's *Frankenstein* (1818):

> It is with considerable difficulty that I remember the original era of my being; all the events of that period appear confused and indistinct. A strange multiplicity of sensations seized me, and I saw, felt, heard, and smelt at the same time; and it was, indeed, a long time before I learned to distinguish between the operations of my various senses.

From Kurt Vonnegut's *Slaughterhouse Five* (1969):

> **Listen:**
> Billy Pilgrim has come unstuck in time. Billy has gone to sleep a senile widower and awakened on his wedding day. He has walked through a door in 1955 and come out another one in 1941. He has gone back through that door to find himself in 1963. He has seen his birth and death many times, he says, and pays random visits to all the events in between.
> He says.

Communication Skills

Writing and Spelling Development

Students progress through several stages of development as they learn to spell and write. You are expected to define each phase and describe the characteristics of each one. The stages, in order of their natural development, are as follows.

In the **picture writing/drawing** stage, students begin to express their thoughts via drawings and pictures. These drawings may not even be recognizable, but they nevertheless represent the critical first stage of writing.

In the second stage of writing development, children begin to draw recognizable shapes and have verbal stories to go with them. This stage is called **scribble writing**.

During the **random letter** stage, students begin to string letters together with their pictures. This may include the student's own name. The words may undecipherable at this point.

After the random letter stage, students begin to use letters to match sounds. They may only use the beginning letter to represent a word. This stage is called **invented spelling**, **semi-phonetic**, or **early spelling**.

Once students begin to write words with correct beginning and ending sounds, they can be considered in the **phonetic** stage. After all, they are beginning to use phonics to write and spell, even though spelling is not a focus for the student at this stage.

During the **transitional** stage, students are beginning to write words based on the way that they sound. The stories that students write may now be a few sentences long and may include punctuation throughout.

By the time students get to the **conventional writing** stage, they are able to spell most words correctly, even if they spell some longer words phonetically. At this point students also begin to use punctuation correctly, as well as proper capitalization.

Stages of the Writing Process

Classroom educators are responsible for helping students develop into strong writers. That involves explaining the steps necessary to build a well-structured essay. The following steps show how a student can create an essay involving a thesis, or a main idea with an argument.

Step 1: Prewriting

The prewriting—or planning—process is essential to developing a clear, organized essay. Prewriting consists of some quick, basic steps: formulating a thesis, brainstorming for examples that will support a student's thesis, and drafting an outline or basic structure for the essay.

A thesis statement should:

- tell the reader what the subject is
- inform the reader about what the writer thinks and feels about the subject
- use clear, active language

Students don't have to waste their time making your thesis statement a masterpiece. They will be able to grab the reader's attention by clearly stating the purpose in simple words. For example, a student wants to write an essay about wearing school uniforms.

The following sentences are *not* thesis statements:

- Many private schools already require school uniforms.
- Some students prefer school uniforms, while others detest them.
- Why do schools use uniforms?

The following *are* thesis statements:

- School uniforms discourage high school students from learning responsibility and developing individuality.
- School uniforms are effective in creating a positive learning environment.

Step 2: Brainstorm for Ideas

Once a student has decided what he or she wants to write about—or what his or her thesis will be—he or she will begin to brainstorm—think up ideas—for support. Students should try to generate about three to five reasons that back up their main idea for a persuasive piece of writing.

Brainstorming is a prewriting process in which you imagine or write down any ideas that come to mind. To brainstorm effectively, students should not judge their ideas initially; they should simply put them down on paper. If they are stuck for ideas, they can try these brainstorming strategies:

- Try the **freewriting** technique, in which they write nonstop for two minutes. They keep their pens to paper and their hand moving. Doubtless, ideas will emerge.
- **List** as many ideas as they can. They don't edit for grammar or structure, just writing down whatever comes to mind.

Step 3: Outline the Essay

To make sure that a student's essay is well developed and organized, the student must draft an outline. An outline will help a student put his or her ideas into a logical order and identify any gaps in supporting details. On your Praxis II, you may see an example of an outline for a student's essay. You may be asked how to help improve the organization of the outline or fill in the gaps in a student's outline with additional information.

Some essays should follow a specific structure. For example, persuasive essays follow a basic three-part structure:

1. **Introduction:** Present your position to your readers. State your thesis.
2. **Body:** Provide specific support for your thesis.
3. **Conclusion:** Bring closure to your essay and restate your thesis.

Where the introduction and conclusion go is obvious. However, a student needs a pattern, or structure, to organize the ideas in the body of the essay. The four most common patterns are **chronological order**, **comparison and contrast**, **cause and effect**, and **order of importance**. The following chart lists each organizing principle's key characteristics and effective uses in writing:

ORGANIZATIONAL PATTERN CHARACTERISTICS AND EFFECTIVE USES
chronological order
uses time as organizing principle; describes events in the order in which they happened
historical texts, personal narratives, fiction
order of importance
arranges ideas by rank instead of time
persuasive essays, newspaper articles
comparison and contrast
places two or more items side by side to show similarities and differences
comparative essays
cause and effect
explains possible reasons why something took place
historical analysis, analysis of current events

Step 4: Writing the Essay

First Impression—The Introduction

Once a detailed outline is completed, a student can begin to draft his or her essay. A student must use clear, direct language to introduce the reader to the thesis and focus. A useful technique for creating a strong introduction is to begin with a thesis and then summarize of the evidence (supporting details) that will be presented in the body of the essay.

Supporting Paragraphs—The Body of the Essay

Working from the detailed outline, a student can begin composing the body of his or her essay. Each paragraph should be treated like a mini essay, with its own thesis (a topic sentence that expresses the main idea of the paragraph) and supporting details (examples). Follow these guidelines for creating supporting paragraphs:

- **Avoid introducing several ideas within one paragraph.** By definition, a paragraph is a group of sentences about the same idea.
- **Use at least one detail** or example to back up each main supporting idea.
- **Aim for about three or four sentences in each paragraph.** If a student writes more sentences for each paragraph, a reader might lose track of the main idea of the paragraph. If a student writes fewer sentences, he or she may not be developing the idea adequately.
- **Use transitions.** Key words and phrases can help guide readers through an essay. Students can use these common transitions to indicate the order of importance of their material: *first and foremost*, *most important*, *first*, *second*, *third*, *moreover*, *finally*, and *above all*. Remind students not to use "firstly," "secondly," or "thirdly"—these forms are incorrect and awkward.

The Conclusion

The last paragraph of a student's essay should sum up the argument. The writer should avoid introducing new ideas or topics. Instead, the concluding paragraph should restate the thesis, but in *new words*. The conclusion should demonstrate that the topic was covered fully and should convince readers that they have learned something meaningful from the argument.

Step 5: Revising and Proofreading the Essay

The goal of proofreading is to give a student's essay a final polish, by checking spelling, correcting grammatical errors, and if needed, changing word order or word choice. The following checklist outlines some basic grammatical problems a student should look out for as he or she proofreads. (All these grammar trouble spots are discussed earlier in this chapter.)

- **Make sure nouns and verbs agree.** The subject of the sentence must match the verb in number. If the subject is singular, the verb is singular. If the subject is plural, the verb is plural.
- **Make sure pronouns and antecedents agree.** Pronouns and the nouns they represent, antecedents, must agree in number. If the antecedent is singular, the pronoun is singular; if the antecedent is plural, the pronoun is plural.
- **Check the modifiers.** Look out for modifiers that are easy to confuse like *good/well*, *bad/badly*, *fewer/less*. Remember: adjectives modify nouns and pronouns; adverbs describe verbs, adjectives, or other adverbs.
- **Keep the verb tense consistent.** Switching tense within a sentence can change its meaning. Generally, a sentence or paragraph that begins in the present tense should continue in the present tense.
- **Check the sentence structure.** Keep an eye out for sentence fragments, run-on sentences, comma splices, or any other issues that prevent the sentence from being understood.

Aspects of Speaking, Listening, and Viewing

About five questions on the Praxis II: Elementary Education: Content Knowledge exam will cover communication skills, including elements of speaking and listening, as well as viewing. Therefore, it is important to review the important concepts of these skills and be sure that you know their role in communication. Keep in mind that teachers must also consider the unique challenges of ELL students in speaking, listening, and viewing.

Speaking

When speaking, students should take into account several different aspects of a speech or a presentation. A dozen different aspects of speaking are listed as follows.

- Consider the audience for the speech.
- Prepare strong opening and closing statements.
- Include details in the story
- Make eye contact with the listeners.
- Include gestures and hand motions during the speech.
- Include humor, if desired.
- Consider the proper pace for the speech.
- Organize the speech with a strong structure and focus.
- Vary the pitch of the speech.
- Consider the appropriate tone.
- Add visuals to a presentation, if possible.
- Increase or decrease the volume as necessary.

Listening

Listening is not a passive process. Students should be fully engaged while listening. To do this effectively, they can and should consider several important aspects of listening. The following list provides a dozen suggestions for improved listening skills.

- Agree or disagree with the speaker.
- Ask questions to improve understanding.
- Create a summary of the main ideas.
- Describe reactions.
- Develop a central idea further.
- Evaluate the tone of the speaker's voice.
- Evaluate the volume of the speaker's voice.
- Focus on the speaker.
- Follow directions carefully.
- Repeat a speaker's words.
- Respond to questions directly.
- Sit upright.

Viewing

In the twenty-first-century classroom, there are many more tools at the teacher's disposal than a chalkboard and textbooks. Many classrooms use a variety of tools that utilize modern technology, such as Smart boards, projectors, or computers. As an educator, you have to consider the implications of these different media.

Some of the implications of the different media include what message the students get from viewing the media or whether the information is more or less understandable as a result of the viewing. For example, ELL students may find that visuals enable them to comprehend some material more easily. You should be expected to evaluate not only the effectiveness of the viewing media but also the techniques used with the media for their use in the classroom.

Test-Taking Tips for the Reading/Language Arts Section

The Reading/Language Arts section of the Praxis II: Elementary Education: Content Knowledge test has 30 multiple choice questions. While you can spend more time on this section than the others, you should expect to spend about 30 minutes for the entire section—or about one minute for each question.

The following tips relate specifically to the Reading/Language Arts section of the test.

Always Consider the Main Idea

The Reading/Language Arts section will include several questions about the main idea of a passage. Those questions may use the term *central idea*, *primary purpose*, or some other similarly worded term that means the same thing. Therefore, always consider the main idea of a passage as you begin to read it.

As you start reading a passage on the test, look for its main idea right away. This will save you time and energy later if you see a question about the main idea. Even if there is no question about the main idea, understanding the purpose of the passage can help you identify other important information—such as supporting details. Therefore, always consider what the main idea of a passage is while you're reading it—rather than having to go back later and figure it out.

Read the Questions about the Passages First

The Reading/Language Arts section will contain about six to eight short passages. These passages may be represented by any style of writing listed in this section, such as poems, excerpts from books, short nonfiction blurbs, or narrative stories. However, one thing will always be true about them: They will be *short*. And there will almost always be only 2 or 3 questions for each passage. So how can you take advantage of this fact?

Read the questions for each passage *before* reading the passage! Because there are only going to be a couple of questions for a passage, you can get an idea of what information you need to look for *before* you dive into the passage. For example, if a question asks for the theme of a poem, you can then read the poem with an eye toward determining its theme. Otherwise, you might not realize that you should be paying attention to the poem's theme.

Know Important Vocabulary

The Reading/Language Arts section of the Praxis II: Elementary Education: Content Knowledge test will test your knowledge of important literary terms. You will be expected to know the bolded words covered throughout this entire section, including the pedagogical strategies. Make sure you are familiar with every one of these terms before taking the test.

Reading/Language Arts Practice Section

Read the following poem, then answer questions 1 through 3.

Down by the Salley Gardens
by William Butler Yeats

(1) Down by the salley gardens my love and I did meet;
(2) She passed the salley gardens with little snow-white feet.
(3) She bid me take love easy, as the leaves grow on the tree;
(4) But I, being young and foolish, with her did not agree.

(5) In a field by the river my love and I did stand,
(6) And on my leaning shoulder she laid her snow-white hand.
(7) She bid me take life easy, as the grass grows on the weirs;
(8) But I was young and foolish, and now am full of tears.

1. The author's phrase "snow-white" was most likely intended to be used as a symbol for
a. an imaginary fairy tale.
b. the innocence of his love.
c. a description of the weather.
d. the fleeting nature of love.

2. Which best describes the tone of this poem?
a. regretful
b. excitable
c. irritable
d. fanciful

3. What rhyming scheme does Yeats use in each stanza of this poem?
a. AABB
b. ABAB
c. ABCD
d. ABBA

4. Which of the following is an example of a complex sentence?
a. Jamaal was a gifted pitcher, fielder, hitter, and base runner.
b. Rebecca turned the lights off in her room, and then she closed the door.
c. Some of the students in Ms. Minkin's class didn't want to write a book report.
d. Marta decided to head home after she spilled punch on her dress.

5. What is the error in the following sentence?

> One of the best camouflaged creatures in the ocean, the leafy sea dragon appear to be a piece of floating seaweed in the water.

a. A pronoun and its antecedent are not in agreement.
b. A comma is included but is unnecessary.
c. The verb and the subject are not in agreement.
d. There needs to be a comma before a preposition.

6. A student writes a story with no definitive thesis statement. The story contains characters and a setting, as well as several events that comprise the plot of the story. There is a climax toward the end of the student's story, followed by a resolution to the problem. Which type of writing did the student best demonstrate with his or her story?
a. expository
b. narrative
c. journal
d. persuasive

7. An English language learner has developed a strong vocabulary and an increased fluency and accuracy with text materials since moving to the United States. However, the student struggles with certain text materials regarding cultural topics when reading independently. Which best explains why the student may struggle with texts regarding those particular topics?
a. The student lacks the requisite prior knowledge to apply to the text materials.
b. The level of vocabulary prevents comprehension of the text materials.
c. The student does not have the ability to progress to the point of full understanding.
d. Text materials involving cultural topics rarely include illustrations for support.

8. A reader is able to demonstrate an ability to think beyond the text if he or she is able to
a. take words apart and put them back together to aid in comprehension.
b. recall the critical information in a text and disregard the unimportant information.
c. scan the text to locate and use a specific piece of information.
d. use the given information to predict what will happen next in a story.

Read the following poem, then answer questions 9 through 12.

Daffodils
by William Wordsworth

I wandered lonely as a cloud
That floats on high o'er vales and hills,
When all at once I saw a crowd,
A host, of golden daffodils;
Beside the lake, beneath the trees,
Fluttering and dancing in the breeze.

Continuous as the stars that shine
And twinkle on the milky way,
They stretched in never-ending line
Along the margin of a bay:
Ten thousand saw I at a glance,
Tossing their heads in sprightly dance.

The waves beside them danced; but they
Out-did the sparkling waves in glee:
A poet could not but be gay,
In such a jocund company:
I gazed—and gazed—but little thought
What wealth the show to me had brought:

For oft, when on my couch I lie
In vacant or in pensive mood,
They flash upon that inward eye
Which is the bliss of solitude;
And then my heart with pleasure fills,
And dances with the daffodils.

9. Which line from the poem represents an example of a simile?
   a. 1
   b. 6
   c. 9
   d. 15

10. What is the mood of the third stanza of the poem?
   a. lonely
   b. frenzied
   c. joyful
   d. pensive

11. Which object is NOT described using personification in the poem?
   a. daffodils
   b. trees
   c. waves
   d. heart

12. William Wordsworth compares the sparkling waves to the dancing daffodils in order to
   a. demonstrate the magnificence of the crashing waves.
   b. provide a setting for the daffodils as being near the seashore.
   c. show that the beauty of the daffodils exceeds even that of the waves.
   d. illustrate how some things are more beautiful than the daffodils.

13. Which action can a teacher follow to best reinforce the meaning of a verbal description?
   a. Combine graphics to the key processes of the descriptions.
   b. Request that a student selected at random repeat the description.
   c. Create a long pause between each of the words within the description.
   d. Translate the verbal description into several different languages.

14. A student writes a speech for the members of her political club. She then wants to prepare the speech in a presentation for her entire class. Which revision should the student most consider for her speech to the class?
   a. Change the pace of the speech so that is much slower for the larger audience.
   b. Alter the speech in response to the change in audience.
   c. Vary the vocabulary to include specific political jargon.
   d. Speak in a monotone voice to avoid offending anyone.

Read the following passage, then answer questions 15 through 17.

While Earth's moon may be little more than a giant rock with few fascinating features, the largest moon of Saturn, Titan, constantly surprised and amazes scientists. Of the 336 known moons, planetlike Titan is the only one to feature a dense atmosphere. It is also the only known celestial body other than Earth with liquid bodies on its surface. And in a revolutionary 2010 discovery, scientists found that a change of methane within the moon's atmosphere could be consistent with the presence of life.

15. The first sentence of the passage provides the readers with a
   a. mystery.
   b. comparison.
   c. history.
   d. contrast.

16. Which type of writing does the passage most likely represent?
   a. fairy tale
   b. science fiction
   c. historical fiction
   d. exposition

17. What was the author's purpose in including the final sentence of the passage?
- **a.** to provide an additional example of Titan's astonishing traits
- **b.** to supply proof of liquid bodies on Titan's surface
- **c.** to make a case that we should return to Earth's moon
- **d.** to disprove the theory that no other life exists outside of Earth

Read the following passage, then answer questions 18 through 20.

The twelfth president of the United States may have been the unlikeliest leader in the country's history. As a child, Zachary Taylor was poorly educated—since there were no schools near his home on the Kentucky frontier. He entered the U.S. Army in 1808 and spent the next 40 years in the U.S. military. Taylor earned distinction as a leader during the Mexican War of the 1840s and was compared to the first president of the United States, another American war hero. Before he was nominated to run for president in 1848, he had never considered a political career. At first Taylor rejected the idea, saying that the idea of him as president "has never entered my head." In fact, Taylor was largely apolitical; he never voted in any election before he ran for president. When he won the election, Taylor became the first U.S. president to never hold elected office before assuming the presidency.

18. Which best describes the organization of the passage?
- **a.** compare and contrast
- **b.** chronological order
- **c.** order of importance
- **d.** cause and effect

19. Which literary device does the author use in the phrase "the first president of the United States, another American war hero"?
- **a.** allusion
- **b.** oxymoron
- **c.** hyperbole
- **d.** metaphor

20. What is the primary purpose of the passage?
- **a.** to describe the improbable ascent of an American leader
- **b.** to detail the military successes from an American soldier
- **c.** to encourage students to stay in school and study hard
- **d.** to illustrate all the different paths there are to the U.S. presidency

21. Which of the following steps is NOT associated with the revising stage of the writing process?
- **a.** get rid of unnecessary words
- **b.** draw a story chart
- **c.** add details if necessary
- **d.** ask peers to suggest improvements

22. A developing speller begins to change from depending on the sound of words for spelling to using knowledge of the structure of words and visual clues. The speller spells the word *eagle* as EGUL and the word *chicken* as CHEKEN. In which developmental stage of spelling is the student?
- **a.** conventional
- **b.** scribble
- **c.** prephonemic
- **d.** transitional

23. Which word or words from the following sentence contains an error?

> Although slow-moving manatees are most frequent seen in the warm waters of Florida, they have been spotted as far north as Cape Cod.

a. frequent
b. of Florida
c. they
d. as far

24. A student is reading the word *chat*. How many distinct phonemes are there in the word?
a. 1
b. 2
c. 3
d. 4

25. Which of the following best verifies a student's comprehension of a story?
a. The student demonstrates no difficulty with the vocabulary in a story.
b. The student is able to retell the story in his or her own words.
c. The student's response to the story is positive.
d. The student applies prior knowledge to the story.

26. Which of the following is NOT a true statement about listening behavior?
a. It can be modified or augmented by instruction.
b. It is a conditioned behavior that can be learned.
c. It requires several different types of learning.
d. It comprises less than one-quarter of communication.

27. Which of the following strategies is least helpful for a student attempting to understand the meaning of an unknown vocabulary word?
a. Read the sentence before the sentence with the unknown word.
b. Identify synonyms or antonyms that signal the meaning of the unknown word.
c. Separate any affixes from the root of the unknown word.
d. Identify the multiple morphemes that comprise the unknown word.

28. What revision should be done to the following sentence to correct an error?

> Each of New York's three largest daily newspapers experienced a dramatic decrease in their circulation between April 2008 and October 2008.

a. Change the pronoun "their" to "its."
b. Remove the apostrophe from "New York's."
c. Change the verb "experienced" to "experiences."
d. Add a comma before the word "and."

29. Which is the best approximation for the total number of phonemes used in the English language?
a. 5
b. 26
c. 44
d. 100

30. Students who spend a great deal of time decoding a written text
- **a.** are frequently unable to determine the meaning of a word.
- **b.** have a significantly lower accuracy rate.
- **c.** often struggle with comprehension of the text.
- **d.** should be using invented spelling to increase the pace.

Reading/Language Arts Practice Section Key

READING/LANGUAGE ARTS KEY					
ITEM	KEY	SUBSECTION	ITEM	KEY	SUBSECTION
1	B	Foundations of Reading	16	D	Language in Writing
2	A	Foundations of Reading	17	A	Language in Writing
3	A	Foundations of Reading	18	B	Language in Writing
4	D	Language in Writing	19	A	Foundations of Reading
5	C	Language in Writing	20	A	Language in Writing
6	B	Language in Writing	21	B	Communication Skills
7	A	Foundations of Reading	22	D	Communication Skills
8	D	Foundations of Reading	23	A	Language in Writing
9	A	Foundations of Reading	24	C	Foundations of Reading
10	C	Foundations of Reading	25	B	Foundations of Reading
11	B	Foundations of Reading	26	D	Communication Skills
12	C	Foundations of Reading	27	D	Foundations of Reading
13	A	Communication Skills	28	A	Language in Writing
14	B	Communication Skills	29	C	Foundations of Reading
15	D	Language in Writing	30	C	Foundations of Reading

Anwers and Explanations

1. **b.** While *Snow White* may be a fairy tale, the author is not using the term as a symbol for the fairy tale. The word *white* is often used as a symbol for purity, and the author is most likely referring to the innocence of his love, choice **b**. It does not refer to the weather, choice **c**, nor the fleeting nature of love, choice **d**.
2. **a.** The author is recalling a young love that passed him by. He refers to himself as "young and foolish" and ends the poem saying that he is "full of tears." The author's tone, therefore, is full of regret, choice **a**.
3. **a.** The first two lines of each stanza rhyme with each other, so they are both A. The next two lines of each stanza rhyme with each other, so they are both B. The rhyming scheme to describe each stanza is therefore AABB, choice **a**.
4. **d.** A complex sentence includes an independent clause and a dependent clause. It also includes a subordinator such as *since*, *after*, *although*, or *because*. Sentence choice **d** fits this description. Sentence choices **a** and **c** are simple sentences because they each contain an independent clause with a subject and a verb. Sentence choice **b** is a compound sentence because it combines two independent clauses.
5. **c.** The subject of the sentence is the leafy sea dragon. That is a singular subject. The corresponding verb is "appear," which is a plural verb. Therefore, the subject and the verb are not in agreement, making choice **c** correct.
6. **b.** The descriptions of the student's story match the parts of a narrative piece of writing exactly. An expository piece of writing, choice **a**, should have a clear thesis statement. A journal, choice **c**, does not have to provide a plot, climax, or resolution. And because the student's story is not attempting to persuade the reader of anything, it does not represent a persuasive text, choice **d**.
7. **a.** Prior knowledge is a critical component for a student's comprehension of a text. Students who move to the United States face a dual challenge of learning the language and learning the culture. Even if a student understands the vocabulary in a text, his or her lack of prior knowledge may inhibit the comprehension. The scenario states that the student's vocabulary is not an issue, so choice **b** is not correct. The statement in choice **c** is never correct; every student has the innate ability to succeed. There is no evidence to suggest that the statement in choice **d** is accurate.
8. **d.** The actions described in choices **a**, **b**, and **c** all reflect ways of thinking within a text. Only choice **d**, predicting, requires students to think beyond the text.
9. **a.** A simile uses the words *like* or *as* to make a comparison. The very first line of the poem compares the author's loneliness to a cloud using the word "as." Therefore, choice **a** represents a simile. Lines 6 and 9 represent personification, a different type of figurative language frequently used in poetry.
10. **c.** The poem begins with a lonely mood, choice **a**, but there is no loneliness in the second stanza. The words in the third stanza—"gay," "jocund," "glee"—describe a joyful mood, **c**; it does not describe any frenzied events, so **b** is not correct. The author mentions a pensive mood, **d**, but only in the fourth stanza—and then only to contrast with the blissful memories of the daffodils.

11. b. In Wordsworth's poem, daffodils, waves, and his own heart are described as dancing. This is a human characteristic given to objects to describe them. The trees are mentioned in the poem—but only as a description for the location of the daffodils. No personification is used on the trees, so choice **b** is correct.

12. c. William Wordsworth says that the waves beside the daffodils danced and sparked, but that the daffodils outdid the waves "in glee." Therefore, he is suggesting that the daffodils are more beautiful than the waves—a comparison represented in choice **c**.

13. a. Research has shown that combining graphics to verbal descriptions aids comprehension of the description, so choice **a** represents the best action for a teacher to take. Repetition, choice **b**, does not necessarily reinforce the meaning of anything. A long pause, choice **c**, can disrupt comprehension. Translating the description can help some ELL students, but for many it will not provide any reinforcement to the meaning of the description.

14. b. A speaker should always consider the audience to whom he or she is speaking. That may involve adjusting the speech in response to a different audience, choice **b**. For example, the speech should be written in a way that provides the greatest interest to the greatest number of people. The student could vary the vocabulary, choice **c**, but only to *reduce* the specific jargon—because fewer students in the larger group will understand it. Speaking in a monotone, choice **d**, is never recommended for effective speaking skills. Similarly, a slower pace, choice **a**, will not engage a large audience.

15. d. The passage may mention some mysteries of Titan, but the first sentence merely contrasts the appeal of largest moon of Saturn to the dullness of Earth's moon. Therefore, choice **d** best represents the purpose of the first sentence of the passage.

16. d. The purpose of an expository piece of writing is to provide readers with background information. For readers unfamiliar with the largest moon of Saturn, this passage provides a great deal of background information. The passage may be scientific, but because it is based in fact and not fiction, choice **b** is not correct. Choice **c** also refers to a fictional account, which does not represent the given passage. A fairy tale, choice **a**, is a short narrative, which is not represented by this passage, either.

17. a. The passage concludes with a potential discovery of life on Titan. Surely this exciting bit of news would provide another example of the moon's "astonishing traits," choice **a**. The sentence does not supply proof of liquid bodies, choice **b**, nor does it make any reference to Earth's moon, choice **c**. While the proof of life on Titan would disprove any theory that life does not exist outside of Earth, choice **d**, this is not the point of the sentence. The entire passage is about how Titan is unique and enthralling; the final sentence acts as a strong piece of evidence to support this thesis.

18. b. The passage tells about the events in Zachary Taylor's life, from his lack of schooling as a child through his election for President in 1848. This type of organization by the time in which the event occurred is called chronological order, choice **b**.

19. a. The author mentions that Taylor was like "another American war hero," but the hero's name is never mentioned. The author merely alludes to the first president, George Washington. Because the author is indirectly describing a person, it is an example of an allusion, choice **a**. The sentence does not contain an example of an oxymoron, a hyperbole, or a metaphor.

20. a. The very first sentence of the passage sums up its main idea: Zachary Taylor was the most unlikely of U.S. presidents. The passage then describes his path from poor student to American leader, which matches the purpose described in choice **a**. The passage mentions Taylor's military success, choice **b**, but that is not the primary purpose. Because Taylor did not attend much school, the passage is not about encouraging students to stay in school and to study hard, choice **c**. While the passage may illustrate one unique path to the U.S. presidency, it is not about all the different paths because only one path is provided.

21. b. At the revising stage of the writing process, writers should be removing any unnecessary words, choice **a**, adding details if necessary, choice **c**, and using the advice of their peers to improve the text, choice **d**. The act of drawing a story chart, choice **b**, is more closely associated with the prewriting stage of the writing process; a story chart helps to organize a text, so it should be used before the drafting stage.

22. d. A student in the conventional stage of spelling, choice **a**, spells most words correctly when he or she writes. In the scribble and prephonemic stages, choices **b** and **c**, a speller is not yet using the knowledge of the structure of words or visual clues to attempt the spelling of a word. This occurs during the transitional stage in which a student might spell the word *eagle* as EGUL and the word *chicken* as CHEKEN. Therefore, choice **d** is correct.

23. a. The word "frequent" is being used to describe how often manatees are seen. Because it describes the verb, it is an adverb—and therefore should be written as "frequently" instead of "frequent."

24. c. A phoneme is the smallest segment of sound in a language. The word *chat* has three distinct basic sounds: the digraph /ch/ sound, the /a/ sound, and then the /t/ sound. There are four letters in the word but only three distinct phonemes.

25. b. A student can understand every word in a story but still be unable to comprehend the story as a whole, which means choice **a** is not correct. It is possible that a student comprehended the story but didn't enjoy it, so choice **c** is not an indication of comprehension. While prior knowledge can aid comprehension significantly, it is not able to verify whether a student understood a story. Retelling the story, choice **b**, is the best strategy to ensure a student's comprehension.

26. d. It is true that instruction can modify listening behavior, so choice **a** is not correct. Listening is indeed conditioned, meaning that it is a learned behavior—making choice **b** incorrect as well. Listening requires a variety of types of learning, so choice **c** is incorrect. Listening should comprise much more than one-quarter of communication, so choice **d** is not a true statement—and therefore the correct answer choice.

27. d. There are many strategies a student can use to identify the meaning of an unknown word. Reading before or after the sentence with the unknown word, choice **a**, can provide the student with context to provide meaning. Sometimes a sentence will provide an antonym or synonym, choice **b**, for the unknown word—thus giving a strong clue to its meaning. Long words can be intimidating for some students; by separating the components of a word, **c**, the root word (and its corresponding meaning) can become apparent. A morpheme is the smallest sound of a word. For example, the word "cat" has three morphemes: /c/, /a/, and /t/; separating an unknown word into its morphemes will not be as useful to determine its meaning as the other three strategies.

28. a. The pronoun *their* in this sentence is referring to the subject *each*. While it may seem like it should be plural—because there are three newspapers—the word *each* itself is singular. Therefore, the pronoun should be singular to agree with the subject; *its* is singular, and so choice **a** is the proper revision.

29. c. The exact number of phonemes is debatable, but the range is usually somewhere in the mid-40s. There are 5 vowels, choice **a**, and 26 letters in the alphabet, choice **b**, but there are more phonemes, such as /ch/ and /sh/, than there are letter sounds. There are not nearly 100 different phonemes, choice **d**.

30. c. Students who spend too much time decoding may be able to still determine the meaning of a word, choice **a**, but the attention that they have allotted to decoding comes at the expense of comprehension, choice **c**. A student can still have a 100% accuracy rate if he or she reads very slowly, so choice **b** is not necessarily true. Invented spelling, choice **d**, relates to writing a text—not reading it.

CHAPTER 4

MATHEMATICS REVIEW

The second section of the Praxis II: Elementary Education: Content Knowledge test is the mathematics section. Of the 120 questions on the test, 30 will cover material from the mathematics section. Each question will be multiple choice with four answer choices.

About the Mathematics Section

The mathematics section of the Praxis II: Elementary Education: Content Knowledge test is designed to ensure that future educators have an appropriate degree of competence with mathematics. As students will be developing their first mathematical concepts in the elementary grades, it is critical that their teachers understand how to help guide the learners with confidence through this stage.

Test takers can expect to see questions that test a wide variety of mathematical content. The greatest percentage of items—about 40%—will cover number sense, including fractions, decimals, and the basic operations (addition, subtraction, multiplication, and division). However, the questions can cover a range of skills from one of four major areas of mathematics.

The four major areas of the mathematics section, and the approximate number of questions that will cover their content, are as follows:

- number sense (12 items)
- algebra (7 or 8 items)
- geometry and measurement (6 items)
- data organization and probability (4 or 5 items)

The elements of each major area are explained in detail in the following sections.

Note: You *are* allowed to use a calculator on the Praxis II: Elementary Education: Content Knowledge test. As you review the material in this chapter and on the 30-question practice section at the end of the chapter, have your calculator handy. This will help model the tools available to you and ensure that you are comfortable working with your calculator when the time comes to take the official test.

You will NOT be provided with a list of important formulas for the mathematics section of the Praxis II: Elementary Education: Content Knowledge test.

Therefore, it is important to memorize the formulas on the following page.

Formulas

Area of a:

square	$A = \text{side}^2$
rectangle	$A = \text{length} \times \text{width}$
parallelogram	$A = \text{base} \times \text{height}$
triangle	$A = \frac{1}{2} \times \text{base} \times \text{height}$
trapezoid	$A = \frac{1}{2}(\text{base}_1 + \text{base}_2) \times \text{height}$
circle	$A = \pi \times \text{radius}^2$; π is approximately equal to 3.14

Perimeter of a:

square	$P = 4 \times \text{side}$
rectangle	$P = 2 \times \text{length} + 2 \times \text{width}$
triangle	$P = \text{side}_1 + \text{side}_2 + \text{side}_3$

Circumference of a circle = $\pi \times$ diameter; π is approximately equal to 3.14

Volume of a:

cube	$V = \text{edge}^3$
rectangular solid	$V = \text{length} \times \text{width} \times \text{height}$
square pyramid	$V = \frac{1}{3} \times (\text{base edge})^2 \times \text{height}$
cone	$V = \frac{1}{3} \times \pi \times \text{radius}^2 \times \text{height}$; π is approximately equal to 3.14

Pythagorean relationship $a^2 + b^2 = c^2$; a and b are legs and c is the hypotenuse of a right triangle

Measures of Central Tendency

Mean = $\frac{x_1 + x_2 + \cdots + x_n}{n}$, where the x's are the values for which a mean is desired, and n is the total number of values for x.

Median = the middle value of an odd number of ordered data, and halfway between the two middle values of an even number of ordered scores.

Simple Interest principal × rate × time

Distance rate × time

Total Cost (number of units) × (price per unit)

Adapted from official GED materials.

Number Sense

Number sense is a general term that refers to a basic understanding of our number system. As a result, the greatest number of questions in the mathematics section of the Praxis II: Elementary Education: Content Knowledge test relate to skills based on number sense. You can expect to see about 12 of the 30 questions in the mathematics section to relate to some aspect of number sense.

The Praxis II: Elementary Education: Content Knowledge test will include questions involving whole numbers, integers, fractions, and decimals. The following sections define each term and demonstrate how to compare and perform operations (addition, subtraction, multiplication, division) with numbers in those systems. You will also learn about other attributes of these numbers, such as prime and composite or factors and multiples.

Whole Numbers

A **whole number** is a nonnegative number that is not expressed as a fraction or a decimal. For example, 0, 4, 39, and 3,318 are all whole numbers. You need to be able to add, subtract, multiply, divide, compare, and order whole numbers.

Comparing and Ordering Whole Numbers

To compare and order whole numbers, it is essential that you are familiar with the place value system. The following table shows the place values for a very large number: 3,294,107.

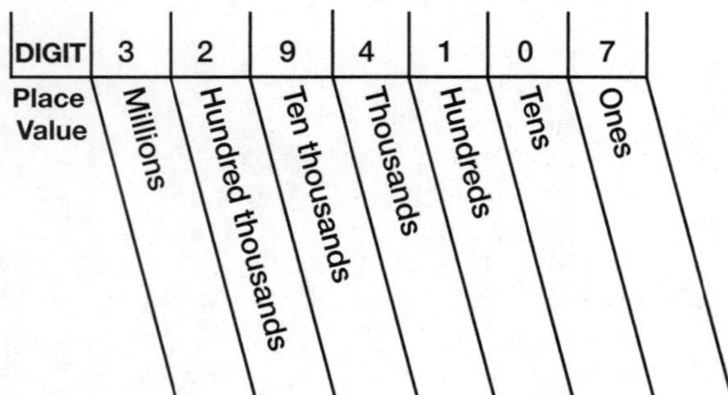

To compare or order whole numbers, you need to look at the digits in the largest place value of a number first.

Example
Compare 3,419 and 3,491.

Begin by comparing the two numbers in their largest place value. They both have the digit 3 in the thousands place. Therefore, you do not know which number is larger. Move to the smaller place values (to the right) of each number and continue comparing. The digit in the hundreds place for each number is 4. You still do not know which number is larger. However, when you compare the digits in the tens places, you see that the 9 is greater than the 1. That means 3,491 is greater than 3,419. This can be represented with the *greater than* symbol: 3,491 > 4,419.

Example
Put the following numbers in order from greatest to least value: 307, 319, 139, 301.

To order these numbers, the digits in their place values must be compared. Three of the numbers have a 3 in the hundreds place, but one number has a 1 in the hundreds place. Therefore, 139 is the smallest number. Next, the digits in the tens places must be compared in the remaining numbers. The tens digit in 319 is 1, and the tens digit in 307 and 301 is 0. Therefore, 319 is the largest number. To order 307 and 301, compare the digits in the ones place. 7 is greater than 1, so 307 is greater than 301.

The correct order of the numbers, from greatest to least, is 319, 307, 301, and 139.

Adding Whole Numbers

Addition is used when it is necessary to combine amounts. It is easiest to add when the addends are stacked in a column with the place values aligned. Work from right to left, starting with the ones column.

Example

Add 40 + 129 + 24.

1. Align the addends in the ones column. Because it is necessary to work from right to left, begin to add starting with the ones column. The ones column totals 13, and 13 equals 1 ten and 3 ones, so write the 3 in the ones column of the answer, and regroup, or carry, the ten to the next column as a 1 over the tens column so it gets added with the other tens:

$$\begin{array}{r} {}^{1} \\ 40 \\ 129 \\ +\ 24 \\ \hline 3 \end{array}$$

2. Add the tens column, including the regrouped 1.

$$\begin{array}{r} {}^{1} \\ 40 \\ 129 \\ +\ 24 \\ \hline 93 \end{array}$$

3. Then add the hundreds column. Because there is only one value, write the 1 in the answer.

$$\begin{array}{r} {}^{1} \\ 40 \\ 129 \\ +\ 24 \\ \hline 193 \end{array}$$

Subtracting Whole Numbers

Subtraction is used to find the difference between amounts. It is easiest to subtract when the minuend and subtrahend are in a column with the place values aligned. Again, just as with addition, work from right to left. It may be necessary to regroup.

Example

If Becky has 52 clients and Claire has 36, how many more clients does Becky have?

1. Find the difference between their client numbers by subtracting. Start with the ones column. Because 2 is less than the number being subtracted (6), regroup, or borrow, a ten from the tens column. Add the regrouped amount to the ones column. Now subtract 12 – 6 in the ones column.

$$\begin{array}{r} {}^{4}\,{}^{1} \\ \not{5}2 \\ -\ 36 \\ \hline 6 \end{array}$$

2. Regrouping 1 ten from the tens column left 4 tens. Subtract 4 – 3 and write the result in the tens column of the answer. Becky has 16 more clients than Claire. Check by addition: 16 + 36 = 52.

$$\begin{array}{r} {}^{4}\,{}^{1} \\ \not{5}2 \\ -\ 36 \\ \hline 16 \end{array}$$

Multiplying Whole Numbers

In multiplication, the same amount is combined multiple times. For example, instead of adding 30 three times, 30 + 30 + 30, it is easier to simply multiply 30 by 3. If a problem asks for the product of two or more numbers, the numbers should be multiplied to arrive at the answer.

Example

A school auditorium contains 54 rows, each containing 34 seats. How many seats are there in total?

1. In order to solve this problem, you could add 34 to itself 54 times, but we can solve this problem more easily with multiplication. Line up the place values vertically, writing the problem in columns. Multiply the number in the ones place of the top factor (4) by the number in the ones place of the bottom factor (4): 4 × 4 = 16. Because 16 = 1 ten and 6 ones, write the 6 in the ones place in the first partial product.

   Regroup or carry the ten by writing a 1 above the tens place of the top factor.

```
   1
  34
× 54
   6
```

2. Multiply the number in the tens place in the top factor (3) by the number in the ones place of the bottom factor (4): 4 × 3 = 12. Then add the regrouped amount: 12 + 1 = 13. Write the 3 in the tens column and the 1 in the hundreds column of the partial product.

```
   1
  34
× 54
 136
```

3. The last calculations to be done require multiplying by the tens place of the bottom factor. Multiply 5 (tens from bottom factor) by 4 (ones from top factor); 5 × 4 = 20, but because the 5 really represents a number of tens, the actual value of the answer is 200 (50 × 4 = 200). Therefore, write the two zeros under the ones and tens columns of the second partial product and regroup, or carry, the 2 hundreds by writing a 2 above the tens place of the top factor.

```
   2
  34
× 54
 136
  00
```

4. Multiply 5 (tens from bottom factor) by 3 (tens from top factor); 5 × 3 = 15, but because the 5 and the 3 each represent a number of tens, the actual value of the answer is 1,500 (50 × 30 = 1,500). Add the two additional hundreds carried over from the last multiplication: 15 + 2 = 17 (hundreds). Write the 17 in front of the zeros in the second partial product.

```
     2
    34
  × 54
   136
 1,700
```

5. Add the partial products to find the total product:

```
     2
    34
  × 54
   136
+ 1,700
 1,836
```

Note: It is easier to perform multiplication if you write the factor with the greater number of digits in the top row. In this example, both factors have an equal number of digits, so it does not matter which is written on top.

Dividing Whole Numbers

In division, the same amount is subtracted multiple times. For example, instead of subtracting 5 from 25 as many times as possible, 25 – 5 – 5 – 5 – 5 – 5, it is easier to simply divide, asking how many 5s are in 25: 25 ÷ 5.

Example
At a road show, three artists sold their beads for a total of $54. If they share the money equally, how much money should each artist receive?

1. Divide the total amount ($54) by the number of ways the money is to be split (3). Work from left to right. How many times does 3 divide into 5? Write the answer, 1, directly above the 5 in the dividend, because both the 5 and the 1 represent a number of tens. Now multiply: since 1(ten) ÷ 3(ones) = 3(tens), write the 3 under the 5, and subtract; 5(tens) – 3(tens) = 2(tens).

$$\begin{array}{r} 1 \\ 3\overline{)54} \\ \underline{-3} \\ 2 \end{array}$$

2. Continue dividing. Bring down the 4 from the ones place in the dividend. How many times does 3 divide into 24? Write the answer, 8, directly above the 4 in the dividend. Because 3 ÷ 8 = 24, write 24 below the other 24 and subtract 24 – 24 = 0.

$$\begin{array}{r} 18 \\ 3\overline{)54} \\ \underline{-3\downarrow} \\ 24 \\ \underline{-24} \\ 0 \end{array}$$

Remainders

If you get a number other than zero after your last subtraction, this number is your remainder.

Example
What is 9 divided by 4?

$$\begin{array}{r} 2 \\ 4\overline{)9} \\ \underline{-8} \\ 1 \end{array}$$

1 is the remainder.

The answer is 2 R1. This answer can also be written as $2\frac{1}{4}$, because there was one part left over out of the four parts needed to make a whole.

Estimating with Whole Numbers

One of the skills required on the Praxis II: Elementary Education: Content Knowledge test is to solve problems using a variety of techniques, including using an estimate. That means you will not need to find the actual answer, but instead an answer that is *close* to the actual answer. One way to solve estimation problems with whole numbers is to use numbers that are easy to work with and are close to the actual numbers.

Example
A television set weighs 21 pounds. About how much will a case weigh if it carries 46 television sets?

The number 21 is close to 20, and 20 is much easier to work with than 21. The number 46 is close to 50, and 50 is much easier to work with than 46. To find the approximate weight of the 46 television sets, you can just multiply 20 by 50. A proper estimate would be 1,000 pounds.

Integers

An **integer** is a whole number or its opposite. A **number line** can be helpful in demonstrating the value of an integer, as well as performing operations with integers. In the following number line, point A is 3 units to the left of the 0, so its value is –3. Point B is 6 units to the right of the 0, so its value is 6.

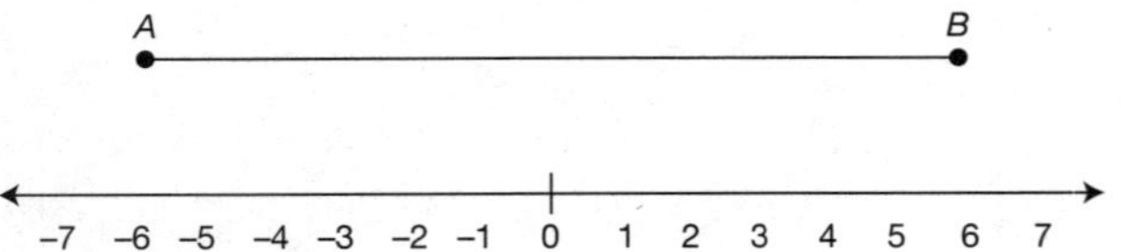

Here are some rules for performing operations with integers.

Adding Integers

Adding numbers with the same sign results in a sum of the same sign:

(positive) + (positive) = positive and
(negative) + (negative) = negative

When adding numbers of different signs, follow this two-step process:

1. Subtract the positive values of the numbers. Positive values are the values of the numbers without any signs.
2. Keep the sign of the number with the larger positive value.

Example

$-2 + 3 =$

1. Subtract the positive values of the numbers: $3 - 2 = 1$.
2. The number 3 is the larger of the two positive values. Its sign in the original example was positive, so the sign of the answer is positive. The answer is positive 1.

Example

$8 + -11 =$

1. Subtract the positive values of the numbers: $11 - 8 = 3$.
2. The number 11 is the larger of the two positive values. Its sign in the original example was negative, so the sign of the answer is negative. The answer is negative 3.

Subtracting Integers

When subtracting integers, change the subtraction sign to addition and change the sign of the number being subtracted to its opposite. Then follow the rules for addition.

Examples

$(+10) - (+12) = (+10) + (-12) = -2$

$(-5) - (-7) = (-5) + (+7) = +2$

Multiplying and Dividing Integers

A simple method for remembering the rules of multiplying and dividing is that if the signs are the same when multiplying or dividing two quantities, the answer will be positive. If the signs are different, the answer will be negative.

(positive) × (positive) = positive $\frac{\text{(positive)}}{\text{(positive)}}$ = positive

(positive) × (negative) = negative $\frac{\text{(positive)}}{\text{(negative)}}$ = negative

(negative) × (positive) = negative $\frac{\text{(negative)}}{\text{(positive)}}$ = negative

(negative) × (negative) = positive $\frac{\text{(negative)}}{\text{(negative)}}$ = positive

Examples

$(10)(-12) = -120$

$-5 \times -7 = 35$

$12 \div -3 = -4$

$15 \div 3 = 5$

Exponents

An exponent indicates the number of times a base is used as a factor to attain a product.

Example
Evaluate 2^5

In this example, 2 is the base and 5 is the exponent. Therefore, 2 should be used as a factor 5 times to attain a product:

$2^5 = 2 \times 2 \times 2 \times 2 \times 2 = 32$

Zero Exponent

Any nonzero number raised to the zero power equals 1.

Examples
$5^0 = 1$ $70^0 = 1$ $29{,}874^0 = 1$

Perfect Squares

The number 5^2 is read "5 to the second power," or, more commonly, "5 squared." Perfect squares are numbers that are second powers of other numbers. Perfect squares are always zero or positive, because when you multiply a positive or a negative by itself, the result is always positive. The perfect squares are $0^2, 1^2, 2^2, 3^2$. . . . Therefore, the perfect squares are 0, 1, 4, 9, 16, 25, 36, 49, 64, 81, 100. . . .

Perfect Cubes

The number 5^3 is read "5 to the third power," or, more commonly, "5 cubed." (Powers higher than three have no special name.) Perfect cubes are numbers that are third powers of other numbers. Perfect cubes, unlike perfect squares, can be either positive or negative. This is because when a negative is multiplied by itself three times, the result is negative. The perfect cubes are $0^3, 1^3, 2^3, 3^3$. . . . Therefore, the perfect cubes are 0, 1, 8, 27, 64, 125. . . .

Concepts of Number Theory

Factors

Factors are numbers that can be divided into a larger number without a remainder.

Example
$12 \div 3 = 4$

The number 3 is, therefore, a factor of the number 12. Other factors of 12 are 1, 2, 4, 6, and 12. The common factors of two numbers are the factors that both numbers have in common.

Examples
The factors of 24 = 1, 2, 3, 4, 6, 8, 12, and 24.
The factors of 18 = 1, 2, 3, 6, 9, and 18.

From the examples, you can see that the common factors of 24 and 18 are 1, 2, 3, and 6. From this list it can also be determined that the *greatest* common factor of 24 and 18 is 6. Determining the **greatest common factor** (GCF) is useful for simplifying fractions.

Example
Simplify $\frac{16}{20}$

The factors of 16 are 1, 2, 4, 8, and 16. The factors of 20 are 1, 2, 4, 5, and 20. The common factors of 16 and 20 are 1, 2, and 4. The greatest of these, the GCF, is 4. Therefore, to simplify the fraction, both numerator and denominator should be divided by 4.

$\frac{16}{20} = \frac{16 \div 4}{20 \div 4} = \frac{4}{5}$

Multiples

Multiples are numbers that can be obtained by multiplying a number x by a positive integer.

Example

$5 \times 7 = 35$

The number 35 is, therefore, a multiple of the number 5 and of the number 7. Other multiples of 5 are 5, 10, 15, 20, and so on. Other multiples of 7 are 7, 14, 21, 28, and so on.

The common multiples of two numbers are the multiples that both numbers share.

Example

Some multiples of 4 are: 4, 8, 12, 16, 20, 24, 28, 32, 36.

Some multiples of 6 are: 6, 12, 18, 24, 30, 36, 42, 48.

Some common multiples are 12, 24, and 36. From the above it can also be determined that the *least* common multiple of the numbers 4 and 6 is 12, since this number is the smallest number that appeared in both lists. The **least common multiple**, or LCM, is used when performing addition and subtraction of fractions to find the least common denominator.

Example (using denominators 4 and 6 and LCM of 12)

$$\frac{1}{4} + \frac{5}{6} = \frac{1(3)}{4(3)} + \frac{5(2)}{6(2)}$$
$$= \frac{3}{12} + \frac{10}{12}$$
$$= \frac{13}{12}$$
$$= 1\frac{1}{12}$$

Odd and Even Numbers

An **even number** is a number that can be divided by the number 2: 2, 4, 6, 8, 10, 12, 14. . . . An **odd number** cannot be divided by the number 2: 1, 3, 5, 7, 9, 11, 13. . . . The even and odd numbers listed are also examples of **consecutive even numbers** and **consecutive odd numbers** because they differ by two.

Here are some helpful rules for how even and odd numbers behave when added or multiplied:

even + even = even and even × even = even
odd + odd = even and odd × odd = odd
odd + even = odd and even × odd = even

Prime and Composite Numbers

A **prime number** is a number that is only evenly divisible by itself and the number 1. For example, 3, 7, and 29 are all prime numbers. The only even prime number is 2. The number 1 is not considered a prime number.

A **composite number** is a number that has more than two factors. For example, the numbers 4, 9, and 100 are all composite numbers because 4 has the factors 1, 2, and 4; 9 has the factors 1, 3, and 9; and 100 has the factors 1, 2, 4, 5, 10, 20, 25, 50, and 100.

Prime factorization is a way to show all the prime numbers that comprise a composite number. For example, the prime factorization of 30 is $2 \times 3 \times 5$. The prime factorization of 24 is $2 \times 2 \times 2 \times 3$, which can be expressed with exponents as $2^3 \times 3$. A factor tree can be helpful in showing all of the prime numbers for a number. The following factor trees show the prime factorization for 60.

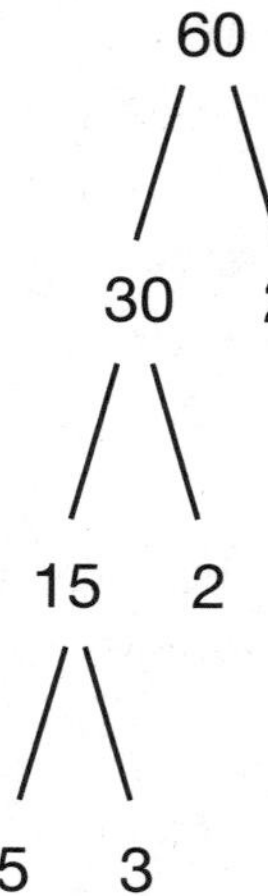

The prime factorization of 60 is $5 \times 3 \times 2 \times 2$, or $5 \times 3 \times 2^2$.

Decimals

It is very important to remember the place values of a decimal. The first place value to the right of the decimal point is the tenths place. The place values from thousands to ten thousandths are as follows:

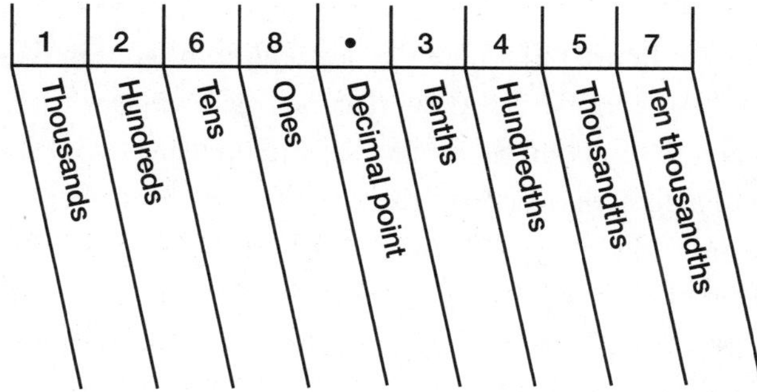

In expanded form, this number can also be expressed as:

$1{,}268.3457 = (1 \times 1{,}000) + (2 \times 100) + (6 \times 10) + (8 \times 1) + (3 \times 0.1) + (4 \times 0.01) + (5 \times 0.001) + (7 \times 0.0001)$.

Comparing and Ordering Decimals

To compare or order decimals, compare the digits in their place values. It's the same process as comparing or ordering whole numbers. You just need to pay careful attention to the decimal point.

Example
Compare 0.2 and 0.05.

Compare the numbers by the digits in their place values. Both decimals have a 0 in the ones place, so you need to look at the place value to the right. 0.2 has a 2 in the tenths place while 0.05 has a 0 in the tenths place. Because 2 is bigger than 0, 0.2 is bigger than 0.05. You can show this as $0.2 > 0.05$.

Example
Order 2.32, 2.38, and 2.29 in order from greatest to least.

Again, look at the place values of the numbers. All three numbers have a 2 in the ones place, so you cannot order them yet. Looking at the next place value to the right, tenths, reveals that 2.29 has the number 2 in the tenths place whereas the other numbers have a 3. So 2.29 is the smallest number. To order 2.32 and 2.38 correctly, compare the digits in the hundredths place. $8 > 2$, so $2.38 > 2.32$. The correct order from greatest to least is 2.38, 2.32, and 2.29.

Rounding Decimals

It is often inconvenient to work with decimals. It is much easier to have an approximation value for a decimal. In this case, you can **round** decimals to a certain number of decimal places. The most common ways to round are as follows:

- To the nearest integer: zero digits to the right of the decimal point
- To the nearest tenth: one digit to the right of the decimal point (tenths unit)
- To the nearest hundredth: two digits to the right of the decimal point (hundredths unit)

In order to round, look at the digit to the immediate right of the digit you are rounding to. If the digit is less than 5, leave the digit you are rounding to alone, and omit all the digits to its right. If the digit is 5 or greater, increase the digit you are rounding by one, and omit all the digits to its right.

Example
Round 14.38 to the nearest whole number.

The digit to the right of the ones place is 3. Therefore, you can leave the digit you are rounding to alone, which is the 4 in the ones place. Omit all the digits to the right.

14.38 is 14 when rounded to the nearest whole number.

Example
Round 1.084 to the nearest tenth.

The digit to the right of the tenths place is 8. Therefore, you need to increase the digit you are rounding to by 1. That means the 0 in the tenths place becomes a 1. Then all the digits to the right can be omitted.

1.084 is 1.1 to the nearest tenth.

Adding and Subtracting Decimals

Adding and subtracting decimals is very similar to adding and subtracting whole numbers. The most important thing to remember is to line up the numbers to be added or subtracted by their decimal points. Zeros may be filled in as placeholders when all numbers do not have the same number of decimal places.

Examples
What is the sum of 0.45, 0.8, and 1.36?

$$\begin{array}{r} \scriptstyle 1\,1 \\ 0.45 \\ 0.80 \\ \underline{+\,1.36} \\ 2.61 \end{array}$$

Take away 0.35 from 1.06.

$$\begin{array}{r} \scriptstyle 0\,\,1 \\ \not{1}.06 \\ \underline{-\,0.35} \\ 0.71 \end{array}$$

Multiplying Decimals

The process to multiply decimals is exactly the same as multiplying whole numbers. Multiply the numbers, ignoring the decimal points in the factors. Then add the decimal point in the final product later.

Example
What is the product of 0.14 and 4.3?

First, multiply as usual (do not line up the decimal points):

$$\begin{array}{r} 4.3 \\ \underline{\times\,0.14} \\ 172 \\ \underline{+\,430} \\ 602 \end{array}$$

Now, to figure out where the decimal point goes in the product, count how many decimal places are in each factor. 4.3 has one decimal place and 0.14 has two decimal places. In order to determine the total number of decimal places the answer must have to the right of the decimal point, add. In this problem, there are a total of three (1 + 2) decimal places. Therefore, the decimal point needs to be placed three decimal places from the right side of the answer. In this example, 602 turns into 0.602. If there are not enough digits in the answer, add zeros in front of the answer until there are enough.

Example
Multiply 0.03 × 0.2.

$$\begin{array}{r} 0.03 \\ \underline{\times\,0.2} \\ 6 \end{array}$$

There are three total decimal places in the two numbers being multiplied. Therefore, the answer must contain three decimal places. Starting to the right of 6 (because 6 is equal to 6.0), move left three places. The answer becomes 0.006.

Dividing Decimals

To divide decimals, you need to change the divisor so that it does not have any decimals. In order to do that, simply move the decimal place to the right as many places as necessary to make the divisor a whole number. The decimal point must also be moved in the dividend the same number of places to keep the answer the same as the original problem. Moving a decimal point in a division problem is equivalent to multiplying a numerator and denominator of a fraction by the same quantity, which is the reason the answer will remain the same.

If there are not enough decimal places in the dividend (the number being divided) to accommodate the required move, simply add zeros at the end of the number. Add zeros after the decimal point to continue the division until the decimal terminates, or until a repeating pattern is recognized. The decimal point in the quotient belongs directly above the decimal point in the dividend.

Example
What is $0.425\overline{)1.53}$?

To make 0.425 a whole number, move the decimal point three places to the right: 0.425 becomes 425. Now move the decimal point three places to the right for 1.53: You need to add a zero, but 1.53 becomes 1,530.

The problem is now a simple long division problem.

$$\begin{array}{r} 3.6 \\ 425\overline{)1{,}530.0} \\ -1{,}275\downarrow \\ \hline 2{,}550 \\ -2{,}550 \\ \hline 0 \end{array}$$

Fractions

A fraction is a part of a whole, represented with one number over another number. The number on the bottom, the denominator, shows how many total parts there are in the whole. The number on the top, the numerator, shows how many parts there are of the whole. To perform operations with fractions, it is necessary to understand some basic concepts.

Simplifying Fractions

To simplify fractions, identify the greatest common factor (GCF) of the numerator and denominator and divide both the numerator and denominator by this number.

Example
Simplify $\frac{16}{24}$.

The GCF of 16 and 24 is 8, so divide 16 and 24 each by 8 to simplify the fraction:

$$\frac{16}{24} = \frac{16 \div 8}{24 \div 8} = \frac{2}{3}$$

Adding and Subtracting Fractions

To add or subtract fractions with like denominators, just add or subtract the numerators and keep the denominator.

Example
$\frac{1}{7} + \frac{5}{7} = 1\frac{5}{7} = \frac{6}{7}$

To add or subtract fractions with unlike denominators, first find the least common denominator or LCD. The LCD is the smallest number divisible by each of the denominators.

For example, for the denominators 8 and 12, 24 would be the LCD because 24 is the smallest number that is divisible by both 8 and 12: $8 \times 3 = 24$, and $12 \times 2 = 24$.

Using the LCD, convert each fraction to its new form by multiplying both the numerator and denominator by the appropriate factor to get the LCD, and then follow the directions for adding/subtracting fractions with like denominators.

Example
$\frac{1}{3} + \frac{2}{5} = \frac{1(5)}{3(5)} + \frac{2(3)}{5(3)} = \frac{5}{15} + \frac{6}{15} = \frac{11}{15}$

Multiplying Fractions

To multiply fractions, simply multiply the numerators and the denominators.

Example
$\frac{2}{3} \times \frac{1}{4} = 2 \times \frac{1}{3} \times 4 = \frac{2}{12} = \frac{1}{6}$

Dividing Fractions

Dividing fractions is similar to multiplying fractions. You just need to flip the numerator and denominator of the divisor, the fraction being divided. Then multiply across, like you would when multiplying fractions.

Example
Solve: $\frac{1}{4} \div \frac{1}{2}$.

Flip the numerator and denominator of the divisor and change the symbol to multiplication.

$\frac{1}{4} \div \frac{1}{2} = \frac{1}{4} \times \frac{2}{1}$

Now, multiply the numerators and the denominators, and simplify if necessary.

$\frac{1}{4} \times \frac{2}{1} = \frac{1 \times 2}{4 \times 1} = \frac{2}{4}$

Because both the numerator and the denominator of $\frac{2}{4}$ can be divided by 2, the fraction can be reduced.

$\frac{2}{4} = \frac{2 \div 2}{4 \div 2} = \frac{1}{2}$

TIP

It can be easy to confuse the processes for multiplying and dividing fractions. It helps to check the reasonableness of a solution by considering it in real-world context. For example, if you are splitting one-quarter of a pizza pie into halves, you need to multiply $\frac{1}{4}$ by $\frac{1}{2}$. You should consider that the solution must be smaller than $\frac{1}{4}$ because that's all the pizza you had when you started. If you got an answer higher than $\frac{1}{4}$, check your math or the process you used to solve.

Comparing Fractions

Sometimes it is necessary to compare the sizes of fractions. This is very simple when the fractions have a common denominator. All you have to do is compare the numerators.

Example
Compare $\frac{3}{8}$ and $\frac{5}{8}$.

Because 3 is smaller than 5, $\frac{3}{8}$ is smaller than $\frac{5}{8}$. Therefore, $\frac{3}{8} < \frac{5}{8}$.

If the fractions do not have a common denominator, multiply the numerator of the first fraction by the denominator of the second fraction. Write this answer under the first fraction. Then multiply the numerator of the second fraction by the denominator of the first one. Write this answer under the second fraction. Compare the two numbers. The larger number represents the larger fraction.

Examples
Which is larger: $\frac{7}{11}$ or $\frac{4}{9}$?

Cross multiply.

$\frac{7}{11} \times \frac{4}{9}$?

$7 \times 9 = 63$ $\quad$ $4 \times 11 = 44$

$63 > 44$; therefore, $\frac{7}{11} > \frac{4}{9}$.

Compare $\frac{6}{18}$ and $\frac{2}{6}$.

Cross multiply.

$\frac{6}{18} \times \frac{2}{6}$

$6 \times 6 = 36 \qquad 2 \times 18 = 36$

$36 = 36$; therefore, $\frac{6}{18} = \frac{2}{6}$.

Percents

Percents are always "out of 100": 45% means 45 out of 100. Therefore, to write percents as decimals, move the decimal point two places to the left (to the hundredths place).

$45\% = \frac{45}{100} = 0.45$
$3\% = \frac{3}{100} = 0.03$
$124\% = \frac{124}{100} = 1.24$
$0.9\% = \frac{0.9}{100} = 0.009$

Here are some common conversions:

FRACTION	DECIMAL	PERCENTAGE
$\frac{1}{2}$	.5	50%
$\frac{1}{4}$	.25	25%
$\frac{1}{3}$	.333 . . .	$33.\overline{3}\%$
$\frac{2}{3}$	.666 . . .	$66.\overline{6}\%$
$\frac{1}{10}$	.1	10%
$\frac{1}{8}$	.125	12.5%
$\frac{1}{6}$	.1666 . . .	$16.\overline{6}\%$
$\frac{1}{5}$	.2	20%

Percent Increase or Decrease

Some questions on the Praxis II: Elementary Education: Content Knowledge test may ask you about an increase or decrease of a number based on a percentage increase or decrease. For example, you may be asked to determine the amount of a 15% tip for a $20.60 bill or the increase in population based on a 4% increase from 22,000. For those types of problems, simply multiply the percentage by the base number, converting the percentage into a decimal first.

Example
The value of a house increased by 8% from 2005 to 2010. If the house was worth $220,000 in 2005, how much was it worth in 2010?

Convert 8% to a decimal by moving the decimal two places to the left: 8% = 0.08. Then multiply that value by the base number: $0.08 \times 220{,}000 = 17{,}600$. The value of the house increased by $17,600. But because the question asked for the value in 2010, you need to add the original value to the amount of the increase: $220{,}000 + 17{,}600 = 237{,}600$. The value of the house in 2010 is $237,600.

Other questions may provide the numbers that demonstrate the increase or decrease but ask you to provide the percentage. In those cases, the easiest way to solve them is to set up a proportion.

Example
An incorporated village had a $1,400 budget to spend on a July 4 celebration. Because of cutbacks, the village now has only $1,232 to spend on the celebration. By what percentage did the budget for the celebration decrease after the cutbacks?

The easiest way to solve this type of problem is to divide the final number by the original number. The quotient will be the percentage of the original number: $1{,}232 \div 1{,}400 = 0.88$. That means 1,232 is 88% of 1,400. In other words, 1,400 decreased by 12% is equal to 1,232. The budget decreased by 12%.

The Order of Operations

There is an order in which a sequence of mathematical operations must be performed:

P: Parentheses/Grouping Symbols. Perform all operations within parentheses first. If there is more than one set of parentheses, begin to work with the innermost set and work toward the outside. If more than one operation is present within the parentheses, use the remaining rules of order to determine which operation to perform first.
E: Exponents. Evaluate exponents.
M/D: Multiply/Divide. Work from left to right in the expression.
A/S: Add/Subtract. Work from left to right in the expression.

This order is illustrated by the acronym PEMDAS, which can be remembered by using the first letter of each of the words in the phrase: **P**lease **E**xcuse **M**y **D**ear **A**unt **S**ally.

Example

$\frac{(5+3)^2}{4} + 27$

$= \frac{(8)^2}{4} + 27$

$= \frac{8}{4} + 27$

$= 16 + 27$

$= 43$

Patterns

The ability to detect patterns in numbers is a very important mathematical skill. Patterns exist everywhere in nature, business, and finance. When you are asked to find a pattern in a series of numbers, look to see whether there is a common number you can add, subtract, multiply, or divide each number in the pattern by to give you the next number in the series.

For example, in the sequence 5, 8, 11, 14 you can add 3 to each number in the sequence to get the next number in the sequence. The next number in the sequence is 17.

Examples
What is the next number in the sequence $\frac{3}{4}$, 3, 12, 48?

Each number in the sequence can be multiplied by the number 4 to get the next number in the sequence: $\frac{3}{4} \times 4 = 3$, $3 \times 4 = 12$, $12 \times 4 = 48$, so the next number in the sequence is $48 \times 4 = 192$.

Sometimes it is not that simple. You may need to look for a combination of multiplying and adding, dividing and subtracting, or some combination of other operations.

What is the next number in the sequence 0, 1, 2, 5, 26?

Keep trying various operations until you find one that works. In this case, the correct procedure is to square the term and add 1: $0^2 + 1 = 1$, $1^2 + 1 = 2$, $2^2 + 1 = 5$, $5^2 + 1 = 26$, so the next number in the sequence is $26^2 + 1 = 677$.

Algebra

Algebra uses letters or symbols, called **variables**, to represent unknown numbers. About 25% of the questions on the mathematics section of the Praxis II: Elementary Education: Content Knowledge test will involve algebraic concepts. This may include algebraic representations, equations, inequalities, or formulas. The algebra questions will also ensure that you are familiar with the properties of numbers, as well as the additive and multiplicative inverses.

Properties of Arithmetic

You should be able to quickly identify each of the following properties of numbers and recognize how they can be used in algebra.

Commutative Property. This property states that the result of an arithmetic operation is not affected by reversing the order of the numbers. Multiplication and addition are operations that satisfy the commutative property.

Examples
$5 \times 2 = 2 \times 5$
$(5)(a) = (a)(5)$
$b + 3 = 3 + b$

However, neither subtraction nor division is commutative, because reversing the order of the numbers does not yield the same result.

Examples
$5 - 2 \neq 2 - 5$
$6 \div 3 \neq 3 \div 6$

Associative Property. If parentheses can be moved to group different numbers in an arithmetic problem without changing the result, then the operation is associative. Addition and multiplication are associative.

Examples
$2 + (3 + 4) = (2 + 3) + 4$
$2(ab) = (2a)b$

Distributive Property. When a value is being multiplied by a sum or difference, multiply that value by each quantity within the parentheses. Then, take the sum or difference to yield an equivalent result.

Examples
$5(a + b) = 5a + 5b$
$5(100 - 6) = (5 \times 100) - (5 \times 6)$

This second example can be proved by performing the calculations:

$$\begin{aligned} 5(94) &= 5(100 - 6) \\ &= 500 - 30 \\ 470 &= 470 \end{aligned}$$

Identities and Inverses

The **additive identity** is the value that, when added to a number, does not change the number. For all integers, the additive identity is 0.

Examples
$5 + 0 = 5$
$-3 + 0 = -3$

Adding 0 does not change the values of 5 and –3, so 0 is the additive identity.

The **additive inverse** of a number is the number that, when added to the number, gives you the additive identity.

Example
What is the additive inverse of –3?

This means, "What number can I add to –3 to give me the additive identity (0)?"

$-3 + \underline{\quad} = 0$
$-3 + 3 = 0$

The answer is 3.

The **multiplicative identity** is the value that, when multiplied by a number, does not change the number. For all integers, the multiplicative identity is 1.

Examples
$5 \times 1 = 5$
$-3 \times 1 = -3$

Multiplying by 1 does not change the values of 5 and –3, so 1 is the multiplicative identity.

The **multiplicative inverse** of a number is the number that, when multiplied by the number, gives you the multiplicative identity.

Example
What is the multiplicative inverse of 5?

This means, "What number can I multiply 5 by to give me the multiplicative identity (1)?"

$5 \times \_\_\_ = 1$

$\frac{1}{5} \times 5 = 1$

The answer is $\frac{1}{5}$.

There is an easy way to find the multiplicative inverse. It is the **reciprocal**, which is obtained by reversing the numerator and denominator of a fraction. In the preceding example, the answer is the reciprocal of 5; 5 can be written as $\frac{5}{1}$, so the reciprocal is $\frac{1}{5}$.

Note: Reciprocals do not change signs.

Note: The additive inverse of a number is the opposite of the number; the multiplicative inverse is the reciprocal.

Linear Equations

A linear equation contains an unknown value, called a **variable**, and an equal sign. The equal sign separates an equation into two sides. You may be asked to find the value of the variable using information in the equation. You may also be asked to identify an equation that represents a given scenario.

The first step is to get all the variable terms on one side and all the numbers on the other side. This is accomplished by *undoing* the operations that are attaching numbers to the variable, thereby isolating the variable. The operations are always done in reverse PEMDAS order: start by adding/subtracting, then multiply/divide.

It is very important to remember that whenever an operation is performed on one side, the same operation must be performed on the other side.

Examples

Solve for k in the equation $3k = 33$.

To get k by itself on the left side of the equation, both sides need to be divided by 3.

$\frac{3k}{3} = \frac{33}{3}$

$k = 11$

The value of k is 11.

Solve for m in the equation $5m + 8 = 48$.

Undo the addition of 8 by subtracting 8 from both sides of the equation. Then undo the multiplication by 5 by dividing by 5 on both sides of the equation.

$-8 = -8$

$\frac{5m}{5} = \frac{40}{5}$

$m = 8$

The variable, m, is now isolated on the left side of the equation, and its value is 8.

Checking Solutions to Equations

To check an equation, substitute the value of the variable into the original equation.

Example

To check the solution of the previous equation, substitute the number 8 for the variable m in $5m + 8 = 48$.

$5(8) + 8 = 48$

$40 + 8 = 48$

$48 = 48$

Because this statement is true, the answer $m = 8$ must be correct.

Linear Inequalities

A linear inequality contains a **variable**, and an inequality sign, such as $<$ or $>$. The inequality sign separates an inequality into two sides. You may be asked to find the value of a variable using information in the inequality. You may also be asked to identify an inequality that represents a given scenario.

There are four inequality signs that you may see on your exam:

- The symbol $>$ means "is greater than." For example, 4 is greater than –5, so $4 > -5$
- The symbol $<$ means "is less than." For example, 3 is less than 8, so $3 < 8$.
- The symbol $\geq$ means "is greater than or equal to." For example 0 is greater than or equal to 0, so $0 \geq 0$.
- The symbol $\leq$ means "is less than or equal to." For example, –1 is less than 1, so $-1 \leq 1$.

To solve an inequality, you follow almost all the exact same steps that are used to solve an equation. You add, subtract, multiply, and divide to both sides of the inequality to isolate the variable on one side. There is only one important difference: When you multiply or divide by a negative number, you must reverse the direction of the inequality symbol.

Example
Solve for a in the following inequality:
$4a + 12 > 40$.

To get a by itself, subtract 12 from both sides of the inequality, and then divide both sides by 4.

$4a + 12 > 40$
$4a > 28$
$a > 7$

The variable, a, is now isolated on the left side of the inequality, and its value can be any number greater than 7.

Checking Solutions to Inequalities

To check an inequality, substitute a possible value of the variable into the original inequality.

Example
To check the solution of the previous inequality, substitute any number greater than 7 for the variable a in $4a + 12 > 40$. For example, you can use the number 10 because it is greater than 7.

$4a + 12 > 40$
$4(10) + 12 > 40$
$40 + 12 > 40$
$52 > 40$

Because this statement is true, the answer $a > 7$ is likely correct.

TIP

If 0 satisfies an inequality, it is an easy number to use to check your answer. When using a number to check your answer with a $\geq$ or $\leq$ symbol, do *not* use a number that is equal to the variable.

Example
Solve for b in the following inequality: $-3b - 10 \geq 20$. Then check your answer.

To get b by itself, add 10 from both sides of the inequality, and then divide both sides by –3. Remember that when multiplying or dividing by a negative number in an inequality, you must flip the direction of the inequality symbol!

$-3b - 10 \geq 20$
$-3b \geq 30$
$b \leq -10$

The variable, b, is now isolated on the left side of the inequality, and its value can be any number less than –10.

To check the solution, substitute any number less than or equal to –10 for the variable b in $-3b - 10 \geq 20$. For example, you can use the number –20 because it is less than or equal to –10.

$-3b - 10 \geq 20$
$-3(-20) - 10 \geq 20$
$60 - 10 \geq 20$
$50 \geq 20$

Because this statement is true, the answer $b \leq -10$ is likely correct.

Geometry and Measurement

About 20% of the questions on the mathematics section—probably six questions in total—will test you on your knowledge of geometry and measurement.

Geometry is the study of shapes and the relationships among them. The geometry you are required to know for the Praxis II will involve the properties of figures in two- and three-dimensional objects, including representations and models. You will also be expected to understand the coordinate grid system and know how to apply transformations of figures on the grid.

The measurement questions on the Praxis II will involve nonstandard, customary, and metric units of measurement. This could involve any type of measurement, including length, weight, time, or temperature.

Geometry

Because you will be tested on your knowledge of two- and three-dimensional figures, it makes sense to review the components of two-dimensional figures—as well as the most common types of two-dimensional figures, polygons.

Angles

An **angle** is formed by an endpoint, or vertex, and two rays.

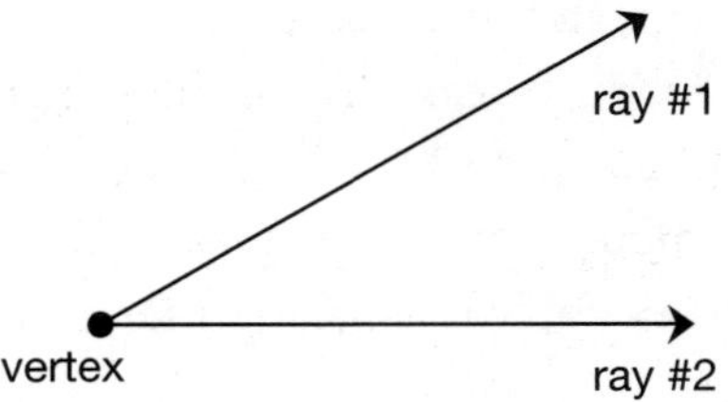

Naming Angles

There are three ways to name an angle.

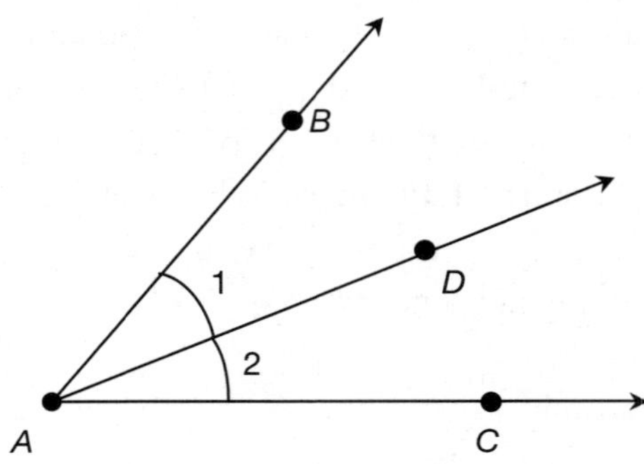

1. An angle can be named by the vertex when no other angles share the same vertex: $\angle A$.
2. An angle can be represented by a number written across from the vertex: $\angle 1$.
3. When more than one angle has the same vertex, three letters are used, with the vertex always being the middle letter: $\angle 1$ can be written as $\angle BAD$ or as $\angle DAB$; $\angle 2$ can be written as $\angle DAC$ or as $\angle CAD$.

Classifying Angles

Angles can be classified into the following categories: acute, right, obtuse, and straight.

- An **acute** angle is an angle that measures less than 90 degrees.

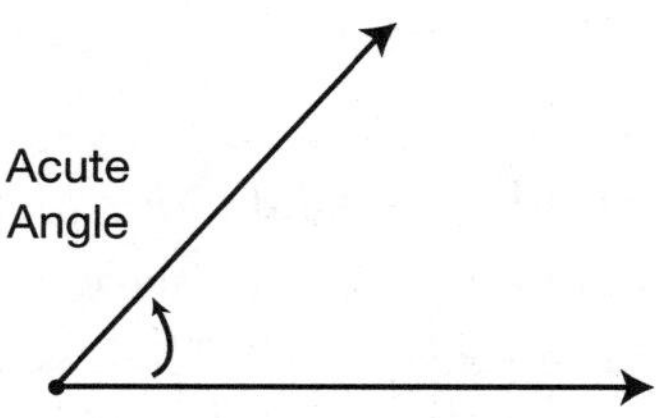

- A **right** angle is an angle that measures exactly 90 degrees. A right angle is represented by a square at the vertex.

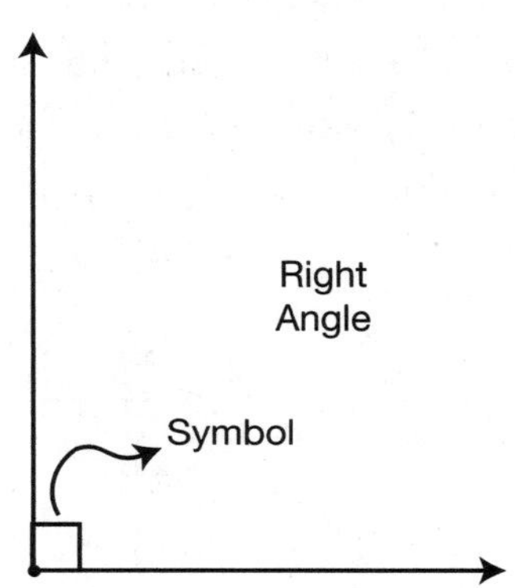

- An **obtuse** angle is an angle that measures more than 90 degrees, but less than 180 degrees.

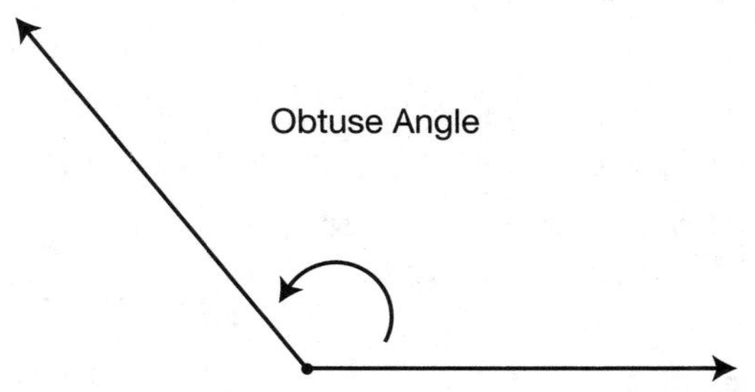

- A **straight** angle is an angle that measures 180 degrees. Thus, both of its sides form a line.

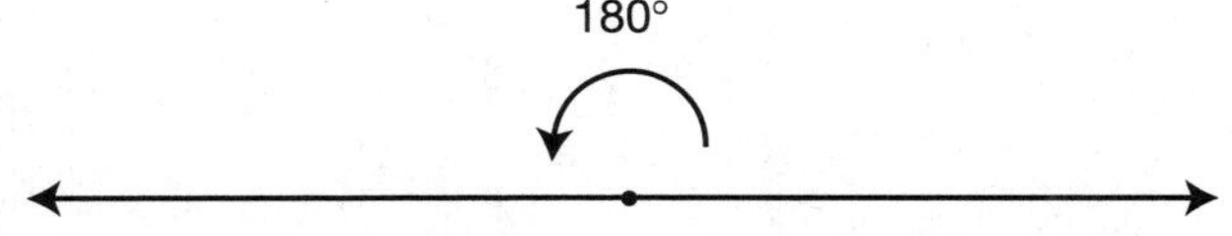

Complementary Angles

Two angles are **complementary** if the sum of their measures is equal to 90 degrees.

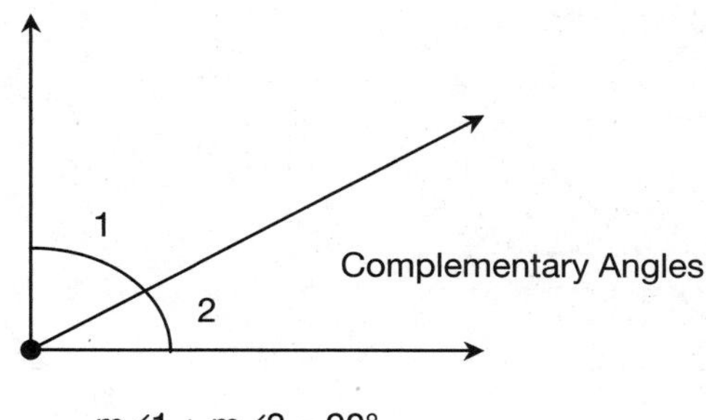

$m\angle 1 + m\angle 2 = 90°$

Supplementary Angles

Two angles are **supplementary** if the sum of their measures is equal to 180 degrees.

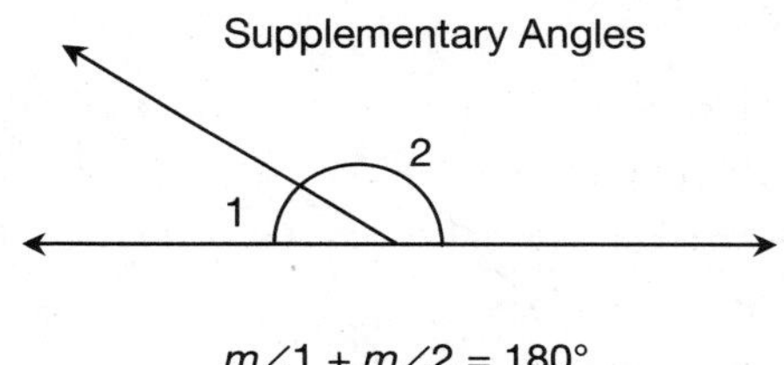

$m\angle 1 + m\angle 2 = 180°$

Adjacent Angles

Adjacent angles have the same vertex, share a side, and do not overlap.

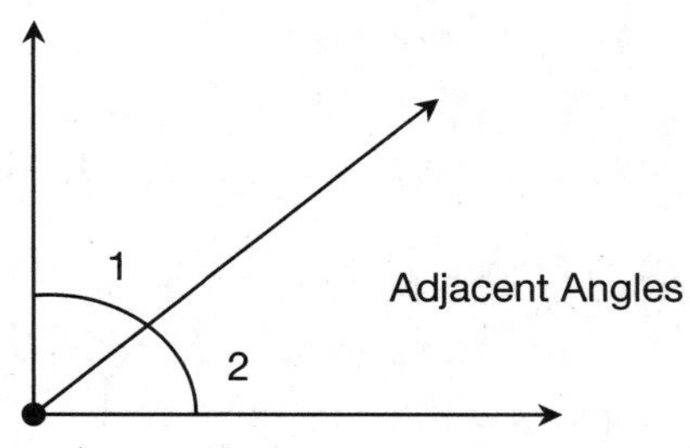

$\angle 1$ and $\angle 2$ are adjacent.

The sum of all of the measures of adjacent angles around the same vertex is equal to 360 degrees.

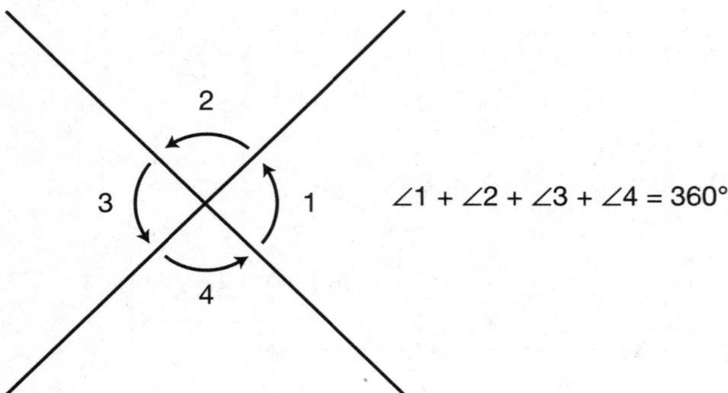

Angles of Intersecting Lines

When two lines intersect, two sets of nonadjacent angles called vertical angles are formed. Vertical angles have equal measures and are supplementary to adjacent angles.

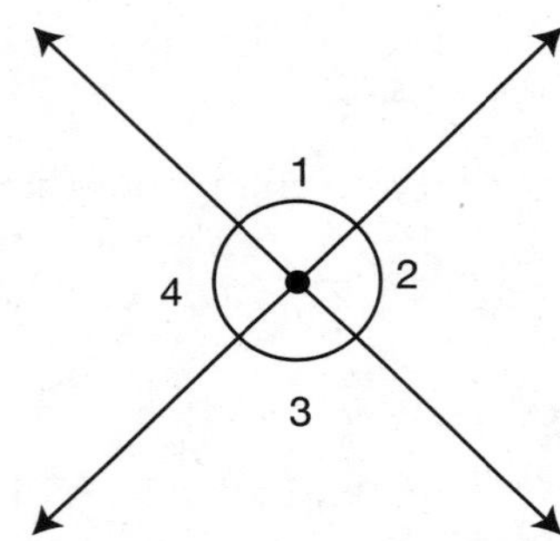

- $m\angle 1 = m\angle 3$ and $m\angle 2 = m\angle 4$
- $m\angle 1 = m\angle 4$ and $m\angle 3 = m\angle 2$
- $m\angle 1 + m\angle 2 = 180$ and $m\angle 2 + m\angle 3 = 180°$
- $m\angle 3 + m\angle 4 = 180$ and $m\angle 1 + m\angle 4 = 180°$

Bisecting Angles and Line Segments

Both angles and lines are said to be bisected when divided into two parts with equal measures.

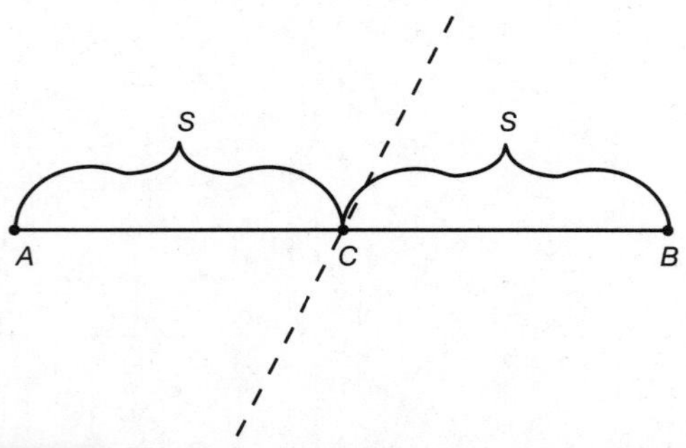

Example

Line segment *AB* is bisected at point *C*.
According to the figure, $\angle A$ is bisected by ray *AC*.

Angles Formed by Parallel Lines

Parallel lines are lines that are always the same distance apart from each other. They never intersect. The symbol for parallel lines is ||.

When two parallel lines are intersected by a third line, vertical angles are formed.

- Of these vertical angles, four will be equal and acute, and four will be equal and obtuse.
- Any combination of an acute and an obtuse angle will be supplementary.

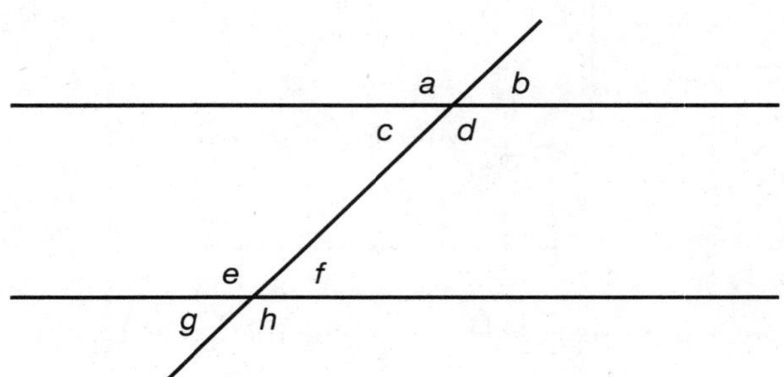

In the previous figure:

- $\angle b$, $\angle c$, $\angle f$, and $\angle g$ are all acute and equal.
- $\angle a$, $\angle d$, $\angle e$, and $\angle h$ are all obtuse and equal.
- Also, any acute angle added to any obtuse angle will be supplementary.

Examples

$m\angle b + m\angle d = 180°$
$m\angle c + m\angle e = 180°$
$m\angle f + m\angle h = 180°$
$m\angle g + m\angle a = 180°$

Example

In the following figure, if $m \| n$ and $a \| b$, what is the value of x?

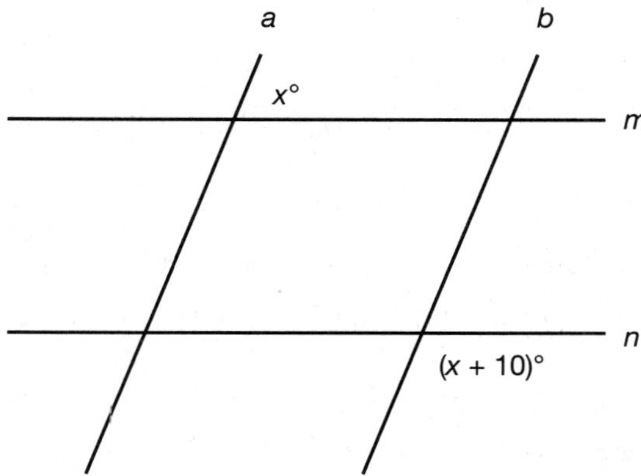

Solution

Because both sets of lines are parallel, you know that $x°$ can be added to $x + 10$ to equal 180. The equation is thus $x + x + 10 = 180$.

Polygons

A **polygon** is a two-dimensional object with straight lines that create a closed figure. Every polygon contains a minimum of three interior angles.

- A **regular polygon** has sides with the same lengths and congruent angles with the same measures.
- An **irregular polygon** does not have sides with the same lengths and congruent angles with the same measures.

You should be prepared to identify the following polygons:

A **triangle** is a polygon with three sides.

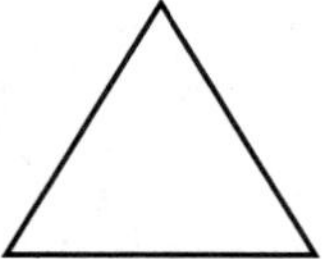

A **quadrilateral** is a polygon with four sides.

A **pentagon** is a polygon with five sides.

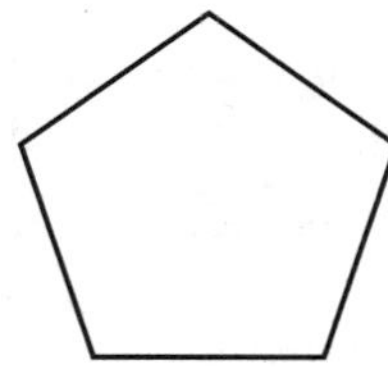

A **hexagon** is a polygon with six sides.

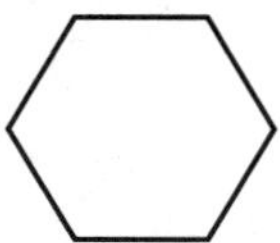

An **octagon** is a polygon with eight sides.

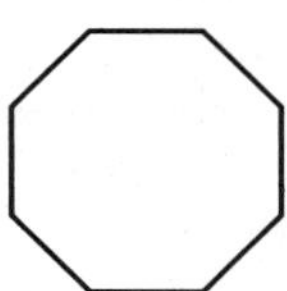

There are also kinds of quadrilaterals that are important to know.

A **trapezoid** is a four-sided polygon with exactly one pair of parallel sides.

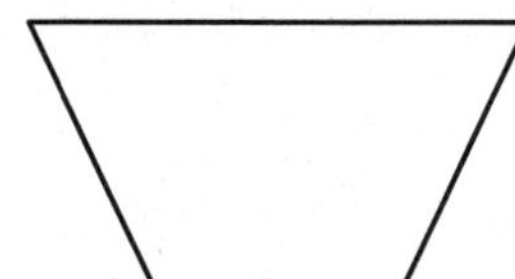

A **parallelogram** is a quadrilateral with two pairs of parallel sides.

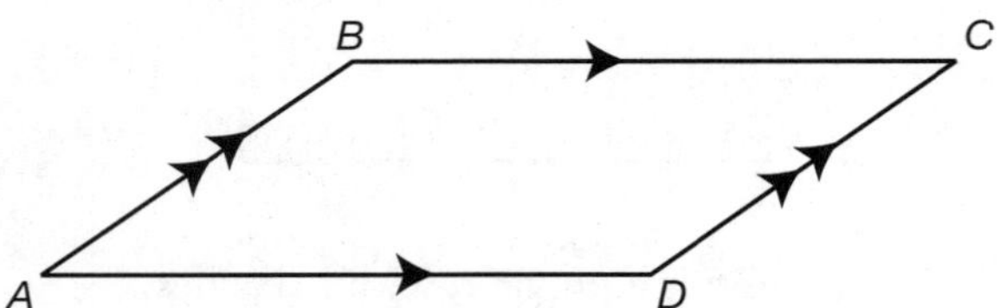

A **rhombus** is a four-sided polygon with four sides of equal length and two pairs of parallel sides. A rhombus is a type of parallelogram.

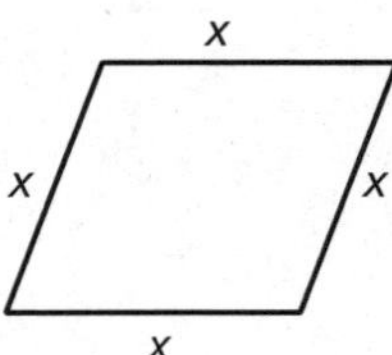

A **rectangle** is a four-sided polygon with four right angles. All rectangles have two pairs of parallel sides. A rectangle is a type of a parallelogram.

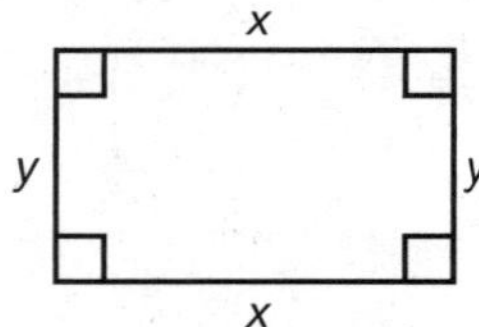

A **square** is a four-sided polygon with four right angles and four sides of equal length. All squares have two pairs of parallel sides. Note that a square is a specific kind of rectangle. It is also a type of rhombus.

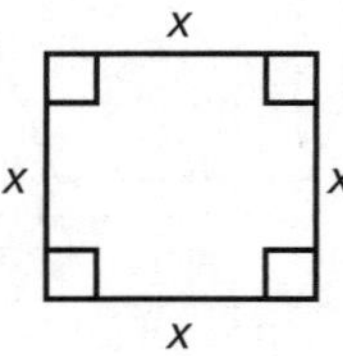

Example

What type of shape is shown below?

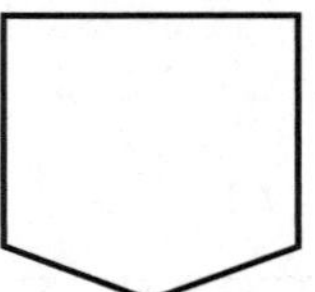

Because the figure has straight lines and makes a closed figure, it is a polygon. Because there are exactly five straight lines, the figure is a pentagon.

Special Triangles and the Pythagorean Theorem

There are special kinds of triangles that are important to know.

An **equilateral** triangle has three sides with the same length. It also has three angles with the same measure (60°).

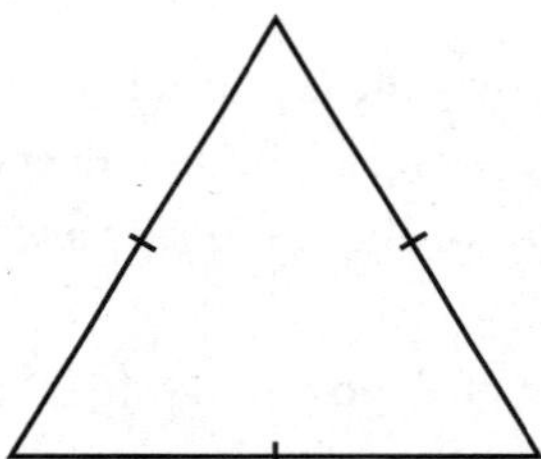

An **isosceles** triangle has at least two sides with the same length. It also has two angles with the same measure.

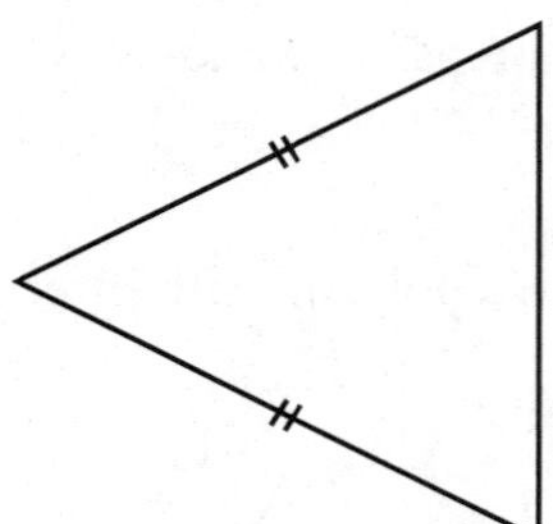

A **scalene** triangle has no sides with the same length.

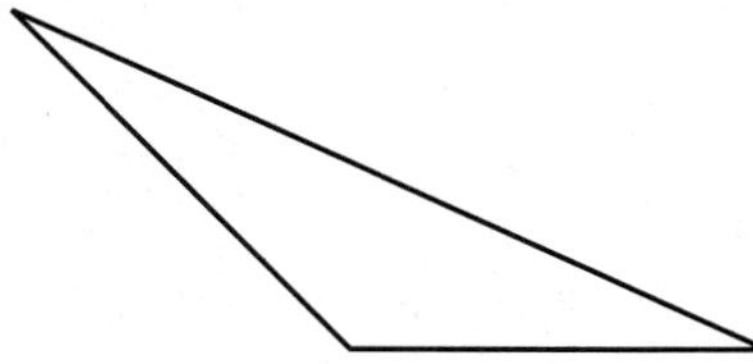

It is also possible to classify triangles into three categories based on the measure of the greatest angle.

	GREATEST ANGLE
Acute	Acute
Right	90°
Obtuse	Obtuse

Angle-Side Relationships

Knowing the angle-side relationships in isosceles, equilateral, and right triangles will be useful.

- In isosceles triangles, equal angles are opposite equal sides.

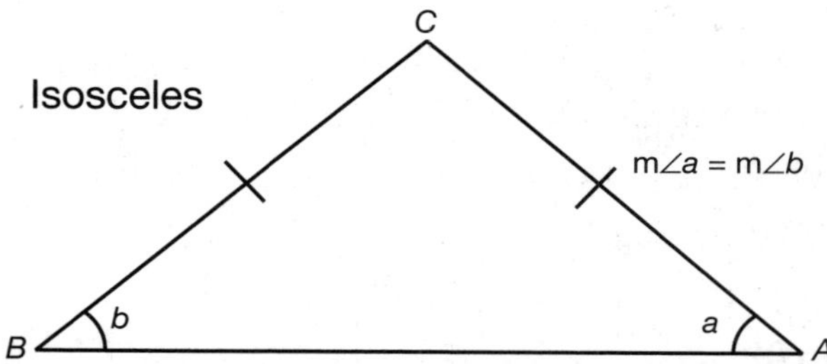

- In equilateral triangles, all sides are equal and all angles are equal.

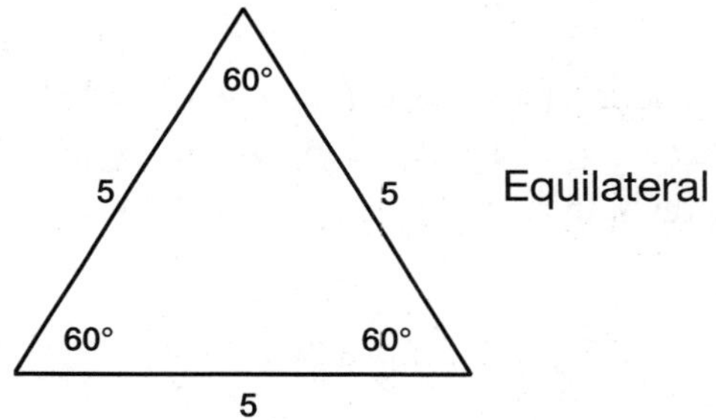

- In a right triangle, the side opposite the right angle is called the **hypotenuse**. This will be the largest side of the right triangle.

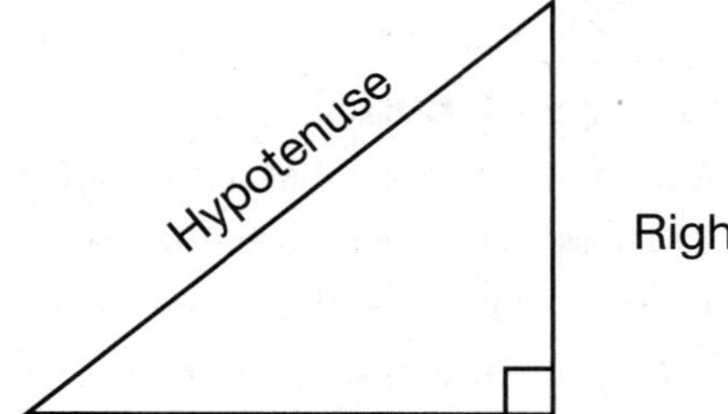

Pythagorean theorem is an important tool for working with right triangles. It states $a^2 + b^2 = c^2$, where a and b represent the legs and c represents the hypotenuse. This theorem allows you to find the length of any side as long as you know the measure of the other two.

$$a^2 + b^2 = c^2$$
$$1^2 + 2^2 = c^2$$
$$1 + 4 = c^2$$
$$5 = c^2$$
$$\sqrt{5} = c$$

Circles

A **circle** is a curved two-dimensional figure in which every point on the circle is the same distance from the center. There are several parts of a circle that you should know.

The **diameter** is a line that goes directly through the center of a circle—the longest line segment that can be drawn in a circle.

The **radius** is a line segment from the center of a circle to a point on the circle (half of the diameter).

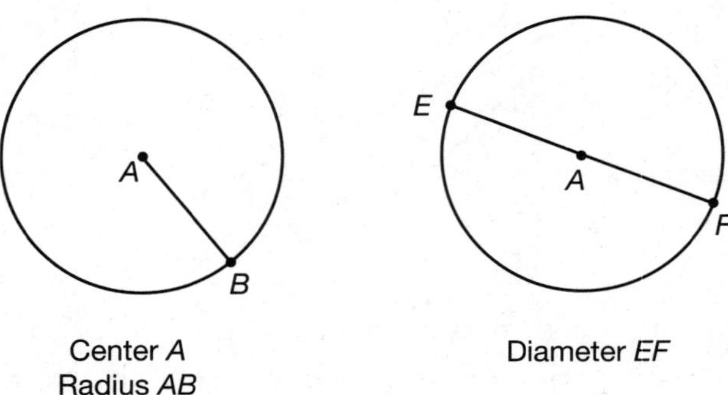

Symmetry

A two-dimensional figure has **symmetry** if it can be divided into two identical parts with one line. This line is called the **line of symmetry**. Some figures have zero lines of symmetry and therefore no symmetry. Others may have many lines of symmetry. Several examples of figures with the lines of symmetry are shown with dotted lines.

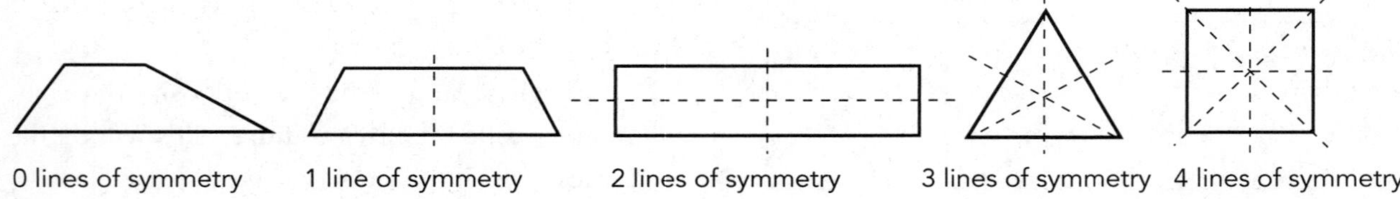

Three-Dimensional Figures

Every three-dimensional shape has a number of faces, edges, and corners. The **faces** are the two-dimensional shapes that comprise the three-dimensional figure. The **edges** are the places where two polygon faces come together to form a line. The **corners**, or **vertices**, are the places where three or more polygon faces come together to form a point.

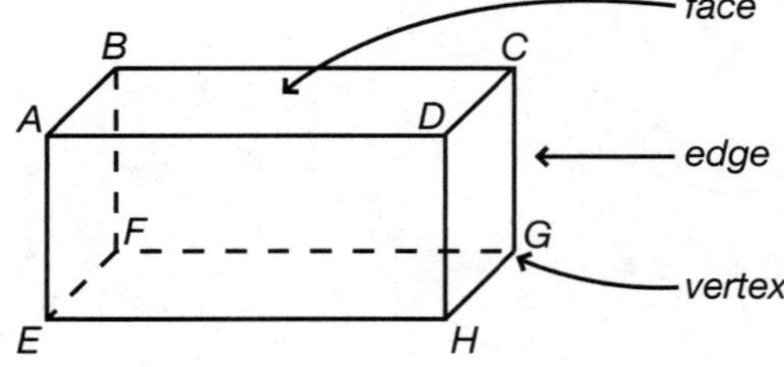

ABCD is a face.
CG is an edge.
G is a vertex.

Following are several of the most common types of three-dimensional shapes.

A **cube** is a three-dimensional figure in which each face is the shape of a square. A cube has six faces, 12 edges, and eight corners.

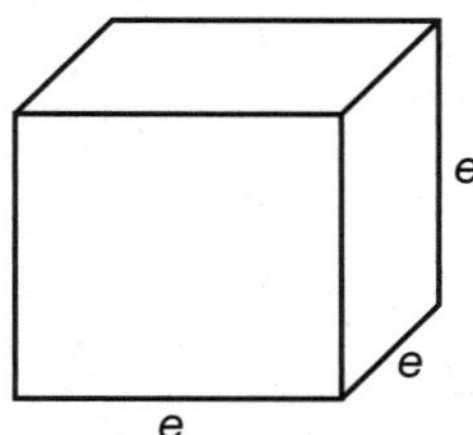

A **rectangular prism** is a three-dimensional figure where each face is the shape of a square. Note that a cube is a specific kind of rectangular prism. A rectangular prism also has six faces, 12 edges, and eight corners.

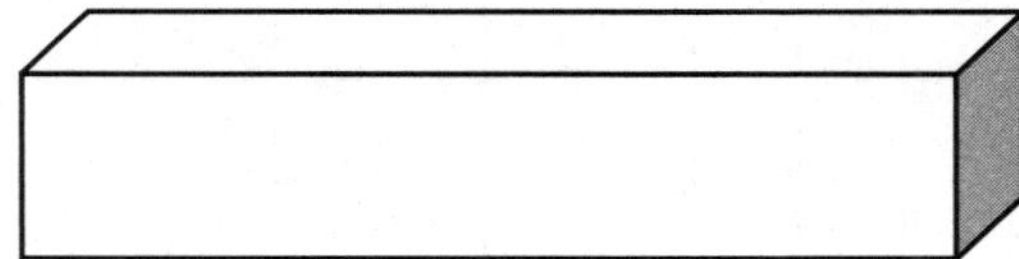

A **triangular pyramid** is a three-dimensional figure in which each face is the shape of a triangle. A triangular pyramid has four faces, six edges, and four corners.

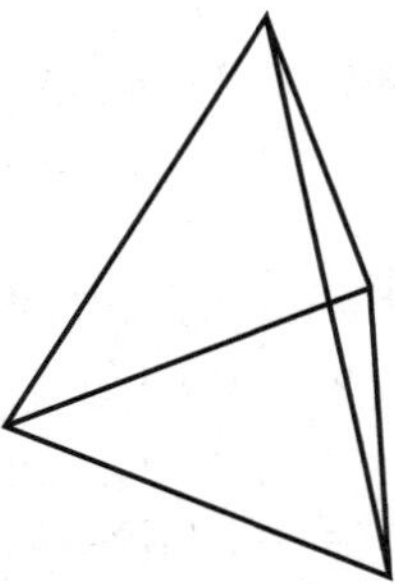

A **rectangular pyramid** is a three-dimensional figure in which the base is the shape of a rectangle and the four sides are in the shape of a triangle. A rectangular pyramid has five faces, eight edges, and five corners.

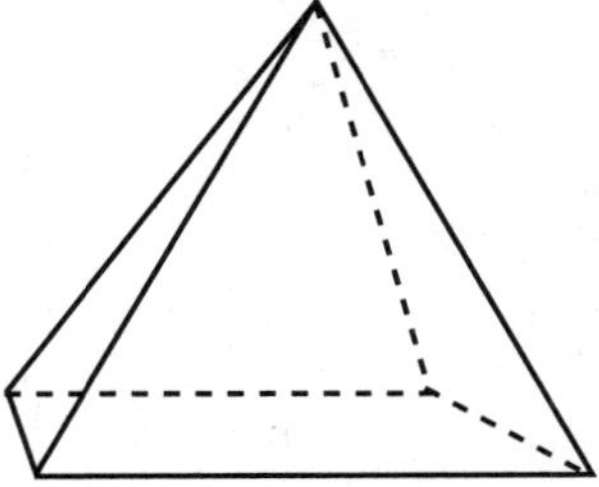

A **cylinder** is a three-dimensional figure with two circular bases.

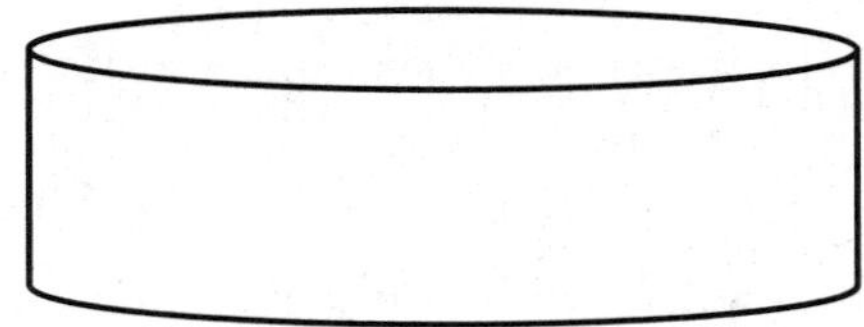

A **sphere** is a three-dimensional figure that is perfectly round, such as a ball.

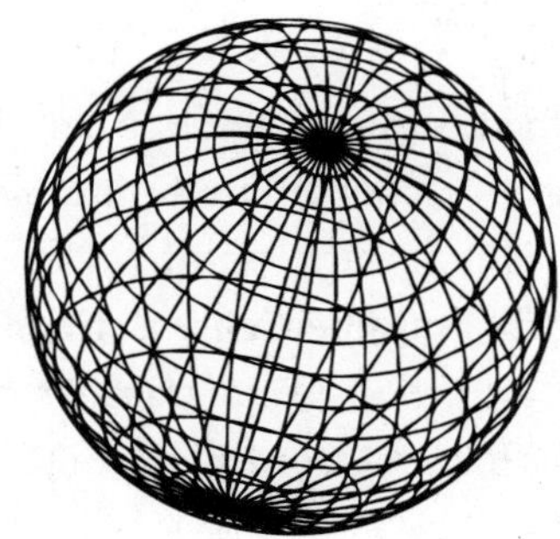

Nets

Nets are two-dimensional representations of three-dimensional objects. A net will show every face of a three-dimensional object in a way that can be used to construct the solid figure. In other words, you can imagine a net as a cardboard box opened up and flattened. The number of two-dimensional figures in a net will always match the number of faces on the three-dimensional figure.

Example
What three-dimensional object can be constructed with the following net?

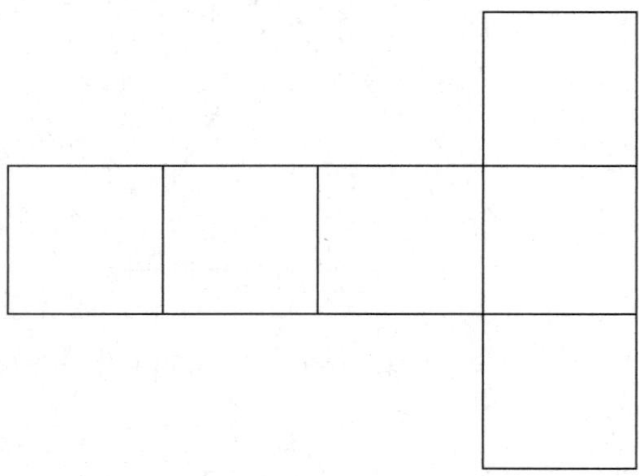

The net is comprised of six square faces. The four squares in the center row could be folded up and over, and the column of three squares could be folded up; the resulting solid figure would be a cube.

Coordinate Geometry

Coordinate geometry is a form of geometrical operation in relation to a coordinate plane. A **coordinate plane** is a grid created by a horizontal x-axis and a vertical y-axis.

These two axes intersect at one coordinate point, (0,0), the **origin**. A **coordinate point**, also called an **ordered pair**, is a specific point on the coordinate plane with the first number representing the horizontal placement and the second number representing the vertical placement. Coordinate points are given in the form of (x,y).

Graphing Ordered Pairs (Points)

The x-coordinate is listed first in the ordered pair and tells you how many units to move to either the left or the right. If the x-coordinate is positive, move to the right. If the x-coordinate is negative, move to the left.

The y-coordinate is listed second and tells you how many units to move up or down. If the y-coordinate is positive, move up. If the y-coordinate is negative, move down.

Example
What is the ordered pair of point X on the following coordinate grid?

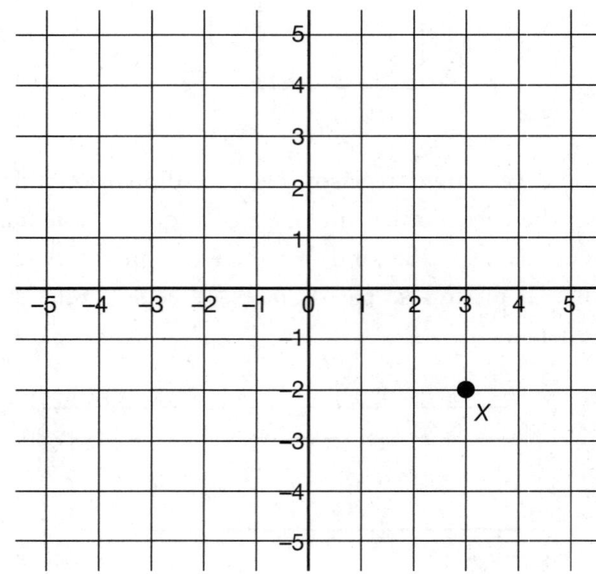

The point on the grid is three units to the right of the origin. Therefore, the first number in the ordered pair is 3. The point on the grid is two units down from the origin. Therefore, the second number in the ordered pair is –2.

The ordered pair for point X is (3,–2).

Transformations

A **transformation** is a movement of a figure that affects each of the points in the figure in the same way. Transformations may or may not appear on a coordinate grid. However, the following examples use coordinate grids because the grids are helpful for demonstrating the action being taken to each figure. There are four transformations that you may see on the Praxis II.

A **reflection** creates a mirror image of a figure over a given line. The line may be the x-axis, the y-axis, or some other line, such as the line of the equation $y = x$. The following graph shows the reflection of a triangle over the y-axis. Notice that the shape and size of the original image do not change. Only the figure's orientation changes. A reflection may also be called a **flip**.

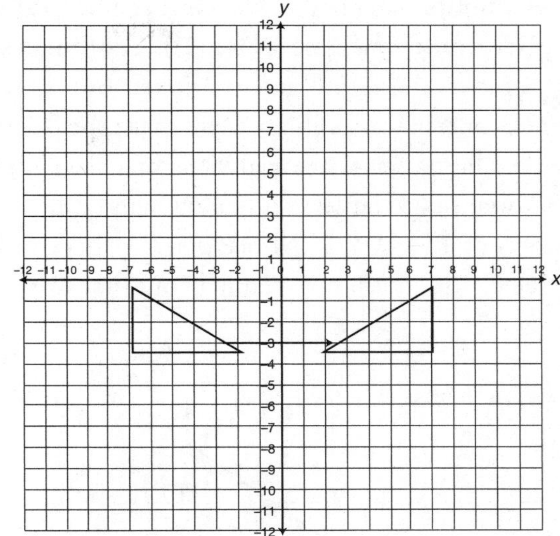

A **rotation** turns a figure over a given point. The point may be a point on the figure or it may be a point on the coordinate grid. The following graph shows the 90-degree counterclockwise rotation of a rectangle over point B in the original figure. Notice that the shape and size of the original image do not change. Only the figure's orientation changes. A rotation is also called a **turn**.

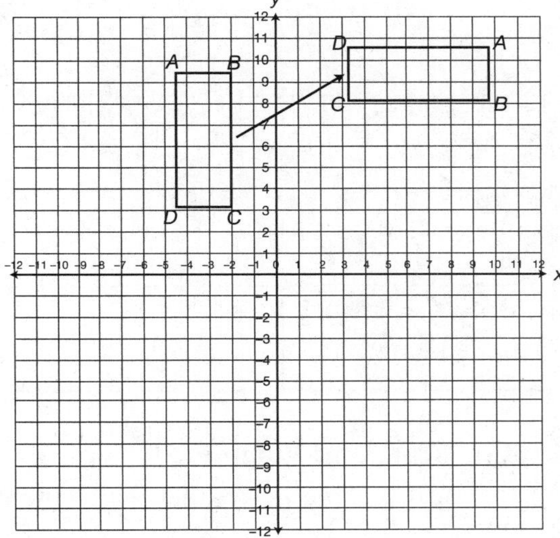

A **translation** moves a figure a given number of points in a certain direction. The translation may move a figure in any direction or a series of directions. The following graph shows a translation of nine units to the right and three units down. Notice that the shape, size, and orientation of the original image do not change. Only the figure's location on the grid changes.

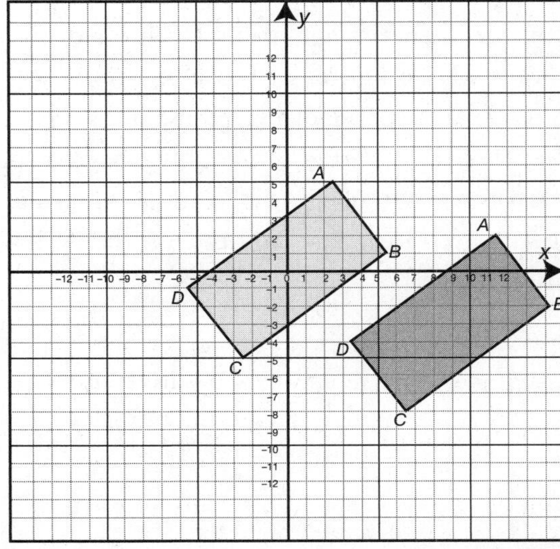

A **dilation** increases or decreases the size of a figure according to a scale factor. The coordinates of each point of the figure are multiplied by the scale factor. A scale factor less than 1 will make the original figure smaller; a scale factor greater than 1 will make the original figure larger. The following graph shows a dilation of 3 for *ABCD*. Notice that the shape of the original figure does not change, but its size *does* change.

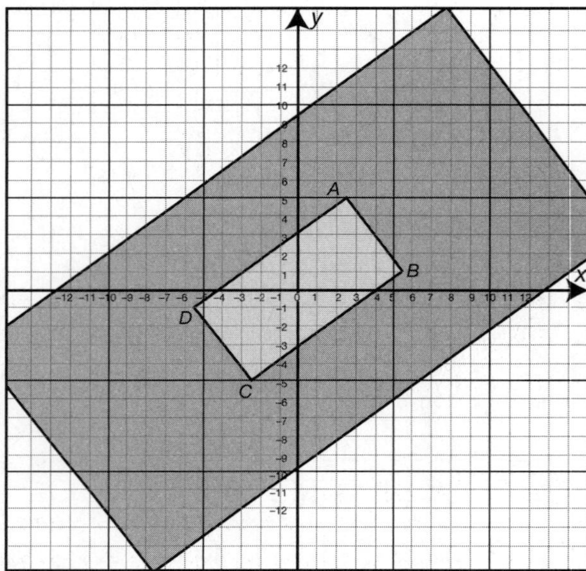

Perimeter, Area, and Volume

One of the most common ways that the Elementary Education: Content Knowledge test will include questions of two- and three-dimensional figures is to ask you for the perimeter, area, or volume of the figure. Some of the figures in those questions will involve unusual shapes. However, these unusual shapes will be comprised of traditional polygons and solids, so it makes sense to review the formulas and rules for the perimeter, area, and volume of the following common shapes.

Perimeter

The **perimeter** of a two-dimensional figure is simply the sum of the lengths of all its sides.

Example

What is the perimeter of the following triangle?

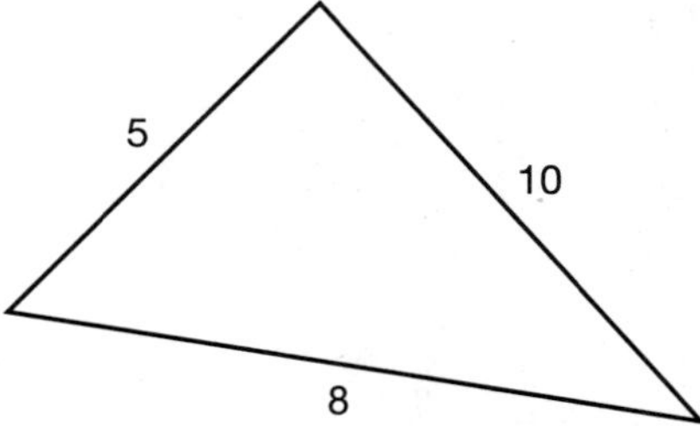

The triangle has side lengths of 5, 8, and 10. The perimeter is therefore the sum of 5 + 8 + 10. The perimeter of the triangle is 23.

Circumference

The **circumference** is the distance around a circle. The circumference can be found by multiplying the diameter of the circle by π (pi), a special number equal to about 3.14. It can also be found by multiplying the radius of the circle by 2 and then by pi. The formulas for the circumference of a circle are circumference = $2r\pi$ or $d\pi$, where r is the radius and d is the diameter of the circle.

Example

What is the circumference of a circle with a radius of 5?

Following the formula area = $2r\pi$, the circumference is equal to $2(5)\pi$, which is equal to 10π.

Area

The **area** is the amount of space inside a two-dimensional shape.

To find the area of a rectangle, you need to multiply the length of the rectangle times the width. The formula is area = length × width, or area = lw.

To find the area of a triangle, you need to multiply $\frac{1}{2}$ times the base of the triangle times its width. The formula is area = base × width, or area = $\frac{1}{2}lw$.

To find the area of a circle, you need to multiply the radius by itself (or square it), and then multiply it by π. The formula is area = πr^2, where r is the radius of the circle.

Example

What is the area of the following rectangle?

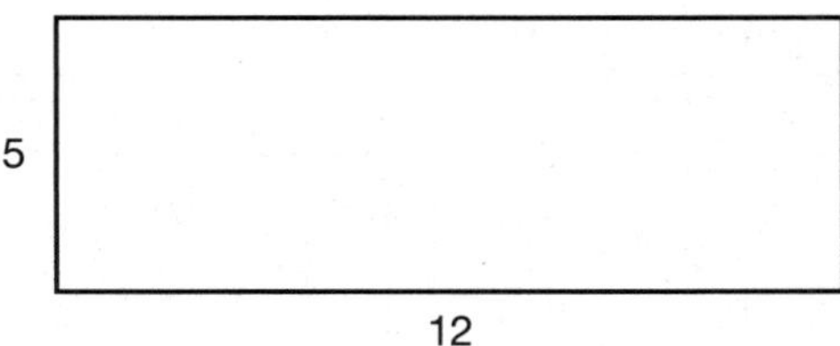

To find the area of a rectangle, the length and the height must be multiplied together. Because the length is 12 and the height is 5, the area is therefore 12 × 5, or 60 square units.

Example

What is the area of the following triangle?

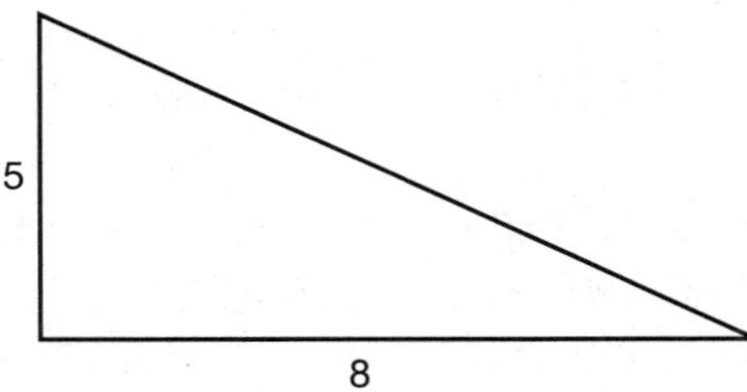

The base of the triangle is 8 and its height is 5. To find the area, just plug in those known values into the formula area = $\frac{1}{2}lw$. You will get area = $\frac{1}{2}(8)(5)$, which is equal to 20. The area is 20 square units.

Example

What is the area of a circle with a radius of 2?

Plug in the value of the radius into the formula for the area of a circle: area = πr^2. You will get area = $\pi(2)^2$, which is equal to 4π.

Volume

Volume is the amount of space inside a three-dimensional shape. To find the volume of a rectangular solid, you need to multiply the length times the width times the height.

Example

What is the volume of the following cube?

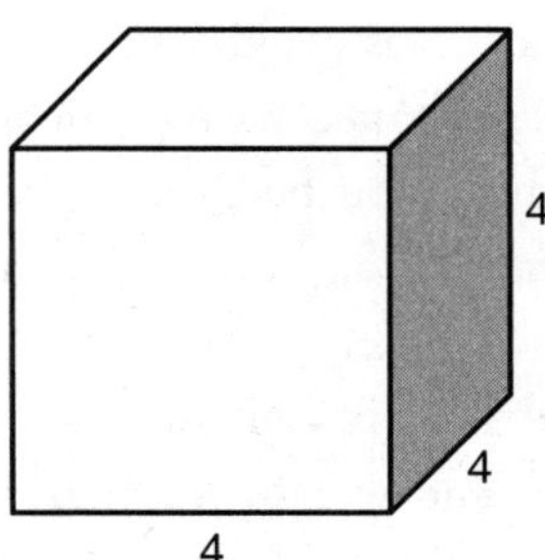

To find the volume, you need to multiply the length times the width times the height. Each dimension of the cube is 4, so the volume is 4 × 4 × 4, or 64 cubic units.

Surface Area

The surface area of an object measures the area of each of its faces. The total surface area of a rectangular solid is double the sum of the areas of the three faces. For a cube, simply multiply the surface area of one of its sides by six.

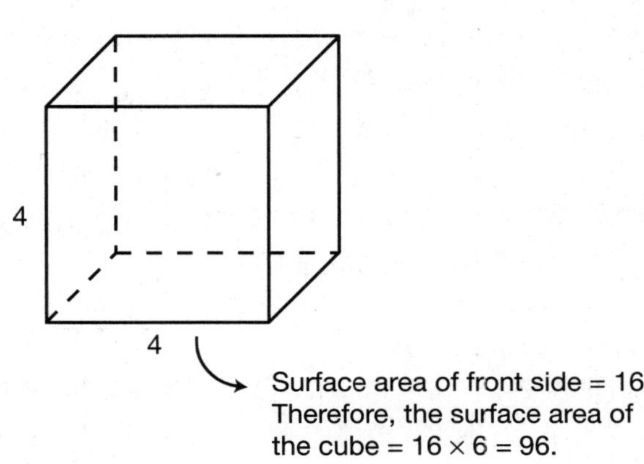

Measurement

This section reviews the basics of measurement systems used in the United States (called the U.S. customary measurement) and other countries, methods of performing mathematical operations with units of measurement, and the process of converting between different units.

The use of measurement enables a connection to be made between mathematics and the real world. For instance, when a fish is caught, it is often weighed in ounces and its length measured in inches. The following lesson will help you become more familiar with the types, conversions, and units of measurement.

Length, Weight, and Volume

Length, capacity, and weight (or mass) can be measured in either the U.S. customary system or the metric system. It is important to know both the U.S. customary and the metric systems of measurement for the Praxis II.

U.S. CUSTOMARY MEASUREMENTS
UNITS OF LENGTH
12 inches (in.) = 1 foot (ft.)
3 feet = 36 inches = 1 yard (yd.)
5,280 feet = 1,760 yards = 1 mile (mi.)
UNITS OF VOLUME
8 ounces* (oz.) = 1 cup (c.)
2 cups = 16 ounces = 1 pint (pt.)
2 pints = 4 cups = 32 ounces = 1 quart (qt.)
4 quarts = 8 pints = 16 cups = 128 ounces = 1 gallon (gal.)
UNITS OF WEIGHT
16 ounces* (oz.) = 1 pound (lb.)
2,000 pounds = 1 ton (T.)

*Notice that ounces are used to measure the dimensions of both volume and weight.

Metric Measurements

The metric system is an international system of measurement also called the **decimal system**. The unit of length is a meter. The unit of capacity is a liter. The unit of mass is a gram.

Prefixes are attached to the basic metric units to indicate the amount of each unit. For example, the prefix *deci-* means one-tenth ([1/10]); therefore, one decigram is one-tenth of a gram, and one decimeter is one-tenth of a meter. The following six prefixes can be used with every metric unit:

KILO	HECTO	DEKA	DECI	CENTI	MILLI
(k)	(h)	(dk)	d	c	(m)
1,000	100	10	$\frac{1}{10}$	$\frac{1}{100}$	$\frac{1}{1000}$

So, for example:

- 1 meter is equivalent to 100 centimeters or 1,000 millimeters.
- 1 gram is equivalent to 1,000 milligrams or $\frac{1}{1000}$ kilogram.
- 1 liter is equivalent to 1,000 milliliters or $\frac{1}{1000}$ kiloliter.

One way to remember the metric prefixes is to remember the mnemonic: "King Henry Died Of Drinking Chocolate Milk." The first letter of each word represents a corresponding metric heading from kilo down to milli: "King"—Kilo, "Henry"—Hecto, "Died"—Deka, "Of"—Original Unit, "Drinking"—Deci, "Chocolate"—Centi, and "Milk"—Milli.

Units of Time

60 seconds (sec.) = 1 minute (min.)
60 minutes = 1 hour (hr.)
24 hours = 1 day
7 days = 1 week
52 weeks = 1 year (yr.)
12 months = 1 year
365 days = 1 year

Converting Units of Measurement

When performing mathematical operations, it may be necessary to convert units of measure to simplify a problem. Units of measure are converted by using either multiplication or division. Note that the test may ask you to convert either metric *or* U.S. customary units. It will not likely ask you to convert *between* units, such as converting a number of inches to centimeters.

Converting Units in the U.S. Customary System

To convert from a larger unit into a smaller unit, *multiply* the given number of larger units by the number of smaller units in only one of the larger units.

For example, to find the number of inches in five feet, multiply 5, the number of larger units, by 12, the number of inches in one foot:

5 feet = ? inches
5 feet × 12 (the number of inches in a single foot) = 60 inches
5 ft = 60 in.

Therefore, there are 60 inches in five feet.

Example
Change 3.5 pounds to ounces.
3.5 pounds = ? ounces
3.5 pounds × 16 ounces per pound = 56 ounces

Therefore, there are 56 ounces in 3.5 pounds.

To change a smaller unit to a larger unit, *divide* the given number of smaller units by the number of smaller units in only one of the larger units.

Find the number of pints in 64 ounces.

64 ounces = ? pints
64 ounces ÷ 16 ounces per pint = 4 pints

Therefore, 64 ounces equals 4 pints.

Converting Units in the Metric System

An easy way to convert within the metric system is to move the decimal point either to the right or to the left, because the conversion factor is always ten or a power of ten. Remember to multiply when changing from a larger unit to a smaller unit. Divide when changing from a smaller unit to a larger unit.

When multiplying by a power of ten, move the decimal point to the right, because the number becomes larger. When dividing by a power of ten, move the decimal point to the left, because the number becomes smaller. Use the table on page 142 to see how many places to move to the left or right.

Example
Change 2 kilometers to meters.

You are changing a larger unit to a smaller unit, so the number must get bigger. You can move the decimal point three places to the right or solve as shown below:

2 kilometers = ? meters
2 × 1,000 meters per km = 2,000 meters

Therefore, 2 kilometers equals 2,000 meters.

Example
Change 520 grams to kilograms.

Changing grams to grams is going from smaller units to larger units and, thus, requires that the decimal point move to the left. Beginning at the unit (for grams), note that the kilo heading is three places away. Therefore, the decimal point will move three places to the left. Move the decimal point from the end of 520 to the left three places. That means you need to place the decimal point before the 5: 0.520.

The answer is 520 grams = 0.520 kilograms.

Converting Units of Time

The Praxis II may ask you to convert units of time. Just like converting U.S. customary or metric units, multiply when changing from a larger unit to a smaller unit and divide when changing from a smaller unit to a larger unit.

Example
A teacher creates a lesson plan for the week that will take 4 hours. How many minutes will the lesson plan take?

Because minutes are a smaller unit than hours, you need to multiply to convert the units. Remember that there are 60 minutes in an hour.

4 hours = ? minutes
4 hours × 60 minutes per hour = 240

Therefore, there are 240 minutes in 4 hours.

Data Organization and Interpretation

To answer the approximately six questions on the Praxis II: Elementary Education: Content Knowledge test on data organization and interpretation, you will need to understand how to interpret graphs and tables, as well as find the mean, median, and mode of a data set. You will need to be able to determine the simple probability of events and determine the total number of outcomes using a variety of counting techniques, including tree diagrams, combinations, and permutations.

Graphs and Tables

On the test you will see graphs, tables, and other graphical forms. You should be able to do the following:

- read and understand graphs, tables, diagrams, charts, and figures
- interpret graphs, tables, diagrams, charts, and figures
- compare and interpret information presented in graphs, tables, diagrams, charts, and figures
- draw conclusions about the information provided
- make predictions about the data

It is important to read tables, charts, and graphs very carefully. Read the information presented, paying special attention to headings and units of measure.

This section covers tables and graphs. The most common types of graphs are pictographs, bar graphs, line graphs, and pie graphs. What follows is an explanation of each, with examples for practice.

Tables

All tables are composed of **rows** (horizontal) and **columns** (vertical). Entries in a single row of a table usually have something in common, and so do entries in a single column. Look at the following table that shows how many cars, both new and used, were sold during the particular months.

MONTH	NEW CARS	USED CARS
June	125	65
July	155	80
August	190	100
September	220	115
October	265	140

Tables are very concise ways to convey important information without wasting time and space. Just imagine how many lines of text would be needed to convey the same information. With the table, however, it is easy to refer to a given month and quickly know how many total cars were sold. It would also be easy to compare month to month. Let's practice by comparing the total sales of July with October.

In order to do this, first find out how many cars were sold in each month. There were 235 cars sold in July (155 + 80 = 235) and 405 cars sold in October (265 + 140 = 405). With a little bit of quick arithmetic it can quickly be determined that 170 more cars were sold during October (405 – 235 = 170).

Bar Graphs

A **bar graph** is a often used to indicate an amount or level of occurrence of a phenomenon for different categories. Consider the following bar graph. It illustrates the number of employees who were absent due to illness during a particular week in two different age groups.

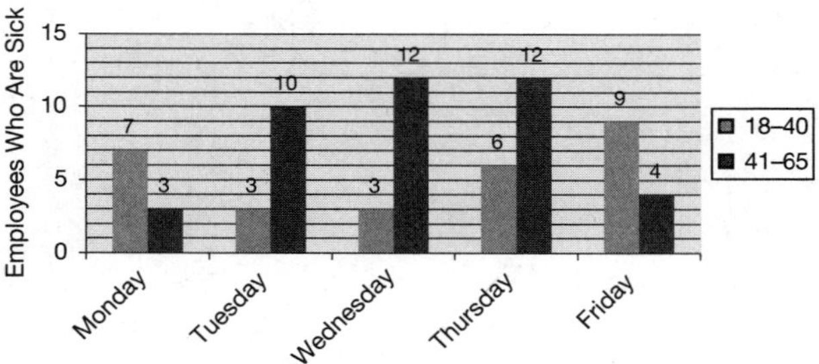

In this bar graph, the categories are the days of the week, and the frequency represents the number of employees who are sick. It can be immediately seen that younger employees are sick before and after the weekend.

There is also an inconsistent trend for the younger employees with data ranging all over the place. During midweek the older crowd tends to stay home more often.

A **histogram** is very similar to a bar graph in that bars are used to measure the quantities. However, the *x*-axis generally represents a range of values, such as 0–10, 11–20, and 21–30; because there is no gap between the numbers in the range, there will be no gap between the bars.

Pictographs

Pictographs are very similar to bar graphs, but instead of bars indicating frequency, small icons are assigned a key value indicating frequency.

Number of Students at the Pep Rally

Freshmen	
Sophmores	
Juniors	
Seniors	

Key: indicates 10 people

In this pictograph, the key indicates that every icon represents 10 people, so it is easy to determine that there were $12 \times 10 = 120$ freshmen, $5.5 \times 10 = 55$ sophomores, $5 \times 10 = 50$ juniors, and $3 \times 10 = 30$ seniors.

Circle Graphs

Circle graphs, also called **pie graphs**, are often used to show what percent of a total is taken up by different components of that whole. This type of graph is representative of a whole and is usually divided into percentages. Each section of the chart represents a portion of the whole, and all these sections added together will equal 100% of the whole. The following chart shows the three styles of model homes in a new development and what percentage there is of each.

Models of Homes

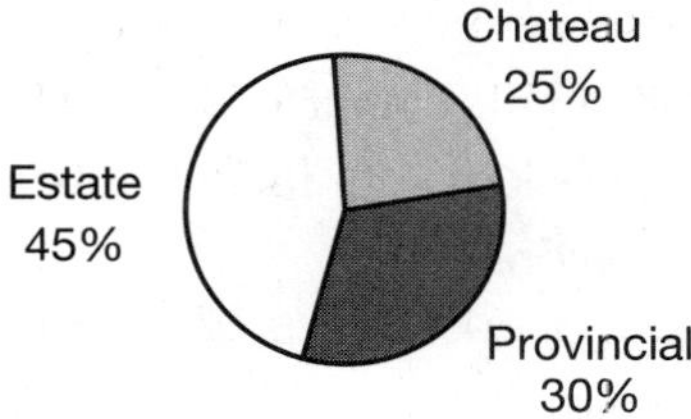

The chart shows the different models of homes. The categories add up to 100% (25 + 30 + 45 = 100). To find the percentage of estate homes, you can look at the pie chart and see that 45% of the homes are done in the estate model.

If you know the total number of items in a circle graph, you can calculate how many of each component. You just need to multiply the percent by the total.

Example

There are 500 homes in the new development. 25% of them are chateaus. How many of them are chateaus?

To calculate the number of components (chateaus) out of the total (500), you need to multiply the percent times the total.

$$25\% \times 500 = 0.25 \times 500 = 125$$

There are 125 chateaus in the development.

Line Graphs

A **line graph** is a graph used to show a change over time. The line moves from left to right to show how the data changes over a time period. If a line is slanted up, it represents an increase, whereas a line sloping down represents a decrease. A flat line indicates no change.

In the line graph shown here, the number of delinquent payments is charted for the first quarter of the year. Each week the number of outstanding bills is summed and recorded.

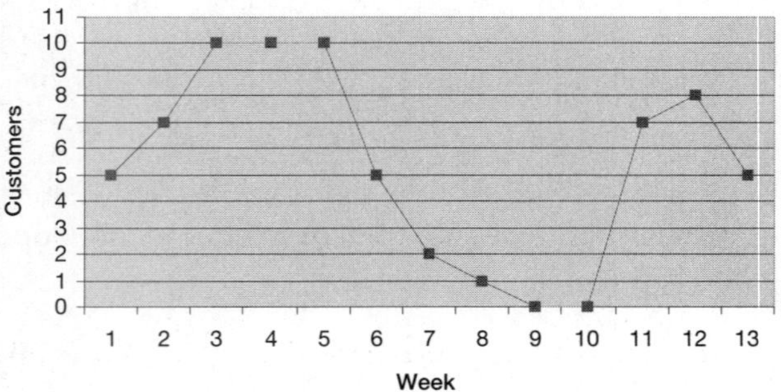

There is an increase in delinquency for the first two weeks and then the level is maintained for an additional two weeks. There is a steep decrease after week 5 (initially) until the ninth week, where it levels off again but this time at 0. The 11th week shows a radical increase followed by a little jump up at week 12, and then a decrease to week 13. It is also interesting to see that the first and last weeks have identical values.

Line graphs are especially useful for identifing trends. A trend exists if the data points show a pattern. For example, see the next line graph.

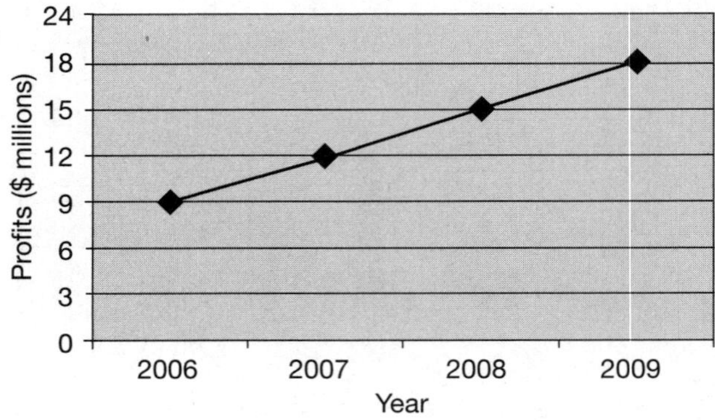

This line graph shows an obvious trend because the points go up as the line moves to the right. That means there is a positive trend. A question on the Praxis II: Elementary Education: Content Knowledge test may ask you to make a prediction based on the trend. Each year the profits of the company go up by about \$3 million. Therefore, if you were asked to predict the profits of the company in 2010, you could add \$3 million to the profits in 2009. An appropriate prediction for the company's profits in 2010, based on the trend in the graph, would be \$21 million.

Scatterplots

Whenever a variable depends continuously on another variable, this dependence can be visually represented in a **scatterplot**. A scatterplot consists of the horizontal x-axis, the vertical y-axis, and collected data points for variable y, measured at variable x. The variable points are often connected with a line or a curve. A graph often contains a legend, especially if there is more than one data set or more than one variable. A legend is a key for interpreting the graph. Much like a legend on a map lists the symbols used to label an interstate highway, a railroad line, or a city, a legend for a graph lists the symbols used to label particular data sets. Look at the following sample graph. The essential elements of the graph—the x-axis and y-axis—are labeled. The legend to the right of the graph shows that diamonds are used to represent the variable points in data set 1, while squares are used to represent the variable points in data set 2. If only one data set exists, the use of a legend is not essential.

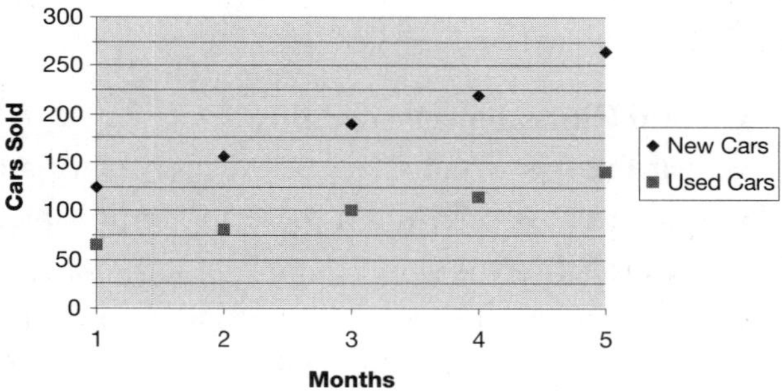

The x-axis represents the months after new management and promotions were introduced at an automobile dealership. The y-axis represents the number of cars sold in the particular month after the changes were made. The diamonds reflect the new cars sold, and the squares show the number of used cars sold. What conclusions can be drawn about the sales? Note that the new and used car sales are both increasing each month at a pretty steady rate. The graph also shows that new cars increase at a higher rate and that there are many more new cars sold per month.

Try to look for scatter plots with different trends:

- increase
- decrease
- rapid increase, followed by leveling off
- slow increase, followed by rapid increase
- rise to a maximum, followed by a decrease
- rapid decrease, followed by leveling off
- slow decrease, followed by rapid decrease
- decrease to a minimum, followed by a rise
- predictable fluctuation (periodic change)
- random fluctuation (irregular change)

Stem-and-Leaf Plots

A **stem-and-leaf plot** is used to display how a set of data falls within certain frequencies. Each value is split by a vertical line. The stem, on the left-hand side of the vertical line, usually acts as the tens digits for the values. The leaf, on the right-hand side of the vertical line, usually acts as the ones digits for the values. For example, the following data set shows the ages of eight customers in a clothing store.

18, 24, 28, 16, 31, 40, 19, 33

The following stem-and-leaf plot shows these values.

STEM	LEAF
1	6 8 9
2	4 8
3	1 3
4	0
key: 4 0 = 40	

There are three leaves in the 1 stem, which means that there are three values in the 10–19 frequency range. There is only one leaf in the 4 stem, which means that there is only one value in the 40–49 frequency range. You can count the total number of values in the data set by counting the number of leaves in the right column of the stem-and-leaf plot. Because there are eight numbers in the right column, there are eight values in the data set.

Venn Diagrams

A **Venn diagram** is a graphical representation that shows the relationships between two or more sets. In a Venn diagram, the sets are represented by closed curves, generally circles—often inside a larger rectangle. Each of the circles represents a set, and all the items that belong within that set are contained within that circle. If an item belongs to two or more sets, then it will be contained within the overlapping section of those circles.

The following Venn diagram shows two sets: even numbers and prime numbers up to 10. The overlapping section represents the area where numbers belong to both sets. The rectangle represents the universe of the entire scenario—which is whole numbers 1 through 10 in this case. The numbers that do not fall into either set fall outside of the circles—but still in the rectangle representing the universe.

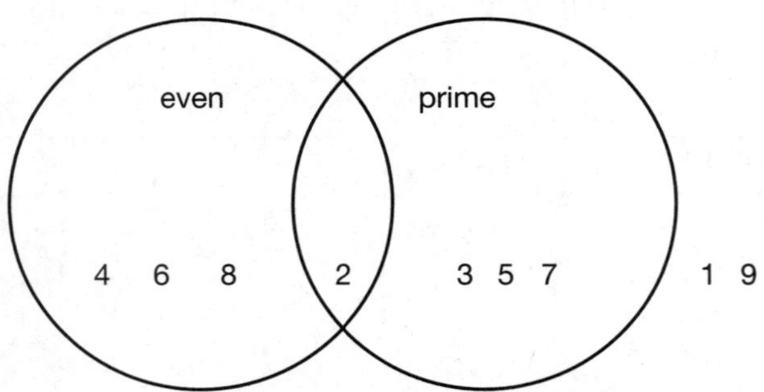

Only the number 2 is both prime and even, so it is the only number in the overlapping area of the circles. The number 1 is not considered a prime number, and it is not even, so it does not belong in either of the circles representing even or prime number sets. The number 9 is also neither prime nor even, so it also belongs outside the circles but inside the rectangle.

Simple Probability

Probability is expressed as a fraction and measures the likelihood that a specific event will occur. To find the probability of a specific outcome, use this formula:

$$\text{probability of an event} = \frac{\text{number of specific outcomes}}{\text{total number of possible outcomes}}$$

Example

If a bag contains 5 blue marbles, 3 red marbles, and 6 green marbles, find the probability of selecting a red marble:

$$\text{probability of an event} = \frac{\text{number of specific outcomes}}{\text{total number of possible outcomes}}$$

$$= \frac{3}{(5+3+6)}$$

Therefore, the probability of selecting a red marble is $\frac{3}{14}$.

Helpful Hints about Probability

- If an event is certain to occur, the probability is 1.
- If an event is certain not to occur (impossible), the probability is 0.
- If you know the probability of all other events occurring, you can find the probability of the remaining event by adding the known probabilities together and subtracting their total from 1.

Outcomes and Events

There are several techniques for counting the number of outcomes.

A **tree diagram** is a graph that illustrates all the ways that an event can happen. It uses branches, like a tree, to show the possibilities. For example, the following tree diagram shows the results of flipping a coin three times. Each H represents heads, and each T represents tails.

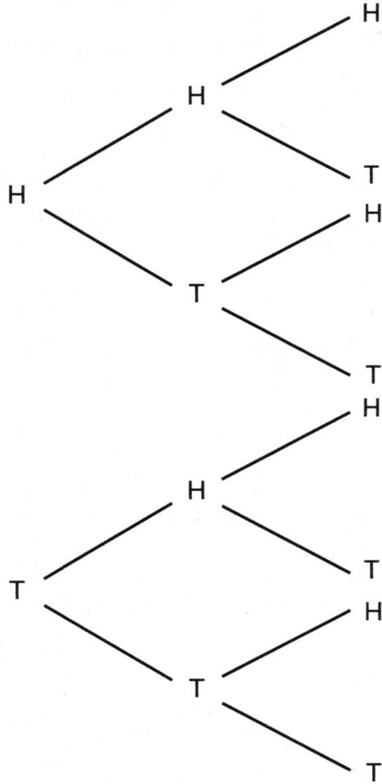

According to the last column of the tree diagram, there are eight possible outcomes.

A **sample space** shows the total list of possible outcomes. From the previous experiment with the three coin flips, the sample space is as follows.

H, H, H	H, H, T	H, T, H	H, T, T
T, H, H	T, H, T	T, T, H	T, T, T

Combinations and Permutations

Combinations and permutations are each used to determine the number of possible outcomes of an event. You should memorize the formulas for both combinations and permutations, as given in the following sections. Each formula uses a **factorial**, represented by the exclamation point. To determine the factorial of a positive integer, multiply the number by each positive integer less than it. For example, $5! = 5 \times 4 \times 3 \times 2 \times 1 = 120$.

A **combination** is used when the order does *not* matter. For example, an ice cream store sells eight flavors of ice creams, and you can choose two flavors to put in a cup. The order of which flavor goes first in the cup does not matter. The total number of possibilities for the two flavors in the cup is determined by using the combination.

The formula for a combination is $\frac{n!}{r!(n-r)!}$, where n is the number of things to choose from, and r is the number of things that are chosen. In this example, you could determine the number of possibilities by plugging in for n and r as shown here:

$$\frac{n!}{r!(n-r)!} =$$

$$\frac{8!}{2!(8-2)!} =$$

$$\frac{8 \times 7 \times 6 \times 5 \times 4 \times 3 \times 2 \times 1}{2 \times 1(6)!} =$$

$$\frac{8 \times 7 \times 6 \times 5 \times 4 \times 3 \times 2 \times 1}{2 \times 1 \times 6 \times 5 \times 4 \times 3 \times 2 \times 1}$$

$$\frac{8 \times 7 \times \cancel{6} \times \cancel{5} \times \cancel{4} \times \cancel{3} \times \cancel{2} \times \cancel{1}}{2 \times 1 \times \cancel{6} \times \cancel{5} \times \cancel{4} \times \cancel{3} \times \cancel{2} \times \cancel{1}} =$$

$$\frac{8 \times 7}{2 \times 1} = \frac{56}{2} = 28$$

There are 28 different ways to pick two flavors of ice cream when there are eight different flavors to choose from—and the order does not matter.

A **permutation** is used when the order *does* matter. For example, 12 runners participate in a race. The first-place finisher gets a trophy, the second-place finisher gets a medal, and the third-place finisher gets a ribbon; the order in this case does matter, and it's not simply an issue of which three runners finished in the top three slots.

The formula for a permutations is $\frac{n!}{(n-r)!}$, where n is the number of things to choose from, and r is the number of things that are chosen. In this example above, you could determine the number of possibilities by plugging in for n and r as shown here:

$$\frac{n!}{(n-r)!}$$

$$\frac{12!}{(12-3)!}$$

$$\frac{12 \times 11 \times 10 \times 9 \times 8 \times 7 \times 6 \times 5 \times 4 \times 3 \times 2 \times 1}{9 \times 8 \times 7 \times 6 \times 5 \times 4 \times 3 \times 2 \times 1} =$$

$$\frac{12 \times 11 \times 10 \times \not{9} \times \not{8} \times \not{7} \times \not{6} \times \not{5} \times \not{4} \times \not{3} \times \not{2} \times \not{1}}{\not{9} \times \not{8} \times \not{7} \times \not{6} \times \not{5} \times \not{4} \times \not{3} \times \not{2} \times \not{1}} =$$

$$\frac{12 \times 11 \times 10}{1} = 1{,}320$$

There are 1,320 different ways that the 12 runners can finish in first, second, and third when the order of the finishers *does* matter.

Mean, Median, Mode, and Range

It is important to understand trends in data. To do that, one must look at where the center of the data lies. There are a number of ways to find the center of a set of data.

Mean

Average usually refers to the **arithmetic mean** (usually just called the **mean**). To find the mean of a set of numbers, add all of the numbers together and divide by the quantity of numbers in the set.

average = (sum of set) ÷ (quantity of set)

Example
Find the average of 9, 4, 7, 6, and 4.

$$\frac{9 + 4 + 7 + 6 + 4}{5} = 6$$

The mean, or average, of the set is 6.
(Divide by 5 because there are five numbers in the set.)

Median

Another center of data is the median. The **median** is the center number if you arrange all the data in ascending or descending order. To find the median of a set of numbers, arrange the numbers in ascending or descending order and find the middle value. If the set contains an odd number of elements, then simply choose the middle value. If the set contains an even number of elements, simply average the two middle values.

Example
Find the median of the number set: 1, 5, 4, 7, 2.

First arrange the set in order—1, 2, 4, 5, 7—and then find the middle value. Because there are five values, the middle value is the third one: 4. The median is 4.

Example
Find the median of the number set: 1, 6, 3, 7, 2, 8.

First arrange the set in order—1, 2, 3, 6, 7, 8—and then find the middle values, 3 and 6.

Find the average of the numbers 3 and 6:

$\frac{3+6}{2} = \frac{9}{2}$ = 4.5. The median is 4.5.

Mode

The **mode** of a set of numbers is the number that appears the greatest number of times.

Example
Find the mode for the following data set: 1, 2, 5, 9, 4, 2, 9, 6, 9, 7.

For the number set 1, 2, 5, 9, 4, 2, 9, 6, 9, 7, the number 9 is the mode because it appears most frequently.

Range

The **range** of a set of numbers is the difference between the greatest number and the smallest number.

Example
The amount of rainfall in a city for each of 12 months is listed here. What is the range of the rainfall in the city during a month?

2.21, 2.49, 5.31, 1.47, 3.33, 4.01, 3.04, 1.11, 5.24, 2.81, 1.91, 4.48

The greatest number in the data set is 5.31. The smallest number is 1.11. The difference is therefore

5.31 – 1.11, which is 4.2. The range of the rainfall in the city during a month is 4.2 inches.

Test-Taking Tips for the Mathematics Section

Here are some specific tips for succeeding on the mathematics section of the Praxis II: Elementary Education: Content Knowledge test.

Use the Answer Choices

Some math problems can be very time-intensive—especially if you are not accustomed to solving those types of problems. However, every question on the Praxis II: Elementary Education: Content Knowledge test will have four answer choices. That means that the correct answer is printed right on the paper, directly below each question. You can sometimes use that information to take a shortcut and save some time. For example, look at the following algebra problem:

1. If $45 - z = 36$, the value of z must be

a. 7
b. 9
c. 11
d. 81

Maybe you forgot the steps needed to solve for a variable (z) in an equation. But you know based on the answer choices that the value of z must be either 7, 9, 11, or 81. It may be easier for you to simply plug the values for z from the answer choices into the equation and see which one fits. The number that makes the equation true is the correct answer choice. In this case, only 9 would fit the equation: $45 - 9 = 36$ is true, so **b** would be correct.

Recognize the Order of the Answer Choices

Chapter 1 of this book covered the usefulness of using the process of elimination. That can be used on any multiple choice standardized test. However, the answer choices on the math section of the Praxis II: Elementary Education: Content Knowledge test will always be in order when they are in numeric form. Most of the time they will be in order from smallest to largest; other times they may be in order from largest to smallest. Either way, you can use this quirk of the test design to your benefit. How? Look at the following question.

2. If $18 + k = 90$, $k =$

a. 98
b. 82
c. 72
d. 5

Notice that the numbers in the answer choices are listed from greatest to least. If you were unsure of how to solve this algebra problem, you could use this order to help save you time. If you are going to plug in a value from the answer choices into the problem, always start with **b** or **c**. In this case, you can start with the number in choice **b**. Using 82 for the value of k results in the following:

$$18 + 82 = 90$$
$$100 = 90$$

Using 82 for k gives you a value that is too high. The value of k must be lower than 82. Therefore, you don't even have to try choice **a**, 98, because it is higher than 82. You can skip right to the number in choice **c**, 72. You were able to eliminate choice **a** without even trying it. This can save you valuable time—especially since you will have to take a whole extra section of the test *after* the mathematics section. The correct answer is indeed choice **c**, 72: $18 + 72 = 90$.

Rewrite the Problem

Some questions will ask you to solve for the sum, difference, product, or quotient of whole numbers, decimals, or fractions. For example, a possible question on the test may look like this:

3. 32.13 + 5.8 =
  a. 26.33
  b. 32.71
  c. 37.21
  d. 37.93

Do NOT try to solve this problem just by looking at it. It's much more difficult to solve a problem written horizontally like this. Rewrite the problem by stacking the numbers to be added, making sure to align them by the decimal value:

$$\begin{array}{r} 32.13 \\ \underline{+\ 5.80} \end{array}$$

Now it's much easier to perform the addition. You can just add the numbers in each place value. You should get 37.93, the number listed in answer choice **d.**

Use Your Calculator *Smartly*

You are allowed to use a calculator on the Praxis II: Elementary Education: Content Knowledge test. Although the questions should not necessarily require the use of a calculator, the calculator will prevent you from making careless errors and help you check your work quickly and efficiently. Therefore, don't feel like you need to use your calculator for every calculation on every problem; use it for what it is—a valuable tool to aid the mathematical process. A calculator won't help if you're not using it properly, so be sure that you've set up a problem the right way before punching numbers into your calculator.

Mathematics Practice

1. Which of the following numbers does NOT represent an integer?
  a. –77
  b. 0
  c. 1.5
  d. 13

2. If $5x - 1 = 6y$, what is the value of x in terms of y?
  a. $\frac{6y+1}{5}$
  b. $\frac{6y}{5} + 1$
  c. $\frac{6y}{5} - 1$
  d. $\frac{6y-1}{5}$

3. Which of the following is a possible solution for b in the inequality shown here?

$$5b - 4 < -14$$

  a. –3
  b. –2
  c. 4
  d. 10

4. A satellite orbits Earth the same number of times each day. After five days, the satellite will have orbited Earth a total of 90 times. How many times will the satellite orbit Earth after one full seven-day week?
  a. 36
  b. 92
  c. 108
  d. 126

5. A bag contains ten marbles of different colors. Ten students in a class pick one marble from the bag each without replacing them in the bag after each pick. Which expression shows the total number of ways that the students in the class can pick the first four marbles from the bag?

a. 10×4
b. $10 \times 9 \times 8 \times 7$
c. 10!
d. 10^4

6. Audrey meets with her math tutor every four days. She also meets with her Spanish tutor every ten days. One day Audrey meets with both her math tutor and her Spanish tutor. In how many more days will Audrey next meet with her math tutor and her Spanish tutor on the same day?

a. 2
b. 14
c. 20
d. 40

7. One inch on a map is equivalent to 50 feet. A rectangular farm on the map has a length of 8 inches and a width of 0.5 inches. What is the area of the farm, in square feet?

a. 4
b. 850
c. 1,000
d. 10,000

8. If the circumference of a circle is 100π cm, the radius of the circle must be

a. 10 cm.
b. 50 cm.
c. 100 cm.
d. 50π cm.

9. A standard deck of cards has 52 cards, 26 of which are red and 26 of which are black. What is the probability that a red card will be drawn from the deck three consecutive times, replacing the card in the deck after each time a card is drawn?

a. $\frac{1}{78}$
b. $\frac{1}{8}$
c. $\frac{1}{6}$
d. $\frac{1}{3}$

10. What is the smallest prime number greater than 20?

a. 21
b. 22
c. 23
d. 29

11. What is the value of k in the following equation?

$$3(6k + 8) = -2(1 \times -3)$$

a. -1
b. $-\frac{1}{9}$
c. 6
d. 18

X	f(x)
7	11
9	15
11	
13	23

12. Which number is missing from the function table shown here?

a. 17
b. 19
c. 21
d. 22

13. Which of the following is the multiplicative inverse of 7*z*?

a. $-7z$
b. $\frac{1}{7z}$
c. $7 - z$
d. $\frac{7z}{1}$

14. The cost of a new car was $21,840, including state sales tax. Without the sales tax, the car was listed as $21,000. What was the percentage of the state sales tax?

a. 0.04%
b. 1.04%
c. 4%
d. 8.4%

15. A student can type at a rate of 30 words per minute. Which expression shows the number of words that he or she can type in *s* seconds?

a. $\frac{s}{30}$
b. $\frac{s}{2}$
c. $2s$
d. $30s$

16. What is the value of 2^6?

a. 26
b. 32
c. 36
d. 64

17. 2, 3, 6

The numbers 2, 3, 6 show the first three terms of a number pattern. The pattern is created by subtracting 3 from the quotient of the product of the previous number and 3. What is the sixth number in the pattern?

a. 15
b. 42
c. 123
d. 126

18. A hardware store sells loose nails in a bin for $0.10 each and loose screws for $0.15 each. One day the store made a total of exactly $1.00 from selling nails and screws from the bin. More screws were sold than nails. How many loose nails did the hardware store sell from the bin during the day?

a. 1
b. 4
c. 6
d. 10

19. Which of the following shows the net for a rectangular prism?

a.

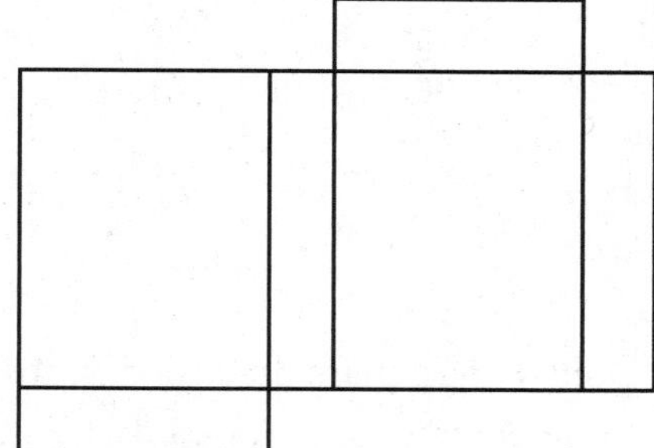

b.

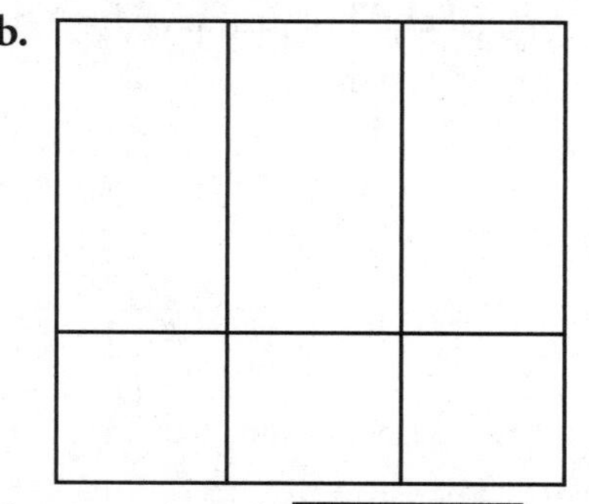

c.

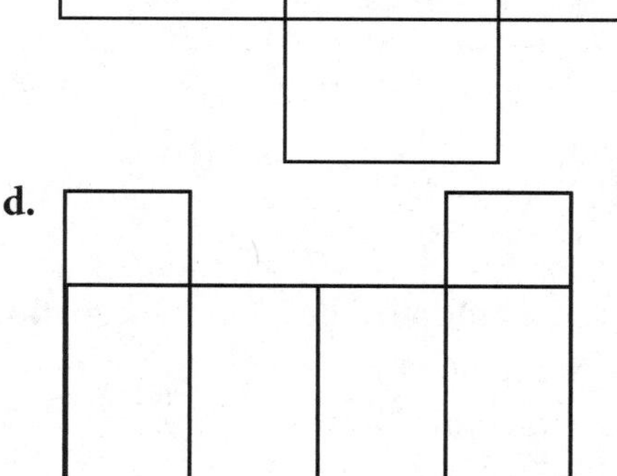

d.

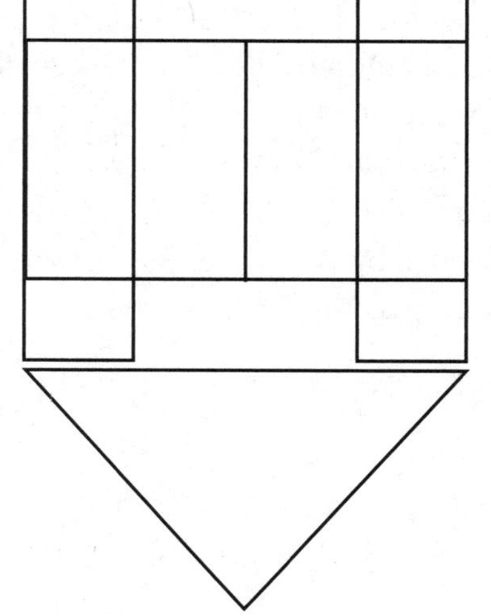

20. The equilateral triangle shown here is rotated so that it looks exactly the same. Which of the following degrees of the rotation could the triangle have been rotated?

a. 60°
b. 90°
c. 180°
d. 240°

21. A band released five albums from the years 2000 to 2010 with an average (arithmetic mean) length of 44 minutes for each album. The first three albums of the decade had lengths of 44, 40, and 38 minutes. Which shows a possible number of minutes for the band's next two albums?

a. 62 and 36
b. 44 and 44
c. 50 and 52
d. 46 and 48

22. Which digit is in the tenths place in the following decimal?

319.078

a. 0
b. 1
c. 7
d. 9

23. An electrician charges $75 for each hour of labor, plus $4.50 for each square foot of installed solar panels. Which equation could be used to represent the electrician's charges based on h number of hours and s number of square feet of solar panels, where c is the total charge?

a. $c = (75 + 4.50)sh$
b. $c = 75s + 4.50h$
c. $c = \frac{75h}{4.50}s$
d. $c = 75h + 4.50s$

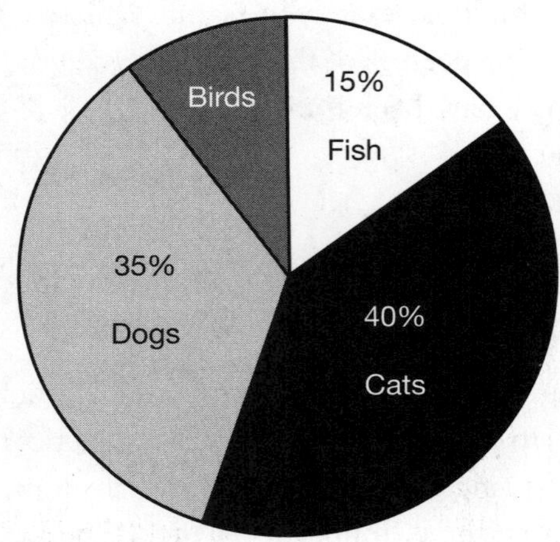

24. The circle graph shows the percentage of students in a middle school who voted for their favorite type of pet. If 20 students voted for birds, how many students voted for cats as their favorite pet?

a. 10
b. 40
c. 50
d. 80

25. To solve an algorithm, Cleveland must follow the steps shown here. Which algebraic expression is equivalent to the algorithm?

First: Set the variable z equal to a specific number.
Second: Add 5 to z.
Third: Multiply the sum by 3.
Fourth: Divide the product by 2.

a. $3\frac{5+z}{2}$
b. $\frac{3(5+z)}{2}$
c. $\frac{3 \times 5 + z}{2}$
d. $5 + z \times \frac{3}{2}$

26. What is the value of the following expression?

$100 \div (5 - 1) \times 5$

a. 5
b. 15
c. 95
d. 125

27. Two points of a square on a coordinate grid have ordered pairs of (–1,4) and (4,9). If the sides are vertical and horizontal, which must also be an ordered pair of the square?

a. (4,1)
b. (–1,–1)
c. (–1,9)
d. (9,4)

28. There are three different kinds of trees in Judith's yard. The ratio of beech trees to elm trees to oak trees is 3:4:1, respectively. If there are a total of 40 trees in Judith's yard, how many beech trees are there in the yard?

a. 3
b. 15
c. 20
d. 30

29. When x is multiplied by –2 in the equation $y = \frac{x}{8}$, the value of y

a. stays the same.
b. is multiplied by –2.
c. is divided by –4.
d. is multiplied by 2.

30. The gray rectangle in the preceding figure is three-quarters the height and three-quarters the width of the surrounding rectangle. If the length of the white rectangle is 12 inches and its width is 6 inches, what is the perimeter of the gray rectangle, in inches?
a. 26
b. 27
c. 36
d. 40.5

MATHEMATICS KEY

ITEM	KEY	SUBSECTION	ITEM	KEY	SUBSECTION
1	C	Number Sense & Numeration	16	D	Number Sense & Numeration
2	A	Algebraic Concepts	17	C	Number Sense & Numeration
3	A	Algebraic Concepts	18	A	Number Sense & Numeration
4	D	Geometry & Measurement	19	A	Geometry & Measurement
5	B	Data Org. & Interpretation	20	D	Geometry & Measurement
6	C	Number Sense & Numeration	21	A	Data Org. & Interpretation
7	D	Geometry & Measurement	22	A	Number Sense & Numeration
8	B	Geometry & Measurement	23	D	Algebraic Concepts
9	B	Data Org. & Interpretation	24	D	Data Org. & Interpretation
10	C	Number Sense & Numeration	25	B	Algebraic Concepts
11	A	Number Sense & Numeration	26	D	Number Sense & Numeration
12	B	Number Sense & Numeration	27	C	Geometry & Measurement
13	B	Algebraic Concepts	28	B	Number Sense & Numeration
14	C	Number Sense & Numeration	29	B	Algebraic Concepts
15	B	Algebraic Concepts	30	B	Geometry & Measurement

Mathematics Answers

1. c. An integer is any positive or negative whole number or zero. If a number is represented by a decimal or a fraction, it is not considered an integer. Therefore, choice **c** is NOT an integer.

2. a. To isolate x on one side of the equation, you first need to add 1 to each side, and then you can divide both sides by 5. The resulting expression is $\frac{6y+1}{5}$. Remember that the entire expression $6y + 1$ needs to be divided by 5—not just $6y$, which is represented by the incorrect expression in choice **b**.

3. a. To solve this question, you need to find a value for b that satisfies the given inequality. The best way to find the correct answer is to try the numbers in the answer choices to find the one that will make it true. Plugging in the value for choice **a**, –3, will give you the following answer:

$5b - 4 < -14$

$5(-3) - 4 < -14$

$-15 - 4 < -14$

$-19 < -14$

Because –19 is less than –14, this is a true inequality. None of the numbers in the other answer choices will provide a correct inequality. –2, the value in choice **b**, would be correct if the inequality symbol < were an equals sign, =, or a greater than or equal to sign, ≥.

4. d. The satellite orbits Earth 90 times in five days. Because it orbits Earth the same number of times each day, you can determine how many times it orbits each day by dividing 90 by 5. $90 \div 5 = 18$. Then you can find out the number of times it will orbit Earth in 7 days by multiplying 18 by 7; the correct answer is 126, choice **d**. Another way to solve this problem is to set up a proportion as shown below:

$\frac{90}{5} = \frac{x}{7}$

You can then cross multiply to find that $5x = 630$, which simplifies to $x = 126$.

5. b. The scenario in the problem represents a permutation because the order of the way that the marbles are picked matters. Therefore, you can multiply the number of possibilities for each place together to find the total number of ways the marbles can be picked. When one marble is selected, there is one fewer marble left in the bag. That means that while there are 10 possibilities for the first marble, there are only 9 possibilities for the second marble. If the question asked for the total number of ways that all ten marbles will be picked, then choice **c**, 10!, would be correct. However, only the first four picks matter, so choice **b** is correct.

6. c. To solve this problem, you need to identify the least common multiple of 4 and 10. While 40, choice **d** is a common multiple of 4 and 10—and Audrey will therefore meet with her math tutor and her Spanish tutor in 40 days—it is not the *least* common multiple and not the *next* time she will meet with both tutors. The least common multiple of 4 and 10 is 20, choice **c**, so Audrey will next meet with her Spanish and math tutors in 20 days.

7. d. According to the map's scale, one inch is equivalent to 50 feet. Therefore, the length of the rectangular farm, 8 inches on the map, is equivalent to 8×50 ft = 400 ft. The width of the map, 0.5 inches on the map, is equivalent to 0.5×50 ft = 25 ft. To calculate the area of any rectangle, multiply the length by the width. In the case of this farm, that would be 400 ft × 25 ft = 10,000 square feet, choice **d**. The perimeter of the farm would be 850 ft, choice **b**.

8. b. To find the circumference of a circle, you need to double the radius and multiply the product by π. Therefore, to find the radius from the circumference, you need to divide by π and then divide by 2. 100π_divided by π and then divided by 2 is 50, so choice **b** is correct. Choice **c** represents the diameter of the circle.

9. b. The probability of picking a red card at random from the deck of cards is $\frac{26}{52}$, or exactly $\frac{1}{2}$. As long as the card is replaced after each pick, the probability will not change. Therefore, you can determine the probability of picking three consecutive red cards by multiplying $\frac{1}{2} \times \frac{1}{2} \times \frac{1}{2}$. The product, $\frac{1}{8}$, is the correct answer.

10. c. A prime number is a number that is divisible only by itself and the number 1. The number 21, choice **a**, is also divisible by 3 and 7, so it is not prime. The number 22, choice **b**, is also divisible by 2 and 11, so it is not prime. The number 23, choice **c**, is only divisible by 1 and 23, so it is the smallest prime number greater than 20. Number 29, choice **d**, is also a prime number, but it is not the smallest prime number greater than 20.

11. a. To find the value of k in the given equation, you can use the distributive property to simplify the value on left side of the equals sign. Then you can find the value inside the parentheses on the right side of the equals sign and multiply by –2.

$3(6k + 8) = -2(1 \times -3)$

$(3 \times 6k) + (3 \times 8) = -2(-3)$

$18k + 24 = 6$

$18k = -18$

$k = -1$

12. b. The $f(x)$ values are related to the x values in the function table. For each value of x, the $f(x)$ value is equal to 3 less than the product of the number and 2. If you don't notice that, perhaps you recognize that the x values increase by 2 and the $f(x)$ values increase by 4. The missing value in the function table is therefore 19, choice **b**.

13. b. The multiplicative inverse of a number is the number that, when multiplied by the original number, results in a product of 1. In the case of $7z$, the multiplicative inverse must be $\frac{1}{7z}$, choice **b**.

14. c. You could solve this problem by plugging in the possible tax rates given in the answer choices to see which one fits the numbers in the situation. Another way to solve it, however, is to set up a proportion as shown below.

$\frac{21{,}840}{21{,}000} = \frac{x}{1}$

You can then cross-multiply to find that $21{,}000x = 21{,}840$. Use your calculator to simplify, and you will get $x = 1.04$. Be careful, however, because this is not the tax rate, choice **b**. The \$21,840 cost is 1.04 times the amount of the \$21,000 cost. That is the result of an increase of 0.04, which is equivalent to 4%, choice **c**.

15. b. Be sure to notice the difference between minutes and seconds in this question. If a student can type 30 words in a minute and there are 60 seconds in a minute, then that means the student can type 30 ÷ 60 words in a second. For one second, this is $\frac{1}{2}$ word. If there are 2 seconds, the student can type $\frac{2}{2}$, or 1 word. The expression that represents this rate is $\frac{s}{2}$, choice **b**.

16. d. To find the value of 2^6, you need to multiply 2 by itself 6 times. $2 \times 2 \times 2 \times 2 \times 2 \times 2 = 64$, choice **d**. If you chose choice **c**, you find the value of 6^2, which is equivalent to 6×6, or 36.

17. c. The numbers in the pattern increase according to the rule "subtract 3 from the quotient of the product of the previous number and 3." The fourth number should therefore be $(6 \times 3) - 3$, or 15. However, the question asks for the sixth number in the pattern, so choice **a** is not correct. The fifth number will be $(15 \times 3) - 3$, or 42, choice **b**. The sixth number will be $(42 \times 3) - 3$, or 123.

18. a. The only possible ways that nails and screws could be sold for the hardware store to earn $1.00 are listed below.
1 nail, 6 screws = $0.10 + 6(0.15) = 1.00$
4 nails, 4 screws = $4(0.10) + 4(0.15) = 1.00$
7 nails, 2 screws = $7(0.10) + 2(0.15) = 1.00$
10 nails = $10(0.10) = 1.00$
The only combination of nails and screws that shows that more screws were sold than nails is the first one. Therefore, only one loose nail was sold at the hardware store that day.

19. a. A rectangular prism has six faces. Therefore, you can eliminate choices **c** and **d** because they show nets with five and eight faces, respectively. While the net in choice **b** has six faces, they cannot be used to form a rectangular prism. The net in choice **a** is the only one that can be used to construct a rectangular prism.

20. d. Any figure will look the same after a rotation of 360°. The equilateral triangle can be rotated by any turn of (360° ÷ 3) and look the same. So a rotation of 120° will make it look the same, as well as a rotation of 240°, choice **d**. The rotations in choices **a**, **b**, and **c** will change the orientation of the triangle.

21. a. If the average (arithmetic mean) length of the 5 albums was 44 minutes, then the sum of the lengths of the 5 albums must be 44×5, or 220 minutes. The given lengths of the albums are 44, 40, and 38 minutes. Therefore, the remaining length of the two albums must be equal to $220 - (44 + 40 + 38)$, which is 98 minutes. Any two album lengths with a sum length of 98 minutes will fit the given scenario. Only the lengths in choice **a** fit and make the mean length equal to 44 minutes.

22. a. The tenths place is the first digit to the right of the decimal point. In the case of 319.078, that digit is 0, choice **a**.

23. d. The electrician's charge of $75 should be multiplied by the number of hours he or she works, *h*. The cost for each square foot of solar paneling, $4.50, should be multiplied by the total number of square feet of solar paneling, *s*. The total cost, then, would be the sum of these two costs. This is represented by the equation in choice **d**. There is no division in the scenario, so choice **c** is not correct. You cannot multiply the variables together, so choice **a** is not correct. Choice **b** has the coefficients mixed up with the variables.

24. d. The total percents representing fish, cats, and dogs is 15 + 40 + 35, or 90%. The percentage of students who voted for birds, therefore, is 10%. Because 20 students voted for birds, you can find out how many voted for cats by setting up a proportion comparing the percents to the actual votes for each animal:

$\frac{10}{20} = \frac{40}{x}$

You can then cross multiply to find that $10x = 800$, which means that $x = 80$. Eighty students voted for cats as their favorite animal.

25. b. According to the steps in this algorithm, the first operation should be adding 5 to z. Parentheses are used to denote that one step should be done first, as shown in the expressions in choices **a** and **b**. However, the fourth step shows that the entire product should be divided by 2—not just the sum of $5 + z$. Therefore, the correct expression is $\frac{3(5 + z)}{2}$, choice **b**.

26. d. To solve this expression, you must follow the order of operations. That means you need to solve for the parentheses first, then the multiplication and division from left to right, and then the addition and subtraction from left to right. The following steps show how to correctly solve the given expression.

$100 \div (5 - 1) \times 5$

$100 \div (4) \times 5$

$100 \div 20$

5

27. c. If two points of a square on a coordinate grid have coordinates at (–1,4) and (4,9), then the lengths of the sides are (9 – 4) or (4 – (–1)), or 5. You can sketch the figure on a coordinate grid to see where the remaining two points must lie.

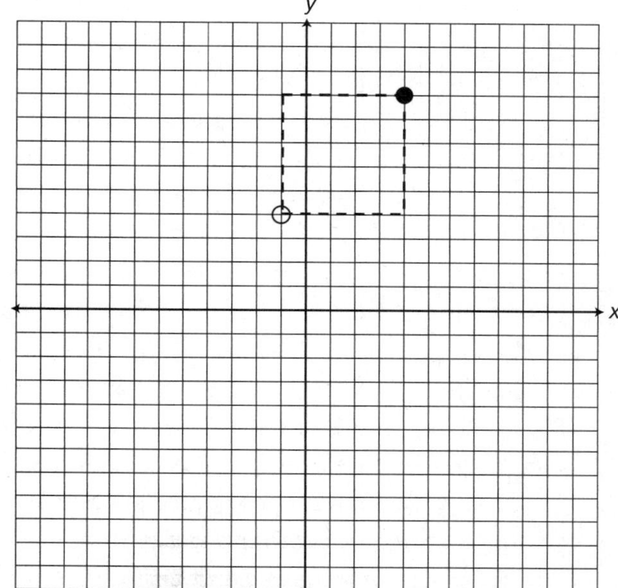

Of the given coordinates in the answer choices, only (–1,9) fits one of the other coordinates of the square.

28. b. The ratio of beech trees to elm trees to oak trees in Judith's yard is 3:4:1, respectively. That means for every 8 trees, 3 are beech, 4 are elm, and 1 is oak. The ratio of beech trees to total trees, therefore, is 3 out of 8. To find the number of beech trees out of 40 trees overall, you can set up a proportion comparing the ratio to the total.

$\frac{3}{8} = \frac{x}{40}$

Then, you can cross multiply to find that $8x = 120$, or $x = 15$. There are 15 beech trees in Judith's yard.

29. b. Whatever is done to one side of the equation must be done to the other to keep it balanced. Therefore, if x is multiplied by -2, then the value of y is multiplied by -2 as well.

30. b. The dimensions of the gray rectangle are exactly three-quarters those of the white rectangle. The length of the white rectangle is 12 inches. The length of the gray rectangle must therefore be equal to $\frac{3}{4} \times 12$, which is 9 inches. The width of the white rectangle is 6 inches. The width of the gray rectangle must therefore be equal to $\frac{3}{4} \times 6$ inches, which is 4.5 inches. Once you know the length and width of the gray rectangle, you can find the sum of the sides to find its perimeter. $9 + 9 + 4.5 + 4.5 = 27$, so the perimeter of the gray rectangle is 27 inches.

CHAPTER 5

SOCIAL STUDIES REVIEW

The third section of the Praxis II: Elementary Education: Content Knowledge test is the social studies section. Of the 120 questions on the test, 30 will cover material from the social studies section. Each question will be multiple choice with four answer choices.

About the Social Studies Section

The social studies section of the Praxis II: Elementary Education: Content Knowledge test will include questions about a wide range of social studies concepts, including not only geography and history but the foundations of government and economics as well. It will even include questions about anthropology, sociology, and possibly psychology.

To succeed on the social studies section, you will need to be familiar with key social studies terminology, facts (including names, dates, and events), conventions, methodology, concepts, principles, generalizations, and theories. This section recaps most of the significant terms, events, and concepts that are likely to be tested on the Praxis II. However, you can research any of the listed subjects further using additional resources, such as college textbooks or encyclopedias.

The questions in this section will fall into one of several major areas of social studies. The major areas of the social studies section, and the approximate number of questions that will cover their content, are as follows:

- geography, anthropology, sociology, and psychology (9 items)
- world history (3 items)
- United States history (9 items)
- government, citizenship, and democracy (3 items)
- economics (3 items)

There will also be about 3 items that test the social studies as inquiry and the processes of social studies. For example, these questions may ask you to interpret information or use tools to gather data and draw valid conclusions. The elements of each major area are explained in detail in the following sections, and the inquiry/processes concepts are interspersed throughout this chapter.

Geography, Anthropology, Sociology, and Psychology

About 30% of the social studies section of the Praxis II: Elementary Education: Content Knowledge test—or about 9 of the 30 questions—will include questions from this very wide-ranging collection of topics. There will likely be a few questions for each of the geography, anthropology, and sociology subgroups. There may also be a question or two relating to psychology. The following four sections focus on each of these topics.

Geography

Many of the geography questions on the Praxis II will simply determine your general knowledge of terms, places, and regions, such as: "In which state is the Grand Canyon?" However, the questions may also involve more in-depth uses of geography, such as reading maps or the way that mankind interacts with and uses its geography.

Physical Geography

Physical geography is the study of the natural features of Earth. While it's impossible to cover every single geographic location and feature that may appear on the Praxis II, it will help significantly if you are familiar with common geographic terminology. What follows are some of the most essential terms.

Archipelago: a chain of islands, such as the islands that largely comprise Indonesia and the Philippines.

Basin: a geographic depression, often filled with water.

Bay: a body of water partially surrounded by land. The land surrounding a bay tends to provide shelter from both harsh weather and military invasion, so bays were historically considered excellent places in which to establish ports.

Delta: a plain at the mouth of a river, often triangular in shape. Rivers deposit sediment in their deltas, which may create especially fertile farmland.

Equator: an imaginary line drawn across the middle of the globe. The equator is the same distance from the magnetic North Pole and the magnetic South Pole. The equator divides the globe into northern and southern hemispheres.

Flood plain: a plain on either side of a river. Flood plains form out of layers of sediment deposited over centuries of flooding. Although regular flooding of these areas may be dangerous, communities often settle in flood plains because the sediment deposited by flooding is rich in minerals and is good farming soil.

Frigid zones: the climate zones of the Arctic and Antarctic Circles. The seasonal cycles of the frigid zones lack any warm summers. In the frigid zones, no month has an average temperature greater than 42° Fahrenheit.

Glacier: a large, slow-moving mass of snow and ice. The movement of glaciers, which advance and retreat over time, can carve valleys out of a stony landscape and deposit mineral resources over an extensive area. Glaciers can also push large deposits of debris to form new land masses. Two of these masses, called moraines, formed the 118-mile-long land mass of Long Island, in New York. Recent climate changes have caused concerns that the glaciers are shrinking.

Hill: a raised area of land under 2,000 feet in height.

Island: an area of land completely surrounded by water.

Isthmus: a narrow strip of land connecting two larger regions. Historically, isthmuses have been important to trade. The fact that they are so narrow compared to the regions they connect made them attractive places to build canals. Even without a canal, overland travel on an isthmus was sometimes cheaper and easier than using sea routes.

Lines of latitude: imaginary horizontal lines that run across the globe. Lines of latitude are measured in degrees, minutes, and seconds. The equator, itself a line of latitude, has a measure of 0°. The north and south poles have measures of 90°N and 90°S, respectively.

Lines of longitude: imaginary vertical lines that run across the globe. Lines of longitude are measured in degrees, minutes, and seconds. The prime meridian, itself a line of longitude, has a measure of 0°. The **International Date Line** (IDL) has a measure of roughly 180°.

Mountain: a raised area of land greater than 2,000 feet in height. The area at the bottom of the mountain is referred to as the **base**. The top of the mountain is the **peak**. When the mountain stretches over a distance, the peak is referred to as a **ridge**.

Mountain pass: a gap between mountains. Historically, early travelers depended on passes to travel through mountainous regions. Even today, road and rail lines are likely to take advantage of natural passes.

Mouth: the point where a river enters a sea or lake.

Peninsula: a region mostly surrounded by water, but still connected to land.

Plateau: a large, flat area raised above the surrounding area. Normally, at least one side of the plateau terminates in a steep slope.

Prime meridian: a line of longitude that, by international agreement, marks 0° longitude. The line passes through Greenwich, England, and divides the globe into eastern and western hemispheres.

Source: the origin point of a river. Water flows from the source to the mouth.

Strait: a narrow body of water between two landmasses.

Temperate latitudes: the climate zones that lie between the tropical latitudes and the polar circles. The northern temperate latitudes exist between the Tropic of Cancer and the Arctic Circle. The southern zone can be found between the Tropic of Capricorn and the Antarctic Circle. The seasonal cycle in the temperate zones includes a distinct spring, summer, fall, and winter.

Tributary: a river or stream that flows into another river. In contrast, a **branch** is a river or stream made when the flow of water leaves a larger river.

Tropic latitudes: the climate zone between the Tropic of Cancer and the Tropic of Capricorn. The seasonal cycle in the tropic includes a hot dry season, a cool dry season, and a rainy season.

Tropic of Cancer: the imaginary line of latitude, at approximately 23° south of the Equator. It marks the point farthest south where the sun can be seen directly overhead.

Tropic of Capricorn: the imaginary line of latitude, at approximately 23° north of the Equator, that marks the point farthest north where the sun can be seen directly overhead.

Valley: a low stretch of land between raised areas of land. Valleys are formed by the action of rivers cutting paths out of the surrounding land. Most rainfall in an area will drain out through the valley.

Human Geography

While physical geography relates to the physical characteristics of the planet, **human geography** refers to the way that humans spread over and interact with Earth. A **population** is any group of individuals that shares some common characteristic. In geography, populations are often defined by geographical proximity and political or ethnic identity. However, numerous traits have been identified, any of which a geographer might use. These include, but are not limited to, birth and mortality rates, age distribution, economic indicators, and public health factors.

The following list identifies some of the core concepts in the study of populations.

Crude birth rate is the annual number of childbirths for every 1,000 people.

Crude death rate is the annual mortality rate, or number of deaths, for every 1,000 people.

Demographic transitions. A population goes through a demographic transition when there is a distinct and drastic change in death and birth rates. Population geographers divide transitions into three major demographic transition models, or DTMs. In the first DTM, a population begins with relatively high birth and death rates. Then the death rate drops. Next, the birth rate drops. Eventually the birth and death rates stabilize again, but at much lower rates than the population experienced before the drop. This pattern describes the typical transitions experienced by Western nations that went through industrialization in the 1800s. In the second DTM, which describes some regions in Central Europe, populations have declines in both birth and death rates, but the death rate continues to drop lower than the birth rate. When the rates do stabilize, the birth rate remains considerably higher than the death rate. Finally, in the third DTM, which describes much of Asia, Africa, and South America, the population will experience declining death rates, but there is no significant decline in birth rates. Population geographers debate what factors might cause the difference in these major transition models.

Development geography. Geographers concerned with development geography study how population dynamics and spatial relationships can affect the standard of living for individuals within a population. This approach often combines geographic techniques with economic and sociological theories.

Economic geography. This term describes the distribution of economic activities. Economic geographers study how different economic activities form links between different regions and populations. One of the critical issues in economic geography is the study of how the natural distribution of resources is exploited and transported.

Infant mortality rate. This figure measures the number of infant deaths for every 1,000 infants within a year. An infant is defined as any child less than one year old. Traditionally, infant mortality rates are used to assess the general state of health care in a population. A population with a high infant mortality rate can be assumed to have poor or no access to health care.

Language demography is the study of the spread of a language. Language demographers attempt to estimate the number of speakers a language has. They also try to distinguish between regional dialects and identify ways in which population changes may impact a language.

Life expectancy is the average age to which the members within a community can be expected to live. For biological and cultural reasons, women tend to live longer than men. To account for this, life expectancies are often given separately for males and females. In the United States, the life expectancy of a male is about 75 years and the life expectancy for a female is about 80 years.

Morbidity rate is the incidence of people contracting a selected illness within a population. Given the differences between diseases, there is no standard unit for morbidity rates and researchers must decide meaningful measures for the problem they wish to study. This should not be confused with **mortality rate**, a measure of the number of deaths in the population.

Population density is a measure of how many individuals of a population exist in a given unit of space. There is no standard measure for population density, so researchers must determine a meaningful unit of space before they can accurately describe population density.

Religious demography is the study of the number and distribution of adherents to various religions or belief systems. There are numerous problems facing religious demographers, notably the sometimes bewildering diversity of belief among religious adherents who identify themselves as members of the same faith.

Urban geography. Geographers have applied tools originally devised to study widespread distributions of populations to densely populated urban environments. The result is the field known as urban geography. Urban geographers study the efficiency of urban development schemes, the way in which social and ethnic groups are distributed through an urban area, and how urban space influences human activities, from employment to crime.

Cartographic Methods

The making of maps is known as cartography. There are three broad types of maps.

Topographic or *topographical maps* are concerned with the accurate depiction of the surface conditions of an area. Topographical maps adhere to the same size scale, will use shading or other graphics to indicate physical features, and include all features and details relevant to the map's scale. Here is a topographical map of San Diego.

Notice that the details are rendered in the same scale. Contour lines indicate elevation changes. Like all topographical maps, this is an effort to render, as realistically as possible, the physical landscape of the area this describes.

Topological maps are maps that have been simplified to the point where only a few pieces of key information stand out. Unlike topographical maps, the point of topological maps is to present essential information to a reader as clearly as possible. Here is a topological map of the New York City subway system.

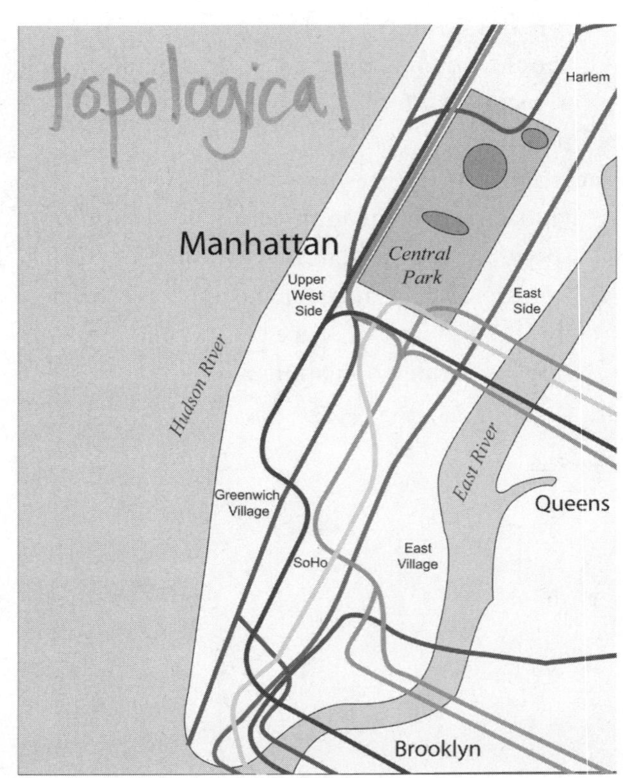

The function of this map is to describe the relative location of subway stops and explain what train lines stop at which stations. To help communicate this clearly, the map ignores all but the most basic physical information. It also eliminates scale. In this map, Manhattan is shown larger than it actually would be if drawn to scale. This is because the density of stops in Manhattan would make the map too difficult to read if it was shown in the proper scale.

Like topological maps, **thematic maps** simplify geographical accuracy in favor of better communicating specific and focused information to the map user. The significant difference between the topological map and the thematic map is in the type of information displayed. Thematic maps display social, political, or otherwise nongeographical data in conjunction with geographical information. For example, the following map shows a rough outline of American coasts; otherwise, it shows the national borders of the United States, indicates the state borders, and uses shading to indicate water usage.

Thematic maps are crucial to the study of cultural geography, or the study of how cultural traits and activities (such as language use, ethnic migration, and industrial diversity) are distributed.

Cartographic Terms

Cartographers have developed a handful of traditional devices and techniques to communicate information to map users. They might appear on any of the three major types of maps. This section details some of the most common ones.

Maps often indicate the cardinal directions—north, south, east, and west—with a **compass rose**. Here is a compass rose that marks the four cardinal points and four intermediate points.

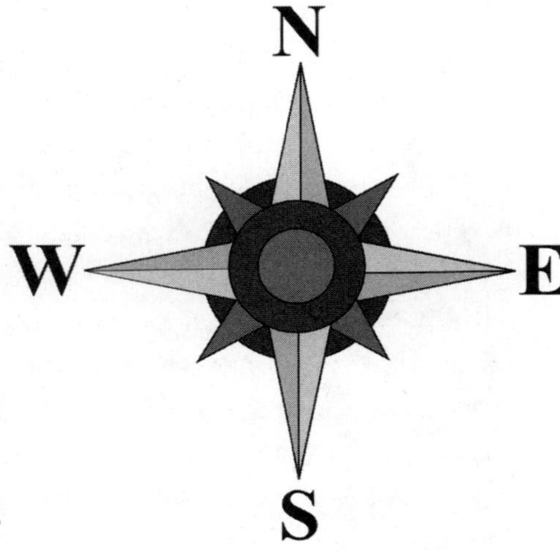

The **key** is a section of the map that explains any representational features, such as symbols or meaningful color usage, to the user. It may also be called the **legend**. Here is a key for a map of North Korea.

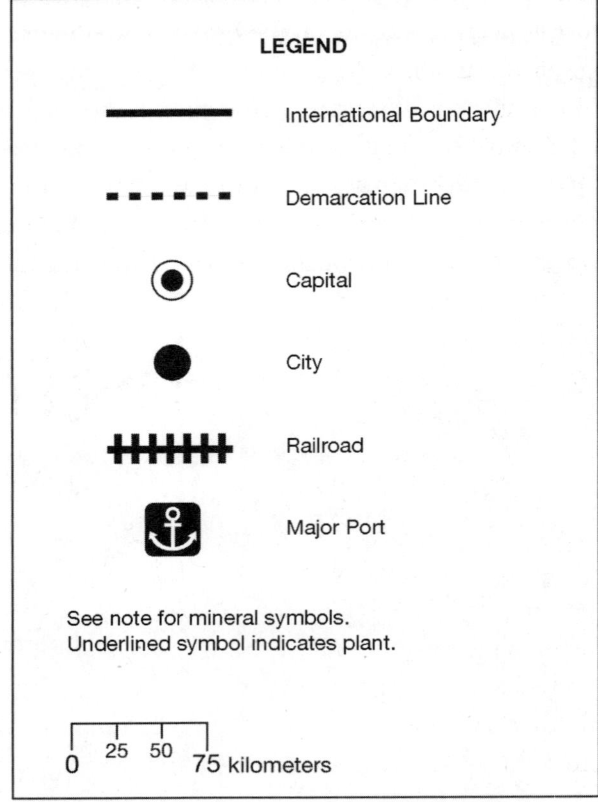

Many maps include a small globe, called a **locator globe**, that highlights the area shown in greater detail on the map. The function of these globes is to orient the map user with regard to a global position.

A **scale** translates the representational differences into their real-world equivalents. Most maps produced in the United States have scales that show distances in both metric and traditional units.

Most maps will have a **title**. With topographical maps, the title will most likely identify the region depicted on the map. The title of topological and thematic maps will usually explain the purpose of the map, giving the user a sense of what information will be presented and what information will be excluded.

Anthropology

Anthropology questions on the Praxis II: Elementary Education: Content Knowledge test may ask you about social institutions, such as communities, organizations, or clubs. Specifically, the test may ask you to interpret these social institutions' customs anthropologically. Additionally, the test may ask you about the many contributions to the continued development of human culture. This may include religion, language, tradition, behavior, or any number of cultural expressions, such as art, dance, music, or even food. However, it's most important to go into the test with a solid understanding of the common anthropological terms that may show up on the exam.

Broadly speaking, **anthropology** is the study of humanity. It is a holistic field, meaning it draws methods and concepts from a broad range of sources. There are several general approaches to the field. For the Praxis II, you should be aware of the cultural and physical branches of anthropology. **Cultural anthropology** studies the cultural organization of a specific group of people. This is what most people think of when they think of anthropology. It relies heavily on qualitative methods and extended observations. **Physical anthropology**, or biological anthropology, focuses on the development of the human race's physical form.

Cultural anthropology has its origins in the rise of the military and economic European powers of the Victorian era. At that time, European anthropologists gathered data from explorers, missionaries, and others involved in the colonial enterprise. They then organized this data, most often looking for similarities in cultural practices and beliefs. The great goal of these early anthropologists was to determine whether there was a single evolutionary path for all cultures and, if there was, to rank existing societies according to their progress on this path.

By the twentieth century, two components of Victorian-era anthropology had fallen out of favor. First, modern anthropologists rejected the notion of a universal path of evolution. The American anthropologist Julian Steward proposed a more nuanced model of cultural evolution called cultural ecology. Stewart proposed that a culture is shaped by its immediate environment. Where there are parallels between cultures, the two cultures must share some environmental element. However, these adaptations are local and can only be found in cultures facing the same environmental challenge. The French anthropologist Claude Lévi-Strauss proposed a non-evolutionary explanation for similarities across societies. Lévi-Strauss was a proponent of a philosophy called structuralism, which holds that humans build meaning out of conceptual differences and oppositions. Some of these oppositions, like life/death or day/night, are so basic as to be universal. Because humans build their culture on top of these oppositions, it is not surprising that some cultural elements, especially those dealing with basic concepts, show some similarities.

The second major development was methodological. The early anthropologists were, for the most part, gatherers of secondhand information. They would sort and sift through reports from sources spread throughout various colonies. By the twentieth century, anthropologists shifted toward what would be the dominant approach of modern cultural anthropology: **ethnography**, which combines insights from multiple disciplines with extensive fieldwork.

Archaeology approaches the study of human history through the examination of material artifacts. The goal of archaeology is to document the development of human evolution and culture. An archaeologist looks at the tools, decorations, art, buildings, and other material remnants of a culture to see what these artifacts reveal about the people who used them.

Sociology

Sociology is the organized study of social phenomena. These phenomena include the ways in which an individual may interact with his or her culture as well as large-scale features that emerge only when people come together to form groups. The Praxis II may test you on some of the basic concepts in sociology, as well as the major sociological paradigms. You may be asked about socialization in society and its negative and positive effects. For example, you should understand the study of populations and how changes to population—such as through immigration or migration—affect a society. You should also be familiar with common sociological terms, such as ethnocentrism and discrimination. While you won't be expected to know about all of the famous sociologists, it will help to be familiar with a few of the individual subjects that have traditionally been important topics for sociological research.

The Major Paradigm of Sociology

The four major sources of sociological theory all appeared, nearly simultaneously, at the latter half of the nineteenth century. Since that time, the field has adopted political ideologies, rejected and rediscovered basic principles, and transformed its methods and ideas to keep pace with the change of society. It would be impossible to cover every shift within the social sciences even in a book twice this size. However, it is possible to follow the general development of sociology's most important schools of thought. This section traces the development of sociology, highlights some of its more important practitioners, and outlines some of the essential sociological theories.

The existence of sociology as a unique branch of study can be traced to **Auguste Comte**, a nineteenth-century French philosopher. Comte not only coined the term *sociology*, but also stressed the importance of empirical research in the study of social phenomena. Unlike the study of philosophy, which advanced through observation and speculation, Comte thought that sociologists had to apply the scientific method to the study of society. In fact, Comte believed that only information gained through the scientific method was worthwhile. Everything else was just speculation.

Comte's **positivism** was attacked almost immediately by others who wanted to push the newly founded science in a different direction. Despite this, Comte's positivism continues to exert a profound influence on the theories and methods of sociology. Most would say that, even today, it is an adherence to a scientific framework that defines and distinguishes sociology.

In contrast to Comte's positivism, the nineteenth-century German philosopher **Karl Marx** and his followers felt that *dialectical materialism* should be the basis of all study of society. Dialectical materialism was a complex set of philosophical positions that, among other things, claimed that societies develop through the conflict of opposites. For Marx, the conflict between social classes was the greatest of these conflicts. Marx saw most of history as the conflict between the haves and the have-nots. Marx further believed that the laboring class was destined to rise up and dominate the upper class.

Marx's ideas were only partially accepted by sociologists. Few modern sociologists are dialectical materialists, but many of the concepts studied by Marx are now an important part of the field. Understanding social conflict, the existence of separate and distinct social classes within societies, and the study of forces that promote or restrict social change are all typical preoccupations of sociologists.

Marxist sociology produced **conflict theory**, a sociological approach that studies the role of power and conflict in social organizations. Much of conflict theory continues to emphasize the struggle between labor and owners that Marx identified as the key driving force in social development, but some sociologists have expanded their focus to include gender, religion, and race as sites of conflict.

Important Sociological Concepts

Sociologists have studied a bewildering array of social organizations, from the mundane to the most exotic. There is no way to range across the entire body of concepts and theories generated by the discipline. There are, however, some concerns that appear again and again. By reviewing these key concepts, we can grasp the issues sociologists seem to perennially revisit.

A **social organization** is any group that organizes its members into roles and provides connections among the various members. Sociologists identify five major social organizations that have been present in civilization: governments, educational institutions, religious institutions, economic systems, and family units. As one might expect, it is common for any individual to have a role in several of these institutions at any given time.

The forms these major institutions might take can vary widely across societies or even within a society. Sociologists have competing theories to explain just why different societies and groups produce different social organizations. One popular nineteenth-century theory of organization and change involved a circular pattern of social growth and decay. This early sociological theory had its roots in classical historical studies that held that civilizations follow a predictable pattern of rise and fall. Modern sociologists now feel that this is too simplistic a model to explain how societies organize themselves and why they change over time. However, some recent studies of population growth rates suggest that some social phenomena, such as birth rates, may follow a general cycle, rising and falling predictably in reaction to a host of external factors.

A nineteenth-century theory that has proven more durable is the **Darwinian model** of social evolution. Herbert Spenser, an early proponent of evolutionary thought, proposed that societies act like a species of animal under the influence of natural selection. The forms a society's social organizations take are the product of natural selection. Organizational forms that were not successful in perpetuating a society's existence failed, and forms that promoted the successful persistence of the society were continued. Early evolutionary sociologists believed that this process of natural selection improved and perfected societies. This bias has been long overturned. Adaptation, it is now believed, is an immediate reaction to the environment and has no long-term goal or end result. This modernized view of social evolution is somewhat similar to the ideas of structural functionalists, who hold that the persistence of any social organization is evidence that it helps maintain the society. This persistence is a morally indifferent fact, and not proof that a society is getting better or improving over time.

Traditional Marxists placed the growth and development of all societies on the same track. According to traditional Marxists, societies grow increasingly complex in order to take advantage of natural resources. The division of labor is an example of this increase in complexity. By specializing in a job, the person doing the job can do it better. However, this increasing complexity creates social inequalities, especially once the concept of private property is developed within a society. Marx felt that these inequalities would destroy a society and, from that destruction, a new order of communal property and collective control of resources would arise. Few modern sociologists believe Marx's predictions are a given. However, many continue to emphasize the ways in which systemic inequalities and conflicts between social groups explain how unique social organizations are created.

Finally, Max Weber, a key figure from the humanistic school, proposed that rationalization was the constant driving force behind the development of society. According to Weber, as societies develop over time, an increasing number of social interactions are shaped by the need for greater efficiency. Influences like traditional values and emotional needs are replaced by the value of increased efficiency. This drive for efficiency eventually remakes the institutional organizations of a society. For example, smaller shops are often pushed out of the market by larger and less personal, but more efficient, so-called big box stores. In turn, these stores feel increasing pressure from even more efficient online stores. Proponents of Weber's theory point to the late twentieth- and early twenty-first-century trend of globalization as evidence of Weber's thesis. However, critics feel Weber overstates his case. Many countries, especially those with theocratic governments, have proved exceptionally resistant to some forms of rationalization. In such cases, the influence of traditional values would seem considerably more powerful than Weber predicted.

Social Stratification

For most societies, some sort of hierarchy of social classes is the norm. (The **norm** itself is a sociological term meaning the typical behavior of a social group.) Describing and explaining this stratification is a common goal of sociologists.

Each major school of sociology has approached the question of social stratification through its own set of assumptions. Structural functionalist sociologists assume that stratification must contribute to the continued persistence of society, or stratification would not be such a common and enduring element of social organizations. The structural functionalist Talcott Parsons theorized that diversification was essential to the survival of societies. Without diversification, societies would not be efficient enough to supply the basic needs of their members. Parson felt that this diversification led inevitably to the creation of imbalances of power, chains of command, and other elements of social stratification.

Where structural functionalists see stratification as a social fact beyond human control, Marxists and conflict theorists stress the role that humans play in actively creating and maintaining social stratification. For these theorists, the labor of the lower classes creates advantages, most typically wealth, for the upper classes. The upper classes then use their advantages to maintain the inequality of power that ensures their privileged status.

Humanistic sociologists tend to agree with Marxists and conflict theorists that stratification is an active process and the product of deliberate action on the part of different members of society. Where they would differ is in the emphasis Marxists and conflict theorists have placed on economic factors. Humanistic sociologists believe that tradition and value systems play an important role in creating and maintaining social hierarchies. For example, the uneven balance of power between a priest and a layperson in a church has little to do with economic factors. Instead, religious conviction, the shared values of the church that bind the priest and layperson, is the source of the power the priest has in the relationship.

Ethnocentrism and Acceptance

Ethnocentrism is the belief that one's own cultural group is superior to others. The concept of ethnocentrism is generally based on **prejudice**, a preconceived belief that frequently casts negative judgments toward other groups. The concept of ethnocentrism has several negative ramifications. It is related to **sociological bias**, which gives favor to one's own society's ideals. It can also create **discrimination**, which refers to a negative behavior toward another group, such as the exclusion or rejection of the people in a group based on class or category. Groups that are frequently the target of discrimination are **minorities**, groups that comprise less than half of a population. Ethnocentrism may also help propagate **stereotyping**, which is a simplified conception that social groups behave in a consistent way—negative or positive.

On the other side of ethnocentrism, **cultural relativism** is the anthropological concept that posits that all cultures are equally valuable and should be studied from a neutral point of view. Rather than disdaining another society's customs, a cultural relativist tries to understand the way another culture acts and behaves and does not try to alter it in any way. Another term that is used for mutual acceptance is **cultural pluralism**, which occurs when small groups with separate cultural identities are accepted by the wider culture within that larger society. A policy of **multiculturalism** embraces **multicultural diversity**, accepting a variety of cultures with the belief that distinct groups should be provided with equitable status within a demographic.

Psychology

Psychology is the study of the mental processes of human beings. It can refer to both the general study of psychological principles in an experimental setting and to the practice of treating patients suffering from psychological disorders. The Praxis II may include a question about psychology; if it does, you may be asked about the basic concepts of psychology, as well as the stages of human development and growth, human behavior, or gender roles and differences.

The following sections cover the four main schools of psychology, including some of the important concepts associated with each school and a few of the notable psychologists. Then the chapter covers some of the crucial concepts in the field and terms you should know. Finally, the stages of human development are covered.

The Four Schools of Psychology

There are four chief schools of modern psychology, which can be arranged in the following rough chronological order: **scientific psychology**, **behaviorism**, **humanistic psychology**, and **cognitive psychology**. This order is helpful, but it should be kept in mind that the schools overlap one another and that the insights of one school are often adopted and adapted by psychologists in other schools.

Scientific Psychology

The dominant period of scientific psychology started in 1879 and lasted roughly until the 1920s. Prior to this period, the study of the mental life of humans was a philosophical or religious endeavor. The scientific psychologists broke with this tradition and tried to replace philosophical speculation with a system of experiments and recorded observations.

In 1879, the first psychology department was founded at Leipzig University in Germany. By 1890, enough progress had been made that American psychologist William James could produce the field's first major textbook, *The Principles of Psychology*.

In Russia, an experimental psychologist named Ivan Pavlov conducted a series of important animal experiments to study how learning happens. The model he developed to explain the learning process is known as **classical conditioning.**

The last important development of the classical period was the explosive rise of Freudian psychoanalysis. Sigmund Freud was an Austrian psychologist who developed a theoretical system of human development, explanations for numerous mental conditions, and a method of treatment called **psychoanalysis**. Freud's ideas were incredibly popular in his time, gaining him and psychoanalysis global recognition. Although research psychologists would criticize Freud for what they perceived as the unscientific basis of his theories, his ideas and method would dominate the clinical practice of psychology from the turn of the century until the 1960s.

The creator of psychoanalysis, **Sigmund Freud** made a strong argument for the existence of an unconscious mind. Operating without conscious control and submerged beneath the threshold of self-examination, the unconscious mind is a repository for ideas too dangerous or painful to be left open to scrutiny in the conscious mind. The process of burying feelings, ideas, and memories in the unconscious is called repression. Repressed ideas and feelings continue to affect the conscious mind, though in obscure and indirect ways. When the conscious mind becomes overwhelmed by these influences, the result is a mental condition. Later, Freud suggested a more complex system of mental elements. Instead of the conscious and unconscious mind, Freud claimed humans possessed an ego, superego, and id. The ego is a sense of self. The superego is an internal censor that represses ideas to protect the ego. The id is the opposite of the superego, an unconscious drive for unregulated pleasure. Freud's numerous theories were all extensions of this basic architecture.

Behaviorism

Many psychologists reacted negatively to what they felt were unscientific assumptions underlying psychoanalysis. Their attempt to get psychology on a more firmly scientific footing created the second major school, **behaviorism**.

Behaviorism was so named because the psychologists who belonged to the movement decided that only observable changes and actions could properly be studied. This restricted what could be researched to external behaviors. Concepts like Freud's id were dismissed as philosophical abstractions. The dismissal of any sort of inner life created an assumption that behavior was also the product of external forces. In the famed nature versus nurture debate, behaviorists were almost entirely on the side of nurture.

Behaviorism was dogged by controversies. The popular application of behaviorist ideas made behaviorists public figures and their provocative statements occasionally overshadowed their work. Pioneer behaviorist B.F. Skinner, for example, dismissed concepts like freedom and dignity as unscientific. Aside from provocative public statements, behaviorists' experiments were sometimes controversial. Noted behaviorist John Watson conducted an experiment to create a rat phobia in an orphan infant known only as "Albert B." By today's standards, his experiment would be considered unethical.

Despite such controversies, behaviorism became the dominant approach to the field in the early twentieth century. This was especially true in America, where its empirical rigor and schematic approach to behavior modification was appreciated by progressive educators, marketing and public relations professionals, and academics in other fields.

Behaviorism ultimately became a victim of its own success. In the search for greater scientific precision, psychologists applied advanced technology to the study of human behavior. This greatly expanded what was now considered observable. Psychologists also used increasingly sophisticated statistical methods to their research. The wealth of new data these advances produced overturned the assumption that external forces were the chief influence on the psychology of an individual. The concerns of behaviorism, if not all the basic assumptions, became the concerns of the cognitive psychologists.

Humanistic Psychology

Just as behaviorism was a reaction to the more philosophical aspects of psychoanalysis, some psychologists reacted to what they felt was the reductive thinking of behaviorism. Less a coherent movement than several contemporary movements with some general similarities, the **existential humanists** reemphasized the role of non-observable, purely mental processes. They also rebelled against some of the basic premises of behaviorism. They rejected the notion that all mental processes could be broken down into smaller independent actions and behaviors. They stressed that all human activity takes place in a complex living context of desires, responsibilities, and negotiations with others. Furthermore, they stressed that humans innately possess self-awareness, creativity, and a drive to find meaning in the world around them.

Another major distinction between humanistic psychologists and their behaviorist predecessors was the emphasis humanistic psychologists placed on the medical practice of psychology. Like some of the earliest scientific psychologists, many humanistic psychologists developed their theories from the observation and treatment of patients. When doing experimental research, a humanistic psychologist was likely to focus on qualitative aspects of the phenomenon being studied rather than quantitative aspects.

Given its emphasis on psychotherapy, it is perhaps unsurprising that the greatest achievements in humanistic psychology came in the form of innovative approaches to treatment. Often these approaches were called holistic treatments, as they were intended to take into account all the needs of a patient and the patient's context in the world. Gestalt therapy was a prominent holistic treatment.

The creation of two German psychologists and one American philosopher, Gestalt theory pulled together elements of psychology, philosophy, Eastern religions, and artistic practices in an effort to create a flexible and all-inclusive approach to therapy. Rather than advancing a particular theory of mental life, Gestalt therapy was a set of practices meant to encourage self-awareness in the patient. Once the patient was aware of unhelpful psychological symptoms, the patient could better avoid negative behaviors and spur positive mental growth.

From its start in the 1950s, humanistic psychology became the dominant school through the 1960s and 1970s. Eventually, **cognitive psychology**, which reemphasized empirical research and the scientific method, replaced it as the dominant model.

Gordon Allport is considered the first psychologist to focus his studies on personality. Allport theorized that all personalities are made up of a collection of traits. These traits are organized into three categories. Secondary traits are traits that appear only in certain contexts or situations. Central traits are the constant elements of personality and they are found in all humans. Cardinal traits are rare traits that act as powerful organizers of an entire personality.

Cognitive Psychology

The biggest single innovation in cognitive psychology was the computer. Computers made it easier for psychologists to use more complicated statistical methods. Computer programmers, finding parallels between the creation of software and the creation of mental faculties, introduced new ideas to the field. Computer-driven imaging technologies allowed psychologists to observe the functioning of the brain at the cellular level. Finally, powerful computers allowed scientists to sequence and study human DNA, unlocking new information about what is and is not innate to our biological being.

Advances in medicine and chemistry also played huge roles in revolutionizing the field. Cognitive psychologists, working with chemists and biologists, revealed the biological and chemical processes that allow the human brain to work. This has created vast new fields of study and powerful, albeit controversial, applications in therapy.

Like humanistic psychology, it is best to think of cognitive psychology less as a movement and more as a collection of research methods and some general common assumptions. As a general rule, cognitive psychologists find that psychology must advance through the scientific method and the use of quantitative data. In this, they differ radically from the humanistic psychologists. However, cognitive psychologists differ from behaviorists in that they believe many, maybe even most, of our mental faculties are innate properties and not the product of external influences. This latter assumption has led to the greatest triumph and most controversial aspect of the primacy of cognitive psychology: the dominance of pharmaceutical treatment.

The discovery of the role various biological and chemical processes play in the role of human psychology led to the development of pharmaceutical treatments for many mental disorders. Although such treatments have been around for as long as psychology has, the late twentieth century witnessed a boom in the number of ailments treated with drugs and an increase in the number of patients currently taking such treatments. Although the positive impact on patients is well documented, detractors say that the scope of these treatments is disturbing and they suggest that such treatments merely suppress symptoms rather than cure patients.

Stages of Human Development and Growth

In general, psychologists divide human development into four stages. While the exact transitions of the stages are debatable, the makers of the Praxis II want you to understand the following four bolded terms. **Infancy** is defined as the period from birth until the child can speak, at which point the child enters babyhood. During infancy, a child undergoes a significant amount of development, although psychologists still disagree about how infants develop their perception abilities, such as object permanence. Generally, at about the point when children enter school for the first time, they enter the **childhood** stage. During this period, children expand their social abilities and responsibilities. The **adolescence** stage begins with puberty and continues until about 18 years old; this volatile period in human development is known for its role in the formation of a social identity. Independence is established during this stage and leads to the fourth and final stage, **adulthood**.

Important Psychological Concepts

Abnormal psychology: the study of behaviors that are rare in the general population, harmful to the subject, unacceptable in the subject's social context, and irrational. Such behaviors are known as **psychopathologies**.

Attachment: the emotional link between an infant and its main caregiver.

Attribution: the action of assigning a cause to a behavior.

***Big Five* theory:** a currently popular theory of the personality that posits five major factors to a subject's personality: openness, conscientiousness, extraversion, agreeableness, and neuroticism. These factors can be identified by the acronym OCEAN.

Cognitive dissonance: a contradiction between thoughts and behaviors.

Defense mechanisms: psychological processes used to protect the ego from the conflict between the id and superego.

Difference (or absolute) threshold: the minimum amount of change in a condition that can be registered by a subject.

Dual-code theory: a theory that holds visual and auditory data are processed in two distinctly different ways.

Encoding: the process of turning data into a memory.

Figure-ground: the distinction made between an object being viewed and the surrounding visual data.

Hueristics: mental rules of thumb that subjects develop to help make sense of the world around them.

Language acquisition device: a theoretical mental architecture that is the source of humans' inherent ability to learn a language.

Locus of control: where a subject believes the dominant force of control of his or her life resides. Subjects with an internal locus believe they control their lives. A subject with an external locus believes outside forces are dominant.

Motivational bias: a tendency to ascribe specific attributions to actions.

Neurotransmitters: chemical actions that allow nerve signals to travel over a synapse.

Perceptual set: a plan of assumptions that helps subjects interpret stimuli.

Plasticity: the capacity of the human brain to adapt its shape over time as a healing process.

Reinforcement schedule: in conditioning, the set of rules that determine when positive and negative reinforcement is applied.

Reflex: actions that require no cognitive process.

Social psychology: the study of the influence of other humans on the development and working of mental processes. The study of interpersonal attraction, the affects of persuasion, and the creation of stereotypes are common areas of study for social psychologists.

Social-cognitive theory: a theory that claims the personality is influenced by internal (ideas and beliefs) and external (the observation of others) behavior.

Socialization: the term for the process of learning about a social group and finding one's role within it. Psychologists emphasize the role of external agents in the process of socialization, especially the family, schools, and peer groups. Other institutions (such as churches) and the mass media may also play a role in socialization.

Synapse: the gap within neurons where nerve signals travel.

Talk therapy: any psychological treatment that relies mainly on regular communication between patient and therapist.

Working memory: a process in which the subject simultaneously processes short- and long-term memories.

Psychological Methods

Questions about the psychological methods may appear in the "Inquiry and Processes" part of the social studies section. It may help to review some of these most common research techniques in the efforts to study human nature. After all, what distinguishes psychology from more philosophical and religious efforts to study human nature is its reliance on agreed-upon scientific methods. To help them understand the human mind, psychologists have developed many different research techniques, several of which are listed here.

Animal studies. Animal subjects have been essential in studying the learning process, memory, and behavior development. Animals, because they can be better controlled, are useful for experiments where limiting the variables on a human subject would be difficult or impossible.

Computer modeling. Many cognitive psychologists find it helpful to simulate mental behaviors through the use of complex computer programs. Computer modeling allows the psychologist total control over the variables involved in an experiment. However, even with modern computers, the number of variables must remain relatively small.

Controlled human experiments. In laboratory conditions, psychologists can apply scientific methods to human research subjects. By using human subjects, the research can avoid having to generalize human behaviors from observed behaviors in other animals. However, the use of human subjects introduces a host of ethical concerns. Most modern researchers comply with an ethical code known as the Declaration of Helsinki. Among other things, this declaration requires subjects be able to give informed consent, allows for subjects to quit an experiment at any time in the process, and requires researchers to always put the welfare of the subject before the consequences of the experiment.

Naturalistic observation. Psychologists may make qualitative and quantitative observations of a subject in an uncontrolled real-world environment.

Neurological observation. Modern technologies, such as MRI scanners, make it possible for scientists to study brain activity on a scale that was impossible before. Using these new technologies, scientists may study the otherwise invisible brain activity of human subjects. A common strategy is to study subjects with known mental impairments to see if their brain activity reveals some distinctly unusual pattern.

Statistical surveys. Using a scientifically determined sample set (a group that represents the broader demographic being studied), psychologists may use interviews, questionnaires, online surveys, or other information-gathering devices. This is the easiest way to get a broad sample, but the researcher loses some control over the quality of the data the subjects choose to report.

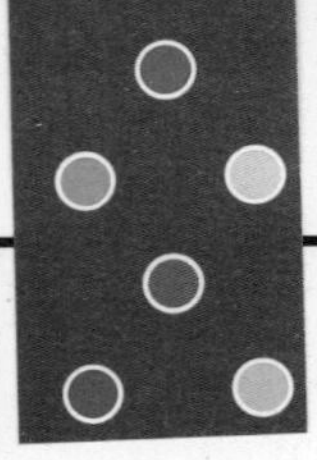

World History

Although the Praxis II: Elementary Education: Content Knowledge test places a greater emphasis on U.S. history than on world history, you will see a handful of questions regarding world history. Those questions could check your knowledge of any era in world history. They may ask you about the contributions of ancient civilizations, such as the Holy Roman Empire, or they could ask about the developments that transformed the world in the twentieth century. Therefore, it helps to have a solid base of the major civilization's beginnings up through the present time. The following sections touch on the key empires and events that you should know heading into the test. To keep things simple and emphasize cause-and-effect relationships, the topics proceed chronologically.

Prehistoric, Early, and Classical Civilizations

For the Praxis II, you may be asked about the characteristics of any of the ancient human societies, ranging all the way back to the first people to use stone tools. You should be familiar with the contributions from all the major prehistoric, early, and classical civilizations. The following sections cover each of these civilizations that may appear on the exam.

Paleolithic and Neolithic Periods: Circa 2.5 m BCE to circa 3500 BCE

The **Paleolithic period**, beginning about 2.5 million years ago, is associated with the first use of stone tools. During the Paleolithic period, societies banded together and existed by hunting and scavenging animals, as well as gathering plants. The societies are therefore referred to as **hunter-gatherers**, since their primary subsistence derived from foraging and hunting edible plants and animals. The several species of humans during the Paleolithic period did not live in permanent constructions. Artwork from this period exists in the form of small sculptures and paintings or designs on the walls inside caves. The advance of agricultural systems marked the end of the Paleolithic period, at about 10,000 BCE.

The end of the Paleolithic period was followed by the start of the **Neolithic period**, sometimes called the New Stone Age, at about 10,000 BCE. The origin of this period in humanity is defined by the use of true farming. This rise of farming created the necessity for permanent settlements, such as villages or tribes of 150 to 2,000 people. In addition to the introduction of agricultural systems, this period is notable for the first use of pottery and the dependence on domesticated animals, such as cattle and pigs. This transition from collecting food to producing food marked a very important change in human culture. It began in the **Fertile Crescent**, a crescent-shaped area that was part of a massive swath of rich farmland that stretched from the Persian Gulf to the Mediterranean Sea. It then spread across Europe and Asia over the next several thousand years. As a result, the period is not defined by a series of precise dates. Its end, however, is marked by the use of metal tools in the Copper Age or Bronze Age. There was only one species of humans during the Paleolithic period, *homo sapiens*.

Egypt and the Middle East: 3200 BCE to 500 BCE

Many of the political and social structures that would reappear in human civilizations throughout history got their start in the ancient kingdoms of the Middle East and Northern Africa. These civilizations both developed in fertile river country. In the Middle East, the Sumerian, Mesopotamian, and other distinct city-states developed along the lush banks of the Tigris and Euphrates rivers (the Fertile Crescent). In Northern Africa, Egyptian culture developed along the banks of the Nile, where seasonal flooding kept the soil rich and productive.

The Sumerians were not a single culture, but a collection of separate states with some common characteristics. All the city-states of Sumer were organized into hierarchies, with the royal family at the top and various civil groups ranked beneath them. They were polytheistic, worshipping many gods. They invented a writing system called cuneiform and are the source of *The Epic of Gilgamesh*, the world's first recorded epic poem. The Sumerians were eventually incorporated into the growing empire of the Mesopotamians. In 2300 BCE, Sargon, ruler of the city of Akkad, launched a campaign to conquer and unify Sumer. He would be the first of several conquerors who would replace one empire with another: the Babylonians, the Hittites, and ultimately, the Persians. During this time, the empires of the Middle East developed civil and criminal law codes, horse-drawn chariots, an early form of a currency economy, and the first written alphabet. One of those law codes, the **Code of Hammurabi**, created in Babylon at about 1790 BCE, lists nearly 300 laws with corresponding punishments for each offense, depending on the social status of the criminal.

In Africa, the two distinct cultures had developed along the Nile: Upper Egypt, which had developed several hundred miles upriver, and Lower Egypt, which developed near the delta of the Nile. In 3100 BCE, these regions were united.

Egyptian history is divided into three periods. The **Old Kingdom** (2575 BCE–2130 BCE) encompasses the time period when the political system of the pharaohs developed. The pharaohs were the absolute power in Egypt. A complex governmental bureaucracy of specialists helped the pharaohs run the kingdom. During this time, the **Great Pyramids** were built. The **Middle Kingdom** (2040 BCE–1640 BCE) was a period of internal strife and hardship. Massive crop failures, political power struggles, and foreign invasions battered the Egyptian people. The **New Kingdom** (1570 BCE–1070 BCE) was an era of resurgence. During this time, Egyptians constructed massive tombs for the burial of their pharaohs and other members of nobility in an area known as the **Valley of the Kings**. Today, the valley is one of the most important and famous archaeological sites in the world. Egypt's first female ruler, Hatshepsut, improved trade and strengthened the Egyptian economy. The rulers after her expanded the boundaries of the kingdom through conquest. Egypt would remain the dominant power in North Africa until the 1100 BCE, when invaders from Persia would conquer the region.

During the long reign of the pharaohs, Egypt developed **hieroglyphics**, a writing system that used pictures and symbols to represent concepts and sounds. The **Rosetta Stone**, an Egyptian artifact, helped provide translations of the hieroglyphics for modern understanding of the symbols. Egyptians were talented scientists, especially in the field of medicine and astronomy. Their visual and written arts were quite advanced as well.

The final group from the region to make a lasting impact on Western culture was the Israelites, who developed a kingdom of their own in Canaan, modern-day Israel. Perhaps the single most significant thing the Israelites contributed to the modern world was monotheism. The belief in a single divine being would form the basis of the three dominant religions of Western culture: **Judaism**, **Christianity**, and **Islam**.

Ancient Greece: 1750 BCE to 133 BCE

In ancient Greece, seafaring cultures developed into a group of diverse city-states. The most influential of these city-states would be **Athens**. In 700 BCE, in response to public discontent, the Athenians began to develop a limited form of democracy. By modern standards, this democracy was extremely limited. However, under the leadership of the statesman Pericles, Athens developed into a direct democracy. Qualified citizens could directly affect government policy, rather than working through elected representatives. This period of direct democracy (460 BCE–429 BCE) was also a period of great financial prosperity and cultural development.

Unfortunately, conflict with other city-states ended Athens's cultural dominance. The prosperity of Athens was oppressive to some of the other Greek city-states. Pro- and anti-Athenian states formed two large alliances. Athens and its allies formed the Delian League. Sparta and other enemies of Athens formed the Peloponnesian League. The war between these two great alliances ultimately ended in defeat for the Athenians. They were stripped of their fleet, which destroyed their economy. The brutality of the war and the loss of Athens as a political anchor sapped Greek culture of its vitality.

Eventually, the Greek city-states were conquered by the Macedonians, who came from the mountainous regions to the north of Greece. The Macedonian leader Phillip II led the invasion. However, this conquest did not extinguish Greek culture. Phillip II was a great admirer of the Greeks and he sought to perpetuate what he thought was best in their arts and sciences. He even went so far as to hire the Greek philosopher Aristotle as the private tutor for his son Alexander. This period of Greek-influenced Macedonian dominance is known as the Hellenistic period.

Under the leadership of the expansionist **Alexander the Great**, the Macedonian Empire spread across eastern Europe, the Middle East, and much of Asia. As Alexander conquered new lands, he brought Greek cultural influences with him. Just as Alexander spread Greek ideas, the ideas of the cultures he encountered and conquered influenced Macedonia. The Macedonian capital was moved to Alexandria in Egypt. This capital city boasted architectural marvels, such as a 440-foot-tall lighthouse and a museum that was a library, zoo, and university all in one. Hellenistic culture also expanded the social role of women. Many women were educated and noblewomen often took leadership positions, such as Cleopatra VII, who ruled after Alexander's death. Hellenistic scholars created the basis of modern geometry, developed the first astronomical theory that stated that Earth revolved around the sun, and discovered many of the basic concepts of modern applied engineering. Hellenistic philosophers developed the philosophy of stoicism, which stressed self-control and reason over emotion and prejudice. This philosophy would later influence the Romans and the early Christians.

The lasting impact of Greek and Hellenistic culture on Western culture is hard to overestimate. The concepts of Greek philosophers like Socrates, Plato, and Aristotle are still studied today. Greek architecture styles are considered the classical forms and, even today, continue to inspire architects. The body of myths of the gods and the natural world devised by the Greeks, once a part of the religion of ancient Greece, is still studied in the form of **mythology**. Perhaps most importantly, democracy, though not exactly as the Greeks practiced it, would become the dominant political system of the Western world.

Ancient Rome: 509 BCE to 476 BCE

The predecessors of the Romans, the **Latins**, were one of several groups living in what is now modern-day Italy. It is believed the Latins migrated to the peninsula prior to 800 BCE. When the various villages of the Latins formed into a single city-state, Rome, the group became known as the **Romans**. In the early days of Rome, the city was ruled by the **Etruscans**, a now extinct cultural group that dominated much of central Italy. In 508 BCE, the Romans overthrew their Etruscan rulers and founded a republic. A unique political system designed to prevent any one person from accumulating too much power, the Roman republic consisted of a 300-member senate. These members were selected from the upper classes. The senate created and passed laws. Each year the senate elected two consuls, who carried out the laws that the senate passed. Those without land could not become senators, but they could vote for tribunes. The tribunes could veto laws made by the senate. This way the upper classes could not pass laws that would be unfair to the lower classes. Finally, in times of crisis, the senate could elect a dictator. Dictators had complete control over the government, but the duration of their rule was limited by the senate.

Rome expanded its borders through a long series of conquests. By 44 BCE, the Roman Empire had expanded west through what is now France and Spain, south to cover a long stretch of the northern coast of Africa, and as far east as modern Syria. This imperialist expansion brought great power and wealth to Rome, but social inequalities ensured the drastically uneven distribution of these gains. This caused civil unrest and led to a series of civil wars. When the dust cleared, the senate was no longer the supreme power in Rome. Instead, powerful leaders transformed the role of dictator into a more permanent position. With power centralized in the role of the emperor and a professional army keeping control over a considerable portion of the known world, the empire entered in a 200-year span of peace and prosperity called the **Pax Romana**, or Roman Peace.

Unfortunately, once power left the hands of the senate, the fortunes of Rome rose and fell with the character of her emperors. Some emperors were effective and just rulers, while others were so violent and irrational as to appear psychotic. Political violence became commonplace. Domestic affairs in the massive empire were ineffectively handled. Eventually, the empire was split into two separate political entities: the Western and Eastern Roman empires. The Western Empire's capital was Rome, while the Eastern Empire was ruled from Constantinople.

It was during this time that Roman legalized Christianity, a breakaway religious sect that had formed in their Jewish colonies. This was significant in that it reflected the growing popularity of the new religion among the Roman upper classes, further divorced traditional Roman political authority from the religious beliefs that justified it, and set the stage for the creation of the powerful Roman Catholic Church.

Although the division of the empire improved conditions for the citizens and resolved many domestic issues, the benefits were temporary. The empire was no longer strong enough to stop foreign invaders, and in 378 CE, Rome itself was attacked and looted. The economy sagged under heavy taxes. Government leaders proved corrupt or ineffective. Still, there was no spectacular fall for the Roman Empire. Rather, it slowly gave way to the next leaders of the Western world.

Medieval History: 500 CE to 1500 CE

In the aftermath of the collapse of the Roman Empire, Europe broke up into smaller nation-states. Despite this collapse, there remained a common thread that helped Europeans keep a transnational Western identity: Christianity. By the time the Roman Empire had completely faded into history, the once outlawed religion had become the dominant faith of Europe. This Christian identity was intensified in the early 700s when Islamic leaders spread their faith throughout the Middle East, Africa, and even into Spain. The existence of these Islamic leaders gave Christian rulers in Europe a shared enemy, and regular religious wars against Islamic kingdoms were often the only thing that brought Christian rulers together in common cause.

During this period, two great empires would rise in Europe. In modern-day France, the Emperor Charlemagne would expand the **Kingdom of the Franks** well into what is now Italy and Germany. Charlemagne envisioned himself as the founder of a new Christianized Roman Empire. Along with his military accomplishments, he encouraged the arts and sciences under his rule. This led to a revival of Latin. Through a system of Christian monasteries, scribes would maintain and copy classical texts, becoming the conduit for the intellectual achievements of Greece and Rome. Charlemagne's empire never attained the scope or permanence of Rome's. After his death in 814, his heirs were unable to maintain the empire and Europe was shattered by repeated invasions and internal conflicts.

The other great European empire of this period was the **Byzantine Empire**. Under Justinian, the Byzantine Empire emerged out of the collapse of the Eastern Roman Empire. Justinian rebuilt Constantinople and established an elaborate code of laws that became a model for other European monarchs. By 1360, the Byzantine Empire had expanded as far west as Italy and, to the south, followed the coast of the Mediterranean as far as the south of Spain.

It was during this time that conflicts between western and eastern Christians reached a breaking point. After a long period of relative unity on points of faith, the differences in opinion had grown so drastic that the church broke into a Western church, which would become the Roman Catholic Church, and an Eastern Church, the Eastern Orthodox Church.

Like Charlemagne's heirs, Justinian's heirs were incapable of maintaining the size and strength of the empire. During the Fourth Crusade, Christian knights going off to fight Muslim forces in the Middle East were convinced by Italian merchants to sack and loot Constantinople. This marked the beginning of the end for the empire. The final blow was delivered by Muslim invaders from modern-day Turkey. The Turks invaded Constantinople in 1453.

After the rise and fall of the second and last great European empire, power devolved to a diverse collection of monarchs who, instead of following imperialistic impulses, tended to focus on building strong nation-states.

Ironically, it was during the rise of local monarchs that the first institutional checks on kings and queens were developed. In England, William the Conqueror, a French-speaking nobleman, gained control. He expanded the king's powers and developed a unified legal code based on the customs of the English people. Years later, these reforms encouraged lesser nobles to demand limitations of royal authority. In 1215, a group of nobles created and forced King John to sign a document called the Magna Carta. The Magna Carta reserved some rights for the nobles. These rights were later extended to commoners as well. These reforms led to the creation of Parliament, which would later become England's chief legislature. In France, Phillip II set up the Estates General in 1302. Made up of nobles, clergy, and commoners, the Estates General was an advisory body. Although it never gained the official force of the Parliament, it acted as an informal check on royal power.

The medieval era was wracked repeatedly by international warfare. There were four different crusades in which soldiers and citizens from multiple nations would march on the Islamic nations to the east in an effort to liberate Jerusalem. More often than not, these campaigns accomplished little more than the depletion of Europe's resources as men and materiel left home on these quixotic efforts. Within Europe, rival powers in France and England fought a long series of bloody conflicts that collectively came to be known as the Hundred Years' War. This protracted conflict introduced the longbow, the crossbow, and the cannon into European warfare.

Another destabilizing factor in medieval life was the **Black Death**, a global plague that swept through Europe from 1347 to 1353. The plague originated in China and was brought to Europe on a trading vessel traveling from the Black Sea to Italy. Likely spread by fleas on rats on these merchant ships, the Black Death spread nearly throughout the entire European continent, including England. By the end of the pandemic, an estimated 25 million people died in Europe. This was roughly a third of the population of the continent. The plague would vanish for a couple centuries before returning in smaller, but still deadly, waves throughout the 1600s.

Three extra features of medieval life demand special attention. First, as the period progressed, **education** spread to the upper and middle classes. After the collapse of the Roman Empire, education was often limited to a small segment of church scholars, many of whom lived isolated monastic lives. Before the end of the Middle Ages, universities were set up for the benefit of people outside the church. The second notable feature is the **feudal system**. Under this system, local lords governed their own lands. These lords owed military service to a higher lord, usually the king, but otherwise were free to do as they pleased. Under each lord lived farmers and peasants who would work the lord's land in exchange for protection and very basic services. The feudal system's tendency to tie up opportunities for non-landowners encouraged many to move to cities to seek their fortune. This led to the development of the third notable feature: a new urban and affluent **merchant class.** The interests of this merchant class, especially their need for efficient trade routes, would help drive the creation of modern Europe and the European colonies abroad.

Other Notable Ancient Civilizations

In addition to the classical and well-known civilizations listed earlier, you may see a question about the characteristics and contributions from one of several other notable civilizations.

The **Indus River Valley Civilization** (circa 2600 BCE–circa 1900 BCE) extended through the modern-day countries of Pakistan and India, though only through northwest areas of the Indian subcontinent. This civilization is known for its sophisticated urban planning, which considered the importance of hygiene in an urban center. Additionally, many of the civilization's cities featured unrestricted access to water and drainage facilities for all the cities' homes. In part because of this access, and also for the rich agricultural lands that surrounded the Indus River, this civilization is also recognized for being one of the early farming cultures in the area.

The Olmec Civilization, in Mesoamerica, flourished from about 1500 BCE to about 400 BCE. The civilization, which greatly preceded any European influences, had its own series of important contributions. It developed its own system of writing and may have been the first civilization in the Western Hemisphere to do so. Much art remains from the civilization, including gigantic sculptures of helmeted heads—the largest of which weighs roughly 50 tons. The Olmec Civilization may also have been responsible for the invention of the concept of zero as a placeholder in the counting system.

The dynasties of **Ancient China** range from about 2100 BCE to 256 BCE This ancient period covers three sovereigns. The earliest was the Xia Dynasty, which lasted until about 1600 BCE. The Shang Dynasty, also called the Yin Dynasty, lasted for about the next five centuries. These cultures believed in ancestor veneration, which required worship of the dead as a religious practice. The final dynasty in Ancient China was the longest-lasting Zhou Dynasty, which went from about 1045 BCE to 256 BCE. It was during this third dynasty that several Chinese philosophers lived, including Confucius and Lao-tzu, founders of Confucianism and Taoism, respectively.

The Rise of Europe

A great focus of world history in American classrooms is European history in the last millennium. As a result, the Praxis II: Elementary Education: Content Knowledge test will likely include at least one question about the European continent during this time. This section reviews all the major events, people, and trends of European history, from the Renaissance through the modern day, that may appear on the Praxis II. Pay special attention to the causes and effects of each of the main events.

The Renaissance and the Reformation: 1300 CE to 1560 CE

The **Renaissance** is a term used to describe a series of profound intellectual and social revolutions that transformed nearly every aspect of life in Europe. Although it is often described as a distinct period, its slow spread means that it overlaps a significant portion of what was considered the medieval era.

The Renaissance began in Italy. There are several reasons for this. First, the great inspiration for Renaissance thought was classical Greek and Roman scholarship. Resources from the past were abundant in Italy. Another reason was the wealth of Italy's merchant classes. Trade and banking generated an enormous amount of wealth for a handful of Italian families. The most famous of these, such as the Medicis of Florence, became financial and political powerhouses. They were also important patrons of the arts and sciences, using their vast fortunes to fund the careers of thinkers and artists.

As the Renaissance spread across Europe, other factors would contribute to its spread. Perhaps no single contribution was more important than the invention of the printing press with movable type. The new printing press encouraged literacy and made a broad range of knowledge available to large audiences all over Europe.

The overall direction of Renaissance thought has been described as *humanistic*. Inspired by classical models, Renaissance thinkers began to make a careful study of the world around them. In the Middle Ages, supernatural and religious doctrines dominated European thought. In the Renaissance, the study of the human experience began to take center stage. Philosophical studies of pragmatic, rather than spiritual, leadership were produced, such as Machiavelli's *The Prince*. Castiglione's *The Book of the Courtier* instructed nobles to not only master ethical virtues, but also gain knowledge of the arts and sciences. In painting, direct observation became tantamount. Visual artists developed perspective to realistically simulate the world around them. Painters and sculptors made a careful study of the human anatomy, a process that prefigured the scientific method's dedication to observational practices. Finally, the literary arts flourished. Poets revived classical form and innovated new styles. It is a sign of how important the artists of this time are to the modern world that at least two Renaissance-era writers, Dante and Shakespeare, are often considered to be the greatest writers ever produced by their respective nations.

The growth of humanism set the stage for the largest break in the Christian religion since the Eastern Orthodox/Catholic schism. Throughout the medieval era, there had been conflicts between church authorities and various groups. Monarchs frequently strained at the extra-national authority the church wielded. Within the church, followers and local leaders often criticized the church leaders. Charges of corruption and differences in doctrine put a strain on the unity of the faith. During the Renaissance, these issues came to a head. The boom in printed materials meant the Bibles could be quickly and cheaply distributed in the native languages of the faithful, rather than the official Latin of the church. This emphasis on the individual led many to question the church's authority over religious matters. In 1517, a German monk named **Martin Luther** publicly posted a list of 95 arguments against the then-common church practice of granting indulgences, essentially an exchange of blessings and grants of forgiveness for money. This act set off a long series of revolts again church authority. Breakaway groups from the church would be known as Protestant faiths and their revolt would be known as the **Protestant Reformation**. A pastor named **John Calvin** was also greatly influential during the Reformation, and he helped devise a new system of Christian theology, later named **Calvinism**.

In England, the Reformation took an unusual shape: The religious revolution was driven by the reigning monarch rather than radical segments within the clergy. Henry VIII was desperate for a male heir, but ran afoul of Catholic bans on divorce. Rather than submit, Henry created the Church of England and appointed himself its pope. The Church of England mixed Protestant and Catholic practices, but eliminated the Catholic Church's power over England's monarch.

The Protestant Reformation gave power to reform-minded activists within the Catholic Church. These Catholics started the Catholic or Counter-Reformation. The church held a council in 1545 to end corruption in the church and affirm certain tenets of the faith. Unfortunately, this also led to the strengthening of the Inquisition. Set up in the Middle Ages, the newly empowered church court used coercive and sometimes brutal methods to enforce church orthodoxy.

Early Modern Europe: 1492 CE to 1648 CE

Throughout the Renaissance and Reformation, Europe's commercial interests were expanding. The need for imported foreign goods and the desire to create new markets for European goods sent explorers and merchants to Africa, the Middle East, and the Far East. Overland routes were well established, but they were slow, and the dangerous political tensions between Christian Europeans and the Islamic kingdoms of Africa and the Middle East made them unreliable. European explorers had discovered a sea route that passed around the southern tip of Africa. However, this route was not much faster or safer than the land routes.

In 1492, **Christopher Columbus**, funded by the Spanish crown, attempted to find a sea route to India by going west and circumnavigating the globe. Instead of establishing a trade route to India, he made landfall in the Caribbean. His voyage started a new phase of global **imperialism** for the European powers. The North and South American continents represented a vast and open commercial opportunity. The development of Atlantic colonies would drive European powers to seek colonies in Africa and Asia as well. Each of these imperialistic exploits forever transformed the African, American, and Asian landscapes.

In Africa, Portugal established forts along the eastern coast. The primary goal of these merchant imperialists was gold, but the trade in slaves ultimately became the most profitable enterprise. Some African leaders resisted the slave trade, but the power of the imperialists and the lure of profits led most African rulers to support it.

In Asia, Portugal established colonies in India. The Dutch displaced the Portuguese, using a combination of business and military methods to push them out of the region. The Spanish conquered the Philippines in 1571.

In Latin America, Spanish conquistadors conquered modern-day Haiti, Santo Domingo, Cuba, and Puerto Rico. From there, they launched campaigns into South America, Central America, and southwestern regions of North America. The conquest of South and Central America was a disaster for the native inhabitants. Mighty empires fell before the Spanish. The Spanish crown established the system of *encomiendas*, which granted conquistadors the right to demand labor and tribute from the native population. This essentially reduced the entire native population to slavery. Portugal established a colony in modern-day Brazil, but their treatment of the native population was no more humane.

France, England, Spain, and the Dutch all clashed over the eastern coast of North America. French colonies were established in what is now Canada. English colonies stretched down the coast of what is now the United States, with the exception of New York, which was a Dutch colony. Spain claimed what is now Florida.

Although some colonists were motivated by their religious beliefs or political necessity, the main reason for the growth of the colonies was economic. And, back in Europe, the economy was transformed by the wealth pouring in from the colonies. Private business was on the rise, making capitalism the dominant economic model for most Europeans. New bookkeeping methods and newly invented business organizations, such as the joint stock company (in which owners purchased stock, representing shares of ownership, in a company) made business more efficient. Inflation, caused by gold and silver from the new world, pushed prices up and made the merchant class extremely wealthy. This gave rise to the mercantilist theory of wealth. Mercantilists believed that a nation's wealth was measured by the gold and silver stores it possessed. Consequently, European nations tried to stop the outgoing flow of precious metals by limiting what they imported. This led to more colonization, as the only way to gain resources and trading partners was to expand the borders of the country.

One of the most profound impacts of the international expansion of the European empires was the environmental impact. The **Columbian Exchange** describes the process by which European plants and animals made their way to America and vice versa. In America, Europeans introduced wheat, sugar, coffee, horses, pigs, and chicken. Colonies sent corn, potatoes, tomatoes, and cocoa to Europe. Unfortunately, viruses also traveled with the colonists. European colonists introduced smallpox and typhus to the

Americas. The native populations had no natural immunities to these diseases, and the results were devastating.

The wealth and conflicts occurring in the so-called **New World** reshaped governments and nations in Europe. The prosperity of Europe translated into approval for European monarchs. Moves to limit the power of monarchs were reversed in several countries. In France and Spain, the national leaders became **absolute monarchs**, or rulers with no checks to their power. England would be one of the few counter-examples to this trend. During this same period, Parliament would grow in strength. Ultimately, this clash would develop into a full-blown civil war that started in 1642 and lasted until 1651.

Spain, fueled by the silver and gold of its new colonies, entered a sustained period of prosperity and political importance. The fearsome Spanish navy, known as the Spanish Armada, defeated many foreign fleets during this period. Ultimately, Spanish designs to build a new European empire were checked when the English navy, under Queen Elizabeth I, defeated the Spanish navy in 1588.

Europe Transformed

In the late 1400s, European governments began an extensive program of overseas colonization. These new colonies provided the European nations with new markets for trade and new sources of revenue. This new prosperity had some drastic effects on the economies and governments of Europe. Some nations turned into absolute monarchies while others began to develop more democratic and liberal modes of government.

During his rule in Spain, King Philip II had spread his influence over several areas in Europe. One of these areas included what is now known as the Netherlands. In the 1560s, riots broke out in the Netherlands against the brutal tactics of the Inquisition, a group Philip II supported. Philip II tried to suppress the rioters. Conflict between Dutch rebels and the Spanish authorities lasted until 1581, when the seven Dutch provinces finally threw off Spanish rule and declared their independence. The Dutch Netherlands were founded as a republic and officially recognized in 1648. Although the government was officially a republic, in practice, nobles were always elected or selected to crucial positions in the government.

In England, political tensions between King Charles I and the Parliament exploded into full-blown civil war. From 1642 to 1651, supporters of the king fought pro-Parliamentary forces. In 1649, King Charles was beheaded. This was the first time a king had ever been executed by his own people. Victorious, the Parliamentary forces founded the English Commonwealth. The Commonwealth was short-lived. In 1660, Parliament voted to install Charles II as king. In 1688, the monarchy was in trouble again. James II, who took the throne after Charles II, was a Catholic. This angered many in the Church of England and they replaced James with the Dutch noble William III in a bloodless coup called the Glorious Revolution. Under William, a governmental system of checks and balances developed in England.

In contrast, the French king Louis XIV used the period of prosperity to consolidate his power. Louis ignored the Estate General, an advisory body made up of representatives from all strata of French society. He developed a complex bureaucracy to help him control all levels of government. He strengthened France's industrial base, helping the economy, but also persecuted non-Catholics, as he viewed Protestants as a threat to his power.

Germany, then a collection of smaller states, became entangled in the ruinous Thirty Years' War. Devastated by the cost in gold and blood, the remaining states signed the Treaty of Westphalia. This brought peace, but left Germany divided into hundreds of separate little states. Eventually, two expansionist kingdoms—the Catholic Austrian and the Protestant Prussian empires—would come to dominate the region.

In Russia, Tsar Peter the Great would undertake a massive project to modernize his nation. Peter took on the powers of an absolute monarch, forcing lesser nobles to accept positions in his government. He brought the church under his control and expanded Russia's borders, stretching the reach of the kingdom all the way to the Pacific Ocean. He built the massive capital city of St. Petersburg and fought naval battles with rival European powers with mixed results.

The dominant economic policy of the day, **mercantilism**, held that the wealth of nations could be measured by the amount of gold and silver they held. Colonial expansion was viewed as a way to increase gold stores while creating new markets that would allow you to trade without giving gold to foreign powers. Consequently, the creation of overseas colonies became a crucial goal for European powers.

These new global empires scattered the once confined populations of Europe. No longer geographically confined, the global population increased. The colonies also encouraged political and religious diversification. Religious and ethnic peoples persecuted in Europe found refuge in the colonies.

During this vast expansion of the European empires, the various governments engaged in shifting alliances to keep the others in check. For example, in 1700, Louis XIV's grandson inherited the throne of Spain. The idea of a single French-Spanish power panicked other European powers. An alliance of English and Dutch forces fought to prevent the unification of the two thrones. In 1713, Louis was forced to sign the Treaty of Utrecht, preventing the unification of the two empires.

The Scientific Revolution

During this time, the sciences underwent a massive shift. Francis Bacon, the English philosopher, is credited with emphasizing the importance of experimentation as a way to advance science. The French philosopher René Descartes emphasized the importance of reason and logic in discovering the truth. Combining these two concepts with the observational methods devised in the Renaissance produced the **scientific method**, a process combining experiments and observations to determine naturalistic explanations for worldly phenomena.

This paradigm shift produced immediate results in the field of medicine. The field of anatomy advanced the human understanding of the body. In 1684, Anton van Leeuwenhoek used a microscope to become the first person to identify red blood cells. William Harvey described the human circulatory system. The chemist Robert Boyle developed the first system of what would become the atomic theory.

In the field of physics, **Isaac Newton** developed the first functional theory of gravity. He and Gottfried Wilhelm Leibniz simultaneously developed calculus, a set of mathematical tools that scientists and mathematicians still use and refine today. Similarly, the discoveries made by astronomers Galileo Galilei and Nicolaus Copernicus changed the way that humans saw themselves in the universe. Galileo improved the telescope to increase the number of observations that could be made in the nighttime sky, including the moons of Jupiter. It was Copernicus who famously proved that Earth rotates around the Sun—and that Earth was not the center of the universe.

The advances of science led many to believe that natural political and moral truths could also be discovered. This link is what connects the scientific revolution to the **Enlightenment** that followed.

The Age of Reason

Central to Enlightenment-era thought is the notion of natural rights. Advanced by **John Locke** and others, this was the notion that some rights are reserved to humans at birth. Locke maintained that humans formed governments to ensure these natural rights. To ensure that governments do not trample on the natural rights they were formed to protect, the philosopher Montesquieu proposed that governing power should be distributed to different branches, guaranteeing no one person or group became too powerful. In England, Mary Wollstonecraft made the case for extending full political rights to women, a group left almost entirely disenfranchised in Europe.

Enlightenment thought affected fields beyond political science. In education, philosophers stressed the importance of encouraging the innate talents of students. In economics, Adam Smith stressed the value of free markets, letting the logic of economic systems operate without economic intervention. In the arts, the new ways of thinking encouraged experimentation and political awareness.

The new ideas of the Enlightenment filtered through society and some monarchs and rulers became relatively liberal and reform-minded. For example, tensions over control of Poland were resolved diplomatically, rather than militarily. In 1772, Russia, Austria, and Prussia partitioned Poland.

However, the largest impact of Enlightenment thought would be felt in the coming revolutions that would topple, rather than reform, monarchies.

Age of Revolutions and the French Empire

Fed by the ideals of the Enlightenment, including those penned by the philosopher **Jean-Jacques Rousseau**, revolution fever spread throughout the colonies of Europe. In 1775, the American colonies began to revolt. Revolutions in Haiti, Paraguay, Chile, Colombia, Mexico, Peru, Brazil, and Bolivia would follow.

In 1789, the citizens of France caught the fever. Economic inequality, government and clerical corruption, and political stalemates over the creation of a constitution all broke into civil violence when angry Parisians stormed the Bastille, a former fortress repurposed as a prison. Urban and rural revolts forced the National Assembly, the French legislature, to create a constitutional monarchy. The royal family was essentially imprisoned in Paris and the church was put under state rule. In 1791, a new constitution was put in place. Foreign monarchies threatened to intervene to protect the French monarchy, but this did not stop radicals from abolishing the monarchy and executing the king and queen in 1793. Under more radical leadership, the French Revolution entered a brutally fanatical phase known as the Reign of Terror. More than 17,000 people were executed for counterrevolutionary crimes at the hands of the new government. The excesses of the Terror left a more moderate, but corrupt government in charge. Facing civil unrest over the poor state of the economy and official wrongdoing, the new government turned to a well-known war hero, **Napoleon Bonaparte**, to act as a figurehead for the new government.

Napoleon, however, was not content to be a figurehead and quickly took control of the new government. During the Revolution, Napoleon became famous for a series of victories against foreign foes. Capitalizing on that popularity, he declared himself the emperor of France and launched an imperialistic campaign in Europe. He conquered and annexed portions of Italy, the Netherlands, sections of Germany, and Poland. He overthrew the king of Spain and put his own brother on the throne.

Ultimately, Napoleon's imperial designs were thwarted. His effort to invade Russia was repelled and his territories in Spain and Austria were constantly in revolt. These failures led to unpopularity at home, and, in 1814, Napoleon abdicated briefly. In 1815, he returned to chase Louis XVIII out of France and take on the British military. At the Battle of Waterloo, the British forces and their allies defeated Napoleon. He was exiled and died on the island Saint Helena in 1821.

After Napoleon's defeat, representatives of the European powers met at the Congress of Vienna in hopes of restoring order to Europe. The Congress reestablished the hereditary throne of France and the Concert of Europe, a system of periodic diplomatic meetings between the heads of state in Europe.

The Industrial Revolution

The relative stability of Europe after the Napoleonic Wars encouraged economic and industrial development. Agriculture was the first sector of the economy to innovate. Cattle breeding, soil and manure experiments, and the development of new mechanized farming practices all contributed to increased yields. Notably, these innovations were the product of farmers themselves and not government reforms.

In industry and transportation, two major technological innovations opened the way for new development: improved steam power and high quality steel. With these improvements in place, the process of **industrialization** began. The process started in England. England had abundant coal sources, which drove the steam engines, and a large skilled workforce. It also had a tradition of business entrepreneurship that drove owners to seek new and more efficient means of production.

The industrial revolution encouraged urban migration as workers moved to be closer to industrial centers. It also created two new social classes: a wealthy class of business owners and a vast class of less wealthy industrial laborers. Life for the laboring class could be hard. Conditions in many factories were brutal and many industrial jobs were dangerous. The positive results of industrialization spurred the growth of philosophies that emphasized limited government regulation, such as utilitarianism. Others were disturbed by the social costs of industrialization and urged reform. One of the most extreme of these reform philosophies was Marxism.

The Rise of Nationalism

In the period after the Congress of Vienna, competing ideas regarding the future of Europe spread across borders and social classes. Concerned about the violence of the French revolution and its role in the rise of Napoleon, conservatives urged a return to monarchal government. Liberals pushed for constitutional governments and stressed democratic processes and free markets. Because of the empire building of the fifteenth and sixteenth centuries, many nation-states spread over a vast area and incorporated diverse populations. Nationalists felt that these empires should be broken up and different cultural groups should be able to form their own nations. Finally, socialists believed that governments should exert greater control over their economies, ensuring a more equitable distribution of wealth. More moderate socialists felt that governments could improve the lot of their citizens by nationalizing just a few key industries. The most radical felt that total control of all industry was required to prevent exploitation and inequality. To a degree, all these philosophies would shape the post-Napoleonic era.

Liberal revolts broke out in several nations. In 1830, the French again revolted. Angry Parisians seized the streets and erected barricades. After the king was replaced with a more acceptable ruler, the unrest died down. The peace was, however, short-lived. Economic hardship and government corruption sent Parisians into the streets again in 1848. The result of this second revolt was the creation of a republican government. It lasted less than a decade. Napoleon III, nephew of the famous emperor, was elected president and, in 1852, he proclaimed himself emperor.

Liberal revolts occurred in several of the German states. Initially it appeared as if these movements would be successful in creating a constitutional monarchy. Fredrick William IV, the Prussian king who ruled the rebellious states, refused the new constitution and the liberal movements collapsed.

In the Austrian empire, Hungarian nationalists revolted in an effort to form an independent government. The Austrian government initially reacted with a series of social reforms, but then the government reversed course and crushed the rebellion.

The Age of Nationalism

In the late 1800s, Otto von Bismarck united the fractious German states into a single nation. Elected prime minister in 1862, Bismarck used military and diplomatic strategies to create a single German state under Prussia. The new state was a constitutional monarchy in which the kaiser, or king, shared legislative power with a two-house legislature.

Italy, like Germany, had long existed as a collection of loosely affiliated states. This fragmentation was exacerbated by the fact that foreign powers—the Austrians, the Prussians, and the French—controlled some of the Italian states. As in Germany, the unification of the nation was largely due to the efforts of a brilliant prime minister: Count Camillo di Cavour, the prime minister of the Italian state of Sardinia. Through a series of alliances with major European powers and the help of Italian nationalist rebels, Cavour completed the process of unification in 1870.

Facing pressure from reformers within and military defeats abroad, the Austrian monarchy formed a dual monarchy with the monarch of Hungary in 1867. Under the new system, Austria and Hungary remained two separate states, each with its own constitution and parliament, but Hungarian monarch Francis Joseph ruled over both. The governments of both nations were rendered ineffective by nationalist revolts and social unrest, specifically from Slavic ethnic groups demanding their own nations.

The once mighty **Ottoman Empire** collapsed as nationalist groups revolted and tossed off foreign rule. While some of these rebellious states, such as Greece, gained their independence, many nationalist breakaway states were quickly assimilated by other European powers. The chaos of the Ottoman collapse left Central Europe with a legacy of conflict that helped spark World War I.

In Russia, social unrest forced Tsar Alexander II to enact widespread social reforms. The benefits of these reforms were mitigated by the abuses of power that followed. Fearful of losing his power, the tsar created a vast secret police network and engaged in campaigns of ethnic and religious persecution. In 1905, antitsarist rebels revolted. Tsar Nicholas II reacted to the revolt by creating a national legislature.

In England, under Queen Victoria, suffrage was greatly expanded. Prior to 1815, less than 5% of the population had the vote. In 1832, reforms gave the vote to a vast majority of the middle class. By the end of the century, most males had the right to vote. Reform campaigns swept through England: antislavery campaigns, campaigns to end capital punishment, and campaigns to improve conditions for workers and the poor. Despite the confidence and liberality of the era, nationalist violence and unrest in Ireland proved an intractable problem. The Great Famine struck Ireland in 1845. This disastrous crop failure killed more than one million people. Another million people emigrated from Ireland to escape "the Great Hunger."

Under Napoleon III, France undertook a ruinous war with Prussia. Napoleon was captured during the war and the French defeat might have been total, had not a citizen army held Paris against Prussian siege in 1870. In 1871, the National Assembly created a new republican government, the third since the French Revolution. That same year the new government violently suppressed a citizens' uprising. Despite this shaky beginning, the Third Republic would act as the French government for more than 70 years.

The Second Imperial Era

Spurred by a mixture of economic, military, and even misguided humanitarian motivations, European powers once again turned their attention to building overseas empires.

European explorers and missionaries had been exploring the continent of Africa for several hundred years. In the early part of the twentieth century, this exploration turned into imperial expansion. Belgium, Britain, France, Germany, Italy, Portugal, and Spain all gained or expanded their colonial holdings. By 1914, the height of imperial expansion in Africa, only two nations remained completely independent: Ethiopia and Liberia.

Throughout the nineteenth century, European powers clashed over control of China. Some nations, like Russia and Britain, actually occupied sections of the country. Most used diplomacy and trade to manipulate local governments, exerting a powerful influence over the Chinese without officially establishing a colony.

By 1850, Britain controlled just over half of India. It also established colonies in Burma. The French established a colony in Indochina (present-day Vietnam) and the Dutch colonized Sumatra, Borneo, and part of New Guinea.

Despite this imperial growth, it was during this period that two of Britain's largest colonies achieved self-rule: Canada gained self-rule in 1867 and Australia gained self-rule in 1901.

World War I

The chaos left behind by the decline of the Ottoman Empire in Central Europe was known as the **Balkan Powder Keg**. In 1914, the powder keg exploded. On June 28, an Austrian noble was assassinated by a Bosnian nationalist in Sarajevo. With the backing of Germany, the Austrian government declared war on Serbia. France and Russia backed Serbia, bringing them in conflict with Germany and Austria. In order to attack France, Germany had to occupy Belgium. Britain, an ally of Belgium, entered the war against Germany and Austria.

Germany and its allies were dubbed the **Central Powers**. Britain, France, and Russia were known as the **Allied Powers**.

As warfare in Europe developed into a bloody stalemate, Europe's overseas colonies were pulled into the conflict. The Ottoman Empire joined Germany and Austria and attacked British colonies in the Middle East and Africa.

In 1917, revolutionary forces overthrew the Russian government. Dominated by communists who felt the war was being fought to perpetuate the oppression of the working class, the new Russian government established peace with Germany and its allies. Russians left the battlefield and began transforming Russia into the core of the **Soviet Union**.

That same year the United States entered the war on the side of France and Britain. Allied troops managed to drive German forces out of France and Belgium in 1918. German military leadership began to view the war as a lost cause. Back in Germany, the wartime economy collapsed and angry citizens rioted in the streets. Germany's military leaders convinced William II, the kaiser of Germany, to step down. A new government was formed and peace-brokering efforts began immediately. Germany's allies also sued for peace. On the 11th hour of the 11th day of the 11th month of 1918, the war officially came to an end.

The war had been disastrous for Europe. More than 8 million soldiers and another 6 to 13 million civilians died as a result of the war. Collectively, the nations involved in the war spent more than $200 billion. The economies of Austria-Hungary, France, and Germany were shattered. To make things worse, the 1918 influenza epidemic added to the misery of the conflict. The flu epidemic would claim 20 million lives worldwide.

In 1919, representatives from the warring nations hammered out the **Treaty of Versailles**. The conditions the Allies placed on the former Central Powers were harsh. The Allies demanded $30 billion in reparations and sections of the treaty were intended to cripple Germany's economic might. The treaty also stripped Germany, Austria-Hungary, and the Ottoman Empire of their overseas colonies. Austria and Hungary were fully divided into individual countries.

The Great Depression and the Rise of the Soviet Union

In Russia, the 1917 revolution became a civil war between communist *reds* and anticommunist *whites*. The communists prevailed and the new government was founded on communist principles. The transition was not easy. Counterrevolutionary elements were brutally suppressed. Differences in political theory were grounds for assassination or deportation, or as in the case of Leon Trotsky, both.

In 1924, Joseph Stalin took control of the Communist Party. He consolidated power under him and became as powerful in Russia as any absolute monarch was in the age of empire.

While the revolution transformed Russia, social upheavals shook European colonies abroad. In India, nationalist leaders, including **Mohandas Gandhi**, began to protest colonial rule. In China, communist revolutionaries under the leadership of Mao Zedong and nationalist leaders began unifying the country and dismantling the system of local rule that Europeans found so easy to influence.

To complicate things, postwar politics crippled the ability of the western democracy to respond to these developments. In France, political corruption and the rise of new political parties meant that governmental administrations obtained and lost power so quickly that no administration could accomplish anything. England was occupied with domestic trouble. Working-class resentment led to the creation of the Labour Party, which caused a conservative backlash in the form of restrictions on workers' rights. In 1922, the Irish Free State was formed. Unfortunately, the peace between the new country and British-controlled Northern Ireland was short-lived and terrorism continued. These domestic troubles contributed to the failure of ambitious foreign policy goals, such as the inability to support a strong League of Nations.

As the 1920s came to a close, a series of financial missteps and crashes created a global economic depression. In 1929, the stock market in the United States crashed. Demand for products and services shrank. To prevent overproduction, jobs were cut. The system of war payments and debts set up at the end of World War I meant that the effects of the crash in the United States spread throughout the global economy. In countries like Germany, where the economy was already crippled from the war years, the impact was severe. In other countries, like Britain, it became the backdrop for a struggle between socialist reformers and more traditional liberal free market leaders.

In Italy and Germany, perhaps the most important result of the **Great Depression** was the rise of fascism. Democratic governments, unable to reverse the economic downturn, were voted out of office and replaced with totalitarian governments. In Italy, the Fascist Party led by Benito Mussolini forced King Victor Emmanuel III to form a new government with Mussolini as prime minister. The **Nazi Party** of Germany, under the leadership of **Adolf Hitler**, was voted into power. Once in power, the Nazis quickly dismantled the democratic institutions of Germany.

The rise of totalitarianism, in Stalin's Russia as well as in Germany and Italy, put democracy on the retreat in Europe. In Russia, Italy, and Germany, purges of scapegoats and political rivals were ruthless and deadly. In Germany, Jewish citizens were persecuted. Eventually, this ethnic persecution led to the Holocaust, Germany's genocidal effort to systematically execute any Jews and other "undesirables" living under Nazi control. More than six million would die in the Holocaust. In Russia, Stalin sent more than four million citizens to labor camps, or *gulags*. When farmers refused to go along with Soviet-style collective production, Stalin used his control of the economy to create famine conditions that killed five to eight million people.

World War II

The totalitarian governments of the post–World War II years had imperial ambitions. In 1935, Italy invaded Ethiopia. In 1936, Germany broke the conditions of the Treaty of Versailles and mobilized troops in an area designated as a demilitarized zone. Germany would support fascist forces in the Spanish Civil War, ensuring their victory. Germany would then invade Austria and Czechoslovakia.

The democratic nations, eager to prevent another global conflict, adopted a policy of **appeasement**—allowing current aggression in the hopes of preventing future aggression.

Italy, Germany, and Japan, which were building an empire in Asia, formed a pact to fight the spread of communism and not interfere with each other's imperial plans. With this agreement in place, these three countries formed the Axis powers.

In 1939, Germany invaded Poland. France and Britain declared war on Germany. This declaration of war began World War II. Germany's allies, Japan and Italy, joined the conflict. Despite a nonaggression pact, Germany invaded the Soviet Union. This caused the Soviet Union to join the war on the side of the Allies, Britain and France. In 1941, Japan attacked the United States. This ended the United States' policy of neutrality and America entered the conflict on the side of the Allies.

After a long string of victories, the Axis powers found themselves suddenly stalled. Germany suffered a long and disastrous defeat at Stalingrad and the naval war in the Pacific Ocean turned against the Japanese. By the end of 1944, Allied troops had conquered Italy. Sensing defeat, Italians rebelled and overthrew the Fascist government. In 1945, the Allies advanced into Germany, and victory over Germany was declared. Before the year was over, the United States dropped two atomic bombs on Japan and ended the war in the Pacific.

Contemporary Europe

In the aftermath of the war, Allied forces divided Germany into zones of control. Two governments, one democratic and one communist, were set up in the divided country.

In 1945, eager to prevent future large-scale conflicts, delegates from 50 nations created the charter for the **United Nations**. Originally conceived as a peacekeeping organization, the UN's mandate would grow to include global health monitoring, the management of refugee services, and the regulation of worldwide environmental initiatives.

In contrast to the international spirit of the UN, one of the other significant effects of the war was the **Cold War**. Once the common enemy of fascism was defeated, the Soviet Union and the western democracies entered into a protracted rivalry. It was a matter of Communist policy that communism should be spread to other countries, either through diplomatic persuasion or military force. By the same token, western democracies wanted to ensure that free markets and democratic governments dominated the globe. In 1949, the Soviet Union developed its first atomic weapon. The threat of nuclear war prevented the western democracies and the Soviet Union from clashing directly. Instead, the Cold War was fought by building alliances, supporting proxy states, and attempting to thwart the expansion of the rival ideology. While the Cold War was primarily a conflict between the Soviet Union and the United States, most of Europe's democracies joined the North Atlantic Treaty Organization (NATO), a military alliance designed to organize a western response to potential Soviet aggression. The Cold War would remain the dominant fact of global diplomacy until the 1980s, when Soviet leaders, facing chronic economic troubles, a failed war in Afghanistan, and social unrest in satellite states, began to dismantle communism. By 1991, Germany was reunified and most of the nations absorbed by the Soviet Union after World War II had formed independent nations.

The collapse of the Soviet Union had a dark side. As Soviet power receded, ethnic and religious hostilities that had been forcefully suppressed by the Communists were unleashed. In Chechnya and the former Yugoslavia, regional conflicts with genocidal aims broke out. The former continues to plague the Russian republic in the form of terror acts, while the latter was resolved only by the UN-led efforts of several member nations.

In a parallel to the decline of communist imperialism, the postwar years marked the decline of imperialism by the western democracies. India and Pakistan both gained their independence in 1947. The Dutch East Indies became free states by 1949. In Africa, once nearly entirely colonized by European powers, every former colony was reconstructed as an independent state by 1990.

As Europe rebuilt, most of the western democracies developed as welfare states—market economies with extensive government intervention in the citizens' social and economic lives. In exchange for generally higher taxes, the citizens in much of Europe had access to universal healthcare and pension programs. Governments also controlled many basic industries, such as power and transportation. This trend toward governmental control would continue until the 1980s, when conservatives in Britain would begin to question the long-term economic impact of the welfare state. Later, citizens in France would also elect politicians who promised less government intervention and more free market capitalism.

In 1956, six nations—West Germany, the Netherlands, Belgium, Luxembourg, France, and Italy—founded the European Community, an organization created to encourage free trade among its member states. The European Community would grow to include new member nations, and eventually it would evolve into the European Union. By the year 2000, most of Western Europe had joined the European Union. In 2002, the European Union introduced the euro, a single currency used by a majority of its member states. Although the citizens in several member states rejected a European Union constitution, the European Union continues to develop as a crucial unifying bond between the nations of Europe.

Other Notable Civilizations

While the European civilizations may dominate classroom curricula, there are many other cultures that may appear on the Praxis II: Elementary Education: Content Knowledge test. The following discussion of non-European civilizations provides a few of the most important civilizations to be familiar with. While the descriptions are brief, you should be familiar with their essential characteristics and be able to make connections that relate to them.

India

The second-most populous nation on Earth, behind China, India today boasts about 1.2 billion residents. The Republic of India was formed officially in 1950 after declaring its independence from Britain in 1947. One of the chief leaders of the Indian independence movement was the spiritual leader **Mohandas Gandhi**, also referred to as Mahatma Gandi. He resisted the tyranny of the imperialistic rulers and helped inspire civil rights through a philosophy called **civil disobedience**, a movement which preached a nonviolent refusal to obey certain laws deemed unfair.

The vast majority of people living in India, about 80%, are Hindu. Similarly, the vast majority of Hindu people, also about 80%, live in India. **Hinduism**, often referred to as the oldest living religion, has no central founder and a very complex system of beliefs about God. Several of the well-known themes in Hindu beliefs include dharma, **Samsāra**, karma, and yoga. **Dharma** represents a Hindu's righteous duty, which can be represented by a wide variety of ideas. **Samsāra** is the continual cycle of life, including reincarnation (or rebirth). **Karma** is the spiritual belief that each action or deed creates a subsequent reaction. The Hindu practice of **yoga** is one of the paths to a spiritual goal. The union and serenity is described in the scripture of the sacred **Bhagavad Gita**, one of the most famous and important texts in literature.

India's societal structure has been known for its **caste system**, which designates social classes within the Indian subcontinent into a system of social stratification. For many years, the caste system restricted millions of people from escaping the class in which they were born and maintained the social hierarchy. However, discrimination based on caste is now illegal, based on the Indian constitution, and the barriers in urban areas have been breaking down. Still, the caste system continues to exist in modern-day India, especially for the nearly three-quarters of the population who live in the rural areas of the country.

Historically, India has been famous for its trade routes that helped propagate its commercial and cultural wealth. For example, many spices, such as pepper, originated from the Indian continent. The **spice trade** between India and Europe was so significant that it helped drive the world economy and inspired the **Age of Discovery**. Although trade no longer plays as significant a role in Indian culture, the country still exports many products, such as textile goods, gems and jewelry, and software, with the United States as its main export destination.

China

One of the first centers of human civilization, China is now the world's most populous nation with more than 1.3 billion residents. China has made several important contributions that may appear on the Praxis II, and there are some features of its government and history that may appear on the test as well.

Among their many inventions, the Chinese are responsible for the inventions of gunpowder, the compass, papermaking, and printing. The People's Republic of China, which was established in 1949, is officially atheist, and it has been known for suppressing religious freedom. However, recognized religions of the state include Buddhism and Taoism, as well as Islam and Christianity.

One of the most notable manmade geographic features of the world is the **Great Wall of China**, built and rebuilt between fifth century BCE and sixteenth century CE. The original purpose of the wall was to protect the Chinese Empire from invaders from the north. Today, the wall stretches for 5,500 miles and up to a height of 16 feet and a maximum width of 30 feet in some places, creating a vast defensive barrier. The colossal barrier is a symbol of China's insularity, though today it is a popular tourist destination.

Japan

You should be familiar with several terms regarding the history of the island nation of Japan. Isolated for centuries, Japan was considered a closed country; its policy from about 1639 through 1853 was that no foreigner could enter Japan, nor could a Japanese citizen leave the country. The penalty for either infraction was death. It was not until 1853, when Admiral **Matthew Perry**, in an attempt to open trade between the United States and Japan, anchored his ships in Tokyo Bay, that Japan was successfully opened to foreigners.

Similar to a religion, **Shinto** is a set of practices followed by more than 100 million Japanese. The purposes of the practices are to connect Japan to its ancient past through shrines. The Buddhist religion was introduced from China throughout the thirteenth century, and it became popular with the **samurai**, Japan's warrior aristocracy.

The military leaders throughout the history of Japan have held the title of **shogun**. Shoguns were in charge of the military system of Japan, and they acted between the leaders of Japan and their protectorates in a system called **feudalism**. The last remaining shogun ruled in 1867. However, the symbol of the state of Japan is its **emperor**, who is also the highest authority of Shintoism, and the emperors have been figureheads of Japan continually for more than 2,500 years.

Sub-Saharan Africa

Although great focus is given to the Egyptian civilization in northern Africa, there are civilizations south of the Sahara Desert that may appear on the Praxis II. The most well-known of them, the **forest kingdoms**, was a coalescence of many villages in the forestlands of western Africa between approximately 1000 and 1500. They may also have formed several centuries earlier. These powerful kingdoms achieved their vast success and wealth not through the traditional route of conquest but through their massive trading empires. These trading routes went north and south through the forestland, and these kingdoms were in a position to control the traffic of goods, most notably gold, from the valley of the Senegal.

Beginning at about 1500 and continuing for about 300 years, the forest kingdoms were incorporated into the European capitalistic activities.

Islamic Civilizations

Islam is a religion followed by more than 1.5 billion adherents, called Muslims. More than 91% of all people from the Middle East and northern Africa are Muslims. Large areas of Asia are populated mostly by Muslims as well, including Indonesia, Pakistan, and Bangladesh. There are also Muslim communities all around the world. After Christianity, Islam is the second largest religion in Europe. Approximately 2.5 million Muslims live in the United States

Muslims believe in one God, as described by the **Qur'an**, or Koran, the Islam holy text. The Qur'an provides knowledge about the founder of Islam, **Muhammed**. Muhammed was born in 570 in the city of Mecca, in modern-day Saudi Arabia, and the origin of Islam was in Arabia. As a result, Mecca is Islam's holiest site. A thriving trading center even in the time of Muhammed, Mecca is now a large city of about 1.7 million people. It is also the destination for millions of Muslims visiting the holy site on an annual pilgrimage called a **hajj**.

Pre-Columbian Mesoamerican Civilizations

There are three Mesoamerican civilizations that may appear on the Praxis II exam. These are often referred to as the three pre-Columbian civilizations because they thrived in the era before Christopher Columbus landed in the Americas. The earliest of those civilizations, the **Maya**, existed mostly in the area now known as Mexico from about 2000 BCE until the arrival of the Spanish, beginning in the sixteenth century. The highly religious Mayan people were known for their advanced written language, as well as their advancements in art, architecture, and mathematics. They used their knowledge of mathematics to create the Mayan calendar, the most accurate calendar in the world at that time. There are still populations of Maya people today that maintain their traditions and beliefs.

The **Aztec** people lived in the area now known as northern Mexico during the late Mesoamerican period. The Aztecs rose to power in the twelfth and thirteenth centuries, and their empire thrived during the late fifteenth and early sixteenth centuries until they were defeated by the Spanish conquistador **Hernando Cortez**. Magnificent temples remain as evidence of the powerful Aztec culture.

The **Inca** civilization, the most recent of the three most famous Mesoamerican civilizations, was based on the west coast of South America, including the modern-day country of Peru. The rise of Incan Empire rose very quickly to become the largest empire in pre-Columbian America, spreading out over nearly 400,000 square miles. Although the Incan civilization was much farther south than the Aztec or Maya civilizations, it too was not immune to the defeat at the hands of the Spanish conquistadors.

The once-thriving Mesoamerican empires were defeated by the Spanish, in part because of the introduction of diseases from the Spanish conquistadors into the Central and South American civilizations. For example, deadly epidemics of smallpox and typhus ravaged the native population, causing the indigenous population of the Valley of Mexico to shrink by more than 80% in the span of a few generations.

United States History

American history on the Praxis II: Elementary Education: Content Knowledge test may cover any period of history from the early European exploration through the colonization of America and Reconstruction to the present. That's a considerable amount of material, and no single chapter could possibly review everything that might appear on the test. However, being aware of broad trends in crucial historical periods will provide a helpful context for the items you might encounter. Because 30% of the social studies section of the test will include questions about U.S. history, you should review the following historical eras in America, including a list of key concepts for each period. This overview and the key concepts will give you the basic structure you will need.

European Exploration and Colonization

Before any European set foot on North American soil, there were many well-developed cultures on the continent. Before reviewing the causes and effects of the European exploration, it is important to consider all the numerous native populations in North America that preceded the exploration.

Early Native Populations

The **Inuit** people, also called Eskimos, have lived in the Arctic and subarctic areas of North America for thousands of years. One of the oldest archeological sites, in Labrador, Canada, is nearly 4,000 years old. Unlike other Native American populations, the Inuit population is believed to have its origins in Asia. Inuit people have adapted to extremely cold environments and continue to live in parts of Alaska in the United States.

The **Anasazi** were a Native American civilization that once existed in the southwestern areas of what is now the United States. The civilization existed from about 100 to 1600 CE, though descendents of the Anasazi comprise current Native American tribes, including the Hopi. The Anasazi constructed buildings into the sides of cliffs, earning them the name of Cliff Dwellers.

The **Kwakiutl** people lived on the west coast of North America, mostly in the area just north of the United States border in what is now British Columbia. As a result of this geographic residence, they are also described with the name **Northwest Indians**. The population of Kwakiutl, mostly fishermen, now numbers fewer than 1,000 individuals.

The Native American peoples who roamed the central plains of North America are named, appropriately, the **Plains Indians**. These populations were mostly nomadic and ranged from the northern border to the southern border of the current United States at the time of the first European contact. The Plains Indians are easily recognizable for their equestrian culture.

The **Mound Builders** were a group of cultures who inhabited North America dating all the way back to 3000 BCE. Their name originates from a series of mounds that they built across the central areas of what is now the United States, including the Ohio River Valley and the areas by the Great Lakes. The Mound Builders, who predated the other Native American populations of North America, existed up until the time of the European explorers, roughly about 1600. However, a violent conflict between the two populations was not the cause of their disappearance. It is theorized that the introduction of European diseases, including smallpox, destroyed what was left of the Mound Builders at the time.

The **Iroquois** people are a group of several tribes that were based in the northeastern United States at the time of the European exploration. The association of the tribes helped them organize together to form a league now known as the Six Nations. The Iroquois people today comprise more than 100,000 people, mostly living in the regions of New York and Canada.

First Explorations

It is usually **Christopher Columbus** who gets the credit for being the first European to discover the Americas with his 1492 voyage in the ships *Santa María*, *Pinta*, and *Niña*. However, a Norse group led by **Leif Ericson** predated Columbus by nearly 500 years. Ericson did not establish a permanent colony in the Americas, however, so it is Columbus's voyage across the Atlantic Ocean that would initiate the significant changes to the North American continent and the Native American groups already living there. And it is Columbus, born in the country now known as Italy, who gets the national holiday in the United States.

After many years of trading with India by land, the route from Europe became unsafe by the 1480s. Therefore, Columbus's voyage in 1492 was an attempt to find the most efficient trade route to India, not to explore new territory. When he landed at an island in the Bahamas, he was under the impression that he had landed in the East Indies. He therefore referred to the people there as "indios,"

Columbus's famous voyages—he took four of them from 1492 to 1502—were also a matter of national imperialism for Spain. France and England were also looking for new territory to colonize, so the purpose of the exploration was not just for better trade routes, but also to help Spain compete with these countries economically and imperialistically.

The Colonial Period

Throughout the fifteenth and sixteenth centuries, the fate of what would eventually become the United

States of America was fiercely contested by European empires, the native cultures of North America, and conflicting groups of colonists.

Spain dominated early exploration of North and South America. The Dutch established the colony of New Amsterdam (later New York). Finally, the French claimed vast stretches of land, but never managed any sustained colonization efforts within the territory that would become the modern United States.

In 1607, England established the first permanent English settlement in North America—the Jamestown colony. The slow-building success of the Jamestown colony inspired the founding of a second colony. In 1620, the Plymouth colony, located in modern Massachusetts, was settled by a combination of Puritans in opposition to the state church of England and economically motivated opportunists. Unlike the disastrous first decades of the Virginian colony, the Plymouth colony was immediately successful. More than 20,000 immigrants, most of them radical Puritans, had arrived in Massachusetts by 1642.

Other colonies soon followed. In 1634, Catholic colonists formed the colony of St. Mary's. This would eventually become the modern state of Maryland. In 1644, Roger Williams, a Puritan who broke with the religious authorities of Massachusetts, established Rhode Island as a haven for unorthodox religious believers. Pennsylvania and Delaware were chartered as colonies in 1681 and 1682. These colonies were home to Quakers and other persecuted religious minorities. The final of the 13 British colonies, Georgia, was founded in 1733 as a utopian experiment.

In 1619, Dutch traders shipped the first slaves to Virginia. As the colonies expanded, the slave trade became an integral part of colonial life. No British colony was free of slavery. In some colonies, such as South Carolina, a majority of the people living in the colony lived in slavery.

Key Concepts for the European Exploration and Colonization

Five Civilized Tribes. The native inhabitants of what is now the southeastern United States, they were called "civilized" because they used advanced farming techniques and lived in settled communities. The five tribes comprised the Choctaw, Creek, Chickasaw, Cherokee, and Seminole people.

Massachusetts Bay Company. Established in 1629, the company funded the colony of Plymouth. In 1684, the company's charter expired and Plymouth became a royal colony. Similar companies established most of the American colonies.

Mayflower Compact. Signed in 1620, the compact was an agreement between the colonists that became the foundation of civil government in Plymouth.

Salem Witch Trials. In 1692, political fears and religious intolerance led to the execution of 19 on charges of witchcraft. The trials have become part of the political lexicon: A *witch hunt* has become a metaphor for a paranoid, politically motivated persecution.

The American Revolution and the Founding of the Nation

As the British colonies grew more prosperous and expanded, violent conflicts arose among these colonies, the native population, and the French colonies. From 1636 to 1763, the colonies found themselves engaged in one bloody conflict after another. These conflicts were devastating to all sides. Some Native American tribes, such as the Yemasee of South Carolina, were completely destroyed. King Philip's War in New England, named for the chief of the Wompanoag tribe, claimed the life of one out of every 16 male colonists of military age.

Although these conflicts left Britain as the uncontested master of colonial North America, they were the beginning of the end of Britain's American rule. The colonists believed these sacrifices entitled them to the status of full legal citizens within the British Empire. This growing dissatisfaction found a philosophical framework in the liberal ideals of Enlightenment thought. Tensions between England and her colonies grew. The anger of the colonists began to focus on a series of taxation measures enacted to help Britain pay for the long series of Native American and

French conflicts. Protests in various colonies turned violent, which provoked a more militaristic lockdown of the northern colonies. By the time representatives from the 13 colonies met to devise a unified response, open warfare between colonial militias and British troops had begun. The colonial representatives adopted the **Declaration of Independence** on July 4, 1776. A year later, the colonial leaders would produce the **Articles of Confederation**, the initial basis for interstate government among the free colonies.

It was not until early 1777 that the rebels could claim any real victories on the field. These successes convinced the French to support the colonial revolutionaries. French support was soon followed by Spanish support. As Washington rallied in the North, fighting in the South degenerated into desperate guerilla-style warfare. In 1781, a combined colonial and French force laid siege to Yorktown, Virginia, and the British forces surrendered. This marked the end of significant combat in the Revolutionary War. The Treaty of Paris officially ended the war in 1783.

The Constitution

The Articles of Confederation rapidly proved inadequate to meet the needs of the newly formed nation. In 1787, 55 delegates from every state in the confederation met in Philadelphia to hammer out a new constitution. Three crucial compromises emerged out of the debates:

1. **The Connecticut Compromise.** In order to strike a balance between larger and smaller states, Roger Sherman, a delegate from Connecticut, proposed that the number of state representatives in the House of Representatives would be determined by a state's population while every state, regardless of size, would get two representatives in the Senate. He also proposed the electoral college system used to elect the president.
2. **The Three-Fifths Compromise.** In order to boost their representation in the House, delegates from the Southern states proposed that slaves be counted as citizens even though they would have no rights as citizens. Ultimately, it was agreed that a single slave would count as three-fifths of a citizen.
3. **The Bill of Rights.** Concerned that the new Constitution would give oppressive power to a centralized federal government, some delegates demanded the addition of a list of rights guaranteed to individual citizens. This list became the first ten amendments to the Constitution and is known as the Bill of Rights.

The Constitution was officially ratified in 1788. A series of political challenges put the new government to the test. In 1789, the Judiciary Act, which established the power of judicial review, was passed. Later, during the two terms of Andrew Jackson, the political franchise was extended to groups that would have made the founding fathers nervous, such as unpropertied men. Finally, the Nullification Crisis, in which the state government of South Carolina threatened to nullify federal law, set the precedent of the primacy of federal law over state law.

Key Concepts for the American Revolution

Benjamin Franklin. A relentless campaigner for colonial unity, Franklin was one of the Founding Fathers and one of the one of five men who drafted the Declaration of Independence. As a scientist and inventor, he was a leader in the Enlightenment movement.

Continental Congress. A legislative body created by the colonies, this group acted as the government during the Revolution. This body produced the Declaration of Independence and the Articles of Confederation.

Founding Fathers. A group of advocates, including George Washington, Benjamin Franklin, Thomas Paine, John Adams, Samuel Adams, James Madison, and Patrick Henry, who signed the Declaration of Independence. These men believed in republican values and acted as a motivating force for the revolution.

Intolerable Acts. Colonists dubbed the series of laws passed by the British in 1774 the "Intolerable Acts." These laws pushed the colonists further toward rebellion.

Loyalists. Colonists who remained loyal to the British government were also called *Tories*. It is estimated that nearly a third of the colonists were loyalists.

Navigation Acts. These laws, which restricted shipping to and from the colonies, were intended to protect the British economy from foreign competition. They became another source of tension between the colonies and Britain. The colonists saw the acts as restrictive and unfair.

The Stamp Act. Taxation laws like the Stamp Act, which taxed paper goods, were a major source of colonial discontent. The Sugar Act and the Townsend Acts were other unpopular tax laws.

Thomas Jefferson. Eventually the third President of the United States for two terms, Jefferson was the primary author of the Declaration of Independence.

The Early Republic and Its Expansion

Not too long after the ratification of the Constitution, the nation experienced explosive growth. It endured wars that tested its strength and dealt with the issues of the native populations and immigration during its expansion. It was torn apart during the Civil War and then struggled to be pieced back together during Reconstruction.

The Early Republic

With the **Louisiana Purchase** of 1803, under the presidency and advocacy of Thomas Jefferson, the country instantly doubled in size. To properly gauge the new resources obtained by this giant purchase of more than 800,000 square miles, Jefferson sent an expedition to explore the new American land. Led by **Meriwether Lewis** and **William Clark**, the expedition would represent the first U.S. expedition to travel to the Pacific coast and return. Aided immensely by the Native American **Sacajawea** in their journeys, Lewis and Clark spent more than two years from 1804 to 1806 traveling from St. Louis to the Pacific Ocean coast of what is now Oregon, and back to St. Louis. The following map shows the route of their expedition, overlaid with the land gained by the Louisiana Purchase.

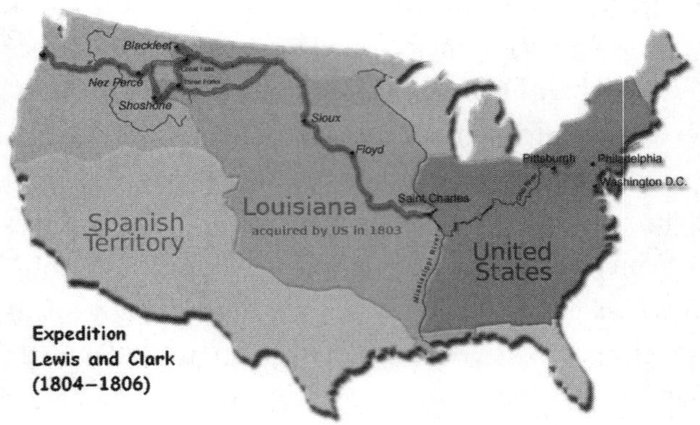

The expansion that was paved by the Louisiana Purchase gave the country access to resources—notably gold, the discovery of which led to the 1849 Gold Rush—that would fuel American growth to the present day. It also ushered in a long period of frequent and bloody struggles with displaced Native Americans. From the date of the purchase until well into the nineteenth century, so-called Indian Wars would break out. For example, Seminole Indians fought to protect their land in Florida and were eventually displaced throughout the mid-nineteenth century.

The forced relocation of the eastern Native Americans as a result of the growing country is called the **Trail of Tears**. Tens of thousands of Native Americans, including members of the Cherokee, Seminole, and Creek nations were displaced from their homelands and sent to new land in Indian Territory, in what is now Oklahoma. Thousands died during the trip from exhaustion, disease, and starvation.

The United States also faced its first major international crisis: the **War of 1812**. This two-year conflict with the British was not a triumph for the nation, but the simple fact that the young nation survived the conflict was enough to establish the United States as a strong presence in international affairs.

Key Concepts for the Early Republic

Slavery Compromises. Throughout the pre–Civil War years, numerous political compromises were made to attempt to defuse the issue of slavery. These compromises included the Missouri Compromise and the Compromise of 1850.

Federalists. one of the first political parties in America, Federalists believed in strong central government. *The Federalist Papers* is a series of essays that presents the Federalist view in the debates over the Constitution. Their opponents were known as anti-Federalists.

Manifest Destiny. This term, coined by a journalist in 1845, described the belief that the United States had a special and divine duty to spread over the entire North American continent.

Monroe Doctrine. This United States policy, declared in 1823, stated clearly that no European nation should intervene with America's growth and colonization within the Western Hemisphere. It also included an agreement that the United States would not interfere with European colonies or in their countries. The doctrine, initiated by the fifth U.S. President, James Monroe, was a defining statement for the foreign policy of the United States.

The Texas Revolution. In 1836, expatriate Americans rebelled in Texas and took the territory by force of arms. The Republic of Texas joined the Union in 1845.

The Civil War and Reconstruction

Slavery became an all-consuming obsession for Americans in the early nineteenth century. The looming crisis was delayed by various compromises and political deals, but the tensions between the North and South eventually overwhelmed the federal government's efforts to keep the peace. Although armed conflict had already started in some sections of the nation, it was the election of **Abraham Lincoln** that proved to be the flashpoint of the war. South Carolina seceded before Lincoln was inaugurated. Mississippi, Florida, Alabama, Georgia, Louisiana, Texas, Virginia, North Carolina, Tennessee, and Arkansas all followed. Calling themselves the **Confederate States of America** and led by **Jefferson Davis** as their president, the rebel states formed a government and began building their military might by seizing United States military installations throughout the South. The explosive situation turned into a shooting war when the soldiers of Fort Sumter refused to surrender to the Confederate forces of South Carolina. Fort Sumter was bombed into submission in 1861 in what most consider the first battle of the Civil War.

The North had superior numbers and was the greater industrial power. Still, ineffective leadership and the lack of will among the northern populace hampered the war effort. In 1862, Lincoln issued the **Emancipation Proclamation**, freeing all slaves in the rebel states. The proclamation's effect on the northern states was to give the war new moral purpose.

The **Battle of Gettysburg** in early July 1863 provided a pivotal point in the war, as the confederate leader, **General Robert E. Lee**, was thwarted in his attempt to continue invading the North. Four and a half months after the success of the Union armies at this location, President Lincoln delivered one of the most famous speeches in American history, the **Gettysburg Address**. In the speech, Lincoln remarked on the importance of the Civil War to create a "new birth of freedom" that would eventually provide equality for all.

General Robert E. Lee surrendered the Army of Northern Virginia to the commander of the Union forces, **General Ulysses S. Grant**, on April 9, 1865. The remaining Confederate forces surrendered just 15 days later. On the eve of the Union's triumph, Abraham Lincoln was assassinated on April 14.

The conclusion of the war left the nation the massive task of reintegrating the South into the United States. Before his death, Lincoln had proposed generous terms of reconciliation intended to quickly mend the nation. After his assassination, the dominant Republican Congress pushed for a more punitive model of Reconstruction. The political fighting over Reconstruction led to the first presidential impeachment: Andrew Johnson was impeached, but his congressional foes were unable to remove him from office. Reconstruction moved ahead sporadically. Organizations were created to help enfranchise the former slaves. Unfortunately, state governments and groups like the Ku Klux Klan undermined these efforts and attempted to maintain the status quo. Federal Reconstruction officially ended in 1876 when Republican lawmakers pulled federal troops out of the South in exchange for the Democrats' concession of the contested 1876 presidential election.

Key Concepts for the Civil War and Reconstruction

Abolitionism. This widespread movement to end slavery was especially strong in the years leading up to the Civil War. Key abolitionists during this period include William Lloyd Garrison, Frederick Douglass, Harriet Beecher Stowe, and Harriet Tubman.

Amendments (13th, 14th, and 15th). In the five years following the conclusion of the Civil War, three amendments were added to the U.S. Constitution. These would be the first amendments in more than 60 years—and the last for another 40. The **Thirteenth Amendment** abolished slavery. The **Fourteenth Amendment** overruled ***Dred Scott v. Sanford*** to allow black Americans to gain citizenship. The **Fifteenth Amendment** stated that the citizens of the United States must not be denied the right to vote based on their race.

Black Codes. Restrictive laws regulating the lives of African Americans passed by Southern states during Reconstruction, they developed into the segregation laws that would last until the 1960s.

Dred Scott v. Sanford. This historical 1857 Supreme Court case declared that black men and women in the United States could never become U.S. citizens.

Frederick Douglass. A former slave, the abolitionist Douglass believed firmly in the equality of all people. After escaping to the northeast, he helped inspire the emancipation through his brilliant writing and speeches, including his best-stelling autobiography.

Free Soil Party. This antislavery party was formed in 1848 and later merged with the fledgling Republican Party.

Fugitive Slave Acts. This series of laws passed from 1787 to 1864 dealt with the treatment of escaped slaves. Enforcing the laws became more and more difficult as the Civil War approached.

Indian Wars. This long series of conflicts with various tribes occurred throughout the nineteenth century. In 1834, the United States set aside territory for Native Americans, but this territory was reduced again and again.

Harriet Beecher Stowe. Stowe was an American abolitionist who authored ***Uncle Tom's Cabin***, which alerted millions of readers to the struggles of slaves during the period of slavery.

Harriet Tubman. An escaped slave like Frederick Douglass, the abolitionist Tubman rescued more than 70 slaves from slavery.

John Brown. Brown was one of the most well-known abolitionists during the mid-19th century, in part because of his violent attempts to try to end the practice of slavery. He was hanged for his involvement in the 1859 raid at **Harpers Ferry** and the murder of five proslavery southerners.

Plessy v. Furgeson. This 1896 Supreme Court decision upheld the segregation that occurred during Reconstruction, allowing for the concept of "separate but equal."

Industrialization during the 1800s

Significant innovations in the fields of agriculture and technology had a great impact on the young nation before the Civil War. The inventions of this era include the steam locomotive and **Robert Fulton's steamboat**, each of which greatly improved transportation and the trade and distribution of goods during the century. **Eli Whitney's cotton gin**, invented at the very start of the nineteenth century, helped turn cotton into a profitable crop and shaped the economy of the American south as a result. **Cyrus McCormick** developed a sophisticated mechanical **reaper** in the 1830s that would greatly improve farming techniques.

The United States continued to undergo a technology-driven industrial revolution after the war. Capitalist enterprises took on new forms, such as the massive Standard Oil monopoly and the national banking network of J.P. Morgan. This new financial order encouraged technological advances. The Transcontinental Railroad, the telephone, the phonograph, the Brooklyn Bridge, the skyscraper, and the first airplane are all products of this era.

These innovations came at a price. Government regulations often failed to keep pace with business development, leading to unethical practices. Conditions for workers were often abysmal. In some cases, such as the Triangle Shirtwaist Company Fire of 1911, these harsh conditions proved deadly.

Key Concepts of Industrialization

Assembly Line. This industrial process involves breaking down a complicated task and having a different worker specialize on each single specific task.

Mass Production. Mass production began in 1798, when standardized parts were first introduced. However, the postwar era saw mass production techniques become a crucial aspect of the growing industrial economy of the United States.

Monopoly. An organization that becomes the sole provider of a product is said to have a monopoly on the product. Monopolies, because they lack competition, can drive up prices without fear of a consumer backlash.

Robber Barons. A derogatory term; robber barons were wealthy and morally questionable businesspersons, specifically those with vast banking or industrial empires.

Trust. This legal device is no longer allowed in American business, but it once allowed the creation of monopolies by placing numerous businesses in the control of a single board of trustees.

The United States in the Twentieth Century

The United States went through unimaginable transformations from the 1890s through the twentieth century. Beginning with the country's imperialism at the start of the century, the United States was involved in several major foreign conflicts that would eventually elevate it to the level of one of the world's superpowers. Its population changed significantly as a result of continued waves of immigration that began after the Civil War. And through the labor movement of the Progressive Era, the conditions and quality of life for those living in America improved significantly.

The Progressive Era

In the decades before World War I, several groups working independently on social reforms managed to make sweeping changes in the practice of democracy, increase the governmental role in social welfare programs, and improve conditions for American workers. Journalists brought unfair labor practices and public corruption to the attention of Americans nationwide. They also reported on conditions in slums, prisons, and asylums, urging readers to press for change. This occasionally led to crucial reforms, such as the Pure Food and Drug Act.

Laborers organized themselves into labor unions. Through collective bargaining and strikes, the unions attempted to improve conditions for the working class. Some of the strikes collapsed, such as the violent homestead strike of 1892. Still, it was the work of the labor unions that ultimately helped establish the idea of the eight-hour day and the weekend.

The federal government was another source of progressive reform. Convinced that monopolies impeded beneficial economic competition, Presidents Theodore Roosevelt and Taft began using antitrust laws to break the corporate empires of monopolies like Standard Oil.

Progressives tackled international concerns, too. In 1898, the United States went to war with Spain.

The short conflict, named the **Spanish-American War**, left the United States in control of several former Spanish territories, including Puerto Rico and the Philippines. Progressives saw this as a form of **imperialism** and campaigned for the independence of both territories. (The Philippines achieved independence in 1946; Puerto Rico is still a territory of the United States.)

An additional example of American imperialism during this time was the construction of the **Panama Canal**. The United States, by supporting an independent Panama in Central America, was granted the right to build the canal when Panama declared its independence in 1903. President Theodore Roosevelt, the driving force behind the construction of the canal, believed in a "Big Stick Diplomacy," which allowed him the right to intervene with small states in Central America. The name of this policy originated from the slogan *Speak softly and carry a big stick*. Roosevelt believed that the Monroe Doctrine should be extended so that the United States could support states like Panama, lest they be interfered with by European nations.

Key Concepts of the Progressive Era

The American Federation of Labor and Congress of Industrial Organizations (AFL-CIO). The American Federation of Labor, founded in 1886, emphasized the organization of skilled workers according to their craft rather than on an industrial basis. In the 1930s, a strong minority group advocating organization according to basic industries formed the Committee of Industrial Organizations. Expelled by the parent organization in 1938, the newly independent Committee became the Congress. In 1955, inresponse to the government's anti-union policies, the AFL and the CIO merged. Today the AFL-CIO is the largest union in the United States.

The Grange Movement. This political movement, organized by farmers in the Midwest and the South, was aimed at regulating railroad companies. The farmers believed they were the victims of illegal price fixing by the railroad.

The Homestead Strike. A blow to the labor movement, this 1892 strike pitted workers against the Carnegie Steel Company. It became a violent conflict and the state militia was called in against the workers. This was followed by another violent and unsuccessful strike: the 1894 strike between railroad workers and Pullman Palace Car Company.

Muckrakers. President Theodore Roosevelt coined the term muckrakers to describe investigative journalists who sought to expose social ills. Famous muckrakers include Jacob Riis, Upton Sinclair, Lincoln Steffens, and Ida M. Tarbell.

World War I

In 1914, the assassination of an Austrian archduke by a Serbian nationalist sent Europe spiraling into war. A complex web of alliance treaties pulled nation after nation into the conflict. President Wilson, reflecting the majority sentiment of the nation, followed a policy of neutrality. This position grew harder to maintain after German submarines sank the passenger liner RMS *Lusitania*, killing 128 American passengers. It became impossible to maintain after the Zimmerman Telegram, a secret communication from Germany proposing a German-Mexican alliance against the United States, was intercepted. The United States entered the war in 1917 and America would lose more than 100,000 soldiers in the war—a loss that was compounded by a worldwide influenza epidemic that started on the filthy battlefields of Europe and eventually claimed the lives of more than 21 million people around the globe.

The United States emerged from the war in a unique position. The nation was now considered a global power on the scale of the European nations. Furthermore, with the Atlantic between it and the ravages of the battlefield, the United States had been spared much of the devastation that wrecked the governments and economies of Europe. Wilson was confident that this newly won status as a global power could be leveraged into a more permanent position of international influence. Wilson lobbied to get the

United States involved in the League of Nations, but Americans instead retreated into a more comfortable isolation.

Key Concepts of World War I

Fourteen Points. President Wilson's 14 principles for peaceful international relations would be worked into the Treaty of Versailles at the end of the war. Unfortunately, the treaty also included punitive measures against Germany that contained the seeds of World War II.

Trench Warfare. One of the characteristics of World War I was protracted fighting between soldiers in heavily fortified trenches.

U-boat. One of many technological inventions used in the war, the U-boats (submarines) were used most famously by Germany, which used them to terrorize shipping lanes. Machine guns, bombers, tanks, and chemical weapons were other recent innovations used on the battlefields of World War I.

The 1920s

Called the Roaring Twenties, the decade after the war was marked by an economic boom. Stock market speculation, driven in part by unstable spending practices, fueled stock values and brought Americans who previously relied on other investments into the market.

This prosperity also brought sweeping social changes. After nearly a century of dedicated suffragette agitation, women were finally given the vote in 1920. This groundbreaking event in the women's suffrage movement was made official with the passage of the Nineteenth Amendment.

Finally, in what is often considered the greatest legislative failure in American history, the creation, importation, sale, and consumption of most alcoholic beverages was outlawed. This national ban, known as **Prohibition**, began with the enforcement of the Eighteenth Amendment in 1920. Violations of the law were rampant and the money to be made in providing illegal bootleg liquor actually encouraged the growth of organized crime. The amendment authorizing Prohibition was repealed in 1933.

This long economic boom came to a sudden halt with the stock market crash of 1929. In one day, stocks lost $14 billion in value, and $30 billion for the week. It was the beginning of a long downward spiral.

Key Concepts of the 1920s

The Harlem Renaissance. This artistic and intellectual revolution in the African American community set the stage for the Civil Rights movement to come. Key players during this time include author Zora Neale Hurston and poet Langston Hughes.

Red Scare. The first of two panics about supposed communist infiltration, this scare led to the deportation of nearly 6,000 people.

Lost Generation. A loose collection of postwar artists and thinkers, the Lost Generation energized the arts by helping introduce modernism to American audiences.

The Great Depression

The exact cause of the global economic depression that caught up the United States for nearly a decade is still debated. Blame has been assigned to the expansion of the money supply, the contraction of the money supply, a decline in international trade, corruption in big business and banking, and the incompetence of government officials. Whatever the cause, the effect was clear. In the United States, unemployment reached 25%. The incomes of those still employed decreased, sometimes by as much as 50%.

President Franklin Roosevelt launched wave after wave of government reforms. Collectively, these reforms are known as the **New Deal**. Work programs like the Civilian Conservation Corps, the Tennessee Valley Authority, and the Works Progress Administration put millions back to work. New regulatory bodies were created, such as the Securities and Exchange

Commission. Price and wage regulations were put in place.

The Agricultural Adjustment Act paid farmers to slow their production in order to stabilize food prices.

The National Industrial Recovery Act outlined codes for fair competition in industry.

The Securities and Exchange Commission was established to regulate stock market.

The Federal Deposit Insurance Corporation insures bank deposits in the case that banks fail.

The Public Works Administration built roads, public buildings, and dams.

The Tennessee Valley Authority brought electric power to parts of the Southeast.

Historians debate the practical effect the New Deal may have had on the severity and duration of the Depression. Regardless, Roosevelt's programs were extremely popular with much of the country and some of his aid programs remain in place today.

Like so much else about the Depression, what ended the crisis is unclear. Some argue that the ups and downs of the economy are cyclical and the Depression ended naturally, as all downturns must. Others feel that the economic crisis was ended by an increase in government spending at the start of an even greater crisis: World War II.

Key Concepts of the Great Depression

Dust Bowl. Poor land management caused crop failures and massive sandstorms in the Midwest. Hard-hit families left their farms and migrated, often to California. Regardless of where they were from, these migrants were often called *Okies* since many (but not all) came from Oklahoma.

Hoovervilles. Large collections of temporary housing created by the legions of homeless during the Great Depression, in the public mind these villages were symbols of government inaction under Hoover (after whom they were named).

Organized Crime. The lasting effect of Prohibition was to organize illegal alcohol producers into large syndicates. Soon the syndicates branched out into other illegal activities. The Federal Bureau of Investigation was created in part to battle these crime syndicates.

World War II

The Great Depression had spurred the growth of fascist and militaristic governments in Europe. The Spanish government fell to fascism in a coup. Then the fascist governments of Germany and Italy began programs of conquest and colonialism. In Asia, the militaristic government of Japan began its own program of expansion.

As it did at the beginning of the previous World War, the United States proclaimed neutrality. However, this neutrality did not prevent the government from lending financial and material aid to democratic countries like England and France. On December 7, 1941, Japanese forces attacked the U.S. naval base at **Pearl Harbor**, Hawaii. The United States entered the war against the Axis powers, with troops fighting on two fronts: Europe and the Pacific. Mussolini, the Italian dictator, was overthrown by his own government in 1943. The Germans, now pushed back to their own capital, surrendered on May 7, 1945. The Japanese surrendered on September 2, 1945, after the United States dropped two atomic bombs, the first on the city of Hiroshima and the other on the city of Nagasaki.

President Harry S Truman's decision to drop the atomic bombs on August 6 and August 9, 1945, had significant consequences. While it led to Japan's formal surrender on August 15, the dropping of the "Little Boy" bomb on Hiroshima from the Enola Gay bomber and the "Fat Man" bomb on Nagasaki killed between 150,000 and 250,000 people in those cities during the first few months, mostly civilians. The bombings followed the **Potsdam Declaration**, which issued the terms of surrender for Japan and was rejected by the country. Truman had said that his decision to drop the bombs was to swiftly end the war.

Key Concepts of World War II

Internment. By executive order, more than 100,000 Japanese-Americans, especially those living on the West Coast, were relocated to camps called *war relocation centers*. Despite this violation of their rights, many Japanese-American citizens fought for America in World War II.

The Lend-Lease Act. Passed prior to the United States entering the war, this act authorized shipping war materials to countries whose defense was considered essential to the United States.

The Manhattan Project. The project to build the first atomic bomb was named after the program's original location on the island of Manhattan in New York City.

The Marshall Plan. Secretary of State George Marshall drew up a massive plan for assisting European reconstruction. More than $13 billion (between $100 and $500 billion at current values) was spent to rebuild Europe.

The 1950s and the Cold War

Just as victory in World War I had led to a period of economic prosperity, the decade after World War II was a boom time. (In fact, the explosive population growth after the war is called the **baby boom**.) However, America's new status as an international superpower meant that it could not retreat into isolationism. America would provide a home for the new United Nations.

The spread of global communism was considered a dire threat to the United States and other democratic countries. Shortly after the destruction of the Axis powers, the Soviet Union (Union of Soviet Socialist Republics, or USSR) emerged as a second superpower. The USSR refused to relinquish control over territories it seized while pushing back the Germans, and invaded Czechoslovakia in 1945. In 1949, communist revolutionaries took control of China and communist dictatorships came to power in several Southeast Asian and Latin American countries.

The United States and its democratic allies decided on a policy dubbed *containment*. President Truman declared that the United States would act to prevent the spread of communism wherever it was deemed a threat to democracy.

In 1950, the United Nations decided to take military action in Korea. North Korean communists, aided by the Chinese, had invaded democratic South Korea. Americans soldiers joined an international force that fought against the Chinese and North Koreans until the cease-fire was agreed on in 1953.

The fear of communism abroad took on a virulent form at home. Senator Joe McCarthy began a second Red Scare. He began exposing alleged communist subversives. His charges are now considered dubious at best, but the lengths to which the senator was allowed to pursue alleged subversives reveals how widespread anxieties about "the red menace" were.

Key Concepts of the 1950s and the Cold War

Brinkmanship. First advocated in 1956, this was the policy of pushing issues with the Soviet Union to the brink of a nuclear exchange on the assumption that the USSR would always back down. This policy's greatest test would come later during the Cuban Missile Crisis.

Brown v. Board of Education of Topeka. This unanimous landmark 1954 Supreme Court decision overturned the decision made more than 50 years earlier with *Plessy v. Ferguson* that permitted segregation. Declaring that "separate but equal" is unconstitutional and that "separate educational facilities are inherently unequal," *Brown v. Board of Education of Topeka* required public schools to integrate black and white students and desegregate their classrooms.

Domino Theory. One of the beliefs of U.S. foreign policy leaders was the domino theory. This held that every country that turned communist set up another country to turn communist. This belief fed into the policy of containment.

The Iron Curtain. Winston Churchill coined the phrase *iron curtain* to describe the barrier of hostility and distrust that existed between democratic and communist countries.

McCarthyism. Inspired by Joe McCarthy's charges, McCarthyism is used to describe the action of making accusations of patriotic disloyalty without evidence.

North Atlantic Treaty Organization (NATO). The North Atlantic Treaty Organization is a mutual defense pact that was meant as a democratic power balance to the Soviets. Although NATO has outlived its original purpose, it still exists today.

The 1960s and 1970s

The 1960s and 1970s were a time a great social upheaval. A combination of international and domestic factors fueled sweeping changes throughout American society.

Pursuing a policy of containment led the United States into its longest and most controversial conflict at the time: the Vietnam War. Since the Korean War, there had been conflicts with communism, notably in Cuba. But the Vietnam War was unique in both its duration—from 1959 to 1975—and the civil unrest it fueled. Protests and acts of civil disobedience aimed at ending the war had the broader effect of politically galvanizing large sections of society.

The public struggle over Vietnam coincided with the largest push for African American rights since the Civil War. Protesting lasting political and social inequalities, civil rights activists managed to move their long struggle into the mainstream consciousness of America. This culminated in the passage of the landmark **Civil Rights Act of 1964**. This had an empowering effect on other minority groups, especially women's rights groups and advocates for the rights of Hispanic laborers.

Finally, the faith many Americans had in their government received two rapid blows. The first was the 1963 assassination of President John F. Kennedy. The second was the resignation of President Nixon after the Watergate scandal. As the 1970s came to a close, the economy suffered a recession and an energy crisis—shortages in gas due to supply restrictions from oil producing countries in the Middle East.

This period also gave birth to a renewed interest in the planet's environment. This movement, called **environmentalism**, was spurred by several environmental catastrophes, including an oil spill off Santa Barbara, California in 1969. The world's first Earth Day was held in 1970, the same year that that the United States created the Environmental Protection Agency (EPA).

Key Concepts of the 1960s and 1970s

Bay of Pigs. An unsuccessful 1961 American-backed invasion of communist Cuba, it was a prelude to the Cuban Missile Crisis of 1962.

Counterculture. An unorganized youth movement with roots in the 1950s and stretching into the 1970s, the counterculture could be understood as an attempt to question, undermine, or provide alternatives to the values of mainstream culture. It was the cultural side of the civil and political unrest of the era.

The Equal Rights Amendment. A proposed amendment would have stated that equal rights could not be abridged because of sex. The power of the growing feminist movement was enough to get it passed by both houses of Congress. However, it was never ratified by enough state governments and failed to become part of the Constitution.

The Great Society. An ambitious collection of social reform packages passed by President Johnson, these reforms included Medicaid, Medicare, and antipoverty measures.

Martin Luther King, Jr. A prominent leader in the civil rights movement, King became an icon for his work to end racial segregation. King's 1963 **March on Washington** and subsequent magnificent "I Have a Dream" speech helped to raise the consciousness of the movement.

Rosa Parks. An African American civil right activist, Parks was made famous for refusing to give up her seat to a white passenger on a Montgomery, Alabama public bus. The 1955 act of defiance helped inspire the **Montgomery bus boycott** and initiated a groundbreaking era of the civil rights movement.

The Late Twentieth Century

The financial stagnation of the 1970s continued until rises in stock values and new markets opened up by the boom gave the economy a needed shot in the arm. Unfortunately, because of a stock crash, a series of recessions, scandals regarding corporate governance, and the overvaluation of Internet-based companies, this rise was not steady after the 1980s.

The social and political turmoil of the 1960s and 1970s led to a conservative backlash. The policy of actively containing communism was left behind. Instead, America and the Soviet Union entered into a costly nuclear arms race. Stung by the loss in Vietnam, America limited the exercise of military power to small, short conflicts (such as the invasion of Grenada) or UN-sanctioned multinational campaigns (such as the first Gulf War).

This conservative backlash was partially to blame for the country's slowness to act when acquired immune deficiency syndrome (AIDS) started to claim the lives of Americans. Cuts to social aid programs meant that the first efforts at combating the spread of the disease were left to private groups. As the century came to a close, the global nature of the health crisis became clear.

This conservative in turn also gave birth to the so-called New Right. This loose coalition of conservative Christians, traditional Republicans, and former liberal neo-conservatives became the political conservative's answer to progressive organizations and coalitions formed in the 1960s and 1970s.

Ironically, the policy of containment was discarded not long before European communism began to crumble. By 1991, Germany was reunited and the Soviet Union had transitioned to an uneasy democracy.

With the end of the Cold War, America had to face the chaos that was left behind as the Soviet Union collapsed. Racial and ethnic tensions once kept in check by the Soviets surfaced again in Europe. African and Middle Eastern regimes that were once propped up by the United States or the USSR fell into totalitarianism and turned to fighting one another, or (in rare cases) started making the slow move toward democracy. From this more chaotic picture would emerge the chief military threat of the early twenty-first century: conflicts with militant ethnic and religious groups.

Key Concepts of the Late Twentieth Century

Black Monday. Largely considered the end of Reagan's economic turnaround, this 1987 stock crash cost investors $870 billion in a single day.

The Iran-Contra Scandal. Members of the Reagan administration were caught illegally selling weapons to Iran and using the profits to illegally support anticommunist rebels in Nicaragua. Three conspirators in the scheme were convicted of crimes, but they were all pardoned by Reagan's successor, George H.W. Bush.

Militia movement. Throughout the 1990s, local and federal law enforcement clashed with domestic terrorists associated with various radical ideologies. The incidents included the Oklahoma City bombing, the Ruby Ridge shootings, the serial bombings of the Unabomber, and the disastrous shootout in Waco, Texas.

Militant Islam. Starting with the Iranian Revolution, led by the theocratic Ayatollah Ruhollah Khomeini, a radical form of Islam has played an increasingly important role not only in the Middle East, but also in Asia. Before the century closed, radical Islamic governments would appear in Libya, Syria, Afghanistan, and elsewhere.

Government, Citizenship, and Democracy

About 10% of the social studies section (approximately 3 questions) will cover content about the U.S. government, citizenship, and democracy. To get these questions right, you need to be familiar with the different levels of government—from the local up to the federal—and you must know their purposes and forms. For example, you will need to know how many

U.S. senators there are, how they get elected, how often they get elected, and what senators do in their role in the U.S. government.

You may also be asked about the documents in U.S. history that helped to define the government. Many of these documents, such as the Bill of Rights or the Declaration of Independence, were covered in the previous section on U.S. history. You may even be asked about speeches, such as presidents' inauguration speeches or the Gettysburg Address. Finally, the citizenship questions will ask you about your civic rights and responsibilities, such as serving for jury duty or in the armed forces.

The following section focuses on the three branches of the federal government. Then, the chapter reviews the tenets of citizenship, including the ways that citizens can get involved with their government. This includes a discussion of parties, interest groups, and the electoral process. This section also provides a list of some of the rights and responsibilities of U.S. citizens. Finally, the section provides a quick overview of the Constitution and the Constitutional ideas and controversies that still impact our government.

The Federal Government

The United States is a **representative democracy**. American citizens elect representatives who then govern for their constituents. In the United States, every state has a limited level of sovereignty. Certain powers, however, are reserved for the federal government, which is empowered to act on a national level and is considered the highest level of government in the country. There are three branches of the federal government: the legislative, the executive, and the judicial branch. The Constitution's division of the government into three branches reflects the influence of the **separation of powers**.

The term **separation of powers** was coined by French philosopher Baron de Montesquieu to describe a model of government where political authority is distributed among many different positions, ensuring that no single official accumulates too much power. In Montesquieu's time, the contrasting system would have been an absolute monarchy—a form of government where all authority resided in the hands of the king or queen.

Another important aspect of the Constitution's separation of power is the system of **checks and balances**. The founding fathers sought to limit the potential for abuse of power by making each branch answerable to the other two branches in some way. Congress makes laws, but the president can veto a bill or the Supreme Court can overturn the new law. The president must obey the law as interpreted by the Supreme Court, but also gets to choose who serves on the Supreme Court, with the consent of the Senate. These institutional limits are a crucial aspect of the founding fathers' vision of how the United States government could operate as a strong central authority without becoming tyrannical.

The Legislative Branch

The United States Congress is the legislative branch of the government. The Congress consists of two different governing bodies: the **House of Representatives** and the **Senate**.

The House of Representatives contains 435 members. Each member of the House represents a single congressional district within his or her home state. Members do not represent the state as a whole.

Each state in the union gets representation proportional to its population. Currently, California seats the greatest number of representatives, 53. Every ten years, census data is used to adjust the number of representatives allotted to each state. Regardless of population, every state gets at least one representative. As of 2010, seven states had only one representative. Representatives are elected for a two-year term. There are no term limitations on representatives.

To qualify as a representative, the candidate must be at least 25 years old. The candidate must have been a citizen for at least seven years prior to his or her election. Candidates must also be residents of the states they represent. Some states require that candidates live in the districts they represent, but this is not a federal law.

From the general pool of representatives, the members of the two parties with the greatest representation select officers. The party with the greatest number of representative picks the **majority leader**, who becomes the ranking member of that party, and the **majority whip**, an officer whose job it is to ensure party loyalty among the party's representatives. The party with the second largest number of representative selects a parallel set of officers: the minority leader and minority whip. The House also elects a speaker. Because this is an elected position, the speaker usually comes from the majority party. The speaker is the presiding officer of the House, serves as the highest-ranking member of the House, and is second in the line of presidential succession, becoming president in the unlikely event that both the president and vice president cannot fulfill the duties of the office.

Along with the state representatives, the House includes several resident commissioners. These elected officials represent constituencies in federal districts (such as Washington, D.C.), U.S. territories, protectorates, and colonies. Resident commissioners do not have the full participatory rights that representatives have.

As one of the two legislative houses, the House of Representatives shares some legislative powers with the Senate. For example, all bills must be passed by both houses of the legislature before being passed along to the president for approval or veto. However, there are some legislative powers that are reserved for the House of Representatives. All taxation legislation must originate in the House. Only the House of Representatives can impeach federal officials. Impeachment is the first of two steps needed to remove a federal official from office. The second step, conviction, is the job of the Senate. Finally, in the case of an electoral election deadlock, the House elects the president.

The Senate is the other house of the legislature. In accordance with the Constitution, every state is represented by two **senators**. These senators represent the entire state rather than the constituents of a single district. The senator who has held office the longest is called the **senior senator**. The other senator is known as the **junior senator**. Senators are elected for a six-year term. There are no term limits on senators.

To qualify for the office, the candidate must be at least 30 years old. The candidate must have been a United States citizen for at least nine years prior to his or her election. Finally, the candidate must reside in the state he or she wishes to represent.

The Senate has two unique officer positions. First, the vice president acts as the president of the Senate. The Senate also elects a president *pro tempore* (Latin for "temporary president") who acts as the president of the Senate when the vice president cannot perform the duties of his or her office. As in the House, the party with the most members in the Senate is called the majority party. The party with the next greatest number is the minority party. In cases of a tie, the party affiliation of the vice president determines which party becomes the majority party. Each party elects a party leader, who acts as the chief spokesperson for the party. Each party also elects a whip, who works to maintain party unity on key votes.

As with the House, some powers are reserved for the Senate. The Senate has the power to "advise and consent" over presidential appointees, meaning the Senate approves or blocks most federal appointees. Only the Senate ratifies treaties with foreign governments. In situations involving a deadlock in the Electoral College, the Senate elects the vice president. Finally, although the House can impeach a federal official, only the Senate may try and convict impeached officials.

The Executive Branch

The president, the vice president, and the majority of the vast bureaucracy of the federal government make up the **executive branch**. It is the single largest branch of the government, employing nearly five million people. It includes the president's cabinet, the members of their departments, the diplomatic corps, the armed services, the park service, the Federal Bureau of Investigation, the postal system—any part of the federal government that does not work for the legislature or the court system.

In the Constitution, the legislative role of the president was clear. The president may sign and approve or veto and reject legislation passed by Congress. The Constitution clearly identified the president as commander in chief of the armed forces. It also gave the chief executive the power to appoint judges, including justices of the Supreme Court, and grant pardons and reprieves. Finally, within the limitations of the Senate's powers to "advise and consent" and ratify treaties, the president can appoint federal officers and make treaties with foreign powers.

All the other powers assumed by the president of the United States come under the relatively ambiguous constitutional mandate that the chief executive "take care that the laws be faithfully executed." As the laws of the nation have expanded, the president's authority and power have increased in direct proportion.

The president is elected indirectly by the **Electoral College**. The Electoral College is discussed in detail in the section on voting. The president is elected on a slate with a vice president. Presidents are elected to a term of four years. The Constitution limits the president and vice president to two terms in office. The vice president can, however, then run for the office of president and, if successful, serve another two terms as president.

To qualify for the office of president, the candidate must be at least 35 years old. The candidate must be a natural-born citizen of the Unite States. Finally, the candidate must have been a resident of the United States for at least 14 years prior to the election. No candidate who held the office previously, but was removed by impeachment and conviction, may hold the office again. The candidate for vice president must possess the same qualifications. Finally, under the Constitution, the president and vice president cannot reside in the same state at the time of election.

Judicial Branch

The **judicial branch** is the federal court system. The federal court system is organized in a hierarchy. At the top is the **Supreme Court**. Underneath the Supreme Court are various courts of appeals. Beneath the courts of appeals are numerous district courts. There are 11 federal court districts. Each district may contain several federal courthouses.

At the lower levels, the judicial branch conducts legal proceedings regarding federal laws. Federal courts also hear cases that arise from United States treaties, cases that involve foreign ambassadors in the United States, cases in which the United States government is a defendant, cases involving complaints between the citizens and governments of two different states, and bankruptcy cases.

The highest court in the land, the Supreme Court, deals with interpretations of the Constitution and acts as a check to the other branches through the power of judicial review. The Supreme Court can strike down or nullify a law deemed unconstitutional.

Judges at all levels of the judicial branch are presidential appointees. They are usually lawyers, state judges, or legal scholars, but there is no requirement for the office other than a presidential appointment. As with all presidential appointees, the appointment of all judges is subject to senatorial review under their power to advise and consent. Nine judges currently sit on the Supreme Court. The Constitution does not specify the number of judges that should sit on the Court, so the number has been left up to Congress to specify. Once appointed, judges may hold office "during good behavior," an archaic way of saying that they hold the position for life unless removed for criminal actions or an ethical breach.

Although originally conceived as a stop on legislative abuses, the power and importance of the judiciary has steadily grown over the years. With its sweeping power to define federal law combined with the constitutional guarantee of "equal protection under the law," a federal court decision, especially a Supreme Court decision, can have a massive effect on the laws of the country. Throughout the 1960s and 1970s, social reformers made extensive use of the federal court system as an instrument for making social policy. Because it was insulated from political pressure and capable of making declarations that can supersede state laws, activists viewed the court system as a more efficient way to refine the law than the legislative process. However, the political direction of the judiciary can change over time.

Other Forms of Government

Federalism is a political philosophy that holds that the government is formed by a voluntary gathering of people who consent to be ruled over by a constitutionally limited central body. In American politics, the contrasting philosophy is often described as *anti-federalist* and places an emphasis on the decentralization of power. Typically, federalists favor a strong national government, while anti-federalists would prefer that the balance of power tip in favor of the states. Historically, the trend in American politics has been one of increasing federal power.

In a **monarchy**, one person from a royal family is the ruler; absolute monarchs have complete authority. A **constitutional monarchy** is a system of government with a monarch and a parliament. The monarch, such as a king or queen, may be the head of the state, but the parliament is provided with authority. Examples of constitutional monarchies in the world include Australia, Canada, Denmark, New Zealand, the United Kingdom, and nearly 20 other countries. A constitutional monarchy is a type of parliamentary system.

An **oligarchy** is a government that is governed by a small upper-class group. In an oligarchy, the leaders are not elected by the people.

A **parliamentary system** is a system of government in which the members of the executive branch are drawn from the legislature. This presents a situation without an obvious separation of powers because the executive branch is therefore accountable to the legislative branch. The head of the parliament is elected by the legislature, for example, not directly selected by the electorate. Compared to the presidential system of the United States, the checks and balances are not as apparent.

Citizenship

The following section discusses the ways in which U.S. citizens can influence their government. This covers voting, party participation, and special interest groups. The section also includes the rights and obligations of U.S. citizens, such as economic rights and the importance of jury duty.

Voting

The most fundamental way a citizen can influence the American government is through **voting**. In the United States, the job of running elections is left to the states. In the United States, citizens 18 years of age or older, who legally reside in any of the 50 states or Washington, D.C., or are legal citizens living abroad have the right to vote. States may make rules regarding the voting rights of convicted felons and the forms of identification that must be presented by voters, but they may not infringe on any citizen's federally protected rights. In most states, voters must register as a member of a political party or as an independent. This affiliation is nonbinding, but it does affect voter participation. Depending on the state and the party, a voter's party affiliation determines whether they may participate in party-specific votes, such as primary elections.

In the United States, voting is voluntary. Elections are generally held on the first Tuesday after November 1, with exceptions for state-specific special circumstance elections and party-specific voting. Voter turnout is usually highest in presidential election years. In 2004, 60% of eligible voters voted in the election. In 2008, as many as 63% of eligible voters participated in the election. In non-presidential election years, voter turnout usually hovers around 40%.

Although presidential elections draw the highest participation levels, they are also subject to one of the most misunderstood political processes: indirect election by the Electoral College. When a U.S. citizen casts a vote for a presidential candidate, what he or she is really doing is voting to send a specific elector to the Electoral College. Then, 41 days after the popular election, these electors gather in Washington or at their individual states' capital buildings to elect the president.

The exact procedures for an electoral election vary from state to state, but all these procedures must get congressional approval to be considered valid. In most states, the electoral vote is **winner-take-all**, meaning that the winner of the electoral voting gets all the electoral votes in the state counted toward his or her total. Only Maine and Nebraska allow their electors to split their state totals between multiple candidates. After the electoral vote is finished, the states send notification to Congress. One month after the popular election, Congress officially declares the winner of the election. The Electoral College currently includes slots for 538 electors. Each state gets a number of electors equal to the number of representatives and senators it has in Congress. Washington, D.C. also gets three electors, the minimum any state can receive. As of 2010, California has the greatest number of electoral votes with a total of 55. To win an election, a presidential candidate needs to receive 270 electoral votes.

Parties can appoint or elect their electors. These electors are pledged to vote for a specific candidate. In many, but not all, states, this pledge is binding. In rare cases, an elector from a state where pledges are not binding will not fulfill his or her pledge. For example, in 2004, one elector cast a presidential vote for vice presidential candidate John Edwards. Despite the possibility of electors reneging on their pledges, no presidential election on record has ever been decided by the votes of so-called faithless electors.

The reason for the Electoral College and its future are matters of debate. The Electoral College was a product of debates among the framers of the Constitution. In early drafts of the Constitution, the president was elected by the legislature. Many of the framers felt this would leave the process of selecting a president too vulnerable to political dealing and trickery. The proposed solution was to let state legislatures send representatives to elect a president. Some members of the Constitutional Convention proposed election by popular vote, but this idea was not met with enthusiasm. It is unclear why the idea was not pursued further. It may have been that the framers felt popular voting should be restricted to the election of members of Congress. Perhaps the technological limitations of the eighteenth century made the idea impractical. Whatever the reason, a majority of the delegates approved the Electoral College system.

Modern Americans appear to be increasingly dissatisfied with the Electoral College system. Many disapprove of the fact that, under the system, the winner of the popular vote is not necessarily going to be the winner of the electoral vote. Others feel that the uneven distribution of electoral slots means that the relative value of a single vote varies from state to state. Others feel that the winner-take-all system adopted by most states minimizes the impact third-party candidates can make. Unless a third-party candidate can take the entire state, the winner-take-all system effectively eliminates any gains he or she might have made in a region.

Still, the system does have its defenders. Proponents of the electoral model argue that the winner-take-all system tends to minimize turnout difference between the states. All a state's electoral votes will be cast regardless of any temporary spikes or dips in voter turnout. Advocates also claim that the electoral vote system forces presidential candidates to appeal to a broad support base and empowers minority voters. Under a winner-take-all system, getting a tiny lead in the popular vote could produce big leads in the electoral vote. Consequently, no voting bloc can be entirely dismissed.

Political Parties

Despite warnings against their pernicious influence from the founding fathers, political parties have become a permanent feature of the American political landscape. For most of the nation's history there have been two dominant parties. The first of the two great parties were the Federalists and the Democratic-Republicans. The two parties that currently dominate the political scene are the Democrats and the Republicans. The Democratic Party, one of the oldest political parties in the world, underwent a major political shift in the 1960s and 1970s. It now represents the more liberal of the two parties. The Republican Party, originally formed as a counterbalance to antislavery political forces, went through a similar realignment in the 1910s and, again, in the 1960s that made it the conservative party of the United States.

There is a long tradition of third parties in the United States. Some of these minor parties coalesce around a specific issue, such as the Anti-Mason Party or Free Soil Party, while others were created to combine the efforts of broad constituencies that, for some reason or another, do not find a home in the major parties. The Populist Party is an example of this kind of broad-based third party. Third parties tend to do better in local elections than on a national level. While third party candidates have won House and Senate seats in the past, none has ever won more than five states in a presidential election.

Parties have a major impact on the American political system. Parties provide major funding for their candidates. They organize the political efforts of their large and often diverse membership. Although there is no constitutional mandate for a two-party system, the two parties are now such an important feature of American politics that many political institutions have developed traditions around their existence. For example, the positions of the majority and minority party officers in the House and Senate reflect the two-party split. Despite how entrenched the party system is, there are some common criticisms of the party system. Some critics have suggested that a two-party system suppresses original political ideas. Because parties must appeal to a broad base of people, parties tend to emphasize non-radical, middle of the road positions. Furthermore, others have suggested that parties, by promoting party insiders, discourage candidates with nontraditional backgrounds.

Special Interest Groups

The right of Americans to attempt to influence their politicians is protected by the First Amendment of the Constitution. When enough people share the same concerns, they may combine their efforts and form a **special interest group**. A special interest group is any coalition of people that attempts to sway the political process to further its own agenda. Special interest groups can be built around a specific issue, to promote a specific candidate, or advance the interest of an affinity group, such as agricultural industries or senior citizens. **Lobbying** is the term given to the influential efforts of the interest groups; more than 17,000 professional lobbyists operate in Washington.

One of the important ways special interest groups can influence politicians is by providing financial campaign assistance. There are extensive laws regulating the amounts interest groups may contribute to candidates or political parties. Still, even with these limitations, the amount of money involved is considerable. In a nine-year span, from 1998 to 2007, the special interest groups representing the finance, insurance, and real estate industries contributed nearly $3 billion to various political campaigns. Each year since 2003, lobbyists from across the spectrum have spent more than $2 billion on campaign financing.

Lobbyists also influence lawmakers through education efforts. Lobbyists spend time communicating to lawmakers the concerns and ideas of the special interest groups they represent. In extreme cases, special interest groups and their lobbyists go as far as to actually draft legislation that lawmakers then submit to Congress.

Though lobbyists are regulated and the rights of special interest groups are well-established, many people have important criticisms of special interest groups and lobbyists. Critics have suggested that the vast sums of money corporate lobbyists can raise cause politicians to give contributing industries preferential treatment. They charge that these campaign contributions are little more than bribes. Others critics feel that the connections between lobbyists and politicians have grown so close as to create a culture of favor swapping that locks out the politicians' real constituents: the voters. The critics often point to the great number of lawmakers who, on leaving office, find jobs as lobbyists. Finally, after a series of public scandals involving illegal financial contributions and under-the-table gift giving, many have argued that current regulations on lobbyists are not strict enough.

The Formation of Political Beliefs

In the 1960s and 1970s, the question of just how citizens develop their political beliefs became a subject of intense interest to sociologists and political scientists. The results of their studies suggest that the two main factors in the development of political identity are the family and education institutions. Families are important vectors of political ideals. According to one study, parents who identify with the Democratic Party have a 66% chance of producing offspring who identify with the Democratic Party. The same is true of households headed by Republican parents: 51% of them are likely to have children who eventually identify themselves with the Republican Party. Even independents pass along a sense of political identity to their offspring. Independent parents have a 53% chance of having children who do not align themselves with either major political party. Along with family members, schools are the second major source of political socialization. Researchers posit that, while family members have a profound influence on ideological outlooks, schools provide citizens with a majority of their practical information regarding American political processes and institutions.

After these two significant sources of political socialization, research suggests that social organizations, like a workplace or church, are significant sources of political socialization. Finally, social context provides a limited but significant source of political socialization. Social scientists also identify three special sources of political socialization: the life-cycle effect, the period effect, and the cohort effect. The *life-cycle effect* is the term used to describe the seemingly predictable ideological changes that occur as a political agent grows older, such as the general correlation between age and conservatism. The period effect describes the broad political shifts that may occur during historically unique periods, such as times of war or economic depressions. Finally, the cohort effect refers to a political shift, specifically an exception to an overall ideological outlook, that occurs in relation to a person's ethnic or cultural identity.

Rights of Citizenship

The First Amendment of the U.S. Constitution guarantees U.S. citizens several very important rights. The exact text of the Amendment is as follows:

> *Congress shall make no law respecting an establishment of religion, or prohibiting the free exercise thereof; or abridging the freedom of speech, or of the press; or the right of the people peaceably to assemble, and to petition the Government for a redress of grievances.*

This 45-word sentence provides the citizens of the United States with protection of religion, meaning they are free to practice whatever religion they choose. It prohibits Congress from limiting the freedom of speech or the press, meaning that citizens are free to criticize their government and that newspapers are allowed to publish whatever they deem important—so long as the speech does not pose a danger (such as yelling "fire" in a theater) or provide an instance of libel. The amendment also guarantees the freedom of assembly, which recognizes the action of association as a human right. It is interpreted to mean an individual's right to assemble as well as to join an association.

The last right listed in the First Amendment states that the citizens of the United States may appeal to the government itself for relief when necessary. This last clause in the amendment may have been inspired by the British Stamp Act, which added a tax to all legal documents—including newspapers and playing cards—in 1765. The American colonists attempted to appeal to the king, but the right of their petition was denied.

The Bill of Rights contains other rights of America's citizens, such as the right to bear arms (Second Amendment) or the right to a fair and speedy trial (Fifth Amendment). The First Amendment, however, sets the tone for the freedoms afforded to the citizens of the United States.

In addition to the rights defined by the Bill of Rights, U.S. citizens are also provided with a series of economic rights. For example, U.S. citizens have the right to own property. They may choose whatever line of work suits them and determine whichever employer they like. They shall enjoy the protection of their ideas, with the ability to copyright and patent their products as necessary. As employees, citizens have the right to join a union and they similarly possess the right to forgo the opportunity to join a union.

Responsibilities of Citizenship

A U.S. citizen does not have to vote. He or she does not have to be informed about the issues and the candidates during a local or federal election. Unlike previous times in American history (such as during the Vietnam War), a citizen does not have to be involved in the military in any capacity, nor does he or she have to volunteer any time or money. However, these are all civic-minded obligations. A citizen *does* have a number of legal obligations to fulfill in order to continue to benefit from the advantages of being an American citizen.

Every U.S. citizen must pay a variety of taxes. They must pay sales tax on purchased goods, of course, but they must also pay local, state, and federal income tax on any money made through employment. Money made through investments is taxable as a result of the capital gains tax. Homeowners must pay taxes to their municipalities to pay for services, such as public education. There are many other kinds of tax, some of which only affect a very small percentage of the population, such as the estate tax. However, it is the duty of the citizen to pay his or her share of taxes, based on current tax laws.

In addition to paying taxes, a citizen must perform his or her duties as a juror on jury duty. After all, the court system in the United States is designed so that a defendant's guilt is determined by a jury of peers. Therefore, a cross-section of the American public should be represented on the jury. There are strict penalties for failure to attend jury duty when summoned, though some people are not selected as jurors during the jury selection process. Jurors' jobs are protected during the time that they may serve on a case.

Economics

About 10% of the social studies section of the Praxis II: Elementary Education: Content Knowledge exam will include questions about economics. Of the 30 questions in the section, that means there will be about three questions on economics. To answer these questions correctly, you should be familiar with many of the key terms of economics, such as the different types of economic systems and concepts such as supply and demand. You will also be expected to understand the effect of economics on a state's population, its government, and its resources.

Economic Systems

An economic system is a governmental system that controls how goods are produced, distributed, and used within a society. Different types of economic systems are in place in different countries across the world. Several of these basic economic systems are discussed here.

The United States uses a **market economy**, which means that the cost of goods and services depends on a free price system. In other words, the government does not dictate what the price of goods or services should be, but instead lets the price be determined naturally by supply and demand. Market economies are therefore considered *hands-off* models, including the specific system type of market economy that is frequently used to describe the United States: **capitalism**.

In a capitalistic economic system, all means of production are privately owned—and decisions determining the supply, demand, and price are determined solely by the free market. All **profit**, the difference between costs and revenue, therefore, goes only to the owners and investors in the businesses. An important term to know that applies to a capitalistic market economy is **laissez-faire**. This French phrase is used to describe an economy that is completely free from state intervention, including any potential government monopolies.

Unlike a market economy, a **planned economy** is directed by the state. This *hands-on* approach dictates the prices of goods or services, as well as their production and distribution. Socialism uses planned economy for its economic system. Examples of planned economies in the world include Cuba, Iran, and North Korea. The former Soviet Union was also a planned economy before its collapse drove it toward a market-based economy. A planned economy is also called a **command economy**.

Communism is a social structure that falls into the category of a planned economy. A communist government owns and controls all means of production without any private interest. Because all the resources, including property, are shared in a communistic system, there is no great disparity of wealth among the citizens.

A **mixed economy** combines elements from both a market economy and a planned economy. While the degrees of economic freedom vary among mixed economies, there is some amount of privately owned industry associated with a market economy and some amount of government regulation associated with a planned economy. Some people even refer to the United States as a mixed economy because its government does include regulation, such as environmental requirements and social welfare for the poor.

A **traditional economy** is an older system of economics that relies on custom and tradition.

The Market

The market is determined by a myriad of factors that affect prices of goods and services. The following section discusses many of these factors. Separate sections on microeconomics and macroeconomics then follow.

Goods are a product that can be bought or sold. The product must be tangible, meaning it has a physical presence. If it is not tangible, then the product is considered to be a **service**. For example, a concert provides a service. T-shirts sold at the concert are examples of goods.

The prices of goods and services are determined in part by **supply and demand**. The amount of some good that is available represents supply. The amount of the good that buyers wish to purchase represents demand. As there is more supply of a good, a price tends to fall. As there is more demand of a good, a price tends to increase. This basic economic model determines that the amounts of supply and demand are equalized by price—meaning that the cost of a good or service will serve as the equilibrium between the quantity produced and the quantity purchased.

The economic model of supply and demand is only true when there is **competition**. Competition, two or more businesses attempting to sell the same or similar goods or services, forces businesses to make their terms as favorable as possible, and it drives new products for the consumer. Without a competitive market, such as is the case with a **monopoly**, there is no reason to provide consumers with improved products.

Goods and services may fall into the categories of **needs** or **wants**. Goods that provide needs are items that ensure survival, such as food or clothing. A want is simply a good or service that is desired but not necessarily required. Consumers are limited by their resources from getting all their wants.

Price is also dictated by the **scarcity** of a good or service. Human needs and wants are great, but a society may be unable to provide all these goods and resources. This fundamental economic problem can increase the cost of a good or service. For example, the most valuable baseball card in history is worth millions of dollars because so few copies of it exist. Scarcity is related to the key economic concept of **opportunity cost**. When scarcity reaches a point where it no longer makes sense to purchase the good or service, the second-best option—the trade-off—is an opportunity cost. Opportunity costs can refer to not only financial costs but also time, pleasure, or any additional benefit.

Labor is defined as work of any kind, such as employment. Workers who are involved in any type of labor are described as employed; workers who want to work and are able to work but cannot find a job are called unemployed. The **labor force** is an entire group that supplies the labor. An **unemployment** percentage represents the percentage of people in a labor force who do not have work. The United States uses the employment and unemployment rates as a measure of its economy.

Laborers in the United States make a wage that is equal to or greater than the **minimum wage**. The minimum wage law was created by the government to prevent workers, especially women and young workers, from getting substandard pay that would not support their cost of living. In the United States, the federal law requires a minimum wage of $7.25 per hour, though some jurisdictions within the country (such as the state of Washington) have a higher rate. The concept of minimum wage is not unique to the United States; most countries have some form of minimum wage.

Microeconomics

Microeconomics focuses on the theories that describe the behavior of individual consumers and business. Microeconomics studies how individuals and businesses use their limited resources in a market economy. Included in this field are the behaviors of competitive markets, the descriptions of common business structures, and how rational agents determine the value of goods based on numerous factors. This section covers crucial concepts in microeconomics that you should know for the Praxis II.

Corporation

The modern business corporation is a business structure that, for legal purposes, is a separate entity apart from the identity of its various members. It is, in the eyes of the law, a person. This status as a legal being gives the corporation some special capacities:

- Corporations can participate in legal proceedings. They may initiate and be the target of lawsuits.
- Like individuals, corporations may own assets. The property of a corporation is understood as belonging to the legal entity of the corporation and not the members of the company.
- A corporation has the right to create its own bylines to regulate its internal activities. These rules are understood to originate from the company and not the members of the corporation.
- The employer/employee relationship is between the individual employee and the legal entity of the corporation. The corporation can hire, fire, promote, or demote employees and other agents.
- Like any human agent, corporations can enter into contracts. Then it is the corporation's legal responsibility to meet its contractual obligations.

For identification purposes, corporations are either **S corporations** or **C corporations**. The former is, for whatever reason, not subject to federal income tax while the latter is. Further, a corporation may also be identified as a limited liability company, or **LLC**. In an LLC, the individual owners enjoy the benefit of an agreement that caps their financial obligations to the company. In short, their financial liability stemming from their involvement with the company can only be accounted to a certain level (usually equal to the value of their investment) regardless of the performance or actions of the company. There are other managerial implications to organizing as an LLC, but it is chiefly the risk-minimizing element of the agreement that makes the LLC such an attractive proposition.

Most modern corporations also include transferable shares of ownership, most likely but not necessarily in the form of stock. The importance of this feature is tied to the corporation's identity as a legal entity. The corporation's identity is not altered by changes in ownership.

Corporations are generally characterized by their capacity to outlast the leadership of any given managers. This is to say that personnel changes, even those at the very highest levels of management, do not change the legal identity of the corporation.

Diminishing Returns

The law of diminishing returns says that, in a production system, each increase in variables intended to increase production yields less actual production in proportion to the amount added. The ultimate result is that producers eventually start investing more and more for smaller and smaller increases in efficiency. Economies of scale describe just the opposite situation.

Economies of Scale

In some situations, increases in the scope of production lead to a drop in the costs of production. There are several reasons this might happen. Increases in the labor pool might allow for greater specialization, which in turn could lead to greater efficiency. The cost of raw materials might decrease when bought in bulk. Economies of scale refute the law of diminishing returns (see the previous section).

Imperfect Competition

A considerable portion of microeconomics assumes perfect competition (see **Perfect Competition**, page 223). However, there are a number of real-world conditions that may create imperfect competition. A restricted number of producers or purchasers will create imperfect competition. A **monopoly**, the sole producer for a specific good, and **oligopoly**, a single purchaser for a good, can exert influence over the pricing of goods that can overwhelm the regular logic of competitive markets.

Pricing strategies might create imperfect competition. Price discrimination, when a single provider offers the same good at different prices to different customers, is one such practice. A company might adopt a policy of predatory pricing or supercompetitive pricing. The former involves slashing prices to a level lower than the market will bear in order to force competitors to make the same damaging move. The latter involves just the opposite: It is a policy of inflating prices past what the market will support. Companies benefiting from unique competitive or legal advances might engage in either strategy and either strategy would result in imperfect competition.

Perhaps the most common cause of imperfect competition is government regulation. Paradoxically, government regulators often work to create both perfect and imperfect competition. When regulators enforce antimonopoly laws, they are acting to promote perfect competition. However, the government also enforces various consumer protection laws, hiring laws, safety laws, and environmental regulations. Any of these might require a company to make noncompetitive policies, the impact of which would be reflected in the cost of the goods it brought to market.

Partnership

A partnership is a business structure in which multiple owners or investors all share in the profits and losses of the company they collectively own. There are three major forms of partnership: general, limited, and limited liability partnership (LLP).

A general partnership is formed between two or more owners, and each and every one of the owners is personally liable for the company's debts and legal troubles. Legally, all the partners are considered equal managers.

In a limited partnership, there are two kinds of partners: general partners and limited partners. General partners have all the rights, authority, and liabilities of partners in a general partnership. Limited partners, on the other hand, benefit from limited liability. The tradeoff is that they also lack any managing authority.

An LLP combines the characteristics of a general partnership and an LLC. All the partners in an LLP benefit from limited liability, but there is no division between general and limited partners. All the partners share management authority. Some states allow limited liability partnerships, but this is still relatively rare.

Perfect Competition

The phrase *perfect competition* describes a theoretical market in which only the logic of supply and demand can influence prices. Most economists assume that perfect competition maximizes the efficient use of resources and maximizes profits.

Perfect competition requires a series of important assumptions. First, perfect competition requires that no single producer or consumer has enough power to influence the market in its own favor. This imaginary market of small and autonomous producers and consumers is called the atomic market. Perfect competition also requires the idea that all similar goods are perfectly interchangeable. In this hypothetical market, all companies produce essentially the same product. This aspect of perfect competition is called homogeneity. In this hypothetical market, every agent knows the price every provider is charging. It assumes that a consumer is never fooled by advertising or false claims about products. The firms involved in perfect competition all have equal access to customers and resources. There are also no barriers to a producer entering the market. Finally, perfect competition assumes all the agents in the market act in full freedom and independence.

Price Elasticity of Demand

Price elasticity of demand (PED) describes the relationship between the price of a good and changes in demand. Goods can be placed on a spectrum of perfectly inelastic to perfectly elastic. If a product is perfectly inelastic, then changes in price do not affect the demand for the good. With goods that are perfectly elastic, even the tiniest rise in price will completely eliminate demand. Few goods are perfectly elastic or perfectly inelastic; however, all products fall somewhere on the spectrum.

One good indication of the elasticity of a good is the possibility of substitution by a consumer. When faced with a rise in price, consumers will try to substitute the now expensive good with something less costly. Inelastic goods are necessary and cannot be replaced. If a sick man needs a specific kind of medicine, he must buy that kind of medicine or go without. There is no possibility of substitution. However, when buying a brand of candy at a movie snack counter, unless the consumer is unusually picky, the consumer can freely trade one treat for another and pick the least costly treat.

Profit

Profit, in economic terms, is wealth an investor gains on his or her initial investment after all the costs of the business he or she has invested in are taken into account. In perfect competition, a business would eventually make what is known as normal profit. The definition of normal profit is a bit tricky. A business is making normal profit when total revenues are equal to the total costs of business. Initially this sounds as if the investors would not be making money. The reason for the confusion is that paying the investors enough return on their investment to ensure their continued support is considered part of the total cost.

It is important to note that accountants use the term *profit* differently than economists. Accountants distinguish among several forms of profit. Gross profit is the amount of wealth gained minus the cost of goods sold (the costs directly related to producing whatever the firm sells). Net profit is the wealth earned after all costs have been paid, including employee wages, administrative costs, and such things.

Finally, optimum profit describes the amount of profit that the owners of the firm have determined is what the firm should be earning. This may or may not match the economists' concept of normal profit.

Revenue

The money a business gets from the normal sale of goods is called revenue. When discussing a particular firm's revenue, it is standard practice to focus only on those activities that are considered a normal part of the firm's business. The reason for this is that revenue is an important consideration in financial planning. If a firm wants to project future economic activity, it would want its projections to be based on the typical revenues of the company. Taking into account atypical or one-time infusions of money would give the firm an unrealistic picture of what normal revenues were.

Macroeconomics

Macroeconomics concerns itself with the behaviors of entire economic systems, often on the national or international scale. This section focuses on essential macroeconomic concepts.

Whereas microeconomics studies the behavior of individual buyers, sellers, and business firms, macroeconomics is the term given to the study of large-scale economic activities. Macroeconomics studies the behavior of nations, entire industries, and global systems. The following section briefly reviews some of the concepts and terms that you should know heading into the Praxis II: Elementary Education: Content Knowledge exam.

Business Cycle

The business cycle describes changes in an economic system's overall performance. The cycle includes several stages:

- **Recovery.** This period of expansion is characterized by an increase in the gross domestic product's (GDP) rate of growth. Typically the unemployment rate decreases as well. This period follows a period of economic contraction.
- **Prosperity.** This is an extended period of economic expansion. It is characterized by sustained growth in the GDP and an unusually low unemployment rate. In times of prosperity, capacity utilization (the ratio of actual production output to potential production output) approaches 1.
- **Recession.** This is a period of economic contraction. Typically, it is characterized by negative GDP growth, a slightly elevated unemployment rate, and a decrease in capacity utilization.
- **Depression.** This is an extended period of economic contraction. It is characterized by sustained negative GDP growth and a decrease in capacity utilization. As a general rule, the distinction between a recession and a depression is that the unemployment rate is even worse in a depression and a depression persists for a long period.

Circular Flow of Income

The circular flow of income is a greatly simplified model of the relationship of production and consumption. The consumer gets wages, goods, and services from producers. Producers get revenue and the capacity to purchase needed supplies, called the *factors of production* in this model. In a perfect world, the flow in both directions would reach equilibrium. In fact, government interventions, foreign trade, and leakages (unexpected, one-time adjustments) insure that equilibrium is never maintained.

Federal Reserve Banking System

In 1913, the United States established the **Federal Reserve** as its central bank system. The intention was to create an organization that could regulate the money supply in an elastic way to meet periodic changes in money demand and act as a last resort lender to commercial banks that were in desperate need of a loan. At the time, its chief function was to defend the nation's banks against bank runs, sudden mass withdrawals from a bank by its depositors.

The Federal Reserve, or Fed for short, is a quasi-public bank system. That means it is a mix of government and privately run institutions. It includes a board of governors appointed by the president of the United States, a financial policy group known as the Federal Open Market Committee, 12 regional federal banks, many privately owned banks, and numerous special advisory committees.

The modern Federal Reserve has four goals. First, it moderates long-term interest rates. Second, it helps create economic growth. Third, it tries to decrease unemployment. And, fourth, it helps stabilize prices.

To achieve these goals, the Fed has three significant tools at its disposal. The first of these is **open market operations**. Open market operations are methods for expanding or constricting the money supply through the sale or loan of government bonds or similar items. The Fed mainly uses an economic tool called an overnight repurchase agreement, which acts like a loan. With these repurchase agreements, the Fed can take money in and out of circulation. The amount of money in circulation has an important impact on inflation (see **Inflation**, page 226).

The Fed can also encourage or discourage spending by adjusting **interest rates** on the loans commercial banks make to one another. Because banks frequently lend money to one another, this rate change is eventually felt at the level of the individual borrower.

Finally, the Fed can set the level of **monetary reserves** all member banks must maintain. Because this money cannot be loaned out or otherwise invested, it is effectively taken out of circulation. If the Fed wishes to shrink the money supply, it raises the level of reserves required. If it wishes to increase the monetary supply, it decreases the mandatory reserve level.

Because it uses interest-generating loans as one of its major tools, the Fed does generate a profit on the loans it makes to its member banks. After paying its operational costs, the Fed's remaining profits are returned to the United States government and included in the federal budget.

There have been numerous criticisms of the Federal Reserve. Some economists have accused the Fed of being too susceptible to short-term economic pressures, arguing that its policies reflect the desires of changing political administrations rather than sound economic thinking. Others allege that any artificial manipulation of the money supply interferes with the logic of the market. Some economists even go so far as to argue that the Fed's manipulation of the money supply is what creates the boom and bust cycles in the economy. Other common criticisms are that the decisions of the Fed are not open to enough public scrutiny and that the tools the Fed uses to control inflation are too imprecise, and their effects too irregular, to provide accurate levels of control.

Fiscal Policy

Generally speaking, the term *fiscal policy* reflects the use of government powers to affect the performance of the national economical system. Fiscal policy is often contrasted with **monetary policy**, which is the effort to affect the economy through the regulation of interest rates and the expansion or contraction of the monetary supply.

If the Fed is the chief agent of monetary policy, the federal government is the United States' chief agent of fiscal policy. The most important tools of fiscal policy are taxation and government spending. These tools impact the economy by altering demand for certain goods and by redistributing wealth among the agents within an economic system.

Unfortunately, a fiscal policy that uses a combination of low taxes and extensive government spending has an important down side: the creation of a **deficit**. When government expenditures overtake the tax revenue, the result is a public debt called the deficit. Eventually, the deficit will have to be paid and this means that, sooner or later, the citizens will have to be taxed enough to raise the money. A good fiscal policy will encourage economic growth while minimizing the debt burden on the government and its citizens. Traditionally, the United States government had simply carried a deficit, spending more than it gains through tax revenues. For a brief period in the twentieth century, the government was actually operating at a **surplus**. If the government spends as much as it gains, the economy is said to be **balanced**. In 2009, the United States government was operating with a deficit of more than $1.4 trillion. This enormous deficit set a record for the largest American deficit—and it was three times larger than the previous record, set in 2008.

Three- and Four-Sector Economy

Some economists like to divide the economy into three or four sectors, depending on the profit motive of the economic agents involved in each sector. The first is known as the private sector and includes for-profit businesses and their customers. The second, or public sector, includes government-owned or state-operated institutions. The third sector encompasses nonprofit and charitable operations. This is known as the social sector.

Finally, some economists like to add a fourth sector to the model. This is called the informal sector and includes exchanges that society does not regulate, such as exchanges between family members or friends. The black market, which includes all illegal transactions, might be considered part of the informal economy.

Transfer Payment

A transfer payment is any payment a government makes to a person without an expectation of a direct exchange of goods or services. In the United States, the money paid out through Social Security and welfare would be considered transfer payments.

Gross National Product (GNP) and Gross Domestic Product (GDP)

The GNP is the market value of all the final goods and services produced by the citizens of a country within a year, no matter where those citizens might be geographically. In contrast, the GDP represents the market value of all the final goods and services produced within a country in a single year. The GDP is often considered the single most important measure in macroeconomics. It represents the ultimate financial restriction on any given national economic system and is the closest thing economists have produced to providing an accurate measure of a nation's real wealth.

Inflation

Inflation is an increase in the average prices in a given economic system. Typically, the term is used to describe consumer price inflation, which specifically refers to an increase in the price of consumer goods. It is often measured in the percentage change of the cost of a selected set of goods.

The most common cause of inflation is an increase in the money supply, literally the amount of money available within an economic system. Changes in the supply of goods may also contribute to inflation. Inflation has many clear negative effects. The oversupply of currency decreases the value of money, thereby reducing the spending power of most agents in an economy. It also pushes up wages (which is helpful for employees, but hurts employers) and distorts the prices of trade goods. Still, some slight inflation is not necessarily a bad thing. It may encourage investment and purchases as money saved becomes less valuable as inflation goes on.

Inflation can be countered in economic systems that have a central bank, like the Federal Reserve Bank. Central banks can slow inflation by raising interest rates and slowing the growth of the money supply. The money supply can also be restricted by altering the exchange rate between money and some other commodity, like gold, or by increasing taxation while cutting government spending. In the United States, the Federal Reserve Bank generally tries to keep inflation under 2%.

The opposite of inflation is **deflation**.

International Trade

The modern economy is now a global phenomenon. In 1944, the International Monetary Fund was established to create a global currency system through the monitoring of exchange rates and balance of payments (payments from any one country to all other countries). In 1995, the World Trade Organization was formed with the purpose of removing barriers to international trade. **Globalization** is the term for the integration that trade, migration, and the spread of technology have brought. The study of international trade is a rich and complex field and this single chapter could not cover every concept and idea international economists have developed, but the concepts that follow are crucial to understanding some of the modern issues surrounding international trade.

Balance of goods and services. Also known as the trade balance, the balance of services and goods equals the value of exports minus the value of imports.

Comparative advantage. Some countries have material or legal advantages in the production of specific goods. This lowers their opportunity cost—not only the cost of producing the good, but also the money lost by not focusing on the production of other goods. It benefits countries to produce items with low opportunity costs and trade for items with high opportunity costs.

Currency appreciation/depreciation. When a currency rises in value in relation to other currencies, it is an example of currency appreciation. A currency depreciates when it loses value relative to other currencies. The value of a currency is related to a number of factors, including the GDP of a country, the volume and direction of the country's international trade, and interest rates within the country. A strong currency would be stable (resistant to inflation) and come from a country with high interest rates (which would make investing attractive to a foreign investor).

Import/export quotas. A government may restrict access to foreign markets or restrict competition by foreign producers by placing a quantity limit on imported and exported goods.

Nontariff barriers. A nontariff barrier is any restriction on international trade that is not a tariff. Environmental regulations that barred the important of certain vehicles would be an example of a nontariff barrier.

Tariffs. Tariffs are taxes on imported goods. Tariffs increase the price of foreign goods and make domestically produced goods more attractive to consumers. They are used by nations to protect domestic producers from foreign competition.

Voluntary export restraints. When two governments agree to limit the volume of a particular exported good, they establish a voluntary export restraint.

Test-Taking Tips for the Social Studies Section

Following are of specific tips for the social studies section of the Praxis II: Elementary Education: Content Knowledge test.

Use Your Knowledge of Dates and Eras

You don't have to memorize exact dates to do well on the Praxis II: Elementary Education: Content Knowledge exam. You should, however, have a firm grip on the major events of different eras in history. This knowledge will come in handy when it's time for you to take the test. Even if you aren't sure about the answer to a specific question, knowing the events of its era can help eliminate incorrect answer choices. For example, look at the following question about the Eighth Amendment:

1. The ratification of the Eighth Amendment to the U.S. Constitution
   a. abolished slavery.
   b. banned cruel and unusual punishment.
   c. ensured the right to bear arms.
   d. prohibited the sale and use of alcohol.

You may not know what the Eighth Amendment does. In fact, you probably don't; it's one of the lesser known amendments. However, it is among the first ten amendments, meaning that it was part of the original Bill of Rights. The Bill of Rights was enacted in 1791, not long after the founding of the United States. This early period in the United States history is not known for the abolishment of slavery, choice **a**, or the prohibition of alcohol, choice **d**. Those events are associated with Reconstruction (after the Civil War) and the Roaring Twenties, respectively. So even if you were not sure what the effect of the Eighth Amendment was, you can eliminate half of the possible answer choices by using your knowledge of basic eras of U.S. history.

Then, perhaps you knew that the Second Amendment provides U.S. citizens with the right to bear arms, in which case choice **c** would also be incorrect. This process of elimination would leave you with only one possible answer, choice **b**, which must be correct. The Eighth Amendment banned the use of cruel or unusual punishment.

Know the Basics

There is a lot of information in this chapter. After all, the test could cover any material from prehistoric civilizations up through the present time. Part of that includes knowing all the major developments in the entire history of the United States. It's nearly impossible to memorize everything, but be sure that you're familiar with the basics. What does that mean? Well, the following bullet points reiterate a handful of the important social studies concepts to know for the Praxis II.

- Know the three branches of government and their purposes. Know how the different men and women attain the positions in those governmental roles—and how long they serve in their jobs.
- Know the basic terms of geography, including not only the definitions of physical characteristics (such as peninsula, archipelago, and isthmus) but the manmade delineations of the globe (such as the equator, the prime meridian, lines of latitude and longitude, and the tropics of Cancer and Capricorn.) You're not going to be able to memorize every possible geographic location in the world, but knowing these terms can help when those geography questions pop up.
- Review the major contributions from the ancient civilizations of Egypt, Greece, and Rome. Other civilizations are listed in this chapter, but those are the "big" civilizations to know.
- Be sure you are very familiar with the key documents of the United States. That includes the Declaration of Independence and the Constitution, as well as the Bill of Rights.

Consider Causes and Effects

History is not a series of isolated events, though it can seem that way if you try to memorize the hundreds of names, dates, and events. The Praxis II: Elementary Education: Content Knowledge exam, however, may not only test you on the isolated events but also their causes and their impact on future history. For example, you may be asked about the causes for initial European exploration of the Americas. Or you may be asked about the repercussions of the Civil War. Therefore, whenever you're asked about an event, consider the other events that led up to it.

A question may ask for the events that led up to World War I. The single event that eventually triggered the war was the assassination of Archduke

Franz Ferninand, but many other factors led to that point—such as the nationalism, imperialism, and militarism of the new alliances.

Furthermore, consider the repercussions of a historical event. When the North won the American civil war in 1865, there were many significant impacts. The obvious answer is that slavery was outlawed and that black people were finally granted the right to be U.S. citizens. However, the defeat of the South also led to massive economic and social transformations in a new era called Reconstruction.

Social Studies Practice Section

1. Which river forms part of the border between the United States and Mexico?
- **a.** the Mississippi River
- **b.** the Rio Grande
- **c.** the St. Lawrence River
- **d.** the Missouri River

2. All the following are reasons for the European powers' policy of appeasement prior to World War II EXCEPT:
- **a.** Hitler's actions were seen as a reasonable response to the overly harsh Treaty of Versailles.
- **b.** Diplomats assumed even fascist nations would act to avoid a highly destructive global conflict.
- **c.** Widespread economic depression would have made an effective military response difficult.
- **d.** Fascist advances stabilized the region and benefited France and England financially.

3. What qualifications does Article I, Section 3 of the Constitution set for becoming a U.S. senator?
- **a.** A senator must be 30 years old and a U.S. citizen for nine years.
- **b.** A senator must be 25 years old and a U.S. citizen for seven years.
- **c.** A senator must be 35 years old and be born in the United States.
- **d.** A senator must be 18 years old and a U.S. citizen.

4. A region in the tropical zone is most likely to experience which of the following weather conditions?
- **a.** tornados
- **b.** monsoons
- **c.** blizzards
- **d.** droughts

5. Which 1803 acquisition of land, made by President Thomas Jefferson, added more than 800,000 square miles to the territory of the United States?
- **a.** the Louisiana Purchase
- **b.** the Alaska Purchase
- **c.** the Texas Annexation
- **d.** the Mexican Cession

6. The advance and retreat of a glacier is likely to produce all the following geographic features EXCEPT a
- **a.** moraine.
- **b.** lake.
- **c.** mountain ridge.
- **d.** valley.

7. Which of the following represents a scenario that would have a negative effect on the supply of a good or service?
   a. An oil company raises the per-gallon price of its product.
   b. A positive review in a technology magazine makes more customers interested in purchasing a specific e-book reader.
   c. A new landscaping company provides another option for mowing lawns in the same town.
   d. A drought causes crops of strawberries to dry out and fail.

8. Which ship was NOT involved with Christopher Columbus's initial visit to the Americas?
   a. Mayflower
   b. Niña
   c. Pinta
   d. Santa Maria

9. Which was most responsible for the reduction of the European population by 25 million during the fourteenth century?
   a. immigration to the Americas
   b. the Black Death pandemic
   c. the advent of birth control
   d. outbreaks of polio

10. All the following are characteristic of fascist governments EXCEPT
   a. strict censorship of the media and artists.
   b. a single-party political system.
   c. commitment to free-market economic policies.
   d. use of political spies and fear to control the population.

11. The Voting Rights Act of 1965 outlawed what voting practice?
   a. literacy tests
   b. the exclusion of female voters
   c. poll taxes
   d. property requirements

12. Animal studies have been used in psychology to study all the following EXCEPT
   a. the learning process.
   b. memory.
   c. circulation.
   d. behavior development.

Study the following map, then answer questions 13 and 14.

Population of Countries

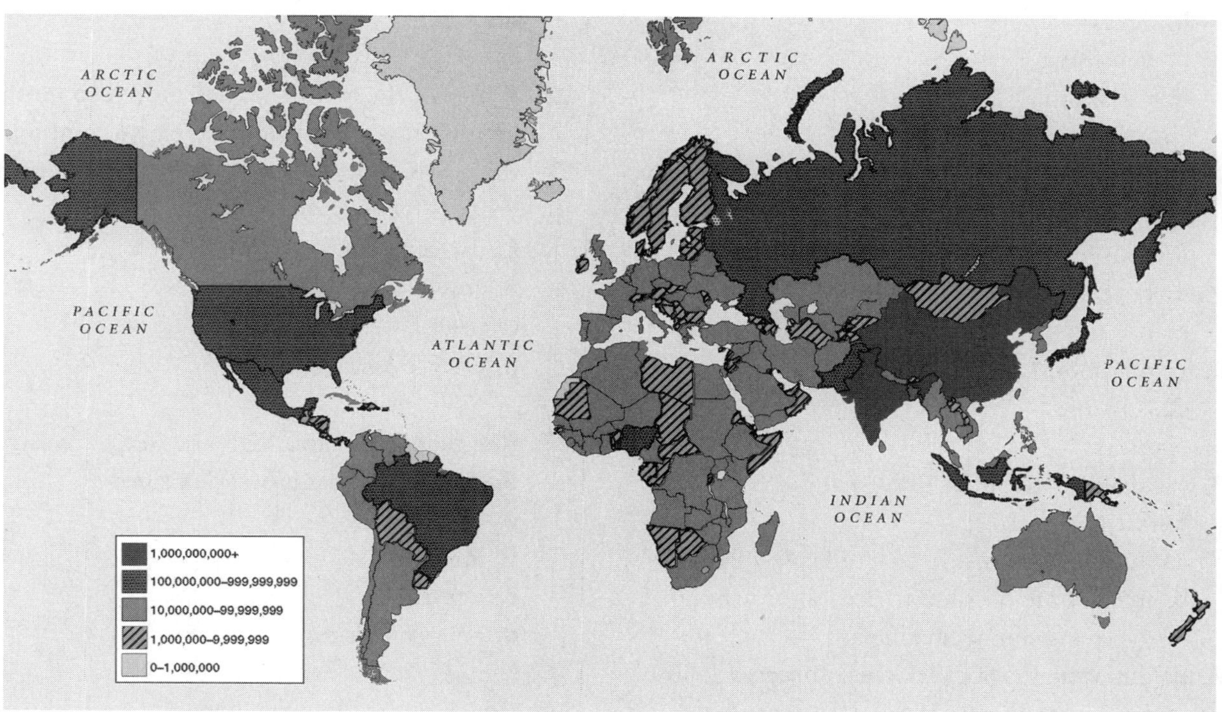

13. Which of the following countries has the greatest number of residents?
- **a.** Canada
- **b.** Egypt
- **c.** Greenland
- **d.** Brazil

14. Which could be the population of Australia?
- **a.** 8,000,000
- **b.** 22,000,000
- **c.** 104,000,000
- **d.** 1,320,000,000

15. The sociological concept of ethnocentrism is most closely defined as
- **a.** the belief that one's own cultural group is superior to others.
- **b.** a group that makes up less than half of a population.
- **c.** the belief that people from different ethnic backgrounds behave in similar ways.
- **d.** the belief that distinct groups should be provided with equitable status within a demographic.

16. The "Trail of Tears" refers to the relocation of Native Americans from their homelands across the United States to an Indian territory that existed in which present state?
   a. Idaho
   b. Texas
   c. Wyoming
   d. Oklahoma

17. Which Civil War battle was the location of a turning point in the war because it prevented the Confederacy's invasion of the North?
   a. Fort Sumter
   b. Lexington
   c. Gettysburg
   d. Concord

18. President Franklin D. Roosevelt did each of the following EXCEPT
   a. leading Congress to enact the New Deal.
   b. making the decision to drop atomic bombs.
   c. declaring war against Japan.
   d. initiating the Social Security program.

19. The First Amendment to the Constitution guarantees each of the following rights EXCEPT
   a. freedom of speech.
   b. the right to form an assembly.
   c. the right to bear arms.
   d. freedom of religion.

20. The landmark Supreme Court case *Plessy v. Ferguson* is best known for
   a. requiring the integration of classrooms across the United States.
   b. declaring that all people of African descent could not be U.S. citizens.
   c. requiring that arrested suspects be told of their rights.
   d. upholding racial segregation under the separate but equal policy.

21. The roots of Islam were in an area that is currently which Middle Eastern country?
   a. Saudi Arabia
   b. Iraq
   c. Egypt
   d. Israel

22. Which of the following tools would be most helpful for an archeologist trying to pinpoint the precise spot of a discovered artifact during an archeological dig?
   a. camera
   b. trowel
   c. level
   d. GPS

23. The geographic area that was used to construct the Panama Canal is best described as
   a. a peninsula.
   b. an isthmus.
   c. a tundra.
   d. an archipelago.

24. Which of the following historic figures during the Civil War era was NOT considered an abolitionist?
   a. Frederick Douglass
   b. Harriet Tubman
   c. Jefferson Davis
   d. Harriet Beecher Stowe

25. Which of the following represents a system of social stratification?
   a. India's caste system
   b. the British House of Commons
   c. the tenets of communism
   d. multiculturalism

26. How did the Cold War achieve its name?

a. It was fought in the frigid climate of northern Russia.

b. There was no direct conflict between the opposing powers.

c. The four countries involved with the conflict began with the letters C-O-L-D.

d. The majority of the war was fought during the last global ice age.

27. Which of the following geographic reasons best explains why Mesopotamia made an ideal cradle of civilization?

a. Its location near the Mediterranean Sea provided convenient access to European trading.

b. Its predictable and temperate weather allowed the ancient population to exist without hardship.

c. Its isolation caused by the neighboring Himalayan Mountains protected it from invasions.

d. Its location between the Tigris and Euphrates rivers allowed for the growth of agriculture.

28. A municipality makes a decision to convert some of its open space to public park space. Which represents a potential opportunity cost of the decision?

a. the theoretical revenue lost from the ability to sell the land to developers

b. the annual costs to maintain the grounds of the public park

c. the amount of money spent by visitors to travel to the public park

d. the time spent by municipal workers to design and create the public park space

29. Which of the following represents an outcome of the War of 1812?

a. The United States annexed the land now occupied by Florida.

b. Trade restrictions were placed on goods exchanged between the United States and Canada.

c. The United States established itself as a strong presence in international affairs.

d. The practice of slavery was outlawed throughout the United States.

30. Which figure from the Scientific Revolution is credited with improving the telescope to achieve greater astronomical observations?

a. Isaac Newton

b. Galileo Galilei

c. Blaise Pascal

d. Nicolaus Copernicus

Social Studies Practice Section Key and Explanations

SOCIAL STUDIES KEY					
ITEM	KEY	SUBSECTION	ITEM	KEY	SUBSECTION
1	B	Geography, Anthrop., Sociology	16	D	United States History
2	D	World History	17	C	United States History
3	A	Gov't, Citizenship & Democracy	18	B	United States History
4	B	Geography, Anthrop., Sociology	19	C	Gov't, Citizenship & Democracy
5	A	United States History	20	D	United States History
6	C	Geography, Anthrop., Sociology	21	A	World History
7	D	Economics	22	D	Inquiry/Processes
8	A	United States History	23	B	Geography, Anthrop., Sociology
9	B	World History	24	C	United States History
10	C	Economics	25	A	Geography, Anthrop., Sociology
11	A	Gov't, Citizenship & Democracy	26	B	United States History
12	C	Inquiry/Processes	27	D	Geography, Anthrop., Sociology
13	D	Geography, Anthrop., Sociology	28	A	Economics
14	B	Geography, Anthrop., Sociology	29	C	United States History
15	A	Geography, Anthrop., Sociology	30	B	Inquiry/Processes

Answers

1. b. The Rio Grande acts as a natural border between Texas and Mexico, so **b** is the right choice. The Mississippi River and the Missouri River, choices **a** and **d**, have their mouths in the Gulf of Mexico, so they do not form a border with Mexico. The St. Lawrence River, choice **c**, acts as part of the boundary between the United States and Canada.

2. d. Before World War II, the European powers attempted to use appeasement to staunch the spread of Hitler's army. It didn't work. But the reasons for attempting the appeasement were many. Germany had been so devastated by the Treaty of Versailles that Hitler's response was tolerated, choice **a**. Diplomats also hoped that even Hitler would have wanted to avoid escalating the war to a global conflict, choice **b**. Furthermore, a depression limited the European powers' ability to fight back, making choice **c** incorrect as well. The Fascist advances did NOT stabilize the region, and France and England did NOT benefit financially from their aggression, making **d** the correct answer choice.

3. a. To be a U.S. senator, a candidate must be 30 years old and have been a U.S. citizen for at least nine years. The qualifications in choice **b** refer to the requirements to be a U.S. representative in Congress. The qualifications in choice **c** refer to the requirements to be a U.S. president. The qualifications in choice **d** refer to the requirements to be a voter.

4. b. Of the weather conditions listed in the answer choices, monsoons are most associated with the tropical zone. The area between the Tropic of Cancer and the Tropic of Capricorn produces monsoons, known to produce great amounts of precipitation in areas like West Africa, India, and Australia.

5. a. The Louisiana Purchase in 1803 added nearly a million square miles of land to the American territory. The Alaska Purchase, the Texas Annexation, and the Mexican Cession all added significant territory to the United States as well, though they all occurred many years after 1803. It was the Louisiana Purchase that was made by Thomas Jefferson and helped define his presidency.

6. c. Glaciers can cause significant effects on the physical geography of a land. They can create moraines, such as Long Island, lakes, or valleys. However, mountain ridges are typically formed by the movement and collision of lithospheric plates. Therefore, **c** is the correct choice.

7. d. The scenario in choice **a** does not affect the supply of oil, though the higher price of a good or service may negatively affect the demand. The scenario in choice **b** will positively affect the demand but will not change the supply one way or another. The scenario in choice **c** will *increase* the supply of a service, not decrease it. Only the scenario in choice **d** represents a decrease in supply because fewer strawberries will be available after the drought.

8. a. Christopher Columbus first traveled to the Americas from Spain with three ships: the Niña, the Pinta, and the Santa Maria. The Mayflower, choice **a**, was the ship used by the Pilgrims who landed at Plymouth Rock in 1620.

9. b. The Black Death, choice **b**, was most responsible for the dramatic reduction in European population during the fourteenth century. Immigration to the Americas, choice **a**, did not begin until several centuries later. Contraceptive practices, choice **c**, actually predate the fourteenth century—though birth control has never been used to reduce a population by such a great percentage in such a short period of time. Polio, choice **d**, has been around since prehistoric times and there have been pandemic outbreaks as recently as the first half of the twentieth century. However, polio is not responsible for the reduction of the European population by 25 million during the fourteenth century.

10. c. Fascist governments employ a censorship of the media, choice **a**, and they have a single-party system, choice **b**. They do NOT, however, believe in a free-market economic system. Fascist governments do not employ a hands-off economic policy that is typified by the free market system.

11. a. The Voting Rights Act of 1965 outlawed literacy tests, choice **a**, which had been used to disenfranchise poor and uneducated voters. Female voters gained the right to vote in the United States in 1920 with the ratification of the Nineteenth Amendment, so choice **b** is not correct. Poll taxes, choice **c**, were abolished by the ratification of the Twenty-Fourth Amendment in 1964. While the requirement of property *was* a voting practice at some time, it was abandoned long before the 1965 Voting Rights Act.

12. c. Psychologists have used animals in studies for many years, in part because the animals can be controlled. These subjects have been essential in studying the learning process, memory, and behavior development, choices **a**, **b**, and **d**. Studying circulation in animals, however, is not something that would be done by psychologists—but rather by biologists or scientists in other fields.

13. d. The country with the greatest number of residents will be the country on the map with the darkest shading. Of the four countries listed in the answer choices, Brazil is the darkest—meaning it has the greatest number of residents.

14. b. The key shows that, based on the shading of Australia in the map, its population will be between 10,000,000 and 99,999,999. The only population listed in the answer choices that falls into this range is 22,000,000, which is choice **c**. This is the estimated population of Australia in 2010.

15. a. Ethnocentrism is best defined as the belief that one's own cultural group is superior to others, choice **a**. A group that makes up less than half of a population is called a minority. The belief described in choice **c** refers to a stereotype; the belief in choice **d** refers to a policy of multiculturalism.

16. d. The Trail of Tears describes the relocation of Native Americans from their home lands to the Indian territory that is represented by modern-day Oklahoma. In fact, the word *Oklahoma*, which means "Red People," is derived from the Native American Choctaw language.

17. c. Fort Sumter was the location where the Civil War began, but it was not a turning point for the war as a victory for the North. Lexington and Concord, choices **b** and **d**, are better known as locations for battles during the Revolutionary War. Gettysburg, choice **c**, was the Civil War battle that prevented the Confederacy's invasion of the North.

18. b. In his first 100 days in office, Franklin D. Roosevelt pushed Congress to enact the New Deal, choice **a**. After the bombing of Pearl Harbor, Roosevelt declared war against Japan, choice **c**, calling it a "date that will live in infamy." The relief programs that he initiated include Social Security, choice **d**. He passed away shortly before the end of World War II, however. Therefore, it was his successor, Harry Truman, who made the decision to drop the atomic bombs on Hiroshima and Nagasaki, choice **b**, effectively ending the war.

19. c. The First Amendment to the Constitution contains several important rights. It prohibits limitations on the freedom of speech, choice **a**. It allows for people to peaceably assemble, choice **b**. It also prohibits any law from interfering with "the free exercise" of religion, choice **d**. The First Amendment makes no reference to the right to bear arms, choice **c**; that right is referenced in the Second Amendment.

20. d. The forced integration of classrooms, choice **a**, was a result of *Brown v. Board of Education of Topeka*, in 1954, which reversed the racist policies of *Plessy v. Ferguson*. The landmark case that declared that all people of African descent could not be U.S. citizens, choice **b**, was the 1857 case *Dred Scott v. Sandford*. Reminding suspects of their rights, choice **c**, is a requirement based on the 1966 Supreme Court case *Miranda v. Arizona*. The separate but equal policy that continued segregation in the United States originated from the results of the *Plessy v. Ferguson* Supreme Court case.

21. a. Islam originated in the area of the Arabian peninsula that is currently Saudi Arabia. The religious center of Islam is Mecca, which is a city in Saudi Arabia.

22. d. Each of the tools listed in the answer choices are used in archeological digs for different purposes. However, only a Global Positioning System (GPS) device, would provide an archeologist with a precise spot of a discovered artifact.

23. b. An isthmus is defined as a narrow stretch of land, usually between bodies of water. This describes the area in Panama perfectly, as it separates the Atlantic and Pacific Oceans with a narrow area of land. A peninsula, choice **a**, is a land mass that is surrounded by water on three sides. An archipelago, choice **d**, is a series of islands. Tundra, choice **c**, is a geographic area that is so cold that the growth of trees is stunted. Panama is tropical, so choice **c** is not correct.

24. c. Frederick Douglass, choice **a**, wrote an autobiography detailing his life as a slave in an attempt to help end the practice of slavery. Harriet Tubman, choice **b**, was also a former slave who was a well-known abolitionist. Harriet Beecher Stowe, choice **d**, authored *Uncle Tom's Cabin*, the famous antislavery book. Jefferson Davis, choice **c**, was the president of the Confederate States of America—and he fought to preserve slavery in the South. Davis was decidedly NOT an abolitionist, so choice **c** is correct.

25. a. A system of social stratification includes a series of hierarchical groups, separated by such factors as wealth or class. The caste system in India is a prime example of social stratification because of its rigid class structures. Communism aims for *no* social stratification, so choice **b** is not correct. Multiculturalism, choice **d**, does not provide an example of social stratification, nor does the British House of Commons, choice **b**.

26. b. There was no actual fighting during the Cold War, which began in the 1950s and lasted until the approximate fall of the Soviet Union. The war earned its name because of that fact. It had nothing to do with the climate, choice **a**, nor was it an acronym, choice **c**. The last ice age ended about 10,000 years ago, so choice **d** is definitely not correct.

27. d. Mesopotamia was an ideal cradle of civilization because of its geographic location between the Tigris and Euphrates rivers, choice **d**. These rivers provided irrigation and drainage, necessary for the growth of agriculture in the area. The rivers also provided food and even building materials such as clay. The ancient civilization of Mesopotamia was not concerned with trading with Europe, so choice **a** is not correct. The weather in Mesopotamia was, in fact, NOT predictable, so choice **b** is not correct. The Himalayan Mountains are far from Mesopotamia and isolation was not a reason that helped make the area a cradle of civilization, so choice **c** is incorrect as well.

28. a. Opportunity cost is considered the trade-off when one economic decision is selected over another. In the case of the public park space, the municipality is no longer able to generate revenue from the land by selling it to a developer, so choice **a** represents an opportunity cost. Choices **b** and **c** do not represent an opportunity cost for the municipality. While opportunity cost can represent intangible products such as time or fun, the time spent by workers to create the park, choice **d**, does not represent a trade-off from NOT building the park.

29. c. The War of 1812 provided an early test for the strength of the young United States. By surviving it, the country established itself as a presence in international affairs, choice **c**. The annexation of Florida, choice **a**, was not associated with the War of 1812. Trade restrictions, choice **b**, were a cause of the War of 1812. The War of 1812 also predated the outlawing of slavery in the United States, choice **d**.

30. b. Each of the individuals listed in the answer choices was an important figure in the Scientific Revolution. However, only Galileo Galilei is credited with the significant improvements to the telescope, which resulted in many important astronomical observations. Isaac Newton, choice **a**, developed the first functional theory of gravity. Nicolaus Copernicus, choice **c**, proved that Earth rotates around the sun—and that Earth is not the center of the universe. Blaise Pascal invented the mechanical calculator and made great contributions to the fields of physics and mathematics, but he is not known for his work in the field of astronomy.

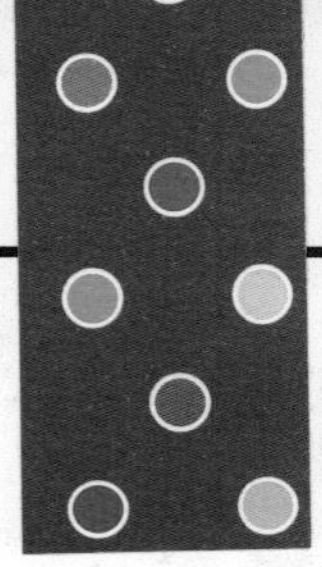

CHAPTER 6 SCIENCE REVIEW

The fourth and final section of the Praxis II: Elementary Education: Content Knowledge test is the science section. Of the 120 questions on the test, 30 will cover material from the science section. Each question will be multiple choice with four answer choices.

About the Science Section

The science section of the Praxis II: Elementary Education: Content Knowledge test will include questions on a wide range of scientific concepts from the three major branches of science: earth science, life science, and physical science. The science section will also include a handful of questions about science in personal and social perspectives (such as the science of personal health), science as inquiry, and the processes of science.

To succeed on the science section, you will need to be familiar with key scientific terminology, processes, principles, and concepts. You won't be expected to be an expert in any one scientific field, but you should have a basic understanding of how science operates in the real world. You should be able to explain a variety of real-life scientific topics to young students.

This chapter is divided into the three major branches of science that are tested on the Praxis II: Elementary Education: Content Knowledge test:

- earth science, such as the history of Earth and the universe
- life science, such as the function of cells, organs, and life cycles
- physical science, such as the states of matter and energy

On the Praxis II, there should be an equal number of questions for each of the major areas of science. There will also be a few questions that test one of the following minor sections of science:

- science in personal and social perspectives, such as personal health (hygiene)
- social perspectives of science, such as a career in science
- science as inquiry, such as proper investigation techniques
- science processes, such as the systems and organization of science

These concepts are covered toward the end of the chapter.

Earth Science

About 30% of the science section of the Praxis II: Elementary Education: Content Knowledge test—or about nine of the 30 questions—will include questions relating to earth science. This includes the history and structure of our planet, as well as the processes, patterns, and cycles of Earth. This section includes not only questions about our home but questions about other celestial objects as well—such as the moon, the sun, other planets, and even other stars and galaxies within our universe. The following subsections cover the information that you should be familiar with to correctly answer the earth science questions on the science section of the Praxis II.

Structure of Earth

Earth has different layers, each with its particular characteristics. Earth's metallic **core** is composed mostly of iron and some nickel, and has a solid inner core and liquid outer core. The circulation of liquid iron in the core generates Earth's magnetic field. Outside of the core is **mantle**. The mantle is mostly solid and comprises about 70% of Earth's volume. The upper layer of the mantle reaches to below 10 to 50 km below Earth's surface and has produced Earth's crust, the rocky outer shell of the planet.

The **lithosphere** consists of a thin upper part of mantle and the outermost crust. Below the lithosphere, the **asthenosphere** contains malleable rock that can move over time. The rock of the lithosphere consists of cooler, brittle rock. The crust under the ocean is about 10 km deep and under the continents is about 50 km thick. The following graphic shows the relationship of the major layers of Earth.

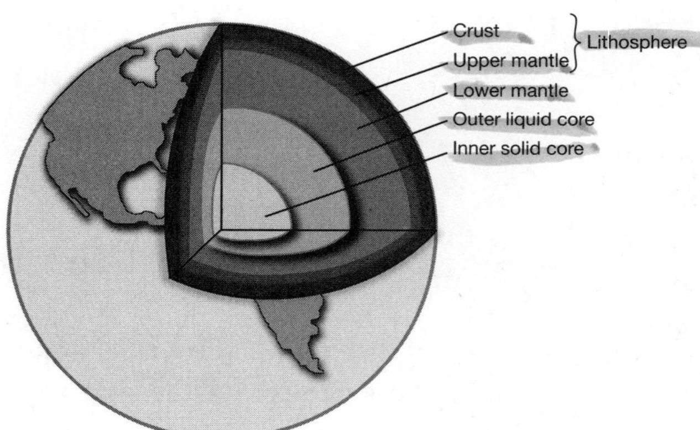

The crust contains a variety of rocks. **Igneous rock** is molten magma that has cooled under the surface of the Earth, and is usually associated with volcanic activity. **Sedimentary rock** is created by underwater sediments in the ocean compacted by pressure as the sediment layer builds up. **Metamorphic rock** is formed when either igneous or sedimentary rock is subject to extreme heat and pressure.

Earth's Atmosphere

The atmosphere has a mixture of gases: nitrogen (78%), oxygen (21%), argon (0.9%), and carbon dioxide (0.038%). Water vapor depends on the climate and ranges from 0.3% to 4%.

The atmosphere is divided into five major layers. The **troposphere** is near the surface of Earth and rises about 15 km. Weather takes place in the troposphere and is the location of almost all clouds. Pressure and temperature decrease with height in the troposphere. The next layer is the **stratosphere,** which spans up to about 50 km. The atmosphere is less dense and temperature increases with height, because ozone in this layer absorbs much of the ultraviolet energy from the sun. The following layer is the **mesosphere**, which extends to about 80 km. Temperature again decreases with altitude and this is where most meteors burn up when entering the atmosphere. Beyond the mesosphere, the atmosphere varies greatly. The air in the **thermosphere** is extremely thin and there is an abundance of ions. Temperature increases within the thermosphere with height and can reach 1,500°C. Above the thermosphere is the outermost layer of the atmosphere, the **exosphere.** At this altitude, this layer has very few particles .

Within those five major layers are several other important atmospheric layers. The **ozone layer**, a layer of the atmosphere with a high concentration of ozone, is located within the lower part of the stratosphere. This layer is known for its ability to absorb nearly 99% of the sun's dangerous ultraviolet light—and the fact that manmade products, such as chlorofluorocarbons, have been responsible for its destruction. The **ionosphere** is the upper part of the Earth's atmosphere and encompasses both the mesosphere and the thermosphere.

Air pressure is the force created by the weight of the air. In Earth's atmosphere, the air weighs less with increasing elevation; as a result, the air pressure also decreased with increasing elevation. The air is so thin and there is so little oxygen above about 8,000 meters that mountaineers refer to that height as the *death zone*. Atmospheric pressure is measured with an instrument called a **barometer**.

The northern and southern lights, known in the Northern Hemisphere as the **aurora borealis** and in the Southern Hemisphere as the **australis borealis**, are natural atmospheric light displays that are visible mostly within the Arctic and Antarctic circles. Formed in the ionosphere, the northern and southern lights are a result of Earth's photons emitting light as they collide with solar wind particles and regain electrons.

Hydrology

Hydrology is the study of all water on Earth, including its movement and distribution. The water cycles are addressed in the following section on the cycles of Earth.

The **hydrosphere** is all the water on Earth's surface, groundwater, and water in the atmosphere. Water is vital to living things and an important factor in climate, weather, and erosion.

The oceans cover about 71% of Earth's surface and contain about 97% of the total water on Earth. The other 3% of the total water on Earth exists mostly as freshwater in lakes, ponds, rivers, and streams. Most plants and mammals require access to freshwater. The ocean acts as a temperature buffer, and ocean currents affect climates by transferring cold and warm air and precipitation to land. Although the oceans are all interconnected in one global body of water, names are given to the major oceanic divisions, such as the Pacific Ocean, the Atlantic Ocean, the Indian Ocean, the Arctic Ocean, and the Southern Ocean.

All the oceans are saltwater bodies, though the average salinity of the oceans varies slightly. The volume of the oceans is massive because the average depth of the oceans is about 3,800 meters. The deepest part of the ocean is nearly 11,000 meters below sea level. The oceans are home to hundreds of thousands of species.

Winds on the surface of bodies of water have the ability to form **waves**. The wind's energy is transferred to the water during this process. Waves can travel thousands of miles in the ocean. When a wave reaches shallow water near land, it is pushed upward. Eventually, it cannot support itself and must break, causing a wave to crash on the shore.

Earth's Processes

Earth is constantly undergoing a series of massive transformations, both below and above the surface. The following sections describe several of the most important processes of change to know for the Praxis II.

Movement of the Tectonic Plates

The uppermost layer of Earth, the lithosphere, is broken up into several **tectonic plates** that shift along the surface of the asthenosphere. As these plates move in relation to each other, the collision or separation of the plates exerts forces that cause several important transformations to Earth's landscape. The continual movement of the tectonic plates causes **continental drift**, which, as its name suggests, refers to the gradual movement of the continents to drift along the surface of the planet. In fact, it is widely accepted that the continents had all once been joined together in a supercontinent known as **Pangaea**.

The movement of the tectonic plates is also responsible for **earthquakes**, destructive releases of energy in Earth's crust caused by seismic waves. As tectonic plates move away from each other or toward each other, the disturbance in the rock releases massive amounts of energy. This generally happens by a **fault**, a fracture between two plates. The location on the surface of Earth directly above the focus of the earthquake is called the **epicenter**. This is generally the area with the strongest earthquake tremors, measured and recorded by instruments called a **seismometer** and a **seismograph**. The Richter scale has been generally used to determine the strength of an earthquake, with a logarithmic scale up to 10 that determines its magnitude.

An earthquake is the most common cause of a **tsunami**, a series of waves that have the potential to devastate coastal regions with massive volumes of water and energy. When the movement of the plates causes a displacement of a large volume of water, the disturbance can shift the water in a series of powerful waves. The massive 2004 Indian Ocean earthquake generated a destructive tsunami that killed more than 200,000 people.

Volcanoes are also frequently formed by the movement of tectonic plates. Wherever the tectonic plates are diverging (moving apart) or converging (moving toward each other), an opening in the crust may be formed. This opening allows for magma, ash, and gases to escape. Most volcanoes, like earthquakes, are found by the fault lines or zones in the areas of tectonic plate movement.

The movement of tectonic plates also has the effect of creating **mountain ranges**. As the plates, which consist of continental and oceanic crust, collide, they push land masses together. As a result, the upper surface may be forced upward. This process is responsible for the creation of the tallest mountain range in the world, the Himalayas. The Indian Plate, home to the Indian subcontinent, was once its own independent land mass. But as it drifted northward, at an approximate speed of about 15 cm per year, it collided with the gigantic Eurasian Plate. When it finally collided about 10 million years ago, the sediments began to crumple into a mountain range. The Indian Plate is still moving north—though less than 7 cm per year—so the Himalayas will continue to grow.

Along the ocean floor, there are areas of deep **ocean trenches** due to the subduction, the sliding of one tectonic plate underneath another as they move toward each other. In other areas, plate tectonics form underwater mountain ranges called mid-ocean ridges.

The following map shows the major tectonic plates in the lithosphere. The circular black dots show the active volcanoes in the world. Notice that the majority of the active volcanoes exist near the major fault lines and that the areas where tectonic plates converge or diverge are known for producing earthquakes.

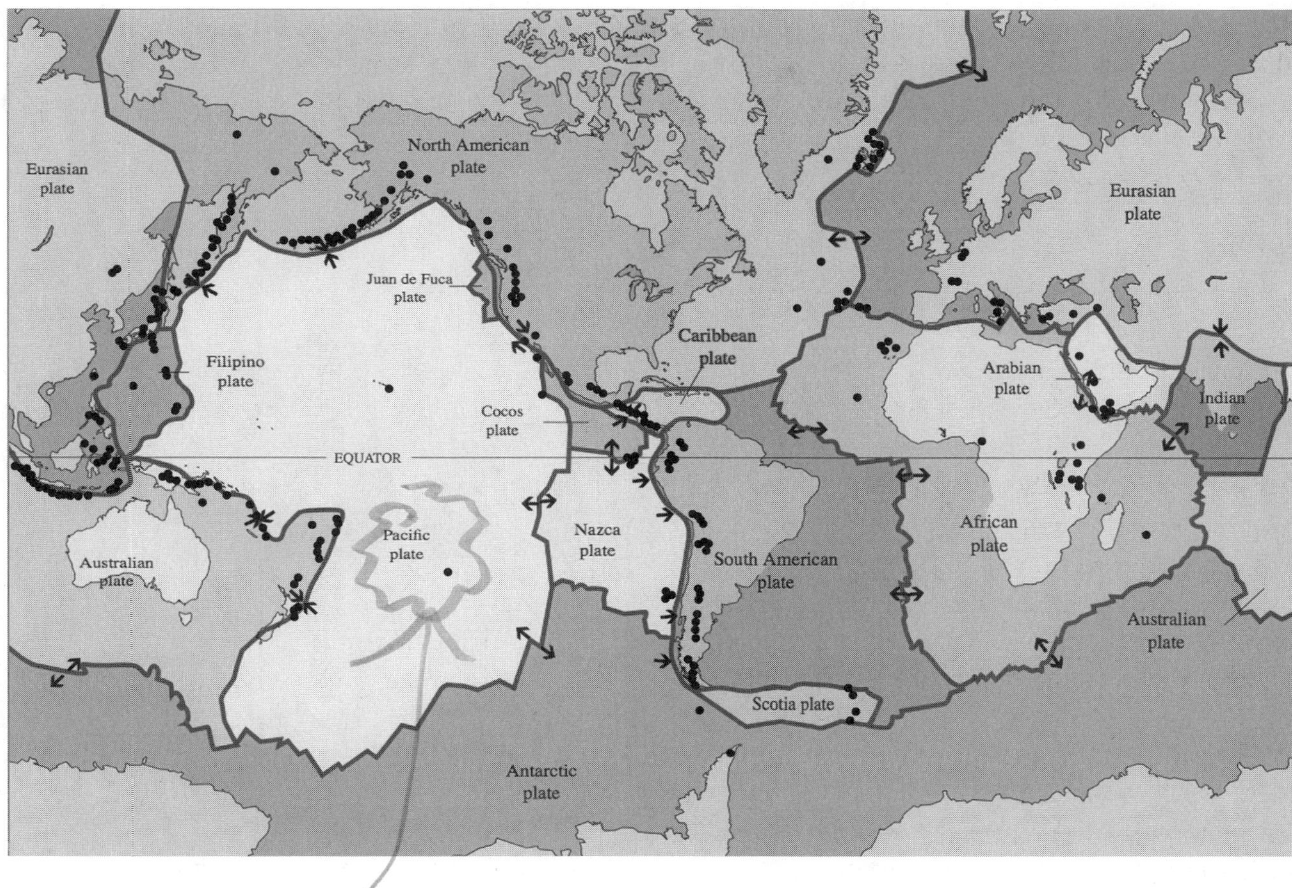

There are almost 500 active volcanoes on the western, northern, and eastern borders of the Pacific Plate, more than everywhere else in the world combined. This volatile area, which is also home to about 90% of the world's earthquakes, is referred to as the **Ring of Fire**.

Erosion and Weathering

A **mineral** is a solid substance that has a specific chemical composition and a crystal structure, which means that its atoms form an orderly structural arrangement. **Rocks**, on the other hand, do not have a specific chemical composition; in fact, rocks are solid substances that may be made up of different types of minerals.

Erosion is the process that changes the surface of Earth by wearing away rock and carrying away soil through agents of current, like wind and water, natural disasters, or chemical erosion, such as acid rain and overuse of fertilizer. **Weathering** is the decomposition of rocks, soil, and minerals through exposure to Earth's atmosphere. This differs from erosion, which requires forces of movement. The impacts of erosion and weathering explain, for example, why some ancient monuments deteriorate more quickly in different climates. For example, the impact of extreme weather changes (weathering) can cause rock to expand and contract, weakening the structure of a monument. Torrential rain and strong winds in other climates (erosion) can further expedite the deterioration process.

Soil is a naturally occurring mixture of broken rock fragments, clay, and decomposing organic matter (humus).

The Water Cycle

Sunlight evaporates the water from the oceans, rivers, and lakes. This evaporation results in the formation of **clouds**, which consist of condensed water droplets frozen in Earth's atmosphere. These clouds then become sources of precipitation. Rain occurs when the air becomes saturated with water vapor, and the water droplets are returned to the surface of Earth.

The following graphic shows the basic stages of the water cycle.

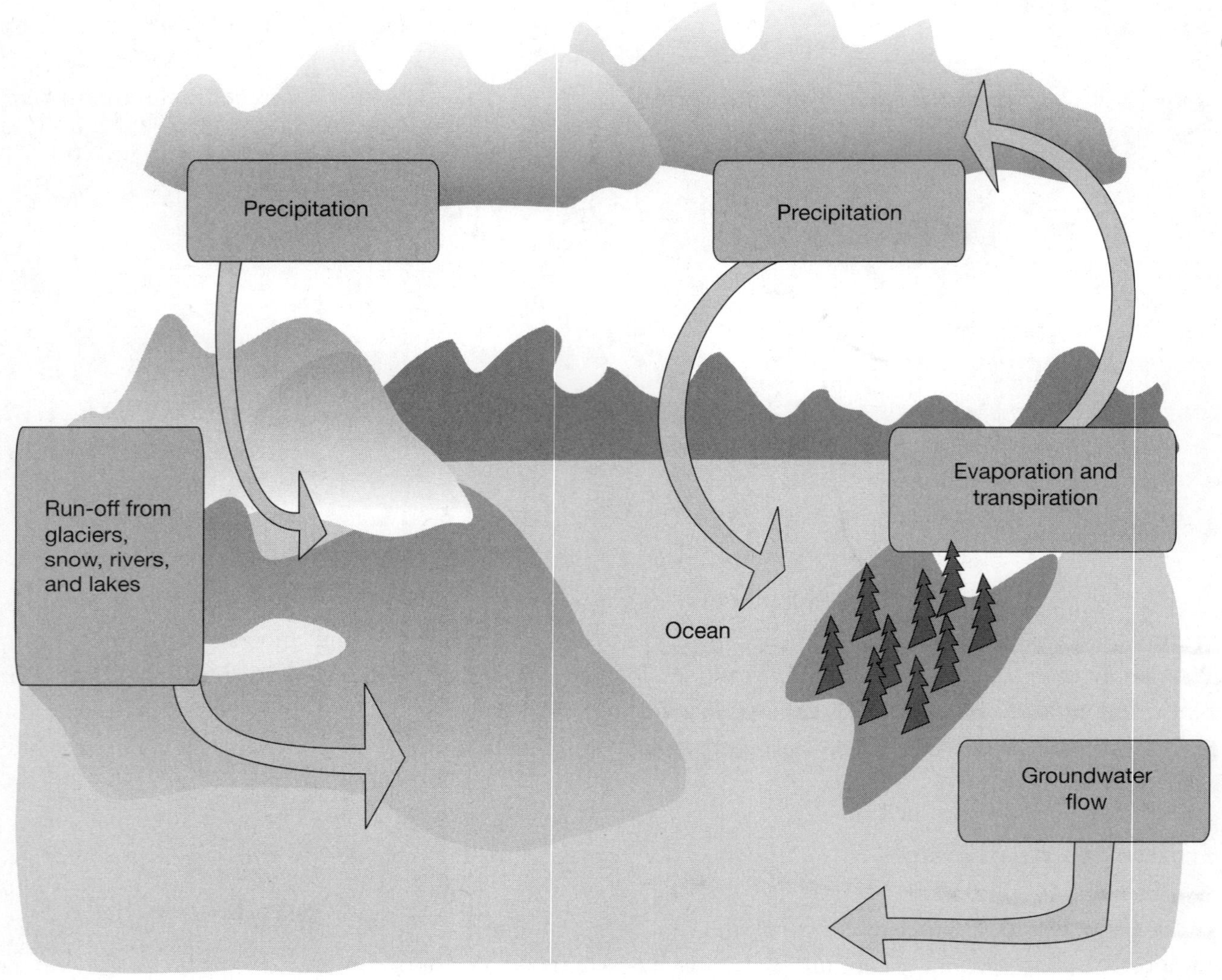

The Carbon Cycle

Carbon is found in the oceans in the form of bicarbonate ions (HCO_3^-): in the atmosphere, in the form of carbon dioxide, in living organisms, and in fossil fuels (such as coal, oil, and natural gas). Plants remove carbon dioxide in the atmosphere and convert it to sugars through photosynthesis. The sugar in plants enters the food chain first reaching herbivores, then carnivores, and finally scavengers and decomposers. All these organisms release carbon dioxide back into the atmosphere when they breathe. The oceans contain 500 times more carbon than the atmosphere. Bicarbonate ions (HCO_3^-) settle to the bottoms of oceans and form sedimentary rocks. Fossil fuels represent the largest reserve of carbon on Earth. Fossil fuels come from the carbon of organisms that had lived millions of years ago. Burning fossil fuels releases energy, which is why these fuels are used to power human contraptions. When fossil fuels burn, carbon dioxide is released into the atmosphere.

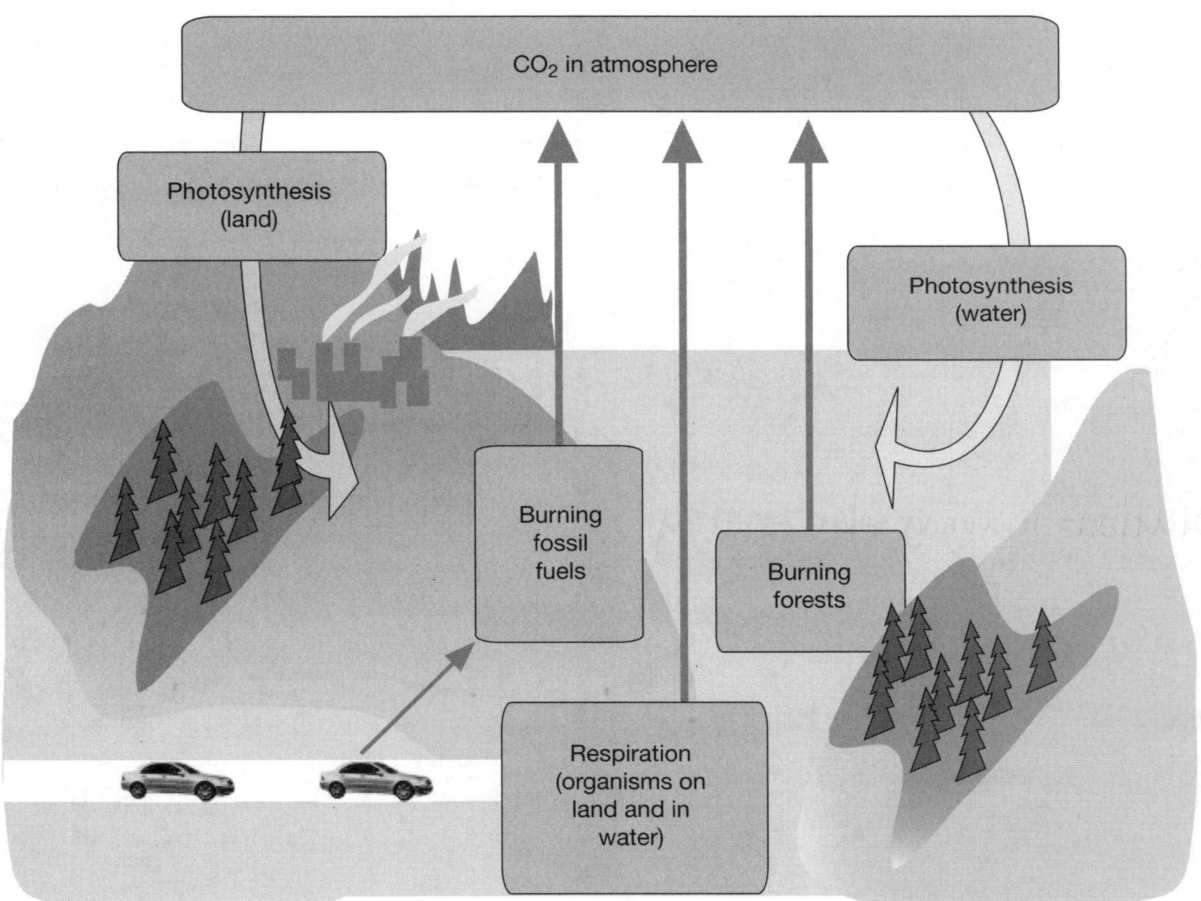

carbon in oceans = bicarbonate ions
carbon in atmasphere = carbon dioxide

Since the Industrial Revolution, people have increased the concentration of carbon dioxide in the atmosphere by 30% simply by burning fossil fuels and cutting down forests, which would otherwise reduce the concentration of carbon dioxide. Carbon dioxide in the atmosphere can trap solar energy—a process known as the **greenhouse effect**. By trapping solar energy, carbon dioxide and other greenhouse gases can cause **global warming**—an increase of temperatures on Earth. In the last 100 years, the temperatures have increased by 1°C. This doesn't seem like much, but the temperature increase is already creating noticeable climate changes and problems. Many species are migrating to colder areas, and regions that normally have ample rainfall have experienced droughts. Perhaps the most dangerous consequence of global warming is the melting of polar ice. Glaciers all over the world are already melting, and the polar ice caps have begun to break up at the edges. If enough of this ice melts, coastal cities could experience severe flooding.

Reducing carbon dioxide concentrations in the atmosphere, either by finding new energy sources or by actively removing the carbon dioxide that forms, is a challenge to today's scientists.

Climate, Weather, and Clouds

Weather consists of the daily conditions of temperature, precipitation, and wind. Weather is largely affected by temperature differences created by incoming solar energy, referred to as **insolation**. Temperature differences result in pressure differences. Winds transport air from high pressure to low pressure, moving weather systems throughout the atmosphere.

Unlike weather, which is based on the specific conditions in a particular area in a short time, **climate** is based on the conditions over a longer period of time. Weather can fluctuate greatly from day to day, whereas climate changes much more subtly over time. Weather is influenced by the seasons, for example.

Pressure Zones

Weather is dependent on pressure zones. A low-pressure zone, characterized by an area of low atmospheric pressure, is associated with high winds, warm air, clouds, and precipitation. Storms such as cyclones are also associated with low-pressure systems. High-pressure zones are characterized by an area of high atmospheric pressure, compared to the area surrounding the system. Compared to a low-pressure zone, a high-pressure zone is associated with clear skies and calm weather. The lack of clouds in a high-pressure system means that there are no clouds to block solar radiation—or to keep the heat from escaping at night. That's why the weather in a high-pressure system is also associated with higher temperatures during the days and lower temperatures during the nights, like in a desert.

Types of Clouds

The Praxis II may test you on your knowledge of cloud types, including which ones are more likely to form storms. There are four basic groups of clouds, each of which has many specific types of clouds within the group.

High-level clouds, also called **cirrus** clouds, are the highest clouds in the atmosphere. Because the temperature is so cold at this high elevation, cirrus clouds are formed mostly with ice crystals. These types of clouds are identified not only by their height in the sky but their white and thin appearance. They are not generally associated with producing precipitation.

Mid-level clouds are usually found in a range from about 6,500 feet to 20,000 feet. These types of clouds, including **altostratus** or **altocumulus** clouds, may or may not be associated with bringing precipitation.

Low-level clouds exist mostly below 6,500 feet above the surface. These low-lying clouds, such as **stratocumulus** or **nimbostratus** clouds, are often associated with rain. However, others, such as cumulus clouds, are not known for bringing rain unless they develop into a bigger storm cloud, such as a cumulonimbus. A low-level cloud that actually comes into contact with the surface is called **fog**.

Vertically formed clouds like the **cumulonimbus** are frequently known as the producer of most thunderstorms. Strong, rotating thunderstorms are called **supercells**. A tornado, one of the most violent weather patterns in the world, is a column of air that usually connects a cumulonimbus cloud with Earth's surface. Storm clouds are formed when convection currents collide, specifically warm, moist air with cooler air.

The following graphic shows the range of several cloud types in the atmosphere:

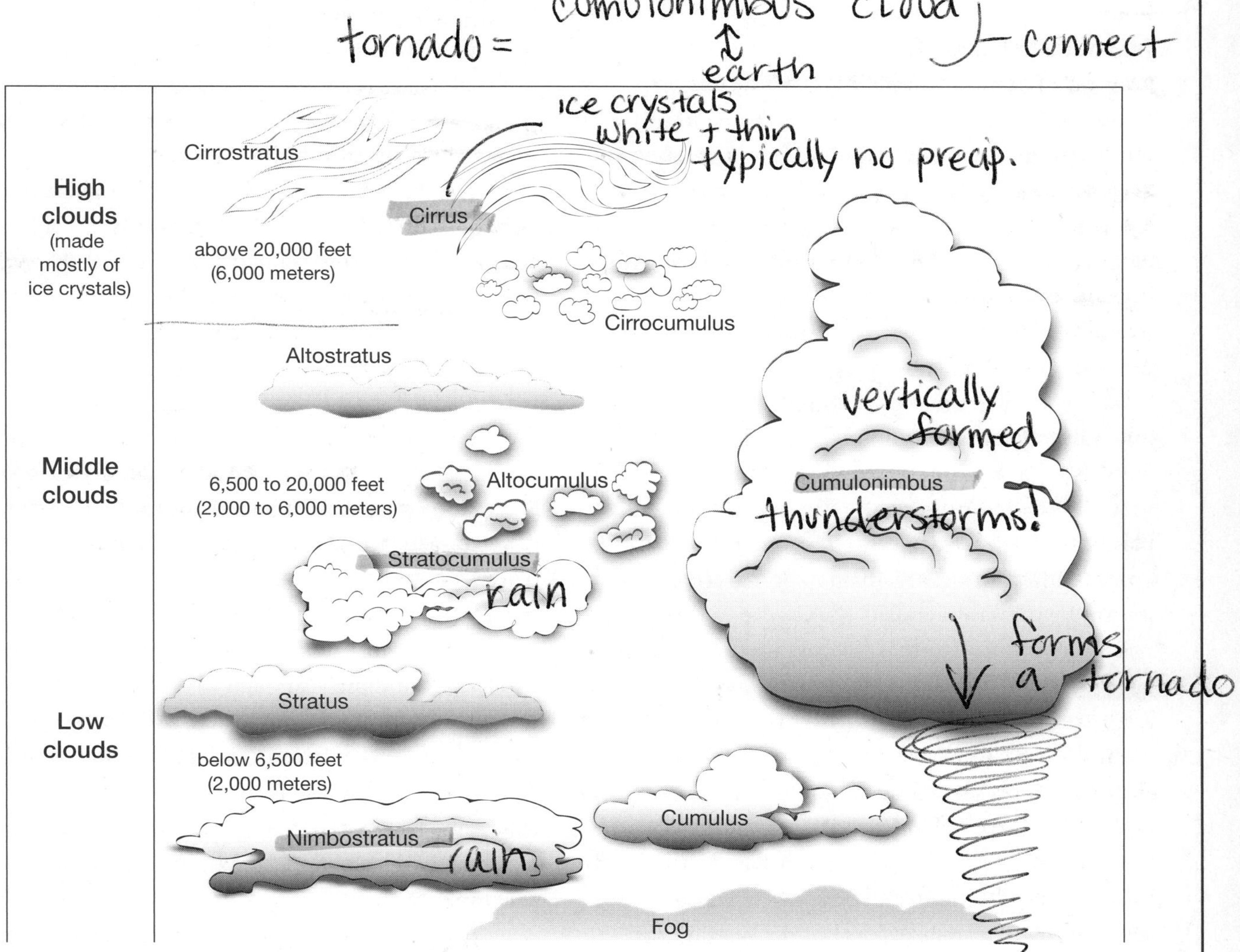

Types of Precipitation

As explained earlier, the water cycle can result in precipitation from clouds. However, this precipitation can appear in several different forms. The most common form is liquid precipitation, or **rain**, which can appear in varying intensities. Liquid precipitation can be measured using a rain gauge, which can then be used to determine the intensity of the rain. When the precipitation is in the form of crystalline water ice, it is considered **snow**. When the precipitation melts and refreezes, it may cause alternate forms of solid precipitation, including **ice pellets** or snow grains. When the precipitation goes through several cycles in the cloud, there is the potential for it to be layered and clumped together. This event occurs when there is a strong upward movement of air with a storm, and the resulting precipitation is called **hail**. Hailstones can be more than 5 inches in diameter during severe thunderstorms.

History of Earth

The age of Earth is about 4.6 billion years. It is believed that our planet formed as a result of dust and gases solidifying into a celestial body. This dust and gas is believed to be remnants from the creation of the sun. For the first 700 million years or so, during what is called the Hadean Eon, the molten earth solidified as it cooled; the crust of the planet was formed during this time. There was no life, however, nor were there even any rocks.

We know a great deal about the history of life on our planet from fossil records. **Fossils** are records of organisms from the distant past. Fossils may show the preserved remains of animals or plants through a variety of preservation methods. For example, an organism may be covered in sediment; the mineral deposits then serve to form a cast of the organism. Another process involves the resin, or amber that is excreted from a plant. This sticky resin can capture insects or other creatures on the plants, which can exist for millions of years. This method of preservation can maintain even some DNA of the original animal. **Paleontologists**, scientists who study prehistoric life on Earth, use fossils to help identify the evolution of life. Fossil records are used to help determine the delineations of the eons, eras, periods, epochs, and stages of Earth's geological timescale.

Life on Earth

Earth's geological time scale is divided into eons, eras, periods, epochs, and stages corresponding to specific life-forms and climate. There are three major geologic eons.

The first life-forms appeared on Earth about 3.9 billion years ago, marking the beginning of the **Archeozoic Eon**. During this time, from about 3.9 to 2.5 billion years ago, single-celled organisms evolved, such as bacteria and algae in the sea.

The second major geologic eon is the **Proerozoic Eon**, which lasted from about 2.5 billion years ago go 540 million years ago. This eon featured the evolution of multicellular organisms, such as sponges. During this time the atmosphere began to fill with oxygen, destroying countless species but providing the atmosphere necessary for future animal life.

The third major geologic eon is the **Phanerozoic Eon**, which began about 540 million years ago and continues to the present day. There are three eras within the Phanerozoic Eon. The first era of the Phanerozoic Eon is the **Paleozoic Era**, which represented an explosion in life-forms, including many marine invertebrates such as trilobites, shellfish, and mollusks. This explosion at the start of the Paleozoic Era is called the **Cambrian Era**, from about 540 to 500 million years ago. It is so significant in the history of life on Earth that everything before it—everything before 540 million years ago—is simply referred to as the **Precambrian era**. During the Paleozoic Era, which lasted from about 540 million years ago to about 250 million years ago, the sea level retreated and advanced over the continents. Marine vertebrates and land plants evolved, and tall forests emerged. There were several ice ages during this time that resulted in mass extinctions. Giant amphibians, early reptiles, and insects appeared by the end of the Paleozoic Era.

The **Mesozoic Era** lasted from 250 million years ago until 65 million years ago. The continents gradually split from Pangaea during this time. The climate was exceptionally warm and many new animal species evolved. During the **Triassic Period**, there was a mass extinction known as the "Great Dying"; most sea and land species became extinct. Dinosaurs dominated the **Jurassic Period** until the **Cretaceous Period**, when there was another mass extinction, most likely caused by a meteor impact—all terrestrial dinosaurs became extinct. Late in the Mesozoic Era, flowering plants appeared.

The **Cenozoic Era** covers the last 65 million years to the present time. This was a time of long-term cooling, significant volcanic activity, and is considered the age of new life. Flowering plants, insects, and birds substantially evolved. Large mammals and the first primates appeared. During the modern **Quaternary Period**, the last ice age occurred. Hominids appeared about 250 million years ago and modern humans evolved about 160,000 years ago. The brief epoch that represents the phase of human civilization is called the **Holocene Epoch**, which began about 11,000 years ago and continues today.

Earth and the Universe

Although the section is technically called "Earth Science," the questions in this section may include content about other celestial bodies, such as the moon, the sun, the planets, and other stars and galaxies in the universe. It's especially important to understand Earth's relationship within the solar system and galaxy.

Earth, Moon, and Sun Basics

Most people know that Earth is round and revolves around its axis in about 24 hours. The rotation of Earth around its axis causes the change between day and night. As Earth rotates, it causes celestial bodies such as the sun and stars to appear as though they are moving across the sky each day and night. The tilt in Earth's axis gives rise to seasons. Earth is a part of the solar system, with the sun in its center. It takes one year for Earth to complete its orbit around the sun. Earth's position changes during this annual orbit around the Sun. Since stars are only visible in the direction away from the sun, people see different stars during different seasons. The following illustration shows this scenario, along with several of the common constellations for each season.

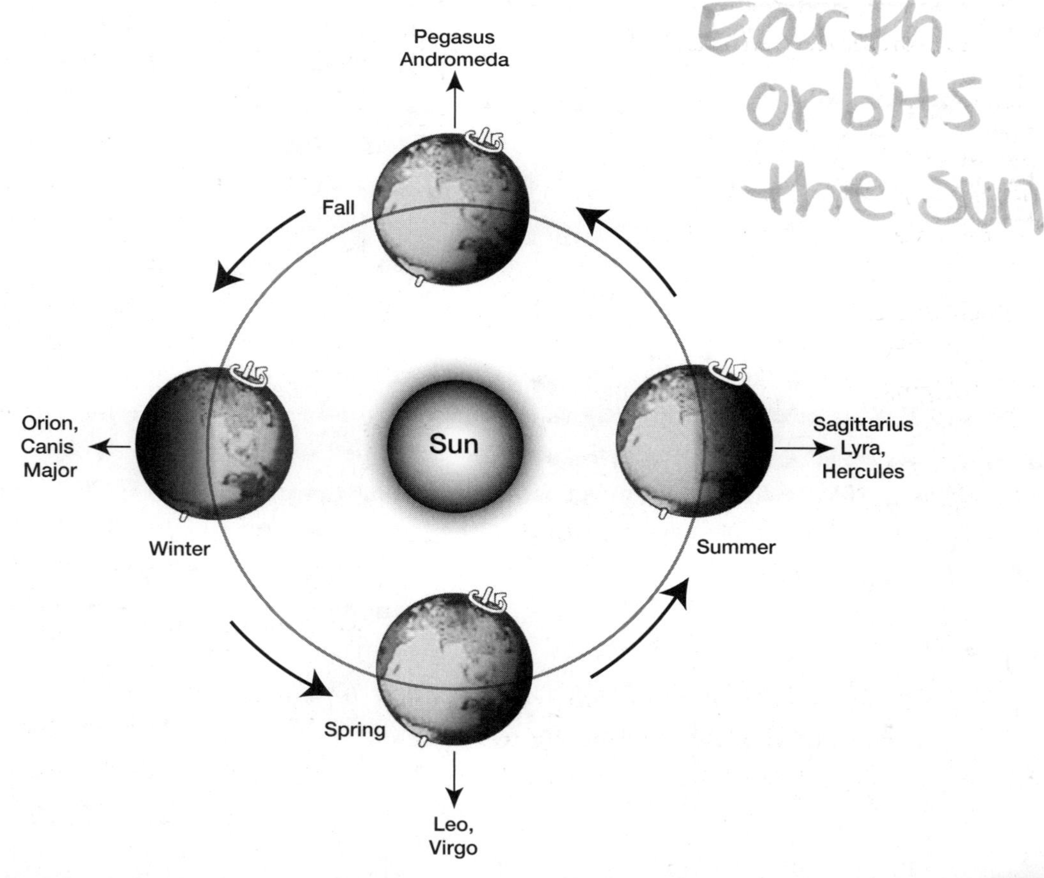

Earth has one moon. As the moon orbits Earth, the same side of the moon is always visible from Earth. This is because of the Moon's synchronous rotation, which keeps it rotating with the same side facing Earth—and the same side (the "dark side") always facing away from Earth. The moon is one of the largest known satellites, and its mass has significant effects on life on Earth. For example, its gravitational force attracts water from Earth's bodies of water, creating the **tides**. This force on the water closest to the moon results in a high tide, with the water at its highest point. The water on the sides of Earth at this time is pulled away, resulting in a low tide at those places. The sun's gravity also influences the tide, but not nearly as much as the moon. The highest tides, therefore, are when Earth, the moon, and the sun are aligned.

While the moon is in its lunar phase, it may appear on the opposite side of Earth from the sun, allowing the sun to illuminate the entire side of the moon facing Earth. This is known as a full moon. When the moon is in its lunar phase, it may appear in between Earth and the sun, allowing the sun to illuminate none of the side of the moon facing Earth. This is known as a new moon.

The origin of Earth's moon is not known, but the accepted theory is that Earth was struck by a giant object and material from the impact was put into orbit, eventually forming the moon. The moon has no atmosphere or water, and has been struck by meteorites that have formed various lunar craters. **Lunar eclipses** occur when the moon passes through some portion of the entire shadow cast by the Earth, blocking the sun's light. **Solar eclipses** occur when the moon passes between Earth and sun, partially or totally blocking the view of the sun.

The Solar System, Stars, and Galaxies

The solar system consists of the eight planets and their moons and three dwarf planets (Ceres, Pluto, and Eris) orbiting the sun. The planets from closest to farthest from the sun are Mercury, Venus, Earth, Mars, Jupiter, Saturn, Uranus, and Neptune. Moons orbit six of the eight planets—all but Mercury and Venus. The first four of these planets (Mercury, Venus, Earth, and Mars) are called the inner planets and are all characterized by their smaller sizes and by their solid surfaces. The four planets farthest from the sun (Jupiter, Saturn, Uranus, and Neptune) are called the outer planets and are all characterized by their bigger sizes and by their gas surfaces. These planets are also called the gas giants. The outer planets also contain rings, though only Saturn's rings are easily observed from Earth.

There are many other small bodies orbiting the solar system. **Comets** are loose collections of ice, dust, and small rock particles that regularly orbit the solar system. On Earth, they are observed as patches of light with long tails. **Asteroids** are small, planetlike bodies in orbit around the sun and in between the orbits of Mars and Jupiter; some may be the remains of comets that have burned out. Smaller particles are considered **meteoroids**, and when they become visible entering Earth's atmosphere, they are called **meteors**. A **meteorite** is a part of the meteoroid that is not destroyed by entering the atmosphere and eventually reaches the ground.

A star is a ball of plasma that shines as a result of fusion in its core. The sun is the star that is closest to Earth. A star initially consists of hydrogen and helium, which are fused together to make heavier elements inside the core of the star. The fusion reactions at a star's core release vast amounts of energy that radiate into outer space. Once the hydrogen fuel at the core is used up, a star can become a red giant and continue fusion of heavier elements. When fusion is no longer possible, the star will either burn out or explode in a supernova. Depending on the size of the star, the supernova can leave a neutron star, or, in the case of the largest stars, a **black hole**. In a black hole, the gravitational forces are so great that not even light can escape from its immediate grasp.

A **galaxy** is a collection of millions of stars bound together by their own gravity. Larger galaxies can have trillions of stars. There are likely more than

170 billion galaxies. Earth's solar system is located in the **Milky Way** galaxy, a spiral galaxy that contains about 200 billion stars.

Origin and Evolution of the Universe

Nobody knows for sure how the universe originated. According to the **Big Bang theory**, the universe started off in a hot dense state under high pressure about 14 billion years ago. The Big Bang theory also postulates that the universe has been expanding since its origination. The universe is still expanding and cooling. Some data suggest that the rate of expansion of the universe is increasing. Whether the universe will continue to expand forever, eventually reach an equilibrium size, or shrink back into a small, dense, hot mass is unknown.

Life Science

About 30% of the science section of the Praxis II: Elementary Education: Content Knowledge test—or about nine of the 30 questions—will include questions relating to life science. This includes the structure of living organisms, such as the functions of the different organs and the components of the cells. The questions from this section will test your understanding of reproduction and heredity, including the growth and development of an organism. You will be expected to know how living things change over time through evolutionary processes such as natural selection or adaptation. Some questions on the test may ask about the behavior and regulation of an organism. Finally, you will be expected to know how different organisms relate to each other in ecosystems. The following subsections cover the information that you should be familiar with to correctly answer the life science questions on the science section of the Praxis II.

The Structure and Function of Living Things

All living things are made up of one or more of the basic functional units called **cells**. Cells differ greatly in their shapes and sizes. Some are circular, like red blood cells. Others are elongated, such as neurons. Some are microscopic, such as bacteria. Others can weigh several pounds, such as eggs. Some living things have one simple cell and other organisms have several specialized types of cells that are responsible for particular functions.

All cells arise from preexisting cells and pass on genetic information in the form of DNA (deoxyribonucleic acid) and RNA (ribonucleic acid) through the process of reproduction. All living things get **energy** for their life functions by either producing or consuming food. The food is digested and broken down into smaller nutrients, the essential building blocks for cellular structure and processes. All living things also regulate their internal environment in order to maintain a stable condition, known as **homeostasis**.

Cell Biology

All cells have a **cell membrane** that regulates the transport of nutrients and wastes in and out of the cell by the processes of diffusion, osmosis, and active transport. **Diffusion** is the movement of molecules from an area of high concentration to one of lower concentration. **Osmosis** is the movement of water across a selectively permeable membrane in order to equalize the concentration (the amount of protein per milliliter of water) on two sides of the membrane. **Active transport** uses proteins and energy to pump material through the cell membrane against a concentration gradient.

Some cells also have cell walls. The membrane surrounds **cytoplasm** where genetic material and cellular structures are located. Many cells contain differentiated membrane-bound structures within the cytoplasm called **organelles**, which are responsible for specific cellular functions. It is important to know the function(s) of each part of a cell, including the organelles.

An organelle whose function is to store DNA is called the **nucleus**. The DNA is stored on structures called **chromosomes**, which are defined in greater detail in the following section on reproduction. Because the nucleus contains the genetic material of the cell, it is often referred to as the control center of the cell. **Prokaryotic cells** (bacteria and cyanobacteria) lack a true nucleus and organelles, though they have a cell wall. **Eukaryote cells** contain organelles, including a nucleus. Almost all larger organisms, including plants and animals, contain eukaryote cells.

All cells contain **ribosomes**, organelles that are responsible for producing proteins from amino acids. **Chloroplasts** are organelles that are used to carry out **photosynthesis**, the process of using sunlight to convert carbon dioxide into organic compounds. As a result, chloroplasts are found only in plant cells or in cells of other organisms containing **chlorophyll** (a pigment used to absorb light). **Mitochondria** are organelles that generate most of the cell's supply of energy. Because of this, mitochondria are often called the "powerhouse" of the cell. The energy created by the mitochondria is in the form of a chemical called adenosine triphosphate, or **ATP**. The **nucleolus** is found in the nucleus and contains RNA and protein; its principle function is to produce and assemble ribosomes. The **Golgi complex**, or Golgi apparatus, is an organelle that processes proteins and other macromolecules for cell secretion. **Lyosomes** contain enzymes used in digestion. Vacuoles are found in the cytoplasm of most plants and some animal cells and serve as storage areas for food, water, or waste.

Tissues, Organs, and Organ Systems

A collection of specialized cells that perform a similar function form **tissue.** These tissues form structures and organs, which compose organ systems that work together to carry out the life functions of an organism.

Plants have **vascular tissue** that transports fluid and nutrients throughout the plant. The primary components of vascular tissue are xylem, which transport water and mineral nutrients from the root up the plant, and phloem, which transports sugars and nutrients to parts throughout the plant. Plants without vascular tissue lack the specialized structures to transport water and are often low-growing and found in moist environments.

Leaves are specialized organs that make food through the process of photosynthesis. Epidermis tissue forms the outer surface of leaves and has pores called stomata that allow carbon dioxide to enter the leaf. The carbon dioxide enters the cell chloroplasts, small structures that contain chlorophyll, which use the sun's energy to produce sugar for food. Plants maintain homeostasis of water content by controlling stomata. Water evaporates from the leaves in a process called **transpiration** when stomata are open, and water loss is reduced by the plant closing stomata.

Most plants grow **flowers** to reproduce. The stamen is the male part of a flower, which contains the anther that produces pollen. To reproduce, pollen attaches to the female part of a flower, the pistil, which contains the ovary and the egg cells. After pollen makes contact with the eggs of the pistil, seeds are made.

Vertebrate animals, including humans, have four types of tissue that compose their organs and organ systems. Epithelial tissue covers organ surfaces, such as skin and the inner lining of the digestive system. **Epithelial tissue** is responsible for protection, secretion, and absorption. **Connective tissue** holds everything together, and includes bone and cartilage, ligaments and tendons, blood, and adipose (fat). **Muscle tissue** is contractile tissue, which provides force and movement, either as motion or movement within internal organs. Muscle tissue includes visceral or smooth muscle, which in found in the inner lining of organs; skeletal muscle, which is attached to bone and provides mobility; and cardiac muscle, which is only found in the heart. **Nervous tissue** makes up the brain, spinal cord, and peripheral nervous system.

Human Organ Systems

Humans have many **organ systems** working together. The **integumentary system** is the outermost organ system covering the body and is its largest organ. It includes the skin and associated glands, hair, and nails. Skin consists of epidermis (thinner, outermost layer) and dermis (thicker, innermost layer). Below the skin is the subcutaneous tissue. The integumentary system cooperates with the immune system to protect against infection and dehydration, regulates body temperature, provides sensation, and synthesizes vitamin D.

The **skeletal system** includes bones, cartilage, tendons, and ligaments, which give the body structural support and protection. With the muscular system, it allows for body movement. Bones store calcium and contain marrow to produce red and white blood cells and platelets. Bones come together at flexible joints, which are held together by ligaments. Muscles are connected to bones by tendons. Cartilage is a flexible yet strong tissue found in the joints, nose, and ears.

The **nervous system** is the command center of the body, consisting of the central nervous system of the brain and spinal cord, and the peripheral nervous system of all the nerves branching from the spinal cord. The brain's functions are broken up into three parts: the cerebral hemispheres responsible for higher functions, like speech and rational thought; the cerebellum, which maintains subconscious activities and balance functions; and the brain stem in charge of automated functions, such as breathing and circulation. Nerve cells called neurons pass along signals through the nervous system. Signals are transmitted through long axons and are received by the dendrites, structures branching out from neurons. The space between axons and dendrites is known as a synapse. Reflexes are unconscious reactions to stimuli that bypass the brain. Sensory receptors are part of the peripheral nervous system and send signals to the brain to be processed as vision, sound, taste, smell, and touch.

The **muscular system** provides force and movement. Muscle tissue can only contract and is generally attached to bone to work in opposing motions. Voluntary muscle (skeletal) is controlled by conscious thought, involuntary muscle (visceral, smooth) is controlled by the nervous system, and cardiac muscle (heart muscle, striated, and smooth) is specialized tissue that contracts spontaneously and is controlled by the nervous system.

The **respiratory system** involves the lungs, nose, trachea, bronchi, and diaphragm. Its primary function is to take in oxygen and eliminate carbon dioxide, a process called **respiration**. Air enters through the mouth or nose and passes through the trachea, which branches into bronchi at the lungs. The bronchi branch off into smaller bronchioles and end with capillary-rich alveoli, which exchange oxygen and carbon dioxide with the circulatory system. The diaphragm is the muscle responsible for expanding and contracting the volume of the chest cavity, which in turn forces air in and out of the lungs.

The **circulatory system** consists of the heart, blood vessels, and blood working together to transport oxygen, carbon dioxide, nutrients, and wastes throughout the body to other organ systems. Arteries and arterioles are blood vessels that carry blood that is oxygen and nutrient rich away from the heart. Veins and venules carry blood that has more carbon dioxide and wastes to the heart. Capillaries are beds of tiny blood vessels found in tissue and are the site of the exchange of gases and nutrients. Arteries are thick-walled because they carry the blood at high pressure, and veins are thin-walled because the blood returns at lower pressure. Blood rate is slowest in the capillaries to allow for material exchange. The human heart has four chambers, two upper atria and two lower ventricles. Blood is pumped from the right ventricle to the lungs by the pulmonary arteries and is returned to the left atrium of the heart through pulmonary veins. This is known as the pulmonary circuit. Blood is then pumped from the left ventricle to all the tissues of the body through the aorta, the largest artery in the body, and is returned to the right atrium of the heart. This is known as the systemic circuit. Red blood cells contain hemoglobin, which carries oxygen and gives blood its red color. White blood cells protect the body from infectious diseases and foreign bodies. Platelets in the blood primarily help blood to clot.

The **endocrine system** is a group of glands and tissues that secrete hormones. Hormones are substances that facilitate communication between the organ systems. Hormones secreted by the pituitary gland regulate growth and stimulate the thyroid. Thyroid hormones help control the rate of metabolism. Hormones produced by the pancreas maintain blood glucose levels; insulin decreases glucose levels and glucagon increases glucose levels. Adrenaline, otherwise known as the fight or flight hormone, is produced by the adrenal glands.

The **immunological system** protects the body from infection. It consists of the lymphatic system, which includes the spleen, tonsils, thymus gland, and bone marrow (producing white blood cells). The lymphatic system is responsible for recycling body fluids and fighting disease. Immunity occurs when the immune system recognizes antigens, harmful pathogens, and produces antibodies to get rid of the antigen. The immune system has the ability to distinguish its own body's molecules from antigens and other foreign bodies. Unfortunately, this means the immune system will attack transplanted tissue from another person. The immune system is able to remember formerly encountered antigens and reacts quickly when exposed again, which is called acquired immunity.

The **digestive** (or **gastrointestinal**) **system** consists of the gastrointestinal tract, which includes the mouth, esophagus, stomach, small intestine, large intestine, and anus. Accessory organs, such as the teeth, tongue, liver, pancreas, and gall bladder, aid in the digestion of food. The function of the digestive system is to break down food, absorb nutrients and energy, and eliminate wastes. Digestion starts in the mouth where the food is broken down into smaller pieces by the teeth and enzymes in saliva begin digestion of carbohydrates. In the stomach, hydrochloric acid and pepsin further digest food. Then food goes into the small intestine, where pancreatic enzymes and bile continue digestion and nutrients are absorbed. Pancreatic enzymes include trypsin to digest proteins, lipase to digest fats, and amylase to digest carbohydrates. The large intestine absorbs water and minerals and eliminates waste as feces through the anus. The liver processes nutrients absorbed by the small intestine and produces bile that emulsifies fats and is stored in the gall bladder. The liver is also responsible for detoxification.

The **renal** (or **excretory**) **system** uses the kidneys to filter blood to remove nitrogenous waste and toxic byproducts and retain necessary nutrients, like glucose and amino acids. The kidneys contain excretory units called nephrons where blood is filtered. This process also allows the renal system to regulate water and salt balance and control blood pH. Waste is passed through the ureters as urine and is stored in the bladder until it is excreted out of the body through the urethra.

The **reproductive system** consists of external genitalia and internal reproductive organs. In males, the scrotum and penis are external genitalia, and the testes, prostate gland, and ducts to transport sperm are internal reproductive organs. In females, the clitoris and two sets of labia are external organs, and the ovaries, fallopian tubes, uterus, vagina, and cervix are the internal system.

The male sperm and female egg (ovum) are gametes, which contain half the correct number of chromosomes. The ovaries contain thousands of eggs, and about once a month, an egg is released from one ovary into the fallopian tube. Sperm is produced in the seminiferous tubules in the testes and travels through the vas deferens and the penis to fertilize an egg in the female uterus. If the egg is not fertilized, menstruation occurs and the cycle continues. If the egg is fertilized, it becomes a zygote with the correct number of chromosomes and attaches to the uterus wall and grows into an embryo. The embryo grows into a baby during a nine-month gestation period and exits the uterus through the cervix and vagina.

Chemistry of Life

All living things need energy to survive. Organisms use a molecule of ATP (adenosine triphosphate) to obtain the energy they need. ATP can be produced from carbohydrates (sugars) or lipids (fats) within an organism's cells. Some organisms, such as plants, are autotrophs because they produce their own energy in the form of glucose (sugar) using the energy of the sun. This process of photosynthesis is represented by the following reaction:

$$6\ CO_2 + 6\ H_2O \rightarrow 6\ O_2 + C_6H_{12}O_6$$

carbon dioxide + water → oxygen + glucose

Plants later use the glucose produced to release energy and form ATP. Organisms that acquire energy by eating food, instead of producing their own food, are **heterotrophs**. Heterotrophs also use glucose digested from food to release energy and make ATP in the process of cellular respiration:

$$C_6H_{12}O_6 + 6\ O_2 \rightarrow 6\ CO_2 + 6\ H_2O + ATP$$

glucose + oxygen → carbon dioxide + water + ATP

This is an aerobic reaction, because oxygen is present to be used in the reaction. If oxygen is not present, organisms release energy from glucose by the anaerobic process of fermentation:

$$C_6H_{12}O_6 \rightarrow 2\ C_2H_5OH + 2\ CO_2$$

glucose → ethyl alcohol + carbon dioxide

Reproduction and Heredity

All living things reproduce to create offspring with similar traits and appearances. As generations of living things reproduce, variations in these traits and appearances arise. **Asexual reproduction** involves one parent and is the primary form of reproduction for single-celled organisms, like bacteria and protists. Some multicellular organisms reproduce asexually also, such as many plants and fungi. **Sexual reproduction** involves the union of genetic information from two parents. Flowering plants and animals reproduce sexually. Asexual reproduction occurs much faster than sexual reproduction. Sexual reproduction results in increased genetic diversity among offspring and parents.

Cells replicate into identical cells in order for an organism to grow and reproduce. **Prokaryotes** (single cell microorganisms) reproduce by binary fission, or division of identical cells. Eukaryote cells follow a more complex process of reproduction described by the cell cycle. Most of a cell's life is spent in interphase, when it grows and replicates DNA. In late interphase, DNA replication produces sister chromatids, identical chromosome strands joined at a centromere. This is followed by **mitosis**, which is divided into prophase, metaphase, anaphase, and telophase. During prophase, DNA condenses into chromosomes, followed by metaphase, when chromosomes are aligned at the central metaphase plate. Next, in anaphase, sister chromatids separate and are pulled apart, forming sister chromosomes. Finally, nuclear membranes form around the sister chromosomes in telophase, creating two nuclei. Now, the cell is ready to split into two daughter cells, known as cytokinesis.

Mitosis

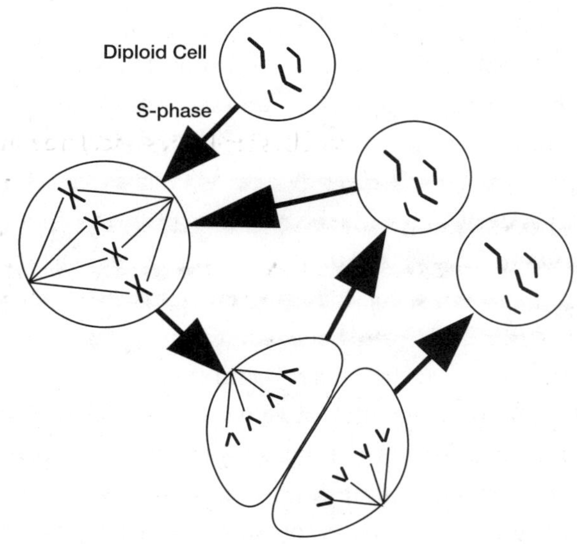

Genetics and Reproduction

Organisms pass on genetic information to their offspring through **chromosomes**, DNA strands that provide the blueprint for cells to build complex proteins that carry out cellular functions. DNA is found in the nucleus of eukaryotic organisms and is composed of two complementary strands of nucleotides that coil around each other forming a **double helix**. The nucleotide strands provide structure through a sugar-phosphate backbone and are held to each other through the hydrogen bonds of complementary bases. For example, adenine pairs with thymine (T) and guanine (G) pairs with cytosine (C).

The sequence of bases on DNA forms genes that represent codes for specific proteins. The code is organized by groups of three bases called codons. In protein synthesis, DNA is read during transcription to produce a complementary copy, messenger RNA (mRNA), which is able travel from the nucleus to the cytoplasm of the cell. Instead of using thymine (T) in mRNA, uracil (U) is used, which bonds to adenine (A). Once in the cytoplasm mRNA attaches to the ribosome, which is the site of protein synthesis. Ribosomal RNA (rRNA) in the ribosome is the main component coordinating the decoding of mRNA to make specific proteins through the process of translation. Transfer RNA (tRNA) contains anticodons that are complementary to the codons of mRNA. tRNA brings amino acids into the ribosome and sequences them into proteins according to the sequences of codons on mRNA.

Organisms that reproduce sexually use haploid **gametes** that have half the required chromosomes as in the diploid eukaryotic cells. During **meiosis**, the diploid cell undergoes one round of DNA replication and two rounds of division (mitosis), forming four haploid gametes. Gametes from male parents are called sperm and from female parents are called eggs, which combined form a diploid zygote. Genetic variation is introducing during the round of DNA replication due to genetic recombination, which occurs when there is chromosomal crossover between chromosomal pairs. This results in gametes with different combinations of genes than their parent cells, leading to genetic diversity and new traits in offspring.

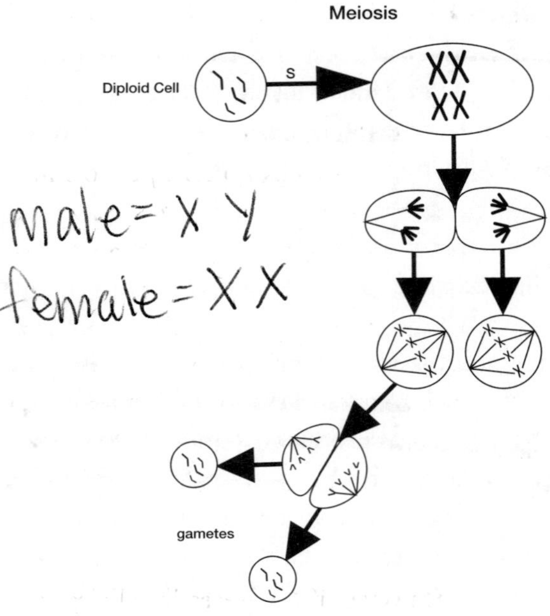

Humans have 23 pairs of chromosomes in their diploid cells—22 pairs of somatic chromosomes and one pair of sex (gender) chromosomes. Males have one X chromosome and one Y chromosome and females have two X chromosomes. Different species have other chromosomes that determine gender.

Unfortunately, there are genetically inherited diseases created by **mutations**, changes in the DNA sequence on chromosomes. Examples include Huntington's disease, Tay-Sachs disease, sickle-cell anemia, hemophilia, and cystic fibrosis. Some genetic mutations are sex-linked, and will be seen more in one gender, as in hemophilia, which is linked to the X chromosome and seen mostly in men. Sometimes, during sexual reproduction, there is an abnormal gain or loss of chromosomes that can lead to genetic disorders. For instance, Down syndrome is usually caused by an extra chromosome 21.

Conditions caused by recessive traits are rare. If a person has one dominant chromosome and one recessive chromosome, the dominant trait will be expressed, but the recessive chromosome will be carried in the cells and may be passed on to its offspring. If two parents pass recessive disorders to their offspring, the genetic condition can become present.

Molecular Genetics

Gregor Mendel is considered the father of classical genetics for the experiments he conducted on the varying traits of garden peas. His work helped formulate the idea that traits are inherited from parents. Earlier ideas of genetics suggested a blending theory of characteristics from parents, much like blending paint colors. However, Mendel's experiments disproved this theory, and heredity is now understood to be controlled by **dominant** and **recessive** traits.

Offspring receive one gene, or allele, from each parent for a specific trait. If the allele is dominant, then the trait will be expressed. The recessive allele can be present and not expressed when it is with a dominant allele. However, if two recessive alleles are present, the recessive trait will be expressed. For example, a mother can express the dominant trait of brown eyes and carry the recessive allele for blue eyes. If this mother gives the recessive trait to its offspring along with the recessive allele from the father, then the offspring will express the recessive trait of blue eyes. The combination of alleles is referred to as genotype, and phenotype describes the observed trait expressed by the two alleles. If the alleles are the same (both dominant or both recessive), an organism is described as being homozygous for that gene. If the alleles are different, it is heterozygous.

A **Punnett square** is used to make predictions of the genotypes of offspring from two parents. In the Punnett square, dominant alleles are represented with uppercase letters and recessive alleles are represented with lowercase letters. For example, Mendel's experiments looked at the colors expressed by pea flowers; purple flowers are the dominant trait (P) and white flowers are the recessive trait (p). In the initial generation (P generation), homozygous dominant plants (PP) were crossed with homozygous recessive plants (pp). The resulting generation (F1 generation) yielded all heterozygous plants (Pp) that expressed the dominant purple flower trait. Plants from the F1 generation were crossed and created mostly dominant plants and some recessive plants in the F2 generation. This is because there is a possibility for offspring to receive one recessive allele from each parent. According to the Punnett square for the F2 generation, 25% will be homozygous dominant (PP), 50% will be heterozygous (Pp), and 25% will be homozygous recessive (pp). In some organisms, it is possible to express incomplete dominance with a heterozygous genotype. For instance, RR for red flowers and rr for white flowers could yield Rr offspring presenting pink flowers.

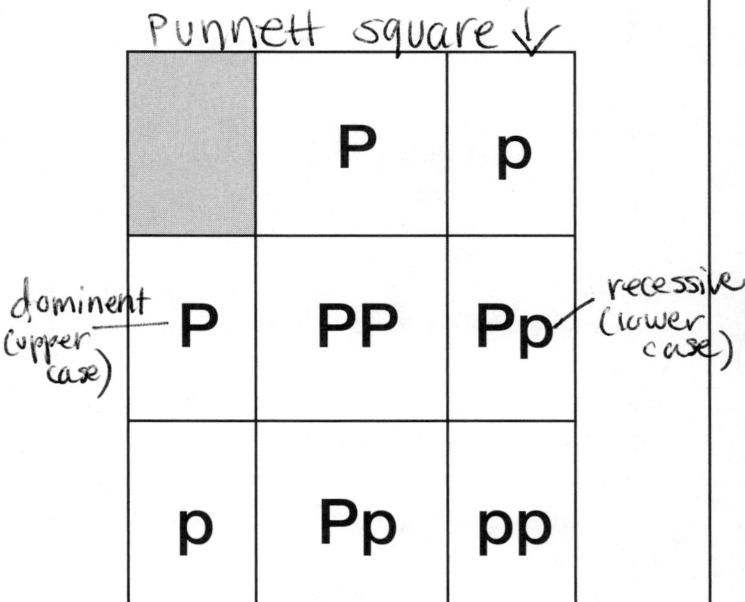

Regulation and Behavior

Living things respond to stimuli, changes in the internal and external environment, so as to maintain homeostasis. For example, a person shivers in a cold environment in order to maintain a constant body temperature. A person sweats in a hot environment in order to maintain that temperature. Pigs do not have the ability to sweat, so they must regulate their temperature during warm weather with water or mud. You should be aware of some of the ways that animals regulate their environments, including through instinctual behavior.

Some species of animals follow an instinctual behavior to deal with changes in their environment. For example, many species of birds travel great distances each year to avoid extreme cold temperatures brought on by winter. This event is called migration. Even though the migration itself may require great amounts of energy, a primary purpose of the behavior is the conservation of energy; the weather in the different climate should require less energy to maintain homeostasis. Animals do not only migrate from their habitat as a result of climate change. Some follow the availability of food. Others, like Atlantic salmon, migrate from the river where they are born as part of their life cycle.

While some animals migrate when the weather gets cold, other animals survive by burrowing into soil or mud and beginning a resting period called **hibernation**. During hibernation, an animal's metabolism slows down. Its body temperature drops and it breathes only a few times a minute. This extended period of inactivity conserves energy—the fat stored in its body—at a time when food may be scarce.

Societal living provides animals with specific means to react to external stimuli as well. For example, most penguins breed and live in large colonies. When they are on land during periods of extreme cold, penguins may huddle together to retain heat and conserve energy. During these huddles, the penguins on the outside of the huddle bear the brunt of the wind while the penguins in the center of the huddle stay the warmest; the penguins rotate so that each animal takes a turn in the center of the huddle and on its perimeter.

Plants react to stimuli as well. For example, plants rely on sunlight for the creation of energy. Despite relatively fixed roots, plants may lean and grow toward the light source. This directional growth is known as **phototropism**. Plants also respond to stimuli by letting their roots run deeper when they need water.

Biological Evolution

There is evidence supporting the theory that the diversity of life is the result of **evolution**, which is a change in the traits of organisms over a series of generations. Mutation is a main cause of evolution because the sequence of a gene is altered, forever changing the species. The other major cause is natural selection. Charles Darwin developed the theory of **natural selection** and proposed that organisms best fit for their environment will survive (survival of the fittest). **Adaptation** is the process by which a population becomes better suited to its environment, possibly through the development of a feature that helps the population survive. Favorable mutations become adaptations that are passed on to offspring and help them survive in their environment.

Fossil records reveal several variations in organs and structures of vertebrate animals. These variations were most likely the result of genetic mutations, changes in genetic code that is passed on to offspring. More favorable mutations help an organism survive, while less favorable mutations are reduced.

During the course of evolution, new species arise. This process is called **speciation**. Organisms that fail to adapt to a changing environment or are unable to compete with superior competition run the risk of extinction, the end of an organism's existence on Earth.

Classification

Organisms are classified by similarity to other organisms and placed in a system of **taxonomy** or hierarchical groups of related organisms. For instance, birds are classified with other organisms that fly, which are classified with other warm-blooded animals, which are classified with other animals. The classification has been revised several times, and currently includes eight levels of classifications: Domain, Kingdom, Phylum (Division for plants), Class, Order, Family, Genus, and Species.

The three **domains** of organisms are archaea, bacteria, and eukaryotes. Archaea are a small group of prokaryotic single-celled organisms. Prokaryotes lack a nucleus and other cellular organelles. Many of these organisms have adapted to live in extreme conditions, like high temperatures and salty environments, but have also been found in all habitats. Bacteria are unicellular prokaryotic microorganisms. Bacteria vary in shape and include spheres, rods, and spirals. Bacteria are found in every habitat on Earth and, when compared with Archaea, have differences in the compositions of their cell membranes, DNA replication, and other structures. All other living things comprise the domain Eukaryota. Eukaryotes are organisms whose cells have a nucleus and specialized organelles, and most eukaryotes are multicellular.

There are six **kingdoms** of living things: Archaebacteria, Eubacteria, Protista, Fungi, Plantae, and Animalae. Archaebacteria and Eubacteria are unicellular prokaryotes. Protists are either unicellular, like amoebas and protozoa, or multicellular without specialized tissue, like algae. There are autotrophs (make their own food) and heterotrophs (find food from other sources) classified as protists, which are found in aquatic environments or in other organisms as parasites. Fungi are multicellular heterotrophs that exist only on land. Fungi reproduce asexually and sexually using pores. Some fungi play an essential role in ecosystems by decomposing dead matter and replacing nutrients in the soil. Plants are multicellular autotrophs that live on land and have cell walls containing cellulose. Plant growth only happens at sites of actively dividing cells, meristems, which are located at the tips and edges of the plant. Bryophytes are nonvascular plants that lack vascular tissue to circulate fluids. Vascular plants have tissue systems that circulate water and nutrients through the plant. These plants are either seedless or have seeds to reproduce. There are two types of vascular seed plants: gymnosperms, with seeds from cones, and angiosperms, flowering plants. Animals are multicellular heterotrophs that live on land and in water, and their cells lack cell walls. Animals are either invertebrates (without backbones) or vertebrates (with backbones). Invertebrate animals include the phyla of sponges, jellyfish, worms, mollusks, arthropods, and starfish. Mollusks include gastropods (snails and slugs), bivalves (clams and mussels), and cephalopods (octopi and squid). Arthropods are animals with hard exoskeletons and have segmented bodies with appendages on at least one segment; insects have six legs and arachnids (spiders and scorpions) have eight legs. Vertebrate animals make up the phylum chordata (along with some closely related invertebrates) and include fish, amphibians, reptiles, birds, and mammals. Birds and mammals are considered warm-blooded, because they can maintain their body temperature while other, cold-blooded, animals cannot. **Mammals** (of which humans are a part) are characterized by having milk-producing glands to feed offspring, growing hair, and giving birth to live young instead of laying eggs (with the exception of the duck-billed platypus).

Viruses are microscopic parasites that are unable to reproduce without a host cell. In order to reproduce, a virus needs to infect an organism and inject its genetic material into a cell for replication. Viruses contain DNA or RNA surrounded by a protein coat, but lack metabolic activity, a nucleus, and other cellular organelles. With this in mind, many scientists consider viruses to be nonliving.

Interdependence of Organisms

The species in communities interact in many ways. They compete for space and resources, they can be related as predator and prey, or they rely on each other as host and parasite. Plants and other photosynthetic organisms harness and convert solar energy and supply the rest of the food chain. Herbivores (plant eaters) obtain energy directly from plants. Carnivores are meat eaters and obtain energy by eating other animals. Omnivores eat both meat and plants. Decomposers feed on dead organisms. The flow of energy can then be represented as follows:

Sun → Photosynthetic organisms →
Herbivores → Carnivores or Omnivores →
Decomposers

The **food chain** is not the only example of the interdependence of organisms. Species often have to compete for food and space, so that the increase in population of one can cause the decrease in population of the other. Organisms also may have a symbiotic relationship (live in close association), which could be classified as parasitism, mutualism, or commensalism. In a **parasitic** relationship, one organism benefits at the expense of the other. For example, a flea feeding from the blood of a dog represents a parasitic relationship. **Commensalism** is symbiosis in which one organism benefits and the other is neither harmed nor rewarded, as with orchids growing on trees. In **mutualism**, both organisms benefit. For example, both organisms benefit when a bird eats nectar from a flower and pollinates the flower at the same time. Under ideal conditions, with ample food and space and no predators, all living organisms have the capacity to reproduce infinitely. However, resources are limited, limiting the population of a species.

Humans probably come closest to being a species with seemingly infinite reproductive capacity. Our population keeps increasing. Our only danger seems to come from viruses and bacteria, which at this point we more or less have under control. When we need more food, we grow more, and when we need more space, we clear some, sometimes modifying ecosystems and destroying habitats through direct harvesting, pollution, atmospheric changes, and other factors.

Organisms are organized into **trophic levels** according to their role in the food chain. Plants and other autotrophs occupy the first level, because they produce energy from sunlight. Herbivores occupy the second level, because they feed off the plants. The third level is for carnivores that eat second-level animals. At the fourth level are carnivores that eat other carnivores. As energy moves up the levels, some of it is used by organisms within the trophic, making it less available for higher-level organisms. As a result, primary producers have the most biomass and top-level carnivores have the least.

Another way to consider the organization of organisms on Earth is to recognize the relationship between producers, consumers, and decomposers. **Producers** are organisms that get their energy from inorganic compounds, such as sunlight, water, and soil. Plants are producers. **Consumers** are organisms that get their energy from other organisms. Human beings, for example, are consumers because they need to consume other organisms (including plants and animals) to sustain life; they can't produce their own energy from inorganic substances. **Decomposers** are organisms that break down other organisms, including producers and consumers, for their energy.

An **ecosystem** is a group of all living organisms (biotic factors) interacting with all the nonliving (abiotic) factors of the environment. For example, all the aquatic animals and plants in a lake, and the water, food, and wastes, make up an ecosystem. Energy and matter move through biotic and abiotic factors according to biogeochemical cycles. For instance, the carbon cycle describes the movement of carbon through the uptake of carbon dioxide by plants and ocean surface reactions, and its release to the atmosphere by respiration of organisms, decomposition of carbon compounds by bacteria and fungi, and combustion of fossil fuels. The water cycle is the movement of water in the ecosystem through the processes of evaporation, precipitation, runoff, and use by organisms. Living organisms rely on the nitrogen cycle for nitrogen to produce proteins, because they cannot use nitrogen abundantly found in the atmosphere. Only specific bacteria can fix nitrogen into a usable form, and are responsible for returning it back into the atmosphere. Other molecules follow cycles in ecosystems and also rely on the food chains between living organisms.

A group of species interacting with each other is called a **population**. The maximum population growth under ideal environmental conditions is considered the population's **biotic potential**. Systems of different species interacting with each other create a **community**. Factors within the community will act to limit a population's actual growth, like food sources, competition, predators, and climate. The number of individuals an ecosystem can support is called its carrying capacity. **Succession** is the process of communities changing over time. When organisms form a new community in previously uninhabited areas, like a lava flow area, it is called primary succession. When an existing community is destroyed by a disturbance, as with a forest fire, it is considered a secondary succession.

Biomes are large geographical areas that share similar types of plants, animals, and climate conditions. Biomes are larger than ecosystems and are similar across the world at the same latitude or similar altitudes. **Tundra** consists of polar regions and alpine locations with a permanently frozen subsoil layer, called permafrost, and tiny plants that grow only during the short summer seasons. The land tends to be boggy in the summer and animals are migratory. Tundra is a very windy area. **Taiga** is characterized by coniferous forest, like spruce and fir, and covers much of the northern hemisphere. Winters are long and cold, and summers are short and dry. **Temperate deciduous forest** consists of trees that lose their leaves each winter, like maple, birch, and oak. There are cold winters and hot summers with plenty of rainfall for trees and plants. There is a great diversity of animal and plant life. **Tropical seasonal forests** and **rain forests** are areas in the tropics that are warm and wet most of the year. Some areas have distinct wet and dry seasons. Biodiversity is at a maximum in these regions, which contain at least half of Earth's land plants and animal species. **Grasslands** and **prairies** have warmer summers than deciduous forests, but with less rainfall. Grasslands have rich soil, which supports farmlands and large populations of grazing animals. Due to hot, dry summers, grasslands experience fires, which is a natural part of this biome. **Deserts** are very dry with little precipitation. Plants and animals have special adaptations to conserve water. Aquatic biomes are freshwater and marine. **Freshwater** includes streams, rivers, ponds, lakes, and wetlands. **Marine regions** include oceans, estuaries, and coral reefs, and have saltwater. Marine life is diverse and their ecosystems are divided into zones: pelagic (open water), benthic (deep water), abyssal (deepest ocean), and intertidal (exposed at low tide).

Physical Science

About 30% of the science section of the Praxis II: Elementary Education: Content Knowledge test—or about nine of the 30 questions—will include questions relating to physical science. This includes the properties of matter, including the atoms and molecules that comprise all matter. You will also be expected to understand forces and motions of objects, including all the different types of motion and the laws relating to motion. Several questions will likely ask you about energy, such as the different forms of energy or how it is transferred or conserved. Finally, you should be familiar with the different ways that energy and matter interact in phenomena such as waves.

Matter

Everything is made up of **matter**. Matter has mass and takes up space. Matter exists in one of three states: **solid**, **liquid**, or **gas**. Solids have distinct shapes and occupy definite volume. The particles making up a solid are packed closely together and maintain fixed positions. Liquids take on the shape of their container and have a definite volume. A liquid's particles are free to move within the boundaries of the liquid within its container. Gases do not have a distinct shape or a definite volume. The particles of gas are in constant motion and are farther apart than liquids and solids. Gas will expand to fill the entire space that contains it, like the air in a room. It is important to remember that gases still have volume and therefore take up space. An empty cup on the surface of Earth will still be occupied by air, which takes up space.

When matter goes from one state to another, it is referred to as a change of state. State changes are controlled by temperature and pressure. As temperature increases, matter will change state from solid to liquid to gas. This is because increasing temperature increases the movement of particles, which is highest in a gaseous state. As pressure is increased, matter moves from gas to liquid to solid. This is because increasing pressure forces particles to get closer; particles are closest in a solid state. The process of moving from a solid state into a liquid state is called **melting**; the temperature at this change is referred to as its **melting point**. Moving from liquid to gas is called **boiling**, and the corresponding temperature is the **boiling point**. When gas changes to a liquid state, it is called **condensation**. When liquid changes to a solid state, it is called **freezing** or **crystallization**, and this corresponding temperature is the **freezing point**. The freezing point is the same as the melting point for any substance. The temperature and pressure at which a substance can exist in equilibrium in its three states of matter is called the **triple point**. When a substance changes state from a solid to gas without first turning into a liquid, it is referred to as **sublimation**. When a substance changes state from a gas to solid without first turning into a liquid, it is referred to as **deposition**.

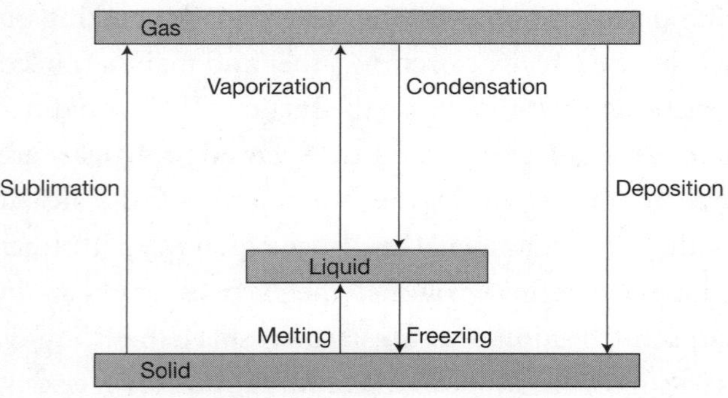

Each of the changes where matter goes from one state to another is a **physical change** of matter. With all physical changes, the change can be undone, meaning that the process can be reversed. For example, water that is frozen to create ice can then be melted to return to its original liquid form.

Atoms and Atomic Theory

Matter is made up of **atoms**. The book you are reading, the neurons in your brain, and the air that you are breathing can all be described as a collection of various atoms. All atoms of a given element are identical. Atoms are made up of subatomic particles: protons, neutrons, and electrons. **Protons** and **neutrons** make up the nucleus of an atom and give an atom its mass. **Electrons** are in motion around the nucleus and have a negligible mass. Electrons are distributed in specific orbitals around the nucleus and each orbital consists of increasing energy levels referred to as shells. Protons are positively charged and neutrons are not charged, leaving the nucleus positively charged. The electrons distributed around the nucleus have a negative charge. If the number of protons is equal to the number of electrons, then the atom will be neutral. Sometimes, an atom will give up an electron or take an electron to become electronically stable, and will have a net positive or negative charge, respectively.

Neil Bohr devised a model to describe the structure of atoms. It depicts electrons as orbiting around the central nucleus. An electron can be excited by a quantum of energy, moving it to an outer orbit (excited level). The electron can then emit radiation (energy) to fall back to its original orbit (ground state). The electrons in the outer orbit are referred to as valence electrons and are in the last energy level. These electrons are loosely held and are responsible for the bonding with other elements and electrons. An element is most stable when it has eight valence electrons.

A representation of a lithium atom (Li). It has 3 protons (p) and 4 neutrons (n) in the nucleus, and 3 electrons (e) in the two electron shells. Its atomic number is 3 (p). Its atomic mass is 7 amu (p + n). The atom has no net charge because the number of positively charged protons equals the number of negatively charged electrons.

The **atomic number** of an element represents the number of protons in its nucleus. The mass number or atomic mass is the sum of protons and neutrons in the nucleus. The atomic number determines the identity of an element. However, an element can have a different atomic mass depending on the number of neutrons in the nucleus. This is called an isotope of an element and most often is an unstable form of the element.

Radioactivity is the spontaneous emission of particles from an unstable nucleus. This radioactive decay can form isotopes or new elements, and can release energy. An alpha particle is a positively charged particle emitted from a heavy nucleus. A beta particle is an electron emitted from an element. During a beta emission, a neutron is converted into a proton, thus increasing the atomic number and changing the identity of the element. Gamma radiation typically occurs with alpha and beta emissions. Gamma rays are high-energy photons that do not change the atomic number or mass of an element.

The **half-life** is the amount of time for half of the atoms of a radioactive sample to decay. This is an important characteristic of isotopes used to determine when radioactive material is safe to handle or to calculate the age of ancient things, as in carbon dating.

Fission is the nuclear reaction of a large isotope breaking apart into two or more smaller elements. This can be accomplished by bombarding the isotope with a smaller unit, usually a neutron. This reaction releases a lot of energy, which has been harnessed in atomic bombs and nuclear power plants.

A **fusion** reaction is essentially the reverse of a fission reaction; two smaller nuclei are fused into one heavier nucleus. This is the same reaction that powers the sun. Fusion reactions release an extraordinary amount of energy. This was first demonstrated detonating the hydrogen bomb, which is approximately 1,000 times as powerful as an atomic bomb. Scientists have tried for several decades to safely harness the energy from a fusion reaction. If this reaction is controlled, it has potential to provide a limitless electricity supply with no pollution.

Elements are categorized by the **periodic table** in order of increasing number of protons. Most periodic tables will provide the symbol for each element and its atomic number (based on the number of protons). For example, the first element in the table is hydrogen, with the symbol H. The 1 in the box represents that its atomic number is 1—and it has 1 proton.

Elements arranged in columns, referred to as families or groups, have the same number of valence electrons and share similar characteristics. Some important families are alkali metals (IA), alkaline earth metals (IIA), halogens (VIIA), and noble gases (VIIIA). The rows of the periodic table are called periods, and the elements of each period do not have any similarities. Moving from left to right along a period the atomic radius increases and the ability to gain electrons increases, referred to as electronegativity. Moving from top to bottom in a family the atomic radius increases and the electronegativity decreases.

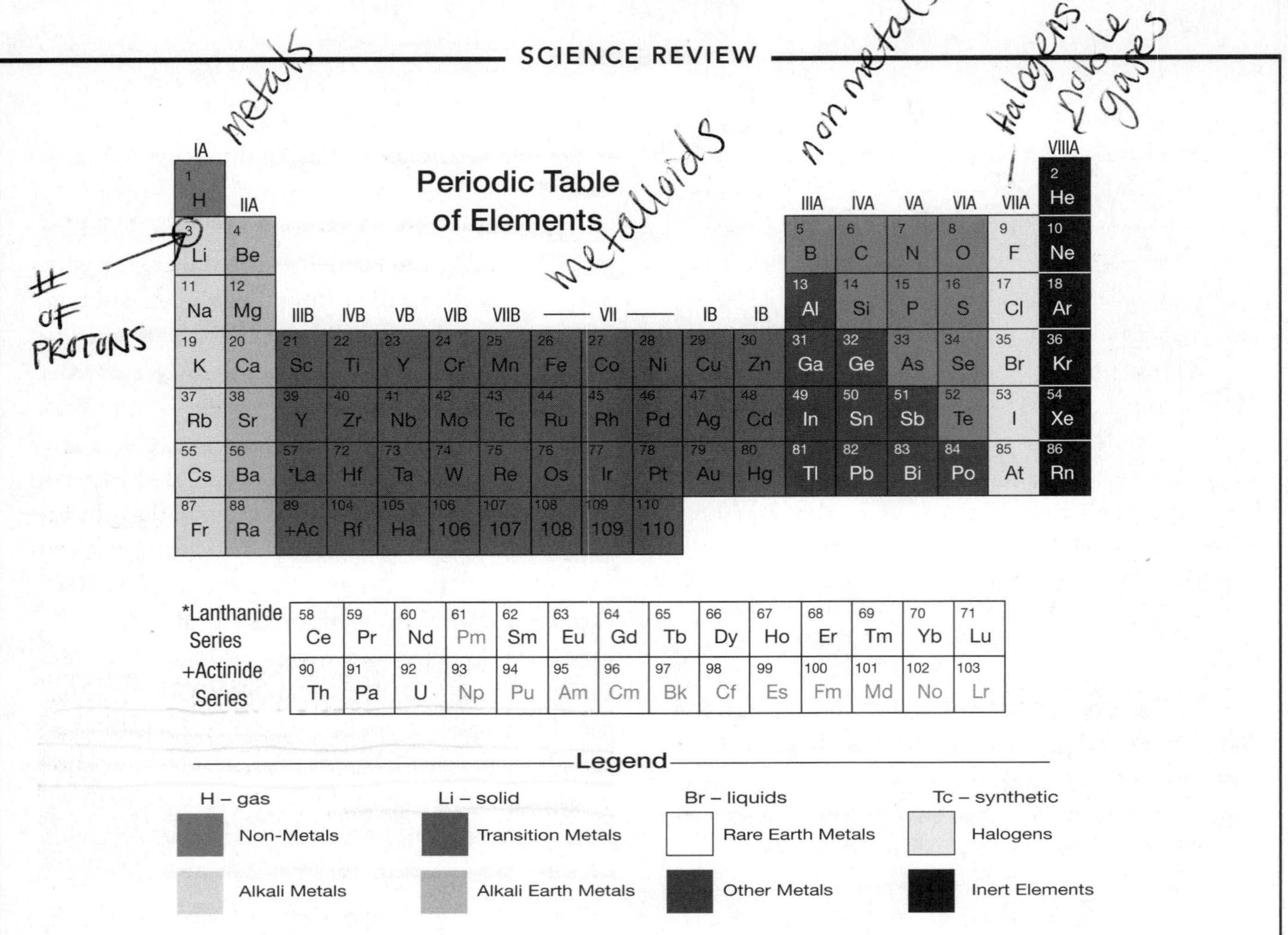

Metals are elements that have high densities, are good conductors of electricity and heat, are shiny and malleable, and are solid at room temperature. Metals have a greater tendency to lose their valence electrons and are grouped in the left side of the periodic table (families I–III). **Nonmetals** are elements that react easily with other substances, are poor conductors, readily accept electrons, and are gaseous at room temperature. Nonmetals are found in the upper right side of the periodic table. **Metalloids** are nonmetallic elements with properties in between those of metals and nonmetals, like semiconductivity. They are found between metals and nonmetals on the periodic table. **Halogens** in family VIIA are nonmetal gases at room temperature that usually exist diatomically, such as Fluorine (F_2). **Noble gases** are in the far right column of the periodic table and have a full number of valence electrons, making them stable and unreactive to other substances.

Compounds and Mixtures

Molecules are two or more atoms bonded together. For example, oxygen in the atmosphere is actually a compound of two atoms of molecule, represented as O_2. A **compound** is a combination of two or more elements and is named according to the bonds that hold them together. Covalent compounds share one or more electron pairs between atoms, and are typically two nonmetal elements. Polar covalent compounds have stronger bonds due to one atom pulling the electron pair more than the other. The resulting molecule has a dipole between the atoms; one end has a negative charge and the other a positive charge. Polar molecules are attracted to other polar molecules and form strong hydrogen bonds between them.

Binary covalent compounds (two elements present) are named according to the number of atoms. Prefixes are used with the name to indicate the number atoms present, such as carbon dioxide (CO_2) and dinitrogen tetroxide (N_2O_4). Ionic compounds tend to be a combination of metal and nonmetal elements. They are named with the metal first, followed by the nonmetal whose ending is changed to *-ide*, such as lithium sulfide (Li_2S). Other times it is a compound of positive or negative polyatomic ions, like ammonium carbonate $(NH_4)_2CO_3$.

A **mixture** is a combination of two or more compounds to form a **solution**. The two substances are not chemically bonded to each other and can be separated out. The liquid of a mixture is called the solvent, and the solute is the compound dissolved into the solvent.

Chemical Reactions

Chemical reactions involve changes in the chemical arrangement of atoms. In a chemical reaction, the atoms of reactants combine, recombine, or dissociate to form products. The number of atoms of a particular element remains the same before and after a chemical reaction. The total mass is also preserved. Similarly, energy is never created or destroyed by a chemical reaction. If chemical bonds are broken, energy from those bonds can be liberated into the surroundings as heat. However, this liberation of energy does not constitute creation, since the energy only changes form—from chemical to heat.

Removing stains from clothes, digesting food, and burning wood in a fireplace are all examples of chemical reactions. During this **chemical change** of matter, the changes cannot be undone. For example, when a piece of steel rusts, the rust represents a chemical reaction between the metal and the oxygen in the atmosphere. Compounds interacted with other chemical compounds to change their composition. The chemical change occurred on a molecular level.

Forces and Motion

A **force** is a push or a pull. Objects move in response to forces acting on them. When you kick a ball, it rolls. A force is also required to stop motion. The ball stops rolling because of the **frictional force**. For example, when you eat, your body first breaks the chemical bonds in the food you have eaten. This supplies your body with energy. You use up some of that energy to kick the ball. You apply a force, and as a result the ball moves, carrying the energy suppplied by your foot. But some of that energy is transferred from the ball to the ground it rolls on, in the form of heat, due to the frictional force it encounters on the surface of the ground. As energy is lost this way, the ball slows down. When all the energy is used up through friction, the ball stops moving. This example illustrates the concept of conservation of energy, as well as **Newton's first law—the Law of Inertia**.

> **LAW OF INERTIA**
>
> The velocity of an object does not change unless a force is applied.

What is the difference between speed and velocity? A speed, such as 30 miles per hour, has **magnitude**. A velocity has **magnitude and direction** (30 miles per hour, north). A similar distinction can be made in considering the difference in the terms **distance** and **displacement**. If you walk 20 feet to your mailbox and 20 feet back, the distance you traveled is 40 feet. Your **displacement** is zero, because displacement compares your ending point to the starting point. **Velocity** is defined as the displacement divided by elapsed time. When you look at the change in velocity divided by the elapsed time, you are looking at **acceleration**. An acceleration that is negative (due to an ending velocity that is less than the starting velocity) is called a **deceleration**. **Momentum** is calculated by multiplying the amount of mass of an object by its velocity.

For velocity of motion to change, either the speed and/or the direction must change and a net or unbalanced force must be applied. To summarize, an object at rest (whose speed is zero) remains at rest, unless some force acts on it—a person pushes it, the wind blows it away, gravity pulls it down. An object that is moving continues to move at the same speed in the same direction, unless some force is applied to it to slow it down, to speed it up, or to change its direction. The amount of acceleration or deceleration is directly proportional to the force applied. The harder you kick the ball, the faster it will move. The mass of the ball will also determine how much it will accelerate. Kick a soccer ball. Now kick a giant ball made of lead with the same force (watch your foot!).Which ball moves faster as a result of an equal kick? These observations constitute **Newton's second law—the Law of Acceleration.**

LAW OF ACCELERATION

The acceleration of an object depends on its mass and on the force applied to it. The greater the force, the greater the acceleration. The greater the mass, the lower the acceleration. Or, mathematically, *force = mass × acceleration* ($F = ma$).

A good way to learn about the laws of motion is to shoot pool. What happens to billiard balls if you miss and fail to hit any of them? Nothing. They stay at rest. What happens when you hit the cue ball with the cue? It moves in the direction you hit it in. The harder you hit it, the faster it moves. Now, what happens when the cue ball collides with another ball? The other ball starts moving. The cue ball slows down. The energy is transferred from the cue ball to the ball it collided with. When an object exerts a force on a second object, the second object exerts an equal force in the opposite direction on the first object. This is **Newton's third law—the Law of Interaction**.

Circular motion is motion with constant speed in a circle. Since the direction of the velocity changes in this case, there is acceleration even though the speed is constant. **Relative motion** takes into account the motion of an object based on the motion of the observer. For example, a ball thrown up and down on an airplane may be traveling 500 miles an hour (along with the airplane), but to a passenger on the plane the ball appears to move in a linear motion. This concept also explains why a slower vehicle may appear to be going backwards when viewed from the faster vehicle.

LAW OF INTERACTION

For every action, there is an equal and opposite reaction.

Types of Forces

Newton's laws do not depend on the type of force that is applied. Some types of forces include gravitational, electromagnetic, contact (including friction), nuclear, and centripetal.

Gravitation is an attractive force that each object with mass exerts on any other object with mass. The strength of the gravitational force depends on the masses of the objects and on the distance between them. When we think of gravity, we usually think of Earth's gravity, which prevents us from jumping infinitely high, keeps our homes stuck to the ground, and makes things thrown upward fall down. We, too, exert a gravitational force on Earth, and we exert forces on one another, but this is not very noticeable because our masses are very small in comparison with the mass of our planet. The greater the masses involved, the greater the gravitational force between them. The sun exerts a force on Earth, and Earth exerts a force on the sun. The moon exerts a force on Earth, and Earth on the moon. As the distance between two objects doubles, the gravitational force between them decreases four times.

What is the difference between weight and mass? On Earth, the acceleration due to gravity, g, is -9.8 m/s^2. Your weight (w) is really a force. The formula $F = ma$ becomes $w = mg$. Since the acceleration,

GRAVITATION

Gravitation is an attractive force that exists among all objects. It is proportional to the masses of the objects and inversely proportional to the square of the distance between them.

g, is $-9.8\ m/s^2$, the overall force (w) is negative, which just means that its pull is in the downward direction: Earth is pulling you toward its center. You weigh less on the moon than on Earth because the gravitational force on the Moon is less than Earth's gravitational force. Your mass, however, would still be the same, because mass is just a measure of how dense you are and the volume you take up.

Electricity and magnetism are two aspects of a single **electromagnetic force**. Moving electric charges produce magnetic forces, and moving magnets produce electric forces. The electromagnetic force exists between any two charged or magnetic objects, for example, a proton and an electron or two electrons. Opposite charges attract (an electron and a proton) while like charges repel (two protons or two electrons). The strength of the force depends on the charges and on the distance between them. The greater the charges, the greater the force. The closer the charges are to each other, the greater the force between them.

Contact forces are forces that exist as a result of an interaction between objects, physically in contact with one another. They include the previously discussed frictional forces, as well as tensional forces and normal forces. The frictional force opposes the motion of an object across a surface. For example, if a glass moves across the surface of the dinner table, there exists a frictional force in the direction opposite to the motion of the glass. Friction is the result of attractive intermolecular forces between the molecules of the surface of the glass and the surface of the table. Friction depends on the nature of the two surfaces. For example, there would be less friction between the table and the glass if the table was moistened or lubricated with water. The glass would glide across the table more easily. Friction also depends on the degree to which the glass and the table are pressed together. Air resistance is a type of frictional force. **Tension** is the force that is transmitted through a rope or wire when it is pulled tight by forces acting at each end. The tensional force is directed along the rope or wire and pulls on the objects on either end of the wire. The **normal force** is exerted on an object in contact with another stable object. For example, the dinner table exerts an upward force on a glass at rest on the surface of the table.

Nuclear forces are very strong forces that hold the nucleus of an atom together. If nuclei of different atoms come close enough together, they can interact with one another and reactions between the nuclei can occur.

Centripetal force is the net force that acts to result in the centripetal acceleration. It is not an individual force, but the sum of the forces in the radial direction. It is directed toward the center of the circular motion.

A reaction has a **reaction rate** related to its activation energy. **Activation energy** is the minimum amount of energy required for reactants to be changed into products. The higher the activation energy needed, the slower the reaction rate will be. Some reactions are reversible; products can transform into reactants. **Equilibrium** occurs when the rates for the forward reaction and reverse reaction are the same.

Energy

Energy is the ability to do work. **Kinetic energy** is energy of motion. For example, a flying airplane, a sprinting runner, and a falling rock all represent forms of kinetic energy. **Potential energy** is stored energy that has potential to be converted into another form of energy. For example, an apple dangling from an apple tree has potential energy; when it falls, the potential energy will be converted to kinetic energy. Other forms of potential energy include elastic potential energy, such as a stretched rubber band, or chemical and electrical potential energy, such as a battery.

Look at the following illustration. As the pendulum swings, the energy is converted from potential to kinetic, and back to potential. When the hanging weight is at one of the high points, the gravitational potential energy is at a maximum, and kinetic energy is at the minimum. At the low point, the kinetic energy is maximized, and gravitational potential energy is minimized.

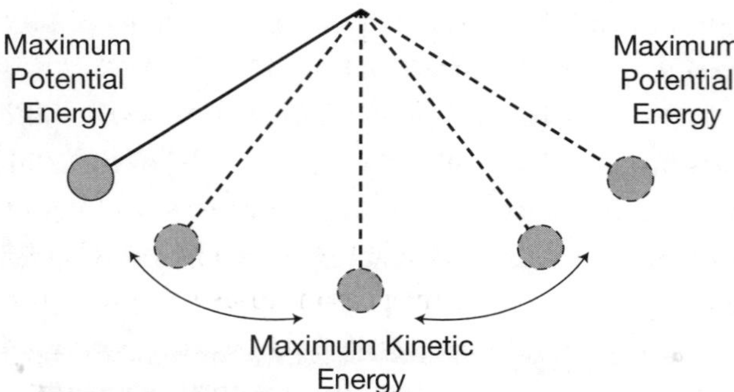

The illustration shows the change of potential energy into kinetic energy, and kinetic energy into potential energy, in a pendulum.

Chemical energy is the energy stored in the bonds between elements. **Thermal energy** is related to temperature and electrical energy is related to the movement of electrons. **Mass energy** refers to the Einstein's Theory of Relativity and is defined as $E = mc^2$, where m is equal to mass and c is equal to the speed of light.

The law of conservation of energy (**first law of thermodynamics**) states that energy cannot be created nor destroyed, but can be transformed into other forms. The **second law of thermodynamics** states that when work is done, some energy is lost as heat. This process increases a system's **entropy**, which is a measure of energy unavailable to do work. Heat is the transfer of energy from areas of high energy (or temperature) to low energy. For example, when you rub your hands together quickly, you will notice that the energy you use creates heat. This is a result of the force of friction, which produces heat. **Conduction** moves heat through matter from areas of high temperature to low temperature. **Convection** transfers heat through the movement of currents within fluids (liquids and gases). The units of heat include the joule (J), British thermal unit (BTU), and calorie (cal).

Measuring potential energy can be difficult. Kinetic energy is easily measured by temperature. A temperature measurement is the average kinetic energy of particles. There are three temperature scales. The Celsius scale is set at 0°C and 100°C for the freezing point and boiling point of water, respectively. The Fahrenheit scale was set at different conditions and is related to the Celsius scale as follows: °F = 1.8°C + 32. The Kelvin scale measures absolute temperature, with 0°K referred to as **absolute zero**, where particles have minimal motion and can be no colder.

Simple Machines

A **simple machine** is a device that uses energy to work. By changing the direction or the strength of a force, a simple machine is able to give its users a mechanical advantage. There are six basic simple machines. An inclined plane is a flat surface at a raised angle that reduces the force required to move an object. A lever uses a solid object with a pivot point to multiply the force to another object. A wedge converts force from its blunt end to its narrow end with its triangular shape. A screw converts a rotational force to a linear force. A pulley changes the direction of a force using a wheel, axle, and a string or rope. Two or more pulleys can be used in conjunction to magnify the mechanical advantage. A wheel and axle rotate around a circle with its center point called the fulcrum. A Ferris wheel is an example of a wheel and axle. The following illustrations show what the six simple machines look like.

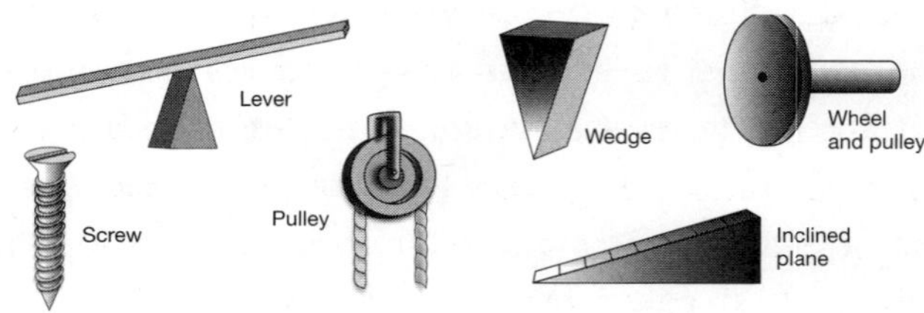

Interactions of Energy and Matter

Energy in all its forms can interact with matter. For example, when heat energy interacts with molecules of water, it makes them move faster and boil. Waves—including sound and seismic waves, waves on water, and light waves—have energy and can transfer that energy when they interact with matter. Consider what happens if you are standing by the ocean and a big wave rolls in. Sometimes the energy carried by the wave is large enough to knock you down. The ocean wave has kinetic energy—sometimes a lot of it!

Waves

Energy is also carried by electromagnetic waves or light waves. All electromagnetic waves travel at the speed of light, roughly 3×10^8 meters per second. The energy of electromagnetic waves is related to their wavelengths. Electromagnetic waves include **radio waves** (the longest wavelength), **microwaves**, **infrared radiation** (radiant heat), **visible light**, **ultraviolet radiation**, **X-rays**, and **gamma rays**.

The wavelength depends on the amount of energy the wave is carrying. Shorter wavelengths carry more energy. All electromagnetic waves are invisible, with the exception of visible light.

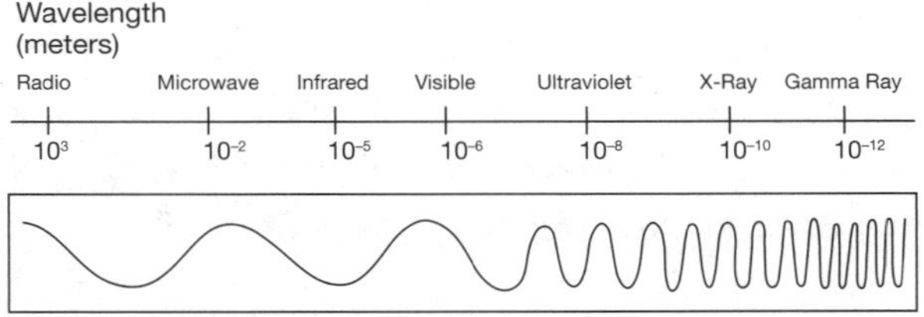

Radio waves are used to broadcast audio, radar, and satellite communications, in addition to other applications. Microwaves, like radio waves, are used for navigation and communication, but they are also known for their ability to heat foods in a microwave oven. Astronomers also use microwave radiation to make discoveries. Ultraviolet (UV) radiation is emitted by the sun, and its waves are responsible for causing sunburns and skin cancer. UV waves, however, are also responsible for many positive effects, including the creation of vitamin D in the human skin. X-ray waves are known for their ability to penetrate through objects, which is why they are used to take images inside objects—such as viewing a broken bone at a doctor's office or inside a passenger's pockets at a security terminal. Celestial objects also emit X-rays, so astronomers study it to learn about our universe. Finally, gamma rays, because they have such short wavelengths and are a form of radiation, are dangerous to human beings. Their energies can cause significant damage at the cellular level. Like many other waves, astronomers study gamma rays emitting from other sources in the universe.

The color that we see on objects depends on what part of the visible light spectrum is being absorbed by the object. For example, an apple may appear red because the apple reflects the red light and absorbs all other frequencies of visible light. Each kind of atom or molecule can gain or lose energy only in particular discrete amounts. When an atom gains energy, light at the wavelength associated with that energy is absorbed. When an atom loses energy, light at the wavelength associated with that energy is emitted. These wavelengths can be used to identify elements.

When a wave hits a smooth surface, such as a mirror, it is reflected rather than being absorbed. That is why a flat mirror provides a reflection without distortion. Matter can also refract or bend waves. This is what happens when a ray of light traveling through air hits a water surface. A part of the wave is reflected, and a part is refracted into the water. A lens also has the ability to refract or bend light waves. By changing the wavelength, a lens can change the focus of an image, helping nearsighted and farsighted people to see more clearly.

Sound waves, which are produced by vibrations, can be reflected as well. The effect of a reflected sound wave is an echo. Keep in mind, however, that a sound wave is not on the electromagnetic spectrum. Like an ocean wave, it must pass through matter—air, in the case of Earth's atmosphere. It is for this reason that you would be unable to hear sounds in space or on the moon; without some matter for the vibrations to travel through, such as air or water, the sound waves cannot be transferred. Sound waves travel at sea level at a speed of about 340 meters per second, which is about 768 miles per hour. This relatively slow speed explains why a bolt of lightning—which travels as visible light at the speed of light—can often be seen much earlier than the sound of the corresponding thunder—which travels as sound waves at only about 340 meters per second.

Electricity and Magnetism

The interaction of the subatomic particles of matter involves **electromagnetic forces**. Electrical forces are either positive or negative. Similar charges repel each other and opposite charges attract each other. The unit for electrical charge is the coulomb (C). Coulomb's law states that the electric force between to electric charges is directly proportional to the product of the magnitudes of each charge and inversely proportional to the square of the distance between them. Normally, objects contain a net charge of zero (equal amounts of positive and negative charges). By applying an external electric field or force on the object, its net charge can be altered to pick up more positive or negative charges. This situation is referred to as **static electricity**.

Conductors easily allow the flow of electron movement or **electrical current**. Insulators resist the flow of electrical current. Semiconductors have properties in between that of a conductor and an insulator. Electrical current is measured by the unit ampere (A) and is equal to the amount of electrical charge per second. The volt (V) is the potential difference across a conductor and can be represented as joules per coulomb (J/C). The electrical resistance between two points of a conductor is measured in ohms (Ω) and is the measure of a substance's ability to oppose electrical current. Ohm's law describes the relationship of electrical current as directly proportional to the voltage and inversely proportional to the resistance ($I = \frac{V}{R}$). A watt (W) measures power, or the ability to do work using electricity, and can be calculated by the product of volts and amperes, $V \times A$.

An **electrical circuit** is a network of electrical current where the current travels in a closed loop within the circuit. The current leads from a voltage source and travels in the loop on wires or some other line of transmission. The following diagram shows a basic circuit: a lightbulb, which converts the electricity from the voltage source into work in the form of light (and heat).

A Basic Current

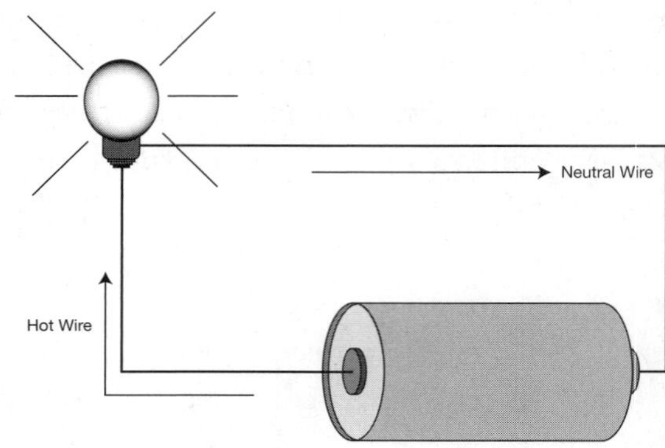

In the diagram of the basic circuit, electrical energy is being converted to light and heat. (Energy efficient lightbulbs tend to give off less heat, making their conversion from energy to light more effective.) However, there are other ways that electrical energy can be converted. A solar cell, for example, converts solar radiation into electrical energy, which can then be used to run an electrical device. A toaster, for example, is used to convert electrical energy to heat. Some new vehicles run on electrical energy, meaning that the energy is converted into motion.

Magnetism is attractive or repulsive forces between objects. Magnetic forces are affected by the charge of the object and its relative motion. Magnetic fields surround electric currents and exert a magnetic force on moving electric charges and magnetic dipoles. A compass, a navigation tool that points to a northerly direction, works because its magnetized pointer aligns to Earth's magnetic field, which is almost exactly in the direction of the planet's geographic North Pole.

Science in Personal and Social Perspectives

Although the majority of the questions in the science section of the Praxis II will include content from life science, earth science, and physical science, you may see one or two questions about science in personal and social perspectives.

Personal Health

Among the questions regarding science in personal and social perspectives, you may be asked about personal health. This topic includes ways to keep your body healthy and fit, as well as keeping safe.

Nutrition and Exercise

The human body requires a balance of vitamins and minerals to maintain its health. The following table lists some of the more important vitamins and minerals to know, their benefits, and several possible sources.

VITAMIN	BENEFIT	POSSIBLE SOURCES
Vitamin A	Keeps eyes healthy, improves skin and immune system	Orange or green vegetables or fruits, dairy products
Vitamin B_1 (Thiamin)	Helps create energy; used by heart and nervous system	Pasta, breads, meat, fish, beans, cereals
Vitamin B_2 (Riboflavin)	Helps create energy; used for vision and making red blood cells	Meat, dairy products, legumes, leafy vegetables
Vitamin B_3 (Niacin)	Helps create energy; maintains skin health and nerve functionality	Cereal, red meat, fish, chicken, peanuts
Vitamin B_6	Aids in red blood cell creation; improves brain and nerve functionality	Fish, dairy products, potatoes, bananas, beans, some cereals
Vitamin B_9 (Folic acid)	Used to make DNA and red blood cells	Legumes, orange juice, liver, leafy vegetables, some cereals and bread
Vitamin B_{12}	Aids in red blood cell creation and function of nerve cells	Fish, meat, dairy products, some cereals
Vitamin C	Strengthens bones, teeth, blood vessels; improves absorption of calcium and iron	Citrus fruits, berries, tomatoes, broccoli, spinach
Vitamin D	Strengthens bones	Manufactured with help of sunlight, fortified product like milk
Vitamin E	Keeps red blood cells healthy; acts as antioxidant	Vegetables, nuts, oils, leafy greens
Calcium	Builds strong teeth and bones	Dairy products, broccoli, leafy vegetables, soy foods
Iron	Helps red blood cells transmit oxygen throughout body	Fish, red meat, chicken, beans, raisins, leafy vegetables, some cereals
Magnesium	Helps create energy; improves function of nerves and muscles, including heart	Whole grains, nuts, beans, avocados, bananas, leafy vegetables
Phosphorus	Aids formation of teeth and bones; helps create energy	Dairy products, meat, fish
Potassium	Builds healthy muscles and nervous system; helps balance of water in body	Bananas, broccoli, citrus fruits, legumes, potatoes, leafy vegetables
Zinc	Improves immunity system and growth	Fish, red meat, dairy products, nuts

It is important to consider that a healthy diet alone does not make a person healthy. **Physical exercise** is also necessary and should be used in conjunction with a healthy, balanced diet. Exercise helps prevent obesity, which can be responsible for high blood pressure and diseases such as diabetes. While exercise obviously benefits many muscles in the human body, the heart is also a major benefactor of regular exercise. Providing the heart with aerobic exercises helps strengthen it and make it a more efficient organ to deliver blood cells throughout the human body.

In addition to all the physical benefits, regular physical exercise has proven mental rewards. The body produces chemicals called **endorphins** during exercise, and this chemical has the ability to prevent depression and help people stay happier.

Diseases

It's not possible to know about every existing type of disease. However, for the Praxis II, you should be aware of some of the common diseases, the ways that they can spread, and ways to prevent their spread.

Common diseases include the cold, influenza (the flu), measles, and chicken pox. These are all infectious types of diseases, which are spread through germs. For the germs to transfer from one person to another, the person with the germ must transmit it through a bodily fluid. Children help spread germs with contact from their eyes, nose, and mouth. Common ways to prevent infection is to keep surfaces clean, ensure proper hygienic habits (such as not putting objects into the mouth), and wash hands often.

Another common way to prevent the spread of some diseases is through a process called a **vaccination**. A vaccine generally contains a weak or dead version of the microbe that is responsible for the disease. When it is injected into the body, the immune system recognizes the microbe and destroys it. By recognizing it, however, it can then destroy any future microbes that enter the body and prevent potential infection. Vaccines can help provide *immunization*, protection for the immune system, from many infectious diseases. For example, vaccination is responsible for the eradication of smallpox—one of the world's deadliest diseases in the twentieth century.

Viruses are microscopic parasites that are unable to reproduce without a host cell. In order to reproduce, viruses need to infect an organism and inject genetic material into a cell for replication. Viral infections usually lead to disease in animals and humans, and require an immune response to overcome. Antibiotics have no effect on viruses (they treat bacterial infections). Antiviral drugs have also been developed to treat viral infections.

Substance Abuse

Different substances have different effects on the human body. For the Praxis II, you should review their possible effects. For example, the long-terms effects of alcohol abuse include damage to the liver and brain. The ingestion of alcohol during pregnancy can result in fetal alcohol syndrome in the child, as well as low birth weight. The long-term effects of tobacco include cancer, lung disease, heart disease, and stroke.

Science in Technology and Society

Science is forever intertwined with technology. For example, breakthroughs in science frequently drive new technologies. At the same time, improvements in technology allow for science to expand, such as through the inventions and modifications of important instruments. When advancements in science create the need for a new tool, a design must be created and implemented—then utilized and evaluated.

Advancements in science are responsible for many positive contributions in society, too numerous to list. However, it is important to consider that not all human activity resulting from the use of science is beneficial. Utilizing the advantages of modern science, human societies have polluted the environment and created stress on the planet's resources. For example, the creation of the internal combustion engine, one of the most important scientific inventions in the last few centuries, is responsible for the release of carbon dioxide and other chemicals. In large quantities, this carbon dioxide contributes to the greenhouse effect and warming of the planet. The generation of electricity has also created acid rain, an acidic precipitation that has the ability to harm plants and aquatic animals.

Science as Inquiry and Science Processes

All sciences are the same in the sense that they involve the deliberate and systematic observation of nature. Each science is not a loose branch. The branches of science connect to the same root of objective observation, experiments based on the scientific method, and theories and conclusions based on experimental evidence. An advance in one branch of science often contributes to advances in other sciences, and sometimes to entirely new branches. For example, the development of optics led to the design of a microscope, which led to the development of cellular biology.

Science as Inquiry

Whatever their discipline, all scientists use similar methods to study the natural world. For the Praxis II, you should consider the abilities that are necessary for scientific inquiry, including the ways to conduct scientific experiments and draw conclusions from the results. For this section, which may comprise one or two questions on the Praxis II, you should also understand the scientific unifying processes, such as their order and organization.

Abilities Necessary to Do Scientific Inquiry

A good scientist is patient, curious, objective, systematic, ethical, a detailed record keeper, skeptical yet open-minded, and an effective communicator. While there are certainly many scientists who don't possess all these qualities, most strive to obtain or develop them.

Patience is a virtue for any person, but it is essential for a person who wants to be a scientist. Much of science involves repetition: repetition to confirm or reproduce previous results, repetition under slightly different conditions, and repetition to eliminate an unwanted variable. It also involves waiting—for example, waiting for a liquid to boil to determine its boiling point, waiting for an animal to fall asleep in order to study its sleep pattern, waiting for weather conditions or a season to be right. Both the repetition and the waiting require a great deal of patience. Results are not guaranteed, and a scientist often goes through countless failed attempts before achieving success. Patience and the pursuit of results in spite of difficulties are traits of a good scientist.

Every child asks questions about nature and life. In some people, this curiosity continues throughout adulthood, when it becomes possible to systematically work to satisfy that curiosity with answers. Curiosity is a major drive for scientific research, and it is what enables a scientist to work and concentrate on the same problem over long periods of time. It's the knowing of the how and the why, or at least a part of the answer to these questions, that keeps a scientist in the lab, on the field, in the library, or at the computer for hours.

Objectivity is an essential trait of a true scientist. By objectivity, we mean unbiased observation. A good scientist can distinguish fact from opinion and does not let personal views, hopes, beliefs, or societal norms interfere with the observation of facts or reporting of experimental results. An **opinion** is a statement not necessarily supported by scientific data. Opinions are often based on personal feelings or beliefs and are usually difficult, if not impossible to measure and test. A **fact** is a statement based on scientific data or objective observations. Facts can be measured or observed, tested, and reproduced. A well-trained scientist recognizes the importance of reporting all results, even if they are unexpected, undesirable, or inconsistent with personal views, prior hypothesis, theories, or experimental results.

Scientists who are effective experimentalists tend to work systematically. They observe each variable independently, and develop and adhere to rigorous experimental routines or procedures. They keep consistent track of all variables and systematically look for changes in those variables. The tools and methods by which changes in variables are measured or observed are kept constant. All experiments have a clear objective. Good scientists never lose track of the purpose of the experiment. They design experiments in such a way that the results are not overwhelming and that the results obtained are not ambiguous. The scientific method, which is described later in this chapter, forms a good basis for **systematic research**.

Good **record keeping** can save scientists a lot of trouble. Most scientists find keeping a science log or journal helpful. The journal should describe in detail the basic assumptions, goals, experimental techniques, equipment, and procedures. It can also include results, analysis of results, literature references, thoughts and ideas, and conclusions. Any problem encountered in the laboratory should also be noted in the journal, even if it is not directly related to the experimental goals. For example, if there is an equipment failure, it should be noted. Conditions that brought about the failure and the method used to fix it should also be described. It may not seem immediately useful, but three years down the road, the same failure could occur. Even if the scientist recollected the previous occurrence of the problem, the details of the solution would likely be forgotten and more time would be needed to fix it. But looking back to the journal could potentially pin down the problem and provide a solution much more quickly. Scientific records should be clear and readable, so that another scientist could follow the thoughts and repeat the procedure described. Records can also prove useful if there is a question about intellectual property or ethics of the researcher.

Reading scientific journals, collaborating with other scientists, going to conferences, and publishing scientific papers and books are basic elements of **effective communication** in the science community. Scientists benefit from exploring science literature because they can often use techniques, results, or methods published by other scientists. In addition, new results need to be compared or connected to related results published in the past, so that someone reading or hearing about the new result can understand its impact and context. As many scientific branches have become interdisciplinary, collaboration among scientists of different backgrounds is essential. For example, a chemist may be able to synthesize and crystallize a protein, but analyzing the effect of that protein on a living system requires the training of a biologist. Rather than viewing each other as competition, good scientists understand that they have a lot to gain by collaborating with scientists who have different strengths, training, and resources. Presenting results at scientific conferences and in science journals is often a fruitful and rewarding process. It opens up a scientific theory or experiment to discussion, criticism, and suggestions. It is a ground for idea inception and exchange in the science community. Scientists also often need to communicate with those outside the scientific community—students of science, public figures who make decisions about funding science projects, and journalists who report essential scientific results to the general audience.

Scientists are trained to be **skeptical** about what they hear, read, or observe. Rather than automatically accept the first explanation that is proposed, they search for different explanations and look for holes in reasoning or experimental inconsistencies. They come up with tests that a theory should pass if it is valid. They think of ways in which an experiment can be improved. This is not done maliciously. The goal is not to discredit other researchers, but to come up with good models and understanding of nature.

Unreasonable skepticism, however, is not very useful. There is a lot of room in science for **open-**

mindedness. If a new theory is in conflict with intuition or belief or previously established theories, but is supported by rigorously developed experiments, and can be used to make accurate predictions, refusal to accept its validity is stubbornness, rather than skepticism.

A good scientist should be an **ethical** scientist. Consider a chemist in the pharmaceutical company who, after much effort, designs a chemical that can cure brain tumors without affecting healthy brain cells. No doubt the scientist is excited about this result and its potential positive impact on humanity. Once in a while, however, experimental rats given this drug die from heart failure within minutes after the drug is administered. But since it happens only occasionally, the scientist assumes that it's only a coincidence, and that those rats that died had heart problems and would have died anyway. The scientist doesn't report these few cases to the supervisor, and assumes that if it's a serious problem, the FDA (Food and Drug Administration) would discover it, and nobody would get hurt. While the scientist has good intentions, such as making the benefits of the new drug available to people who need it, failing to report and further investigate the potential adverse effects of the drug constitutes negligent and unethical behavior. Scientists are expected to report data without making up, adjusting, downplaying, or exaggerating results. Scientists are also expected to not take credit for work they didn't do, to obey environmental laws, and to consider and understand the implications of the use of scientific knowledge they bring about.

Why study science? A scientist seeks to observe, understand, or control the processes and laws of nature. Scientists assume that nature is governed by orderly principles. They search for these principles by making observations. The job of a scientist is to figure out how something works, or to explain why it works the way it does. Looking for a pattern, for cause and effect, explanation, improvement, and developing theories based on experimental results are all jobs of a scientist.

The Scientific Method

There are many ways to obtain knowledge. Modern scientists tend to obtain knowledge about the world by making systematic observations. This principle is called **empiricism** and is the basis of the **scientific method**. The scientific method is a set of rules for asking and answering questions about science. Most scientists use the scientific method loosely and often unconsciously.

However, the key concepts of the scientific method are the groundwork for scientific study, and we review those concepts in this section.

The scientific method involves:

- asking a specific question about a process or phenomenon that can be answered by performing experiments.
- formulating a testable hypothesis based on observations and previous results (i.e., making a guess).
- designing an experiment, with a control, to test the hypothesis.
- collecting and analyzing the results of the experiment.
- developing a model or theory that explains the phenomenon and is consistent with experimental results.
- making predictions based on the model or theory in order to test it and designing experiments that could disprove the proposed theory.

The Question

In order to understand something, a scientist must first focus on a specific question or aspect of a problem. In order to do that, the scientist has to clearly formulate the question. The answer to such a question has to exist and the possibility of obtaining it through experiment must exist. For example, the question "Does the presence of the moon shorten the life span of ducks on Earth?" is not valid because it cannot be answered through experiment. There is no way to measure the life span of ducks on Earth in the absence of the moon, since we have no way of removing the moon from its orbit. Similarly, asking a general question, such as "How do animals obtain food?" is not very useful for gaining knowledge. This question is too general and broad for one person to answer.

Better questions are more specific—for example, "Does each member of a wolf pack have a set responsibility or job when hunting for food?" A question that is too general and not very useful is "Why do some people have better memories than others?" A better, more specific question, along the same lines, is "What parts of the brain and which brain chemicals are involved in recollection of childhood memories?" A good science question is very specific and can be answered by performing experiments.

The Hypothesis

After formulating a question, a scientist gathers the information on the topic that is already available or published, and then comes up with an educated guess or a tentative explanation about the answer to the question. Such an educated guess about a natural process or phenomenon is called a **hypothesis**. A hypothesis doesn't have to be correct, but it should be testable. In other words, a testable hypothesis can be disproved through experiment, in a reasonable amount of time, with the resources available. For example, the statement "Everyone has a soul mate somewhere in the world" is not a valid hypothesis. First of all, the term *soul mate* is not well defined, so formulating an experiment to determine whether two people are soul mates would be difficult. More important, even if we were to agree on what *soul mate* means and how to experimentally determine whether two people are soul mates, this hypothesis could never be proved wrong. Any experiment conceived would require testing every possible pair of human beings around the world, which, considering the population and the population growth per second, is just not feasible. A hypothesis can be a suggested explanation or an educated guess. Keep in mind that it doesn't need to be correct—it only has to be testable.

Disproving a hypothesis is not a failure. It casts away illusions about what was previously thought to be true, and can cause a great advance—a thought in another direction that can bring about new ideas. Most likely, in the process of showing that one hypothesis is wrong, a scientist may gain an understanding of what a better hypothesis may be. Disproving a hypothesis serves a purpose. Science and our understanding of nature often advance through tiny incremental pieces of information. Eliminating a potential hypothesis narrows down the choices, and eliminating the wrong answers sometimes leads to finding the correct one.

The Experiment

In an experiment, researchers manipulate one or more variables and examine their effect on another variable or variables. An experiment is carefully designed to test the hypothesis. The number of variables in an experiment should be manageable and carefully controlled. All variables and procedures are carefully defined and described, as is the method of observation and measurement. Results of a valid experiment are reproducible, meaning that another researcher following the same procedure should be able to obtain the same result.

A good experiment also includes one or more controls. Experimental controls are designed to provide an understanding of the observed variables in the absence of the manipulated variables. For example, in pharmaceutical studies, three groups of patients are examined. One is given the drug, one is given a placebo (a pill containing no active ingredient), and one is not given anything. This is a good way to test whether the improvement in patient condition (observed variable) is due to the active ingredient in the pill (manipulated variable). If the patients in the group that was given the placebo recover sooner or at the same time as those who were given the drug, the effect of pill taking can be attributed to patient belief that a pill makes one feel better, or to other ingredients in the pill. If the group that was not given any pill recovers faster or just as fast as the group that was given the drug, the improvement in patient condition could be a result of the natural healing processes. An experimental control is a version of the experiment in which all conditions and variables are the same as in other versions of the experiment, but the variable being tested is eliminated or changed. A good experiment should include carefully designed controls.

The Analysis

Analysis of experimental results involves looking for trends in the data and correlation among variables. It also involves making generalizations about the results, quantifying experimental error, and correlation of the variable being manipulated to the variable being tested. A scientist who analyzes results unifies them, interprets them, and gives them a meaning. The goal is to find a pattern or sense of order in the observations and to understand the reason for this order.

Models and Theories

After collecting a sufficient amount of consistently reproducible results under a range of conditions or in different kinds of samples, scientists often seek to formulate a theory or a model. A **model** is a hypothesis that is sufficiently general and is continually effective in predicting facts yet to be observed. A **theory** is an explanation of the general principles of certain observations with extensive experimental evidence or facts to support it.

Scientific models and theories, like hypotheses, should be testable using available resources. Scientists make predictions based on their models and theories. A good theory or model should be able to accurately predict an event or behavior. Many scientists go a step beyond and try to test their theories by designing experiments that could prove them wrong. The theories that fail to make accurate predictions are revised or discarded, and those that survive the test of a series of experiments aimed to prove them wrong become more convincing. Theories and models therefore lead to new experiments; if they don't adequately predict behavior, they are revised through development of new hypotheses and experiments. The cycle of experiment-theory-experiment continues until a satisfactory understanding that is consistent with observations and predictions is obtained.

Unifying Processes

Whether they are chemists, biologists, physicists, or geologists, all scientists seek to organize the knowledge and observations they collect. They look for evidence and develop models to provide explanations for their observations. Scientists depend heavily on measurement and developed devices and instruments for measuring different properties of matter and energy. Scientists also use units to make the quantities they measure understandable to other scientists. Questions that come up in every science are:

- What causes change?
- What causes stability?
- How does something evolve?
- How does something reach equilibrium?
- How is form related to function?

Systems, Order, and Organization

What happens when an Internet search produces too many results? Clearly, having some results is better than having none, but having too many can make it difficult to find the necessary information quickly. If scientists didn't systematically organize and order information, looking for or finding a piece of data or making a comparison would be as difficult as looking for one specific book in a huge library in which the books are randomly shelved. In every science, knowledge is grouped into an orderly manner.

In biology, an organism is classified into a domain, kingdom, phylum, class, order, family, genus, and species. Members of the same species are the most similar. All people belong to the same species.

People and monkeys belong to the same order. People and fish belong to the same kingdom, and people and plants share the same domain. This is an example of **hierarchical classification**—each level is included in the levels previously listed. Each species is part of an order, and each order is part of a kingdom, which is a part of a domain.

Another example of hierarchical classification is your address in the galaxy. It would include your house number, street, city, state, country, continent, planet, star system, and galaxy.

Here is another example of organization in biology. Each organism is made of cells. Many cells make up a tissue. Several tissues make up an organ. Several organs make up an organ system. In chemistry, atoms are sorted by atomic number in the periodic table. Atoms that have similar properties are grouped.

Scientists also classify periods of time since Earth's formation 4.6 billion years ago, based on the major events in those eras. Time on Earth is divided into the following eras: Precambrian, Paleozoic, Mesozoic, and Cenozoic. The eras are further divided into periods, and the periods into epochs.

Evidence, Models, and Explanation

Scientists look for evidence. The job of a scientist is to observe and explain the observations using factual evidence, and develop models that can predict unobserved behavior.

Scientific evidence should:

- be carefully documented and organized
- be quantified as much as possible
- be reproducible by other scientists

Scientific explanations should:

- be consistent with observations and evidence
- be able to predict unobserved behavior
- be internally consistent (two statements in the same explanation should not contradict each other)

Scientific models should:

- be consistent with observations
- be consistent with explanations
- be able to predict unobserved behavior
- cover a wide range of observations or behaviors

Equilibrium and Change

A favorite pastime of scientists is figuring out why things change and why they stay the same. For instance, many systems seek to establish equilibrium. In organisms, this equilibrium is called **homeostasis**. It is the tendency of organisms to maintain a stable inner environment, even when the outside environment changes. When people sweat, they are trying to cool off and maintain their equilibrium temperature.

Contrary to a common misconception, equilibrium is not a state of rest at which nothing happens. At chemical equilibrium, reactants continue to form products, and products continue to form reactants. However, the rate of formation of reactants is the same as the rate of formation of products, so that no net change is observed. Equilibria are fragile states, and a little change, a tiny force, is often enough to disturb them. Think of a seesaw in balance. A little puff of wind, and the balance is gone.

The same is true of chemical equilibrium—increase the pressure or temperature, and the equilibrium will shift. Your body is pretty good at keeping a steady temperature, but when you get sick, you are thrown out of balance; up goes your temperature, and out the window goes your homeostasis. A change is often a response to a gradient or a difference in a property in two parts of a system. Here are some examples of common gradients and the changes they drive.

- Difference in **temperature** causes heat to flow from a hotter object (region) to a colder object (region).
- Difference in **pressure** causes liquid (water) or gas (air) to flow from a region of high pressure to a region of low pressure.

- Difference in **electric potential** causes electrons to flow from high potential to low potential.
- Difference in **concentration** causes matter to flow until concentrations in two regions are equalized.

Measurement

An established principle in science is that observations should be quantified as much as possible. This means that rather than reporting that it's a nice day out, a scientist needs to define this statement with numbers. By *nice*, two different people can mean two different things. Some like hot weather. Some like lots of snow. But giving the specifics on the temperature, humidity, pressure, wind speed and direction, clouds, and rainfall allows everyone to picture *exactly what kind* of a nice day we are having. For the same reason, a scientist studying the response of dogs to loud noise wouldn't state that the dog hates it when it's loud. A scientist would quantify the amount of noise in decibels (units of sound intensity) and carefully note the behavior and actions of the dog in response to the sound, without making a judgment about the dog's deep feelings. Now that you are convinced that quantifying observations is a healthy practice in science, you will probably agree that instruments and units are also useful.

In the following table are the most common properties scientists measure and common units these properties are measured in. You don't need to memorize these, but you can read them to become acquainted with the ones you don't already know. You should also be familiar with the following devices and instruments used by scientists:

- **balance:** for measuring mass
- **graduated cylinder:** for measuring volume (the bottom of the curved surface of water should always be read)
- **thermometer:** for measuring temperature
- **voltmeter:** for measuring potential
- **microscope:** for observing very small objects, such as cells
- **telescope:** for observing very distant objects, such as other planets

COMMON UNITS OF MEASURE	
Length or distance	meter (about a yard) centimeter (about half an inch) micrometer (about the size of a cell) nanometer (often used for wavelengths of light) angstrom (about the size of an atom) kilometer (about half a mile) light-year (used for astronomical distances)
Time	second, hour, year, century
Volume	milliliter (about a teaspoon), liter (about $\frac{1}{4}$ of a gallon)
Temperature	degree Celsius, degree Fahrenheit, or Kelvin
Charge	coulomb
Electric	potential volt
Pressure	atmosphere, mm Hg, bar
Force	newton

Evolution

Most students tend to associate evolution with the biological evolution of species. However, **evolution** is a series of changes, either gradual or abrupt, in any type of system. Even theories and technological designs can evolve. Ancient cultures classified matter into fire, water, earth, and air. This may sound naive and funny now, but it was a start. The important thing was to ask what matter is, and to start grouping different forms of matter in some way. As more observations were collected, our understanding of matter evolved. We started out with air, fire, earth, and water, and got to the periodic table, the structure of the atom, and the interaction of energy and matter.

Consider how the design of cars and airplanes has changed over time. Think of a little carriage with crooked wheels pulled by a horse and a plane with propellers. The car and the plane have evolved as well. So did our planet. According to theory, 200 million years ago all the present continents formed one supercontinent. Twenty million years later, the supercontinent began to break apart. Earth is still evolving, changing through time, as its plates are still moving and the core of Earth is still cooling.

Form and Function

There is a reason why a feather is light as a feather. In both nature and technology, form is often related to function. A bird's feathers are light, enabling it to fly more easily. Arteries spread into tiny capillaries, increasing the surface area for gas exchange. Surface area and surface to volume ratio are key issues in biology and chemistry. A cell has a relatively large surface to volume ratio. If it were larger, this ratio would increase. Through the surface, the cell regulates the transport of matter in and out of the cell. If the cell had a bigger volume, it would require more nutrients and produce more waste, and the area for exchange would be insufficient. Notice the difference between the leaves of plants that grow in hot dry climates and the leaves of plants in cooler, wetter climates. What function do the differences in form serve? Did you realize that a flock of birds tends to fly forming the shape much like the tip of an arrow? Several years ago, curved skis were brought onto the market and have almost replaced traditional straight-edge skis. There are countless examples of how form develops to serve a useful function. Your job is to open your eyes to these relationships and be prepared to make the connections.

Test-Taking Tips for the Science Section

Below are a handful of specific tips for the science section of the Praxis II: Elementary Education: Content Knowledge test.

Know the Basics

The Praxis II: Elementary Education: Content Knowledge exam can test you on a wide variety of scientific concepts and terms from the elements of an atom up to the properties of galaxies. It can be very difficult to memorize all the terms in this chapter, so at least make sure that you're familiar with some of the more basic concepts that are likely to appear on the test. The following bullet points reiterate a handful of the important concepts to know for the science section of the Praxis II.

- Know the layers of Earth and its atmosphere.
- Memorize the parts of a cell (the organelles) and each of their functions.
- Make sure you know the difference between kinetic energy and potential energy.
- Make sure you know the difference between chemical changes and physical changes.
- Review Newton's laws.
- Check that you know the terms relating to reproduction and heredity, including mutations, adaptations, and natural selection.
- Review the roles of different organisms in an ecosystem, including producers, consumers, and decomposers.

Use the Images

Several questions on the science section of the Praxis II will contain some type of image, such as an illustration or a table containing data. In most cases, the information you need to solve the problem will be contained within the image. For example, a table may include data about the eight planets of the solar system, including their diameters and densities. A corresponding question may ask you to identify the planet with the densest mass. To answer that question correctly, you simply need to review the information in the density column of the table and pick the largest number. You wouldn't be expected to know that kind of information on your own.

Use Common Sense to Eliminate Wrong Answer Choices

You may encounter difficult terms or concepts on the Praxis II, but that doesn't mean that you have to guess wildly. In fact, you can often get rid of one or more incorrect answer choices simply by using common sense. For example, a question may ask you about the gravitational force of the moon, as shown below.

1. The moon's gravitational force is
  a. greater than Earth's gravitational force because of the moon's large deposits of iron.
  b. less than Earth's gravitational force because the moon's mass is less than Earth's mass.
  c. less than Earth's gravitational force because the moon's distance from the sun is greater than Earth's distance from the Sun.
  d. greater than Earth's gravitational force because the moon's mass is greater than Earth's mass.

You may not know what the moon's gravitational force is, or whether it is greater or less than Earth's gravitational force. However, the answer choices lead to some clues that can help you to narrow the possibilities. Answer choice **c** says that the moon is farther from the sun than Earth. The moon orbits Earth while both of them orbit the sun togethe Even if the moon's gravitational force is less tha Earth's gravitational force, the explanation fo choice **c** doesn't seem to make sense. Choice **d** state that the moon's gravitational force is greater thai Earth's because its mass is also greater. Does th moon have a greater mass than Earth? You may no know the exact numbers, but this would essentially mean that the moon is bigger than Earth. That's certainly not true, leaving choices **a** and **b** as the only possible answer choices. Because the moon has less mass than Earth, its gravitational force is less than Earth's; choice **b** is correct.

Science Practice

1. The following diagram represents which of the following events?

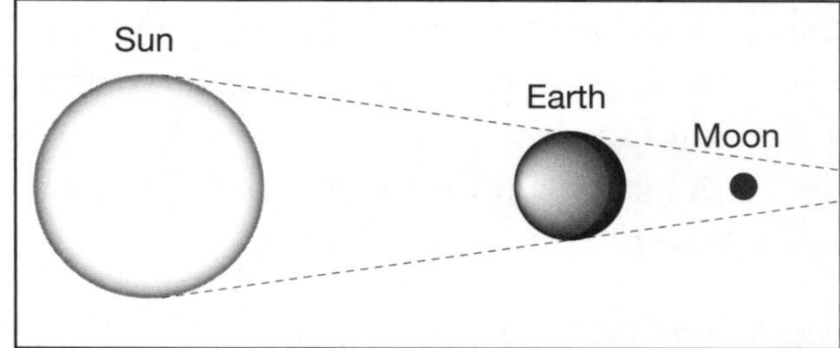

  a. solar eclipse
  b. lunar eclipse
  c. new moon
  d. apogee

2. In the early nineteenth century, almost all peppered moths collected by biologists in the United Kingdom were pale and mottled. Only rarely was a collector able to find a dark peppered moth. After the industrial revolution, when furnaces filled the air with dark soot, the light peppered moth became rare and the dark peppered moth was most common in industrial cities. A reasonable explanation for this change is that the dar

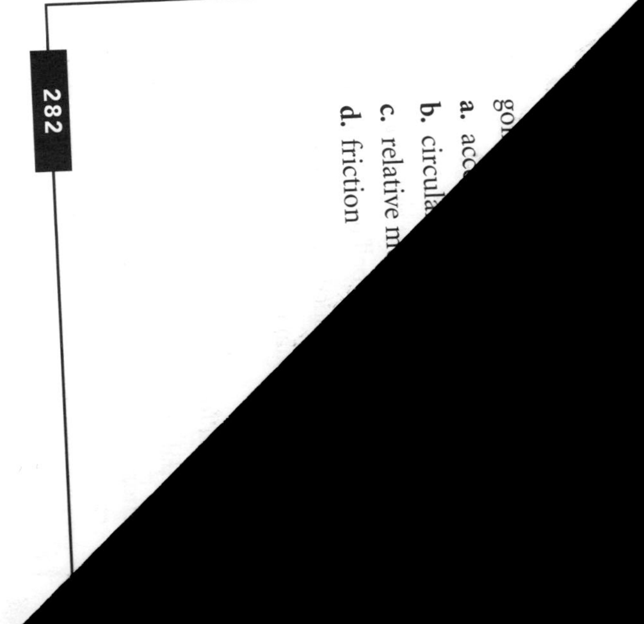

4. Which of the following situations represents an example of potential energy without kinetic energy?

a. A cannon is loaded and stuffed with gunpowder.
b. A pitcher throws a baseball 100 miles an hour.
c. A ripple on a pond travels from one side to the other.
d. A roller coaster picks up speed as it goes down.

5. Which organ is NOT part of the human digestive system?

a. esophagus
b. stomach
c. small intestine
d. heart

6. Which layer of Earth's atmosphere is responsible for the creation of the aurora borealis?

a. ionosphere
b. ozone layer
c. troposphere
d. exosphere

7. Two auto drivers are racing next to each other at identical speeds on a racetrack. Eventually, one driver begins to slow down in her car. From the perspective of the other driver, that car appears to be going backwards. What type of motion describes the appearance of the car [illegible]ing backwards from the other driver?

[illegible]eleration
[illegible]r motion
[illegible]otion

8. Which scientific phenomenon is demonstrated by the illustration shown here?

a. phototropism
b. speciation
c. etiolation
d. skototropism

9. Which is NOT a similarity between all the outer planets of Earth's solar system?

a. They all have rings.
b. They all have gaseous surfaces.
c. They are all bigger than Earth.
d. They all have exactly one moon.

10. The table gives some data about solar system asteroids.

Asteroid	Diameter (km)	Mass (10^{15} kg)	Rotation Period (hr.)	Orbital Period (Yr.)
Ceres	~950	875,000	~9	~4.6
Pallas	~500	318,000	~9	~4.6
Juno	~250	20,000	~7	~4.4
Vesta	~550	300,000	~5	~3.6

Which asteroid has the shortest "day"?

a. Ceres
b. Pallas
c. Juno
d. Vesta

11. Brown eyes represent an example of a dominant trait. Blue eyes represent an example of a recessive trait. Whether an eye color is brown or blue is determined from two alleles, one taken from each parent. Which scenario represents a case where the offspring *must* have blue eyes?

a. The father has brown eyes and the mother has blue eyes.
b. The father has brown eyes and the mother has brown eyes.
c. The father has blue eyes and the mother has brown eyes.
d. The father has blue eyes and the mother has blue eyes.

12. The following image shows a graduated cylinder that is being used to measure the volume of a liquid mixture.

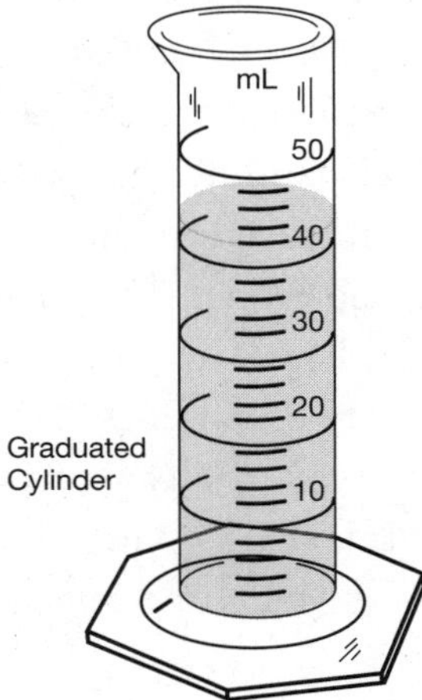

What is the most accurate measurement of the volume of the liquid mixture?

a. 35 mL
b. 37 mL
c. 38 mL
d. 40 mL

13. Which of the following waves travel most slowly?

a. gamma rays
b. sound waves
c. visible light
d. radio waves

14. Each of the following must be true about a scientific hypothesis EXCEPT that it

a. must be factually correct.
b. must be testable.
c. must be based on information that is already available.
d. must be able to be proved wrong through experimentation.

15. A satellite is launched from Earth toward the outer edge of the solar system. Its speed and direction, once leaving Earth's orbit, remains nearly unchanged for hundreds of millions of miles and several years. At no point during the satellite's journey is fuel used to propel the satellite. Which best explains how the satellite manages to maintain its speed and direction?

a. The velocity of an object does not change unless a force is applied.
b. The satellite is able to utilize the solar winds from the sun for energy.
c. Newton's Law of Interaction states that every reaction has an equal and opposite reaction.
d. The friction caused by the satellite's movement generates heat for the travel.

16. Which is the best description of the Pacific Ring of Fire?

a. the warm climate of the countries by the Pacific Ocean
b. the volatile faults bordering the Pacific Plate
c. a western region susceptible to dangerous monsoons
d. a dry area of Japan known for deadly wildfires

17. Which of the following categories describes the narrowest range of organisms within the biological taxonomy?

a. genus
b. family
c. phylum
d. species

18. The following table shows the approximate diameters and masses of the four outer planets of our solar system.

PLANET	DIAMETER (IN KM)	MASS (IN KG)
Jupiter	142,984	1.90×10^{27}
Saturn	120,536	5.69×10^{26}
Uranus	51,118	8.66×10^{26}
Neptune	49,532	1.03×10^{26}

Based on the data in the table, which planet would have the greatest gravitational force?

a. Jupiter
b. Saturn
c. Uranus
d. Neptune

19. Which of the following events represents a chemical change?

a. Snow melts and forms a puddle.
b. Liquid hydrogen evaporates into the air.
c. A fire turns a log of wood into ash.
d. Salt is mixed with water, forming a mixture.

20. The following equation shows a model for photosynthesis, but one part of the equation is missing.

$$6\ CO_2 + \square \rightarrow 6\ O_2 + C_6H_{12}O_6$$

What is missing from the equation?

a. H_2O
b. $6\ HO_2$
c. $3\ H_4O_2$
d. $6\ H_2O$

21. Which of the following types of clouds generally has the highest elevation in the atmosphere?
- **a.** fog
- **b.** cirrus
- **c.** stratus
- **d.** cumulus

22. Which layer of Earth's structure is responsible for the majority of the planet's volume?
- **a.** inner core
- **b.** mantle
- **c.** asthenosphere
- **d.** crust

23. Which biome is characterized for having the greatest amount of biodiversity?
- **a.** tundra
- **b.** desert
- **c.** tropical rainforest
- **d.** grasslands

24. The following instrument works because

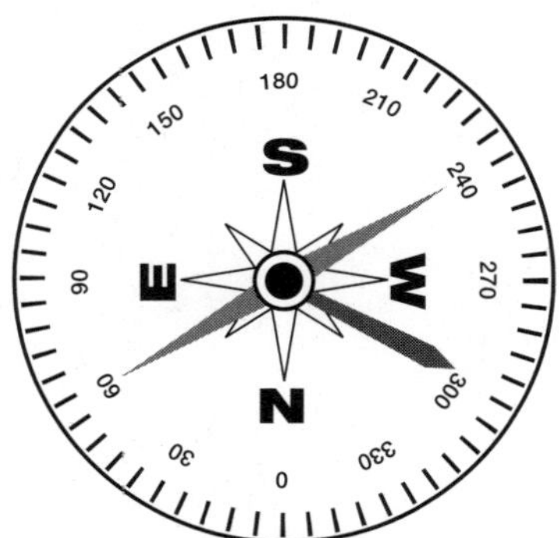

- **a.** the temperatures on Earth's poles are very low.
- **b.** the needle points to the direction of minimum pressure.
- **c.** the needle changes position depending on the position of the sun.
- **d.** Earth has two magnetic poles.

25. Which of the following vitamins or minerals is most useful for the creation and maintenance of healthy bones and teeth?
- **a.** riboflavin
- **b.** vitamin A
- **c.** calcium
- **d.** vitamin E

26. Which answer provides the best explanation of why only one side of the moon is visible from Earth?
- **a.** The moon orbits around Earth with a synchronous rotation.
- **b.** The sun's light does not reach the dark side of the moon.
- **c.** The moon rotates on its axis at a 90-degree angle.
- **d.** The moon's gravitational force is less than Earth's gravitational force.

27. Which of the following organelles is most essential to carrying out the process of photosynthesis?
- **a.** vacuole
- **b.** ribosome
- **c.** chloroplast
- **d.** golgi apparatus

28. Which of the following statements is NOT true about an animal during hibernation?
- **a.** The animal's rate of breathing slows.
- **b.** The animal's heart rate drops.
- **c.** The animal uses more energy to maintain homeostasis.
- **d.** The animal's internal body temperature is lowered.

29. In the following diagram, the dotted and solid lines indicate the changes from one form of rock to another.

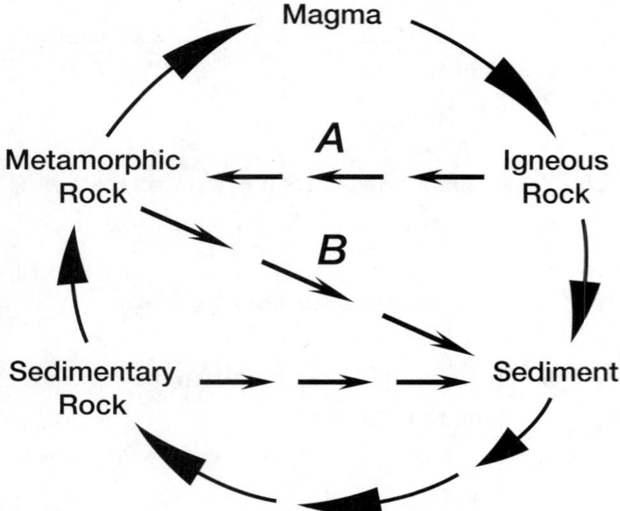

Which type of rock can change directly into sediment?

a. igneous rock
b. igneous, metamorphic, and sedimentary rock
c. sedimentary rock
d. magma and sedimentary rock

30. Which best explains why the sound of thunder may often be heard several seconds after the appearance of its corresponding lightning?

a. The lightning and thunder originate from two distinctly different locations.
b. The human eye processes the light nearly instantaneously, whereas the sound of the thunder may take several seconds to process.
c. The sound waves of the thunder travel significantly slower than the speed of the visible light of the lightning.
d. The air that the thunder and the lightning travel through is much more efficient when transmitting light than transmitting sound.

Science Practice Section Key and Explanations

SCIENCE KEY					
ITEM	KEY	SUBSECTION	ITEM	KEY	SUBSECTION
1	B	Earth Science	16	B	Earth Science
2	B	Life Science	17	D	Life Science
3	A	Physical Science	18	A	Physical Science
4	A	Physical Science	19	C	Physical Science
5	D	Life Science	20	D	Life Science
6	A	Earth Science	21	B	Earth Science
7	C	Physical Science	22	B	Earth Science
8	A	Life Science	23	C	Life Science
9	D	Earth Science	24	D	Physical Science
10	D	Earth Science	25	C	Personal/Social Perspectives
11	D	Life Science	26	A	Earth Science
12	B	Science as Inquiry/Processes	27	C	Life Science
13	B	Physical Science	28	C	Life Science
14	A	Science as Inquiry/Processes	29	B	Earth Science
15	A	Physical Science	30	C	Physical Science

Answers

1. **b.** In a solar eclipse, choice **a**, the moon blocks the Sun's light from reaching Earth and casts a shadow that has the potential to turn daytime into darkness. This is not what the diagram shows, however. The diagram shows Earth's shadow blocking the sunlight from reaching the moon. This is indicative of a lunar eclipse, choice **b**. A lunar eclipse can only occur during a full moon stage, so choice **c** cannot be correct. Choice **d**, apogee, is a term that refers to a time when the Moon is at its farthest distance from Earth. This is not represented by the diagram.
2. **b.** Natural selection, choice **b**, is the process whereby the members of the species who are best able to survive and reproduce in an environment thrive, passing their genes on to next generations. The pollution in the environment during the early nineteenth century in the United Kingdom selected for a new advantageous trait: the dark color of peppered moths.
3. **a.** The ball, while at rest on a flat surface, must be pushed (by a force) to start moving. Once the ball is in motion, it will stay in motion unless a force acts to stop it. An object in motion will stay in motion, and an object at rest will stay at rest unless a force is applied. Thus, choice **a** is the correct answer choice.
4. **a.** Potential energy is stored energy that has potential to be converted into another form of energy. Kinetic energy is the energy of motion. The only situation that does NOT include some form of kinetic energy (movement) is in answer choice **a**, a cannon loaded with gunpowder. The other situations better represent kinetic energy.
5. **d.** The esophagus, choice **a**, stomach, choice **b**, and small intestine, choice **c** are all essential organs of the human digestive system. The heart, choice **d**, plays no essential role in the digestive process; it is part of the circulatory system, which works to transport oxygen, carbon dioxide, nutrients, and wastes throughout the body to other organ systems.
6. **a.** The aurora borealis is formed in the upper layers of Earth's atmosphere. Specifically, the aurora borealis can form in either the mesosphere or the thermosphere, which are collectively part of the ionosphere, choice **a**. The troposphere, choice **c**, is near the surface of Earth. The exosphere, choice **d**, has very few particles and is the outermost layer of the atmosphere.
7. **c.** Relative motion takes into account the motion of an object based on the motion of the observer. In the scenario in the given problem, one car appears to be going backwards from the perspective of the other driver. This describes relative motion, choice **c**, perfectly.
8. **a.** Plants will lean toward a light source because the light is necessary for photosynthesis. In the given illustration, the plant is leaning toward a window on the side of the box, which is its source of sunlight. The term that describes this phenomenon is phototropism, choice **a**. Speciation, choice **b**, refers to the birth of new species during the course of evolution. Etiolation, choice **c**, is the growth of a plant in very low or no light. Skototropism, choice **d**, is actually the growth away from light.

9. d. The outer planets of Earth's solar system include Jupiter, Saturn, Uranus, and Neptune. Each of these planets contains rings, choice **a**, even though Saturn's rings are most pronounced. All four of these planets are gas planets larger than Earth, so choice **b** and choice **c** are incorrect. The number of moons for each planet varies, but they each have more than one moon, making choice **d** correct.

10. d. The rotation period is equivalent to a "day" and Vesta has the shortest day. Choice **a** is incorrect because Ceres has the longest day. Choice **b** is incorrect because Ceres and Pallas have the longest "year," not the shortest day. Choice **c** is incorrect because Juno's rotational period is greater than Vesta's rotational period.

11. d. If the father has brown eyes and the mother has blue eyes, choice **a**, the offspring may get the brown eye color allele from the father, making the offspring's eyes brown. But the offspring may also get the blue eye color allele from the mother and a recessive blue eye color allele from the father. This would make the offspring's eyes blue. Therefore, it cannot be determined with certainty what the eye color of the offspring will be in scenario choice **a**. Scenario choice **c** represents a similar case with mixed parents, so it is also not correct. In the scenario in choice **b**, the father and mother can both provide the offspring with their recessive blue eye color allele, which would mean that the offspring would have blue eyes. Of course, as long as one brown color allele was passed down, then the offspring would have brown eyes. Therefore, choice **b** also represents a scenario where the eye color of the offspring is unknown. If both parents have blue eyes, choice **d**, then there cannot be any brown color alleles in either parent (because the brown eye color allele is dominant.) Both parents will therefore pass on blue eye allele, and the offspring *must* have blue eyes.

12. b. A graduated cylinder is measured by reading the lowest portion of the liquid level. Even though the liquid mixture appears to touch the 38 mL measurement of the cylinder, choice **c**, the lowest portion is at 37 mL, which means choice **b** is correct. Choices choice **a** and choice **d** do not represent an accurate measurement of the liquid mixture.

13. b. Gamma rays, choice **a**, visible light, choice **c**, and radio waves, choice **d**, are all different wavelengths on the electromagnetic spectrum. All waves on the electromagnetic spectrum travel at the speed of light. Sound waves, choice **b**, are NOT on the electromagnetic spectrum; at sea level on Earth, sound waves travel at about 340 meters per second—considerably slower than the other waves listed in the answer choices.

14. a. A hypothesis does NOT have to be correct. It should be based on information that is already available, choice **c**, however. A key attribute of a hypothesis is the ability for it to be proved wrong through experimentation and testing, which makes choice **b** and choice **d** true—and therefore incorrect answer choices.

15. a. Newton's first law, the Law of Inertia, states that the velocity of an object does not change unless a force is applied. With this in mind, a satellite will continue with its velocity—which is the combination of speed and direction—unless interfered with by a force such as gravity or friction. Choice **a** best describes this phenomenon. Solar winds, choice **b**, do not provide the best explanation for the inertia of the satellite. The Law of Interaction, choice **c**, also does not fully explain why the satellite would continue in its path without changing speed of direction. Without matter, there can be no friction, so choice **d** is not correct.

16. b. The Ring of Fire is the volatile faults bordering the Pacific Plate, choice **b**. This area is responsible for the majority of Earth's active volcanoes and large earthquakes. It has nothing to do with the climate of the countries, choice **a**, nor is it directly responsible for monsoons, choice **c** or wildfires, choice **d**.

17. d. A species provides the narrowest range of organisms within the biological taxonomy. From broad to narrow, the terms are kingdom, phylum, class, order, family, genus, and species.

18. a. The gravitational force of a celestial body is based on its mass. It is possible that a planet with a greater diameter than another planet has a smaller mass than the other planet, based on the densities of the planets. However, Jupiter has both the greatest diameter and the greatest mass in our solar system. Therefore, its gravitational force is also the greatest. A 150-pound person would have a weight of about 355 pounds on Jupiter, based on the gas giant's massive gravitational force.

19. c. A chemical change cannot be undone and there is a reaction between the atoms of the elements. When snow melts, choice **a** or when liquid hydrogen evaporates, choice **b**, it is an example of matter changing phase from solid to liquid or liquid to gas. Each of these events can be undone with a change of temperature. They reflect physical changes, therefore, and not chemical changes, so choice **a** and choice **b** are not correct. Choice **d** is also a physical change because there is no chemical reaction taking place; the salt can still be removed from the water mixture. A fire, choice **c**, does represent a chemical change because the ash cannot be reconstructed to form the log of wood; the chemical change forever altered the substance.

20. d. Missing from the equation representing photosynthesis is 6 molecules of water, or 6 H_2O. Remember that photosynthesis requires carbon dioxide and water, and a molecule of water is represented with two atoms of hydrogen and one atom of oxygen, H_2O. If you were unsure of the missing part of the equation, you could have counted the atoms of carbon, oxygen, and hydrogen on the right side of the equation. Just as in math, both sides of the equation need to be balanced. That means each side needs the same number of carbon, oxygen, and hydrogen atoms. Only choices **c** and **d** have the missing 12 atoms of hydrogen and 6 atoms of oxygen, though the molecules in choice **c** do not represent molecules of water.

21. b. Fog, choice **a**, is a cloud that comes into contact with the surface of Earth. It is therefore has the lowest elevation in the atmosphere and is not correct. Stratus and cumulus clouds, choices **c** and **d**, are mid-level clouds. Cirrus clouds, choice **b** are upper level atmospheric clouds, so choice **b** is the correct choice.

22. b. The mantle comprises about 70% of Earth's volume, making **b** the correct answer choice. Both the asthenosphere, choice **c** and the crust, choice **d**, represent relatively thin layers of Earth's structure.

23. c. Tundra and desert, choices **a** and **b**, are not known for having a great amount of biodiversity. Not many plants grow in either tundra or a desert, and animals require special adaptations to adjust to the extreme cold and heat. Tropical rainforests, choice **c**, and grasslands, choice **d**, each have more biodiversity. The rainforest, in part due to its warm and wet climate, is known for having the greatest biodiversity in the world.

24. d. The instrument shown in the diagram is a compass. The needle on the compass responds to Earth's magnetic poles, so the correct choice is choice **d**.

25. c. Vitamin A, choice **a**, is not known for building strong bones; it helps the body's eyes and skin, as well as its immune system. Riboflavin, choice **b**, is an important mineral that is used for the creation of energy, as well as improved function for nerves and muscles. Calcium, choice **c**, is the mineral that strengthens and maintains bones, and teeth. A steady diet of calcium can prevent deterioration of bones which can happen with osteoporosis. Vitamin E, choice **d**, is known for its ability to act as an antioxidant and keep red blood cells healthy.

26. a. As the moon orbits Earth, the same side of the moon is always visible from Earth. This is because of the moon's synchronous rotation, which keeps it rotating with the same side facing Earth—and the same side (the dark side) always facing away from Earth. Despite the name, the dark side of the moon, choice **b**, does get sunlight; it simply never faces Earth. The moon's axis, choice **c**, and its gravitational force, choice **d**, have nothing to do with why the same side of the satellite always faces Earth.

27. c. A vacuole, choice **a**, serves as a storage area for food, water, or waste. A ribosome, choice **b**, produces proteins from amino acids Chloroplasts are the organelles that are used to carry out photosynthesis, so choice **c** is the correct choice. The Golgi apparatus, choice **d**, processes proteins and other macromolecules for cell secretion.

28. c. Hibernation is a resting period during which an animal's metabolism slows down. While the animal is inactive, its body temperature, its heart rate, and its rate of breathing all drop. Therefore, choices **a**, **b**, or **d** cannot be correct. The animal uses less energy during this time, so choice **c** is not true.

29. b. The dotted and solid lines show igneous, metamorphic, and sedimentary rock changing into sediment. Choices **a** and **c** are incorrect because igneous and sedimentary rock are only two of the three rocks that can change directly into sediment. Choice **d** is incorrect because magma does not change directly into sediment.

30. c. When lightning strikes, the sound of the thunder originates from the same relative location, so choice **a** does not explain the disparity between hearing the sound of thunder and seeing the lightning. It does not take the human ear several seconds to process a sound, so choice **b** is not reasonable, either. Sound waves travel at about 340 meters per second at sea level. Light waves, however, travel at the speed of light (about 300,000,000 meters per second). Therefore, choice **c** is correct. While it is true that air may be more efficient at transmitting light than sound, it does not provide the best explanation for the discrepancy between the times. Sound waves travel faster in water and in steel than they do in air, but even those faster speeds are nowhere near the incredibly quick speed of light.

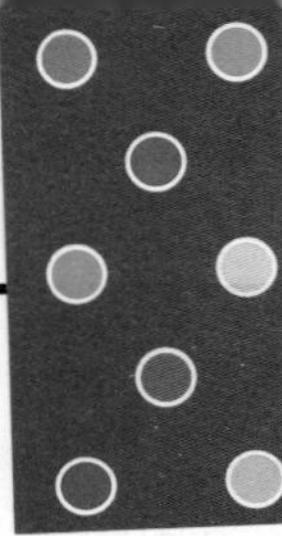

CHAPTER

PRACTICE TEST 1

Praxis II: Elementary Education: Content Knowledge Practice Test 1

You have 120 minutes to take the entire 120-question Praxis II: Elementary Education: Content Knowledge practice test. There are four sections of the test: Reading/Language Arts, Mathematics, Social Studies, and Science. You can spend more time on one section than the other. You can go back to any section of the test at any time. Take the diagnostic test with a timer or stopwatch to familiarize yourself with the 120-minute time limit. You may use a scientific or four-function calculator.

Use the answer sheet on the following page to record your answers to the 120 questions.

Reading/Language Arts

Read the following poem, then answer questions 1 and 2.

Bivouac on a Mountain Side
by Walt Whitman

I see before me now, a traveling army halting;
Below, a fertile valley spread, with barns, and the orchards of summer;
Behind, the terraced sides of a mountain, abrupt in places, rising high;
Broken, with rocks, with clinging cedars, with tall shapes, dingily seen;
The numerous camp-fires scatter'd near and far, some away up on the mountain;
The shadowy forms of men and horses, looming, large-sized flickering;
And over all, the sky—the sky! far, far out of reach, studded, breaking out, the eternal stars.

1. The poem reflects primarily on the author's perspective of
a. the eternal stars.
b. the Civil War.
c. a beautiful mountain.
d. horseback riding.

2. Walt Whitman describes the setting in line 2 in order to
a. contrast the violence of the war with the calm of the country.
b. provide a tranquil setting for a peaceful narrative.
c. depict the lush eighteenth-century American countryside.
d. compare the natural American beauty to the European landscape.

Read the following poem, then answer questions 3 through 5.

My mistress' eyes are nothing like the sun;
Coral is far more red than her lips' red
If snow be white, why then her breasts are dun;
If hairs be wires, black wires grow on her head.
I have seen roses damask'd, red and white,
But no such roses see I in her cheeks;
And in some perfumes is there more delight
Than in the breath that from my mistress reeks.
I love to hear her speak, yet well I know
That music hath a far more pleasing sound;
I grant I never saw a goddess go;
My mistress, when she walks, treads on the ground:
And yet, by heaven, I think my love as rare
As any she belied with false compare.
—William Shakespeare

3. This poem is an example of a
a. cinquain.
b. haiku.
c. limerick.
d. sonnet.

4. Line 11 in the poem provides an example of which literary device?
a. metaphor
b. hyperbole
c. alliteration
d. simile

5. In what way does Shakespeare compliment his mistress in the poem?
a. He compares her eyes to the beauty of the sun.
b. He takes pleasure in the music that she creates.
c. He says that he enjoys hearing her talk.
d. He states that her lips are redder than coral.

Read the following passage, then answer questions 6 through 8.

The Cambrian Period was a period on Earth when life diversified from mostly single-cell organisms to more complex animal groups, some of which still exist today. Ranging from about 542 to 488 million years ago, the period represented an explosion of innovative life-forms. In fact, the term *Cambrian explosion* is often used to describe the rapid diversification of species on our planet. Although scientists are enthralled by this evolutionary epoch, they don't agree on the reasons for the immense increase of life.

6. The first sentence of the passage provides the readers with a
- **a.** comparison.
- **b.** contrast.
- **c.** definition.
- **d.** symbol.

7. Which type of writing does the passage most likely represent?
- **a.** exposition
- **b.** historical fiction
- **c.** science fiction
- **d.** tall tale

8. What was the author's purpose in including the final sentence of the passage?
- **a.** to explain a scientific phenomenon
- **b.** to mention an unexplained aspect of the period
- **c.** to provide additional information about the time period
- **d.** to disprove a common claim about a scientific theory

9. What is the importance of a phoneme in a student's literacy development?
- **a.** It is the smallest segment of sound in a language.
- **b.** It is a method of reading using the fundamental sounds of syllables.
- **c.** It is a blend of two consecutive letters to form a single sound.
- **d.** It is a letter that is not said but changes the pronunciation of a word.

10. A running record of student's reading will do all the following EXCEPT
- **a.** ensure that the student has comprehended the meaning of a text.
- **b.** reveal the types of reading errors made by a student.
- **c.** indicate whether a text is at the right level for a student.
- **d.** provide an accuracy rate for a student's reading abilities.

11. A student is unfamiliar with a word in a book. Which of the following would NOT help a student decipher its meaning?
- **a.** analyzing the prefix or suffix of the word
- **b.** looking up the word in a dictionary
- **c.** reading the few lines before and after the word
- **d.** identifying literary devices in the sentence

12. What is the error in the following sentence?

The bald eagle, one of the symbols of the United States, is easily recognized by their white heads and hooked beaks.

- **a.** The subject and verb are not in agreement.
- **b.** The pronoun does not match the subject.
- **c.** The words "heads" and "beaks" should include apostrophes.
- **d.** Both of the commas should not be included.

13. Which of the following best defines active listening?
- **a.** listening without talking
- **b.** listening for meaning
- **c.** agreeing with the speaker
- **d.** sitting up straight in a chair

14. A group of students is working independently to write about a topic. Which of the following steps would NOT help them in their prewriting?
- **a.** brainstorming about the different topics that interest them
- **b.** clustering the ideas into smaller groups
- **c.** checking for spelling errors or grammatical mistakes
- **d.** considering the audience and the purpose of the writing

15. Which part of the following sentence contains an error?

The decision to rest his best player weighed heavy on the manager's shoulders.

- **a.** to rest
- **b.** weighed
- **c.** heavy
- **d.** manager's

16. The elected officials of a township are considering passing a bill that would convert some natural land in the town into a series of condominiums. This would help the town to generate revenue, which could be used to support the town library. Some of the students in a classroom feel strongly that the loss of the natural land would not be worth the short-term financial gain for the town. The students intend to write a letter to the elected officials in their town to express their position on the possible bill.

What type of letter should the students work to create?
- **a.** fictional
- **b.** expository
- **c.** narrative
- **d.** persuasive

17. Which of the following actions for a classroom library would *least* encourage the students in the class to use and enjoy the library?
- **a.** involving the students in the organization of the books in the library
- **b.** including as many appropriate books as possible, including copies of the popular books
- **c.** displaying the books so that the covers are visible, changing the display periodically
- **d.** providing only leveled books based on the reading abilities of the students

18. Which of the following would be most beneficial to an ELL student when a teacher asks the student a question about a text?
- **a.** asking the question more loudly
- **b.** providing the student with increased wait time
- **c.** letting the student write the answer on the board
- **d.** supplying the student with several possible choices

Read the following passage, then answer questions 19 through 21.

My brother and I both have short, brown, curly hair. We're both about the same height. We both enjoy sandwiches. But the similarities end there. Last weekend was one of the most beautiful weekends of the year. Between riding my bike around town, walking to my friend's house, and playing roller hockey, I spent a total of three minutes indoors throughout the entire weekend. I don't even know whether my brother left the living room. He told me he's enjoying his new book about arachnids. I can't even look at a spider; the last thing in the world I'd want to do is spend a beautiful weekend reading about them. Of course, the fact that he's a pale-faced spider nerd doesn't make me love him any less. He's my brother, after all.

19. Which best describes the organization of the passage?
- **a.** cause and effect
- **b.** chronological order
- **c.** order of importance
- **d.** compare and contrast

20. Which literary device does the author use in lines 7, 8, and 9?
- **a.** allusion
- **b.** hyperbole
- **c.** foreshadowing
- **d.** oxymoron

21. What is the primary purpose of the passage?
- **a.** to make fun of a boy who never leaves the house
- **b.** to demonstrate that even spiders can be interesting if there is a good book about them
- **c.** to show that differences don't interfere with the bond between brothers
- **d.** to describe two children as having nearly the same height and hair style

22. Which of the following is an example of a compound sentence?
- **a.** Jane went to the store to buy milk, eggs, vanilla, and flour for the cake.
- **b.** Maria dressed herself slowly, and then she headed down the stairs.
- **c.** After walking for a few minutes to warm up, Jonathan began to jog.
- **d.** Ivan and Meredith both knew that something was wrong when they walked outside.

23. What is the most beneficial reason to include video screens in a classroom?
- **a.** The teacher can relax while he or she is screening a video.
- **b.** All students prefer to watch videos in a classroom.
- **c.** Video screens are the most dependable medium for learning.
- **d.** A video may aid students' understanding of a certain topic.

24. Which of the following could a teacher do to best support an English Language Learner (ELL) who is struggling with understanding the teacher?
- **a.** use pictures and nonverbal clues when talking
- **b.** ask a classmate to repeat the teacher's words
- **c.** tell the ELL to write the teacher's words on a piece of paper
- **d.** explain that the ELL will begin to understand eventually

25. Research has shown that accessing a student's prior knowledge can improve reading comprehension. Which of the following is NOT considered a prior knowledge connection to improve comprehension?
- **a.** text-to-self
- **b.** text-to-world
- **c.** self-to-world
- **d.** text-to-text

26. Students can benefit from using graphic organizers in reading and language arts in all the following ways EXCEPT that graphic organizers

a. can help students visualize how knowledge is connected.
b. are quickly constructed and are always an efficient use of time.
c. can help students learn to make meaning from the text.
d. have been proven to improve a student's vocabulary.

27. Research has determined that the best predictor of a student's early decoding ability is his or her

a. vocabulary.
b. phonemic awareness.
c. listening comprehension.
d. positive attitude.

28. Which of the following statements provides the best reason to have young students read nonfiction texts?

a. They expose students to a wide variety of literary devices.
b. Students enjoy playful stories such as those with talking animals.
c. They help teach students about the world around them.
d. They are much easier to read than fiction texts.

29. A teacher should consider each of the following attributes of speech when speaking to a group of students EXCEPT

a. purpose.
b. volume.
c. tone.
d. punctuation.

30. What rhyme scheme does the following children's poem use?

Old Mother Twitchett had but one eye,
And a long tail which she let fly;
And every time she went through a gap,
A bit of her tail she left in a trap.

a. AABB
b. ABAB
c. ABCD
d. ABBA

Mathematics

31. What is the value of 5^5?

a. 2,500
b. 3,025
c. 3,125
d. 55,555

32. Which of the following numbers represents a whole number?

a. –5
b. 0
c. 0.75
d. $\frac{9}{10}$

33. The numbers shown here are the first three terms of a number pattern. The pattern is created by subtracting 1 from the product of the previous number and 2. What is the sixth number in the pattern?

3, 5, 9, . . .

a. 32
b. 65
c. 66
d. 72

34. If $3a - 49 = 5b$, what is the value of a in terms of b?

a. $5b + 49$
b. $\frac{5b + 49}{3}$
c. $3(5b + 49)$
d. $\frac{5b - 49}{3}$

35. A stationery store sells pencils for $0.75 each and pens for $1.00 each. One day the store made a total of $6.00 selling pens and pencils, and at least one pen and one pencil were sold. How many pencils did the store sell during the day?

a. 1
b. 3
c. 4
d. 8

36. Which of the following is a possible solution for s in the following inequality?

$$3s + 6 < 12$$

a. –3
b. 2
c. 6
d. 20

37. Which of the following shows the net for a cube?

a.

b.

c.

d.

38. Jorge measured the temperature when he woke up at 7 A.M. and found that it was 66°F. The temperature changed by the same rate throughout the day. At 2 P.M. Jorge measured the temperature again and found that it was 87°F. What was the temperature at noon?

a. 69°F
b. 71°F
c. 81°F
d. 84°F

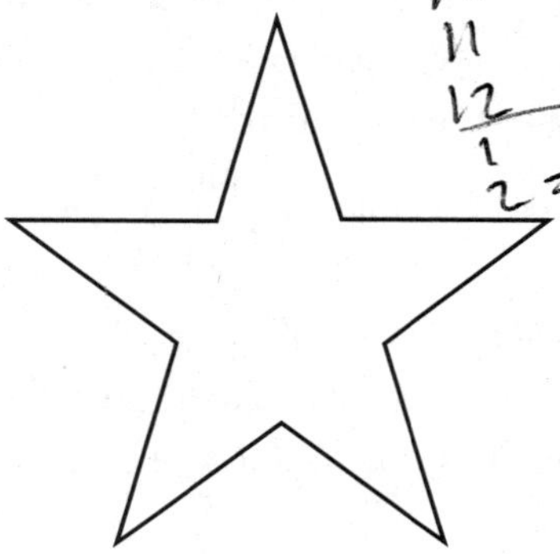

39. The figure shown here is rotated so that it looks exactly the same. Which of the following degrees of rotation could the figure have been rotated?

a. 90°
b. 142°
c. 180°
d. 288°

40. Twelve students are participating in a race. A 1st-place trophy, a 2nd-place medal, and a 3rd-place ribbon will be awarded to the top three finishers of the race. Which expression shows how many possible ways the prizes can be awarded to the runners?

a. $12 \times 11 \times 10$
b. 3×12
c. $12 \times 12 \times 12$
d. 12!

41. A basketball player has an average (arithmetic mean) of 22 points in five games. The player scored 18, 16, and 20 points during the first three games. Which shows a possible number of points that the basketball player scored in the next two games?

a. 22 and 22
b. 24 and 28
c. 27 and 29
d. 30 and 36

42. Annabelle takes a piano lesson every 8 days. She also takes a swimming lesson every 10 days. One day Annabelle has both a piano lesson and a swimming lesson. In how many more days will Annabelle next have a piano lesson and a swimming lesson on the same day?

a. 2
b. 20
c. 40
d. 80

43. Which digit is in the hundredths place in the following decimal?

438.591

a. 1
b. 4
c. 5
d. 9

44. One centimeter on a map is equivalent to 200 meters. A rectangular park on the map has a length of 3.5 centimeters and a width of 4 centimeters. What is the area of the park, in square meters?

a. 1,100
b. 2,800
c. 280,000
d. 560,000

45. A cab driver earns a fare by charging his customers a flat rate of \$1.50 plus \$0.40 for every one-fifth of a mile driven. Which equation could be used to represent the cab driver's fare based on the distance driven in miles where *m* is the number of miles driven and *f* is the total fare?

a. $f = 1.50 + (5\text{m} \times 0.40)$
b. $f = 1.50 + (0.40 \times \frac{1}{5}m)$
c. $f = 0.40 + (5m \times 1.50)$
d. $f = \frac{1}{5}m(1.50 + 0.40)$

46. If the radius of a circle is 8 inches long, the circumference of the circle must be

a. 8 inches.
b. 16 inches.
c. 16π inches.
d. 64π inches.

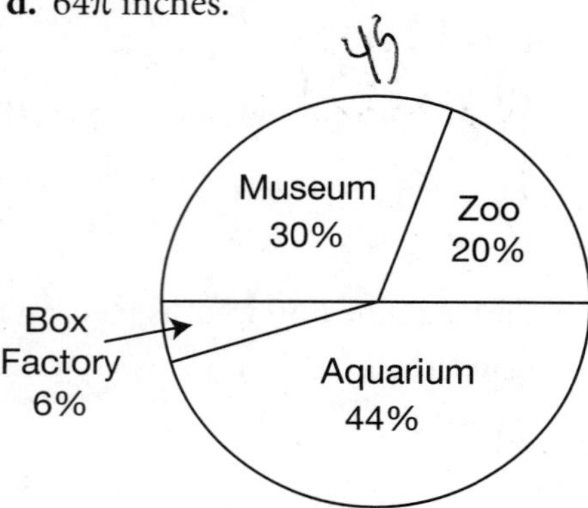

47. The circle graph shows the percentage of students in a middle school who voted for each of four possible field trips. If 45 students voted for the museum, what is the total number of students who voted for the four field trips?

a. 67
b. 115
c. 150
d. 250

48. A game player rolls a pair of number cubes that are each numbered from 1 through 6. The player needs the number cubes to land with the same number facing up. What is the probability that this will happen?

a. $\frac{1}{1}$
b. $\frac{1}{6}$
c. $\frac{1}{12}$
d. $\frac{1}{36}$

49. To solve an algorithm, Ella must follow the steps shown here. Which algebraic expression is equivalent to the algorithm?

First: Set the variable *x* equal to a specific number.
Second: Divide *x* by 4.
Third: Subtract 10 from the quotient.
Fourth: Multiply the difference by 2.

a. $2(\frac{x}{4} - 10)$
b. $(\frac{x}{4} - (2 \times 10)$
c. $2(\frac{4}{x} - 10)$
d. $2(10 - \frac{4}{x})$

50. The product of two prime numbers will always be a(n)

a. composite number.
b. odd number.
c. irrational number.
d. even number.

51. What is the value of the following expression?

$10 + (18 - 4) \times 3$

a. 16
b. 42
c. 52
d. 72

52. What is the value of z in the following equation?

$$5(3z - 12) = 3(5 \times 2)$$

a. –2
b. $2\frac{4}{5}$
c. 6
d. 90

53. Three points of a rectangle on a coordinate grid have ordered pairs of (–2,7), (6,4), and (–2,4). Which must be the ordered pair of the fourth point of the square?

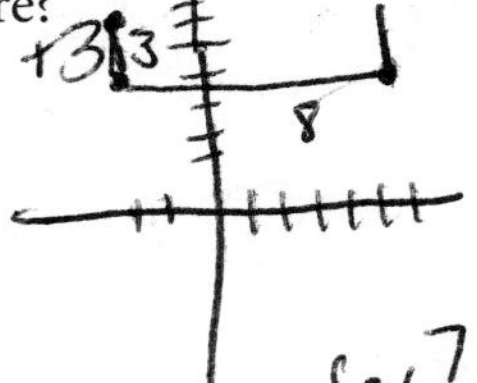

a. (7,6)
b. (2,–7)
c. (–6,7)
d. (6,7)

54. Which number is missing from the function table?

x	f(x)
1.5	12
2.5	20
3.5	28
5	

a. 36
b. 36.5
c. 38
d. 40

55. There are three different styles of houses in Andy's neighborhood. The ratio of ranch houses to Victorian houses to colonial houses is 4:1:7, respectively. If there are a total of 600 houses in Andy's neighborhood, how many Victorian houses are there in his neighborhood?

a. 50
b. 60
c. 100
d. 200

56. Which of the following is the multiplicative inverse of $x + 8$?

a. $x - 8$
b. $\frac{1}{x+8}$
c. $-(x + 8)$
d. $\frac{1}{x} + 8$

57. When x is multiplied by –4 in the equation, the value of y

$$y = -5x$$

a. is multiplied by –4.
b. is multiplied by –20.
c. is divided by –4.
d. is multiplied by 20.

58. The cost of a family dinner was \$42.50, not including a tip. With the tip, the family paid \$50.15. What percentage of the original cost of the dinner did the family leave for a tip?

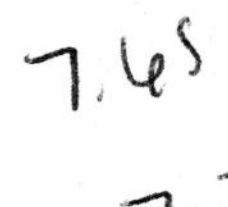

a. 0.18%
b. 7.65%
c. 15%
d. 18%

59. The gray square in the figure is half the height and one-quarter the width of the surrounding rectangle. If the perimeter of the gray square is 16 feet, what is the perimeter of the entire rectangle, in feet?

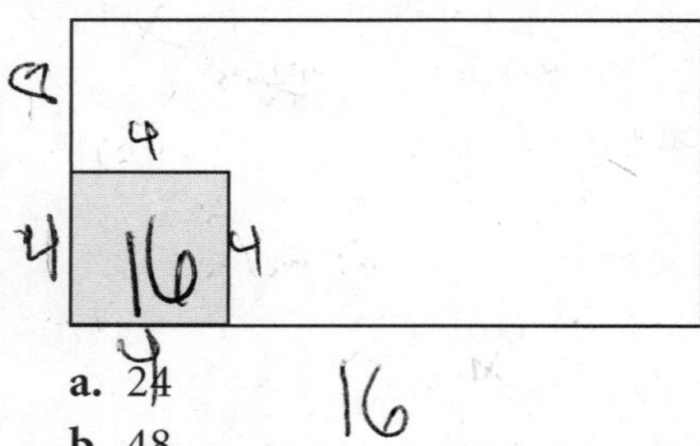

a. 24
b. 48
c. 96
d. 128

60. A shoe shiner at the airport can shine a pair of shoes in 5 minutes. Which expression shows the number of pairs of shoes that he or she can shine in h hours?

a. $\frac{h}{5}$
b. $5h$
c. $10h$
d. $12h$

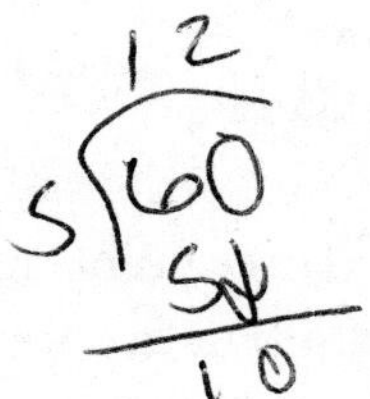

Social Studies

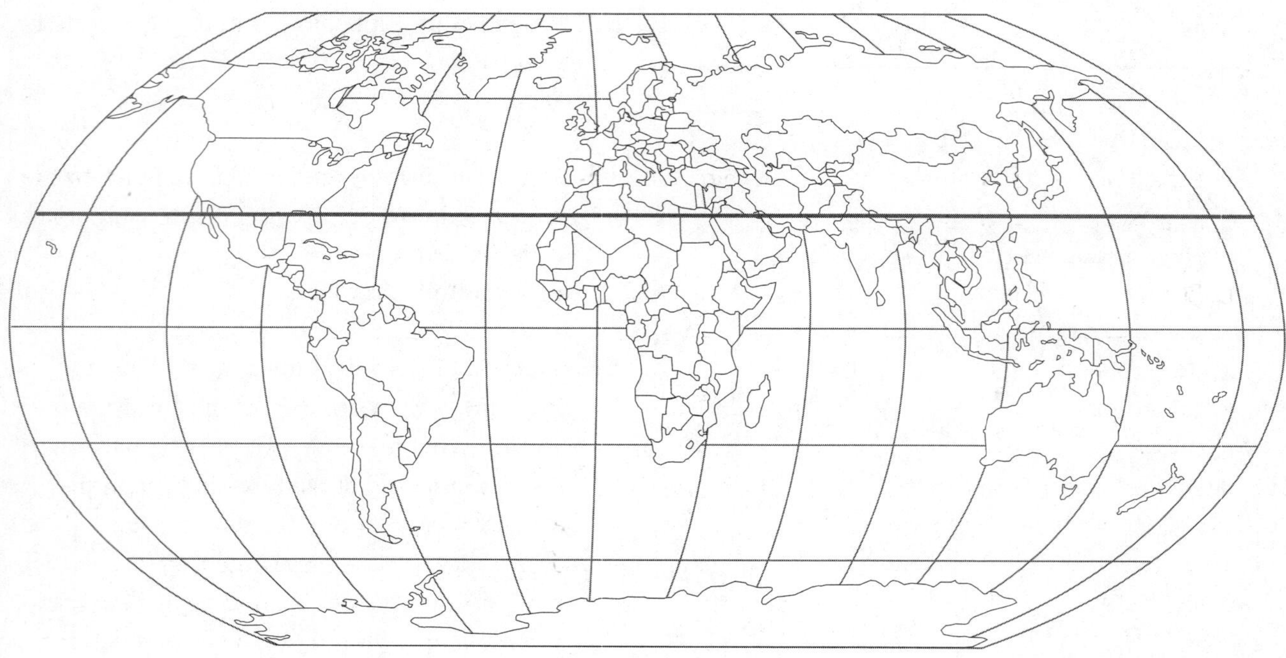

61. The solid line drawn on the preceding map represents the
a. equator.
b. Tropic of Cancer.
c. prime meridian.
d. Tropic of Capricorn.

62. While bodies of water separate most of the continents, the people in Europe and Asia have been separated by
a. Russia.
b. the prime meridian.
c. the Ural Mountains.
d. the Red Sea.

63. What is the minimum age to be eligible to be U.S. president, according to the constitution?
a. 18
b. 25
c. 30
d. 35

64. Euclid, a mathematician also known as the Father of Geometry, revolutionized the field of mathematics about 2,300 years ago, in the ancient civilization of
a. Egypt.
b. Rome.
c. Angkor Wat.
d. Mesopotamia.

65. The aspect of the Ford Model T that transformed the American automobile industry was its
a. style.
b. high speed.
c. affordability.
d. safety measures.

66. The economic principles of laissez-faire state that a government should
a. prevent industrial monopolies from developing.
b. provide healthcare to all of its citizens.
c. tax its wealthier residents at a higher rate.
d. allow industry to bloom without intervention.

67. Which was the deadliest U.S. war in terms of American lives lost?
a. the Revolutionary War
b. the Civil War
c. World War I
d. World War II

68. Which of the following countries was never colonized by a European country?
a. India
b. Thailand
c. Laos
d. Australia

69. Each of the following events contributed to the American colonies initiating the Revolutionary War EXCEPT
a. the Boston Massacre.
b. the passage of the Stamp Act.
c. the Louisiana Purchase.
d. the passage of the Tea Act.

70. The construction of the Hoover Dam in the early 1900s was most important for the development of the American West because it
a. prevented the annual flooding of Lake Mead.
b. encouraged the growth of the populations of several native fish.
c. created a route for automobiles to cross the Colorado River.
d. provided electric power to the western states.

71. A student wants to use primary sources to learn about the American Revolutionary War. Which of the following sources could the student use?

a. a series of letters written by George Washington during the war
b. the book *1776*, written by famous historian David McCullough
c. a Revolutionary War reenactment organization
d. a college-level history textbook about the American Revolutionary War.

72. Which of the following groups reached the Americas before the others?

a. Christopher Columbus and his expedition
b. the Pilgrims from England
c. the Vikings from Scandinavia
d. Ponce de Leon and his expedition

73. A government that is defined as oligarchic

a. is controlled by a single ruler for life.
b. believes in the abolishment of the class system.
c. is governed by a small group of elites.
d. has free and open elections.

74. The Northwest Passage refers to the

a. direct route over the North Pole taken by aircraft seeking the shortest distance to a destination.
b. sea route through the Arctic Ocean, made more navigable by the melting ice created by climate change.
c. ancient trade routes developed to facilitate business between Southeast Asia northwest toward Europe.
d. the first cross-continental rail line connecting the eastern and western United States.

Source: http://lcweb4.loc.gov/ammem/collections/continental/images/photo01.jpg

75. The political cartoon shown here was used to

a. inspire the American colonists to unite against the British rule.
b. encourage enlisters to join the army for World War I.
c. persuade the Confederacy to unify with the northern states after the Civil War.
d. influence additional countries to join NATO following the end of World War II.

76. In a capitalistic system, demand and price are generally set by

a. market forces.
b. elected leaders.
c. leading economists.
d. private companies.

77. The expansive stretch of land between the east and west coasts of Australia is largely uninhabited by people because of

a. dangerous dingo populations.
b. jails set up in the areas.
c. overgrazing from farm animals.
d. low and inconsistent rainfall.

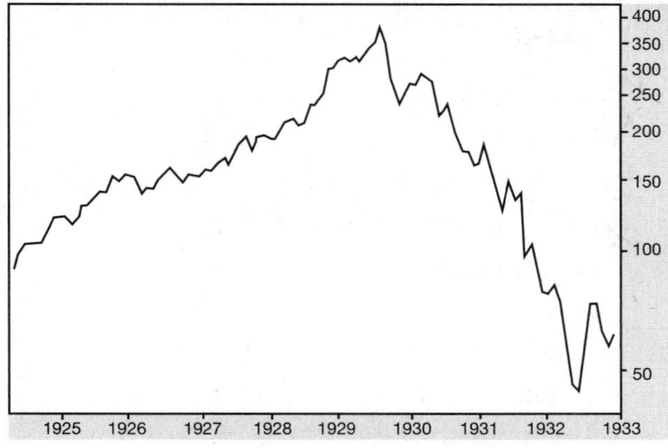

78. The graph shown here is missing its title. Which title fits the information it provides?
  a. Total Immigration to the United States
  b. Dow Jones Industrial Average
  c. Land Area of the United States
  d. Casualties of WWI

79. The poll tax was outlawed by the Twenty-Fourth Amendment because
  a. the revenue generated from the tax was insignificant.
  b. a tariff interferes with a citizen's right to vote.
  c. elections had become efficient enough to not necessitate their own tax.
  d. U.S. leaders wanted to continue to disenfranchise poor voters.

80. For about 47 years, from 1912 to 1959, the official design of the United States flag did not change. How many stars did the flag have during this period?
  a. 47
  b. 48
  c. 49
  d. 50

81. Which of the following events triggered United States involvment in the World War II conflict?
  a. the German invasion of Poland
  b. the assassination of Archduke Ferdinand
  c. the attack on Pearl Harbor
  d. the dropping of the atomic bomb on Hiroshima

82. The basic tenet of the New Deal was to
  a. provide relief for America's poor and unemployed.
  b. split the railroad monopolies to protect public interest.
  c. forcibly integrate America's public schools.
  d. limit the numbers of immigrants entering the United States.

83. One drawback to a Eurocentric curriculum in a social studies classroom is that it
  a. does not provide students with enough information about the British monarchy.
  b. places too much emphasis on dates and names and not on social studies as inquiry.
  c. overly stresses the lesser important leaders of Asia and the Americas.
  d. does not reflect the sociocultural realities of society.

84. Angkor Thom, once the thriving capital of the Khmer Empire, is located in which Southeast Asian country?
  a. Thailand
  b. Cambodia
  c. Vietnam
  d. Laos

85. The cost of fruits and vegetables in Japan can be higher than in other countries. The best explanation for this is that

a. the country does not possess the technology to harvest the fruits and vegetables efficiently.
b. the seeds for the fruits and vegetables do not exist on the island nation of Japan.
c. not much land is available for crops, so Japan must import the fruits and vegetables from other places.
d. the Japanese population does not eat the same fruits and vegetables as people do in other countries, so they are specialty items.

86. On July 20, 1969, the United States became the first country to land a man on the moon. What was the name of the first American astronaut to walk on the moon?

a. Buzz Aldrin
b. John Glenn
c. Alan Shepherd
d. Neil Armstrong

87. The conclusion of World War II led to the formation of which of the following countries?

a. Czechoslovakia
b. Israel
c. USSR
d. Italy

88. Which of the following countries initially used the island of Australia as a penal colony for its criminals?

a. New Zealand
b. the United States
c. Great Britain
d. Russia

89. One of the grandparents of a student in a classroom is a Vietnam veteran and has volunteered to share information about his time as a soldier with the class. Which technique should the teacher encourage his or her students to use to gain the most from the experience?

a. ask the veteran pertinent questions about his wartime experiences
b. memorize the dates of the soldier's enrollment with the U.S. army
c. record the veteran's conversation and transcribe his words on a computer
d. determine whether the veteran's statements are factually correct

90. The formation of Long Island, the largest island in the contiguous United States and the country's most populous island, is largely a result of

a. rocks created from volcanic overflow.
b. land left over after the retreat of glaciers.
c. receding sea waters from the Long Island Sound.
d. landfill created by early settlers to the New York City area.

Science

91. The primary function of the ribosome in an animal cell is to

a. create protein from amino acids.
b. convert the energy from food into cellular energy.
c. protect the cell from potentially dangerous substances.
d. carry waste material out of the cell.

92. Which is the thickest layer of Earth?
a. the crust
b. the inner core
c. the outer core
d. the mantle

93. How many chromosomes does a normal human cell contain?
a. 23
b. 45
c. 46
d. 47

94. Which of the following can be used to calculate the amount of momentum of an object?
a. multiply mass by velocity
b. multiply weight by mass
c. multiply speed by acceleration
d. multiply gravity by weight

95. A person on Earth can only see one side of the moon, regardless of the time of day or location on the planet. Which explains this phenomenon that keeps the dark side of the moon hidden from people on Earth?
a. The dark side of the moon always faces toward the sun.
b. The rotation of the moon is equal to its orbit around Earth.
c. The moon rotates on its axis at exactly 90 degrees.
d. The electromagnetic field of the dark side of the moon is repulsed by Earth.

96. During the Apollo 15 mission, an astronaut on the moon conducted an experiment by dropping a hammer and a feather at the same time. Both the hammer and the feather hit the surface of the moon at the same time. Which is a reasonable conclusion that can be made from the astronaut's experiment?
a. The feather and the hammer have the same mass.
b. The gravitational force on the moon is less than that on Earth.
c. Distance from the sun affects the way an object falls.
d. Objects fall at the same rate regardless of mass.

97. Which of the following do human beings produce from sunlight?
a. vitamin A
b. vitamin B_1
c. vitamin C
d. vitamin D

98. Which of the following is NOT an example of a physical change?
a. A piece of paper is cut into hundreds of pieces.
b. An iceberg melts into the ocean.
c. An apple rots on a kitchen table.
d. Liquid mercury is boiled to a gas.

99. Which of the following elements of an atom is NOT contained within the nucleus?
a. electron
b. proton
c. neutron
d. quark

100. About 250 million years ago, the continents of Earth were joined as one supercontinent. What is the name attributed to this ancient continent?

a. Oceana
b. Pangaea
c. Hadean
d. Panthalassa

101. Which statement is NOT true for all mammals, without exception?

a. Mammals are warm-blooded.
b. Mammals have a backbone.
c. Mammals give birth to live young.
d. Mammals have hair.

102. Although some machines may appear complex, each machine is comprised of one of the simple machines defined by scientists. How many simple machines are there in total?

a. 3
b. 6
c. 10
d. 42

GALILEAN MOONS OF JUPITER

MOON	DIAMETER (IN KM)	AVERAGE DISTANCE FROM JUPITER (IN KM)	ORBITAL PERIOD (IN EARTH DAYS)	YEAR DISCOVERED
Io	3,636	422,000	1.77	1610
Europa	3,130	670,900	3.55	1610
Ganymede	5,268	1,070,000	7.15	1610
Callisto	4,806	1,883,000	16.7	1610

Using the preceding table, answer questions 103 and 104.

103. All the Galilean moons are roughly spherical. Which Galilean moon has the greatest circumference at its equator?

a. Io
b. Europa
c. Ganymede
d. Callisto

104. Which is an accurate conclusion to make about the four Galilean moons of Jupiter?

a. The closer the moon is to Jupiter, the shorter its orbital period.
b. The farther the moon is from Jupiter, the greater its diameter.
c. The larger Galilean moons were discovered first.
d. The smaller the moon's diameter, the farther the moon is from Jupiter.

105. As an ambulance approaches a person, the sound of the siren is high pitched. However, when the ambulance drives away from the person, the sound of the siren becomes lower pitched. Which describes the effect on the pitch of the sound?

a. Doppler effect
b. sonic boom
c. resonance
d. butterfly effect

106. Which of the following is a vestigial organ of the human body?

a. kidney
b. appendix
c. skin
d. gallbladder

107. The chemical compound carbon dioxide, one of the greenhouse gases responsible for climate change, has which of the following chemical formulas?

a. H_2O
b. C_2O
c. C_2O_2
d. CO_2

108. According to Newton's First Law of Motion, which of the following affects the motion of an object while it is in motion?

a. a simple machine
b. an opposite reaction
c. an external force
d. gravity

109. A meteorologist predicts the weather using a combination of data, including temperature, air pressure, wind speed, and humidity. Which instrument can the meteorologist use to determine the air pressure of the atmosphere?

a. thermometer
b. hygrometer
c. barometer
d. anemometer

110. Which best explains the cause of a lunar eclipse?

a. The sun moves between Earth and the moon.
b. Earth moves in between the sun and the moon.
c. The moon moves between Earth and the sun.
d. The moon moves between Earth and Mars.

111. Which of the following is NOT a reason why pigs spend much of their time wallowing in mud?

a. Pigs use the mud to attract a potential mate during mating season.
b. Pigs lack sweat glands and need the mud to regulate their body temperature.
c. The mud protects their skin from getting burned by the sun.
d. The mud acts as a natural barrier from insect bites.

112. The population of a species may, over time, develop more common traits that help the species reproduce and thrive within an environment. The name of this process is

a. mutation.
b. population decline.
c. natural selection.
d. diversification.

113. Which of the following represents an example of potential energy?
a. An ocean wave crashes on the seashore.
b. A rubber band is stretched to capacity.
c. Sound waves echo in a concert hall.
d. A microwave heats a frozen dinner.

114. Producers, consumers, and decomposers each play a pivotal role in the forest community. Which of the following represents a decomposer?
a. shelf fungus
b. pine tree
c. grizzly bear
d. wood log

115. According to Einstein's theory of relativity that connected mass to energy, energy is equivalent to
a. mass times the speed of light.
b. mass times velocity.
c. mass plus half the speed of light.
d. mass times the speed of light squared.

116. Which of the following shows the life cycle of a butterfly in correct chronological order?
a. egg, pupa, larva, adult
b. adult, pupa, larva, egg
c. egg, larva, adult, pupa
d. egg, larva, pupa, adult

117. The climate in the United Kingdom is warmer than its northern position on the globe might suggest. Which of the following has the greatest warming effect on the island nation?
a. the prime meridian
b. the North Atlantic current
c. great amounts of rainfall
d. population density

118. Which of the following atmospheric conditions is most likely to form a tornado?
a. cirrus clouds
b. a contrail cloud
d. cool, dry air
d. a supercell

119. The process of asexual reproduction is characterized by
a. cell division in which the number of chromosomes per cell is halved.
b. the fertilization of gametes outside of the body.
c. the duplication of an organism with a single parent.
d. the development of babies in the pouch of the mother.

120. Sedimentary rocks, which comprise about 5% of the volume of Earth's crust, are formed by
a. the deposits of materials that are compacted together.
b. the cooling and hardening of liquid magma.
c. rocks that change their state through a combination of extreme temperature and pressure.
d. the shifting of continental plates.

READING/LANGUAGE ARTS KEY					
ITEM	KEY	SUBSECTION	ITEM	KEY	SUBSECTION
1	B	Foundations of Reading	16	D	Language in Writing
2	A	Foundations of Reading	17	D	Foundations of Reading
3	D	Foundations of Reading	18	B	Communication Skills
4	C	Foundations of Reading	19	D	Language in Writing
5	C	Foundations of Reading	20	B	Foundations of Reading
6	C	Language in Writing	21	C	Language in Writing
7	A	Language in Writing	22	B	Language in Writing
8	B	Language in Writing	23	D	Communication Skills
9	A	Foundations of Reading	24	A	Communication Skills
10	A	Foundations of Reading	25	C	Foundations of Reading
11	D	Foundations of Reading	26	B	Foundations of Reading
12	B	Language in Writing	27	B	Foundations of Reading
13	B	Communication Skills	28	C	Foundations of Reading
14	C	Language in Writing	29	D	Communication Skills
15	C	Language in Writing	30	A	Foundations of Reading

MATHEMATICS KEY					
ITEM	KEY	SUBSECTION	ITEM	KEY	SUBSECTION
31	C	Number Sense & Numeration	40	A	Data Org. & Interpretation
32	B	Number Sense & Numeration	41	C	Data Org. & Interpretation
33	B	Number Sense & Numeration	42	C	Number Sense & Numeration
34	B	Algebraic Concepts	43	D	Number Sense & Numeration
35	C	Number Sense & Numeration	44	C	Geometry & Measurement
36	A	Algebraic Concepts	45	A	Algebraic Concepts
37	B	Geometry & Measurement	46	C	Geometry & Measurement
38	C	Geometry & Measurement	47	C	Data Org. & Interpretation
39	D	Geometry & Measurement	48	B	Data Org. & Interpretation

MATHEMATICS KEY *(continued)*

ITEM	KEY	SUBSECTION	ITEM	KEY	SUBSECTION
49	A	Algebraic Concepts	55	A	Number Sense & Numeration
50	A	Number Sense & Numeration	56	B	Algebraic Concepts
51	C	Number Sense & Numeration	57	A	Algebraic Concepts
52	C	Number Sense & Numeration	58	D	Number Sense & Numeration
53	D	Geometry & Measurement	59	B	Geometry & Measurement
54	D	Number Sense & Numeration	60	D	Algebraic Concepts

SOCIAL STUDIES KEY

ITEM	KEY	SUBSECTION	ITEM	KEY	SUBSECTION
61	B	Geography, Anthrop., Sociology	76	A	Economics
62	C	Geography, Anthrop., Sociology	77	D	Geography, Anthrop., Sociology
63	D	Gov't, Citizenship & Democracy	78	B	Economics
64	A	World History	79	B	Gov't, Citizenship & Democracy
65	C	United States History	80	D	United States History
66	D	Economics	81	C	United States History
67	B	United States History	82	A	United States History
68	B	World History	83	D	Inquiry/Processes
69	C	United States History	84	B	Geography, Anthrop., Sociology
70	D	Geography, Anthrop., Sociology	85	C	Geography, Anthrop., Sociology
71	A	Inquiry/Processes	86	D	United States History
72	C	United States History	87	B	World History
73	C	Gov't, Citizenship & Democracy	88	C	Geography, Anthrop., Sociology
74	B	Geography, Anthrop., Sociology	89	A	Social Studies Inquiry/Processes
75	A	United States History	90	B	Geography, Anthrop., Sociology

SCIENCE KEY					
ITEM	KEY	SUBSECTION	ITEM	KEY	SUBSECTION
91	A	Life Science	106	B	Life Science
92	D	Earth Science	107	D	Physical Science
93	C	Life Science	108	C	Physical Science
94	A	Physical Science	109	C	Science Inquiry/Processes
95	B	Earth Science	110	B	Earth Science
96	D	Science Inquiry/Processes	111	A	Life Science
97	D	Science in Personal/Social	112	C	Life Science
98	C	Physical Science	113	B	Physical Science
99	A	Physical Science	114	A	Life Science
100	B	Earth Science	115	D	Physical Science
101	C	Life Science	116	D	Life Science
102	B	Physical Science	117	B	Earth Science
103	C	Earth Science	118	D	Earth Science
104	A	Earth Science	119	C	Life Science
105	A	Physical Science	120	A	Earth Science

Reading/Language Arts Answers

1. b. Walt Whitman was a nurse during the Civil War and used his poetry to portray the horrors of the war. He mentions eternal stars, choice **a**, a mountain, choice **c**, and horses, choice **d**, but the poem is not reflecting on his perspective of those subjects.

2. a. The first line of the poem mentions an army, but the second line of the poem provides a serene setting. The purpose of this line is to contrast the setting of the war, so choice **a** is the best choice. Whitman may be providing a tranquil setting, choice **b**, or a lush countryside, choice **c**, but that is not the purpose of the line. There is no mention of the European landscape, so choice **d** is not correct.

3. d. Cinquains and limericks are 5-line poems, so choice **a** and choice **c** are not correct. A haiku is even shorter, as it must be limited to 3 lines. A sonnet must be 14 lines, and the poem is an example.

4. c. Line 11 has three words that begin with the "g" sound. Alliteration is the repeated sound at the beginning of the words. Therefore, choice **c** represents the literary device used in line 11.

5. c. In this poem, Sonnet 130, Shakespeare does not actually use exaggerations to compliment his mistress. He says that her eyes are *not* like the sun and that coral is redder than her lips, so choices **a** and **d** are incorrect. Shakespeare states in line 9 that he enjoys hearing her talk, so choice **c** is correct. He also says, however, that music is more pleasing than hearing her talk; the mistress is not creating the music, though, so choice **b** is not correct.

6. c. Nothing is being compared or contrasted in the first sentence of the passage, so choices **a** and **b** are not correct. The first sentence provides the readers with a meaning of the Cambrian Period, so a definition, choice **c**, is the best answer. It does not provide a symbol, which might be found in a poem, so choice **d** is not correct, either.

7. a. A fictional story uses made-up information, whereas this passage is fact-based. Therefore, choices **b** and **c** are not correct. The passage is an example of exposition, the purpose of which is to provide readers with background information. A tall tale also uses made-up information, so choice **d** is not correct.

8. b. The author tells the readers in the last sentence of the passage that scientists don't agree on why life diversified so greatly during the Cambrian Period. Therefore, choice **b** makes the most sense. The author does not explain a scientific phenomenon or disprove a claim, so choices **a** and **d** are not true, either. Because the author is simply saying that scientists don't exactly know why the explosion of life occurred, no other information is being provided, making choice **c** incorrect.

9. a. A phoneme is the smallest unit of sound in a language. The description in choice **b** describes phonics, not a phoneme. The description in choice **c** describes a digraph. The description in choice **d** describes a silent letter, so it is not the correct answer choice.

10. a. A running record assesses a student's reading abilities by counting the number and types of errors made. However, it does not measure any aspect of a student's comprehension of the text. Therefore, choice **a** represents one result that is not provided by a running record.

11. d. There are many ways a student can work to identify the meaning of an unknown word. The prefix or suffix of the word may provide some clues to its meaning, so choice **a** is not correct. A dictionary will surely help a student learn its meaning, so choice **b** is not correct. Looking for context before and after the word is one of the best strategies, so choice **c** is not correct either. Identifying a possible literary device, such as alliteration, will not help a student understand the meaning of the word. Therefore, choice **d** is the right answer.

12. b. The subject of the sentence is the bald eagle, which is singular. The corresponding verb, *is*, is also singular. That means they are in agreement and choice **a** is not correct. The pronoun, *their*, is plural, however. That means they do not match and choice **b** is correct. The words *heads* and *beaks* are plural words and therefore should not have apostrophes, cso choice **c** is not correct. Both commas are necessary in the sentence to set off the interruption, so choice **d** is not correct.

13. b. Active listening involves many qualities. An active listener should listen without talking, choice **a**, but that does not define the purpose of active listening best. The purpose of active listening is simply to listen for meaning—to understand what the speaker is saying. Therefore, choice **b** is correct. The listener does not have to agree with the speaker, so choice **c** is not right. And while a seated listener should sit up straight, that is not mean that the listener is necessarily listening for meaning, so choice **d** is not right.

14. c. Prewriting involves several steps. Its purpose is to get students to decide what subject they want to write about and how they want to organize it, so choices **a** and **b** are not correct. They should also consider the purpose of their writing, so choice **d** is not correct. They should not be concerned with spelling or grammar at this stage, so choice **c** is correct.

15. c. The word *heavy* is being used in the sentence to describe how the decision weighed on the manager's shoulders. Therefore, it is being used as an adverb and should include -ly at the end of the word: heavily. Because the shoulders belong to the manager, an apostrophe should be used to show possession. There are no errors in the others parts of the sentence.

16. d. The students feel strongly that the bill should not be passed because of the loss of the natural land. There are trying to convince the elected officials in their town of this position. That means they should be writing a persuasive letter, choice **d**, in an attempt to persuade the officials.

17. d. According to Regie Routman's *Reading Essentials*, "When students help create the library, they use it more." Therefore, choice **a** would be an effective action to get students to use the library. An exceptional classroom library should have more than 1,000 books. Additionally, having copies of some of the more popular books ensures that students will always have access to them. Therefore, choice **b** is not right. Just as a bookstore features its bestsellers with the front of the book facing out, so too should the books be displayed in a classroom library; choice **c** is therefore not correct. Leveled books can be very helpful, but students should not be limited to only the books that are at their level. Students should learn how to select books at their own level without being handed only books at that level. Therefore, choice **d** is correct.

18. b. ELL students need the additional time to process the language in addition to processing the question itself. Therefore, additional wait time, choice **b**, would be the most beneficial to an ELL student. Asking the question more loudly, choice **a**, may not help and, in fact, may create anxiety in the student. While some ELL students are more comfortable writing their answers on the board, many have greater conversational language proficiency. Therefore, choice **c** is not right. Providing students with choices, choice **d**, may prevent them from expressing their own opinions on a text; it may be detrimental to ELL students if they are not allowed to provide their own answers.

19. d. The passage begins by mentioning some of the similarities between two brothers. Then it mentions how they are very different. Therefore, the organization of the passage is compare and contrast, choice **d**.

20. b. The author of the passage says that he spent three minutes indoors all weekend. Unless he camped outside and didn't use a bathroom indoors, this is surely an exaggeration. A hyperbole is another word for an exaggeration. Therefore, choice **b** is the correct answer.

21. c. The passage describes the differences between two brothers, one of whom spends most of his time outdoors, while the other spends most of his time indoors. But the primary purpose isn't simply to make fun of one of the boys, even though they author does poke some fun at his brother. The author says at the end of the passage that his brother's behavior doesn't affect the way he feels about him. Therefore, the primary purpose is to show that differences don't interfere with a brotherly bond, choice **c**. The children may have the same height and hairstyle, choice **d**, but that is only a detail in the story, not its primary purpose.

22. b. Choices **a** and **d** are simple sentences. Choice **c** is an example of a complex sentence. Choice **b** is a compound sentence because it connects two independent clauses.

23. d. A teacher should use a video screen as a tool to improve the learning experience for his or her students. Video offers the unique ability to demonstrate certain topics with images and sound, thus giving students a new way to learn. Therefore, choice **d** is correct. The intention of screening a video should not be to allow the teacher to relax, nor is that the reason it is most beneficial to students, so choice **a** is not correct. Some students may prefer to watch videos, but not all of them do, so choice **b** is not right either. Video screens may be getting more reliable, but they still require technological proficiency and are dependent on electricity. Compared to books and other media, video is not the most dependable medium, so choice **c** is not correct.

24. a. Pictures and nonverbal clues can greatly improve an ELL's ability to understand meaning. Therefore, choice **a** is correct. None of the choices listed in choice **b**, choice **c**, or choice **d** will better help the ELL student improve his or her understanding of the teacher.

25. c. When students make personal connections to a text, it increases their comprehension of the material. Students can connect the text to their own experiences (self), the events in the world around them (world), or to other texts they have read (text). That is why choices **a**, **b**, and **d** are incorrect. Comparing the students to the world around them does not involve the text, so choice **c** does not make a connection to improve comprehension.

26. b. Graphic organizers are terrific aids for teachers. By connecting the major ideas of a text in a map, students can help see how the knowledge is connected. Graphic organizers also help students to make meaning of the text and, amazingly, increase their vocabulary skills. One potential drawback to using graphic organizers is that they can take a lot of time to create. For students who are already comfortable with the text, this may feel like a waste of time. Therefore, choice **b** is the only choice that does not necessarily represent a benefit.

27. b. Research has demonstrated compellingly that a student's phonemic awareness, choice **b**, is the best predictor of a student's early reading acquisition abilities. The other choices represent positive attributes for early reading comprehension, but they are not as important as a student's phonemic awareness.

28. c. It is very important for classroom libraries to provide students with nonfiction texts. However, fictional texts are more likely to provide literary devices, so choice **a** is not correct. Choice **b** represents a trait of a fictional text as well, so it is not correct. Choice **c** explains one reason why nonfiction texts should be read by students; it helps them to make connections with their world, which in turn leads to improved informational writing. Choice **d** is not necessarily true since both fiction and nonfiction can be easy or challenging.

29. d. A speaker with good communication skills should always consider the purpose, volume, and tone of the speech when addressing a group. Punctuation, choice **d**, relates only to the symbols of written language, so it cannot be considered when speaking.

30. a. The rhyme scheme of a poem uses letters to show how the lines rhyme. Because the first two lines of the poem rhyme, they share the same letter: A. Because the second two lines of the poem rhyme, they share the same letter: B. Therefore, the correct rhyme scheme is AABB, choice **a**.

Mathematics Answers

31. c. The value of a number with an exponent is equal to that number times itself the number of times shown in the exponent. 5^5 is therefore equal to $5 \times 5 \times 5 \times 5 \times 5$, which is 3,125.

32. b. A whole number is any positive integer or zero. Therefore, choice **b** is the only choice that represents a whole number.

33. b. Following the rule of the pattern, the fourth number in the pattern should be 1 less than the product of 9 and 2, which is 18 – 1, which is 17. The fifth number will be 1 less than the product of 17 and 2, which is 34 – 1, which is 33. The sixth number will be 1 less than the product of 33 and 2, which is 65.

34. b. To find the value of *a*, you need to isolate it on one side of the equation. That means you first need to add 49 to both sides of the equation to get $3a = 5b + 49$. Next, you need to divide both sides of the equation by to isolate *a* by itself. $\frac{3}{a} = \frac{5b + 49}{3}$, which means that *a* is equal to $\frac{5b + 49}{3}$, choice **b**.

35. c. There are three possible ways for a store to sell \$0.75 pencils and \$1.00 pens to earn \$6. Either the store sells 6 pens and no pencils, 8 pencils and no pens, or 3 pens and 4 pencils. Because the problem says that at least one pen and one pencil were sold, the store must have sold 3 pens and 4 pencils. The question asks for the number of pencils sold during the day, so choice **c** is correct.

36. a. To solve the given inequality, first subtract 6 from both sides.

$3s + 6 < 12$

$3s + 6 - 6 < 12 - 6$

$3s < 6$

Then you can divide both sides of the inequality by 3 to isolate the variable s on one side.

$3s < 6$

$3s \div 3 < 6 \div 3$

$s < 2$

Because the < symbol means "is less than," the value of s must be less than 2. The only number in the answer choices that could be a possible solution is –3, choice **a**.

37. b. A cube has six square sides. Its net, which shows the two-dimensional representation of a solid, must therefore have six squares. Only choices **b** and **d** have six sides. However, the net in choice **d** cannot be used to construct a cube. The net in choice **b** can.

38. c. The difference between 7 A.M. and 2 P.M. is 7 hours. The difference between 66°F and 87°F is 21 degrees. To find the change in temperature each hour, divide the change in degrees by the change in hours: $21 \div 7 =$ 3 degrees per hour. Choice **a**, 69°F, shows the temperature only one hour after 7 A.M. There are 5 hours between 7 A.M. and noon, so the difference in temperature is 3 degrees per hour × 5 hours, or 15 degrees. If you chose choice **b**, you may have made a regrouping error when adding 15 to 66. The correct answer is choice **c**. Choice **d**, 84°F, shows the temperature six hours after 7 A.M., so it is not correct.

39. d. The figure is in the shape of a star with five points. It can be rotated one-fifth at a time and will look the same. One-fifth of 360° is 72°. A rotation with any multiple of 72° will make the figure look exactly the same. The only answer that is a multiple of 72° is 288°, choice **d**. Choice **a** will turn the star to the right and choice **c** will turn the star upside town; in both cases, the star would not look exactly the same.

40. a. The scenario in the problem represents a permutation because the order of the finishers matters. Therefore, you can multiply the number of possibilities for each place together to find the total number of ways the prizes can be awarded. However, one runner cannot win more than one award, which means that while there are 12 possibilities for the 1st-place trophy, there are then only 11 possibilities for the 2nd-place medal—and then only 10 possibilities for the 3rd-place ribbon. That is why the expression is not $12 \times 12 \times 12$, choice **c**, but instead $12 \times 11 \times 10$, choice **a.**

41. c. If the basketball player scored an average of 22 points in 5 games, that must mean that he or she scored a total of 22×5 points in total during the games. The player scored 18, 16, and 20 points during the first three games for a total of 54 points. The player must have then scored a total of $110 - 54$ points in the next two games to average 22 points. That is 56 points, which is represented by the number of points listed in choice **c.** If the player scored 22 points in each of the next two games, only the mode would be 22 points, so choice **a** is not correct. If the player scored 24 and 28 points in each of the next two games, only the median would be 22 points, so choice **b** is not correct. If you chose choice **d**, you may have made a regrouping error.

42. c. To solve this problem, you need to find the least common multiple for 8 and 10. The number 2 is the greatest common factor, not the least common factor, so choice **a** is not correct. 20 days, choice **b**, is only a multiple of 10 and not also 8, so it is not a common multiple. Choices **c** and choice **d** both represent common multiples of 8 and 10, but choice **c** is the least common multiple. The next time Annabelle will have a piano lesson and a swimming lesson on the same day will be in 40 days, choice **c.**

43. d. The hundredths place is the second digit to the right of the decimal point. In the decimal 438.591, the digit in the hundredths place is therefore 9. The digit 1 is in the thousandths place, 4 is in the hundreds place, and 5 is in the tenths place.

44. d. The first step you have to take is to convert both sides of the park from centimeters into meters. Because 1 centimeter is equal to 200 meters, you can multiply each side of the park, which is given to you in centimeters, by 200 to find out their values in meters. $3.5 \times 200 = 700$ and $4 \times 200 = 800$. Next, you need to find the area of the park. Area = length × width, so Area = $700 \times 800 = 560{,}000$, or choice **d.** If you selected choice **b**, then you calculated the area of the park before you converted each side, which is incorrect.

45. a. The cab driver earns exactly \$1.50 for each fare regardless of the number of miles driven. Therefore, the \$1.50 amount should not be multiplied by any variable, eliminating choices **c** and choice **d**. Additionally, the driver charges \$0.40 for every fifth of a mile driven. That means the number of miles, *m*, should be multiplied by 5 and also by 0.40 to find the cost of driving each mile. The equation that represents this is choice **a**. Remember that each mile driven is worth 5 times 0.40, not one-fifth times 0.40.

46. c. The circumference of a circle is equal to the diameter of the circle multiplied by pi. The radius of a circle is one-half of the circle's diameter. Therefore, the radius should be doubled and then multiplied by pi to find the circumference of the circle. 8 inches $\times$ 2 $\times \pi = 16\pi$ inches, choice **c**.

47. c. The 45 students who voted for the museum represent 30% of the total number of students who voted for one of the four field trips. To determine the total number of students who voted, you can set up an equation comparing the percents to the numbers. You can use x for the unknown number.

$\frac{30}{45} = \frac{100}{x}$

You can then cross multiply to find that $30x = 4{,}500$, which means that $x = 150$. There were 150 students who voted in total.

48. b. Regardless of which number the first number cube shows, the second number cube has six numbers, one of which would satisfy the game player's requirements. Therefore the probability of the number cubes landing with the same number facing up will be $\frac{1}{6}$.

49. a. $\frac{x}{4}$ represents the second step because it shows x divided by 4. When 10 is subtracted from the quotient, it should be represented by $\frac{x}{4} - 10$. To multiply that difference by 2, you would need to put the entire expression $\frac{x}{4} - 10$ in parenthesis first. The answer choice that represents these steps in listed in choice **a**.

50. a. A prime number is a number that has only two factors: itself and 1. When you multiply two prime numbers, the resulting product must be evenly divisible by at least one additional number. For example, 3 and 7 are both prime numbers. $3 \times 7 = 21$, which is a composite number because it has more than two factors: 1, 3, 7, and 21. When prime numbers are multiplied, the product does not have to be even or odd, and it cannot be an irrational number.

51. c. When solving an expression with multiple operations, you need to follow the order of operations. Perform any operation within parentheses first, then solve multiplication and division from left to right, and then solve addition and subtraction from left to right.

$10 + (18 - 4) \times 3 =$

$10 + (14) \times 3 =$

$10 + 42 =$

52

If you chose choice **a**, you disregarded the parentheses. If you chose choice **b**, you may have forgotten to add 10 or you made a regrouping error. If you chose choice **d**, you solved the expression from left to right without considering the order of operations.

52. c. To solve for z in the given equation, you need to first distribute the numbers in the expressions on either sides of the equals sign.

$5(3z - 12) = 3(5 \times 2)$

$15z - 60 = 3(10)$

$15z - 60 = 30$

Then you can add 60 to both sides of the equation and divide both sides by 15 to isolate z on one side of the equation.

$15z - 60 = 30$

$15z = 90$

$z = 6$

53. d. Two points on the rectangle are at (–2,4) and (–2,7). Therefore, the line that connects those two points has a length of 3 and is vertical. A rectangle has parallel and congruent opposite sides; the other two points must also be vertical with a length of 3. If one of those points is (6,4), the fourth point must be (6,7), choice **d.**

54. d. Try to identify the pattern in the table and recognize the relationships between the numbers in the x column and the $f(x)$ column. Each $f(x)$ value is 8 times greater than its x corresponding value. Therefore, the $f(x)$ column for $x = 5$ should be $5 \times 8 =$ 40.

55. a. The ratio of ranch houses to Victorian houses to colonial houses is 4:1:7, respectively. Therefore, for every 12 houses in his neighborhood, there will be 4 ranch houses, 1 Victorian house, and 7 colonial houses. You can set up an equation comparing the number of Victorian houses out of 12 to the number out of 600. Use x for the unknown number.

$\frac{1}{12} = \frac{x}{600}$

If you cross-multiply, you will get $12x = 600$, or $x = 50$. There are 50 Victorian houses in Andy's neighborhood.

56. b. The multiplicative inverse of a number is the number that, when multiplied by the original number, will result in a product of 1. Whatever the value of x may be, $x + 8$ multiplied by $\frac{1}{x+8}$ will be equal to 1. Therefore, choice **b** is correct.

57. a. Whatever is done to one side of an algebraic equation must be done to the other side. Therefore, if the right side of the equation is multiplied by –4, then the left side must also be multiplied by –4. Therefore, the value of y will be multiplied by –4 as well.

58. d. To calculate the percent increase from \$42.50 to \$50.15, you can divide the difference by the original cost of the dinner. The difference, of the amount of the tip left, is equal to 50.15 – 42.50, or 7.65. Divide that difference by 42.50 to find the amount of the tip: $\frac{7.65}{42.50} = 0.18$. The question asks for the percent tip, which can be found by moving the decimal point two places to the right and adding a percent sign: 0.18 = 18%.

59. b. If the gray square has a perimeter of 16 feet, each side has a length of 16 feet ÷ 4, or 4 feet. If each side of the square has a length of 4 feet, then the rectangle has a height of 8 feet and a width of 16 feet. A rectangle with a height of 8 feet and a width of 16 feet has a perimeter equal to 2(8 feet + 16 feet). This is equal to 48 square feet, so choice **b** is correct.

60. d. If the shoe shiner can shine a pair of shoes in 5 minutes, that means he or she can shine 60 ÷ 5, or 12 in every hour. To find the number of pairs of shoes that can be shined in h hours, just multiply h by 12. That's the expression in answer choice **d.**

Social Studies Answers

61. b. The solid line on the map goes through Mexico, just south of the United States. This is too far north to be the equator, choice **a**. It is the Tropic of Cancer, choice **b**. The prime meridian, choice **c**, goes north-south, not east-west. The Tropic of Capricorn, choice **d**, is south of the equator, so it is not correct either.

62. c. The European and Asian continents are separated not by a body of water but by a mountain range—the Ural Mountains, choice **c**. Russia occupies both sides of the mountain range, but the country does not separate the continents itself.

63. d. According to the U.S. Constitution, a president must be 35 years old. A person must be 18 to vote, 25 to serve in the House, and 30 to serve in the Senate.

64. a. Euclid was a Greek Mathematician who studied, taught, and published the most famous textbook in history, *Elements*, in Alexandria, in Egypt.

65. c. Henry Ford designed an automobile that, with the efficiency of the assembly line, was affordable for more people than any other car before it. It may have been stylish for its time, and it may have been able to attain high speeds, but it was its low price that revolutionized the automobile industry.

66. d. The loose translation of the French term *laissez-faire* is "let it be" or "leave alone." Therefore, the best description of a laissez-faire government is one that allows industry to bloom *without intervention*, choice **d**. That's the only description that implies that the government is purposefully not getting involved.

67. b. By far, the deadliest U.S. war was the Civil War, with more than 500,000 lives lost. Of course, part of the reason for the high death toll was that the people fighting on both sides were Americans.

68. b. India and Australia were both colonized by England, so choices **a** and **d** are not correct. Laos was a French protectorate until 1949, so choice **c** is not correct, either. Thailand, choice **b**, is the only country in Southeast Asia that was never colonized.

69. c. The Boston Massacre, the Stamp Act, and the Tea Act were all contributing factors to the origins of the Revolutionary War. Each event helped to further distance the colonists from their British rule. The Louisiana Purchase, choice **c**, occurred in 1803—long after the end of the Revolutionary War.

70. d. The Hoover Dam prevented the annual flooding of the Colorado River, but Lake Mead did not exist until after the Hoover Dam was built. Therefore, choice **a** is not correct. The dam actually decimated the native fish populations, so choice **b** is not right, either. While the Hoover Dam does provide a route across the Colorado River, this is not the most important reason for its existence. It is more important to provide electric power to the western states, choice **d**. The Hoover Dam provides immense power for California, Nevada, and Arizona.

71. a. A primary source is some material that was created by a direct witness to an event. A photograph, autobiography, and an interview with an eyewitness are all examples of primary sources. The only primary source listed in the answer choices is the series of letters from George Washington, choice **a**.

72. c. While Christopher Columbus is said to have discovered the Americas in 1492, the Vikings from Scandinavia actually arrived in the New World about 500 years earlier. The Pilgrims did not land in the Americas until the 1600s. Ponce de Leon first journeyed across the Atlantic on Christopher Columbus's second trip from Spain, so his group was not the first to reach the Americas, either.

73. c. The description in choice **a** defines a monarchy, not an oligarchy. Communism aims to abolish the class system, but an oligarchic government does not. An oligarchy is a form of government that is controlled by a small group, so choice **c** is correct. An oligarchy does not have elections, so choice **d** is not correct either.

74. b. The Northwest Passage is the name of the sea route that goes north of Canada, recently exposed as a possible trade route with the shrinking of the Arctic icepack. Therefore, choice **b** is correct.

75. a. Benjamin Franklin created this famous political cartoon in the 1750s. Although it was used for a different purpose prior to the American Revolution, it was spread throughout the colonies around the time of the Stamp Act. with the intention of uniting the colonists against tyrannical British rule. Therefore, choice **a** is correct.

76. a. With few exceptions, market forces naturally determine the demand and price of goods in a capitalistic system. That is one of the major tenets of capitalism, though leaders have occasionally intervened to set the prices of goods.

77. d. Large parts of inland Australia, often called the Outback, is classified as a desert. That is because the amount of rainfall is very low. Therefore, choice **d** is the best answer.

78. b. The line graph shows a steep drop beginning in late 1929. This represents the approximate time of the Great Crash, the stock market collapse of 1929. The Dow Jones Industrial Average (DJIA) shows the prices of stocks, so this graph is in fact a representation of the DJIA. Immigration to the United States also went down during the period following 1929, but the scale on the *y* axis would be way too low to match total immigration numbers. The land area of the United States did not go down during this period, so choice **c** is not correct. World War I was over by the time the 1920s began, so this graph cannot represent casualties from the war, making choice **d** impossible as well.

79. b. A poll tax charges voters a fee to vote. For poor voters, this can interfere with their ability to cast a ballot. Therefore, the Twenty-fourth Amendment was ratified in part to protect those citizens' right to vote. Choice **b** is correct. Some U.S. leaders may have wanted to continue to disenfranchise voters, choice **d**, but that does not explain why the poll tax was outlawed.

80. b. The United States flag never had 47 states. Arizona and New Mexico were admitted to the union in early 1912 as the country's 47th and 48th states. The flag then displayed 48 stars until 1959, when the admission of Alaska required an additional star. Therefore, choice **b** is correct. The U.S. flag has had exactly 50 stars since July 4, 1960.

81. c. The German invasion of Poland elevated the war, but it did not cause the United States to become engaged in the conflict. Choice **a** is therefore not correct. The assassination of Archduke Ferdinand triggered the start of World War I, not World War II. It was the attack on Pearl Harbor by the Japanese in 1941 that finally forced the United States to become involved, so choice **c** is correct. The United States dropped an atomic bomb on Hiroshima in 1945 in the final stages of the world war.

82. a. Franklin D. Roosevelt established the programs of the New Deal in an effort to help the millions of Americans suffering from the effects of the Great Depression. The economic programs of the New Deal were designed specifically to aid the poor and unemployed, choice **a**.

83. d. A Eurocentric curriculum in a social studies classroom presents information that focuses on European contributions to society. There are many problems with this type of common curriculum. Because it focuses on Europe, the problem is not that it doesn't provide enough information about the British monarchy, choice **a**. Similarly, the problem is not that it overly stresses the leaders of Asia and the Americas, choice **c**; if anything, it's the opposite. Many social studies curricula overly emphasize dates and names, but that is not a result of a Eurocentric curriculum specifically, choice **b**. A Eurocentric curriculum does not fairly represent the contributions from all the cultures of the world, which is why choice **d** is correct.

84. b. Angkor Thom was the last and greatest capital of the Khmer Empire. The ruins of Angkor Thom can be found in modern-day Cambodia, choice **b**.

85. c. Fruits and vegetables can be costly in Japan, but it is not because the country lacks the technology to harvest them, choice **a**. The problem is also not that the seeds don't exist in Japan, choice **b**, because seeds can be easily imported. Japan is a fairly small but populous island nation with a small amount of arable land. Therefore, it must frequently import fruits and vegetables from other places, choice **c**.

86. d. Buzz Aldrin, choice **a**, was the second man to walk on the moon. John Glenn, choice **b** was the first American in space, but he never walked on the moon. Alan Shepherd, choice **c**, walked on the moon as well, but he was not the first American astronaut to do so. Neil Armstrong, choice **d**, was the first person to walk on the moon.

87. b. Czechoslovakia formed in 1918 when it declared independence from the Austro-Hungarian Empire. Therefore, its formation is more closely associated with World War I, and choice **a** is not correct. The Jewish people were granted land following World War II; the land would officially become Israel in 1948. The formation of the Union of Soviet Socialist Republics (USSR) occurred in 1924 as a result of the Russian Revolution seven years earlier. Like Czechoslovakia, the USSR was dissolved in the 1990s. Italy voted to become a republic after the end of World War II, but it had been a country since the mid-1800s.

88. c. While New Zealand, choice **a**, may be the closest country to Australia among the choices, it never housed its criminals in Australia. Remarkably, it was the nation of Great Britain, choice **c**, that sent criminals halfway around the world to be kept in penal colonies in Australia.

89. a. One of the key attributes for students to employ social studies as inquiry is for them to ask questions. While the other techniques may be useful, they will not be as helpful as asking the veteran pertinent questions. Therefore, choice **a** would help students to gain the most from the experience with the Vietnam War veteran.

90. b. During the previous two ice ages, large glaciers pushed rocks and sediments down from Canada and New England. The glaciers advanced as far as the current location of Long Island. When the glaciers retreated, the materials were deposited, forming the 118-mile-long island now named Long Island.

Physical Science Answers

91. a. The primary function of the ribosome is to create protein from amino acids, so choice **a** is correct. The description in choice **b** is the function of the mitochondrion. The description in choice **c** is the function of the cell membrane. The description in choice **d** is the function of the vacuoles.

92. d. Extending below Earth's crust nearly to a depth of 3,000 kilometers, the mantle is the thickest layer of our planet. The crust, choice **a**, by comparison, is less than 100 km thick.

93. c. A normal human cell contains 23 pairs of chromosomes for a total of 46 chromosomes. People with 45 or 47 chromosomes usually have a disorder, and those cells do not reflect a traditional human cell.

94. a. To calculate the momentum of an object, physicists use the simple formula $p = mv$, where p is momentum, m is mass, and v is velocity. Therefore, momentum is the product of mass and velocity, choice **a**.

95. b. Because the moon rotates around Earth at the same rate as the planet's orbit, the same side of the moon always appears from Earth. Therefore, choice **b** best explains the cause for a hidden, dark side of the moon.

96. d. Galileo had concluded that objects should fall at the same rate hundreds of years ago. However, air resistance on Earth can slow some objects down, such as feathers. The astronauts on the moon had a unique opportunity to test Galileo's hypothesis because the moon has no atmosphere. Both the feather and the hammer landed at the same time, proving that choice **d** is correct.

97. d. One of the essential vitamins, vitamin D is manufactured from sunlight, choice **d**. The reason that vitamin D is often added to staples such as milk is to ensure that people get their allotment even if they don't spend enough time outdoors.

98. c. A physical change can change the state of a substance. Ripping paper, choice **a**, an iceberg melting, choice **b**, and boiling a metal, choice **d**, are all examples of a substance changing its form or state. Each of those examples can be undone. An apple rotting, however, represents a chemical change and cannot be undone. Therefore, choice **c** is NOT a physical change.

99. a. The proton and neutron are both contained within the nucleus of an atom. A quark is a sub-nucleonic particle that can make up a proton or neutron. Therefore, quarks are also contained within the nucleus of an atom. Only an electron, choice **a**, is NOT contained inside the atom's nucleus.

100. b. The supercontinent on Earth has the name Pangaea, choice **b**. Panthalassa, choice **d**, refers to the ocean that surrounded the single continent.

101. c. All mammals are warm-blooded, choice **a**, and they all have a backbone, choice **b**. Almost all mammals give birth to live young, with the exception of monotremes, so the statement in choice **c** does not apply to *all* mammals. All mammals have some hair, even if they lose it later in their lives.

102. b. There are six simple machines: the lever, wheel and axle, pulley, inclined plane, wedge, and screw.

103. c. A circumference is determined by multiplying a diameter by pi. Therefore, the moon with the greatest diameter will also have the greatest circumference. Ganymede, choice **c**, is Jupiter's largest moon and has the greatest circumference.

104. a. As the Galilean moon gets closer to Jupiter, it orbits the giant planet in less time. This fact is represented by the statement in choice **b**. There is no relationship between the size of the moon and its distance from the planet; therefore, choices **b** and **d** represent statements that cannot be supported. According to the table, each of the Galilean moons was discovered in 1610. Therefore, the statement in choice **c** cannot be determined, either.

105. a. The Doppler effect is responsible for the change in the pitch of a sound as it approaches and moves away from a source. As the ambulance travels toward a source, the sound waves are compressed—making the pitch higher. As it travels away from a source, the waves are further apart—making the pitch lower.

106. b. A vestigial organ is an organ that no longer serves any purpose or serves a minimal function after the evolution of the species. In the human body, the appendix, choice **b**, fits this description. Human beings may have two kidneys and can survive with only one, but that does not define a vestigial organ. The skin and the gallbladder both serve important functions, so they are not vestigial, either.

107. d. The compound carbon dioxide is comprised of a molecule with one atom of carbon, C, and two atoms of oxygen, O. The word *dioxide* literally means "two atoms of oxygen." Therefore, choice **d** represents this molecule structure.

108. c. Newton's First Law of Motion states that a body will remain in motion unless acted upon by another force, making choice **a** correct. It is Newton's Third Law that relates to every action resulting in an equal and opposite reaction, so choice **b** is not correct. A gravitational force is an example of an external force, but it is too specific for Newton's Law; there are other forces that can affect the motion of an object.

109. c. A thermometer, choice **a**, measures temperature. A hygrometer, choice **b**, measures humidity. An anemometer, choice **d**, measures wind speed. Because a barometer is used to measure air pressure, choice **c** is correct.

110. b. A lunar eclipse occurs when the moon moves into Earth's shadow and seems to disappear. Therefore, it is Earth that is between the moon and the sun in a lunar eclipse, making choice **b** the correct explanation.

111. a. It is true that pigs lack sweat glands, so the behavior of wallowing in mud helps control their body temperature. The mud also serves to protect the skin from sunburn and insect bites. It is not proven that the mud is used to attract a mate, so choice **a** is correct.

112. c. Natural selection describes the process by which a species develops certain traits to help it survive. Mutation, population decline, and diversification describe different processes that can effect an organism or species.

113. b. Waves are examples of kinetic energy, and the examples in choices **a**, **c**, and **d** all use waves. Only the stretched rubber band represents potential energy—because the energy is stored in the tension of the mechanism.

114. a. A decomposer is an organism that breaks down dead organisms or waste from living organisms. Decomposers are especially important in a forest where dead trees and animals need to be broken down for food for other organisms. The shelf fungus, choice **a** is an example of a decomposer. A pine tree, choice **b** is a producer. A grizzly bear, choice **c**, is a consumer. A wood log is not alive and does not perform the role of producer, consumer, or decomposer in a community. Decomposers such as fungi use the log as food, however.

115. d. Einstein connected the relationship between mass and energy with a simple and extraordinary equation: $E = mc^2$. In this equation, E represents energy, m represents mass, and c represents the speed of light. Therefore, choice **d** is correct.

116. d. A butterfly begins its life as an egg, and then it goes through a larval phase. The pupa stage represents its transformation. Finally, it becomes an adult. This sequence is correctly described in choice **d**.

117. b. The prime meridian is a man-made and arbitrary line that connects the two poles; it has no impact on weather, so choice **a** is not correct. The North Atlantic current brings warm waters from the Gulf of Mexico across the Atlantic Ocean toward the United Kingdom; this has a great warming effect on the country, so choice **b** is correct. Contrary to popular opinion, the United Kingdom is not extremely wet, so choice **c** is not correct.

118. d. Cirrus clouds exist in the upper atmosphere and are too wispy to form tornadoes. Contrails are clouds formed by the water vapor emitted by aircraft, and they cannot form tornadoes. Tornadoes most likely form in warm, moist air, so choice **c** is not correct, either. Supercells are storms that are best known for forming tornadoes; about 30% of all supercells result in a tornado, making choice **d** the correct choice.

119. c. The process described in choice **a** reflects meiosis. The process in choice **b** represents external fertilization, which is still a type of sexual reproduction. All asexual reproduction involves a single parent, so choice **c** is the correct choice. The description in choice **d** represents a trait of marsupials, such as kangaroos, and is not representative of asexual reproduction.

120. a. Sedimentary rocks are formed by the deposits of materials that are compacted together with a force such as gravity, choice **a**. The process in choice **b** describes igneous rocks. The process in choice **c** describes metamorphic rocks.

CHAPTER 8

PRACTICE TEST 2

Praxis II: Elementary Education: Content Knowledge Practice Test 2

You have 120 minutes to take the entire 120-question Praxis II: Elementary Education: Content Knowledge practice test. There are four sections of the test: Reading/Language Arts, Mathematics, Social Studies, and Science. You can spend more time on one section than the other. You can go back to any section of the test at any time. Take the diagnostic test with a timer or stopwatch to familiarize yourself with the 120-minute time limit. You may use a scientific or four-function calculator.

Use the answer sheet on the following pages to record your answers to the 120 questions.

Reading/Language Arts

The following passage is the first stanza of Edgar Allan Poe's "The Raven." Read the stanza, then answer questions 1 through 3.

Once upon a midnight dreary, while I
pondered, weak and weary,
Over many a quaint and curious volume of
forgotten lore,
While I nodded, nearly napping, suddenly there
came a tapping,
As of some one gently rapping, rapping at my
chamber door.
"'Tis some visitor," I muttered, "tapping at my
chamber door—
Only this, and nothing more."

1. The first stanza of Edgar Allan Poe's poem, "The Raven," employs several literary techniques, including
- **a.** alliteration, rhyme, and repetition.
- **b.** alliteration, dissonance, and repetition.
- **c.** rhyme, connotation, and dissonance.
- **d.** alliteration, consonance, and resolution.

2. Which rhyme scheme does Poe use for this stanza of his poem, not considering any internal rhyme?
- **a.** ABCABC
- **b.** ABCDDD
- **c.** ABCBAB
- **d.** ABCBBB

3. Which best describes the tone that Edgar Allan Poe sets in the first stanza of "The Raven"?
- **a.** merry
- **b.** melancholy
- **c.** musical
- **d.** quaint

4. Which explanation best describes the value for a student in indentifying the root of a vocabulary word?
- **a.** The root of a vocabulary provides essential context clues for meaning within a text.
- **b.** By identifying the root, a student can recognize other words that share the same ending sound.
- **c.** The root can help a student understand the core meaning of the vocabulary word.
- **d.** The root of a vocabulary word is the key to decoding the word's sound segmentation.

5. A teacher uses a running record to evaluate a student's accuracy rate when reading a book aloud. Which accuracy rate percentage shows that the level of the text is "instructional," which means the student has the ability to read the book with the help of the teacher?
- **a.** 72%
- **b.** 84%
- **c.** 92%
- **d.** 99%

6. Which of the following sentences can be described as interrogative?
- **a.** The color of the truck was darker than the car.
- **b.** Watch out that you don't burn yourself!
- **c.** Even though Jackson had never tried it.
- **d.** Why did the bird fly away from the tree?

Read the following passage, then answer questions 7 through 9.

While Pablo Picasso became perhaps the greatest painter of the twentieth century with his surreal and abstract images, Chuck Close established his greatness with an uncanny ability to recreate the detail of a photograph with paint. An American painter, Close created large-scale portraits that appeared to be as accurate as photographs, even when viewed from a close vantage point. This genre of painting is understandably referred to as photo-realism.

Close suffered a paralyzing event in 1988 that left him wheelchair bound with limited mobility of his hands and arms. Using a brush strapped to his wrist, Close continued to create lifelike portraits using larger strokes within grids, similar to pixilation. Viewed from up close, his modern works may appear haphazard, though the effect of photo-reality can be observed from farther away. Close's paintings since 1988 are different but no less astounding than his earlier works. The paralysis merely challenged him to rethink his artistic process.

7. The author's purpose in writing the first sentence of the passage is to provide the readers with a

a. solution.
b. definition.
c. comparison.
d. contrast.

8. Which type of writing does the passage most likely represent?

a. exposition
b. fiction
c. elegy
d. legend

9. Which best describes the function of the last sentence of the passage?

a. to show that a disability does not have to end an artist's career
b. to provide details that show the difficulties Close faced as an artist in a wheelchair
c. to explain that Close's paralysis shifted the artist's style but not his talent
d. to describe the processes that Close needed to invent to continue his profession

10. During a writing development period in kindergarten, a student creates the following image. The student then orally tells a story about the horse, including characters who interact with it and events that happen with the horse.

Which stage of writing development best describes the student who drew the horse and told the corresponding story?

a. picture writing
b. scribble writing
c. random letter
d. invented spelling

11. A K-W-L chart is an effective tool to aid in a student's comprehension. What does the "W" stand for in the acronym?

a. what I know
b. why it is
c. when it happened
d. want to learn

Read the following poem, then answer questions 12 and 13.

Maid Quiet
by William Butler Yeats
Time drops in decay,
Like a candle burnt out,
And the mountains and woods
Have their day, have their day;
What one in the rout
Of the fire-born moods
Has fallen away?

12. Which type of literary device is used in line 1 of the poem?
a. simile
b. metaphor
c. personification
d. onomatopoeia

13. How does the author use a simile in the poem?
a. to compare time to an extinguished candle
b. to give human characteristics to the mountains and woods
c. to pose a hypothetical question
d. to contrast the light of a candle with the darkness of the woods

14. A student struggles with reading the word "shop." The teacher suggests breaking the word into its distinct phonemes. How many phonemes are in the word "shop"?
a. 1
b. 2
c. 3
d. 4

15. Which of the following must have exactly five lines?
a. haiku
b. sonnet
c. couplet
d. limerick

16. Which of the following sentences does NOT contain a conjunction?
a. Dogs are not allowed in any of the county's public parks.
b. Jackson and Owen scored the same number of points in the game.
c. I have not had a donut since I was 12 years old.
d. We can visit the professor during her office hours on Tuesday or Thursday.

17. Text-to-self connections are especially powerful for improving a student's comprehension of a text because they
a. require students to apply the information in the book to their own personal experiences in their lives.
b. require students to process all the major events and characters of a text that they have read.
c. force students to make their own personal predictions about what they think will happen next in a story.
d. force students to make comparisons from a text to previous texts that they have read.

18. Which of the following is the least effective behavior for improved listening?
a. repeating a speaker's words
b. evaluating the tone and volume of the speaker
c. sitting upright if seated, and remaining focused
d. remaining completely still and quiet

19. The freewriting technique for writing is most closely associated with which stage of the writing process?
a. publishing
b. prewriting
c. revising
d. outlining

20. Eduardo has to make a speech to his classmates about his favorite type of pet. He wants to begin his speech with a thesis statement that tells the listeners what he thinks and feels about the subject. Which of the following sentences best represents a possible thesis statement to begin Eduardo's speech?

a. Many different types of animals can be kept as pets.
b. Which is your favorite animal to keep as a pet?
c. Considering all their great attributes, dogs are the best pets.
d. Cats sharpen their claws on furniture and can ruin a couch.

21. Which of the following is the most advanced developmental stage of writing development?

a. conventional
b. transitional
c. derivational
d. phonetic

22. Metacognition is important for the reading process of students because it

a. requires them to think about what will likely happen next in a story.
b. helps them think about the way that they read and understand the material.
c. is supported with the guidance of a literary instructor.
d. helps them to map out the main idea and supporting details of a passage or text.

Read the following passage, then answer questions 23 through 25.

In 1911, Roald Amundsen became the first person to reach the South Pole. However, the exploration of Antarctica was not yet complete. Sir Ernest Shackleton left England in 1914 with the goal of being the first to cross the entire Antarctic continent by land. During the Antarctic summer of 1914–1915, however, Shackleton's ship *Endurance* was slowly enveloped by increasingly dense pack ice, like a fog closing in on a city. By April 1915, the ship was completely trapped by the ice. As the cold winter months hardened the ice, the pressure on the ship became tremendous. Crunch! The frozen ice squeezed the ship's hull. The hull cracked, and water spilled in to the ship. In October 1915, the crew abandoned the ship and set out to camp on the ice. What followed over the next year was one of the greatest stories of survival and endurance in history.

23. A student reads the passage and is unsure of the meaning of the word "enveloped," Which of the following techniques would be most useful to help him or her understand the word's definition?

a. identifying the individual phonemes that comprise the unknown word
b. retelling the main idea and supporting details of the given passage
c. reading the sentence before and after the word looking for synonyms or antonyms
d. identifying the suffix and considering vocabulary words that share the same suffix

24. Which of the following resources would be most valuable in obtaining a primary account of the event in the story?
a. letters and journals from Shackleton's crew
b. newspaper accounts of the expedition from the 1910s
c. a biography of Sir Ernest Shackleton
d. an atlas showing the geographic details of Australia

25. Which literary device does the author use in line 13 of the passage?
a. metaphor
b. onomatopoeia
c. hyperbole
d. allusion

26. The following diagram represents the plot of a fictional story.

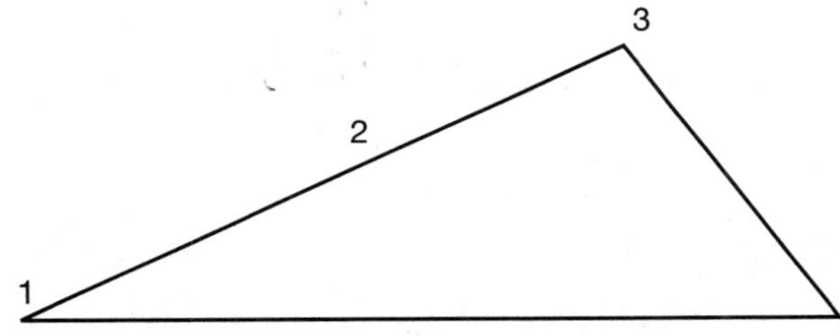

Which part of a story most likely occurs at point 3 on the diagram?

a. resolution
b. complication
c. exposition
d. climax

27. Which type of text is most often told from the first-person point of view?
a. fable
b. short story
c. memoir
d. fantasy

28. What type of error is included in the following sentence?

The squirrel was dodging from place to place grabbing acorns, stuffing them into their cheeks, and rushing back to its home to stash the treasures away.

a. subject-verb agreement
b. noun-pronoun agreement
c. adverb form
d. dangling modifier

29. Read the following sentence.

The large, gray canine and the little, scrawny, white dog bark incessantly.

This is an example of a
a. simple sentence
b. compound sentence
c. complex sentence
d. compound-complex sentence

30. Which action would most improve the following sentence?

The reason that I was late was because I had to stop for three trains, I had a flat tire, and five people called me on my cell phone.

a. removing the words "The reason that" and "was"
b. changing the word "was" to "were"
c. removing the words "was because"
d. changing "that I was" to "for my being"

Mathematics

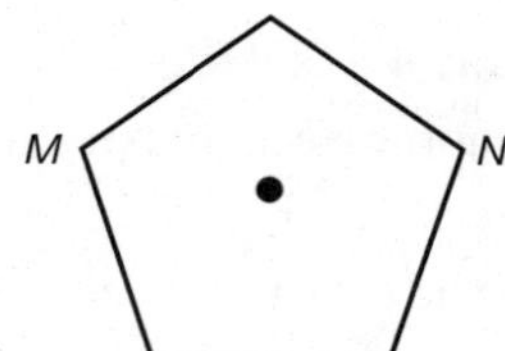

31. The regular pentagon has two points labeled M and N on its corners, as shown. The figure is rotated about its center, shown with the dot inside the pentagon. How many degrees must the figure be rotated clockwise for point M to move to the location occupied by point N?

a. 72°
b. 144°
c. 180°
d. 216°

32. Which of the following is a possible solution for z in the following inequality?

$4z + 8 > 16 - 4$

a. –1
b. 0
c. 1
d. 2

33. Erik bought four items at the grocery store: eggs, juice, bread, and a pineapple. Not including tax, the average (arithmetic mean) of the items was $2.95. He bought a dozen eggs for $2.75, a gallon of juice for $3.80, and a loaf of bread for $2.25. What was the cost of the pineapple, not including tax?

a. $2.85
b. $2.95
c. $3.00
d. $3.10

34. A distance of 3 inches on a topographical map is equivalent to 100 miles. The distance between two mountain peaks on the map is 5 inches. Which is the most accurate length of the distance between the two mountain peaks?

a. 60 miles
b. 102 miles
c. 160 miles
d. 167 miles

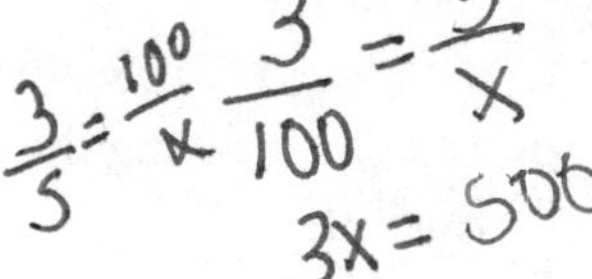

35. If the circumference of a circle is 100π centimeters, the radius of the circle is

a. 10 centimeters.
b. 50 centimeters.
c. 100 centimeters.
d. 50π centimeters.

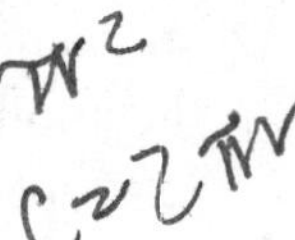

36. What is the product of the two smallest prime numbers greater than 10?

a. 24
b. 132
c. 143
d. 187

37. What is the value of the following expression?

$20 - (15 - 6) \div 3$

a. $-\frac{1}{3}$
b. 3
c. $-\frac{11}{3}$
d. 17

38. Which of the following expressions is the multiplicative inverse of $10y$?

a. $\frac{1}{10y}$
b. $-10y$
c. $-\frac{1}{10y}$
d. $10x$

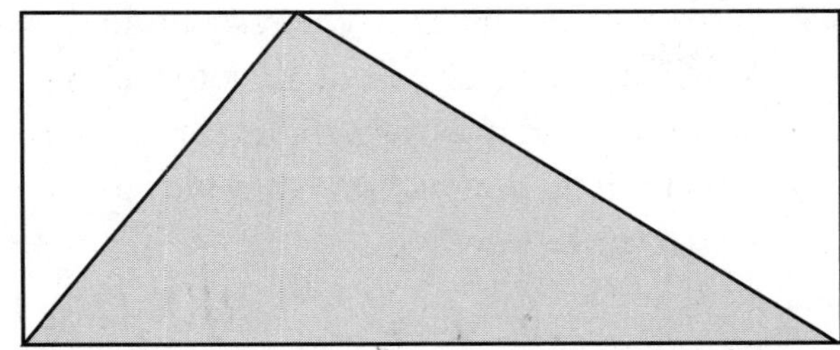

39. What is the area of the shaded triangle?

a. 30 sq. cm
b. 36 sq. cm
c. 60 sq. cm
d. 72 sq. cm

x	f(x)
5	14
7	20
9	26
11	

40. Which number is missing from the function table shown here?

a. 20
b. 28
c. 32
d. 34

41. The cylinders in an engine rotate 2,400 times in a period of 1 minute. Which expression shows the number of rotations of the cylinders in *s* seconds?

a. $\frac{1}{60}2{,}400s$
b. $(60)2{,}400s$
c. $2{,}400 + s$
d. $\frac{2{,}400}{60s}$

42. JoAnne packs a box with hardcover and paperback books. Each paperback book weighs 2 pounds. Each hardcover book weighs 5 pounds. The weight of the box is 18 pounds. There is at least one paperback book and one hardcover book in the box. How many paperback books are in her box?

a. 2
b. 4
c. 8
d. 9

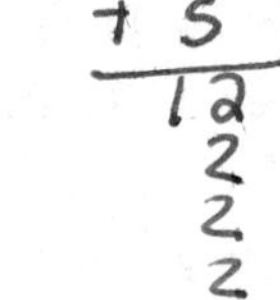

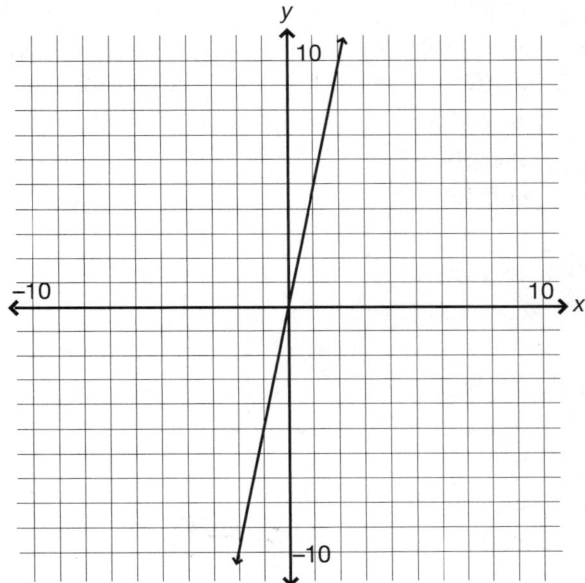

43. Which of the following equations could represent the line on the coordinate graph shown here?

a. $y = 3x$
b. $y = 3$
c. $y = \frac{1}{3}x$
d. $y = -3x$

44. What is the value of 1^5?

a. 0
b. 1
c. 5
d. 6

45. Which of the following values can NOT be expressed as an integer?

a. –5
b. 0
c. 0.5
d. $\frac{5}{1}$

46. There are nine different classes in an elementary school. The school is raising money by having each class sell baked goods and art. The class that makes the most money wins a pizza party. The class that makes the second-most money wins a plaque. The class that makes the third-most money will win a banner. Which expression shows how many possible ways the prizes can be awarded to the different classes in the school?

a. $9 \times 8 \times 7$
b. $9 \times 9 \times 9$
c. 9×3
d. $9 \times 8 \times 7 \times 6 \times 5 \times 4$

47. When the value of r is –5 in the equation shown, what is the value of q?

$$10q + 5 = r$$

a. –45
b. –10
c. –1
d. 0

48. Ms. Posada sold her home for $400,000. However, she had to give her realtor a percentage of the sale price for finding the buyer. If Ms. Posada paid her realtor $14,000, what percentage of the sale price of the home did she give?

a. 0.35%
b. 3.5%
c. 14%
d. 28.57%

49. There are three different colored pens in Ming's drawer. The ratio of black to blue to red pens is 5:2:1, respectively. If there are a total of 40 pens in his drawer, how many blue pens does Ming have?

a. 2
b. 5
c. 10
d. 20

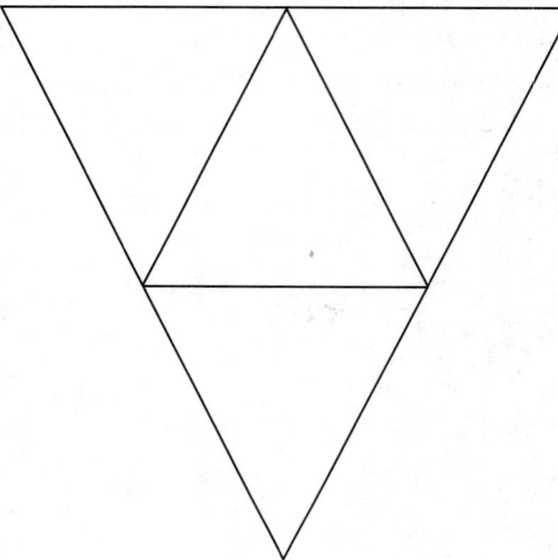

50. Which solid figure can be constructed from the net shown?

a. pentagonal prism
b. triangular prism
c. square pyramid
d. triangular pyramid

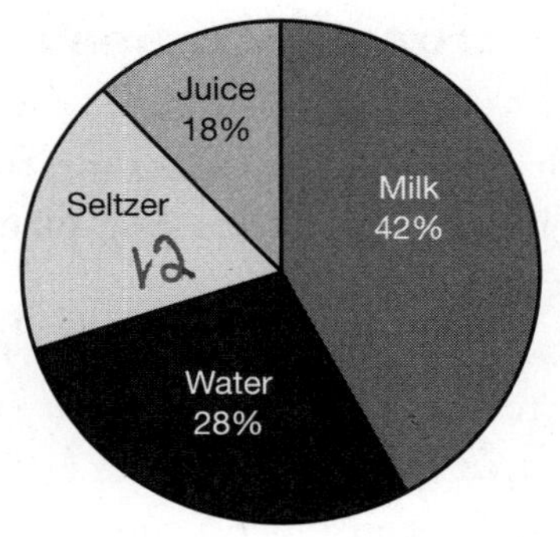

51. This circle graph shows the beverages sold in a school cafeteria during the month of November. If a total of 500 beverages were sold in the cafeteria in November, how many seltzers were sold?

a. 12
b. 50
c. 60
d. 110

52. A lighthouse beam flashes every 6 seconds. Robert's watch is set to beep every 10 seconds. Robert's watch beeps and the lighthouse beam flashes at the exact same time. How much time will elapse before Robert's watch beeps and the lighthouse beam flashes at the same time again?

a. 2 seconds
b. 16 seconds
c. 30 seconds
d. 1 minute

53. Which of the following equations represents the associative property of addition?

a. $3 + (4 + 6) = (3 + 4) + 6$
b. $3 + 7 = 4 + 6$
c. $5(3 + 8) = (5 \times 3) + (5 \times 8)$
d. $6 + (2 + 2) = (6 + 6) + 2$

54. A guitar instructor comes to her customers' homes to give private lessons. She charges her customers according to the following formula, where C is the total cost in dollars, h is the number of hours of the lesson and t is the travel time, in hours, that the instructor spends getting to and from her customer's home.

$$C = 30t + 50h$$

What does the instructor charge for a private lesson that lasts for 1.5 hours if she also spends 30 minutes getting to and from the customer's home?

a. \$70
b. \$80
c. \$90
d. \$975

55. The numbers shown are the first four terms of a number pattern. The pattern is created by finding the sum of the previous two terms. What is the seventh term in the pattern?

1, 2, 3, 5,

a. 8
b. 13
c. 19
d. 21

56. A game player rolls a pair of number cubes that are each numbered from 1 through 6. The player needs the number cubes to land in a way that their sum is equal to 3. What is the probability that this will happen?

a. $\frac{1}{36}$
b. $\frac{1}{18}$
c. $\frac{1}{12}$
d. $\frac{1}{8}$

First: Set the variable z equal to a specific number.
Second: Multiply z by 3.
Third: Add 12 to the product.
Fourth: Divide the sum by 2.

57. To solve an algorithm, Jeremiah must follow the preceding steps. Which algebraic expression is equivalent to the algorithm?

a. $\frac{3z+12}{2}$
b. $\frac{3+12z}{2}$
c. $3z + \frac{12}{2}$
d. $\frac{2}{3z+12}$

58. A whole number is multiplied by an unknown real number. The product is a positive number less than 1. The unknown number must be a(n)

a. integer.
b. negative number greater than –1.
c. decimal value with digits in the tenths and hundredths places.
d. fraction with a denominator greater than its numerator.

59. If $2m + 22 = 6n$, what is the value of m in terms of n?

a. $3n + 11$
b. $6n - 11$
c. $6n + 22$
d. $3n - 11$

60. Which digit is in the tenths place in the following decimal?

174.56

a. 4
b. 5
c. 6
d. 7

Social Studies

61. Which of the following economic measures is NOT indicative of a recession in the economic system?

a. negative GDP growth
b. decrease in capacity utilization
c. reduced unemployment rates
d. decreased consumer spending

62. Which of the following would be the best indication for the number of time zones used within a country?

a. range of longitude degrees within the country
b. distance of the country from the equator
c. range of latitude degrees within the country
d. population density of the country

63. A U.S. senator who served for three full terms spent how many years in the Senate?

a. 3
b. 6
c. 12
d. 18

64. Federalism describes a system of government in which

a. a monarch rules as a figurehead of the state, but a separate parliament utilizes the authority over the land.
b. the government is formed by a voluntary gathering of people who consent to be ruled by a constitutionally limited central body.
c. an emphasis is placed on the decentralization of power with more power given to smaller political units, such as states.
d. the government owns and controls all means of production and does not allow any private interest to generate profits.

65. Which nineteenth-century term is used to describe the American belief that the United States was fated to control the land between the Atlantic and Pacific oceans?
a. Monroe Doctrine
b. Manifest Destiny
c. Magna Carta
d. Bill of Rights

66. Which president was known for using the political slogan "Speak softly and carry a big stick"?
a. Harry S Truman
b. Franklin D. Roosevelt
c. John F. Kennedy
d. Theodore Roosevelt

67. Each year millions of Muslims travel to Mecca for an annual pilgrimage called a Hajj. In which country is Mecca located?
a. Egypt
b. India
c. Iraq
d. Saudi Arabia

68. Which period of human history is defined by the use of agricultural systems and domestic animals?
a. Neolithic period
b. Paleolithic period
c. Copper Age
d. Stone Age

69. What was the historical significance of the discovery of the Rosetta Stone?
a. It helped provide translations for Egyptian hieroglyphics.
b. It provided a series of laws and standardized the penalties for breaking each.
c. It proved that the invention of writing occurred in Mesopotamia.
d. It helped identify the sun as the center of Earth's orbit.

70. Which American innovation does NOT represent an important technological or agricultural advancement in the pre–Civil War era?
a. invention of the cotton gin
b. improvements to the mechanical reaper
c. construction of the first airplane
d. development of the first steamboat

71. A person becomes a justice of the United States Supreme Court by
a. being nominated by the president of the United States and confirmed by the Senate.
b. being elected by a majority of congressional vote.
c. being elected by the popular vote of the court's constituents.
d. being appointed by the Senate Judiciary Committee.

72. Which of the following research tools would most likely provide the most accurate information about a historical event?
a. a peer-reviewed journal
b. a series of diary entries
c. a movie adaptation of the event
d. a work of historical fiction based around the event

73. Which of the lines on the following graph best represents how a demand curve affects price in economics?

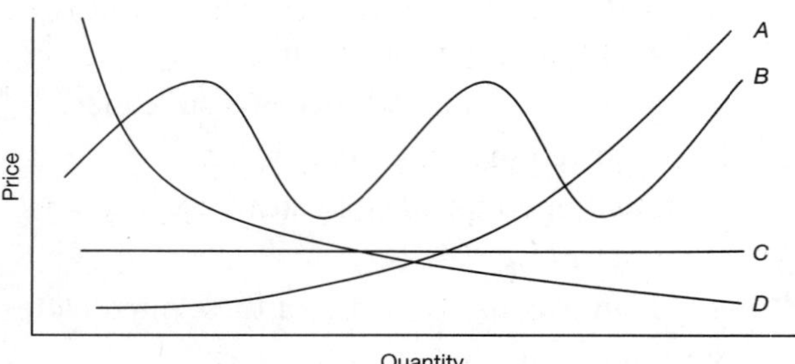

a. line *A*
b. line *B*
c. line *C*
d. line *D*

74. The tallest mountain in the world, based on height from sea level to peak, is part of which mountain range?
a. Himalaya
b. Rockies
c. Andes
d. Alaska

75. Which geographic term best describes the 17,508 islands that comprise the nation of Indonesia?
a. peninsula
b. isthmus
c. shoal
d. archipelago

76. Which Native American is best known for helping act as a guide and translator during Lewis and Clark's successful expedition to the Pacific Ocean, following the completion of the Louisiana Purchase?
a. Sacajawea
b. Geronimo
c. Pocahontas
d. Sitting Bull

77. Which of the following is associated with physical anthropology?
a. the development of the written language
b. the discovery of early stone tools
c. the development of the human body
d. the study of religion, traditions, and beliefs

78. Which of the following was an outcome of the Three-Fifths Compromise?
a. Former slaves were only allowed to own three-fifths as much land as white owners.
b. Three-fifths of the slave population would count toward representation and taxes.
c. The votes of slaves would only count three-fifths as much as the votes of white voters.
d. All income earned by former slaves would be taxed at an elevated rate of three-fifths.

79. Which manmade waterway was built to connect the Mediterranean Sea with the Red Sea, providing a passageway from Europe to Asia without requiring navigation around Africa?
a. Panama Canal
b. Erie Canal
c. Suez Canal
d. Black Sea

80. Which figure was most responsible for the spread of Greek culture between 400 and 300 BCE?
a. Socrates
b. Alexander the Great
c. Euclid of Alexandria
d. Aristotle

81. The famous Russian psychologist Ivan Pavlov performed experiments in behavioral psychology with which animals to develop the concept of conditioned reflex?

a. dogs
b. cats
c. mice
d. horses

82. Which provides the best explanation for the decade of the 1920s in the United States being referred to as the "Roaring Twenties"?

a. It was defined by a rise in popularity of zoos and the introduction of exotic creatures, including lions.
b. Wartime attacks included thunderous raids that affected large segments of urban populations.
c. The Wall Street Crash forced millions out of work and into an economic depression.
d. Economic boom times provided a setting for cultural, technological, and artistic dynamism.

83. A geographic area off the coast of Cape Cod, MA, was chosen to be the location for a renewable energy development because of the area's

a. high-speed and frequent winds.
b. enormous supply of natural gas.
c. near-constant exposure to the sun.
d. massive tidal swings.

84. The spread of the Black Death throughout Europe in the 1300s was most likely initially caused by

a. the introduction of domestic animals to European farming.
b. disease-carrying fleas and rats aboard merchant ships from Asia.
c. the dense urban centers of the European capital cities.
d. a native population that had been unexposed to such deadly bacteria.

85. Who was the civil rights activist who helped to inspire the Montgomery Bus Boycott by refusing to vacate a seat to a white passenger on the bus?

a. Martin Luther King, Jr.
b. Jim Crow
c. Rosa Parks
d. Malcolm X

Study the map, then answer questions 86 and 87.

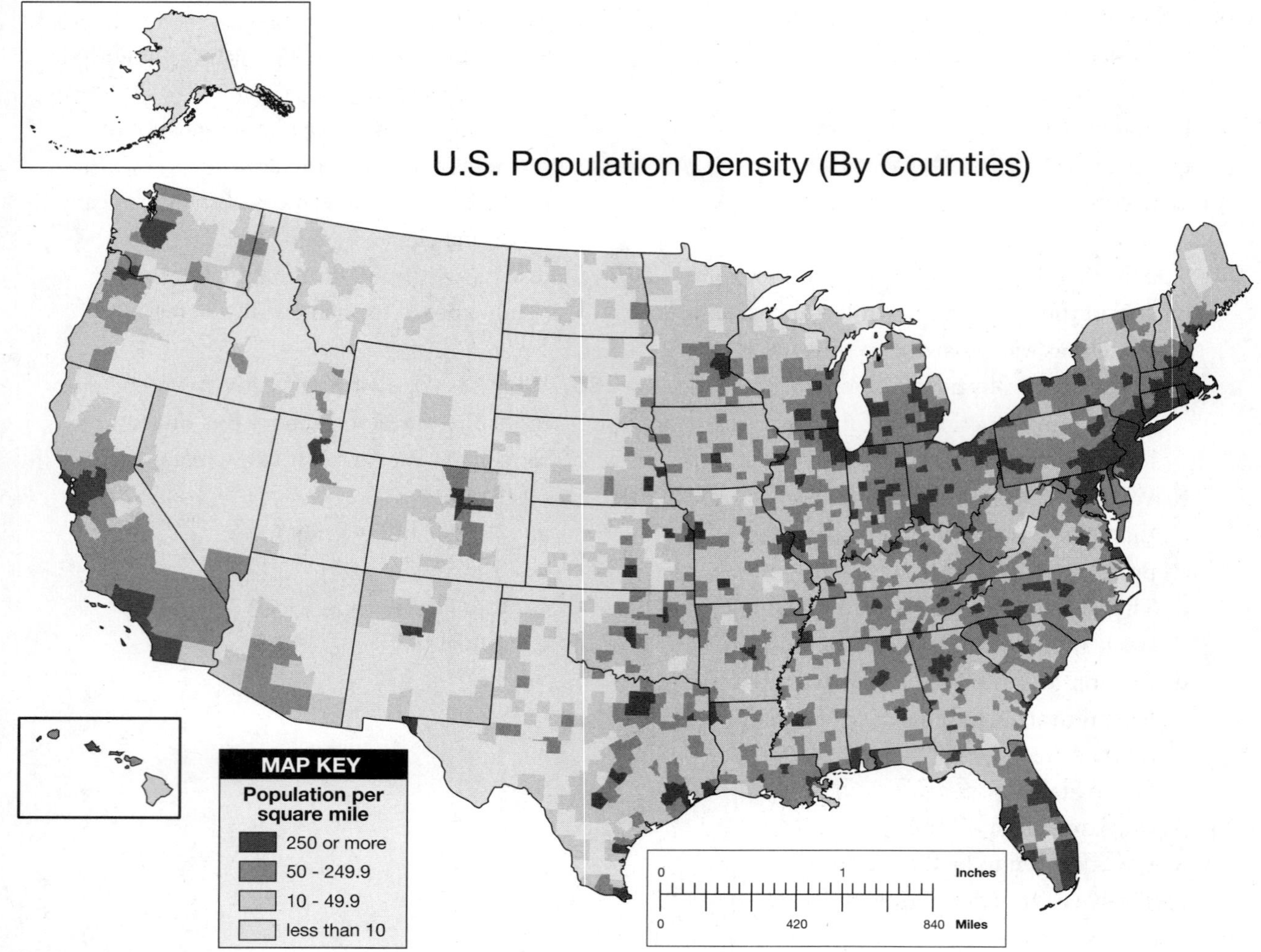

Source: U.S. Census

86. Which state has a population density of at least 250 people per square mile for the greatest percentage of its land?

a. California
b. Alaska
c. New York
d. New Jersey

87. What is the approximate distance between the densely populated El Paso County, in the western corner of Texas, and the densely populated San Diego County, in the southwest corner of California?

a. 300 miles
b. 700 miles
c. 1,200 miles
d. 2,000 miles

88. Which of the following was NOT a reason why Christopher Columbus sailed west from Spain in 1492?

a. Columbus wanted to find a more efficient trade route to India.
b. The Spanish king and queen wanted to enter the profitable spice trade.
c. Columbus wanted to discover a new trading partner with which to exchange European goods.
d. Tensions between Christian Europeans and the Islamic kingdoms of the Middle East made overland travel dangerous.

89. The historic Supreme Court case *Dred Scott v. Sanford* was notable for its impact on civil rights in the United States because it

a. maintained that racial segregation was acceptable as long as separate facilities provided equal amenities.
b. declared that black men and women in the United States could never become U.S. citizens.
c. desegregated public school classrooms for the first time.
d. provided freed slaves the opportunity to become U.S. citizens.

90. Which country's population follows a set of practices known as Shinto?

a. Japan
b. India
c. Israel
d. China

Science

91. A solar eclipse occurs when the moon blocks our view of the sun. Select the diagram that best represents the position of the sun, Earth, and the moon during a solar eclipse (not drawn to scale), as well as the correct orbits.

a.

Moon
Earth
Sun

b.

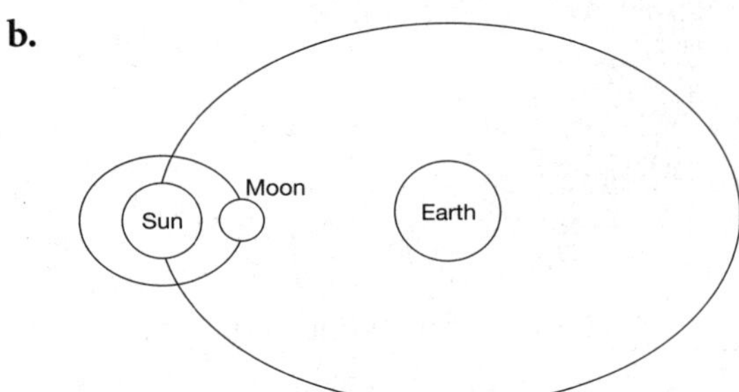

c.

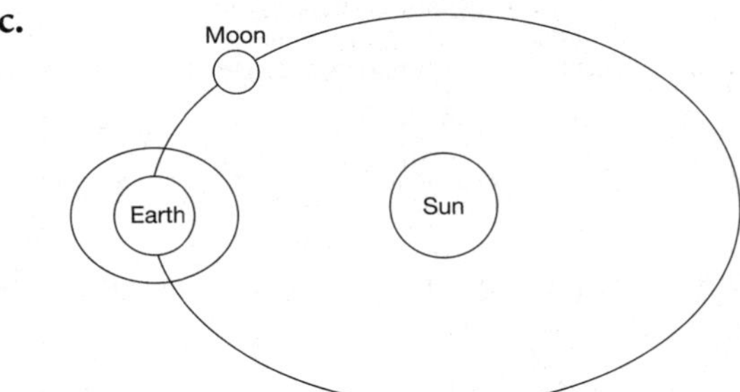

d.

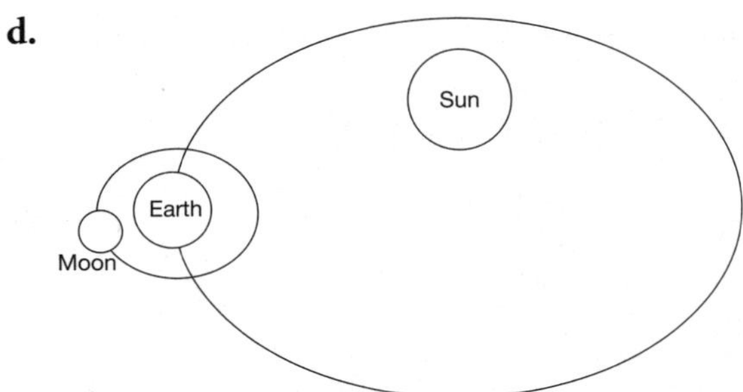

Study the following diagram, then answer questions 92 and 93.

$$6CO_2 + 12H_2O + \text{energy} \rightarrow C_6H_{12}O_6 + 6O_2 + 6H_20$$

92. What reaction is summarized in the box?
- **a.** respiration
- **b.** oxidation
- **c.** fermentation
- **d.** photosynthesis

93. Where does the energy in the first part of the reaction come from?
- **a.** heat
- **b.** water
- **c.** light
- **d.** oxygen

94. Which of the following is the correct order of the layers of Earth's interior, starting with Earth's surface?
- **a.** crust, lithosphere, mantle, inner core, outer core
- **b.** crust, lithosphere, mantle, outer core, inner core
- **c.** inner core, outer core, mantle, lithosphere, crust
- **d.** mantle, outer core, inner core, lithosphere, crust

95. The following diagram shows the anatomy of a flower.

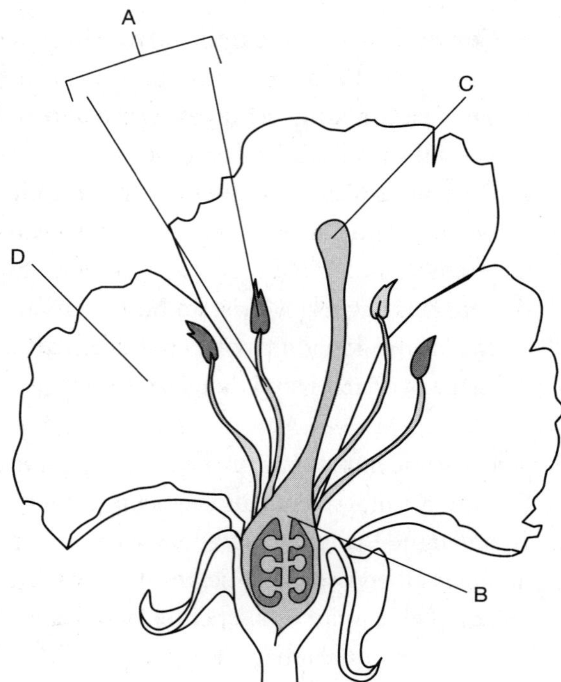

Which part of the flower represents the stamen?
- **a.** A
- **b.** B
- **c.** C
- **d.** D

96. What is the primary function of the nucleus of a cell?
- **a.** act as a protective wall
- **b.** pack proteins for export to other cells
- **c.** digest organic material
- **d.** house the DNA of the cell

97. Which gas is most prevalent in Earth's atmosphere?
- **a.** oxygen
- **b.** nitrogen
- **c.** carbon dioxide
- **d.** water vapor

98. Which of the following scientific advancements had the greatest effect on the eradication of smallpox?
  a. the increasingly popular use of antibacterial gels and liquids
  b. the forced isolation of patients infected with the disease
  c. the advent and mass production of a smallpox vaccine
  d. the destruction of the smallpox environment through radiation

99. Which is the best explanation for why a ripe banana appears yellow when viewed in sunlight?
  a. The banana absorbs the yellow light and reflects all other frequencies of visible light.
  b. The sunlight provides only a yellow range of visible light, which is then reflected by the banana.
  c. The air in between the banana and the viewer scatters all wavelengths of visible light except yellow.
  d. The banana reflects the yellow light and absorbs all other frequencies of visible light.

100. At which of the following temperatures is there the least amount of kinetic energy in a molecule?
  a. 0°C
  b. 0°K
  c. 0°F
  d. 100°C

101. A boulder falls from a mountain, creating vibrations when it hits the ground in a valley. The vibrations travel through the air in waves and are reflected on the other side of the valley. This reflection can be described as
  a. convection.
  b. an echo.
  c. conduction.
  d. a current.

102. What type of information can a fossil record provide about conditions on Earth millions of years ago?
  a. whether two ancient species existed at the same point in time
  b. whether ancient hominids mapped constellations
  c. the distance between Earth and Venus
  d. the percentage of herbivorous dinosaurs that laid infertile eggs

103. Several children are participating in a go-cart race. The racers line up at point A in the following diagram and continue toward point D, the finish line in the race.

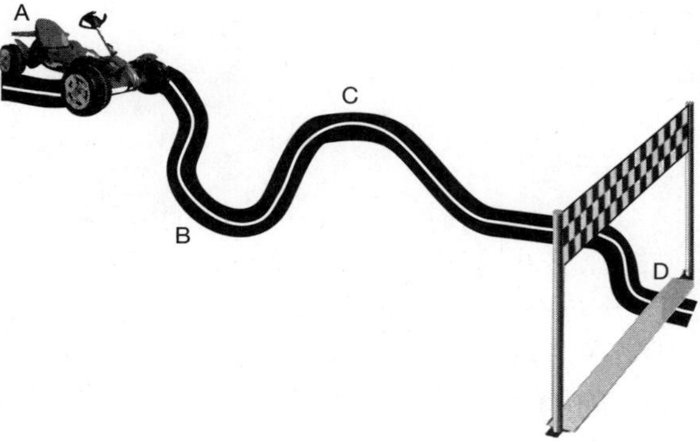

At which point in the race will a go-cart racer have the greatest amount of potential energy?
  a. point A
  b. point B
  c. point C
  d. point D

104. Which of the following produce(s) energy through the process of photosynthesis?

a. I only
b. II only
c. II and III only
d. I, II, and III

105. What aspect of the following diagram of Earth and the moon is MOST inaccurate?

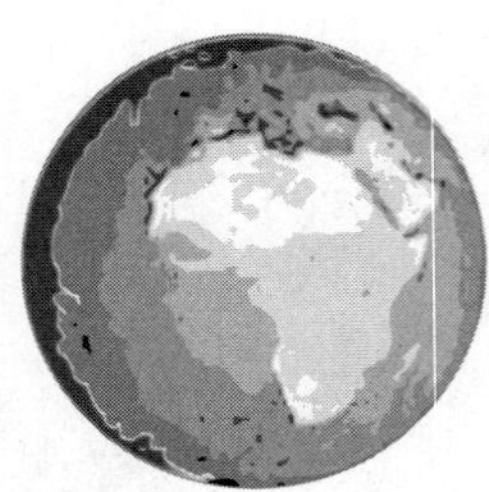

a. the proportion of the diameter of the moon to the diameter of Earth
b. the relationship between the shapes of Earth and its moon
c. the distance of the moon from Earth relative to its diameter
d. the proportion of the circumference of the moon at its equator to the circumference of Earth at its equator

106. Which of the following terms can NOT be used to describe a plant?
a. autotroph
b. producer
c. photosynthetic organism
d. herbivore

107. Which of the following is NOT an example of a simple machine?
a. wedge
b. calculator
c. pulley
d. wheel and axle

108. Visible light is comprised of all of the colors of the rainbow. An instrument that separates the various colors that comprise visible light is called
a. a prism.
b. a microscope.
c. a telescope.
d. a Geiger counter.

109. Which attribute of a star best defines how great its gravitational force will be?
a. mass
b. radius
c. brightness
d. diameter

110. Which of the following *must* be true about an organism that reproduces asexually?
a. It is a single-celled organism.
b. It reproduces with the use of a single parent.
c. It combines genetic information from another organism to reproduce.
d. It does not have the physical capability to reproduce.

111. During which time in Earth's history did the first life forms appear on the planet?
a. Phanerozoic Eon
b. Cambrian Era
c. Archeozoic Eon
d. Mesozoic Era

112. Four groups of mice consume different amounts of artificial sweetener in their food. The control group is the one that receives
- **a.** 10 mg/day of sweetener.
- **b.** 50 mg/day of sweetener.
- **c.** no sweetener.
- **d.** milk instead of water.

113. Which of the following does NOT represent a physical change?
- **a.** A sugar tablet is dissolved in a cup of water.
- **b.** A glass is shattered into hundreds of pieces.
- **c.** The temperature of oxygen is lowered to form a liquid fuel.
- **d.** Vinegar is mixed with baking soda, creating bubbles.

Study the following diagram, then answer questions 114 and 115.

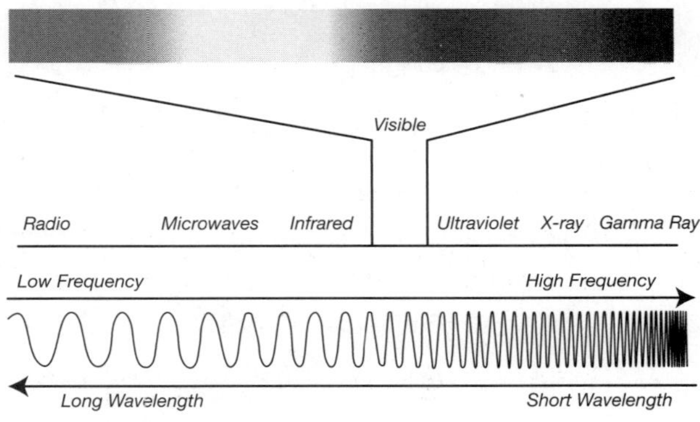

114. The wavelength of a microwave is approximately 1 centimeter. Which of the following lengths could represent the wavelength of a radio wave?
- **a.** 0.1 millimeter
- **b.** 0.5 centimeter
- **c.** 1 centimeter
- **d.** 1 mile

115. The frequency of an X-ray is approximately 10^{18} Hz. Which of the following could be the frequency of a gamma ray?
- **a.** 10^{20} Hz
- **b.** 10^{18} Hz
- **c.** 10^{16} Hz
- **d.** 10^{4} Hz

116. Which of the following is NOT caused by the movement of tectonic plates?
- **a.** earthquakes
- **b.** monsoons
- **c.** tsunamis
- **d.** volcanoes

117. The following isobar weather map shows bands of atmospheric pressure centered over Michigan.

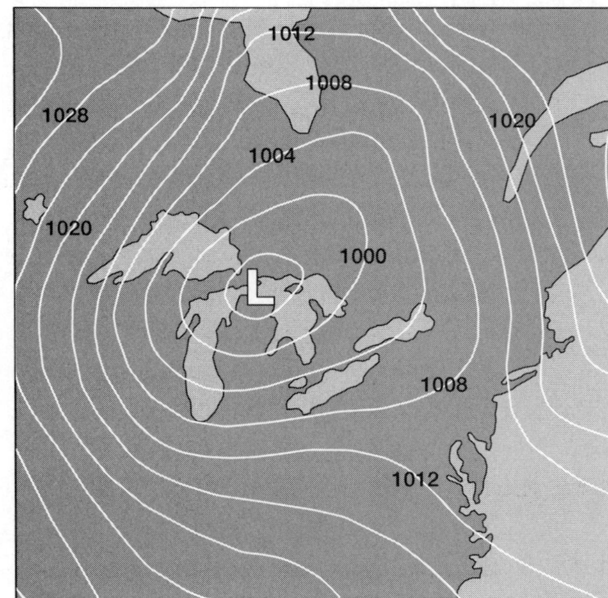

Which of the following words describes the most likely weather condition in Michigan during this time?
- **a.** cold
- **b.** cloudy
- **c.** hail
- **d.** calm

118. Which provides the best explanation why the stars in the sky appear to rise in the east and set in the west?
- **a.** Earth spins on its axis from west to east.
- **b.** The Milky Way rotates in a spiral formation.
- **c.** Earth spins on its axis from east to west.
- **d.** Earth faces different directions as it orbits the sun.

119. The primary difference between a meteoroid and a meteorite is that only a meteorite
- **a.** contains life-forms.
- **b.** orbits the Sun.
- **c.** touches Earth's surface.
- **d.** contains frozen water.

120. Which organ is most associated with its role in the excretory system of a human being?
- **a.** stomach
- **b.** heart
- **c.** esophagus
- **d.** kidney

READING/LANGUAGE ARTS KEY

ITEM	KEY	SUBSECTION	ITEM	KEY	SUBSECTION
1	A	Foundations of Reading	16	A	Language in Writing
2	D	Foundations of Reading	17	A	Language in Writing
3	B	Foundations of Reading	18	D	Communication Skills
4	C	Foundations of Reading	19	B	Communication Skills
5	C	Foundations of Reading	20	C	Foundations of Reading
6	D	Language in Writing	21	A	Communication Skills
7	D	Language in Writing	22	B	Foundations of Reading
8	A	Language in Writing	23	C	Foundations of Reading
9	C	Language in Writing	24	A	Foundations of Reading
10	B	Communication Skills	25	B	Foundations of Reading
11	D	Communication Skills	26	D	Foundations of Reading
12	C	Language in Writing	27	C	Foundations of Reading
13	A	Language in Writing	28	B	Language in Writing
14	C	Foundations of Reading	29	A	Language in Writing
15	D	Foundations of Reading	30	A	Foundations of Reading

MATHEMATICS KEY

ITEM	KEY	SUBSECTION	ITEM	KEY	SUBSECTION
31	B	Geometry & Measurement	46	A	Data Org. & Interpretation
32	D	Algebraic Concepts	47	C	Algebraic Concepts
33	C	Data Org. & Interpretation	48	B	Number Sense & Numeration
34	D	Geometry & Measurement	49	C	Number Sense & Numeration
35	B	Geometry & Measurement	50	D	Geometry & Measurement
36	C	Number Sense & Numeration	51	C	Data Org. & Interpretation
37	D	Number Sense & Numeration	52	C	Number Sense & Numeration
38	A	Algebraic Concepts	53	A	Algebraic Concepts
39	A	Geometry & Measurement	54	C	Algebraic Concepts
40	C	Number Sense & Numeration	55	D	Number Sense & Numeration
41	A	Algebraic Concepts	56	B	Data Org. & Interpretation
42	B	Number Sense & Numeration	57	A	Algebraic Concepts
43	A	Geometry & Measurement	58	D	Number Sense & Numeration
44	B	Number Sense & Numeration	59	D	Algebraic Concepts
45	C	Number Sense & Numeration	60	B	Number Sense & Numeration

SOCIAL STUDIES KEY

ITEM	KEY	SUBSECTION	ITEM	KEY	SUBSECTION
61	C	Economics	70	C	United States History
62	A	Geography, Anthrop., Sociology	71	A	Gov't, Citizenship & Democracy
63	D	Gov't, Citizenship & Democracy	72	B	Inquiry/Processes
64	B	Gov't, Citizenship & Democracy	73	D	Economics
65	B	United States History	74	A	Geography, Anthrop., Sociology
66	D	United States History	75	D	Geography, Anthrop., Sociology
67	D	Geography, Anthrop., Sociology	76	A	United States History
68	A	World History	77	C	Geography, Anthrop., Sociology
69	A	World History	78	B	United States History

SOCIAL STUDIES KEY *(continued)*					
ITEM	KEY	SUBSECTION	ITEM	KEY	SUBSECTION
79	C	Geography, Anthrop., Sociology	85	C	United States History
80	B	World History	86	D	Geography, Anthrop., Sociology
81	A	Inquiry/Processes	87	B	Geography, Anthrop., Sociology
82	D	United States History	88	C	United States History
83	A	Geography, Anthrop., Sociology	89	B	United States History
84	B	Geography, Anthrop., Sociology	90	A	World History

SCIENCE KEY					
ITEM	KEY	SUBSECTION	ITEM	KEY	SUBSECTION
91	A	Earth Science	106	D	Life Science
92	D	Life Science	107	B	Physical Science
93	C	Life Science	108	A	Science as Inquiry/Processes
94	B	Earth Science	109	A	Physical Science
95	A	Life Science	110	B	Life Science
96	D	Life Science	111	C	Earth Science
97	B	Earth Science	112	C	Science as Inquiry/Processes
98	C	Personal/Social Perspectives	113	D	Physical Science
99	D	Physical Science	114	D	Physical Science
100	B	Physical Science	115	A	Physical Science
101	B	Physical Science	116	B	Earth Science
102	A	Earth Science	117	B	Life Science
103	A	Physical Science	118	A	Earth Science
104	C	Life Science	119	C	Earth Science
105	C	Earth Science	120	D	Life Science

Reading/Language Arts Answers

1. **a.** Alliteration is the repetition of initial sound of a word. "While I nodded, nearly napping" is a perfect example of alliteration. Rhyme is the likeness of sounds existing between two or more words. This poem uses rhymed at the ends of the lines, such as "lore" and "door." However, the poem also contains internal rhythm with words within the same line, such as "dreary" and "weary" in the first line. Repetition is repeating the same word or phrase, such as "chamber door" in lines 5 and 6. Choice **b** is incorrect because dissonance indicates there are disagreeing sounds within the passage. Choice **c** is incorrect because connotation is the emotions and thoughts that a phrase or word can cause. Choice **d** is incorrect because the stanza does not have resolution. Nothing is resolved. The only answer choice in which the literary techniques are included in the first stanza is **a**.
2. **d.** The ends of the first three lines of the stanza do not share the same ending sounds, so they do not rhyme. Therefore, the lines can be assigned the different letters A, B, and C. The fourth, fifth, and sixth lines all rhyme with the second line, B. The correct rhyme scheme for this stanza, therefore, is ABCBBB, choice **d**. If you chose **b**, you may not have recognized that the last three lines of the stanza rhyme with the second line of the poem.
3. **b.** The tone of a poem is constructed through descriptive words that provide an overall atmosphere. Although "The Raven" has many stanzas, Edgar Allen Poe begins to set the tone even in the first stanza. Words like "weary" and "dreary" provide a dark and tired tone. The act of an unexpected stranger knocking at the door adds to the mystery. There is nothing to indicate a merry tone, choice **a**. A better description of the tone would be melancholy, choice **b**. While the reading of the poem itself may be musical, choice **c**, the tone refers to the feeling of the poem. There is nothing musical occurring in the story during the first stanza. While the word quaint, choice **d**, is used in the first stanza, it refers to a book that the narrator is reading. It is not the best description of the tone of the poem thus far.
4. **c.** The root of a word is the main part of a word that gives it the meaning. Therefore, choice **c** provides the best explanation for the value of identifying the root of a vocabulary word. Context clues, choice **a**, are found in the sentence that contains the vocabulary word, as well as in the sentences immediately preceding and following the word. The context does not come from the middle of the word. Words with the same ending sounds, choice **b**, are called rhyming words. The root of a word may be unrelated to the ending of a word if the word contains a prefix, so **b** is not the best choice. Sound segmentation, choice **d**, requires a student to separate the sounds in a word by speaking each of the sounds separately in the order they appear in the word. While the root of the word is important, all the phonemes of a word are important in sound segmentation—including phonemes from a prefix or suffix.

5. c. If a student's accuracy rate is between 95% and 100%, the student can read the text on his or her own and the text is called independent. If the accuracy rate is between 90% and 95%, the student can read with help, and the text is called instructional. If the accuracy rate is below 90%, the student can't read the book yet, and the text is called frustrational. Of the given percentages in the answer choices, only 92%, choice **c**, represents an instructional text in which the student has the ability to read the book with the help of the teacher.

6. d. An interrogative sentence asks a question. The only sentence in the answer choices that asks a question is in choice **d**. You can tell because it ends with a question mark. The sentence in choice **a** makes a declaration and ends in a period, which means it is a declarative sentence. The sentence in choice **b** ends with an exclamation point, which means that it is an imperative sentence. Answer choice **c** presents a dependent clause and is therefore not even a complete sentence.

7. d. The first sentence of the passage contrasts the opposing styles of the two famous twentieth-century painters. It does not provide a solution, choice **a**, or a definition, choice **b**, because there is nothing to solve yet and no definition is provided. A comparison, choice **c**, compares similarities between two things. Because Picasso and Close's differences are being contrasted, choice **d** is correct.

8. a. A work of fiction, choice **b**, uses made-up information, whereas this passage is fact-based. Similarly, a legend, choice **d**, is a story that is most likely a fictional tale. One may consider Chuck Close to be a legend in the world of art; the passage itself would not be referred to as a legend, so choice **d** is not correct. An elegy, choice **c**, is a poem that laments the loss of someone or something. Because Chuck Close is alive as of 2010 and the passage does not appear to be lamenting his loss, choice **c** is not correct. The passage is an example of an exposition, choice **a**; its purpose is to provide readers with background information.

9. c. It is true that a disability does not have to end an artist's career, choice **a**, but that is not the function of the last sentence of the passage. The last sentence does more than simply say that Close continued painting; its point is that the disability forced him to change his artistic process. This is best summed by the explanation provided in choice **c** because there was a shift in style, but not in talent. The sentence does not provide any specific details about Close's difficulties, choice **b**, or of the Close's invented process to continue painting, choice **d**.

10. b. Although the student created a picture as part of this early writing process, the images created during the picture writing stage, choice **a**, are generally less recognizable than during the second stage, the scribble writing stage, choice **b**. In addition, accompanying verbal stories are associated with the scribble writing stage of writing development, so **b** is the correct choice. During the random letter stage, choice **c**, students begin to string letters together with their pictures. During the invented spelling stage, choice **d**, students begin to use letters to match sounds. Because the image shows no attempt to create letters—let alone match them to sounds—choices **c** and **d** cannot be correct.

11. d. The useful K-W-L chart stands for **K**now, **W**ant to Learn, **L**earned. Before reading a text, students fill out the K column of the table to show what they know already about the topic. Then they fill out the W column, representing what they want to learn. When the reading is complete, students work to fill out the L column to show what they learned.

12. c. Personification gives human characteristics to an animal or an inanimate object. While "time" is not an animal or an object you can touch with your hand, it can still be given human-like attributes. Saying that time "drops in decay" gives it an animated description that it is not generally associated with. It is not a simile or a metaphor, choice **a** or **b**, because there is no comparison being made in the first line of the poem. Onomatopoeia is a word that sounds like its meaning; since no example of onomatopoeia is given in line 1 of the poem, choice **d** cannot be correct.

13. a. The first two lines of the poem say that time drops "like a candle burnt out." A simile is a comparison using the words "like" or "as." The author, William Butler Years, is therefore using the simile to compare time to the candle. Giving human characteristics to inanimate objects, **b**, would be an example of personification rather than a simile. A simile is not used to pose a question, choice **c**, or contrast the candle with the woods, choice **d**.

14. c. A phoneme is the smallest segment of sound in a language. The word "shop" has three distinct basic sounds: the digraph /sh/ sound, the /o/ sound, and then the /p/ sound. The word has one syllable, choice **a**, with four letters, choice **d**, but includes only distinct phonemes, choice **c**.

15. d. A haiku must have exactly three lines, so choice **a** is not correct. A sonnet must have exactly 14 lines, so choice **b** is not correct. A couplet is a pair of rhyming lines, so choice **c** is not correct. A limerick is a type of poem with exactly five lines.

16. a. A conjunction is a part of a sentence that joins two words or phrases. Common conjunctions include "and," "but," and "or." Other conjunctions include "because," "since," and "so." The sentences in answer choices **b**, **c**, and **d** all contain conjunctions. Because choice **a** does not contain a conjunction, it is the correct choice.

17. a. A text-to-self connection helps a student to consider how the book relates to events that have encountered in his or her life. These personal experiences match the description given in choice **a**. Choice **b** more closely matches a comprehension strategy called retelling. Choice **c** is also a comprehension strategy, but it requires a student to make inferences, not make text-to-self connections. Choice **d** represents a text-to-text connection.

18. d. There are many behaviors that can aid in the listening process. Repeating the speaker's words, choice **a**, can help reinforce the meaning of the speech. The tone and volume of the speaker, choice **b**, are important attributes of a speech that should be considered for improved listening. Sitting upright and remaining focused, choice **c**, is certainly an effective behavior for improved listening. Remaining completely still and quiet is not, however, a recommended behavior for improved listening. A listener should feel free to move, such as by nodding in agreement; staying quiet is important, but a listener should also be willing to ask questions to improve understanding or to agree or disagree with the speaker

19. b. The purpose of freewriting is to help students develop ideas for writing. During freewriting, students should not yet be concerned with writing, revising, or publishing their work. This technique should therefore be employed during the prewriting stage, choice **b**.

20. c. A thesis statement, whether in writing or speech, should inform the reader or listener what the speaker or writer thinks about the subject. It should be active and clear—and it needs to lay out exactly what the rest of the essay or speech will be about. Choice **a** could lead to the thesis statement, but by itself the sentence does not say anything about Eduardo's purpose or beliefs. Choice **b** is a question that might be asked; a thesis should be a declarative statement. Choice **c** clearly states that dogs are the best pets, so it is the best option for Eduardo's thesis. Choice **d** provides a reason why cats may not be the best pets. This could be support for a thesis statement, but by itself the sentence does not declare the purpose behind Eduardo's speech.

21. a. The stages of writing development progress from picture writing/drawing to scribble writing to random letter, then invented spelling, phonetic, transitional, and finally the conventional stage. The most advanced stage of the development is therefore the conventional stage, choice **a**.

22. b. Metacognition is, literally, thinking about thinking. Metacognition is important in reading comprehension because students need think actively about their own reading process. Understanding how the reading process works is important for students to improve their comprehension abilities. Metacognition is not about making predictions, choice **a**. It does not require the guidance of a literary instructor, choice **c**. A graphic organizer is a tool for mapping out the main idea and supporting details of a passage of text, so choice **d** is not correct.

23. c. There are several strategies that students can employ to determine the meaning of an unknown word. Identifying the individual phonemes of the word, choice **a**, would not be the most useful strategy, however. A phoneme is the smallest individual unit of sound. Because phonemes by themselves have no meaning, identifying them may not be the best technique to decipher meaning of a larger word. Retelling the main idea and supporting details, choice **b**, is a good strategy to aid in comprehension, but it does not support vocabulary enhancement. Reading the sentence before and after the unknown word, choice **c**, can provide clues for meaning, especially when looking for synonyms and antonyms. There are several clues that can aid a student unsure of the word "enveloped"; it's similar to a fog "closing in" on a city, and eventually the fog made the ship "completely trapped." The suffix *-ed* can be used to show that the unknown word is in the past tense, but otherwise it does not by itself help identify the word's meaning. The best technique in this example is to read the sentence before and after the word looking for synonyms and antonyms, choice **c**.

24. a. Primary sources are materials that are generated from direct witnesses of an event. Although each of the resources listed in the answer choices would provide more information on Shackleton's expedition, only letters and journals from his crew would provide a primary account of the event.

25. b. A metaphor makes a comparison between two things without using the words "like" or "as." There is no comparison being made in this line, so choice **a** is not correct. Onomatopoeia is a word that sounds like its meaning. Because the word "crunch" sounds like its meaning, it is an example of onomatopoeia, choice **b** is correct. A hyperbole is an extreme exaggeration. There is no instance of a hyperbole in this passage, so choice **c** is not correct. An allusion, choice **d**, is a reference to another person or text, and there is no reference in the given line.

26. d. Exposition, choice **c**, introduces readers to the people, places, and basic circumstances or situation of the story; this is represented by point 1 on the diagram. Complication, choice **b**, represented by point 2, is the series of events that build up to the climax. The climax itself is the highpoint and turning point of the story, and so it is represented by point 3 on the diagram, choice **d**. The resolution, choice **a**, is the conclusion of the story and is therefore represented by point 4.

27. c. A first-person point of view means that the narrator is telling a story from his or her own point of view using I. This is a very personal point of view. Both fiction and nonfiction texts can be written in the first-person. When nonfiction books are written in the first-person, it means that the author is also the narrator. This can be represented in the form of an autobiography or a memoir, so choice **c** is the best choice. Fables, short stories, and fantasies may or may not include a first-person point of view, but a memoir is almost assured to be writing from that perspective.

28. b. The subject in this sentence is "the squirrel," which is a singular subject. The corresponding verbs are all in alignment with the subject, so choice **a** is not correct. The acorns are being stuffed into the squirrel's cheeks. Because the squirrel is singular, the corresponding pronoun should also be singular; "their cheeks" refers to multiple squirrels, so there is an error in noun-pronoun agreement, choice **b**. There is no adverb in the given sentence, so there cannot be an error in the adverb form of a word, choice **c**. A dangling modifier is a word or phrase that modifies a word or phrase in a sentence. An error can occur if the modifier is left without a word to modify, but there is no dangling modifier in the given sentence.

29. a. Although the sentence may seem to have a lot of words, many are simply adjective and adverbs that do not affect the type of sentence. A simple sentence, choice **a**, has one independent clause and no dependent clauses. A compound sentence, choice **b**, would require at least two independent clauses. A complex sentence, choice **c**, has one independent clause and at least one dependent clause. A compound-complex sentence, choice **d**, combines multiple independent clauses in the sentence, as well as at least one dependent clause. The given sentence has one independent clause and no dependent clauses, so choice **a** is correct.

30. a. Removing the words "The reason that" from the original sentence results in a shorter, simpler sentence that still has the same meaning as the original. An answer choice that eliminates wordiness will frequently be correct. Choice **b** incorrectly changes the verb tense. Choice **c** deletes the verb and leaves the sentence incomplete. The revision suggested in choice **d** would result in another wordy sentence.

Mathematics Answers

31. b. A figure can be rotated 360° for it to return to its original orientation. The regular pentagon has five equal sides and angles. Therefore, each time the pentagon rotates (360° ÷ 5), the location of one corner will move to the other corner. That's a rotation of 72°. Two clockwise rotations of 72° will move point M to the location occupied by point N. The correct answer is therefore 144°, choice **b**. Choice **d** would represent the counterclockwise rotation to move point M to the location occupied by point N.

32. d. To solve this problem, you can either solve the inequality algebraically and solve for z or plug in the values in the answer choices to see which one provides a correct solution. To solve it algebraically, you need to isolate z on one side of the inequality. The steps are shown as follows:

$4z + 8 > 16 - 4$

$4z + 8 - 8 > 16 - 4 - 8$

$4z > 4$

$z > 1$

If z must be greater than 1, the only choice that could correctly solve for the inequality is 2, choice **d**. If you plugged in the different values from the answer choices into the original inequality, only 2 would provide a solution.

33. c. The four items that Erik bought had an arithmetic mean (average) of \$2.95, which means that he spent a total of \$2.95 × 4, or \$11.80, at the grocery store, not including tax. The cost of the eggs, juice, and bread cost a total of \$2.75 + \$3.80 + \$2.25, or \$8.80. The difference between \$11.80 and \$8.80 is the amount he spent on the pineapple, not including tax. The difference is \$3.00, choice **c**.

34. d. The easiest way to solve this scale problem is to set up a proportion. To correctly set up the proportion, you need to compare the known relationship of 3 inches : 100 miles to 5 inches : x miles.

$$\frac{3 \text{ inches}}{100 \text{ miles}} = \frac{5 \text{ inches}}{x \text{ miles}}$$

Once the proportion is set up, you can cross multiply to get 3 inches × x miles = 5 inches × 100 miles. This is equivalent to $3x = 500$. Dividing both sides of the equation then by 3 provides the answer $x = 166.6$. The most accurate length in the answer choices is 167 miles, choice **d**.

35. b. The formula for the circumference of a circle is $C = 2r\pi$ or $d\pi$. Therefore, to find the radius of a circle from its circumference, you can divide the circumference by 2π. Because 100π centimeters $\div 2\pi =$ 50 centimeters, choice **b** is correct. If the area of the circle were 100π square centimeters, then its radius would be 10 centimeters, choice **a**. The diameter of the circle would be 100 centimeters, choice **c**. If you selected choice **d**, you forgot to divide by pi to determine the radius.

36. c. Prime numbers are whole numbers that are only evenly divisible by itself and 1. The two smallest prime numbers greater than 10 are 11 and 13. Their product is 143, choice **c**. If you chose choice **a**, you may have confused the terms sum and product. To find the sum of two numbers, you add them together; to find their product, you must multiply them. If you chose choice **b**, you may have considered 12 to be a prime number; however, 12 is evenly divisible by 2, 3, 4, and 6, so it is not prime. If you chose choice **d**, you may not have realized that 13 is a prime number and multiplied 11 by 17—two prime number greater than 10 but not the smallest prime numbers greater than 10.

37. d. When solving an expression with several operations, you need to follow the order of operations. Any operation within parentheses should be solved first, followed by multiplication and division. Therefore, the following steps should show how to solve for the expression.

$20 - (15 - 6) \div 3$

$20 - 9 \div 3$

$20 - 3$

17

If you chose answer choice (A), you solved from left to right without considering the order of operations. If you chose choice **b**, you neglected to consider the parentheses but knew that division comes before subtraction. If you chose choice **c**, you knew to solve for the operation in parentheses first, but you then solved from left to right instead of solving the division first.

38. a. The multiplicative inverse of a number is the number that, when multiplied by the original number, will result in a product of 1. When you multiply $10y$ by $\frac{1}{10y}$, the resulting product will be 1, so choice **a** is correct. $-10y$, choice **b**, is the additive inverse of $10y$. When you add $10y$ to $-10y$, the sum will be 0; when you multiply them, however, the product will be $-100y^2$. Choice **c** would result in a negative product, so it cannot be correct, and choice **d** does not include the same variable so it cannot be the multiplicative inverse.

39. a. The formula for the area of a triangle is $\frac{1}{2}bh$, where b is the base of the triangle and h is its height. In the given figure, the base of the triangle is 12 cm and its height is 5 cm. (The side labeled 6 cm does not represent the height.) The area of the triangle is therefore $\frac{1}{2}(5)(12)$, which is 30 sq. cm, choice **a**.

40. c. For each value in the x column of the function table, the corresponding value in the $f(x)$ column is one less than three times larger. If you didn't recognize that pattern in the numbers, you may have noticed that every time the x value increases by 2, the $f(x)$ value increases by 6. Either way, the missing number in the function table will be 32, answer choice **c**.

41. a. The number of rotations of the cylinders in an engine is given for 1 minute. To determine the number of rotations in a second, you would need to divide the rotations by 2,400. Then, for s number of seconds, you can multiply by s. The expression that matches this is $\frac{1}{60}2{,}400s$, choice **a**. If you were unsure of which expression to choose, you could substitute values for s into the expression to see which fits the problem. In 60 seconds, for example, there should be 2,400 rotations. In 1 second, there should be 40 rotations. The only expression that fits these numbers is in choice **a**.

42. b. Each paperback book weighs 2 pounds, and each hardcover book weighs 5 pounds. There is at least one paperback book and one hardcover book in the box, which weighs 18 pounds. If there were one hardcover book in the box, then the weight of the paperback books would need to be 18 – 5 pounds, or 13 pounds. Because 13 is not evenly divisible by 2, there must be more than one hardcover book in the box. If there were two hardcover books in the box, then the weight of the paperback books would need to be 18 – (2 × 5) pounds, or 8 pounds. Because 8 is evenly divisible by 2, there could be two hardcover books in the box. If there were three hardcover books in the box, then the weight of the paperback books would need to be 18 – (3 × 5) pounds, or 3 pounds. Because 3 is not evenly divisible by 2, there cannot be exactly three hardcover books in the box. Any more than three hardcover books, however, would result in a weight greater than 18 pounds. There must be exactly two hardcover books in the box, which would weigh 10 pounds. To find the number of paperback books, divide the remaining weight, 8 pounds, by the weight of each paperback, 2 pounds: 8 ÷ 2 = 4, choice **b**.

43. a. The line on the coordinate graph has a positive slope that is steep. The equation in choice **a** represents a slope of 4 units up for every unit 1 unit to the right which seems to fit the graph. The equation in choice **b** represents a vertical line, so it cannot be right. Choice **c** represents a line with a very steep slope which goes 1 unit up for every 4 units across. Choice **d** represents a line with a negative slope, which means it goes down as it moves to the right. The only equation that could be represented by the graph is $y = 3x$, in choice a.

44. b. To calculate the value of an exponent, you need to multiply the base number by itself a number of times based on the power. In the case of 15, 1 is the base and 5 is the power. To solve, you need to multiply 1 by itself 5 times. $1 \times 1 \times 1 \times 1 \times 1 = 1$, so choice **b** is correct. Choice **c** would be correct if the exponent was 5^1 instead of 1^5.

45. c. An integer is a whole number, its opposite, or 0. In other words, an integer cannot be a fraction or a decimal. –5 and 0 are both examples of integers, so choices **a** and **b** are incorrect. Choice **c** is a decimal and cannot be expressed as an integer, so it is correct. Choice **d**, is in the form of a fraction but can also be expressed as 5, an integer.

46. a. The scenario in the problem represents a permutation because the order of the finishers matter. Therefore, you can multiply the number of possibilities for each place together to find the total number of ways the prizes can be awarded. However, one class cannot win more than one award, which means that while there are 9 possibilities for the pizza party, there are then only 8 possibilities for the 2nd-place plaque—and then only 7 possibilities for the 3rd-place banner. The expression $9 \times 8 \times 7$, choice **a**, therefore represents the possible ways the prizes can be awarded to the different classes in the school.

47. c. If you plug the value –5 for r in the given equation, the value for q will provide the correct answer.

$10q + 5 = r$
$10q + 5 = (-5)$
$10q + 5 - 5 = -5 - 5$
$10q = -10$
$q = -1$

If you selected choice **a**, you may have plugged –5 for q into the equation and then solved for r. If you selected choice **b**, you may have found that $10q = -10$ but then forgotten to simplify to find the value of q. If you selected choice **d**, you may have added 5 to the right side of the equation to isolate $10q$ by itself on the left side.

48. b. To determine the percentage of her sale that Ms. Posada gave to her realtor, you can divide the payment by the sale price of the home: $14{,}000 \div 400{,}000 = 0.035$. However, this does not yet represent the percentage. To convert 0.035 to a percentage, you need to move the decimal place two places to the right: $0.035 = 3.5\%$, choice **b**. If you selected choice **d**, you may have divided the sale price of the home by the payment to the Realtor.

49. c. The ratio of black to blue to red pens in Ming's drawer is 5:2:1. That means for every 5 black pens, there are 2 blue pens and 1 red pen. Another way to consider that is for every 8 pens, there are 5 black pens, 2 blue pens, and 1 red pen. If the ratio of blue pens is 2 out of every 8, you can set up a proportion to find how many blue pens he has out of 40. Use x for the unknown number of blue pens out of 40.

$\frac{2}{8} = \frac{x}{40}$

By cross multiplying, you will find that $8x = 80$, which means that $x = 10$. There are 10 blue pens in Ming's drawer, choice **c**.

50. d. The net shown in this problem has 4 faces, each of which is a triangle. The only solid figure made up of polygons that has as few as 4 faces is a triangular pyramid, choice **d**. The sides of the net could be folded up from the center triangle, which would act as the base. The resulting solid is a triangular pyramid.

51. c. The percentages of the sections in a circle graph must add up to 100%. The given percentages for milk, water, and juice have a sum of 42 + 28 + 18, or 88%. The remaining percentage for seltzer is represented by (100 – 88), or 12%. To find 12% of 500 beverages sold, you can multiply them. Remember that 12% is equal to 0.12. The product of 0.12 and 500 is 60, choice **c**. If you chose **a**, you identified the remaining percentage for seltzer and not the number of seltzers sold. If you chose **d**, you may have made a regrouping error while finding the sum of the other percentages.

52. c. The lighthouse beam flashes every 6 seconds. Robert's watch beeps every 10 seconds. They beep and flash at the same time. To find the next time when this will happen, you need to find the least common denominator (LCD) of the two numbers. The LCD of 6 and 10 is 30, which means that the watch will beep and the lighthouse bea, will flash together the next time in 30 seconds, choice **c**. Choice **a**, 2 seconds, represents the greatest common factor (GCF) of the two numbers, which would not be useful in identifying the next time a repeated event will occur. While Robert's watch will beep and the lighthouse beam will flash together in 60 seconds, or 1 minute, choice **d** does not represent the next time that this will happen. It will happen earlier, at 30 seconds.

53. a. The associative property of addition states that the order of the addends does not matter. This is demonstrated with the expression in choice **a**, where 4 and 6 are added first on the left side of the equation but 3 and 4 are added first on the right side of the equation. While the equation in choice **b** is correct, the numbers are different. The equation in choice **c** represents the distributive property, not the associative property. Choice **d** does not represent a correct equation since the two sides of the equation are unequal; choice **d** is therefore not representative of a property of addition.

54. c. To correctly use this formula, substitute the given numbers for the variables. Because the instructor spends 30 minutes traveling and the formula is given in terms of hours, you need to convert 30 minutes to 0.5 hours before plugging in.

$C = 30t + 50h$

$C = 30(0.5) + 50(1.5)$

$C = 15 + 75$

If you selected choice **a**, you may have confused the variables and assigned the cost of traveling to the instruction time and assigned the cost of the instruction to the travel time. If you chose choice **b**, you may have made a regrouping error. If you chose choice **d**, you may have neglected to convert the 30 minutes to 0.5 hours and instead plugged in 30 for the value of *t*.

55. d. The fifth term in the pattern will be the sum of the two previous terms: 3 and 5. Because $3 + 5 = 8$, the fifth term will be 8, choice **a**. The sixth term will then be the sum of the two previous terms: 5 and 8. Therefore, the sixth term will be $5 + 8$, or 13, choice **b**. The seventh term is the sum of the fifth and sixth terms, 8 and 13, which is 21, choice **d**.

56. b. There are 36 possible distinct outcomes when two number cubes are rolled. That's because each number cube has 6 different numbers, and the possibilities are multiplied when they are rolled together. There are two possible outcomes for the sum of the number cubes to equal 3: One cube can show a 2 and the other can show a 1 or one cube can show a 1 and the other can show a 2. Any probability is found using the fraction [number of successful options/total number if possibilities]. In this case, the probability is $\frac{2}{36}$, which can be reduced to $\frac{1}{18}$.

57. a. Multiplying z by 3 and adding 12 to the product is equivalent to $3z + 12$. To divide the sum by 2, you need to divide the entire $3z + 12$ expression. The expression in choice **a** demonstrates these steps perfectly. The expression in choice **b** combines 12 and 3 before multiplying by z, but the multiplication needs to come before addition so choice **b** cannot be correct. The expression in choice **c** only divides 2 by 12 and not by the sum of $(3z + 12)$. If you chose choice **d**, you reversed the denominator and numerator of the answer.

58. d. A whole number is any positive number that does not contain a fraction or decimal, such as 1, 2, or 10. To multiply a whole number by an unknown number and have the product be a positive number less than 1, the unknown number has to be less than 1. It cannot be an integer, choice **a**. If the unknown number were negative, then the product would also be negative, so choice **b** cannot be correct. A decimal may be the unknown number, but it does not have to have digits in the hundredths place, choice **c**. For example, 4×0.1 would satisfy the scenario without using a decimal that goes beyond the tenths place. The unknown number must be a positive real number less than 1, which means that it can be expressed as a fraction. A fraction is only less than 1 if its denominator is greater than its numerator, so choice **d** is correct.

59. d. To find the value of m in terms of n, you need to isolate m on one side of the equation. To do that, you need to subtract 22 from both sides of the equation and then divide both sides by 2, as shown.

$$2m + 22 = 6n$$
$$2m + 22 - 22 = 6n - 22$$
$$2m = 6n - 22$$
$$\frac{2m}{2} = \frac{6n - 22}{2}$$
$$m = 3n - 11$$

Because the value of m is identified as $3n - 11$, choice **d** is the correct answer.

60. b. The tenths place in a decimal is the digit directly to the right of the decimal point. In the number 174.56, the digit 5 is in the tenths place, making **b** the correct choice. The tens place is 7, choice **d**. The one places is 4, choice **a**. The hundredths place is 6, choice **c**.

Social Studies Answers

61. c. Indicators that an economic system is undergoing a recession include a negative GDP growth, choice **a**, a decrease in capacity utilization, choice **b**, and decreased consumer spending, choice **d**. During a recession, unemployment rates generally increase, so choice **c** is correct.

62. a. The more that a land mass stretches from east to west, in terms of degrees, the greater the disparity there is between the sunrise and sunset within the country. That's why most large countries, including the United States, have time zones. Generally speaking, for every change of 15 degrees longitude, there should be one hour increased or decreased to the time. Because the time zones are bounded by lines of longitude, answer choice **a** is correct. The indications in choices **b** and **c** would describe a land mass from north to south—which would not necessitate a time change. Population, choice **d**, can modify the borders of a time zone slightly, but it is not the best indicator.

63. d. Senators enjoy six-year terms in the U.S. Senate. Therefore, a senator who serves for three full terms will spend a total of 18 years in the Senate. Representatives in Congress have two-year terms, so a three-term representative would serve for a total of six years, choice **b**. Governors have four-year terms, so a three-term governor would serve for a total of 12 years, choice **c**.

64. b. Federalism describes a government, such as the United States, where the government is formed by people who are then ruled by a central body, choice **b**. The description in choice **a** describes a constitutional monarchy. A federalist government does contain power that is divided between a central body and smaller units, such as states; however, the emphasis is not on the decentralization of power, choice **c**. The description in choice **d** is associated with communism, not federalism.

65. b. The term used to describe the American belief that the United States was destined to control the land between the Atlantic and Pacific oceans was Manifest Destiny, choice **b**. The Monroe Doctrine, choice **a**, was a nineteenth century U.S. policy that stated that no European nation should intervene with America's growth and colonization within the western hemisphere. The Magna Carta, choice **c**, was a charter that was issued centuries before Christopher Columbus landed in the Americas. Choice **d**, the Bill of Rights, is the first ten amendments to the U.S. Constitution.

66. d. It was Theodore Roosevelt, choice **d**, who adopted the slogan "Walk slowly and carry a big stick" as his "Big Stick Diplomacy." This policy provided Roosevelt with the right to intervene in some foreign affairs, including those of small states in Central America.

67. d. Mecca, the religious center of Islam, is the destination for millions of Muslims each year. During their pilgrimage, called a Hajj, these travelers visit Saudi Arabia, choice **d**, the Middle Eastern country where Mecca is located.

68. a. The Neolithic period, choice **a**, is defined by the use of agricultural systems and domestic animals. The Paleolithic period, **b**, preceded the Neolithic period and is not known for the use of agriculture or the dependence on domestic animals. The Copper Age, choice **c**, followed the Neolithic period; as its name suggests, it is better known for the advent of metal tools. The Stone Age, choice **d**, is an ancient period in human history in which the first stone tools were used; the human species was not yet advanced enough to utilize agricultural systems.

69. a. The Rosetta Stone is an Egyptian artifact that helped provide translations of the hieroglyphics for modern understanding of the symbols, making **a** the correct choice. Choice **b** is associated with the Code of Hammurabi. The Rosetta Stone is not associated with Mesopotamia, choice **c**, or the astronomical concept that Earth revolves around the sun, choice **d**.

70. c. The invention of the cotton gin, choice **a**, the improvements to the mechanical reaper, choice **b**, and the development of the first steamboat, choice **d**, all represented significant technological or agricultural advancement in the pre–Civil War era. The construction of the first airplane, however, did not occur until several decades *after* the end of the Civil War, so it is not included among the advancements of that age.

71. a. The president of the United States has the important task of nominating a Supreme Court justice. It is one of the greatest responsibilities of the president because Supreme Court justices can serve for decades, influencing a country long after the president has stepped down. Before a nominee can become a member of the highest court, however, he or she must be confirmed by the Senate. These steps match the description provided in answer choice **a**. Choice **b** is incorrect because the members of Congress cannot elect a Supreme Court justice. Choice **c** is incorrect because the people of the United States do not elect justices to the Supreme Court. Choice **d** is incorrect because the Senate Judiciary Committee has the job of investigating whether a person is suitable to become a Supreme Court justice. The Senate Judiciary Committee does not formally determine who will become a Supreme Court justice.

72. b. Primary sources from historical events are known to provide the most accurate information, since they are not influenced by the details being passed from one person to another. A peer-reviewed journal, choice **a**, may be generally trustworthy, though it still represents an example of a secondary source. Neither a movie adaptation, choice **c**, nor a work of historical fiction, choice **d**, provide a primary source for a historical event, making them less likely to provide accurate information than a series of diary entries. Diary entries, choice **b**, are written as a first-person account of an event.

73. d. The basic principles of supply and demand dictate that the price of a good or service decreases when a supply of the good or service increases. The only line that decreases consistently as it moves from left to right along the *x*-axis (representing "Quantity") is line *D*, making choice **d** the correct choice.

74. a. Mount Everest, the highest peak in the world, exists in the Himalaya mountain range, which is located on the north end of the Indian subcontinent. The Andes and Rockies mountain ranges, choices **b**, and **c**, do not have peaks as high as the Himalaya range. The Alaska Mountain Range, choice **d**, is home to Denali, the highest peak in the United States—but not the highest peak in the World.

75. d. An archipelago is defined as a series of tectonically formed islands. The nation of Indonesia represents perhaps the largest archipelago in the world, with approximately 17,500 islands. A peninsula, choice **a**, represents a land mass that is surrounded by water on three sides, such as Florida. An isthmus, choice **b**, represents a narrow land mass that likely has water on both sides, such as Panama. A shoal, choice **c**, is also referred to as a barrier beach or a sandbar. Some islands can act as shoals, but only if they serve to protect a mainland.

76. a. Sacajawea served as a guide and translator for Meriwether Lewis and William Clark during their 1804–1806 expedition to the Pacific coast and back. Sacajawea was instrumental in the expedition's success, and her likeness is now immortalized by the U.S. mint on a $1 coin.

77. c. Physical anthropology, or biological anthropology, focuses on the development of the human race's physical form. Therefore, choice **c** is the only description that is associated with physical anthropology.

78. b. The Three-Fifths Compromise of 1787 was a compromise between the North and South regarding the counting of slaves. The purpose of counting them was for the distribution of taxes and for determining the apportionment for the U.S. representatives in Congress. The Compromise was not about black land ownership, choice **a**, or the tax rate for their income, choice **b**. Slaves did not have the ability to vote, so choice **c** is not correct either.

79. c. The Suez Canal, choice **c**, connects the Mediterranean Sea and the Red Sea. Completed in 1869, the canal is one of the world's most important manmade waterways. The Panama Canal, choice **a**, is one of the other important manmade waterways, but it connects the Atlantic and Pacific oceans. The Erie Canal, choice **b**, connects the Great Lakes to the Hudson River. The Black Sea, choice **d**, does connect to the Mediterranean Sea, but it is not manmade, nor does it connect to the Red Sea.

80. b. Of Alexander the Great's many achievements, the spread of the Greek culture is one of the most lasting and significant. Socrates and Aristotle, choices **a** and **d**, were Greek philosophers, but they are not as well known as Alexander for spreading the Greek culture. Euclid of Alexandria is known as the Father of Geometry, but he is not known for the spread of Greek culture in the same way as Alexander the Great.

81. a. The subjects used in Ivan Pavlov's experiments were dogs, choice **a**. While doing an experiment on dogs' saliva, Pavlov noticed that the dogs would secrete saliva even when they were expecting to eat food. This helped him to study and develop the concept of conditioned reflex.

82. d. The Roaring Twenties is a reference to the decade after the war that was marked by an economic boom. The period is also known for a cultural, technological, and artistic explosion, choice **d**. There were no attacks on the United States during or after World War I, so choice **b** is incorrect. The Wall Street Crash of 1929 effectively ended the roaring twenties, so choice **c** is not correct. There is no evidence to support choice **a**.

83. a. The area off the coast of Cape Cod, MA, was chosen as the site on which to build a massive wind farm, based on the fact that it is an outstanding source for power, due to its high and frequent winds, choice **a**. Natural gas is not a renewable energy source, so choice **b** could not be correct. Solar energy, choice **c**, is renewable, but exposure to the sun is not the reason for the development off the coast of the Cape. There are tidal swings near Cape Cod—and people have tried to harness the energy from the movement of the water, especially farther north by the Bay of Fundy. However, it is a wind farm that was approved to be built in that area, so choice **d** is not correct.

84. b. It is widely believed that the spread of the Black Plague was introduced to Europe from the merchant ships from Asia and spread by fleas and rats aboard them. Native populations have been decimated as a result of their lack of exposure to bacteria, such as the destruction of the Native American populations due to smallpox, introduced by the conquistadors. However, this was not the likely cause of the Black Plague. Domestic animals, choice **a**, and urban centers, choice **c**, were not the cause of the spread of the Black Death. However, walled cities at the time were especially vulnerable to the plague.

85. c. Rosa Parks is best known for her refusal to give her seat to a white passenger on a bus in Montgomery, Alabama, in December 1955. The act of defiance inspired the Montgomery Bus Boycott, which involved Martin Luther King, Jr., choice **a**. Parks' defiance also went against the segregation laws at the time, referred to as Jim Crow laws. Malcolm X, choice **d**, a human rights activist, was not involved with this important event in civil rights history.

86. d. The areas with a density of 250 or more people per square mile are presented on the map in the darkest shade. Several states have parts that have this darkened shade. However, almost the entirety of New Jersey is this shade, meaning that almost all its counties have a population of at least 250 people per square mile. California, choice **a**, has the greatest overall population in the United States, but it is not the most densely populated state. Alaska, choice **b**, is almost entirely shaded in the lightest color, and it is in fact the least densely populated state in the country. Large portions of New York, choice **c**, are densely populated, but only the area of New York City and Long Island shows the darkest shade. Choice **d**, New Jersey, is the best choice.

87. b. To correctly answer this question, you will need to estimate the distance from the western end of Texas to the southwestern corner of California. You must read the given scale in the map which shows that $1\frac{1}{4}$ inches is equal to about 700 miles. Based on that scale, the distance is about 700 miles, choice **b**. The other answer choices represent distances that are either much too short or much too long.

88. c. In the years leading up to Christopher Columbus's voyage to the Americas, tensions between Christian Europeans and the Islamic kingdoms of the Middle East made overland travel dangerous, choice **a.** However, the only way to sail from the Mediterranean Sea to India, before the creation of the Suez Canal, was to sail completely around Africa. This forced traders to try to find new and more efficient routes to trade with India, choice **a.**The Spanish king and queen were willing to finance to journey because they knew that the spice trade with India was especially lucrative, choice **b.** While Columbus may have discovered a new trading partner, choice **c**, his intention was NOT to discover new partners but to find a better way to connect with existing trading partners. Therefore, choice **c** represents the only reason why Columbus did NOT sail west in 1492.

89. b. The 1857 Supreme Court case *Dred Scott v. Sanford* was notable because it formally declared that black men and women in the United States could never become U.S. citizens, choice **b.** This racist decision would not be overturned until the ratification of the Fourteenth Amendment after the Civil War, which declared that former slaves could become citizens, choice **d.** The outcome described in choice **a** refers to the ramifications of the 1896 Supreme Court case *Plessy v. Ferguson. Plessy v. Ferguson* would be overturned in 1954 with the Supreme Court case *Brown v. Board of Education of Topeka*, which desegregated public school classrooms, choice **c.**

90. a. Shinto is a set of practices followed by more than 100 million Japanese, so choice **a** is correct. The majority of people living in India, choice **b**, are Hindu. Israel, choice **c**, was designated as a Jewish state. China, choice **d**, has no official religion, but Buddhism and Taoism are practiced there, as well as Islam and Christianity.

Science Answers

91. a. The diagram in choice **a** corresponds to the correct arrangement of Earth, the moon, and the sun during a solar eclipse. The moon is located between Earth and the sun, blocking Earth's view of the sun. It also corresponds to the correct orbits, with the moon orbiting around Earth, and Earth around the sun. Choice **b** is incorrect because it shows the sun orbiting around Earth, and the moon around the sun. Choice **c** is incorrect because Earth, the moon, and the sun are not aligned as they should be during an eclipse, and the moon is not orbiting around Earth. Choice **d** shows correct orbits, but the moon is not blocking the sun from Earth's view. In fact, choice **d** may correspond to a lunar eclipse.

92. d. The diagram shows the chemical process of photosynthesis, choice **d.** In photosynthesis, plants use light energy to convert carbon dioxide (CO_2) and water (H_2O) to glucose ($C_6H_{12}O_6$), oxygen (O_2), and water (H_2O). In aerobic respiration, glucose and oxygen are converted into water, carbon dioxide, and energy. In fermentation, glucose is converted into carbon dioxide and alcohol or lactic acid.

93. c. Light from the sun is captured by plants to drive the process of photosynthesis. Different pigments in the plant absorb different wavelengths of light in photosynthesis. Water, oxygen, and carbon are involved in photosynthesis in different ways, but light is the primary energy source driving the reactions.

94. b. The outermost layer of Earth is the crust, which means that answer choices **c** and **d** cannot be correct. Beneath the crust, in order of the depth beneath the surface, are the lithosphere, mantle, outer core, and inner core, choice **b**. Choice **a** reverses the order of the inner and outer core. Choice **c** lists the order of the layers of Earth's interior *ending* with Earth's surface.

95. a. The stamen is the male part of a flower that contains the anther that produces pollen and the filament. The stamen is represented by the part on the diagram labeled A, which makes choice **a** correct. Part B of the diagram represents the ovary, part C represents the stigma, and part D represents the petal.

96. d. The primary function of the nucleus is to store the genetic information (DNA) of the cell.

97. b. Earth's atmosphere has a mixture of gases: nitrogen (78%), oxygen (21%), argon (0.9%), and carbon dioxide (0.038%). Water vapor depends on the climate and ranges from 0.3% to 4%. By far, the most prevalent gas in Earth's atmosphere is nitrogen, choice **b**.

98. c. Smallpox was once one of the world's most deadly diseases. It was the first human infectious disease to be completely eradicated from the planet. This was a result of the use of the smallpox vaccine, choice **c**, which inoculated enough of the population from the disease that it was unable to spread. None of the other choices are either true or a primary cause for the eradication of smallpox.

99. d. The color that we see on objects depends on what part of the visible light spectrum is being absorbed by the object. Whatever is not absorbed is reflected. A yellow banana, therefore, appears yellow because it reflects the yellow part of visible light and absorbs all other wavelengths of light. This is best described by the explanation in choice **d**.

100. b. Absolute zero is the temperature at which particles have minimal motion and can be no colder. Because of this minimal motion, there is minimal kinetic energy in the molecules at this temperature. Absolute zero is 0° on the Kelvin scale, –273.15° on the Celsius scale, or –459.67° on the Fahrenheit scale. Because 0°K represents absolute zero, there is the least amount of kinetic energy in a molecule at that temperature. Choice **d**, 100° C, is the boiling point of water, and there would be the most kinetic energy in a molecule at that temperature.

101. b. The effect of a reflected sound wave is an echo, choice **b**. Convection, choice **a**, transfers heat through the movement of currents within fluids (liquids and gases). Conduction, choice **c**, moves heat through matter from areas of high temperature to low temperature. A current, choice **d**, can refer to the flow of electron movement, as well as air currents or ocean currents; either way, it does not reflect the scenario given in the problem.

102. a. Fossils are records of organisms from the distant past. There are ways to tell how old they are, so fossils could determine whether two species existed at the same point in time, choice **a**. Ancient cave drawings could tell whether ancient hominids mapped constellations, choice **b**, but this would not be an example of a fossil. Similarly, fossils do not provide the kind of astronomical information provided in choice **c**. While dinosaur eggs may create fossils, scientists would not be able to determine which eggs were fertile or infertile from the remains left by the fossils.

103. a. Potential energy is stored energy that has potential to be converted into another form of energy. The higher an object is off the ground, the farther it can fall—meaning that it has more potential to be converted into kinetic energy. The point on the go-cart race with the greatest potential energy will be the highest point on the hill. This is represented by A on the diagram, choice **a**. Choice **b** may have the greatest kinetic energy if the go-cart is traveling with the most momentum at this point.

104. c. Of the pictures shown, only the tree and the flower are able to produce energy by way of photosynthesis. Mushrooms get their energy through a process of decomposition.

105. c. In the given diagram of Earth and the moon, Earth is about 3.67 times larger in terms of their radii and diameters. Their circumferences will therefore also be in proportion to each other. This is accurate to the actual scale of the two bodies, making choices **a** and **d** incorrect. The diagram shows that Earth and the moon are roughly spherical, which would be accurate—even if Earth is slightly elongated at its equator—so choice **b** is not correct. The distance from Earth to the moon is about 400,000 km. The moon has a diameter of 3,475 km. Therefore, the distance between them should be much greater if the illustration were to scale. Choice **c** is correct.

106. d. An autotroph, choice **d**, produces its own energy in the form of glucose (sugar) using the energy of the sun. This fits the characteristics of a plant. Another name for an organism that produces its own energy supply from inorganic materials is a producer, choice **b**. Any organism that converts sunlight into energy is a photosynthetic organism, choice **c**. An herbivore, choice **d**, relates to an animal that eats only plants, such as a deer. An herbivore cannot be used to describe a plant, so choice **d** is correct.

107. b. There are six simple machines: an inclined plane, a lever, a wedge, a screw, a pulley, and a wheel and axle. Each of these simple machines uses energy to work. A calculator, choice **b**, is not considered to be among the simple machines.

108. a. A glass prism separates white visible light into the visible array or spectrum of all the colors of the rainbow. Choice **c** is incorrect because a telescope is a device that focuses and concentrates radiation from distant objects. A microscope, choice **b**, is incorrect because it is designed to magnify objects smaller than the naked eye's detection capabilities in close proximity. A Geiger counter, choice **d**, is incorrect because it is an instrument that detects radiation and measures its intensity.

109. a. The strength of a gravitational force depends on the mass of the object. A star generally has a great deal of mass, and so its gravitational force will be significant as well. In fact, our own Sun's gravitational force, due to its size, is responsible for keeping Earth and all the other planets in orbit.

110. b. While asexual reproduction is the primary form of reproduction for single-celled organisms, some multi-cellular organisms reproduce asexually as well. Therefore, choice **a** is not necessarily true. Asexual reproduction, by its definition, involves one parent, choice **b**. Sexual reproduction involves the union of genetic information from two parents, so choice **c** is not correct. Whether an organism reproduces asexually or sexually, it still has the physical capability to reproduce.

111. c. The Phanerozoic Eon began about 540 million years ago and continues to the present day. Life began about 3.9 billion years ago on Earth, so choice **b** is incorrect. The Cambrian Era at the beginning of the Phanerozoic Eon, from about 540 to 500 million years ago, is known for an explosion of life; however, it is not known for the planet's first life forms. The Archeozoic Eon, choice **c**, is marked by the first life forms about 3.9 billion years ago. From about 3.9 to 2.5 billion years ago, the range of the Archeozoic Eon, single-celled organisms evolved, such as bacteria and algae in the sea. The Mesozoic Era lasted from 250 million years ago until 65 million years ago and is known for the dominance of dinosaurs during the era, not the birth of life.

112. c. A control group experiences or is exposed to all the same variables as the experimental or test group except for the variable being tested, in this case the effect of artificial sweetener. Choices **a** and **b** are just variations on the variable being tested. Choice **d** is a variable as well, but has nothing to do with the variable being tested.

113. d. When matter goes from one state to another, it represents a physical change. Therefore, choice **c** represents a physical change. The event in choice **a** is also a physical change because it can be undone; there is no chemical reaction between the sugar and the water that cannot be undone. Glass shattering, choice **b**, may create a mess, but it does not represent any chemical reaction within the matter. Bubbles often represent a chemical reaction, and vinegar and baking soda, choice **d**, will indeed combine to form a chemical reaction.

114. d. According to the given diagram, the wavelength of a wave increases from right to left on the electromagnetic spectrum. Radio waves are to the left of microwaves on the diagram. Therefore, a radio wave has a greater length than a microwave. The question tells you that the length of a microwave is approximately 1 centimeter. The only length that is greater than 1 centimeter is stated in choice **d**, 1 mile. Believe it or not, a radio wave can have a wavelength of 1 mile!

115. a. According to the given diagram, the frequency of a wave increases from left to right on the electromagnetic spectrum. The only type of wave with a greater frequency than an X-ray is the only type of wave to its right: gamma rays. The question tells you that the frequency of an X-ray is approximately 10^{18} Hz. The only greater frequency among the answer choices is 10^{20} Hz, choice **a**. This could represent the frequency of a gamma ray.

116. b. The movement of tectonic plates is responsible for some of the most devastating natural disasters on Earth. The shifting of the plates at the faults causes vibrations on the surface of Earth known as earthquakes, choice **a**. If these earthquakes occur in water, the plates can cause a displacement of water which can reach landfall as a tsunami, choice **c**. Volcanoes, choice **d**, are formed by the opening in Earth's crust caused by the movement of tectonic plates. Monsoons, choice **b**, are seasonal changes that bring great amounts of precipitation. Since a monsoon is a weather event, it is not affected by the movement of tectonic plates.

117. b. The isobar weather map shows a low pressure zone centered over Michigan. A low pressure zone, characterized by an area of low atmospheric pressure, is associated with high winds, warm air, clouds, and precipitation. It is not indicative of cold, choice **a**, or calm weather, choice **d**. Hail, choice **c**, is possible because a low-pressure zone is associated with precipitation, but hail is a somewhat less predictable event. It is most likely that the area in Michigan will be cloudy, choice **b**.

118. a. Earth rotates on its axis from west to east. As a result, the stars—which are largely stationary from Earth—appear to move from east to west. This is why choice **a** is correct and choice **c** is not correct. The movement of the Milky Way galaxy does not provide the best explanation for the apparent movement of the stars in the sky each day. The explanation in choice **d** refers to why different stars are visible during different seasons. It does not explain why stars seem to rise in the east and set in the west.

119. c. Small particles of debris that orbit the sun are considered meteoroids. When they become visible entering Earth's atmosphere, they are called meteors. A meteorite is a part of the meteoroid that is not destroyed by entering the atmosphere and reaches the ground. The presence of life-forms or frozen water, choices **a** and **d**, have nothing to do with these definitions. Since meteorites orbit the sun, choice **b** is not correct either.

120. d. The stomach and esophagus, choices **a** and **c**, are key organs in the digestive system of a human being. The heart, choice **b**, is known as the central organ in the human circulatory system. It is the kidney, choice **d**, that is most associated with its role in the excretory system of a human being. During the excretory process, the kidneys filter blood to remove nitrogenous waste and toxic byproducts.

ADDITIONAL ONLINE PRACTICE

Whether you need help building basic skills or preparing for an exam, visit the LearningExpress Practice Center! On this site, you can access additional practice materials. Using the code below, you'll be able to log in and take an additional practice exam. This online practice exam will also provide you with:

- **Immediate scoring**
- **Detailed answer explanations**
- **Personalized recommendations for further practice and study**

Log on to the LearningExpress Practice Center by using the URL: **www.learnatest.com/practice**

This is your Access Code: **7700**

Follow the steps online to redeem your access code. After you've used your access code to register with the site, you will be prompted to create a username and password. For easy reference, record them here:

Username: ______________________ **Password:** ______________________

With your username and password, you can log in and answer these practice questions as many times as you like. If you have any questions or problems, please contact LearningExpress customer service at 1-800-295-9556 ext. 2, or e-mail us at **customerservice@learningexpressllc.com**

NOTES

NOTES

NOTES